Economic Policy Reform

Economic Policy Reform
The Second Stage

Edited by **Anne O. Krueger**

The University of Chicago Press

Chicago and London

ANNE O. KRUEGER is the Herald L. and Caroline L. Ritch Professor
of Economics, senior fellow of the Hoover Institution, and director
of the Center for Research on Economic Development and Policy
Reform at Stanford University, and a research associate of the
National Bureau of Economic Research.

The University of Chicago Press, Chicago 60637
The University of Chicago Press, Ltd., London
© 2000 by The University of Chicago
All rights reserved. Published 2000
Printed in the United States of America
09 08 07 06 05 04 03 02 01 00   1 2 3 4 5
ISBN: 0-226-45447-9 (cloth)

Library of Congress Cataloging-in-Publication Data

Economic policy reform : the second stage / edited by Anne O.
    Krueger.
        p. cm.
    Includes bibliographical references and index.
    ISBN 0-226-45447-9 (cloth : alk. paper)
        1. Developing countries—Economic policy—Case studies.
    I. Krueger, Anne O.

    HC59.7 .E3123 2000
    338.9′009172′4—dc21

                                                        00-029932

Contents

Foreword

The future of developing countries and those in transition is critically linked to their success in reforming economic policies to assure more rapid and sustainable growth and higher living standards, especially for the poor. Experience has demonstrated the extent to which an appropriate economic policy environment can enhance economic performance while inappropriate policies can stifle economic growth and lead to stagnation.

However, changing policies has not always succeeded, in significant part because the problems inherent in altering policies have not been well understood. As experience has mounted rapidly over the past decade, a basis has been laid for researchers to examine policy reform efforts and to analyze the determinants of their success or failure and the ways alternative reforms feed into improved economic performance.

When development efforts got under way after the Second World War, most people in developing countries lived in rural areas and derived their livelihood from agriculture. Agricultural development was therefore a key issue in improving living standards, and Stanford University was proud to support the Food Policy Research Institute in its research on the determinants of agricultural output and rural income.

As developing countries transformed their economies from an almost entirely rural base to one with a preponderance of economic activity in urban areas, they simultaneously built labyrinths of government interventions, regulations, and controls, which increasingly hampered economic activity in all sectors of the economy. Stanford University has therefore shifted its support for research on the critical problems of developing economies to the Center for Research on Economic Development and Policy Reform.

The center was formally established in January 1997. As an inaugural activity, it seemed appropriate to assess the state of knowledge about economic policy reform and to set forth a research agenda. To that end, leading researchers in many fields of development were invited to review the state of knowledge with respect to their individual fields, and to provide their judgments as to priority areas for future research. Other leading academics and policymakers were invited to the conference to participate in the discussions that followed each paper.

This volume represents the product of that conference. As will be seen in the first and last chapters, there is a surprising convergence of researchers' views on the challenges facing would-be reformers, and the ways in which fruitful research can inform that effort. Research is now under way at the Center for Research on Economic Development and Policy Reform and elsewhere on many of these key issues. This volume provides a guide to the current state of thinking about economic policy reform and the resolution of difficult issues that would improve prospects for poor people and poor countries throughout the world.

Gerhard Casper
President, Stanford University

Acknowledgments

The papers in this volume were initially prepared for the first conference held by Stanford's new Center for Research on Economic Development and Policy Reform. As a new center, it seemed appropriate that the first conference focus on the state of knowledge, and needed research, in the subject area of the center's purpose.

The most important supporters of the conference, and the individuals to whom the greatest thanks are owed for making the center possible, are President Gerhard Casper and then provost Condollezza Rice, who devoted much time and support to the center at its inception. I am also indebted to Charles Kruger and Jacqueline Wender for their able efforts in making the center a reality.

The second most important debt is to the contributors to this volume. All of the authors not only delivered excellent papers but did so in a timely fashion and cooperated well in achieving the deadlines. Their contributions and cooperation made the editing of this volume a relatively simple and pleasant task.

Sajjid Chinoy, of the Stanford Economics Department, provided expert and conscientious research assistance in the preparation of this volume. Slavi Slavov, also of the Economics Department, filled in ably during Sajjid Chinoy's absences. Nicholas Hope, deputy director of the center, helped facilitate many of the arrangements for the conference, as well as participating in the conference and contributing to the volume.

Funds for the conference and the editing of the volume came from the President's Fund of Stanford University, the Mellon Foundation, the Koret Foundation (through its support for the Stanford Institute for Economic Policy Research), and the center's own unrestricted funds. I am grateful to them all.

Last but certainly not least, I would like to thank Deniece Frazier, center administrator, for her work in overseeing conference arrangements and coordinating the support for the work involved in preparation of the volume. Thanks are also due to Lawrence J. Lau, director of the Stanford Institute for Economic Policy Research, Deborah Carvalho, institute administrator, and the rest of the SIEPR staff for their support of the conference.

Anne O. Krueger
Director, Center for Research on Economic
Development and Policy Reform

I

Overview

Introduction

Anne O. Krueger

Since the mid-1980s, a number of developing countries and economies in transition have been engaged in unprecedented efforts to alter their economic policy regimes. It has become widely recognized that earlier policies, which had been based on state control of most large-scale economic activity, had not served their intended purposes. By the late 1990s, most developing countries outside south central Asia and some economies of sub-Saharan Africa had attempted policy reform. Efforts to change course, and alter economic policies, have been under way with varying degrees of commitment, political support, and thoroughness. In some countries, reforms have been limited to removal of the worst and most visibly costly controls. In other countries, reforms have begun but are in their initial stages. In still others, reforms have radically altered the economic environment for private decision makers and government officials alike.

Even the most reform-minded countries, however, still have considerable agendas for further reform. In those countries where "big picture" changes—removal of quantitative restrictions on imports and major reductions in the heights of tariffs, privatization of key state-owned enterprises and changes in the regulatory regime for the private sector, removal or significant reduction of subsidies, reform of the welfare system, and so on—have been accomplished, there remain a host of "second stage" re-

Anne O. Krueger is the Herald L. and Caroline L. Ritch Professor of Economics, senior fellow of the Hoover Institution, and director of the Center for Research on Economic Development and Policy Reform at Stanford University, and a research associate of the National Bureau of Economic Research.

The author is indebted to Sajjid Chinoy for valuable comments on this chapter as well as research assistance. In addition, the author thanks all of the contributors to this volume for their prompt and careful reading of the first draft of this chapter, and for their thoughtful comments.

forms that would further increase economic efficiency and enhance growth prospects for all socioeconomic groups.

First-stage reforms are in general politically and administratively easier to implement for a variety of reasons. Their very success, however, generates the need for second-stage reforms, without which the full benefits of first-stage reforms cannot be realized. For example, an infrastructure adequate to support economic activity under an import substitution regime is usually entirely inadequate to permit the rapid growth of exports and accelerated growth of real GNP that is possible after first-stage reforms have been implemented.

Second-stage reforms tend to encounter more political resistance (as, e.g., with labor market reforms), and in addition, more "technical" bureaucratic and administrative work must usually be done, first, to obtain parliamentary approval for reforms and, second, to implement them once enabling legislation is passed.

But enough countries have progressed far enough in the reform process that it is meaningful to discuss the second stage of reforms. This second stage entails the implementation of particulars—the details of a tax reform program, the development of a new regulatory regime for formerly government-owned and now privatized enterprises, and so on. In most instances, the broad thrust of policy is already set, but many inefficiencies remain. Some remain because their solution requires careful planning and presentation of plans to legislatures and meets political resistance. Some remain because policymakers have been sufficiently absorbed in the first-stage reforms that they have not had the resources (including able technocrats) needed to address other topics as well. Still others remain because not enough is yet known about the benefits and costs of alternative approaches to reform.

The theme of attention to particulars, and analysis of alternative ways of achieving given ends, recurs surprisingly often throughout the papers in this volume. Vito Tanzi, for example, focuses on the need for careful work on the details of fiscal reform, and especially implementation, in achieving more efficient use of resources within the public sector. Michael Kremer discusses alternatives for achieving more within the educational sector with given resources. Aaron Tornell addresses issues that arise when privatization takes place without the necessary attention to managerial control and other requisites for successful functioning of newly privatized firms. In some markets, of which labor may be the most notable, reforms have barely begun, as Paul Schultz notes. In part, this is because of political resistance, but the lack of reform also reflects in Schultz's view the lack of agreed-upon orders of magnitude of payoffs for alternative reforms. The same point arises in an analysis of telecommunications, for which Roger Noll points out that many countries have made some efforts to reform the sector but none has gone far enough to achieve attainable efficiencies, and further changes in regulatory structure and incentives are called for. Matusz and Tarr address questions surrounding trade liberalization, analyzing how it may be achieved with smaller costs to those adversely affected in the short run. Stiglitz, in his assessment of the state of policy reform, worries that poorly implemented, ill-thought-out first-stage reforms may have soured the political atmosphere for further needed efforts.

Each of the papers in this volume addresses a key issue in economic policy reform. All of the authors examine the progress of reforms to date in the markets they are considering and then analyze the issues that arise for the second stage of policy reform (although the second stage is further advanced for some types of reforms than for others). They then consider the sorts of research that can serve to inform policymakers in the choices they make with regard to second-stage reforms.

The volume has five parts. Parts 1 through 4 cover economic policy reforms viewed topically. Part 5 contains reflections by Joseph Stiglitz on the present state of economic policy reform, and then a concluding chapter sets out a research agenda, drawing on insights from the individual papers.

Part 1 provides an overview of economic policy reform to date. Chapter 2, by Stephan Haggard, examines the political context in which reforms take place. In chapter 3, Vittorio Corbo evaluates progress to date in Latin America and assesses the second-stage reform agenda and research that can support it. T. N. Srinivasan then analyzes the progress of four countries of South Asia with economic policy reform. They are generally much less advanced in the reform process, and Srinivasan provides some important insights as to the reasons.

Haggard starts by noting the voluminous work on the political economy of economic policy reform but also indicates its "balkanization." He then focuses on a central issue that seems to divide analysts regardless of field (such as corruption, central banking, privatization, and regulatory reforms): some analyses of economic policy reform are couched primarily in terms of social preferences and interest groups, while others regard institutional arrangements as crucial. The first approach regards reform as a process of coalition building. This style of analysis focuses on strategic and tactical questions: how quickly to reform, how to build support from winners, and how to compensate, or finesse, losers. In the second approach, institutions themselves matter, and their reform may be key to the pursuit of wider economic policy objectives. Haggard then examines these two approaches and their implications by considering a number of key issues, such as the role of governmental form (democracy or dictatorship, parliamentary or presidential system) and the linkages between the politics of reform and the ways in which social protection can contribute to political sustainability of reform.

In his comment, Abhijit Banerjee concurs with the need to analyze institutions but questions whether they are as exogenous as Haggard's paper suggests. He also notes that reforms are most likely to take place when the usual political constraints have been relaxed, if not removed, because of crisis or for other reasons. He suggests that institutional change may speed reforms by permitting innovation and new forms of doing things, such as town and village enterprises in China, and points to the need for, but difficulty of, empirical testing of these questions.

In his paper, Corbo notes that for many Latin American countries, the first stages of reform are largely complete, although there are opportunities for further reform, with an estimated 2.5 percentage point increase in the rate of economic growth if these were accomplished. He reports that most progress has been achieved in fiscal adjustment, trade regime reform, and financial reforms, with less but still considerable reform achieved in privatization. The least progress has been made in labor market and pension reform.

That macroeconomic reforms came first should not be surprising, given the height of inflation experienced in many Latin American countries. Corbo notes that the generally poor economic performance of individual countries was a major motivation for the start of the reform process: some had hyperinflation (Bolivia, Peru, Argentina, and Nicaragua); some had successive economic crises (Brazil and Mexico); still others had highly unsatisfactory growth performances (Argentina, Chile, Colombia, El Salvador, Guatemala, and Venezuela). He also credits the success of the Chilean reforms with spurring reform efforts in other Latin American countries. Other contributing factors were the collapse of the former Soviet Union and the emergence of a group of highly trained technocrats in most Latin American countries.

The areas of second-stage reform where he believes needs are most pressing include delivery of health, education, nutrition, and judicial services. In these arenas, there are significant problems of reforming existing services. Corbo calls attention to the inefficiency of existing allocations of educational expenditures, with many countries allocating sizable shares of their educational budgets to tertiary education and leaving many primary-school-age children with no access to schooling. The same dilemmas apply to the delivery of health care. Corbo points to research issues that can better inform these reforms, a subject addressed in the final chapter of this volume.

Interestingly, in his comment Miguel Savastano does not take issue with Corbo's second-stage reform agenda but rather raises questions about the efficacy of inflation targeting and speculates about the reasons for what appears to be political resistance to second-stage reforms. He posits in particular that policymakers are overloaded with suggestions and that further work prioritizing the issues requiring attention might have a sizable payoff.

T. N. Srinivasan first surveys the state of policies and reforms undertaken thus far in various South Asian countries. He notes the large number of well-intentioned programs, such as India's efforts at redistribution, that have "contributed only modestly to the equally modest reduction in poverty alleviation" and emphasizes the need for reforms in order to achieve higher rates of economic growth as "the only efficacious long-term solutions to the problem of poverty."

But despite the pressing needs, the subcontinent seems far behind Latin America in its reforms. Srinivasan reports on a number of reforms for which initial policy decisions have been made but there has thus far been little implementation—privatization, tax reform, and financial reforms are among them. In many instances, it is the nuts and bolts of existing institutions—such as center-state relations—that must be understood if reforms are to have their intended effects. In many of these areas, as in Latin America, political pressure groups mount strong opposition to reforms.

Srinivasan concludes that for the moment, the reform process is stalled on the subcontinent, with the possible exception of Sri Lanka. Nonetheless, he sets forth a reform agenda and identifies issues on which research could guide policy formulation. These issues are addressed in the final chapter.

In moving from government-led and -directed economic development to greater reliance on "user-friendly" policies and incentives to achieve social objectives, one major effort has been to shift to the private sector economic activities that the public sector was not performing well and that the private sector might perform better. These privatizations and denationalizations have taken many forms. In some instances, ownership has been shifted outright to the private sector. In others, concern over the potential abuse of monopoly power has led governments to shift control subject to regulation, to retain partial ownership, or to "corporatize" state-owned enterprises, giving managers incentives similar to those faced by managers in the private sector.

Establishing policies to make previously state-owned and state-operated enterprises more efficient is among the most difficult issues confronting economic policy reformers. Finding appropriate means to achieve the desired results is still a major challenge. Three papers in part 2 address aspects of that challenge. In chapter 5, Aaron Tornell considers privatization, primarily from the vantage point of seeking efficiency in firms that are transferred to outright private ownership and where concerns about private monopoly do not dominate. In chapter 6, Roger Noll considers reforms in telecommunications, a sector in which until very recently very few developing or developed countries had carried reform very far because of the enormous political and economic power of incumbent monopoly carriers as well as the complexities of developing effective regulatory regimes to manage the transition from state-owned monopoly to privatized competition. In chapter 7, Noll, Mary Shirley, and Simon Cowan address alternative means of improving the delivery of water. In contrast to telecommunications, where reforms have not proceeded far and little empirical work has been done, Noll, Shirley, and Cowan analyze six separate experiences with reform efforts for water. In his comment, Takatoshi Ito emphasizes how technological changes that have reduced fixed costs, and demand changes that have necessitated innovative management, have contributed to the successful deregulation and privatization of many goods traditionally considered "public." In the case of water systems, however, Ito wonders if enough political, technological, and institutional change has occurred to justify privatization.

In his paper, Aaron Tornell considers lessons from the first wave of privatizations and questions for further research. He notes that privatization of small shops has gone reasonably smoothly: competition is already in place, returns can be fairly readily estimated, so it is relatively straightforward to divest the state of these firms. In the case of "behemoths," the issues are much more difficult. If behemoths operate in industries where there is domestic competition or where imports can provide competition, problems arise but they are more or less surmountable.

The real difficulties for privatizers come when unitary control within the candidate firms is lacking, when the new owners do not face hard budget constraints, or when the judicial system does not ensure transparent bankruptcy procedures. When unitary control is lacking, the newly privatized firm does not have management and control to enable changes in its mode of operation. When there is no hard budget constraint (such as when a newly privatized firm can count on the government to underwrite new bank loans, provide protection, or provide subsidies to keep the firm afloat), incentives for the owners to reform the firm in ways that will contribute to economic efficiency and economic growth are lacking. Likewise, when bankruptcy procedures are drawn out or ineffective, incentives to new owners are not satisfactory.

These issues are especially difficult when natural monopoly is involved, as happens when there is networking or in some public utilities (see the discussion of water below). But even when natural monopoly is absent, large companies often are the sole producer of goods within countries, and issues of control and hard budget constraints are crucial. In addition, there are other issues: What is the objective of privatization: should the enterprise be transferred to those paying the highest price, or should issues concerning social and distributive justice enter? How can one efficiently auction off public sector enterprises in a way that is seen to be fair? Should enterprises be restructured before or after privatization? And so on.

Tornell discusses these, and related, issues and points to some of the dilemmas involved. He also points to experience with privatization carried out with a variety of techniques. But there are many thorny issues. Tornell ends by calling for a great deal of additional research, which forms part of the research agenda discussed in the concluding chapter.

In his comment, Nicholas Hope discusses the relevance of Tornell's conditions for successful privatization in the context of China's state-owned enterprises.

Whereas Tornell focuses on the need to privatize in ways that provide incentives for managers and owners to respond to market signals and at the same time induce firms to behave in economically efficient and socially desirable ways when the competitive environment alone does not achieve that end, Roger Noll delves deeply into a vital industry where achieving competition is indeed difficult: telecommunications.

Telecommunications is an interesting case for analysis of economic policy reform in developing countries because these countries are beginning to attempt the same reforms at the same time as developed countries, but from a very different starting point. Developed countries have in place a regulatory regime developed when technology was very different and led to a "natural monopoly" in the industry. As Noll notes, developing countries are just beginning to address the issue, but many of these countries did not inherit the earlier regulatory regime to the same extent as developed countries. In a sense, the second stage of policy reforms for telecommunications has already arrived, although the first was never really undertaken.

The issue of telecommunications reform is pressing because all private sector firms in any economy need good telecommunications to make efficient use of resources. But it is also very complicated because of some of the underlying technical complexities of telecommunications, including its component parts and especially the issues pertaining to interconnections between carriers. Noll analyzes these issues, highlighting the complexities and dilemmas that deregulators and reformers face. To date, there has been little empirical analysis of experience with reforms, which leads Noll to sketch a road map of the issues and possible measures that can address them.

Interestingly, telecommunications in most developing countries prior to the 1950s (which, for many, means prior to independence) were privately owned, usually by foreign firms. But a wave of nationalizations in the 1940s and 1950s (with a few, such as Mexico, earlier) resulted in the first stage of telecommunications policies in developing countries. After a brief period when telecommunications services improved after nationalization, Noll states that "the ubiquitous, depressing fact about telecommunications during the nationalized era was its deterioration." Delays in obtaining service or repairs and significant probabilities of failing to get a dial tone or complete a call characterized most nationalized systems in developing countries. Inefficiencies arose because of the high cost of capital, underpricing of services so that maintenance and investment could not be financed out of earnings, and overstaffing of labor. Noll points out that unstable governments had every incentive to seek popularity by underpricing telecommunications services and few incentives to maintain systems because they did not expect to be long in power.

Telecommunications reforms then began for two reasons. First, the era of reforms was sweeping developing countries after the crises of the 1970s and 1980s, although as Noll notes, these reforms focused largely on other issues. Second, the poor performance of nationalized communications industries gave rise to additional pressures for change.

Fixing the problems within nationalized entities would have been difficult at best, but reform confronted two essentially political economic problems: it would have required greatly reduced staffing of nationalized enterprises, and at the same time, additional investment would have had to increase by 10 or more percent of government investment budgets. Because investment funds were scarce and the political costs of reduced staffing unacceptable, privatization, especially to foreign investors, was a means of addressing both problems in a way that was at least partly depoliticized. Even so, resistance from labor unions to necessary retrenchment is considerable and often leads to the sale of equity to raise funds but without surrender of control.

However, political constraints usually prevented governments from resorting entirely to that solution. The compromise was generally to permit foreign investment, but often at less than 50 percent ownership, and with governments often retaining an ownership share. Shares were often given to domestic residents at low cost. These measures increased the political feasibility of reform but diluted control and returns to foreign investors, with costs in terms of long-run performance potential. In some cases, all that happened was that government-owned telecommunications enterprises were corporatized, taking day-to-day managerial control out of government hands.

These compromises impaired performance, although performance appears to be systematically better, even under corporatized state-owned enterprises, than under direct state control. In this second stage, only Chile has achieved a competitive environment in its telecommunications.

However, in the same period when poor performance was providing a political imperative for reform, the technology of telecommunications was changing dramatically in both developed and developing countries. In an important sense, developing countries were confronted with the challenges of reforming their inefficient state-owned systems into competitive systems at the same time as developed countries were grappling with the problem of how to create an appropriate regulatory framework for a competitive telecommunications industry. As Noll points out, the question of whether telecommunications will be privatized, simply because it is no longer a natural monopoly, is not an easy one to answer even in developed countries, "in the presence of a powerful, entrenched monopoly." But most strategies tried by monopolists to maintain their position constitute "regulatory challenges in managing the transition to competition," and Noll demonstrates why the arguments against introducing competition into telecommunications are, in fact, "bad economics" and concludes that creating a competitive industry should be the objective of reform.

The challenge for the reformer, therefore, is to prevent the incumbent monopolist from extracting monopoly rents from consumers while creating conditions for a competitive industry. To complicate reform further, governments need to adopt and to commit to policies that investors will find credible and that will induce them to invest.

Noll's analysis of the challenges of finding an appropriate policy set starts with the observation that telecommunications is highly capital intensive, and historical failures to maintain investment in almost all developing countries have led to poor service. The first challenge, then, is to find mechanisms that promote adequate expenditure on equipment and maintenance so that service will improve in both quality and coverage. Of the three chief mechanisms available—price caps, cost of service, and franchising agreements—Noll concludes that for developing countries, most regulation will take a form very close to price-cap regulation. He proposes joint regulatory authorities that could regulate monopolies in several industries and several countries at the same time, although this has not yet been tried anywhere.

Noll then turns his attention to political constraints on good regulatory outcomes and considers ways in which likely difficulties can be reduced, focusing on the structure of the regulatory authority and its independence, although he also raises questions about the likelihood of finding an appropriate framework in poor developing countries.

A key issue in rate setting is cross-subsidization, the practice of setting high rates for some services to enable below-cost provision of services to favored groups. Noll explains why this practice is inconsistent with permitting entry (because entrants will "cherry pick" the high-price market) and hence with encouraging competition.

But to achieve competition, the difficult problem is to assure interconnection on reasonable terms to potential entrants, something the incumbent is naturally reluctant to do. Entrants can be thwarted by high connection charges or by inferior network service. No country has yet fully solved the service quality problem, and Noll surveys possible solutions. As he notes in his conclusion, because it is probably impossible to reform telecommunications into a perfectly competitive industry, we need empirical analyses of the benefits and costs of alternative reform efforts to ascertain which come closest to achieving efficient delivery of telecommunications services to users.

In contrast to telecommunications and other utilities, water supply (in conjunction with sewage) has important health and environmental externalities. Capital investments associated with the development of water supply systems are exceptionally long lived, making the problems associated with the credibility of government commitments even more intractable than for other utilities. Moreover, water sources vary widely from place to place, and when usage rates are high enough relative to water resources, water takes on the characteristics of a depletable resource. This consideration is pertinent when considering how much competition can be generated in the provision of safe water.

Noll, Shirley, and Cowan point out that when there is enough water to allow natural replenishment after water use, the problem of pricing amounts to charging enough that maintenance and delivery can be sustained. When, however, water resources are limited (as in the extreme case of Mexico City), pricing must charge for use of the depletable resource and induce usage at a rate that is sustainable given the rate at which water supplies are replenished.

Noll, Shirley, and Cowan analyze and contrast efforts to reform water supply pricing and operation in Abidjan, Côte d'Ivoire; Buenos Aires, Argentina; Conakry, Guinea; Lima, Peru; Mexico City, Mexico; and Santiago, Chile. Lima (because of water-borne disease) and Mexico City (because the water table underneath the city is sinking as it becomes depleted) have very high costs because of externalities, whereas water is plentiful for Abidjan and Buenos Aires. In Lima and Mexico City, reform was abandoned as too costly. In Conakry, "weak governance institutions" resulted in far smaller benefits than could otherwise have been achieved. In the three other cities, reforms resulted in significant savings.

The authors proceed to analyze these cases, noting that none attempted privatization (although it was tried in three of the fifty-three efforts at water supply reform listed in the World Bank's database). Service quality varied widely in the six cities, with underinvestment in maintenance and replacement having led to leakage, low pressure, and disruptions of service in some, especially Buenos Aires. Low pricing led to very high consumption per capita (e.g., 351 liters per day in Buenos Aires compared to 150 to 200 liters per day consumption in Europe).

Reforms varied, both in structure and in results, with the nature of the preexisting situation. In Buenos Aires, for example, the prereform operator had barely covered the costs of bad service but had been so inefficient that the new operator was able to invest considerably and yet earn a profit.

One of the chief issues in reforming water supply delivery systems pertains to politics. In Buenos Aires, where there was political pressure for reforms, they were carried out promptly; in Santiago and Lima, by contrast, decisions to reform were taken, but implementation began only very slowly and was finally abandoned. One difficulty was that large price increases would have been necessary, with significant political costs.[1] The

---

1. It should be noted, however, that poor service also entails political costs. Constituencies favoring improved service may, however, have less political influence than those opposing cost increases.

authors then assess the extent to which reforms were successful and estimate their net benefits, which were sizable even when the reforms were far from ideal. They note that their analysis covers very few cases of water supply reform and urge further analysis of these issues.

Part 3 of this volume covers "human issues" in economic policy reform. A first concern is labor markets. These important markets have two crucial and somewhat contradictory aspects: on one hand, labor is a critically important factor of production; on the other hand, workers are the people whose satisfaction is the objective of economic activity. A poorly functioning labor market can both thwart economic growth and prevent large groups of people from sharing in the gains from what economic growth there is.

Chapter 8, by Paul Schultz, therefore focuses on labor markets. Chapter 9, by Michael Kremer, assesses the ways in which education may be reformed. The dual nature of education is once again crucial: improving the quality of the labor force through more and better education can accelerate economic growth and the rate of improvement in living standards; it can also empower people, especially poor people, to obtain better earnings streams.

Chapter 10 is by Steven Matusz and David Tarr. One area where reforms started early enough that even some aspects of second-stage reforms are well understood is trade policy. Trade liberalization has taken place in a large number of countries, and there appears to be wide acceptance that trade liberalization is desirable in the early part of the reform process. Some degree of liberalization is relatively easy because it is accompanied by exchange rate depreciation that offsets the impact on import-competing firms.

Much has been learned about the trade liberalization process, but questions remain about the impact of trade liberalization on the costs of adjustment. Are these costs high enough to justify the fears of policymakers regarding trade liberalization? Matusz and Tarr focus on these issues, examining the ways in which trade liberalization can be effected with minimal impact on the relatively poor in society. Chapter 11 is by Jonathan Morduch, who examines policies to alleviate poverty and the degree to which these policies are consistent with accelerating growth. Several decades ago, many policymakers took the view that poverty alleviation conflicted with accelerating growth; today the vast majority in the development community accept that over the longer run, more rapid growth will enable more people to escape from poverty to rising and adequate standards of living. Morduch notes, however, that little research exists on such basic questions as to how to formulate policies in ways that will bring more households into growth processes. He then illustrates by examining two cases in which these questions are critical, microfinance and health policy.

Schultz's paper examines labor market regulations, other policies affecting employment and productivity, and their effects. As he points out, labor market regulations affect not only the efficiency with which the workforce is allocated at any point in time but also the degree to which there can be dynamic responses to changes in incentives. In the case of policy reform, this has an important implication: the ability of an economy to improve its performance once policies are reformed in other areas (such as trade) depends heavily on the extent to which labor is attracted to newly profitable endeavors.

But the needs for "static" efficiency and an ability to adjust to new incentives are only two reasons for concern with labor markets. The third reason has to do with equity considerations. Compensation differentials determine the returns to investment in human capital and set incentives for moves from less productive to more productive employment. But they also affect the plight of the very poor, and there are trade-offs between the efficiency—both static and dynamic—properties of an economy and the ways in which equity considerations may be handled.

Paul Schultz discusses these issues in the context of policy reform for labor markets in developing countries. Because the extent of empirical work is limited, Schultz draws on the experience of industrial countries, as well as economies in transition and developing countries, in setting forth the issues. These pertain not only to compensation differentials and the effects that taxation of labor in the formal sector has on allocation of labor but also to such issues as conditions governing layoffs and hours of work.[2] In many developing countries, unions appear to be as strong as, if not stronger than, their counterparts in developed countries. Labor laws protecting union rights to organize and bargain give unions a great deal of economic power. In poor countries, where many workers are excluded from unionized activities, the result is an apparent wedge of considerable magnitude between the remuneration of employees in the "formal sector," where employers are subject to labor legislation, and the "informal sector," where each employer has many fewer workers and most employers can safely ignore labor legislation. Workers in unionized sectors have become a "labor aristocracy," with unions defending the privileged position of

---

2. In most countries, there are taxes on employment (social security taxes, e.g., in the United States) where the intended use of the funds is to allocate expenditures in ways designed to increase workers' welfare. This raises the costs of hiring labor to employers in the "formal" sector of the economy. If workers receive goods and services that they value at the full amount of the tax paid, then presumably they would be indifferent between working in an establishment where they receive lower wages (by the amount of the taxes) and working in firms where no taxes are paid toward workers' benefits. But, as Schultz points out, in many countries, tax rates can be as high as 50 percent, while workers value the benefits at 10 to 20 percent of their take-home wages. The additional 30 to 40 percent cost to employers can be viewed, and acts, as a tax on employment in those sectors of the economy subject to that tax.

their members at the expense of workers excluded from opportunities in unionized sectors.

Other wage regulations—such as minimum wage legislation, prohibitions against the firing of workers, or the requirement that separated workers be very generously compensated—can also affect the functioning of the labor market in all three dimensions. Schultz points to the absence of a conclusive body of empirical research that identifies the relative costs to the economy of various interventions, and Julie Schaffner, in her comment, fully concurs with his conclusion that there would be a very large payoff for policymakers if we could better understand the costs and benefits of particular kinds of regulations in the three dimensions he outlines. Their research agenda is reviewed in the final chapter of this volume. Mario Blejer, by contrast, considers Schultz's comment that labor market reforms seem to be among the most difficult to instigate. He then provides an interesting account of Argentina's attempt to implement labor market reform.

As Schultz notes, a major determinant of the productivity of the labor force, and therefore of real wages, is the amount of human capital embodied in the labor force. Human capital can be acquired through formal schooling and through other mechanisms, including on-the-job training. Its importance has long been recognized. And as Michael Kremer points out, economists have long noted the desirability in many countries of increasing emphasis on education, especially at the primary and secondary levels. But as we enter the second stage of reforms, it is also important to learn how to improve the quality of education. Kremer's paper focuses on these second-stage issues.[3] While it may be desirable to increase educational expenditures, it is also important to use available resources effectively. Kremer reports on research attempting, among other things, to evaluate the effects of substituting more textbooks for more teachers, the effects of wall charts on performance, and the effects of provision of courses by radio, which seems to have improved mathematics education in Latin America.

Kremer then reports on aspects of school governance and the ways they affect education. Noting a high rate of teacher absenteeism (about 66 percent in India and 41 percent in Kenya), he discusses ways to improve teacher effort: providing teachers with incentive pay and providing parents and children with school choice. Kremer examines some of the difficulties and trade-offs involved in provision of teacher incentives: pay scales based on student test performance run the risk that weaker students will be forced to drop out or that teachers may choose to teach in "better"

3. In many countries, educational expenditures in the public sector appear to be heavily biased toward universities, while many children still have no access to primary education. Whether the reallocation of expenditure toward primary education is a first- or a second-stage issue is unclear.

schools, for example. He then examines experience with vouchers and notes that given their theoretical superiority (especially in light of problems with teacher incentives), "it is something of a mystery" that vouchers are not more frequently used. He therefore considers the political economy of public provision of education, including sociological possibilities, such as the need to teach children both cognitive skills and values[4] or the desire for instruction in a common language (where minority groups, if permitted to self-segregate by vouchers, might opt for instruction in their own languages). Kremer concludes by calling for much greater research efforts to understand both the determinants (and trade-offs between inputs) of educational outcomes and the factors affecting the preference for public schooling.

In discussing Kremer's paper, Anjini Kochar takes issue with the proposition that we know enough about the determinants of human capital acquisition. She focuses on a set of significant questions, aimed at better understanding behavior with respect to school enrollments and the quality of educational outcomes, the answers to which could prove extremely helpful in enabling policymakers to make informed choices among alternatives aimed at improving educational quality, quantity, and outcomes. These suggestions are discussed further in the final chapter.

In his discussion, Paul Schultz offers the human capital approach as an alternative to Kremer's emphasis on improving quality for a given cost. In the human capital approach, rates of return for schooling of different types are calculated, and Schultz gives a brief indication of the range of these studies as well as of some of the questions they raise. These rates of return are then used to evaluate how resources might be reallocated between various categories of schooling to increase total returns. As Schultz concludes, the two approaches are complementary, and each has something to offer educational policy reformers.

In their paper, Matusz and Tarr focus on a key second-stage issue for trade liberalization. They note the strong consensus emerging in favor of the proposition that trade liberalization benefits growth and is obviously worthwhile in the long run. But they also point out the reluctance of policymakers to embark on trade liberalization. They believe this reluctance is explained by concern over the costs of transition from a protectionist regime to a more open trade regime.

But the costs and benefits of trade liberalization are themselves functions of how trade liberalization is undertaken, what other policies are in place during the liberalization process (especially in the labor market), and what kind of social safety net (such as unemployment compensation) is in place. Once again, policymakers are by now well aware of the desir-

---

4. Kremer notes that there may also be practical difficulties, such as "kickbacks" by schools to parents sending their children there with vouchers.

ability of trade liberalization, but second-stage research is needed to learn more about the relative effectiveness of alternative policies supporting liberalization policies.

Matusz and Tarr start by discussing the analytical framework they use for estimating adjustment costs. They then marshal the available evidence on adjustment costs after trade liberalization. Much, but certainly not all, of the evidence comes from industrialized countries. Almost all individual studies show that adjustment costs are small relative to the present value of benefits—benefit-cost ratios are generally over 20:1. Interestingly, concerns about unemployment of displaced workers seem somewhat overblown, as the evidence indicates that manufacturing employment reaches or exceeds its level at the time of trade liberalization within a year.

Much less research has been done on adjustment costs in developing countries, but what there is supports the same general conclusions (see the final chapter for more on these needed research directions). Matusz and Tarr then turn to macroeconomic issues surrounding trade liberalization and examine the literature on outcomes in the short run—the time period during which they believe adjustment costs would be incurred—for macroeconomic stability, including inflation. They note that all observers recognize the importance of achieving an appropriate exchange rate regime and reining in fiscal deficits if trade liberalization is to be successful and accompanied by macroeconomic stability. Matusz and Tarr end their paper by calling for more research on adjustment issues, a subject addressed in the final chapter of this volume.

In her comment, Julie Schaffner takes issue with some of Matusz and Tarr's conclusions. In particular, she believes that longer run costs of trade liberalization might include worsening income inequality, especially in middle-income countries unable to compete with much poorer countries in world markets for unskilled-labor-intensive products. She believes that research is needed to ascertain the long-run costs of trade liberalization if it entails an increase in inequality of the income distribution.

Morduch's examination of health and microfinance regimes first demonstrates that overall economic growth is generally shared by the poorest groups in society; nonetheless there are significant opportunities for orienting reforms in ways that bring the poor into the growth process more rapidly. He notes the strong associations between GDP per capita and child health, but these same analyses show that direct investments have also been able to make big differences. Morduch contrasts different approaches to health care that focus on saving the greatest number of lives at least expense. These include improving education, combating virulent communicable diseases, encouraging preventive care, and improving infrastructure (especially sanitation). He then points to the large number of questions these prescriptions raise in terms of implementation alternatives. Likewise, with microfinance, examination of programs to date indicates that microfinance has failed to meet expectations with respect to poverty alleviation, especially because most programs have failed to cover their costs, and there are serious doubts as to whether the benefits of these interventions exceed those of alternative uses of the same funds. Finally, Morduch raises important questions about the definition of poverty that is most meaningful from the viewpoint of research and policy actions and asserts the need for new poverty measures.

In her comment, Anjini Kochar agrees with Morduch that a major means for improving the lot of the poor is economic growth. She questions some of the details of his discussion and policy conclusions on health care and microfinance, in particular, and believes that part of the reason for inaction has been lack of agreement among researchers. In addition, she sets forth additional questions that should form part of the second-stage agenda.

In part 4 of this volume, macroeconomic policies are addressed. In the first generation of reforms, these issues would almost certainly have been placed at the beginning of the volume, as central to any reform effort. But by now, it is well accepted that some degree of macroeconomic stabilization is an essential prerequisite for the success of many other reforms, and a great deal has been learned in the first generation.

Each of the chapters in this part starts by acknowledging progress in the first stage of reforms and our understanding of it. However, as Vito Tanzi notes in chapter 12, while the idea of budgetary reform is accepted in principle, attention must turn to how reforms may be implemented in other than ideal circumstances. Tanzi assumes for the purposes of his paper that the national budget reflects national objectives. But he proceeds to identify a variety of ways in which difficulties arise. Center-state relations may complicate the budgetary process enormously, as has happened in a number of countries. Fiscal institutions may be highly inefficient at collecting tax revenue, at maintaining records for welfare payments, or at other tasks. Moreover, a number of practices, such as "directed lending," are quasi-fiscal in nature and thwart the efficient operation of fiscal institutions.

In chapter 13 Sebastian Edwards and Miguel Savastano examine what we know and what we need to learn about exchange rates and exchange rate regimes. Most countries, developed and developing alike, adhered to (nominal) fixed exchange rate regimes for the first several decades after the Second World War, although many developing countries used quantitative restrictions on imports and exchange controls to regulate their balance of payments. Only with trade liberalization and the elimination of quantitative restrictions in the 1970s and 1980s did exchange rate regimes begin to be seen as key to the efficient allocation of resources between tradable and nontradable sectors of the economy.

Edwards and Savastano then review the alternative forms of exchange rate regime, ranging from a "pure" float at one extreme to a complete elimination of domestic currency and "dollarization" at the other extreme. In between are such regimes as "nominal anchor" exchange rate policies (under which the authorities may adjust the nominal exchange rate but do so by a proportion less than the inflation differential between themselves and the rest of the world as a means of reducing domestic inflation), "crawling pegs" (under which the exchange rate is adjusted in proportion with inflation differentials to maintain a constant real rate), and currency boards (under which the domestic currency is fully backed by foreign exchange). Edwards and Savastano also examine the behavior of exchange rates during policy reform periods as well as in the longer term. Despite the volume of research to date, they conclude that a great deal has still to be learned about the determinants of exchange rate behavior under alternative macroeconomic regimes and institutions. Their research agenda is discussed in the final chapter of this volume.

The final paper in part 4 covers a topic to which the attention of policymakers and academics alike has forcefully been turned since the Asian crisis. Frederic Mishkin assesses financial sector reform and what we need to learn about it in chapter 14. He starts by considering the role of asymmetric information as a rationale for government intervention in financial markets, focusing on the roles of adverse selection, free riders, and moral hazard as problems confronting anyone considering the organization and functioning of a financial system.

He then considers alternative policies that can mitigate these problems. Increased information and disclosure from financial institutions can let individuals better monitor these institutions, but there are limits, especially since the free-rider problem will lead to underresearch by individuals. Capital adequacy requirements (set by risk class of asset) can be used to reduce incentives for taking on risk. But of course, a safety net is still needed, which in turn entails other dilemmas that create a need for supervision.

There are also issues pertaining to the prevention of financial crises, some of which are particularly relevant because financial crises have been linked, at least in the minds of some, to financial and capital market liberalizations. Linkages between the financial sector and lending booms and currency crises are then considered, as well as the effect of devaluation from a fixed nominal exchange rate on the position of banks. Mishkin then addresses the various components of financial sector reform: adequate resources and authority for bank regulators, adequate independence but with accountability for regulatory agencies, prompt corrective action where needed, means to assess risk management, limits on the too-big-to-fail instincts of regulators, restrictions on connected lending, appropriate accounting and disclosure standards, adequate legal and judicial systems including bankruptcy provisions, and market-based incentives for financial institutions. He also considers issues associated with the entry of foreign banks and with the use of capital controls. A final issue, which was an important contributor to several of the East Asian crises, concerns the appropriate regime within which debt in foreign currencies may be incurred. Clearly, recovery from crisis (especially if devaluation is part of the reform package, as it often must be) is easier if there is little or no foreign-denominated debt. Structuring incentives to discourage the use of foreign-denominated debt is therefore also part of any policy reform package. Mishkin then briefly addresses issues of monetary policy, exchange rate regime (discussed by Edwards and Savastano), and financial deregulation in the context of his earlier arguments, concluding with his agenda for future research.

Part 5 contains two papers, one by Joseph Stiglitz and the other by Anne Krueger. In chapter 15 Joseph Stiglitz views economic policy reform from the perspective of the World Bank and concludes that while there is great need for additional reforms, much of the world is suffering from "reform fatigue" caused in part by partial and ill-thought-out first-stage reforms.

Chapter 16 then synthesizes analyses from the earlier chapters to formulate an agenda for research. As should be evident from the brief descriptions of papers given above, much of the emphasis is on the effects of various institutions and incentives on responses to alternative policies and on issues of implementation in a second-best world.

2

Interests, Institutions, and Policy Reform

Stephan Haggard

The literature on the political economy of policy reform is now vast, unwieldy, and, in typical academic fashion, increasingly balkanized.[1] In addition to a growing body of work on the political economy of long-term growth (which I will for the most part ignore), there are now literatures (and even review essays) on a range of specific policy issues from fiscal and monetary policy (Perotti 1997) and central banking (Eijffinger and de Haan 1996), to trade policy reform (Nelson 1988, 1998; Milner 1998), to privatization (Waterbury 1993; World Bank 1995, chap. 4) and regulatory reform (Levy and Spiller 1996). While some of these literatures have primarily addressed the OECD countries, particularly those on macroeconomic policy, the findings are of increasing relevance to new democracies in Eastern Europe, Latin America, Asia, and Africa as well. A number of collective research projects have implicitly rejected the analysis of particular policies by examining broader reform packages through comparative case studies (Nelson 1990; Bates and Krueger 1993; Bresser Pereira, Maraval, and Przeworski 1993; Dornbusch and Edwards 1993; Haggard and Webb 1994; Williamson 1994; Nelson 1994; Haggard and Kaufman 1995). Interesting debates are continuing or newly launched on a variety of factors that affect the policy reform process, such as democracy and democratization (Haggard and Webb 1994; Haggard and Kaufman 1995), corruption (Rose-Ackerman 1998), and federalism (Weingast 1995). Moreover, this work is taking place across disciplines, and while there are important signs

Stephan Haggard is professor in the Graduate School of International Relations and Pacific Studies at the University of California, San Diego.
1. Two particularly good reviews of the literature are Rodrik (1996) and Tommasi and Velasco (1996).

of convergence, differences in intellectual style and method persist among economists, political scientists, and sociologists.

Confronted with this complexity, some strategy of simplification is required, and I have chosen a particularly gross one; I distinguish approaches to policy reform that focus primarily on the role of social preferences and interest groups and those that emphasize the importance of institutional arrangements. The modeling of any political system requires an integration of these two key elements, but there is some utility in this distinction, including in organizing the lessons that can be drawn from recent scholarship.

Approaches that emphasize the role of interests see policy reform as a coalition-building process (Waterbury 1989). Successful reform results from the formation of a minimum winning coalition and the defeat, or at least acquiescence, of those groups opposed to reform. These theories naturally direct our attention to issues of strategy and tactics; the great debates center on how the design of the reforms themselves affects political support for the program and thus successful implementation and stability. These theories also raise the thorny question of why policy preferences might shift, for example, as a result of crises or of learning.

Those looking at institutions focus more attention on constitutional design, the decision-making process, and the incentives facing politicians. An advantage of this work is to see the politics of reform not simply in terms of discrete policy changes but as requiring institutional and administrative reforms that will ensure that policy making is decisive, efficient, and credible over the longer run. The great debate in this area centers on the advantages of concentrated authority and the "insulation" or "autonomy" of government as opposed to decision-making processes that provide for multiple veto gates ("checks and balances") and consultation of various sorts.

2.1   Interest Groups and Economic Reform

The distortionary effects of interest group pressures are at the heart of a number of political models by economists, including the literature on rent seeking (Krueger 1974), capture models of regulation (Peltzman 1976), and endogenous tariff theory (Nelson 1988). Political scientists have proceeded along similar lines (Bates 1981, 1983 on African agricultural pricing policy; Frieden 1991 on exchange rates; Frieden and Rogowski 1996 on trade). However, no name is more closely associated with the perspective that interest groups drive and distort economic policy than Mancur Olson (1982). Although well known, the logic of Olson's *Rise and Decline of Nations* makes a good starting point.

Drawing on his earlier work, Olson argued that interest groups could serve their members either by making society as a whole more productive, which would allow the income of the group to rise even if its share remained the same, or by obtaining a larger share of output for itself. Olson's pessimistic conclusion is that the second strategy typically dominates the first. Only under the relatively restrictive condition that interest groups are relatively "encompassing" will they internalize the costs of their behavior (see also Olson 1993).

The interest group approach raises two central problems, one theoretical and one empirical. The theoretical problem is that Olson's setup can imply that groups favor policies that not only lower aggregate social welfare but their own welfare as well. If I know that rent seeking on the part of a number of groups can have systemic effects, for example, on macroeconomic stability, it calls into question the rationality of rent seeking in the first place. Much effort has been spent on solving this problem, typically by invoking collective action problems of various sorts. For example, interest groups may be unable to agree on how to share the costs of stabilization. Legislators may be unable to agree on how to "divide the dollar" or share spending cuts.

The attention thrown at this issue immediately raises a second one: if interest groups are such potent barriers to policy change, how do we explain the near ubiquity of reform that has taken place in the developing and former socialist economies over the past two decades? Interest group analysis is typically static; it explains why a given policy regime constitutes an equilibrium, implying that all agents have optimized over their political as well as economic strategies. But reform is about changes in policy regime and thus requires the introduction of some dynamics. These have been supplied in a number of ways, including through the introduction of bargaining among groups, crises, and corresponding changes in the cost of the status quo. Particular attention has also been paid to how the design of reform packages, including their speed, comprehensiveness, and the extent of compensation, affects the dynamics of political support over time.

2.1.1   Collective Dilemmas among Interest Groups and the Role of Crises

The first wave of papers on the political economy of reform by economists in the 1990s was preoccupied with the question of why stabilizations were delayed. These papers were motivated by the unsustainable accumulation of public debt in Latin America in the 1980s and the very high or hyperinflations in Argentina, Brazil, Peru, and Bolivia. These papers rejected any suggestion that actors were myopic, as well as the common argument that reform is delayed because it is costly in the short run. As Alesina (1994, 48) pointed out, this too is irrational since the longer a country waits, the more costly stabilization becomes.

The critical papers that established the broad outlines of the new approach were Alesina and Drazen's (1991) model of a "war of attrition," models of fiscal policy as a commons problem, and a body of work on the economic consequences of political instability. In the Alesina and Drazen model, delay is the result of conflict between groups over how the costs of stabilization will be allocated. It is assumed that these costs will be borne unequally, with one group paying a higher share of the taxes or lost income than the other. The groups are also heterogeneous in their preferences; one group bears a higher cost from macroeconomic instability than the other, but that information is private. Given asymmetric information, the group experiencing greater costs from failure to stabilize has no incentive to reveal its identity; rather, it is rational to wait, hoping that the other will concede first. Stabilization occurs when one group "throws in the towel," which happens when the marginal costs of conceding are equal to the marginal costs of holding out (see also Labán and Sturzenegger 1994a; Drazen 1996).

Models of fiscal policy as a common pool problem by Velasco (1994, 1998) and Tornell (1995) have a slightly different structure, but the same general flavor. Two rent-seeking groups treat public revenue—raised through taxes on a third, unorganized "group"—as a commons and decide how much to "graze." They can either extract a large amount from the fisc, in which case public debt increases, or they can exercise restraint, in which case the government's net wealth remains unchanged. As in the tragedy of the commons, each group has an incentive to overgraze because restraint will simply be exploited by the other party. Overgrazing dominates until there is nothing left to take; at that point, the equilibrium strategy shifts to self-restraint, that is, policy reform. Tornell's (1995) version has a nastier, *sauve-qui-peut* element; as fiscal resources diminish, each group may be willing to pay a cost to actively block the access of the other group to rents. If both groups attempt this strategy, both lose influence to the state, which gains autonomy and can then act in the interests of the unorganized by instituting reform.

A cognate class of models extends the collective action problem across time. Governments representing different interest groups or classes alternate in power. The time horizon of each government is shortened by the prospect that it will at some point be replaced by another government representing opposed interests. The greater the likelihood of a change in government in the next period, the more divergent the preferences of actors, and the shorter the period between changes of government, the more inflationary macroeconomic policy will be (see, e.g., Cukierman, Edwards, and Tabellini 1992; Roubini 1991). These models also offer an explanation for the inflation-stabilization cycles that appeared in some Latin American countries (Dornbusch and Edwards 1993) and now seem to be plaguing Russia and several former Soviet republics as well.

It is worth digressing briefly on the informational assumptions in these models, since the logic of interest group analysis hinges critically on how groups understand and update their preferences.[2] The common pool models of Velasco and Tornell are full information models. Alesina and Drazen, Drazen and Grilli, and other models in the war-of-attrition vein rely on asymmetric information to get their results. Groups are certain about their own payoffs, but uncertain about the reservation points of their opponents, and it is this uncertainty that induces groups to hold out. It is equally plausible that the distribution of costs from the reform are not known precisely, and that this general uncertainty plays a role in delaying reform. Fernandez and Rodrik (1991) developed this insight formally (see also Labán and Sturzenegger 1994a). Fernandez and Rodrik showed that trade liberalization can fail if ex post winners are uncertain ex ante about their identity as winners.

How do we assess the utility of these models? First, it is important to note that despite the invocation of collective action problems, the key mechanism generating reform in the war-of-attrition, common pool, and instability models is economic deterioration; groups change their policy preferences as a result of the rising cost of the status quo. This insight has led to a series of papers that have tried to identify more precisely the way crisis affects veto-wielding groups. In Drazen and Grilli (1993), monetization of the budget deficit (a distortionary tax) leads to high inflation and more rapid agreement among the contending parties on the necessity of reform (nondistortionary tax increases). Several papers on trade policy have made similar arguments. Frieden and Rogowski (1996) argued that exogenous technological changes have brought about a reduction in the cost of trade, thus increasing the opportunity costs of protection for those groups that are potential beneficiaries of liberalization, such as capitalists and skilled workers in advanced industrial states and unskilled workers in the developing world.

Rodrik (1994) used crisis to explain another stylized fact: that stabilization has frequently been accompanied with a wider package of reforms, including trade liberalization. Broader reform is possible according to Rodrik because the benefits of stabilization swamp the redistributive effects of trade reform. Rodrik did not really explain why negatively affected groups would go along with such packages; they would presumably prefer that policies be unbundled. But if one assumes that reformers within the government have some agenda-setting power—which interest group models typically do not—policies that interest groups want, such as stabilization, can be traded for those that reformers want. Kaufman, Bazdresh, and Herredia (1994) found compelling evidence of just such a bargain in their analysis of Mexico's reforms.

An empirical test of the crisis-begets-reform proposition by Bruno and Easterly (1996) found that the proposition holds, but only when "crisis"

2. The following is indebted to Nelson (1998).

is defined in terms of inflation, and then only if inflation is particularly high (over 40 percent); slow growth, even where persistent, does not appear to lead to reform. Indeed, Anne Krueger (1992) has developed a model of a "vicious circle" of economic deterioration in which misguided government policy and corresponding poor performance spawns interest groups that lobby for ever more distortionary interventions in the misguided belief that they will offset the deleterious effects of the previous ones. In this model, poor performance breeds, not reform, but more poor performance. Similar observations are of long standing in the trade policy literature; economic downturns are associated with increasing pressures for protection, not further liberalization (e.g., Cassing, McKeown, and Ochs 1986).

There are several ways to reconcile these competing arguments about the effects of crisis. It may be easier for firms and households to adjust to a slow deterioration in aggregate output than to a sharp change in the price level; the latter may generate more protest (the "IMF riot"), but also more tacit support for reform. We clearly need more survey work to reach firmer conclusions on how economic conditions affect political attitudes. The handful of studies we do have reach surprisingly ambiguous results that call into question any simple relation between economic performance and attitudes. Przeworski (1994) showed that support for reform in Poland was negatively correlated with unemployment. However, a study of Mexico by Kaufman and Zuckerman (1998) using survey data found no connection between support for reform and self-assessments of either current well-being or future economic prospects. Rather, support for reform was a function of party identification; citizens who identified themselves with the PRI supported reform even if they thought that it might affect them negatively. It should also not be assumed that poor economic conditions necessarily translate in an unambiguous way into political behaviors and attitudes. Ekiert and Kubik examined various forms of collective action in Eastern European countries and found that "Poland had a higher magnitude of protest than Slovakia and Hungary, although its economy performed better than the economies of the other two countries and although *Poles were far more satisfied* than were Slovaks or Hungarians with the results of the post-communist economic reforms" (1998, 571; emphasis in original).

If the explanation of reform is simply that groups change their policy preferences, then the puzzle that the "delayed stabilization" literature sets out to solve may be less than puzzling. The evidence is now overwhelming that stabilization and macroeconomic stability yield positive benefits in terms of aggregate growth not only in the long run but often quite rapidly. Is it really that surprising that high or hyperinflation would generate widespread support for stabilization even among those who had benefited from fiscal and monetary profligacy in the past?

The political implications are clear, but underresearched; although the assumption is widespread that initiating reform is politically costly, we have few studies that systematically test the proposition. Those that we do have show that reformers may be taking fewer risks than is commonly thought. In a sample of fourteen "intensive adjusters" with competitive electoral systems, Nelson (1992) found that only half of the parties initiating reform suffered electoral defeat as a result. Geddes (1994) found a similar rate of defeat in a sample of eleven middle-income countries in which working class incomes fell following reform.

In sum, crises do change interest group dynamics, but perhaps not in the way suggested by the models under review. Crises may weaken interest groups; there is a substantial literature in political science noting the quiescence of labor in the face of wide-ranging reform (see, e.g., Greskovits 1998 on Eastern Europe; Nelson 1994 on Latin America and Eastern Europe). But a more convincing model may be that crises lead to Bayesian learning about the appropriate model of the world, a recognition of the unsustainability of the status quo, and corresponding changes in preferences (Krueger 1992; Tommasi and Velasco 1996).

Second, the decision-making process in these models requires close scrutiny. In most war-of-attrition and common pool models, all groups hold veto power over the reform, which therefore can only come when all but one "concedes" by agreeing to pay the costs of adjustment.[3] But such consensus is not in principle required in a democracy to change the policy status quo, and a number of reform mongers, most notably Roger Douglas (1990) and Jeffrey Sachs (1994), have warned about the costs of seeking it. In the crudest model of democratic rule, all that is required is a minimum winning coalition; depending on electoral rules, this may not even entail a majority. As Alesina himself admitted, the concept of a "concession" may encompass not only a rejection of confrontational tactics on the part of interest groups but electoral defeat of the party or parties favoring the status quo (1994, 51).

The idea that reform comes when status quo incumbents are replaced by new reformist governments suggests a subtly different political dynamic than that in the interest group models just reviewed. As Geddes (1994), Heller, Keefer, and McCubbins (1998), and Schamis (1999) have argued, policy can change as a result of a change in ruling coalition that represents a different group of interests (see also Rodrik 1994, 81) or a change in the support base of the existing coalition, *even if the overall configuration of interest groups remains unaltered.*

These points have been made in a number of monographs on particular

---

3. In Tornell's succinct, if tautological, formulation, government can stabilize or initiate trade reform "only if it does not encounter opposition from interest groups that have the power to block the reform" (1995, 54).

countries, but studies of Zambia by Bates and Collier (1993), of Chile by Silva (1993), and of Argentine and Mexican populism by Gibson (1997) illustrate the point. Bates and Collier showed that the barriers to economic reform in Zambia did not reside in the structure of interests per se. Important productive forces in the country—indeed nearly *all* of the productive forces in the economy, including farmers, businessmen, and those who drew incomes in their enterprises—would have benefited from reforms. The crucial point is that these groups were marginalized within the ruling party; reform could only come from a regime change that empowered alternative groups. Silva (1993) made the same point with respect to the Pinochet reforms, tracing how alliances between technocrats and particular segments of the domestic private sector shaped the nature of policy with respect to banking reform and the opening of the capital account. Edward Gibson's (1997) study of how historically populist governments in Argentina and Mexico initiated wide-ranging reforms proceeded along a similar path. Gibson showed how demographic and occupational changes, including rural to urban migration and a decline in the proportion of workers linked to party-dominated unions, forced the Peronists and the PRI to reforge new "metropolitan" coalitions. These coalitions included large businesses and even portions of the labor movement who were beneficiaries of at least some of the reforms.

More generally, the conception of interest groups as veto players who oppose reform is limiting and makes policy change more, rather than less, mysterious. In a setting characterized by a myriad of distortions, an interest group that seeks a large share of total output for itself does not necessarily reduce efficiency as Olson contended; to the contrary, responding to the demands of exporters, agricultural producers, the informal sector, and labor-intensive manufacturers would improve aggregate social welfare and probably the distribution of income as well. The problem is thus not that there are too many interest groups but that there are too few, of the wrong sort, and facing too little effective competition from groups with divergent social interests.[4] Olson would have argued that the skewed distribution of interest groups is endogenous to the logic of group formation and that an efficiency-enhancing interest group is an oxymoron. But as Schamis (1999) argued forcefully, exogenous shocks and crises can change the relative power of interest groups. And as I will argue below, the entire interest group logic ignores the role of political entrepreneurs and institutions in organizing broader coalitions of interests.

The policy implications of this class of models are far from clear. Few would subscribe to the radical notion that the way to generate reform is to spawn crises. The most important policy lesson is that uncertainty

---

4. See Becker (1983) for a theoretical argument on why competition among interest groups serves to reduce rents.

about the distribution of costs can be an important barrier to reform. For example, in Alesina and Drazen (1991), the more unequally the costs of stabilization are distributed, the greater the incentive to wait and thus the greater the delay in supporting reform. If costs are shared equally, stabilization would occur immediately since there is no gain from being the "winner." Fernandez and Rodrik (1991) reached somewhat similar conclusions; if uncertainty were reduced, there would be less resistance to reform.

These observations suggest that reforms have elements of an assurance game, in which groups will contribute to the costs of the reform effort but only if they know that others are doing the same. Escaping the costly conflicts that are implicit in wars of attrition and commons problems requires coordination, credible signals, and assurances, which various institutional arrangements and compensatory policies can provide.

2.1.2 Tactical Approaches: Speed, Comprehensiveness, and Compensation

The models described so far take the nature of the reform as given and focus on some highly stylized distributive consequences that flow from it. But the design of reforms is not a given; fiscal adjustment can take place via tax increases or spending cuts, trade reform is an almost infinitely divisible good, and countries have experimented with privatization schemes with more or less involvement on the part of incumbent management and workers. Three broad lines of inquiry have emerged in the discussion of program design. The question of *sequencing* centers on whether reforms are best launched all at once in the form of packages of policies or need to be introduced in some particular order to be most effective. *Speed* refers to the question of whether any particular reform should be introduced rapidly or gradually. Despite the utility of this distinction, issues of sequencing and speed can be discussed together since positions on the two tend to converge; those arguing for gradualism are also likely to see political benefits in a sequencing of reforms. The third general issue is the role *compensatory mechanisms* play in the reform process. Drawing on the Western European experience, social democrats argue that the transition to the market will avoid undesirable political consequences and be more equitable and therefore sustainable over the long run if accompanied by appropriate social policies (Przeworski 1991; Bresser Pereira et al. 1993).

Much of the debate about the speed and sequencing of reforms centers on purely economic issues, such as the complementarity of different reforms, but the political advantages of rapid as opposed to gradual and sequenced reform has constituted an important leitmotif in the literature on the transition from socialism. Sachs and his coauthors and collaborators were early in making the argument for rapid reform, based largely on the Polish case (Lipton and Sachs 1990; Berg and Sachs 1992; Sachs 1994). Portes (1991), Murrell (1992), and Aghion and Blanchard (1994) expressed concerns and urged gradualism. On both sides, political economy arguments were invoked.

Formal theoretical treatments followed. Papers by Dewatripont and Roland (1991, 1992, 1995) and Wei (1998) made the case for gradualism, while Murphy, Shleifer, and Vishny (1992), Rodrik (1995), Roland and Verdier (1994), and Martinelli and Tommasi (1997) pointed out its drawbacks. It is important to underscore that both sides of the debate were largely in agreement on the desirability of rapid economic transformation; they differed on the question of what strategy would achieve this objective *taking into account the possibility that any reform initiative was subject to the possibility of political reversal.*

These papers also relied on an interest group logic, but several general features distinguished them from those discussed in the previous section. First, although Martinelli and Tommasi (1997) explicitly adopt the veto player approach, most other work in this vein saw reform as requiring support (or at least acquiescence) typically modeled as a simple majority in a referendum. In such a setup, groups—even "powerful" groups—do not wield vetoes over policy; opponents of reform can be politically defeated. The central trick is therefore to show how support for reform evolves over time under alternative strategies, and to identify the conditions under which it becomes irreversible.

The second important feature of these models is that policy is not fully endogenous. This is particularly true for big bang approaches, which ignore altogether what Roland (1994) has called ex ante political constraints. The government is assumed to have some freedom of choice in the first period, which might be thought of as the power to set the agenda, to write the language in a referendum, or to decree a policy that can only be vetoed by a majority vote ex post. This initial policy then sets in train structural changes in the economy, which have dynamic effects on patterns of support and the subsequent course of policy. Rather than policy being the result of interest group pressures, actors' preferences over time are partly explained by policy choices.

Several examples provide the flavor of the models supportive of gradualism and sequencing. Wei's model posits an economy with three sectors: an export sector and two import-competing ones. A proposal for liberalization of both import-competing sectors would be voted down, but the removal of trade barriers in one of the import-competing sectors could garner support from the other two sectors. A key feature of Wei's model is that partial reform does not stall because of the reallocation of labor and changing policy preferences following the partial reform. In the second period, the export sector is larger, and the first import-competing sector to be liberalized now supports liberalization of the second import-competing sector. Liberalizing both import-competing sectors at once would have been politically impossible, but sequencing or gradualism allows for the full opening of trade.

In contrast to Wei, the models by Dewatripont and Roland rely on informational asymmetries (1991, 1992) or on general uncertainty (1995) about the outcome of reforms. With respect to speed, they noted that the difficulty of reversing reforms once taken is often cited as an advantage by advocates of big bang. However, such irreversibility makes reforms more difficult to launch if there is uncertainty about their effects; gradualism allows reversal at lower cost and thus broader support ex ante. Dewatripont and Roland also tackled a second argument of big bang advocates: that it is important to package reforms because of complementarities among them. They made a case for gradualism even in the presence of complementarities. They assumed that following any initial reform, the existence of complementarities implies that publics have a choice either to reverse the reform of the previous period or to accept new ones. If the first reform is successful, publics will accept further reform, even if there is some uncertainty about its effects, if not doing so implies a high reversal cost; by contrast if the first reform does not succeed, the reform process stops or shifts into reverse.

The most important empirical defenses of gradualism come from analyses of the Chinese case (McMillan and Naughton 1992; Gelb, Jefferson, and Singh 1993), and they also contain an implicit political economy logic. The basic idea is that in an economy characterized by a range of policy-induced distortions, partial reform can generate pressures for further reform. McMillan and Naughton (1992), for example, explored the consequences of a policy mix that included delayed privatization, a two-track pricing system, and free entry for private firms. Given pricing policy, private entry was highly attractive and profitability of private firms was high. These conditions in turn encouraged both investment and saving. Managers of uncompetitive state-owned firms responded by seeking further subsidies, but this was not altogether bad since it provided a social safety net during the early stage of the transition. Managers of potentially profitable state-owned firms responded by making productivity improvements (the market response) but also by lobbying for greater managerial autonomy (the political response); both the market and political responses propelled reform forward.

A number of papers on China have added a spatial dimension to this analysis by looking at the effects of uneven reform across jurisdictions, a particular form of gradualism. In an analysis of Chinese-style federalism by Montinola, Qian, and Weingast (1995), for example, firms in one jurisdiction face restrictions (which might be thought of as a tax) while those in the second jurisdiction do not. Firms from the first jurisdiction lose market share, and both capital and labor move to the less regulated jurisdiction. This in turn pushes firms and politicians in the first jurisdiction to lobby for deregulation (see also Shirk 1993).

If defenses of gradualism showed how it could permit the initiation of reform or lead to greater political support over time, critics pointed out

various ways in which partial reform had perverse economic consequences, including continuing opportunities for rent seeking and slower
growth, which in turn have the political effect of slowing support for further reform over time (Murphy et al. 1992; Rodrik 1995).

In an important paper that combines electoral and interest group logic,
Joel Hellman (1998) argued that postsocialist governments that remained
in the hands of Communist parties or strongmen are more likely to undertake only partial reforms, which then makes them more vulnerable to capture by nomenklatura capitalists and newly rich oligarchs; it is not the
losers from reform that constitute the barriers to a more complete transition to the market but the "winners" from partial reform. Critics of the
Chinese model make similar arguments. The virtuous circle outlined by
the gradualists has now run its course, and powerful political forces are
blocking important reforms, for example, of the legal system, that are required for China to continue to grow over the long run (Sachs 1993; Woo
et al. 1994; Sachs and Woo 1994).

Proponents of rapid reform also argue that it too generates political
support, particularly where macroeconomic instability is great. It is not
coincidental that the defense of rapid reform approaches has typically
drawn on cases with high or hyperinflation, such as Bolivia, Poland, and
Russia. For proponents of speed and comprehensiveness, good economics
makes for good politics; the more quickly reforms are undertaken, the
more rapid the return to growth and the broader the political support for
the reforms. Much of the debate among economists on the politics of reform is therefore reduced to the issue of whether the reforms have the
desired effect on aggregate economic performance.

However, defenders of rapid transition also recognize that it is not just
aggregate growth that matters but the distributive implications of the
reform, the corresponding level of support that they garner (Przeworski
1991), and what Roland (1994) called ex post political constraints—the
fact that an initiative once taken can be reversed. These considerations do
not necessarily defeat the case for moving quickly, however. Roland and
Verdier (1994) argued that the sustainability of reform (they used the case
of privatization) rests on a "critical mass"; if the level of privatization is
not high enough at the outset, the profitability of private entry drops and
investment is deterred by fears of policy reversal. Martinelli and Tommasi
(1997) offered an argument not just for speed with respect to a particular
reform but for comprehensiveness and the packaging of reforms as well.
If packaged appropriately, measures that hurt a particular group can be
offset by gains from other measures so that all groups are made net beneficiaries.

Finally, "large" reforms may have important signaling and credibility
effects quite apart from their other advantages. In a game in which investors are unsure of the real identity of the government, Rodrik (1989) ar-

gued that "overshooting" can be used to reveal a true reformist identity and thus generate a stronger investment and supply response to reforms than would otherwise be the case.

Given the prima facie plausibility of these arguments on both sides, much hinges on the empirical literature. Ideally, we would want to know the answer to three simple questions: What are the economic consequences of different strategies? Do those different strategies and their economic consequences generate different levels of political support? Does the level of political support affect the extent and integrity of the reform effort? However, there is surprisingly little systematic evidence on the second and third questions, which for our purposes are the most important.

Economists have spent a considerable amount of time debating the first question, but with surprisingly little consensus and even bitter disagreement on the relevance of the Chinese experience. Part of the problem is that the empirical referents of "rapid reform" and "gradualism" are far from clear. Anders Aslund's (1995) book *How Russia Became a Market Economy* provides an example. As the title suggests, Aslund believed that Russia became a market economy some time in the early 1990s, and he attributed that achievement to rapid market-oriented reform, particularly with respect to privatization. But to any disinterested reader, his empirical chapters are case studies of political vacillation and hesitation, driven by the opposition of very powerful groups to the real and perceived costs of rapid adjustment. Does Russia provide evidence of the political advantages of a big bang (the creation of a private sector with a long-term interest in stable property rights), evidence of an unsuccessful big bang (misguided attempts at radical reform creating a political backlash that stalled subsequent reform), or in fact not a big bang at all (inadequate government commitment to key reforms and ample evidence of misguided commitment to gradualism in areas such as fiscal policy where it was not appropriate)? The debate about the Chinese reforms has taken on a similar character. Is China a case of successful gradualism (high growth since the introduction of partial reforms), unsuccessful gradualism (many of the most difficult problems such as the disposition of loss-making state-owned enterprises and the legal framework remaining unresolved), or in fact not gradualism at all (a number of key reforms, such as agricultural pricing policy and the opening of the south China coast, that were not really gradual)?

Some purported tests of the proposition that rapid reform is superior are misleading if not downright disingenuous. For example, it has become common to point out that "early" reformers have fared better than "late" or "partial" reformers; this stylized fact is then invoked to buttress the superiority of rapid and comprehensive approaches. However, it demonstrates no such thing; it only proves that countries that undertake reform do better than those that do not. Similarly, episodes of political immobilism, such as those we are currently witnessing in Russia, are chalked up as exemplary of the failures of gradualism, as if anyone would advocate complete policy deadlock as a strategy.

It is far beyond the scope of this essay to resolve this dispute, but several points might help reconcile the contending positions to some extent. First, the speed with which it is possible to move may have less to do with political circumstances than it does with the nature of the issue area under consideration. In the early transition period, a number of decisions could in principle be taken by the finance minister acting alone; devaluations and trade liberalizations can be implemented by the stroke of a pen, and reforms of this nature seem to drive most of the modeling by economists. But a number of so-called second-stage reforms (Naím 1994) imply fundamental changes in organizational routines or the creation of altogether new institutions, such as regulatory agencies, central banks, treasuries, and tax collection agencies, or fundamental changes in existing bureaucratic organizations, such as reforms of health care and education. Even if initiated quickly, they are likely to require some time to reach fruition. However, a number of cases, including New Zealand, suggest that success of first-stage reforms can provide the basis for more profound institutional change, and further research is needed on these dynamics (see Kornai, Haggard, and Kaufman, forthcoming).

That important caveat aside, there is little evidence to support the contention that radical reform is less politically sustainable than gradualism. Critics of big bang policies predicted not only a derailing of economic reform but mass protest and even a breakdown of democracy. As Greskovits (1998, chap. 1) detailed in a withering review of the Eastern European experience, these predictions—and they were legion—did not materialize (see also Fish 1998). Where adverse political consequences have arisen in the transition to the market, they appear to result not from overly radical reform but from continuing deterioration associated with the failure to achieve macroeconomic stability. Nor have predictions of "reform fatigue" leading to a fundamental derailing of reform proved valid. In a review of sixteen highly studied reforming countries, Tommasi and Velasco (1996) found only one (Venezuela) where reforms were reversed and another three where they slowed; in fifteen of sixteen case studies, reforms were continued in successor governments even if the party initiating the reform was defeated at the polls (see also Haggard and Kaufman 1995, chap. 10; Fish 1998).

The Chinese and a number of other favorite reform cases, including Korea and Taiwan, provide evidence for the possibility of gradual reform. The appropriate question then becomes, Under what circumstances are rapid and gradualist strategies likely to be politically feasible? Rapid strategies assume away ex ante political constraints. They are thus more likely to emerge and be successful (in the narrow political sense, at least) when such constraints are in fact minimal; this may occur as a result of crisis, when new governments come to power, or when interest groups are weak or poorly organized, as they initially were in Eastern Europe and the former Soviet Union. By contrast, gradualism requires a "strong" and highly credible government since it must be able to limit concessions that undermine the integrity of the reform.

Another answer to the question is supplied by looking at economic structure, and its implications for the power of interest groups. China did not face the same macroeconomic crises as a number of former socialist countries, but it also had a very different economic structure; the larger size of the agricultural sector and the comparatively small size of the uncompetitive industrial sector arguably facilitated a gradual reform process (Sachs and Woo 1994; but see also Naughton 1995). These observations about economic structure have important, but potentially discouraging implications for the politics of reform, and particularly for interest group approaches. They suggest that the level of resistance to reform may have to do less with strategy than with history and more long-standing structural factors that predate the initiation of reform.

Three strands of recent literature have moved in this more determinist, structuralist direction. First, a number of economists have focused on the debilitating effects of inequality on growth; political economy plays a role in these arguments, since inequality increases political polarization, instability, and disagreements over sharing the costs of reform (Alesina and Rodrik 1994). Second, Ranis and Mahmood (1992) have developed the argument that resource endowment is fate; countries with relatively rich endowments of natural resources face greater political difficulties in undertaking reforms than countries without such endowments. The latter have fewer choices and are more likely to exploit their comparative advantage. Finally, Michael Shafer (1995) has brought attention to how the nature of production in leading sectors affects not only policy preferences but the ability to organize. Certain sectors, such as mining, tend to create highly concentrated economic interests that become powerful opponents of reform. The greater degree of prereform concentration in industry in Russia makes it more difficult to marketize than under more decentralized patterns of socialist organization such as in China. It also results in highly oligopolistic political as well as economic structures when privatization and marketization do occur.

Finally, a brief word should be said about the politics of compensation. Over the long run, there is a deep and convincing literature outlining how various forms of social protection contributed to the political sustainability of market economies in the West. To cite but several examples, Alvarez, Garrett, and Lange (1991) and Calmfors (1993) have shown that European social democracies with strong links to centralized and encompassing union organizations fared better with respect to both macroeconomic management and growth than their center-right counterparts; one reason was the ability to extend credible guarantees to workers that their long-term interests would be accommodated. Similar arguments have been made with respect to trade policy. David Cameron (1978) was among the first to note the positive correlation between economic openness and the size of government, and Peter Katzenstein (1985) among others developed the argument that this was related to political arrangements that incorporated and accommodated labor. Bates, Brock, and Tiefenthaler (1991) showed that the level of protection was negatively correlated with the extent of worker protection, and Rodrik (1997) has recently restated the political case for social protection in the context of increasing globalization.

The theoretical case for compensation is airtight; if a reform will raise aggregate welfare but harm certain groups, compensatory schemes can transform the reform into a Pareto-improving one. However, we do not have convincing cross-national evidence that compensation does in fact contribute to the political success of reform. The most detailed study of the subject, Carol Graham's (1994) study of reform in six countries, provides evidence that successful reform was facilitated by compensatory measures. Haggard and Webb (1994) also provided evidence of the role of compensation in securing support, but they stressed that the nature of this compensation was elastic and in some cases included political as well as economic concessions. Moreover, they distinguished between compensation in the form of complementary policies that have other positive benefits, which may help offset the effect of reforms, and direct subsidies and transfers, which are subject to capture by the politically powerful rather than the poor (Nelson 1992).

2.1.3   Theoretical Reprise

It is easy to find cases of failed or partial reform that can be attributed to the influence of interest groups. But such analysis is frequently ad hoc, and the general approach has great difficulty explaining why the past twenty years has witnessed such a wide-ranging move toward the market. The two dominant answers to this question are that crises have changed groups' strength and even policy preferences, and that losers have been finessed or weakened through getting strategy and tactics right. But the latter explanation begs the question of why reformers were able to get policies right; presumably if groups can foresee the effects of policy, they, rather than some benevolent social planner, will be dictating the course of policy. These problems can be resolved in part by focusing greater attention on the institutional setting in which policy is made, and on the conditions under which the policymaker—a neglected actor in interest group approaches—has incentives to respond to the collective good.

2.2   Political Institutions and Economic Reform

Just as households and firms face incentives structured by the markets in which they operate, so politicians and bureaucrats face incentives associated with the political institutions in which they operate, including the representative institutions that link them to constituents. These incentives can make policy more or less decisive, more or less coherent, more or less subject to reversal, and thus more or less credible.

I begin with a brief discussion of the debate about the performance of democratic and authoritarian regimes, focusing on reasons why democracy and democratization not only is compatible with reform but under some circumstances may be a crucial prerequisite for it. I argue that much depends on the nature of the new democratic institutions. By way of illustration I look briefly at the effect of the constitution of executive authority, and characteristics both of the party system and the internal organization of parties, on the prospects for reform.

2.2.1   Authoritarianism, Democracy, Democratization, and Policy Reform

Over the past two decades, the developing and formerly socialist worlds have witnessed epochal changes in the direction of greater democracy. The dictatorships of southern Europe were the first to fall. Beginning in the late 1970s, Latin American militaries started to withdraw from power. Over the next decade, political transitions began in a number of Asian countries as well, including Korea, Taiwan, Thailand, the Philippines, Turkey, and Pakistan. This wave of democratization crested in the late 1980s with the stunning collapse of Communist governments in Eastern Europe, the breakup of the Soviet Union, and increasing pressure on authoritarian regimes in Africa and the Middle East.

The debate over the effects of regime type on economic performance need not be rehearsed in detail here except to note that the growing body of cross-national empirical work generally reaches ambiguous results. Some studies suggest that democratic governments perform less well (e.g., Barro 1996), some argue that democracies perform better (e.g., Devarajan and Lindenberg 1993; Maraval 1997), but most reviews reach the conclusion that there is no significant relation one way or the other (for reviews, see Sirowy and Inkeles 1990; Przeworski and Limongi 1993; Helliwell 1994).

That said, there is a lingering authoritarian undertone to some of the reform literature that springs directly out of the interest group approach just surveyed. If policymakers face collective action problems, groups and electorates with short time horizons, and the pull of particularistic interest groups, then an argument can be made for a "strong" government that "solves" these problems through decisive action. Moreover, the deeper these problems are, the stronger the government presumably needs to be. Economists rarely make this argument explicitly, although Roger Douglas (1990) and Jeffrey Sachs (1994) have made a forceful case for decisive leadership (although not authoritarianism!) even in the absence of consensus or public support for reforms.

However, the argument for authoritarianism is implicit in the cases economists hold up as models of successful reform. First among these are the East Asian newly industrializing countries (Haggard 1990a). Taiwan was a dominant-party state led by the KMT and Hong Kong until 1997 was a no-party administrative government under British rule. Most interesting are the histories of Korea and Singapore, since they show clearly how social polarization, authoritarian installations, and economic reform can be related. After the fall of Syngman Rhee in Korea in 1960, a weak but reformist democratic government took office (the Second Republic), but it proved unable to act in the face of serious political and social divisions. There is a substantial debate over the nature of the reforms associated with the South Korean miracle, but both orthodox and heterodox interpretations trace the takeoff to policies launched under the military government that took office in 1961. Singapore was also a politically polarized society in the second half of the 1950s and early 1960s. The export-oriented strategy based on attracting multinationals emerged following the defeat of the leftist Barisan Socialis and the consolidation of dominant-party rule. Similar political stories could be told about the initiation of economic reform in Indonesia (1965), Chile (1973), and Turkey, where reforms initiated under civilian government in 1980 were pushed forward following a military coup in that year.

But we also know that other authoritarian regimes—typically personalist dictatorships of various sorts—provide examples of economic decline not found in any democracy: Haiti under the Duvaliers, Zaire under Mobutu, North Korea under Kim Il Sung, and Romania under Ceaucescu. In these and many other authoritarian systems, reform is only likely when incumbent politicians associated with the ancien régime are fully replaced. The reasons reside in the fact that it is not only social interest groups that constitute barriers to reform but the state apparatus itself: the political leaders, bureaucrats, and party functionaries that loom so large in authoritarian settings. Examples of this problem can be seen in efforts to reform socialist systems. For a complex set of reasons, the Chinese Communist Party was able to launch extensive, but still incomplete reforms from above. But as Maraval (1997) argued, Communists in Poland, Hungary, and Czechoslovakia ultimately proved unable to do so; Aslund (1995, chap. 2) made a similar argument with respect to the political limits on Gorbachev's reforms. Structural reforms, even partial ones, ran into stiff opposition from within the party and bureaucracy, while the questionable political legitimacy of the party made the government surprisingly hesitant in undertaking difficult measures such as fiscal adjustments, price increases, or wage discipline; indeed, efforts at partial political reform, such as those undertaken in the Polish roundtable negotiations, were designed precisely to secure opposition support for measures the government feared undertaking on its own. Similar stories can be told about the problems of reform in authoritarian governments with strong "crony," patrimonial, or clientelist structures, such as the Philippines under Marcos (Haggard 1990b), Indonesia under Suharto, and a number of African governments (Bratton and van de Walle 1997).

In a wide-ranging effort to explain the determinants of economic reform in the post-Communist world, M. Steven Fish has argued that the outcome of the initial posttransition election (whether reformers or Communists triumphed) and the extent of democratization (whether there even were elections and how competitive they were) prove to be the single most important determinant of subsequent propensity to reform. He traced this effect through a number of channels, including elite turnover, the development of independent loci of political as well as economic power, and the greater stability of the political system under democratic rule (see also Hellman 1998).

Bienen and Herbst (1996) and van de Walle (1994) provided equally wide-ranging reviews of the African experience in the first half of the 1990s, and they found that political liberalization in Africa has not had the salutary effects found in the former Communist countries. But this was precisely because democratization had been limited in various ways, had not brought new leaders to power, and had not occurred in such a way as to force politicians to be responsive to constituencies who benefit from reform.

In sum, although the design of new democratic institutions matters, democratization itself can provide the political foundation for reform by exposing groups privileged under the old order to competition and scrutiny and widening the range of constituencies to which politicians must respond.

2.2.2   The Design of Democracies I: The Constitution of Executive Authority

Political scientists are converging on a theory of the state as a complex chain of principal-agent or delegation relationships (Cox and Mc-Cubbins 2000). Building on the contractual theory of democratic rule that goes back to Hobbes, Locke, and Hume, the sovereign people delegate decision-making power to a government (through a constitution) and monitor its subsequent behavior through elections. Electoral rules, in turn, can vary substantially and are one important influence on the nature of the party system. A second step in the delegation process centers on the internal constitution of the government itself, including the rules governing the relations between the executive, the cabinet, the legislature, and legislative committees.[5] Of particular interest is the question of how many veto gates exist in the policy-making process; the more veto gates, the more difficult policy is to change, but therefore the more stable and credible it tends to be (Tsebelis 1995). Finally, the executive and legislature delegate to ministries, bureaus, and agencies the power to implement, but also often to make, policy; administrative procedures set the terms of this delegation (McCubbins, Noll, and Weingast 1987).

The emerging theory of public policy centers on how the design of these institutions affects the *incentives* facing politicians, their *capabilities,* and as a result various features of policy itself. The question of incentives goes to the heart of the interest group approach to politics, which stumbles on the issue of when government policy would be responsive to narrower or broader interests. The institutionalist approach suggests that this may have to do with the design of government. Some political systems encourage responsiveness to the median voter while others provide strong incentives for politicians to respond to the interests of narrow groups, resulting in policy distortions of various sorts (Myerson 1993). The question of capabilities is particularly important for understanding policy reform: can policymakers take decisive action when required, and can they implement decisions once taken? These issues were generally assumed away in the extensive literature on strategy and tactics, in which executives had agenda-setting or even decree powers.

One of the dilemmas of the new institutionalist literature is that the range of features that may affect policy outcomes is quite large, including whether the political system is presidential or parliamentary, the electoral rules, the party system, and more specific characteristics of the different institutions of government: the powers of the executive, the organization and powers of the legislature, and the capacity of the courts to undertake judicial review. Moreover, discrete elements of constitutional design cannot be viewed in isolation but interact in complex ways. However, the general flavor of this rapidly growing literature can be captured by focusing on three institutional factors that have affected policy reform: the constitution of executive authority, including the executive's relation with the legislature; the nature of the party system; and the internal organization of parties.

As advocates of a big bang approach recognize, centralized executive authority plays a pivotal role in overcoming the collective action problems and distributive conflicts associated with the initiation of comprehensive economic reforms. In the early phase of a reform, key decisions about the design of policy and political and legislative strategy are usually taken by

5. Questions of federalism also arise here: the relation between the central and other levels of government.

the president or prime minister on the basis of counsel from a hand-picked team of advisors or "change teams" (Waterbury 1993), usually operating outside normal bureaucratic channels. The ability of the executive to act aggressively is partly a function of economic factors. One reason why crisis is associated with reform is not the nature of interest group conflict or changes in their policy preferences, but a greater willingness during times of crisis for legislators and publics to expand the discretionary authority of the executive. Executives are also empowered by the electoral cycle and honeymoon effects; many instances of dramatic reform—for example, under Menem in Argentina or Collor in Brazil—came in the wake of electoral victories that gave political leaders mandates, albeit broad and undefined ones, for policy change (Haggard and Webb 1994; Rodrik 1994). In tandem, these observations reinforce the advantages of speed and comprehensive reform in democratic governments, but for somewhat different reasons; acting swiftly at the outset of an administration allows the government to absorb transition costs prior to the next electoral contest and increases the likelihood that politicians will be able to profit from recovery.

In addition to the effects of crisis and electoral cycles on executive power, institutions have also been explicitly designed to buttress central authority or to insulate decision making from political interference. In analyzing the powers of the executive, it is important to distinguish between those powers that belong to the executive by constitutional right and those that are explicitly delegated (Shugart and Carey 1992, chap. 7). In presidential systems, the former typically include a veto (of varying scope and with differing provisions for legislative override) that provides some check on legislative power and can limit debilitating logrolls (Shugart and Haggard 2000). Presidential authority also typically includes certain legislative or decree powers that grant presidents more direct control over the policy agenda. These powers can be extremely important for the initiation of reform and for the conduct of economic policy more generally. For example, in Chile the president introduces the budget and the legislature has no power to increase spending; it may only shift expenditures between categories and reduce spending (Baldez-Carey and Carey 2000); similar rules pertain in Korea. In Brazil, presidential authority to issue "urgent" laws was used by the Collor administration to initiate reform legislation, though not always successfully.

These powers must be distinguished from those that are explicitly delegated to the executive by the legislature. Prime ministers and their cabinets in parliamentary systems are typically quite powerful. In contrast to presidents, who must rely on securing the support of a separate branch, parliamentary governments can in principle legislate at will; this observation has given rise to an extensive debate on the relative merits of parliamentary versus presidential rule for policy reform, one that remains to this date inconclusive (critics of presidentialism include Linz 1993a, 1993b;

Linz and Valenzuela 1994; Horowitz 1993; skeptics include Shugart and Carey 1992, 28–54; Mainwaring and Shugart 1997; Haggard and Kaufman 1995; Shugart and Haggard 2000). The existence of multiple veto gates in a separately elected president and legislature (and frequently two houses as well) create the possibility of divided government and policy deadlock, as Russia in 1998 reminded us once again. But the decisiveness of parliamentary systems rests on the backing of a majority in parliament, either of the dominant party or a coalition, and coalitions can be difficult to form and fractious. For example, the Turkish governments of the late 1970s were notoriously divided, and the first democratic Hungarian government's "gradualism" was in part attributable to intracoalitional dynamics that resulted in the postponement of difficult fiscal decisions (Haggard, Kaufman, and Shugart, forthcoming). Conversely, legislators in presidential systems may delegate quite substantial decree power to the president on a temporary basis; such powers were important in the initiation of reforms in Argentina and Peru.

A second feature of the executive that can have important implications for the conduct of economic policy is the delegation of decision-making authority to specialized agencies. Such delegation can substantially alter the political calculus, and even the very organization, of interest groups. The best researched examples are the creation of independent central banking institutions (Cukierman, Webb, and Neyapti 1992; Eijffinger and de Haan 1996), quasi-judicial structures for the management of trade policy issues (Hall and Nelson 1992), and centralization of the budgetary process (Alesina and Perotti 1996; Perotti 1997). Of course, no institution in a democracy can altogether escape legislative and electoral oversight and control, and there is thus always the problem of endogeneity; why would groups disfavored by a given institutional arrangement agree to it? But the answer is easily supplied if we move away from the mistaken idea that disfavored interest groups exercise vetoes over institutions. Winning coalitions can lock in their policy preferences by creating institutions that raise the costs of policy reversal and thus enhance both the coherence and credibility of policy.

The establishment of independent agencies or authorities serves to limit the access of groups to decision making or fundamentally alter the way in which they exercise influence. The establishment of quasi-judicial procedures for the management of unfair trade practices may provide access for aggrieved parties with protectionist intent; indeed, legislators design them with this in mind. Yet such procedures also protect legislators against protectionists since they demand that petitioners demonstrate that their cases are in conformity with statute. Such a process differs fundamentally from a lobbying relation with a legislator.

Though constitutional arrangements and processes of delegation can strengthen the hand of the executive by expanding the discretionary power to initiate policy or by insulating decision making from short-term political pressures, such mechanisms do not necessarily provide an effective basis for policy coordination and the management of distributive conflict over the long run. First, strong executive discretion can weaken the incentives for party, legislative, and interest group leaders to provide political support for policy initiatives (Shugart and Carey 1992, 174–93). Legislators with limited influence over policy are likely to distance themselves from the chief executive, including during times of economic distress; this is especially true in presidential systems and where parties are weak. Efforts to insulate decision making can also backfire. The purpose of such institutional arrangements is to offset threats to policy continuity and coherence from the opposition, particularly in countries with long histories of polarization and social conflict over economic issues. Countries that made gradual transitions to democratic rule, such as Turkey and Thailand, demonstrate that an insulated executive is not sufficient to prevent opposition to reform as barriers to political contestation fall; indeed, insulated government agencies may become the focus of opposition attention.

Such processes of delegation may run particular risks in weakly institutionalized democracies. Take, for example, the recent tendency in Latin America for legislators to grant executives substantial powers for the purpose of undertaking economic reform measures, a process Bresser Pereira et al. (1993) have labeled "decretism." It is not clear that the decisions taken under such conditions are necessarily optimal or even politically sustainable. Critics also raise the question of whether decretism leads to a plebiscitarian political style and the atrophy of the core representative institutions; while this has not generally been the case, Peru and Russia provide discouraging counterexamples.

Nonetheless, the process of delegation is a central one in all democratic systems; modern democracy would be impossible without it. Thus the issue is not whether or not to delegate, but how delegation can be structured to maximize both efficiency and accountability. There are two competing conceptions of how such institutions can be strengthened and given more independence. One is to increase their "capacity," a concept that has appealed to the international financial institutions (Grindle 1996). This technocratic strategy has some merit. By increasing salaries, attracting and training high-quality personnel, and injecting greater expertise through training, agencies gain political weight.

The record of the recent past suggests that such a technocratic strategy is inadequate by itself. For agencies to sustain themselves over time, they must also build on bases of constituent support. For example, recent research on central banks is beginning to reveal that these institutions gain "independence" not from statute, but by maintaining close relationships with those groups favorable to the conduct of stable monetary policy (Maxfield 1997). The task for institutional design is therefore to consider how new policy-making bodies can enfranchise and strengthen the hand of proreform groups that have previously been underrepresented.

2.2.3 Party Fragmentation and Polarization

Even if executives are able to play an agenda-setting role in initiating reform, legislatures must ultimately pass the supporting legislation to ratify reform decisions and guarantee that they are implemented and sustained over time. In many cases, even the initiation of reform requires legislation, and thus support from some coalition of legislators. The party system constitutes a critical determinant of politicians' behavior in this regard.[6]

A number of features of party systems are salient for understanding political behavior and resulting policy outcomes, but fragmentation and polarization have received the most sustained attention. Fragmentation is typically defined simply by the number of effective parties (Sartori 1976, 185 ff.; Powell 1982, 80–84). Polarization is defined by the ideological distance between the extreme parties in the system (Sartori 1976, 132–37). Fragmentation can be measured easily (see, e.g., Roubini and Sachs 1989 on fiscal policy), but it is notoriously difficult to gauge the extent of ideological distance among parties. The problem is compounded in developing countries, where party cleavages do not always fall along a clear left-right dimension. Several indicators are likely to point to polarization, however. The first is the presence of left and populist parties that have historically mobilized followers around anticapitalist or antioligarchic protests; some of the Communist successor parties would fall in this category. It is also useful to consider the strength of "movement parties" that exhibit the sectarian characteristics of a social movement and rest on strong loyalties among party activists; the Italian fascists constitute an historical example, as do the Peronists at several points in Argentine history.

Nonpolarized party systems, by contrast, are characterized by a low level of ideological distance among parties, typically meaning that left and populist parties are weak or nonexistent. Nonpolarized systems rest on "pragmatic" parties in which ties between leaders and followers are largely instrumental and rest on shared interests in obtaining political office rather than strong ideological commitments.

Fragmentation creates impediments to the coordination required both to initiate and to sustain policy changes; more cohesive systems, by contrast, are more likely to generate the stable electoral and legislative support that are a prerequisite for consolidating economic reform. However, fragmentation alone says nothing about the underlying preferences of the contending political forces in the system or about the extent of cleavage among them. We expect that reform will be more difficult in polarized

---

6. This subsection and the following draw on Haggard (1997).

systems in which strong left, populist, and movement parties are competing, both because of their effects on partisan conflict and because of their influence on the stance of interest groups, particularly the labor movement and the popular sector.

The principal effect of fragmentation on the conduct of policy is the difficulty it poses for coordination: within the ruling coalition, between executive and legislative branches, and among different levels of government. How these effects operate will depend in part on whether the system is presidential or parliamentary. In parliamentary systems based on proportional representation with high proportionality, a multiplicity of parties increases the difficulty of forming and sustaining coalition governments. The division of cabinet posts among contending parties that is required to form such coalitions can undermine the capacity of central authorities to undertake the coordinated implementation of reform programs; policy becomes a logroll. When such governments are formed, small coalition partners can hold veto power over policy decisions (Roubini and Sachs 1989).

As Scott Mainwaring (1989) has argued, party fragmentation in presidential systems compounds the chances that executives will become politically isolated and powerless to pursue their agenda. The incentives for small parties to cooperate with the government are weaker than in a parliamentary system, since there is no ability to threaten early elections, and the temptations to legislative blackmail are correspondingly greater.

The effects of fragmentation on policy making will also depend on whether the system is simultaneously polarized. Thailand in the late 1980s had a highly fragmented party system but showed no signs of polarization. In the absence of strong left or populist parties, the principal coordination problems centered on the struggle for pork: with multiple contenders and weak party organizations, there were few constraints among politicians in the competition for patronage and pork-barrel expenditures. To the extent that Thailand did escape this trap, it was due to enduring features of the executive and the bureaucracy, and to some extent a new round of reforms launched under a brief military coup (Doner and Laothamatas 1994).

Coordination becomes even more difficult, however, when the centrifugal pressures in fragmented systems are compounded by strong ideological polarization or sectarian tendencies such as those we are witnessing in Russia. First, parties in such systems are more likely to engage in programmatic "bidding wars" in order both to differentiate themselves from opponents and to maintain the allegiance of relatively narrow constituencies. Second, and for very similar reasons, fragmented and polarized systems amplify the distributional demands coming from antiadjustment interest groups.

The combination of polarization and fragmentation also affects economic management by exacerbating political business cycles (Alesina

1987). Not only do elections in such systems invite opportunistic behavior and encourage the delay of adjustment efforts, but the combination of an unstable and volatile party landscape with deep programmatic or partisan antagonisms among contenders increases the uncertainty surrounding elections due to the potential for large policy swings between successive governments. Argentina, Bolivia, Brazil, and Peru all experienced profound economic collapses in the run-up to elections.

In cohesive party systems, competition is organized between a smaller number of larger parties. At the time of its transition to democracy, the Philippines was probably the most cohesive party system among new developing country democracies; the transitional election was fought between two blocs consisting of the pro- and the anti-Marcos forces. In subsequent elections, the weakness of party organizations and the tendency to personalism and fragmentation were revealed more clearly, but these tendencies were constrained at least to some extent by the centripetal incentives associated with single-member electoral districts for the lower house. Chile, Korea, and Taiwan also showed low levels of fragmentation, as both moved toward the formation of broad-based political blocs. Korea even evolved "past" a two-party system toward a dominant-party model along Japanese lines. Argentina and Uruguay were also relatively cohesive. Turkey constitutes an ambiguous case; at the time of the transitional election in 1983, the country had less than three effective parties, but this was the result of a military ban on full party participation. By the late 1980s, the Turkish party system had become both more fragmented and more polarized, which helps explain the growing incoherence of economic policy. Russia also provides an obvious example of this process.

2.2.4   Internal Party Organization

Some important barriers to reform reside not in the nature of competition among parties, but in the incentives different party organizations create for individual politicians to engage in pork-barrel spending, rent seeking, and other forms of particularism. A key variable in this regard is the relative strength of the party leadership vis-à-vis the individual politician. Where party leaderships are strong, there is greater prospect of enforcing programmatic discipline on followers and less likelihood that programs will be dominated by geographic or other constituent interests. Party strength is likely to be reflected not only in intraparty organization but in the design of legislative institutions themselves. Strong parties are more likely to favor rules and institutions that further buttress party discipline, such as strong oversight or control committees, extensive agenda-setting and committee assignment powers for party leaders, and weak policy committees.

The strength of the party leadership is, in turn, contingent on the extent to which electoral rules encourage politicians to cultivate personal reputations. Where politicians have incentives to cultivate the personal vote, they are more likely to seek to develop narrow constituent bases of support and to press for particularistic policies at the expense of party platforms. As Shugart and Nielson put it, with Colombia, Japan, and Brazil in mind, "In personalistic systems, party programs are constantly being scavenged by individual politicians for their idiosyncratic interests—they seek to break up national policies into localized or issue-specific parcels in appeal to narrow groups" (1994, 18). These particularistic policies take the form of patronage, pork, and the drafting of statutes that are cast in general language but are in fact designed to appeal to narrow constituent—and even individual!—bases of support; the growth of American tax expenditures provides an example of the last stratagem.

Among the institutional factors that encourage party control are, first and foremost, the control that party leaders exercise over access to the ballot and the order in which candidates are elected. Open and decentralized nomination procedures weaken party control. In an open list system, the electorate effectively orders the ballot. Open lists allow entrants to free-ride on the party label while simultaneously encouraging them to curry personal reputations for the provision of particularistic goods. A closely related feature of the electoral system that determines politicians' behavior is whether they are competing against members of their own party in large multimember districts. As the magnitude of the district goes up, and the individual politician is competing with more members both of the opposition and her own party, this competition becomes more fierce. The party label is of no use in competition with members of one's own party; the only way to conduct such rivalry is by stressing personal traits that differentiate the candidate. In effect, politicians are encouraged to pursue what Ramseyer and Rosenbluth (1993) called a "niche" strategy based on instrumental promises to followers and the provision of personal services rather than to stand up for the public good.

A third related feature of the electoral system is whether voters choose parties or candidates. If voters choose parties, then the politician has little incentive to differentiate himself from the party platform; his fate rises or falls with the party's. If voters choose individual candidates, there are, again, incentives to cultivate a personal vote. A final factor is the control of campaign finance. Where individual politicians have responsibility for raising their own campaign money and subsequently control their own purses, there is an incentive to cultivate personal reputations. Donors in such settings typically provide candidates with money for the purpose of realizing particular objectives.

It is important to underscore that centralized control is certainly not a guarantee of good economic policy. Centralized parties might well have ideological platforms that are hostile to economic reform. The distribution of private goods is also of use even in a centralized system. Party leaders still have an interest in maintaining the loyalty of both legislators and voters and will use patronage and pork to that end. Venezuela, for example, is a country with highly centralized party institutions, but ones that have been riddled with corruption and patronage. However, if the distribution of private goods is controlled through centralized monitoring mechanisms either within the party or through legislative delegation, it may actually have a salutary effect in the reform process in line with theories of gradualism and compensation already outlined (Shugart and Nielson 1994). The distribution of a certain amount of patronage and pork provides a mechanism for building support, including among previously excluded groups, and of partially compensating losers. The key issue is guaranteeing that pork is distributed in a relatively efficient way. One way of achieving this is through electoral reforms that reduce intraparty competition, such as the formation of single-member districts or delegation of greater authority to the executive.

2.2.5   Theoretical Reprise

The new institutionalist literature has generated many hypotheses about the functioning of political systems. An unfortunate feature of this literature is that the number of institutions that may matter is quite large, and the effects of each one individually is subject to the standard ceteris paribus caveat. However, several general conclusions emerge from this discussion. First, the initiation of reform is facilitated by concentrated executive authority, although this may itself require legislative delegation. Institutional analysis also draws our attention to how the decision-making process itself can be reorganized and institutionalized to increase coordination and reduce the types of collective action problems among groups noted in the first section of this paper; this can be accomplished through the development of insulated agencies with a mandate to be responsive to broad interests in such areas as monetary policy, trade policy, and the budget process.

Over time, these policies must sustain party support, which in turn is contingent on the nature of the party system. In general, I have argued in favor of systems that reduce the tendency to polarization and fragmentation and that increase the discipline of central party leaders over backbenchers. It may seem farfetched to argue that constitutions should be changed to make economic policy more efficient, but on closer reflection it is not at all farfetched and has motivated at least in part recent constitutional changes in Japan and Colombia; other systems, such as Russia, could obviously benefit from constitutional change as well.

2.3   Some Concluding Reflections: The Research Frontier and the Determinacy Paradox

This survey has attempted to provide a broad overview of the literature on the political economy of reform. What emerges is not altogether flattering; numerous modeling efforts have gone untested, or rest on unobservables, and numerous case studies, or worse yet "stylized facts," are invoked to support one theory or another. Yet on a number of the most important and contested claims, such as the role of interest groups or the political virtues of radical versus gradual reform, there are surprisingly few consistent tests, either in the form of tightly structured case studies undertaken within a common framework or through cross-national quantitative designs.

Clearly much work remains to be done, but where should researchers place their bets? What lines of research are likely to be most fruitful for policy purposes? First, we need to know much more about the dynamics of support and opposition to reform, using both attitudinal surveys and studies of particular organized groups. Much theoretical work to date focuses on the (presumed) reactions of interest groups and voters, but until we have more systematic information, it is difficult to draw conclusions about the all-important question of appropriate strategy and tactics.

A second, related issue is the political logic of compensation. The logic of compensation is theoretically compelling. Some reforms may be Pareto-improving only in the presence of appropriate transfers; in short, they involve losers as well as winners. In these instances, compensatory policies may be necessary to buy support. However, compensation raises interesting moral as well as practical problems. For example, if reforms hurt politically powerful or even middle-income groups, should they be compensated? Will opening a discussion of compensation necessarily introduce new distortions or delay reform? What, more generally, is the politics of compensation?

Finally, one major disability of the literature is that it has focused on a particular class of reforms, particularly macroeconomic stabilization and trade reform, that may have distinctive properties. At least in principle, these reforms can be undertaken relatively quickly. Macroeconomic stabilization issues, in particular, have the advantage of arising during crises, which generate both interest group and institutional effects that can be favorable to reform.

The literature on privatization has already come to grips with the fact that institutional reforms are of a different nature. Reforms of the legal system, of the bureaucracy, of regulatory agencies, of courts, and of service delivery institutions such as health care systems necessarily involve much more complex questions of institutional and organizational design.

Institutional design should be an area in which political economists have a comparative advantage. The issue is not simply mechanism design; it is also a question of ensuring that the design of those mechanisms is compatible with the political incentives of actors. In the shift to the market, a particularly important role will be played by regulatory agencies of various sorts: this is true in communications, transportation, power, water, and finance to name but a few important sectors. How do we design a credible regulatory agency, given certain constitutional constraints? How do we ensure public checks on agency discretion? While there is much normative work on regulation, there is much less on how to design regulatory institutions.

Finally, a brief word should be said about what Bhagwati, Brecher, and Srinivasan (1984) have called the "determinacy paradox." If we have fully elaborated models of the political economy, what then happens to normative economics? Policy choice will be endogenous to some political economy logic, and giving advice or trying to persuade would make no sense— like asking the San Andreas fault to be quiet, as O'Flaherty and Bhagwati have put it recently (1997). This problem is not a trivial one; some of the models and findings we have outlined here, for example, about crises, polarization, or the influence of powerful interest groups and constitutional design, may be of interest to outsiders, such as investors or the international financial institutions, but they are either altogether irrelevant from the standpoint of the policymaker or are nearly so because the parameters that matter cannot be manipulated. Philosophically, there appear to be no completely satisfying exits from this paradox.

We are very far from having anything resembling a general equilibrium political economy model, and even if we did, it would be difficult to persuade the politician that the model was right; economists and political scientists have credibility problems too. The paradox is created in part by strong rationality assumptions, even a kind of hyperrationality, in which each actor is assumed to maximize across all political and economic strategies. However, agents are rational subject to some informational constraints, and it is in the interstices of those constraints that advice can make a difference. Political economy models that deal with strategy and tactics and with the design of institutions can assist those in power to more fully realize their objectives as long as there is something about the way the world works that the policymaker does not yet know. When the policymaker is informed of that thing, there will be, because of the evolution of human knowledge, some new thing that he will not know, and so on. My own suspicion is that a good politician probably understands the political constraints under which she operates better than a good political economist, but that just demonstrates that the gains from trade can run in two directions.

References

Aghion, P., and O. Blanchard. 1994. On the speed of transition in Central Europe. In *NBER macroeconomics annual,* ed. S. Fischer and J. J. Rotemberg. Cambridge, Mass.: MIT Press.

Alesina, A. 1987. Macroeconomic policy in a two-party system as a repeated game. *Quarterly Journal of Economics* 101:651–78.
———. 1994. Political models of macroeconomic policy and fiscal reforms. In *Voting for reform,* ed. Stephan Haggard and Steven B. Webb. New York: Oxford University Press.
Alesina, A., and A. Drazen. 1991. Why are stabilizations delayed? *American Economic Review* 81, no. 5 (December): 1170–88.
Alesina, A., and R. Perotti. 1996. Budget deficits and budget institutions. NBER Working Paper no. 5556. Cambridge, Mass.: National Bureau of Economic Research.
Alesina, A., and D. Rodrik. 1994. Distributive politics and economic growth. *Quarterly Journal of Economics* 109, no. 2 (May): 465–90.
Alvarez, R. M., G. Garrett, and P. Lange. 1991. Government partnership, labor organization and macroeconomic performance. *American Political Science Review* 85:541–56.
Aslund, A. 1995. *How Russia became a market economy.* Washington, D.C.: Brookings Institution.
Baldez-Carey, L., and J. Carey. 2000. The budgetary process in Chile. In *Presidents, parliaments, and policy,* ed. Stephan Haggard and Mathew McCubbins. New York: Cambridge University Press, forthcoming.
Barro, R. 1996. Democracy and growth. *Journal of Economic Growth* 1, no. 1 (March): 1–28.
Bates, R. 1981. *Markets and states in tropical Africa: The political basis of agricultural policies.* Berkeley: University of California Press.
———. 1983. The nature and origins of agricultural policies in Africa. In *Essays on the political economy of rural Africa,* by R. Bates. Berkeley: University of California Press.
Bates, R., P. Brock, and J. Tiefenthaler. 1991. Risk and trade regimes: Another exploration. *International Organization* 45, no. 1 (winter): 1–18.
Bates, R., and P. Collier. 1993. The politics and economics of policy reform in Zambia. In *Political and economic interactions in economic policy reform,* ed. Robert Bates and Anne Krueger. Cambridge, Mass.: Blackwell.
Bates, R., and A. Krueger, eds. 1993. *Political and economic interactions in economic policy reform.* Cambridge, Mass.: Blackwell.
Becker, G. 1983. A theory of competition among pressure groups for influence. *Quarterly Journal of Economics* 98, no. 3 (August): 371–400.
Berg, A., and J. Sachs. 1992. Structural adjustment and international trade in Eastern Europe: The case of Poland. *Economic Policy* 14:117–73.
Bhagwati, J., R. Brecher, and T. N. Srinivasan. 1984. DUP activities and economic theory. In *Neoclassical political economy,* ed. D. Colander. Cambridge, Mass.: Ballinger.
Bienen, H., and J. Herbst. 1996. The relationship between political and economic reform in Africa. *Comparative Politics* 29, no. 1 (October): 23–42.
Bratton, M., and N. van de Walle. 1997. *Democratic experiments in Africa: Regime transitions in comparative perspective.* New York: Cambridge University Press.
Bresser Pereira, L. C., J. M. Maraval, and A. Przeworski. 1993. *Economic reforms in new democracies.* New York: Cambridge University Press.
Bruno, M., and W. Easterly. 1996. Inflation's children. Washington, D.C.: World Bank. Unpublished manuscript.
Calmfors, L. 1993. Centralisation of wage bargaining and macroeconomic performance: A survey. OECD Economics Department Working Paper no. 131. Paris: Organization for Economic Cooperation and Development.

Cameron, D. 1978. The expansion of the public economy: A comparative analysis. *American Political Science Review* 72:1243–61.

Cassing, J., T. McKeown, and J. Ochs. 1986. The political economy of the tariff cycle. *American Political Science Review* 80:843–62.

Cox, G., and M. McCubbins. 2000. Political structure and economic policy: The institutional determinants of public policy. In *Presidents, parliaments, and policy,* ed. Stephan Haggard and Mathew McCubbins. New York: Cambridge University Press, forthcoming.

Cukierman, A., S. Edwards, and G. Tabellini. 1992. Seignorage and political instability. *American Economic Review* 82 (3): 537–55.

Cukierman, A., S. B. Webb, and B. Neyapti. 1992. The measurement of central bank independence and its effect on policy outcomes. *World Bank Economic Review* 6:353–98.

Devarajan, S., and M. Lindenberg. 1993. Prescribing strong economic medicine: Revisiting the myths about structural adjustment, democracy, and economic performance in developing countries. *Comparative Politics* 25, no. 2 (January): 169–82.

Dewatripont, M., and G. Roland. 1991. Economic reform and dynamic political constraints. *Review of Economic Studies* 59:703–30.

———. 1992. The virtues of gradualism in the transition to a market economy. *Economic Journal* 102:291–300.

———. 1995. The design of reform packages under uncertainty. *American Economic Review* 85:1207–23.

Doner, R., and A. Laothamatas. 1994. The political economy of structural adjustment in Thailand. In *Voting for reform: Democracy, political liberalization, and economic adjustment,* ed. S. Haggard and S. Webb. New York: Oxford University Press.

Dornbusch, R., and S. Edwards, eds. 1993. *The macroeconomics of populism.* Chicago: University of Chicago Press.

Douglas, R. 1990. The politics of successful structural reform. *Wall Street Journal,* 17 January.

Drazen, A. 1996. The political economy of delayed reform. *Policy Reform* 1: 25–46.

Drazen, A., and V. Grilli. 1993. The benefit of crisis for economic reforms. *American Economic Review* 83 (3): 598–607.

Eijffinger, S., and J. de Haan. 1996. The political economy of central bank independence. Special Paper in International Finance no. 19. Princeton, N.J.: Princeton University, Department of Economics.

Ekiert, G., and J. Kubik. 1998. Contentious politics in new democracies: East Germany, Hungary, Poland and Slovakia, 1989–93. *World Politics* 50, no. 4 (July): 547–81.

Fernandez, R., and D. Rodrik. 1991. Resistance to reform: Status quo bias in the presence of individual-specific uncertainty. *American Economic Review* 81, no. 5 (December): 1146–55.

Fish, M. S. 1998. The determinants of economic reform in the post-Communist world. *Eastern European Politics and Societies* 12, no. 1 (winter): 31–78.

Frieden, J. 1991. Invested interests: The politics of national economic policies in a world of global finance. *International Organization* 45 (4): 425–51.

Frieden, J., and R. Rogowski. 1996. The impact of the international economy on national policies. In *Internationalization and domestic politics,* ed. R. Keohane and H. Milner. New York: Cambridge University Press.

Geddes, B. 1994. Challenging the conventional wisdom. In *Economic reform and democracy,* ed. Larry Diamond and Marc Plattner. Baltimore: Johns Hopkins University Press.

Gelb, A., G. Jefferson, and I. Singh. 1993. The Chinese and Eastern European routes to reform. In *NBER macroeconomics annual 1993,* ed. O. J. Blanchard and S. Fischer. Cambridge, Mass.: MIT Press.

Gibson, E. 1997. The populist road to market reform: Policy and electoral coalitions in Mexico and Argentina. *World Politics* 49, no. 3 (April): 339–70.

Graham, C. 1994. *Safety nets, politics and the poor.* Washington, D.C.: Brookings Institution.

Greskovits, B. 1998. *The political economy of protest and patience: East European and Latin American transitions compared.* Budapest: Central European University Press.

Grindle, M. 1996. *Challenging the state: Crisis and innovation in Latin America and Africa.* Cambridge: Cambridge University Press.

Haggard, S. 1990a. *Pathways from the periphery: The politics of growth in the newly industrializing countries.* Ithaca, N.Y.: Cornell University Press.

————. 1990b. The political economy of the Philippine debt crisis. In *Economic crisis and policy choice,* ed. Joan Nelson. Princeton, N.J.: Princeton University Press.

————. 1997. Democratic institutions, economic policy, and development. In *Institutions and economic development,* ed. Christopher Clague. Baltimore: Johns Hopkins University Press.

Haggard, S., and R. Kaufman. 1995. *The political economy of democratic transitions.* Princeton, N.J.: Princeton University Press.

Haggard, S., R. Kaufman, and M. Shugart. Forthcoming. The politics of Hungarian fiscal policy. In *Reforming the state,* ed. J. Kornai, S. Haggard, and R. Kaufman. New York: Cambridge University Press.

Haggard, S., and S. Webb, eds. 1994. *Voting for reform: Democracy, political liberalization, and economic adjustment.* New York: Oxford University Press.

Hall, H. K., and D. Nelson. 1992. Institutional structure and the political economy of protection: Legislated vs. administered protection. *Economics and Politics* 4 (1): 61–76.

Heller, W. B., P. Keefer, and M. McCubbins. 1998. Political structure and economic liberalization: Conditions and cases from the developing world. In *The origins of liberty: Political and economic liberalization in the modern world,* ed. P. Drake and M. McCubbins. Princeton, N.J.: Princeton University Press.

Helliwell, J. F. 1994. Empirical linkages between democracy and economic growth. *British Journal of Political Science* 24 (2): 225–48.

Hellman, J. 1998. Winners take all: The politics of partial reform in postcommunist transitions. *World Politics* 50, no. 2 (January): 203–34.

Horowitz, D. L. 1993. Comparing democratic systems. In *The global resurgence of democracy,* ed. Larry Diamond and Marc F. Plattner. Baltimore: Johns Hopkins University Press.

Katzenstein, P. 1985. *Small states in world markets: Industrial policy in Europe.* Ithaca, N.Y.: Cornell University Press.

Kaufman, R. R., C. Bazdresh, and B. Herredia. 1994. Mexico: Radical reform in a dominant party system. In *Voting for reform,* ed. S. Haggard and S. Webb. New York: Oxford University Press.

Kaufman, R. R., and L. Zuckerman. 1998. Attitudes toward economic reform in Mexico: The role of political mediations. *American Political Science Review* 92, no. 2 (June): 359–76.

Kornai, J., S. Haggard, and R. Kaufman. Forthcoming. *Reforming the state: Fiscal and welfare reform in post-socialist countries.* New York: Cambridge University Press.

Krueger, A. 1974. The political economy of the rent seeking society. *American Economic Review* 83 (June): 291–303.

———. 1992. *Economic policy reform in developing countries.* Oxford: Blackwell.

Labán, R., and F. Sturzenegger. 1994a. Distributional conflict, financial adaptation and delayed stabilization. *Economics and Politics* 6, no. 3 (November): 257–78.

———. 1994b. Fiscal conservatism as a response to the debt crisis. *Journal of Development Economics* 45:305–24.

Lange, P., and G. Garrett. 1985. The politics of growth: Strategic interaction and economic performance in the advanced industrial democracies, 1974–1980. *Journal of Politics* 67:792–827.

Levy, B., and P. Spiller. 1996. *Regulations, institutions, and commitment: Comparative studies in telecommunications.* New York: Cambridge University Press.

Linz, J. J. 1993a. The perils of presidentialism. In *The global resurgence of democracy,* ed. Larry Diamond and Marc F. Plattner. Baltimore: Johns Hopkins University Press.

———. 1993b. The virtues of parliamentarism. In *The global resurgence of democracy,* ed. Larry Diamond and Marc F. Plattner. Baltimore: Johns Hopkins University Press.

Linz, J. J., and A. Valenzuela. 1994. *The failure of presidential democracy.* Baltimore: Johns Hopkins University Press.

Lipton, D., and J. Sachs. 1990. Creating a market economy in Eastern Europe: The case for Poland. *Brookings Papers on Economic Activity,* no. 1:75–147.

Mainwaring, S. 1989. Presidentialism in Latin America. *Latin American Research Review* 25:157–79.

Mainwaring, S., and M. Shugart, eds. 1997. *Presidentialism and democracy in Latin America.* New York: Cambridge University Press.

Maraval, J. M. 1997. *Regimes and markets: Democratization and economic change in southern and eastern Europe.* New York: Oxford University Press.

Martinelli, C., and M. Tommasi. 1997. Sequencing of economic reforms in the presence of political constraints. *Economics and Politics* 9, no. 2 (July): 115–31.

Maxfield, S. 1997. *Gatekeepers of growth: The politics of central banking in developing countries.* Princeton, N.J.: Princeton University Press.

McCubbins, M., R. Noll, and B. Weingast. 1987. Administrative procedures as an instrument of political control. *Journal of Law, Economics and Organization* 3:243–77.

McMillan, J., and B. Naughton. 1992. How to reform a planned economy: Lessons from China. *Oxford Review of Economic Policy* 8, no. 1 (spring): 130–43.

Milner, H. 1998. The political economy of international trade. New York: Columbia University. Unpublished manuscript.

Montinola, G., Y. Qian, and Barry Weingast. 1995. Federalism, Chinese style: The political basis of economic success in China. *World Politics* 48, no. 1 (October): 50–81.

Murphy, K., A. Shleifer, and R. Vishny. 1992. The transition to a market economy: Pitfalls of partial reform. *Quarterly Journal of Economics* 107, no. 3 (August): 889–906.

Murrell, P. 1992. Conservative political philosophy and the strategy of economic transition. *East European Politics and Society* 6, no. 1 (winter): 3–16.

Myerson, R. 1993. Incentives to cultivate favored minorities under alternative electoral systems. *American Political Science Review* 87 (4): 856–69.

Naím, M. 1994. Latin America: The second stage of reform. *Journal of Democracy* 5, no. 4 (October): 33–48.

Naughton, B. 1995. China's economic success: Effective reform policies or unique conditions? In *The evolutionary transition to capitalism,* ed. K. Z. Poznanski. Boulder, Colo.: Westview.

Nelson, D. 1988. Endogenous tariff theory: A critical survey. *American Journal of Political Science* 32, no. 3 (September): 796–837.

———. 1998. The political economy of trade policy reform: The problem of social complexity. New Orleans: Tulane University, Murphy Institute of Political Economy. Unpublished manuscript.

Nelson, J., ed.1990. *Economic crisis and policy choice.* Princeton, N.J.: Princeton University Press.

———. 1992. Poverty, equity, and the politics of adjustment. In *The politics of adjustment: International constraints, distributive conflicts and the state,* ed. S. Haggard and R. Kaufman. Princeton, N.J.: Princeton University Press.

———, ed. 1994. *Intricate links: Democratization and market reforms in Latin America and Eastern Europe.* Washington, D.C.: Overseas Development Council.

O'Flaherty, B., and J. Bhagwati. 1997. Will free trade with political science put normative economists out of work? *Economics and Politics* 9, no. 3 (November): 207–19.

Olson, M. 1982. *The rise and decline of nations.* New Haven, Conn.: Yale University Press.

———. 1993. Dictatorship, democracy, and development. *American Political Science Review* 87, no. 3 (September): 567–76.

Peltzman, S. 1976. Toward a more general theory of regulation. *Journal of Law and Economics* 19, no. 2 (August): 211–40.

Perotti, R. 1997. The political economy of fiscal consolidations. New York: Columbia University. Unpublished manuscript.

Portes, R. 1991. The path of reform in central and eastern Europe: An introduction. *European Economy,* special issue no. 2:3–15.

Powell, G. 1982. *Contemporary democracies: Participation, stability, violence.* Cambridge, Mass.: Harvard University Press.

Przeworski, A. 1991. *Democracy and the market: Political and economic reforms in Eastern Europe and Latin America.* New York: Cambridge University Press.

———. 1994. Public support for economic reform in Poland. *Comparative Political Studies* 29:520–43.

Przeworski, A., and F. Limongi. 1993. Political regimes and economic growth. *Journal of Economic Perspectives* 7, no. 3 (summer): 51–69.

Ramseyer, J. M., and F. M. Rosenbluth. 1993. *Japan's political marketplace.* Cambridge, Mass.: Harvard University Press.

Ranis, G., and A. Mahmood. 1992. *The political economy of development policy change.* Oxford: Blackwell.

Rodrik, D. 1989. Promises, promises: Credible policy reform via signaling. *Economic Journal* 99:756–72.

———. 1994. The rush to free trade in the developing world: Why so late? Why now? Will it last? In *Voting for reform: Democracy, political liberalization, and economic adjustment,* ed. S. Haggard and S. Webb, 61–88. New York: Oxford University Press.

———. 1995. The dynamics of political support for reform in economies in transition. *Journal of the Japanese and International Economies* 9:403–25.

———. 1996. Understanding economic policy reform. *Journal of Economic Literature* 34 (March): 9–41.

———. 1997. *Has globalization gone too far?* Washington, D.C.: Institute for International Economics.

Roland, G. 1994. The role of political constraints in transition strategies. *Economics of Transition* 2 (1): 27–41.

Roland, G., and T. Verdier. 1994. Privatization in Eastern Europe: Irreversibility and critical mass effects. *Journal of Public Economics* 54:161–83.

Rose-Ackerman, S. 1998. Corruption and development. In *Annual World Bank conference on development economics 1997*, 35–68. Washington, D.C.: World Bank.

Roubini, N. 1991. Economic and political determinants of budget deficits in developing countries. *Journal of International Money and Finance* 10:549–72.

Roubini, N., and J. Sachs. 1989. Political and economic determinants of budget deficits in the industrial democracies. *European Economic Review* 33:903–38.

Sachs, J. 1993. *Poland's jump to the market.* Cambridge, Mass.: MIT Press.

———. 1994. Life in the emergency room. In *The political conditions for economic reform*, ed. John Williamson. Washington, D.C.: Institute for International Economics.

Sachs, J., and W. T. Woo. 1994. Structural factors in the economic reforms of China, Eastern Europe, and the Soviet Union. *Economic Policy* 18 (April): 102–45.

Sartori, G. 1976. *Parties and party systems.* New York: Cambridge University Press.

Schamis, H. 1999. Distributional coalitions and the politics of economic reform in Latin America. *World Politics* 51, no. 2 (January): 236–68.

Shafer, M. 1995. *Winners and losers.* Ithaca, N.Y.: Cornell University Press.

Shirk, S. 1993. *The political logic of economic reform in China.* Berkeley: University of California Press.

Shugart, M., and J. M. Carey. 1992. *Presidents and assemblies.* New York: Cambridge University Press.

Shugart, M., and S. Haggard. 2000. Institutions and public policy in presidential systems. In *Presidents, parliaments, and policy,* ed. Stephan Haggard and Mathew McCubbins. New York: Cambridge University Press, forthcoming.

Shugart, M., and D. Nielson. 1994. A liberal dose: Electoral reform and economic adjustment in the wake of the debt crisis. Paper presented at the annual meeting of the American Political Science Association, New York, September.

Silva, E. 1993. Capitalist coalitions, the state, and neoliberal economic restructuring: Chile, 1973–1988. *World Politics* 45, no. 4 (July): 526–59.

Sirowy, L., and A. Inkeles. 1990. Effects of democracy on economic growth and inequality: A review. *Studies in Comparative International Development* 25 (1): 126–57.

Tommasi, M., and A. Velasco. 1996. Where are we in the political economy of reform? *Journal of Policy Reform* 1:187–238.

Tornell, A. 1995. Are economic crises necessary for trade liberalization and fiscal reform? The Mexican experience. In *Reform, recovery, and growth: Latin America and the Middle East,* ed. R. Dornbusch and S. Edwards. Chicago: University of Chicago Press.

Tsebelis, G. 1995. Decision making in political systems: Veto players in presidentialism, parliamentarism, multicameralism, and multipartyism. *British Journal of Political Science* 25 (3): 289–325.

van de Walle, N. 1994. Political liberalization and economic policy reform. *World Development* 22, no. 4 (April): 483–500.

Velasco, A. 1994. The state and economic policy: Chile, 1952–1992. In *The Chilean economy: Policy lessons and challenges,* ed. B. Bosworth, R. Dornbusch, and R. Labán. Washington, D.C.: Brookings Institution.

———. 1998. The common property approach to the political economy of fiscal policy. In *The political economy of reform,* ed. F. Sturzenegger and M. Tommasi. Cambridge, Mass., and London: MIT Press.

Waterbury, J. 1989. The political management of economic adjustment and reform. In *Fragile coalitions: The politics of economic adjustment*, ed. J. Nelson. New Brunswick, N.J.: Transaction.

——. 1993. *Exposed to innumerable delusions: Public enterprise and state power in Egypt, India, Mexico, and Turkey.* Cambridge: Cambridge University Press.

Wei, S.-J. 1998. Gradualism versus big bang: Speed and sustainability of reforms. In *The political economy of reform*, ed. F. Sturzenegger and M. Tommasi. Cambridge, Mass., and London: MIT Press.

Weingast, B. 1995. The economic role of political institutions: Market-preserving federalism and economic development. *Journal of Law, Economics and Organization* 11 (1): 1–31.

Williamson, J., ed. 1994. *The political economy of policy reform.* Washington, D.C.: Institute for International Economics.

Woo, W. T., W. Hai, Y. Jin, and G. Fan. 1994. How successful has Chinese enterprise reform been? Pitfalls in opposite biases and focus. *Journal of Comparative Economics* 18, no. 3 (June): 410–37.

World Bank. 1995. *Bureaucrats in business: The economics and politics of government ownership.* New York: Oxford University Press.

Comment on the Paper by Stephan Haggard
Abhijit V. Banerjee

Stephan Haggard starts with a premise that I wholeheartedly agree with: that it is not always useful to think of reforms as outcomes of interest group conflicts. He suggests (and once again I concur) that major reforms that involve the transformation of entire systems are perhaps only possible when something like a crisis opens up a space between the interest groups where a range of policy options suddenly become available.

The author goes on to argue that it is precisely this space that allows institutions to have a role to play. This too I agree with. But I am less sure that I entirely agree with the author about the role that institutions play in this process.

The author suggests that institutional facts such as whether it is a presidential or a parliamentary system, the extent of delegation of decision-making powers to specialized agents, and the nature of the internal organization of the ruling party may have important effects on the reform process. This is because policy changes are easier to block or derail or delegitimize under some of these institutional arrangements than under others.

These are indeed interesting hypotheses, though for reasons I will elaborate later I am not entirely sure they are pertinent to concerns about what enables the kinds of very large scale reforms the paper mainly talks about. Before I come to that, however, let me point out some difficulties with empirically evaluating such hypotheses.

Abhijit V. Banerjee is professor of economics at the Massachusetts Institute of Technology.

The basic problem is that most of these institutions are likely to be endogenously selected: countries often switch from parliamentary to presidential systems because those in power think that this change will give them more power; delegation to specialized agents often reflects the fact that the executive has lost its credibility; lack of inner party democracy may reflect a broader authoritarian strain in the political culture. Ideally, of course, one would like to find instruments: exogenous sources of variation that, once one puts in the appropriate controls, do not by themselves affect the progress of the reform. But I am not sure where to look—or even what theory to use—when arguing for exogeneity. The next best alternative is probably detailed case studies that are sensitive to the issue of exogeneity (rather than cross-country regression studies that put institutions on the right-hand side), but I know too little about the field to judge the adequacy of these studies.

However, my more basic concern is theoretical: even if the author is right about the role played by institutional arrangements in structuring the political process, it seems to me that many reforms take place exactly when politics-as-usual is at least partly in abeyance. The magnitude of the crises that both necessitate and enable the reforms are often such that almost everyone feels the need for something to change—it is, after all, exactly that shared feeling that clears a space inside the logjam of interest group politics. Therefore, while I agree that institutions play an important role in enabling reforms, the most important institutions may be those that serve a very different function.

Before saying anything about what these institutional imperatives might be, I need to emphasize that I have a very specific view of large-scale reforms: I hold that up to a first approximation, large-scale reforms have to be seen as systemic innovations. This is not just because economies differ—they sometimes do and sometimes do not—but also because histories differ and the set of existing institutions with real legitimacy differs and the capabilities of the reforming leadership differ. Even where the basic economics is clear and the medicine is well known, reforms may fail because the relevant people did not understand what was to happen to them, or because they did not believe (perhaps rationally, given their past history) that what was announced would actually happen, or because they did not believe that others would believe that what was announced would actually be carried out, or for a host of other reasons. In other words, reforms necessarily involve cobbling together a package that is only part economics—which is itself often not very well understood because of the many important complementarities that are involved. The rest of it is part institutional design, part public relations, part rhetoric. A successful reform involves coming up with the right combination of all these things in the context of the particular country. No wonder it looks like a lot of intuition and guesswork even where the rhetoric of the leaders is one of economic science. Who could have guessed that the strange institution of a town and village enterprise would be the engine of one of the greatest growth miracles of all time or that Russian privatization would have gone the way it did?

If this view of reforms is correct, then the role of institutions in the reform process may be very different from that envisaged by the author. Their most important contribution may be to facilitate innovation: that is, to allow the system to adopt new untried ideas relatively easily, to discard old failed ones quickly, and to capitalize on the few ideas that in the end turn out to work. A free press may be a vital institution from this point of view: the diffusion of reliable information about what is working and what is not is clearly essential in determining what to discard and what to push. Moreover, an independent and reputable press may play a crucial role in building a consensus in favor of one reform and against another. For very similar reasons, having a statistical apparatus that can gather relevant data quickly and reliably and an academic community capable of correctly interpreting the available data may be very important. This also suggests a reason why countries with well-functioning welfare systems might find it easier to reform:[1] quick changes may be easier when people are relatively confident they will not lose too much.

All this is of course very speculative. I do not claim to know how one would even begin to empirically assess this view of reforms and institutions and compare it with the view espoused by the author. But I do feel it is a step we need to take.

1. The author suggests a related but different reason.

Economic Policy Reform in Latin America

Vittorio Corbo

3.1 Introduction

During the past decade the focus of economic policies in Latin America has shifted radically, away from a disregard for basic macroeconomic balances and efficiency in the use of resources, toward restoring macroeconomic stability and increasing the role of markets in the allocation of resources. Policy and institutional change has been so radical that the overall model of development has been turned upside down. The new model emphasizes macroeconomic stability, competitive market structures, integration into the world economy (outward orientation), and a new role for the government sector. In the new model the government sector is responsible for establishing the institutions necessary for achieving and maintaining macroeconomic stability and for the proper functioning of a market economy. But this is not all. The government has been given additional responsibilities in providing public goods and in improving the access of the poorest groups in the population to social services.[1]

These are major changes. Up to the mid-1980s, most Latin American economies were characterized by very restrictive trade regimes, very intrusive and large government sectors, and severe macroeconomic imbalances. Those imbalances took the form of high and sometimes accelerating infla-

Vittorio Corbo is professor of economics at Pontificia Universidad Católica de Chile (the Catholic University of Chile) and current vice president of the International Economics Association.

The author thanks Andrés Elberg and Francisco Gallego for very efficient research assistance. He also thanks Anne O. Krueger, Miguel Savastano, and an anonymous referee for comments on previous versions of the paper.

1. For an assessment of the consensus on policy reforms, see Williamson (1989) and Corbo and Fischer (1995).

tion and large current account deficits. Throughout the region, economic policy typically included price controls, a very protective and highly distorted trade regime (with a high mean tariff in a context of great variance in nominal import tariffs and a wide variety of nontariff barriers), multiple exchange rate systems, a distorted process of credit allocation, and very restrictive labor practices.

The old development model not only led to a highly distorted and inefficient economy but also failed to achieve the ultimate objectives of sustainable improvement in output growth, reduced income distribution inequality, and significant reduction in poverty. Failures on this front were due to both the inefficient economic system created in the process and the lack of policies targeted to improve the opportunities of the poorest groups in the population. A clear example of the latter is the complete lack of focus of education expenditures. Thus a substantial part of the education budget was spent on tertiary education, while the quality and coverage of primary and secondary education remained very poor.

The debt crisis of the early 1980s set the stage in Latin America for the introduction of widespread reforms that drastically changed the traditional import substitution-cum-government intervention development model, which most Latin American countries had pursued since the Second World War. As the debt crisis unfolded, one by one the countries in the region found their access to commercial loans severely curtailed. In these circumstances, adjustment was inevitable. Typically, the country suffering an external crisis also had a large and unsustainable fiscal deficit and, in many cases, was experiencing very rapid inflation. Thus macroeconomic problems were at the root of the crisis, and macroeconomic adjustment programs were at the forefront of the adjustment effort.

The adjustment programs of the 1980s, designed in the middle of a profound crisis, had to find quick ways to reduce current account deficits while simultaneously creating the basis for future growth. In the short run, to reduce current account deficits (which are equal to the difference between domestic expenditures and national income) it was necessary to focus policy measures more on expenditure reduction than on boosting output, as the latter type of policy produces results much more slowly. Thus adjustment programs were dominated by stabilization components, often with the support of the International Monetary Fund (IMF) and other international financial institutions.

The adjustment programs included drastic reductions in public sector deficits, monetary and exchange rate policies geared to produce real depreciation while avoiding an acceleration of inflation, and the privatization of public enterprises operating at a loss. Once the worst of the crisis was over, countries initiated more profound policy and institutional reforms to complement stabilization policies, with a view to creating conditions for achieving sustainable growth and reducing poverty. These changes in policy and institutions emphasized actions that maintained macroeconomic stability and established the conditions needed to make markets operate more efficiently and to reduce government interference. Measures to enhance the role of markets included the creation of more open trade regimes, the development of competitive market structures, and the restructuring of the public sector.

In the process, most Latin American countries have experienced drastic changes in economic policy during the past decade, moving decisively toward more stable and more open market systems. New policies have been introduced in the areas of inflation stabilization, fiscal reform, trade and financial liberalization, privatization and regulation of newly privatized enterprises, and the transition from pay-as-you-go to individually capitalized social security systems.

Once the first-generation reforms were consolidated, several countries made incursions into a second generation of policy and institutional reform by tackling long overdue improvements in the delivery of health, education, nutrition, and judicial services. Pursuing this type of reform much later has to do both with the increasing awareness of the role it can play in raising the benefits of the first generation of reform and with the greater difficulty of designing and implementing this type of reform. Part of the difficulty is related to opposition from interested pressure groups that are obtaining rents from the current state of affairs.

These reforms have gone hand in hand with a sharp rise in the quality of the policy debate in the region, where technical arguments have replaced ideology. A new generation of highly trained economists, many of them graduates of first-rate academic programs in North America and Europe, has played a key role in the design and implementation of these policies and in selling them to society at large. While the first generation of reforms benefited from accumulated knowledge, much remains to be learned about the most appropriate way to implement this second generation of reforms. Moreover, progress in this area is central to making further progress with regard to reducing poverty and improving income distribution.

The rest of the paper is divided into four sections. Section 3.2 reviews the analytical underpinnings and results of the first generation of reforms introduced in the 1980s. Section 3.3 reviews the Latin American experience with this type of reform. Section 3.4, studies the second generation of reforms that would be necessary to increase the payoff of the first generation of reforms. Finally, section 3.5 presents the main conclusions.

3.2 First Generation of Economic Policy Reforms: Setting Conditions for Sustainable Growth

With macroeconomic problems so endemic to the region, it is not surprising that the first policy reforms were intended to get macroeconomic fundamentals in place. However, policymakers soon realized that there were major opportunities available to them in addressing, early on, other, more structural impediments to growth. Thus the first generation of policy reforms addressed stabilization, efficiency, and growth objectives concurrently. The analytical underpinnings for these types of reforms have been provided by work in applied open economy macroeconomics (Dornbusch 1980; Corden 1994; Corbo and Fischer 1995), applied trade and welfare (Krueger 1984; Krugman 1987; Bhagwati 1991), and applied industrial organization (Jacquemin 1987; Scherer and Ross 1990; Vickers and Yarrow 1988).

The movement toward more liberal economic policies was initiated in Chile, in the mid-1970s, and subsequently spread to most countries in the region.[2] Many factors contributed to this change of model, but it is possible to single out a few as being of central importance. First, most countries suffered from poor economic performance in the post-1970 period, including open hyperinflation (Bolivia 1985, Peru 1989, Argentina 1987–89, and Nicaragua 1988–89) and a string of economic crises (Brazil 1985–93 and Mexico 1982 and 1987). Second, other countries wished to remove obstacles to sustainable growth (Argentina since 1991, Chile 1973–76, Colombia 1990, El Salvador 1990, Guatemala 1995–98, and Venezuela 1989). Third, the transformation of the Chilean economy was successful. Fourth, the socialist model in Eastern and Central Europe and in the former Soviet Union collapsed. Fifth, a critical mass of well-trained economists existed, with the capacity to evaluate the welfare effects of existing policies and to propose alternatives.[3] Finally, the intensity of the crisis diminished the political power of the rent-seeking groups that had benefited from earlier policies and had previously resisted this type of reform and, at the same time, increased the demand for reform.

The winds of reform led the UN Economic Commission for Latin America and the Caribbean (ECLAC)—once the major advocate of the import substitution model—to endorse the new development strategy. ECLAC (1992) proposed a new development model, based on restoring and maintaining macroeconomic balances, increasing outward orientation, broadening the role of market forces, and introducing social programs targeted toward the poorest groups in the population.

Structural reforms were necessary to promote higher, sustainable growth by improving the efficiency of resource allocation and improving the environment for physical and human capital accumulation. However, the supply response to this type of reform takes time, because the new

2. For a review of economic policies in Latin America from a historical perspective, see Corbo (1988) and Diaz-Alejandro (1983).

3. In many countries, this new breed of professional economists working in universities and think tanks had prepared specific proposals for alternative policies that later were used as blueprints by reformist governments.

policy environment must become credible and this credibility must be earned through overall consistency and persistence of policy. Furthermore, the supply response will also often require increased investment rates and the development of new products for external markets. Both types of initiatives take time to materialize once the new policy framework becomes credible. The supply response is also limited by the quality of human capital and of the legal framework.

In the area of structural reforms there is a broad base of knowledge on both the theory and the practice of policy reform. It was this accumulated knowledge and experiences with the previous policies that led most governments in Latin America to ease trade restrictions by lifting nontariff barriers and reducing the mean and variance of import tariffs. Opening to trade also included a radical reexamination of the treatment of direct foreign investment (DFI). In the 1960s and the 1970s DFI was discriminated against through restrictions on profit remittance and sectors of destination (DFI had restricted access to manufacturing and to "strategic" sectors), as well as on license payments and on property structure. However, during the 1980s and 1990s the doors were opened wide to DFI.

The rediscovery of the allocation role of markets led to the privatization of public enterprises that were engaged in the production and distribution of goods and services in markets where competition was present or could be developed. In the case of public utilities, where competition had to be developed, preparation of regulations that would promote a competitive environment went hand by hand with the privatization of public utilities. The principle of letting markets work was also behind the deregulation of labor and financial markets.

However, we still have much to learn about timing, comprehensiveness, sequencing, and reducing opposition to reforms by groups of vested interests that will be affected negatively by the reforms (Corbo and Fischer 1995; Graham and Naím 1998). We also need to learn how to put together a reform package that will maximize the synergy it generates. The payoff from trade reform will be severely reduced if macroeconomic stability is absent, if labor markets are highly regulated, and if port and highway infrastructure is deficient. In this case, to improve the supply response to the reforms, one must work on all fronts simultaneously. Recent empirical support for this idea is presented in Aziz and Wescott (1997). Much needs to be learned about efficient ways to reduce opposition and mobilize groups that benefit from the reforms. Given that reforms are a positive-sum game, some of the benefits could be invested in reducing the opposition of short-term losers.

The stabilization programs typically introduced in Latin America during the 1980s usually included fiscal consolidation, monetary contraction, and exchange rate adjustments. The starting point was often an external deficit target, based on the availability of external financing, including assumptions about debt service. This involved the necessary adjustment of domestic absorption relative to domestic output. Absorption was often reduced through direct cuts in government spending and restrictive monetary and fiscal policies aimed at reducing private spending. Real depreciation was most often accomplished by combining a nominal devaluation, flexible real wages, and contractionary aggregate demand policy. In most cases, fiscal adjustment included the introduction of an economywide value-added tax (VAT).

Analyses of the two components of structural adjustment—stabilization and macroeconomic adjustment and structural or microeconomic adjustment—are not generally dealt with simultaneously. And even on the macroeconomic side, the economics of stabilization are generally dealt with separately from the analysis of saving, investment, and growth, which are addressed once stabilization has been achieved.[4]

For an economy with restricted access to external financing, the effects of demand reduction programs are likely to be most apparent in the short run. As domestic expenditures are reduced, the real exchange rate must depreciate to avoid creating an excess supply of nontradable goods and unemployment. Unemployment will result if the real exchange rate is, for whatever reason, not allowed to rise, for example, due to insufficient adjustment (or none at all) of the nominal exchange rate or through real wage resistance.

Some countries have gone one step further in the development of institutions to support stabilization and adjustment. In particular, two types of institutional reforms have become popular: first, making central banks more independent and, second, enacting budgetary procedures more conducive to fiscal discipline.

Assessing the effects of reforms on macroeconomic outcomes is not easy because one needs to have an acceptable model and to control for other factors that also affect outcomes but are not related to the reforms. A simplistic evaluation procedure is to examine outcomes before, during, and after the introduction of the reforms. Using this procedure, the results of the first generation of reforms in terms of inflation and growth have been impressive. Tables 3.1 and 3.2 present the inflation and growth performances of the main countries in Latin America. As shown in table 3.1, three countries experienced triple-digit annual inflation in 1980–85 and in 1986–90. However, Bolivia moved to double-digit annual inflation during the second period, while Peru shifted from double-digit to quadruple-digit annual inflation. In contrast, during the 1991–97 period, only one country had an average annual inflation rate in three digits, Brazil. However, in 1997, Brazil reached an annual inflation of only 6 percent.

---

4. On the macroeconomic aspects of economic policy reforms, see Corbo and Fischer (1995).

Table 3.1   Inflation Rate (percent)

Country	Average			1996	1997
	1980–85	1986–90	1991–97		
Argentina	335.6	1,192.7	30.8	0.2	0.8
Bolivia	2,249.9	68.0	11.8	12.4	4.7
Brazil	141.9	1,056.9	823.6	15.5	6.0
Chile	23.8	19.4	11.9	7.4	6.2
Colombia	23.1	25.0	23.9	20.8	18.5
Mexico	56.4	75.7	20.8	34.4	20.6
Peru	97.4	2,341.4	83.8	11.6	8.6
Latin America and the Caribbean	107.1	321.9	110.11	22.3	13.1

Sources: Burki and Perry (1997) and IMF (1998a). Computed using yearly averages.

Table 3.2   Real GDP Growth Rate (percent)

Country	Average[a]			1996	1997
	1980–85	1986–90	1991–97		
Argentina	−1.1	0.4	2.6	4.2	8.4
Bolivia	−1.4	2.3	4.0	4.1	4.3
Brazil	2.5	2.0	3.0	2.8	3.0
Chile	2.3	6.5	7.4	7.2	7.1
Colombia	2.6	4.6	4.0	2.0	3.2
Mexico	3.1	1.5	2.9	5.2	7.0
Peru	0.6	−0.8	5.4	2.6	7.5
Latin America and the Caribbean	1.8	3.4	3.7	3.5	5.0

Sources: Burki and Perry (1997) and IMF (1998a).
[a]Unweighted average.

Table 3.2 shows that while inflation was being reduced and structural reforms were being implemented, the rate of growth was increasing in most countries. This is not surprising if one considers that the literature has shown that inflation has a negative effect on growth and that these costs are highly nonlinear in the rate of inflation.[5]

One key component of the first generation of reforms was a macroeconomic component aimed at achieving a drastic reduction of inflation and reducing the large current account deficits. Many factors were involved in this frontal attack on macroeconomic disequilibria.

First, the poor inflation record of the 1980s was overwhelming, as was

5. On the negative effects of inflation on growth, see Fischer (1993) and Corbo and Rojas (1993); on the nonlinear cost of inflation, see Bruno and Easterly (1994) and Sarel (1995).

the evidence of the high political and economic costs arising from that inflation. Second, theoretical and empirical evidence had accumulated that attempts to reduce unemployment through monetary policy result, eventually, in an acceleration of inflation without a permanent effect on the unemployment rate.[6] That is, the short-term Phillips curve trade-off between inflation and unemployment—so popular in the 1960s and early 1970s—tends to vanish in the long run. Third, awareness had increased that with future-oriented expectations and credible policies, the costs of reducing inflation are much lower than had been previously thought (Sargent 1982). Fourth, a widespread consensus had been reached among economists that macroeconomic stability is a precondition for sustainable growth and, thus, the best contribution monetary policy can make to long-term growth is to make low and predictable inflation possible.[7] Fifth, awareness had increased that inflation gives rise to a very regressive tax regime that affects mainly the poorest groups in the population, who have an unusually high ratio of non-interest-earning monetary assets to income (Bulir and Gulde 1995).

In most countries it was well understood that in order to reduce high inflation, the monetization of high public deficits had to be stopped. Thus the reform of public finances, to achieve low levels of deficits, had to be introduced as a core component of any inflation reduction program. The reduction of high inflation was pursued using two models: a money anchor strategy, followed clearly by Bolivia (1985) and Peru (1989), and an exchange rate anchor strategy, used in Argentina (1991) and in part in Brazil (1993).

Deficit reduction was based on both revenue enhancement and expenditure reduction measures. Revenue measures had to be introduced also to compensate for the reduction in trade taxes. On the revenue side, the introduction of a tax on value added was a standard feature, while reduction in government expenditures relied on the reduction of subsidies and the privatization of money-losing public enterprises.

Once enough progress had been made in lowering inflation, from the very high levels of the 1980s, most countries began to introduce programs aimed at reducing their inflation to single-digit annual levels and in some cases toward the levels observed in industrial countries. Three types of

6. For a recent references to these developments, see Goodhard (1994), Fischer (1995), and Bernanke et al. (1999).

7. Some of these factors have also been behind policy change in developed countries geared toward achieving price stability (Fischer 1996). The consensus is on the final objective of monetary policy but, as is the case in industrial countries, there is much disagreement about the transmission mechanisms of monetary policy and the length of lags involved. This is not surprising because the profession at large does not agree on a unique macroeconomic model. Contrary to what is claimed by my discussant, this is also a problem in industrial countries (see, in particular, Mishkin 1996 and the symposium in the *Journal of Economic Perspectives* 1995).

programs have been used to reduce inflation toward single-digit levels: monetary anchor, exchange rate anchor, and inflation target anchor.[8] Stabilization programs that rely on a money anchor or an inflation target anchor and, simultaneously, use a narrow band for the exchange rate face the potential problem of promoting capital inflows to take advantage of interest rate differentials. In that scenario, the authorities face a dilemma. If they sterilize the inflow, the resulting accumulation of reserves will result in a quasi-fiscal deficit and, at the same time, generate expectations of real exchange rate appreciation, which will encourage even larger volumes of capital inflow. If they do not sterilize the inflow, then the monetary expansion will be incompatible with achieving the monetary target or the inflation target.

The exchange rate anchor strategy usually takes the form of a predetermined path for the rate of currency devaluation. In extreme terms, this rate of change could be fixed at zero, while it can also be built into a stronger institutional framework, as in Argentina's currency board system. However, this system has some disadvantages. The first drawback is that one loses the freedom to implement an independent monetary policy. A country that pegs its currency to that of another country loses the ability to use monetary policy to respond to domestic shocks. Given that fiscal policy is very difficult to change and works with a substantial lag, this is not a minor problem. Furthermore, with free capital movements, the use of an exchange rate anchor exposes the country to speculative attacks. These could be costly in terms of the potential unemployment costs of defending the peg or in terms of the consequences of abandoning the peg when it results in a devaluation (Obstfeld and Rogoff 1995).

But this is not all. Fixing the exchange rate also makes it necessary to abandon other indexation mechanisms in the economy and to develop the appropriate institutional framework to protect the financial system from an eventual exchange rate correction.

Table 3.3 shows the inflation strategies used by several Latin American countries today to reduce inflation—gradually or otherwise—toward a single-digit annual level. All countries have as their main objective reducing inflation toward industrial country levels. To achieve this ultimate objective they use a combination of strategies, with some more important than others. Thus today Chile, Colombia, and Mexico use inflation targeting, and Brazil is in the process of doing so. However, at times Brazil's, Chile's and Mexico's exchange rate policies have been adjusted to ensure a trajectory of the exchange rate consistent with the inflation target, in the process relying also on the exchange rate as a nominal anchor for inflation.

---

8. Bernanke et al. (1999) discussed recent experiences with the use of inflation targeting in both industrial and semi-industrialized countries and compared them with the use of monetary and exchange rate targeting.

Table 3.3   Latin American Strategies for Reducing Inflation, 1990s

Country	Traditional		Other: Inflation Targeting
	Monetary Anchor	Exchange Rate Anchor	
Argentina		Main	
Bolivia	Main		
Brazil		Main	
Chile		Secondary	Main
Colombia			Main
Mexico	Main	Secondary	
Peru	Main		Secondary

Indeed, up to the end of 1998 Brazil pursued the objective of low inflation using all the instruments available, but the main instrument was the exchange rate.[9] Following the devaluation and the ensuing currency crisis of January 1999, Brazil shifted from the use of an exchange-rate-based nominal anchor toward an inflation target nominal anchor. Cases where a second nominal anchor is also used are presented in table 3.3, with the main anchor and the secondary anchor indicated. This classification is not foolproof, because at times the importance of the nominal anchors changed. Bolivia uses monetary targets as the main nominal anchor and does not have an explicit target for inflation. However, in Bolivian programs supported by the IMF, an inflation forecast has increasingly been playing the role of a nominal anchor. Peru uses a monetary target that takes the form of a ceiling on the expansion of net domestic assets, but it also announces an inflation target and, lately, has been moving from the explicit use of a monetary target to an inflation target. However, Peru and Mexico today use flexible exchange rate systems.

A common problem with the three types of stabilization strategies, in the case of the free movement of capital, is the impact of the chosen policy on the trajectory of the nominal and real exchange rates. In particular, a country that uses an inflation target or money target as a nominal anchor occasionally faces a dilemma insofar as the monetary policy enacted to reach the target could result in excessive nominal appreciation. This nominal appreciation, in the presence of inertia in the inflation rate, could result in a pronounced real appreciation that could jeopardize export growth and eventually threaten the sustainability of the external account, when economic agents begin to anticipate that it may be necessary to reverse the initial appreciation. Although this situation does not invalidate the consensus about how to conduct monetary policy to achieve long-term

9. Dornbusch went as far as stating that "Brazil has no explicit inflation target or nominal exchange rate commitment" (1997, 391); although there is no clear commitment, the active crawling peg plays, in part, the role of a monetary anchor.

objectives, it indicates the sort of dilemma about how to conduct monetary policy in the short run that has sometimes given rise to conflicts between central banks and finance ministries.[10] The trajectory of the real exchange rate is a much more important issue for small open economies than for large economies (Krugman 1999). The concern centers on the medium-term trajectory of the real exchange rate rather than on its observed value period by period. The problem here is that with two objectives—the inflation or money target and the real exchange rate (or the size of the current account deficit)—one needs two instruments and monetary policy provides only one.

The dilemma is well illustrated by recent Chilean experience. Chile has used inflation targeting since 1991, and from then to the present, it has also used an exchange rate band (Zahler 1997). Given the exchange rate system, as long as the observed value of the exchange rate is well within the band, the uncovered interest rate parity condition links the interest rate and the nominal exchange rate. In particular, when the exchange rate is well within the band, any adjustment in the domestic interest rate results in a movement in the opposite direction in the nominal exchange rate. Therefore, for all practical purposes, exchange rate policy has not been independent. Conflicts between the independent central bank and the Ministry of Finance have arisen when sharp nominal and real exchange rate appreciation has occurred, as a result of increases in domestic interest rates brought about to sterilize the inflationary effects of capital inflows. Similar problems have emerged in Colombia, when the central bank found it necessary to tighten monetary policy to undo the expansionary effects of very loose fiscal policy. It is claimed that during 1992–93, Peru was forced to decelerate the rate of reduction of inflation to avoid excessive real appreciation (Favaro 1996). In these cases, the way out of the dilemma is to select a second instrument that can be quite effective in helping to achieve a real exchange rate target. To this end, an effective instrument is fiscal adjustment.

Much remains to be learned about how to supplement monetary policy with fiscal and other policies to avoid too abrupt a real appreciation, which could result in an unsustainable current account deficit.[11] One could consider the development of automatic triggers, in the form of adjustments in the VAT or in the sequence of the execution of public investment projects, to achieve a current account deficit and a trajectory of the real exchange rate more sustainable over time. A potential problem, inherent in the introduction of temporary tax increases, is a political economy one. Temporary increases in the VAT, introduced when the economy overheats,

10. I thank Miguel Savastano for suggesting that this short-run monetary management point needs to be recognized explicitly.

11. The problem is aggravated by the finding that in general, fiscal policy has been procyclical, thus exacerbating the expansionary effects of capital inflows (Gavin et al. 1996).

are usually difficult to reverse because the authorities find reasons to maintain the higher tax to finance a higher permanent level of public expenditure. The way out of this impasse could arise during a period when the economy is growing below potential; in this case, the authorities could use a temporary decrease in the VAT, instead of a decrease in interest rates, to stabilize the economy. This action could open the door for a more balanced use of monetary and fiscal policy to stabilize the economy, while simultaneously avoiding the broad swings in the nominal (and real) exchange rates that accompany sharp changes in domestic interest rates not associated with movements in international interest rates. It could be claimed that under Ricardian equivalence, fiscal policy is ineffective. However, much empirical evidence shows that in developing countries, the null hypothesis of Ricardian equivalence is strongly rejected (Corbo and Schmidt-Hebbel 1991; Edwards 1995b; Masson, Bayoumi, and Samiei 1998).

In the other areas encompassing the first generation of reforms the general principle has been to promote competition as a means of improving resource allocation. In trade reforms the mean and variance of import tariffs have been reduced, nontariff barriers have been replaced by tariffs, and multiple exchange rate systems have been unified. In some countries opening to trade has been pursued in a multilateral way, while in others it has been done through regional trade agreements. In the area of financial reforms, interest rate controls have been lifted, target credit allocation schemes abandoned or notably softened, reserve requirements reduced, and financial institutions privatized. However, although some progress has been made in the development of an appropriate regulatory and supervisory framework for the financial system, much still has to be done in this area. Furthermore, the series of financial crises experienced throughout the region in recent years has been facilitated by this weakness.

The restructuring of the public sector has been done in two stages. First, it has been disengaged from the production and distribution of private goods and from the allocation of credit. Second, it has become involved more fully in the creation of the institutions needed by a properly functioning competitive market economy and in the provision of public goods. The latter function involves improving the access of the poorest groups in the population to education, health, and nutrition services.

In the area of privatization, the state has moved away from the production of private goods traded in competitive markets. In the case of public utilities, privatization has been preceded by the development of appropriate competition-promoting regulations. However, this is also an area where much work remains. Creating a competitive framework for newly privatized public utilities has proved difficult. The new model also recognizes a positive role for DFI in the transfer of technology, access to financing and marketing channels, and the incorporation of modern managerial capabilities. It further recognizes that DFI flows are a more stable source of financing than highly volatile short-term financial flows.

Labor reforms have been aimed at increasing the mobility of labor and the flexibility of wages. Traditional labor legislation in Latin America was intended to assure job stability and protect workers from the risks associated with unemployment, illness, and old age. The side effects of this legislation were high labor turnover, widespread use of informal labor contracts, and, ultimately, high unemployment. In this area, reforms have reduced labor taxes and severance payments, but progress has been much slower than in other areas. Social security reforms have replaced old pay-as-you-go systems with private individual capitalization systems (Edwards 1995a; Inter-American Development Bank [IDB] 1996).

The current international crisis has put some stress on economic policies in the region. In particular, the crisis has resulted in a sharp drop in terms of trade, a substantial increase in spreads, and a sudden reduction of capital flows. The drop in capital flows has resulted in a drastic correction in equity markets and has put pressures on exchange rate regimes, forcing the introduction of restrictive fiscal and monetary policies. Although the model has received wide acceptance, some voices question the potential benefits of opening the capital account (Bhagwati 1998; Krugman 1998a).

Much is to be gained by integration into world capital markets (Obstfeld 1998). Gains here are similar to gains from trade in goods and nonfactor services, although the risks are much higher. To maximize gains and reduce potential costs, the best strategy a country can pursue is to begin by getting its economic fundamentals in place. These fundamentals include macroeconomic stability—including a competitive real exchange rate—and a sound and safe financial system. The financial system must be well supervised, regulated, and capitalized. Lending to connected firms must be restricted, risks must be controlled and appropriately priced, and institutions in charge of supervision and regulation must be politically and financially independent and have well-trained staffs (Villanueva and Mirakhor 1990; Stiglitz 1994; Mishkin 1997, chap. 14 in this volume).

The importance of a safe and sound financial system cannot be minimized, as various countries have suffered costly and disruptive financial crises (Mexico, Paraguay, Ecuador, Venezuela, and Bolivia). Problems have emerged as a result of weaknesses in the regulation and supervision of financial institutions, which has led to undue risk taking with inappropriate assessment of the risks involved. This has been especially the case with exchange rate and maturity risks. Moreover, the running of such institutions requires a great deal of specific business knowledge and experience. They are also difficult to evaluate, in particular because undercapitalized institutions can run for some time without their problems becoming evident. Thus it is necessary to have in place the appropriate regulatory and supervisory capacity in an independent superintendent of banks, or a similar organization, before liberalizing. Regulations should require that banks have enough capital to deal with the large shocks to their portfolios that are typical of emerging markets. Indeed, Argentina has gone further that the Basle criteria, requesting banks to hold a level of capital above the 8 percent cutoff included in the Basle Accord.

The importance of having well-capitalized banks and appropriate regulation and supervision of the financial system has been emphasized by the recent discussion of the causes of the Asian crisis. Although many causes of the crisis have been identified by different authors, one common factor singled out in most interpretations of the crisis is weakness in the financial system and in the resulting investment allocation process (Corsetti, Pesenti, and Roubini 1998; Krugman 1997).

However, even for a country with the right fundamentals in place, problems can develop if too sudden an increase in capital inflows triggers overheating in the economy. This overheating results in a large increase in the current account deficit and an increase in the price of assets. Both effects will eventually have to be reversed but at very high cost.

Moreover, with the ongoing financial crisis in emerging markets, some consequences of the stabilization strategies followed in the 1990s have become much too evident. In particular, Chile and Colombia have become vulnerable to changes in the sentiments of foreign investors as a result of the large current account deficits and large appreciation built by those countries while they attempted to reduce inflation with restrictive monetary policies. Of course, this vulnerability grew when both countries suffered severe terms-of-trade losses and emerging market risk increased.

Another source of weakness relates to the defense of a rigid exchange rate system. The high interest rates required to withstand attacks on the currency could result in a deterioration in the quality of loans and a sharp slowdown of the economy, leading financial markets to conclude that the rigid exchange rate system must eventually be abandoned. In the process, the loss of reserves and high interest rates—to compensate for the expectations of a depreciation—could set the stage for a major financial and exchange rate crisis. Here too an externality could arise if a large country that follows this strategy ends in a crisis that ultimately engulfs a whole region (Glick and Rose 1998).

After the Asian crisis, and the current sudden shift in market sentiment toward Latin America, it has become commonplace to praise capital controls for their role in restoring the effectiveness of monetary policy as a stabilization tool. The endorsement of capital controls also embraces their role in reducing the vulnerability of a country subject to a sudden reversal in capital flows, such as those that have been recently observed (Krugman 1998b). Here one needs to be careful, and much still must be learned.

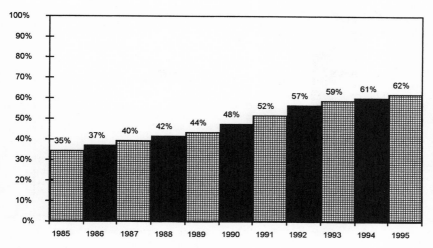

Fig. 3.1   Progress of overall reforms, 1985–95
Source: IDB (1997).

Some studies have claimed that thanks to controls on capital inflows, Chile and Colombia avoided "tequila"-type effects (IMF 1995, 1998b; Budnevich and Le Fort 1997). However, Valdés and Soto (1996) have shown that taxes on capital inflows change the composition but not the total amount of the inflow or the trajectory of the real exchange rate. Also, capital controls imposed for too long generate distortions and opportunities to invest resources in order to evade them. Controls on outflows are even worse because they generate incentives that discourage capital inflows of a more permanent nature (Dornbusch 1998; Labán and Larraín 1993).

3.3   Progress with First-Generation Policy Reforms

Much progress has been made in the past decade in implementing the first generation of policy reforms. IDB (1997) presented an index of the degree of progress with the first generation of reforms since 1985.[12] Based on the IDB work, progress with this first generation of reforms at the regional level is presented in figures 3.1 through 3.7. Figure 3.1 shows overall progress made with the first generation of reforms; the policy reforms considered are tax, trade, privatization, financial, and labor. As indicated in the figure, progress has been continuous throughout the period with acceleration in the early 1990s. Figure 3.2 indicates advances made

12. It should be mentioned at the outset that these indicators are highly subjective because they weigh a set of factors associated to each type of reforms. But other work done at the World Bank, reported in Burki and Perry (1997), provides a similar picture of progress with the reforms.

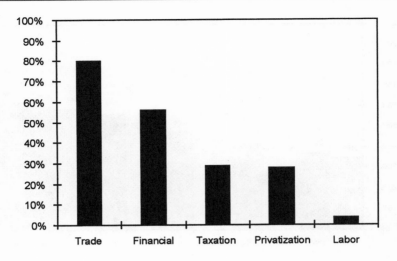

Fig. 3.2   Progress of structural reforms, 1985–95
Source: IDB (1997).

in individual areas. Progress on these measures is assessed by taking the difference between the 1995 and 1985 values and dividing by one minus the 1985 value. That is, they compare the progress made with how much overall was still left to liberalize. By these measures the most progress has been achieved in fiscal adjustment, trade reform, and financial reform, followed by privatization, while the least progress has been achieved in labor market reforms.

This is not surprising because labor and pension reforms have faced strong opposition from the power groups, and the introduction of pension reforms has to deal with financing the transition from pay-as-you-go to a fully funded individual capitalization system. The fiscal costs of financing this transition have often proved to be one of the main obstacles to further progress on social security reform (IDB 1997).

Looking at individual countries during the post-1982 period, major reform programs have been introduced in Mexico starting in 1983 but increasing since 1985, in Uruguay starting in 1984, in Bolivia since 1985, in Argentina and Peru since the early 1990s, in Venezuela starting in 1989 but abandoned soon thereafter, in El Salvador since the early 1990s, and in Costa Rica starting in 1985. Chile first, and then Mexico, Costa Rica, Bolivia, Venezuela, and lately El Salvador and Honduras have also made major inroads into the liberalization of foreign trade. Good progress in restructuring the public sector and reducing the role of the public sector in the production and distribution of private goods has been made in Argentina, Chile, Peru, Bolivia, and Mexico (see IDB 1996).

During the 1990s, Peru, Argentina, and El Salvador undertook the most radical reform programs in the region, while Brazil, since early 1994, has made great progress in reducing inflation and is initiating profound reforms of its overall economic system. Nicaragua not only eliminated its hyperinflation but also undertook a major reform effort geared to restoring a market economy. In recent years, Argentina has continued with reforms aiming at achieving fiscal consolidation and has made major progress in getting the private sector involved in the operation and construction of infrastructure, including ports and airports. Brazil has made progress in the privatization of public utilities. Chile has made advances in introducing a particular form of BOT (build, operate, and transfer) arrangement in highway infrastructure. Lately, Venezuela, which had been a major exception to the rule of introducing reforms, has also initiated adjustment efforts.

Table 3.4 shows overall progress with the first generation of reforms in individual countries. As indicated in the table, Chile made the most progress in the pre-1990 period; however, in the 1990s the countries that made the most progress were Peru and Argentina.

Figures 3.3 through 3.7 show the progress made in the different areas of reform by individual countries. The tax policy reform index in figure 3.3 is based on the efficiency of the tax on value added and the rates of corporate and personal income tax. In all countries but Chile much progress has been made in tax reform over the 1990s. In Chile progress has been minor because radical tax reforms had already been introduced in the 1970s and early 1980s.

Figure 3.4 shows the status of trade reform through time. Trade reforms have included unification of multiple exchange rate systems, replacement of nontariff barriers by tariffs, and reduction in the mean and dispersion of protection rates. According to the index of progress with trade liberalization, by the early 1990s most Latin American countries were very open to trade. The most progress was made in Brazil and Colombia.

Table 3.4   **Progress with Reforms by Country**

Country	1985–90	1991–95	Progress
Argentina	37.8	62.5	24.7
Brazil	40.7	56.1	15.4
Chile	56.8	61.4	4.6
Colombia	47.7	59.3	8.0
Mexico	41.2	59.3	18.1
Peru	25.6	61.9	36.3
Venezuela	30.4	42.5	12.1

Source: Author's calculations from data in Lora (1997).
Note: Table reports percentage of reforms achieved out of total that should be done.

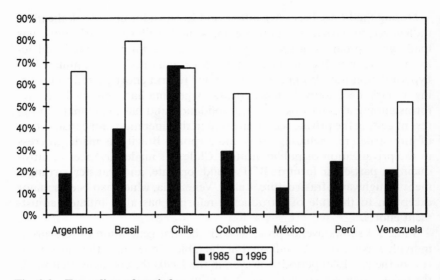

Fig. 3.3 Tax policy reform index
Source: Built using the methodology of Lora (1997), using data from Lora (1997) and Loayza and Palacios (1997).

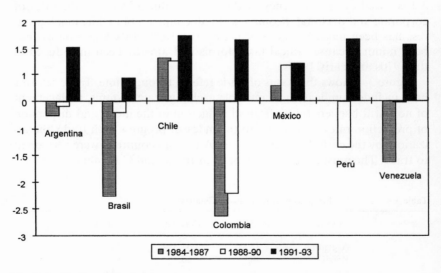

Fig. 3.4 Trade reform index
Source: Loayza and Palacios (1997).

Trade policy during the 1990s has made increasing use of trade agreements. It could be claimed that use of this mechanism is a step backward on the road to trade liberalization. However, the trade agreements of the 1990s are very different from those implemented in the 1960s and 1970s. The old agreements were extensions of the import substitution development model, while the new agreements are part of an outward-oriented development model. As an indication of the movement toward integration into the world economy, it is important to observe that today twenty-five countries in the region belong to the World Trade Organization (IDB 1996). Thus the opportunities for trade diversion are now much smaller because trade barriers against countries outside the agreement are much lower. The most important of the regional trade agreements is MERCOSUR. It includes Argentina, Brazil, Paraguay, and Uruguay as full members and Chile and Bolivia as associated members. Trade agreements are not a substitute for overall integration into the world economy, but they could complement this strategy by improving access to neighboring countries. Indeed, the most important benefits of MERCOSUR are expected to come from the promotion of trade through improvements in infrastructure, speedy movement of goods through customs, liberalization of transport services, and so forth. Mexico used its privileged relation with the United States to sign a trade agreement that also includes Canada: the North American Free Trade Agreement (NAFTA). NAFTA has given Mexico freer access to the all important North American market and played an important role in the export-led recovery of Mexico following the tequila crisis. Because the United States was already Mexico's most important trade partner and the import barriers of the United States and Canada are fairly low by international standards, the room for trade diversion in NAFTA is fairly limited while the room for trade creation in Mexico is fairly large.

These agreements, in general, include both the granting of preferential treatment to member countries and an exclusion list of products in which trade will be liberalized much later. The net result of these agreements has been the creation of a very differentiated and opaque tariff structure, in which the same good is subject to many levels of import tariffs depending on the country of origin. This tariff structure increases the costs of implementing country-of-origin regulation and creates opportunities for corruption through manipulation of the country classification of the origin of imports. As a result, the variance of the Latin American tariff structure has increased from 6.7 in the period 1990–93 to 8.5 in 1995 (Burki and Perry 1997).

Moving away from MERCOSUR, the recent proliferation of bilateral trade agreements among Latin American countries is most likely a movement in the wrong direction. Potential gains are very small, and these trade agreements have multiplied the opportunities for triangulation of

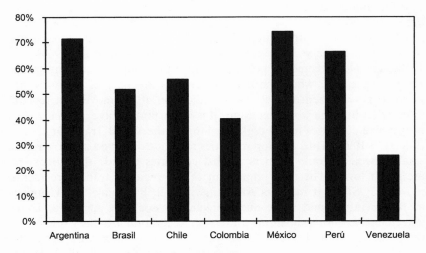

Fig. 3.5   Progress of privatization index, 1985–95
Source: Built using the methodology of Lora (1997), using data from Loayza and Palacios (1997).

trade and for trade diversion while the opportunities for trade creation are minimal. Furthermore, given the small sizes of the markets involved, one cannot claim that this type of agreement could have hidden benefits arising from increasing returns or dynamic advantages.

Figure 3.5 shows progress with privatization. The index takes into account the number of privatizations, the ratio of private investment to total investment, and the share of privatization revenues in GDP. By this measure the most progress in privatization was made by Mexico, Argentina, and Peru.

Figure 3.6 shows the status of financial liberalization across countries. Financial liberalization includes the privatization of banks and the lifting of restrictions on interest rates and on sectoral and regional credit allocation. It also includes the reduction or elimination of credit subsidies. The index is built by comparing an index of financial sector liberalization with the average value of this index for the group of countries considered. Using this indicator Chile, Mexico, and Brazil had the most liberalized financial systems in 1995.

Finally, figure 3.7 shows the status of reforms in the labor market. Labor market reforms include measures that increase labor mobility and wage flexibility. Reforms in this area include reductions in the causes for payment and the amount of payment for labor dismissal. They also include the reduction of labor taxes in connection to contributions to the social

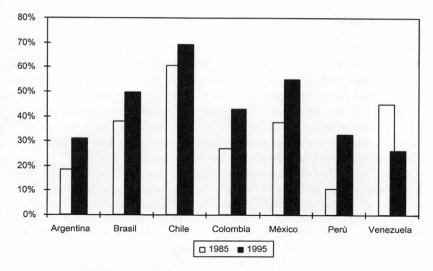

Fig. 3.6 Financial reform index
Source: Built using the methodology of Lora (1997), considering the Stock Market Development Index and the Banking Development Index of Loayza and Palacios (1997).

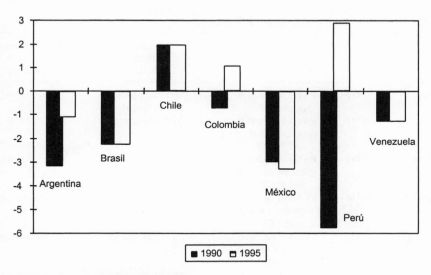

Fig. 3.7 Labor market reform index
Source: Loayza and Palacios (1997).

security system and to general government revenues. According to the index of the degree of labor market liberalization, by 1995 Peru, Chile, and Colombia had the most competitive labor markets.

The status of reforms of pension systems is presented in table 3.5. Most countries have moved away from pay-as-you-go state-run systems toward fully funded systems administered by the private sector but with government regulation and supervision. Reforms in this area have built on the Chilean model introduced in 1981. Private dedicated institutions have been created to administer pensions, with individuals having freedom of choice with respect to the administrator of their funds.

Concerning DFI the change in policy has been substantial. The main purpose of policy reforms in this area has been to get the benefits of DFI in terms of access to markets, technology, organization, and potential externalities from spillovers to local firms. Policy reform in this area has been radical, going all the way from the previous system of outright discrimination against DFI for ideological and political reasons to the new system of open competition among countries to attract DFI. Reforms in this area include the elimination of restrictions on sectors of destination and profit remittances and equal treatment with investment by locals. Some countries have gone further by offering stability with respect to tax

Table 3.5   Pension Reforms in Latin America

Country	Year	Kind[a]	Role of Public Sector	Relation between Public and Private Sectors
Chile	1981	PAYG replaced by private FF	Minimum pension, social assistance	Public sector subsidiary
Peru	1993	PAYG replaced by option between FF and PAYG	Social assistance	Competition
Colombia	1994	PAYG replaced by option between FF and PAYG	Minimum pension, social assistance	Competition
Argentina	1994	Division between private FF and public PAYG	Minimum and fixed pension	Complementarity
Uruguay	1996	Division between private FF and public PAYG	Basic pension for all	Complementarity
Mexico	1997	Public PAYG replaced by private FF (only for private sector workers)	Minimum pension, social assistance	Public sector subsidiary

Source: IDB (1996).
[a]PAYG, pay-as-you-go system; FF, fully funded system.

treatment. Chile, Argentina, Peru, and later Venezuela give more liberal treatment to DFI, while Mexico and Brazil keep some important restrictions. Table 3.6 presents the status of DFI regulation in the main countries of the region.

Because of the better business environment resulting from the reforms, the privatization programs, the introduction of equity swap schemes, and the lifting of restrictions on DFI, the share of DFI in GDP has increased substantially throughout the region (fig. 3.8).

Although much progress has been made in terms of the implementation of the first generation of reforms, there are still many impediments to growth related to policies and institutions in these areas of reform. These impediments provide opportunities for efficiency-enhancing reforms. Among these opportunities can be singled out reforms aimed at increasing labor mobility and improving the operation of ports, airports, and roads. Thus Fernández-Arias and Montiel (1997) found that an intensification of reform of the first-generation type could raise the rate of growth of GDP by as much as 2.5 percent per year.

Many opportunities also exist to increase efficiency and to reduce poverty and improve the distribution of income in the area of second-generation reforms, which are discussed in the following section.

3.4   Second Generation of Economic Policy Reforms

As the crisis of the early 1980s was left behind and sufficient progress was made in the implementation of the first generation of reforms, country after country began to focus on removing those obstacles that reduced the payoff of the first-generation reforms or limited the opportunities of the poorest groups in the population. This so-called second generation of policy reforms has focused on public sector reforms, judicial reforms, regulatory reforms, decentralization reforms, and education and health reforms.

The motivation for intensifying and extending the coverage of the reforms varies. For some, the first generation of reforms did not raise the growth rate high enough to permit substantial improvement in living standards. It has been claimed that with the first generation of reforms, the rate of growth of potential output could reach only 3.8 percent per year, a rate considered too low to permit substantial reduction of poverty and to increase support for the reforms (Lora and Barrera 1997). It has also been found that controlling for economic and political factors associated with differences in long-term growth, the growth rate of GDP per capita in Latin America is 1.5 percent lower than the growth rate in more advanced countries. It is claimed that policy and institutional weaknesses are the main factors behind this difference in growth rates (World Bank 1997).

It has also been claimed that a second generation of reforms is needed to raise output growth, to improve equity, to increase opportunities for

Table 3.6   **Regulations on DFI in Latin America, through 1994**

Country	Sectors Restricted to State	Sectors Restricted to Nationals	Controlling Interest by Foreigners Allowed?	Restrictions on Profit Remittances	Privatization Financed by Debt-Equity Swaps?
Argentina	None	None	All sectors	None	Yes
Brazil	Oil, gas, telecommunications	Banking, transport, media, health	Yes, except in computers	None	Yes
Chile	None	None	All sectors	None	No, program canceled early 1993
Colombia	Alcoholic beverages	Defense, toxic material disposal	All sectors	None, up to registered investment	No
Mexico	Petroleum, hydrocarbons, nuclear energy	Transport, media	Most sectors	None	No
Peru	None	None	All sectors	None	Yes
Venezuela	None	None	All sectors	None	n.a.

Source: Edwards (1995a).

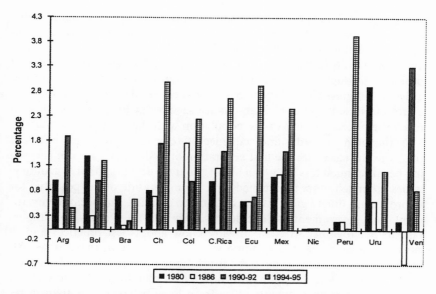

Fig. 3.8   Ratio of FDI to GDP in selected Latin American countries (percent)

the poorest groups in the population to advance in society, and, in this way, to assure the sustainability of the overall reform effort (Edwards 1995a). The importance of this point should not be dismissed, as there are groups ready and waiting for the failure of the reform process, namely, intellectuals and unreformed government bureaucracies (Edwards 1998).

The problem with the second generation of policy reforms is that no blueprint for these reforms is available, as there was for the first generation of reforms. Much must still be learned. For example, while there is a considerable body of knowledge on the theory and practice of trade policy reforms that has a bearing on policy design, the same is not the case for the design of policies to improve the quality and coverage of education and health services. Even more difficult problems emerge in the design of judicial reforms. "While there is increasing consensus on the need for institutional building and reform, and governments and multilateral banks are beginning to designate substantial amounts of resources towards these objectives, there is little intellectual clarity about how to achieve them. . . . There is even less clarity about the wide range of political dynamics that underlie institutional failure or underperformance. The scope of sectors is extremely broad, ranging from education to telecommunications to the judiciary" (Graham and Naím 1998, 323).

However, the need to improve the quality of services in these areas is so pressing that government after government in Latin America has decided to increase social expenditures (expenditures on education, health, nutrition, and pensions). If proper care is not taken to choose the "right" policies, there is the risk that a unique opportunity to improve policies in this area could be lost, and even worse, the attempt to solve these types of problems through increasing use of financial resources could put in jeopardy the progress made in achieving fiscal consolidation. The important issues are how to produce high-quality services at low cost and how to reach the poorest groups in the population with these types of services.

In this area the order and sequence of reforms is much less clear-cut than was the case with the first generation of reforms. This is not surprising because much less is known about program design, political economy issues are much more entrenched, and the magnitude of the potential for improvement differs greatly from country to country. But because government after government has decided to move into these areas, it is important to put together what we already know about best practices and to rush the research agenda to improve our knowledge in these areas. Although the international financial institutions have also focused their research and lending programs on these types of reforms, the interest of Latin American governments arose from local needs, rather than in response to an obscure Washington agenda as is claimed by my discussant. Indeed, it would be insulting to a political leader and to Latin America's intelligence to claim that these problems were discovered in Washington.

In the area of public sector reforms, on top of privatization of firms that produce private goods efforts have been made to improve the efficiency of public administration. Progress here includes the introduction of performance criteria in government programs and better definition of responsibilities and tasks within the public sector. However, changing the government model also requires completely overhauling the public sector, upgrading its regulatory capacity and downsizing its interventionist capacity. There are complex issues of worker redundancy, severance payments, and the introduction of a wage scale consistent with the need to improve the quality of civil servants. Important progress has been made in Argentina, Mexico, and Nicaragua, but much remains to be done (Burki and Perry 1997).

In the area of education, much progress has been made in the past twenty years in expanding enrollment at all levels. However, major deficiencies remain in the average level of academic achievement and in the opportunities offered to different groups in society. Because these problems have existed for a long time one observed consequence is that the average educational attainment of the labor force in Latin America lags behind those in other regions.

Improving education is not simply a problem of resources because extensive evidence exists that expenditures in this area are allocated in highly inefficient ways and that in spite of major expenditure increases, standard measurements of school performance and parental satisfaction have not improved much (IDB 1997; World Bank 1998). Moreover, school attendance is low and the time spent in school is short. The most pressing problem is the quality of education, which is still poor or mediocre in many countries. There is also much inequity in the quality of education to which poor people have access, while preprimary school coverage for girls and for the poorest groups in the population is very low, especially in rural areas.

Some simple reforms would increase inputs going into the school system: school buildings, books, and standard supplies. More inputs would permit the coverage of preprimary and secondary education to be increased, especially in rural areas, and the school day to be lengthened throughout the educational system. However, much must still be learned about the most efficient ways to improve education. This is not surprising because informational problems are endemic in this area. There are informational problems in assessing the quality of services provided and in enhancing the information set of parents, who are the ones making most choices about primary and secondary school. Policy reforms in the area of education (and health) services have to address (1) giving more authority to those with more information—users and local providers—by way of decentralizing, (2) improving information on school quality and making this information more accessible, and (3) using knowledge about curricula and new technologies to improve quality (World Bank 1998).

Some countries are moving in directions different from those suggested by research findings. Thus Hanushek (1995) and Kremer (1995, chap. 9 in this volume) have found that contrary to standard beliefs, class size is not an important and significant determinant of school performance. The same studies have found that the experience and education of teachers have positive—but not too important—effects on performance. In contrast, the quality of school facilities is an important determinant of performance. This literature has also found evidence in favor of institutional arrangements that decentralize the choice of school inputs to an accountable group far removed from central authorities (Kremer 1995; Pritchett and Filmer, forthcoming). Recent work by Kremer (chap. 9 in this volume), using experimental rather than econometric techniques, has shown that the quality of education depends on teaching techniques (audiovisual systems, radio, TV, etc.), the quality of the schools, and the incentive system facing the agents involved in the production of education.

It is surprising that contrary to what has been done in other areas, not much progress has been made in introducing competition into the provision of education, although there are some well-known techniques to promote private provision. It has been found, for example, that the use of vouchers, by increasing competition in the provision of school services, improves the quality of education.[13]

One can also say that reforms in this area have become very difficult for political economy reasons (Graham and Naím 1998). Teachers' trade unions and groups of intellectuals have opposed the introduction of freedom of choice and of private initiatives in the provision of school services. Typical arguments used to oppose this type of reform include the following: that they discriminate against poor children, that they do not promote national values, that parents do not make well-informed choices, and so on. Although some of these problems could be real, the alternative is a public monopoly that has all the problems listed above and many more.

Although we are far from having a unified view of how best to produce "good" education, the problems are so acute that it is necessary to proceed with methods that could make an obvious contribution now, even if they can be improved upon later. Among the methods that have proved effective are (1) extending the school day from half a day to a full day, (2) extending the coverage of preprimary school to girls and the poorest groups in the population (this strategy is especially recommended for rural areas), (3) improving basic school infrastructure, (4) investing in teacher training, and (5) decentralizing provision through appropriate incentives and regulations. One problem with the introduction of reforms in this area has been the lack of incentives to pursue alternative paths. In particular, the central government bureaucracy in charge of public education does not want to give power away by encouraging private provision, and it is not interested in trying alternative and (to it) unknown methods and procedures. A summary of recent educational reforms carried out in Latin America is presented in table 3.7.

In the case of health services, although progress in medicine has made it possible to reduce infant mortality and increase life expectancy, current provision is very inefficient and the degree of user satisfaction remains very low, in spite of substantial increases in the amount of resources spent. Furthermore, there is serious inequity in access to and quality of health services. The problem is not lack of resources. Latin America spends US$234 per patient while Asia spends only $21. However, access to health services is very limited for the poor and the rural population (IDB 1996). Furthermore, it has been found that given the low quality of the services provided, the poor in Latin America spend on health services more than twice of what is spent by comparable groups in other parts of the world (Londoño and Frank 1996).

---

13. West (1997) presented evidence in this direction based on the experience with this system in Milwaukee, but see Carnoy (1997) for a critique. It has been found that the voucher system also increases the motivation and commitment of parents to be involved with the schooling of their children (Witte, Thorn, and Prichard 1995 presented this type of evidence for Milwaukee).

Table 3.7   Educational Reforms in Latin America and the Caribbean

Country	Year of Initiation of Reform	Evaluation of Students	Systems of Information Management	Parental Participation	Decentralized Administration
Argentina	1994	X	X		X
Brazil					
Minas					
Gerais	1991	X	X	X	X
Parana	1995	X	X	X	X
Chile	1991	X	X		X
Colombia	1989				X
Dominican					
Republic	1990	X	X	X	X
El Salvador	1992	X	X	X	X
Mexico	1991	X	X	X	X
Nicaragua	1992	X	X	X	X
Paraguay	1995			X	X

Source: Academy for Educational Development, *Educational Reform Projects Supported by the World Bank, the IADB, and the USAID in Latin America and the Caribbean* (Washington, D.C., 1996).

Today most ministries of health and social security systems finance and provide health care through their own networks of hospitals and clinics. Such systems have a host of problems: service providers are not accountable, they have rigid staffing and little freedom in how to use their budget, and they are often highly inefficient. It has been found that in the allocation of the health budget, a large share goes to treatment and a much smaller portion to prevention. More than changing incentives, what is required is a major change in the microeconomic organization of the provision of services, separating the funding of services from their provision and strengthening the responsibilities of the funding agencies (Oxley and MacFarlan 1994). Also responsibility for provision should be given to local units, and the private sector should become involved in the provision of services (Gertler and Hammer 1997).

Political economy factors are as important in the health sector as in the educational sector (Graham and Naím 1998). The strongest opposition to reform in this sector comes from trade unions, medical associations, and intellectuals who claim that health care should be a universal service. It is the collapse and profound inequities of the current system that is forcing reform.

In designing the second generation of reforms some experiences are beginning to emerge in the use of demand subsidies instead of direct public provision of education and health services. Chile and Colombia have gone far in this direction, by introducing demand subsidies in education and health services and, in this way, promoting the participation of the private sector in the production of these services. In particular, for improving the access of the poorest groups in the population, a system like that in Colombia of targeting expenditures through the use of vouchers is an interesting innovation.

Private sector participation in the provision of health and education has been made possible by decentralizing production. For example, granting state subsidies (per student or per patient), once the production of services had been decentralized into the private sector, has encouraged the provision of these services to the poorest groups, who would otherwise have gone without them.

The justice system plays a key role in a market economy through many channels: defining and enforcing property rights, reducing transactions costs, limiting the discretion of the public sector, and reducing corruption in society at large.

It is widely acknowledged that the current judicial system is highly unpredictable, very slow, and very costly; that it provides very poor access to the poorest groups in the population; and that it is subject to widespread political intervention. Reforms must address the independence of the judicial system, the training of judges, and a major overhaul of the judicial process.

Another area being covered by the second generation of reforms is the introduction of regulations promoting competition in public utilities. Now that substantial progress has been made throughout the region in the privatization of energy, telecommunications, ports, and water services, problems have arisen in the operation of the system that were not envisaged when regulations were created at the time of privatization. There is a wide consensus now that the regulatory capacity of the state must be improved in order to promote competition in the production and distribution of these services. Modern regulatory theory provides the analytical underpinnings for efficient regulation. However, much remains to be done with regard to improving the training and qualifications of the regulators and ensuring that regulators are more independent of the political process.

A major challenge is to carry out this second generation of reform while preserving the newly gained macroeconomic prudence that is necessary to increase the payoffs of the first and second generations of reforms. Moreover, as the fiscal adjustment programs of the 1980s reduced the size of public sectors, they also reduced the capacity of these sectors to invest in infrastructure and human capital. For the public sector to be able to invest in upgrading its infrastructure and human capital base (which have the character of public goods), it will be necessary to allow the private sector to become involved in the production of these types of services. But this is not all. A framework must also be developed to permit private sector investment in infrastructure that belongs more properly to the category of private goods (i.e., high-density roads, ports, airports, and other things). Progress has been made recently in developing an efficient regulatory framework for the participation of the private sector in infrastructure, including roads and port facilities (Engel, Fischer, and Galetovic 1997).

As reductions in poverty slowed and, in some countries, even reversed, the new programs of the 1990s have adopted as an explicit objective the reduction of poverty. Progress on this front requires not only achieving sustainable growth at rates high enough to increase per capita income but also improving the access of the poorest groups in the population to government transfers and basic social services. Bolivia and Chile have made the most progress in this direction in Latin America.

3.5 Conclusions

Some observers of the Latin American situation have called the 1980s the "lost decade." However, the 1980s was also the decade of reckoning because the crisis created a unique opportunity to introduce radical reforms. The crisis not only made reforms more urgent but reduced the power of pressure groups opposed to change.

Policy and institutional changes introduced in the region are much more consistent with the lessons derived from mainstream economics than policies followed during the heyday of the import substitution-cum-government intervention model of the previous forty years.

Reforms have included drastic reductions in public sector deficits, opening of the economies to foreign trade, promotion of competition through openness to trade, elimination of discrimination against direct foreign investment, deregulation or privatization of public utilities, and radical redefinition of the role of the state. However, although much progress has been made in these areas, there is still much to be done.

Current problems in emerging markets emphasize the importance of having the right policies—in particular, a sound and solid financial system—maintaining low current account deficits, and reducing distortions that may encourage short-term capital inflows.

As a result of the reforms, the state has reduced its role as a producer and distributor of private goods and has increased its role in macroeconomic management, provision of public goods, and improvement of access to social services by the poorest groups in the population.

However, at the regional level, with the exception of Chile and Bolivia, poverty has not been significantly reduced. As a result, increasing attention is being given in the 1990s to a second generation of reforms aimed at increasing overall growth and reducing poverty. These reforms have as their main objectives improving provision and distribution of social services, judicial services, physical infrastructure, and competitiveness of public utilities.

For the second generation of reforms much remains to be learned about how to improve the quality of services in the most efficient way. In the case of education this includes teaching methods, input relations, and the industrial organization of the sector. Similar problems emerge in the case of health care.

References

Aziz, J., and R. Wescott. 1997. Policy complementarities and the Washington Consensus. IMF Working Paper no. 97/118. Washington, D.C.: International Monetary Fund, September.

Bernanke, B., T. Laubach, F. Mishkin, and A. Posen. 1999. *Inflation targeting.* Princeton, N.J.: Princeton University Press.

Bhagwati, J. 1991. *Political economy and international economics.* Cambridge, Mass.: MIT Press.

———. 1998. The capital myth: The difference between trade in widgets and dollars. *Foreign Affairs* 77, no. 3 (May/June): 7–12.

Bruno, M., and W. Easterly. 1994. Inflation crises and long-run growth. Washington, D.C.: World Bank, November. Mimeograph.

Budnevich, G., and G. Le Fort. 1997. Capital account regulations and macroeconomic policy: Two Latin American experiences. Working Paper no. 6. Santiago: Central Bank of Chile, March.

Bulir, A., and A. M. Gulde. 1995. Inflation and income distribution: Further evidence on empirical links. IMF Working Paper no. 95/86. Washington, D.C.: International Monetary Fund, August.

Burki, S., and G. Perry. 1997. *The long march: A reform agenda for Latin America and the Caribbean in the next decade.* Washington, D.C.: World Bank.

Carnoy, M. 1997. A comment on West. *World Bank Research Observer* 12, no. 1 (February): 105–16.

Corbo, V. 1988. Problems, development theory and strategies of Latin America. In *The state of development economics: Progress and perspectives,* ed. G. Ranis and T. P. Shultz. London: Blackwell.

Corbo, V., and S. Fischer. 1995. Structural adjustment, stabilization and policy reform: Domestic and international finance. In *Handbook of development economics,* vol. 3, ed. J. Behrman and T. N. Srinivasan. Amsterdam: Elsevier.

Corbo, V., and P. Rojas. 1993. Investment, macroeconomic stability and growth: The Latin American experience. *Revista de Análisis Económico* 8 (1): 19–35.

Corbo, V., and K. Schmidt-Hebbel. 1991. Public policies and saving in developing countries. *Journal of Development Economics* 36:89–115.

Corden, W. 1994. *Economic policy, exchange rates and the international system.* Chicago: University of Chicago Press.

Corsetti, G., P. Pesenti, and N. Roubini. 1998. What caused the Asian currency and financial crisis? Revised version of paper presented at 1998 LACEA conference. Available at http://equity.stern.nyu.edu/~nroubini/referen.htm.

Diaz-Alejandro, C. 1983. Stories of the 1930s for the 1980s. In *Financial policies and the world capital market: The problem of Latin American countries,* ed. P. Aspe et al. Chicago: University of Chicago Press.

Dornbusch, R. 1980. *Open economy macroeconomics.* New York: Basic.

———. 1997. Brazil's incomplete stabilization and reform. *Brookings Papers on Economic Activity,* no. 1:367–404.

————. 1998. Capital controls: An idea whose time is gone. Cambridge: Massachusetts Institute of Technology, March. Mimeograph.

ECLAC (UN Economic Commission for Latin America and the Caribbean). 1992. *Equidad y transformación productiva: Un enfoque integrado.* Santiago: UN Economic Commission for Latin America and the Caribbean.

Edwards, S. 1995a. *Crisis and reform in Latin America: From despair to hope.* Oxford: Oxford University Press.

————. 1995b. Why are saving rates so different across countries? An international comparative analysis. NBER Working Paper no. 5097. Cambridge, Mass.: National Bureau of Economic Research.

————. 1998. El fin de las reformas latinoamericanas? *Estudios Públicos* 69 (summer): 69–84.

Engel, E., R. Fischer, and A. Galetovic. 1997. Highway franchising: Pitfalls and opportunities. *American Economic Review* 87, no. 2 (May): 68–72.

Favaro, E. 1996. Peru's stabilization under floating exchange rate. Washington, D.C.: World Bank. Mimeograph.

Fernández-Arias, E., and P. Montiel. 1997. Reforma y crecimiento en América Latina: Mucho ruido y pocas nueces? Washington, D.C.: Inter-American Development Bank, February. Mimeograph.

Fischer, S. 1993. The role of macroeconomic factors in economic growth. *Journal of Monetary Economics* 32 (3): 485–512.

————. 1995. Central bank independence. *American Economic Review* 85, no. 2 (May): 201–6.

————. 1996. Why are central banks pursuing long-run price stability? In *Achieving price stability,* symposium sponsored by the Federal Reserve Bank of Kansas City. Kansas City: Federal Reserve Bank of Kansas City.

Gavin, M., R. Hausmann, R. Perotti, and E. Talvi. 1996. Managing fiscal policy in Latin America: Volatility, procyclicality and limited creditworthiness. IDB Working Paper no. 326. Washington, D.C.: Inter-American Development Bank.

Gertler, P., and J. Hammer. 1997. Strategies for pricing publicly provided health services. Policy Research Working Paper no. 1762. Washington, D.C.: World Bank, May.

Glick, R., and A. Rose. 1998. Contagion and trade: Why are currency crises regional? San Francisco: Federal Reserve Bank of San Francisco; Berkeley: University of California, August. Mimeograph.

Goodhard, C. 1994. Central bank independence. In *The central bank and the financial system,* by C. Goodhart. Cambridge, Mass.: MIT Press.

Graham, C., and S. Naím. 1998. The political economy of institutional reform in Latin America. In *Beyond tradeoffs: Market reform and equitable growth in Latin America,* ed. N. Birdsall, C. Graham, and R. Sabot. Washington, D.C.: Brookings Institution.

Hanushek, E. 1995. Interpreting recent research on schooling in developing countries. *World Bank Research Observer* 10, no. 2 (August): 227–46.

Inter-American Development Bank (IDB). 1996. *Progreso económico y social en América Latina.* Washington, D.C.: Inter-American Development Bank.

————. 1997. *Progreso económico y social en América Latina.* Washington, D.C.: Inter-American Development Bank.

International Monetary Fund (IMF). 1995. *World economic outlook.* Washington, D.C.: International Monetary Fund, May.

————. 1998a. *World economic outlook.* Washington, D.C.: International Monetary Fund, May.

————. 1998b. *World economic outlook.* Washington, D.C.: International Monetary Fund, September.

Jacquemin, A. 1987. *The new industrial organization: Market forces and strategic behaviour.* Cambridge, Mass.: MIT Press.

Journal of Economic Perspectives. 1995. 9, no. 4 (fall).

Kremer, M. 1995. Research on schooling: What we know and what we don't. A comment on Hanushek. *World Bank Research Observer* 10, no. 2 (August): 247–54.

Krueger, A. 1984. Trade policies in developing countries. In *Handbook of international economics,* ed. R. Jones and P. Kenen. Amsterdam: North-Holland.

Krugman, P. 1987. Is free trade passé? *Journal of Economic Perspectives* 1 (2): 131–44.

———. 1997. Bubble, boom, crash: Theoretical notes on Asia's crisis. Cambridge: Massachusetts Institute of Technology. Mimeograph.

———. 1998a. Curfews on capital flight: What are the options? Cambridge: Massachusetts Institute of Technology. Mimeograph.

———. 1998b. The eternal triangle. Cambridge: Massachusetts Institute of Technology. Mimeograph.

———. 1999. *The return of depression economics.* New York: Norton.

Labán, R., and F. Larraín. 1993. Can a liberalization of the capital outflows increase net capital inflows? Working Paper no. 155. Santiago: Pontificia Universidad Católica de Chile, Instituto de Economía.

Loayza, N., and L. Palacios. 1997. Economic reform and progress in Latin America and the Caribbean. Washington, D.C.: World Bank, June. Mimeograph.

Londoño, J., and J. Frank. 1996. Structured pluralism: A new model for health reform in Latin America. LATD Working Paper. Washington, D.C.: World Bank.

Lora, E. 1997. Una década de reformas estructurales en América Latina: Qué se ha reformado y cómo medirlo. Washington, D.C.: Inter-American Development Bank, February. Mimeograph.

Lora, E., and F. Barrera. 1997. Una década de reformas estructurales en América Latina: El crecimiento, la productividad y la inversión ya no son como antes. Washington, D.C.: Inter-American Development Bank, February. Mimeograph.

Masson, P., T. Bayoumi, and H. Samiei. 1998. International evidence on the determinants of private saving. *World Bank Economic Review* 12 (3): 483–501.

Mishkin, F. S. 1996. The channels of monetary transmission: Lessons for monetary policy. *Banque de France Bulletin Digest* 27 (March): 33–44.

———. 1997. Understanding financial crises: A developing country perspective. In *Annual World Bank conference on development economics,* ed. M. Bruno and B. Pleskovic. Washington, D.C.: World Bank.

Obstfeld, M. 1998. The global capital market: Benefactor or menace? NBER Working Paper no. 6559. Cambridge, Mass.: National Bureau of Economic Research, May.

Obstfeld, M., and K. Rogoff. 1995. The mirage of fixed exchange rates. *Journal of Economic Perspectives* 9 (fall): 73–96.

Oxley, H., and M. MacFarlan. 1994. Health care reform: Controlling spending and increasing efficiency. OECD Working Paper no. 149. Paris: Organization for Economic Cooperation and Development.

Pritchett, L., and D. Filmer. Forthcoming. What education production functions really show: A positive theory of education expenditures. *Economics of Education Review.*

Sarel, M. 1995. Nonlinear effects of inflation on economic growth. IMF Working Paper no. 95/56. Washington, D.C.: International Monetary Fund, May.

Sargent, T. 1982. The end of four big inflations. In *Inflation: Causes and effects,* ed. R. Hall. Chicago: University of Chicago Press.

Scherer, F., and D. Ross. 1990. *Industrial market structure and economic performance,* 3d ed. Boston: Houghton Mifflin.

Stiglitz, J. 1994. The role of state in financial markets. In *Annual World Bank conference on development economics*, ed. M. Bruno and B. Pleskovic. Washington, D.C.: World Bank.

Valdés, S., and M. Soto. 1996. Es el control selectivo de capitales efectivo en Chile? Su efecto sobre el tipo de cambio real. *Cuadernos de Economía* 33 (98): 77–108.

Vickers, J., and G. Yarrow. 1988. *Privatization: An economic analysis.* Cambridge, Mass.: MIT Press.

Villanueva, D., and A. Mirakhor. 1990. Strategies for financial reforms: Interest rate policies, stabilization and bank supervision in developing countries. *IMF Staff Papers* 37 (3): 509–36.

West, E. 1997. On education vouchers. *World Bank Research Observer* 12, no.1 (February): 83–103.

Williamson, J. 1989. *Latin American adjustment.* Oxford: Oxford University Press.

Witte, J., C. Thorn, and K. Prichard. 1995. *Fourth year report: Milwaukee Parental Choice Program.* Madison, Wisc.: State Department of Public Instruction.

World Bank. 1997. *World development report 1997: The state in a changing world.* New York: Oxford University Press.

———. 1998. Estudios del Banco Mundial sobre América Latina y El Caribe: Más allá del concenso de Washington, La hora de la reforma institucional. Washington, D.C.: World Bank.

Zahler, R. 1997. La política macroeconómica de Chile en los años noventa: La visión del banco central. Santiago: UN Economic Commission for Latin America and the Caribbean, December. Mimeograph.

Comment on the Paper by Vittorio Corbo
Miguel A. Savastano

Vittorio Corbo has written a comprehensive and useful overview of the progress on and agenda for economic policy reform in Latin America. A one-sentence summary of the central message of the paper could be the following: Latin America has come a long way in the process of economic reform (especially on the trade and macroeconomic fronts) but still has a long way to go (especially on the other reform fronts). This message is fundamentally correct, and I know of few people in the profession or in the region who would, or could, disagree with it. The message also has a familiar ring because, as is clear from the charts and references in the paper, this is pretty much the message that the international financial institutions (IFIs) have been giving to Latin America for a number of years— in fact, one may think of it as the late 1990s edition of the "Washington consensus." But something about this message is not entirely satisfactory, and more important, the message does not seem to be coming across too well. My conjecture is that this has to do with serious problems in the way

Miguel A. Savastano is a deputy division chief in the Research Department of the International Monetary Fund.

The opinions expressed in this comment are exclusively those of the author and do not represent those of the IMF.

the message is being delivered by the IFIs, policymakers, and influential observers, especially when it comes to the important issues of prioritizing the items and reforms pending on the agenda and of conveying a sense of the expected gains from implementing those reforms. I will come back to these issues later.

I have three main comments on Corbo's account of economic policy reform in Latin America. The first is a point of clarification. The second is a comment related to a misconception about the role of monetary policy that is widely held among Latin American economists. And the third, rather than a specific comment, is a general reflection on the way the profession and the IFIs are delivering the message on the need for and gains from *further* economic policy reform in Latin America.

The point of clarification has to do with the portrayal of the disinflation strategies followed by seven Latin American economies in the 1990s that is summarized in table 3.3. I found the taxonomy presented in the table, and its discussion in the text, a bit confusing. The main problem is that the table combines strategies that were employed by (the majority of) those countries to bring down inflation from very high levels to more tolerable rates (the "traditional" columns) with inflation targeting, which is a framework for conducting monetary policy in low-inflation environments rather than a strategy for stopping high inflation.[1] The discussion in the text makes this distinction somewhat more clearly, by noting that many of the countries switched nominal anchors over time as disinflation took hold, but not clearly enough. Because the policy issues and dilemmas are so different, I think it would have been preferable to follow the more standard practice of discussing the strategies followed to stop high inflation separately from the strategies used to conduct monetary policy in low(er) inflation environments.

The second comment is to question whether there is a *consensus* in Latin America about what monetary policy should do and about how to gear it toward that goal. In my opinion no such consensus exists, certainly not to a degree comparable to the one that exists in advanced economies. Consensus is needed about the main objectives of monetary policy, about the relative effectiveness of policy instruments and the horizons over which they operate, about key features of the transmission mechanism of monetary shocks, and about the modeling of monetary policy. It so happens that for the advanced economies there is in fact a considerable degree of agreement about these issues based on the available evidence. For example, many countries now mandate that the primary objective of monetary policy should be to attain and maintain low and stable inflation (which is widely understood to consist of rates of inflation that deliver

---

1. For a discussion of inflation targeting and its relevance for developing countries, see Masson, Savastano, and Sharma (1997).

"operational price stability"—i.e., annual rates of inflation in the 1 to 3 percent range). Furthermore, policymakers in most countries believe central bank interest rates to be more effective than monetary aggregates as instruments or operating targets of monetary policy. The evidence also shows that it takes somewhere between eighteen and twenty-four months for changes in monetary policy instruments to have their full effect on the rate of inflation, and that the best way of modeling monetary policy is through the use of some variant of an output gap or NAIRU type of model. A comparable degree of consensus about any of these aspects of monetary policy in Latin America, and more generally in developing countries, simply does not exist (see Masson et al. 1997).

A good example of the Latin American disarray about what monetary policy should do is given by what has become known as the "capital inflows problem," which is discussed at some length in section 3.2 of the paper. What is the essence of this "problem"? That a surge in foreign capital inflows to a developing country may give rise to (or exacerbate) a trade-off or conflict between the objectives of external sustainability and inflation control—that is, the inflows will tend to unleash inflationary pressures but will also provoke a real exchange rate appreciation that may weaken the country's external position. What is the standard policy prescription? Many analysts seem to be saying that the primary goal of monetary policy in Latin America should be to strike a period-by-period balance between two competing goals (with the time frame covered by the "period" often left conveniently vague). This view rests on the premises not only that monetary policy in Latin America is not subject to "long and variable lags" of uncertain duration and strength but that we actually know the (approximate) nature and size of the short-run effects of monetary policy on inflation, the real exchange rate, and the external balance. There is simply no evidence to support those claims, and the ground is fertile for good empirical research on these important questions.

Furthermore, the policy prescription to the capital inflows problem comes from the opposite side of the "rules versus discretion" debate that persuaded academics and practitioners around the industrial world that the overriding goal of monetary policy has to be the control of inflation. In fact, those advocating intervention seem to be arguing that the role of monetary policy in the latter economies should be to strike a period-by-period balance between the competing objectives of inflation and unemployment. Many prominent Latin American economists do not (want to) see the irony behind the fact that their preferred response to the capital inflows problem entails giving considerably more discretion to the central bank than would be afforded by a monetary policy rule or a transparent framework such as inflation targeting, which they also advocate; but the irony is there.

Bringing fiscal policy into the picture as the second instrument that avoids overburdening monetary policy in the face of capital inflows, a suggestion often made by the IFIs and other influential observers (including Corbo), is not a satisfactory solution. Not only is fiscal policy more difficult to control than monetary policy in the short term but its effects on the real exchange rate and on the current account are, to say the least, uncertain. In sum, while it may be the case that Latin American countries do need to strike some kind of period-by-period balance between their external and inflation objectives, I do not think it can be argued that there exists anything resembling consensus about how to strike that balance in a context of high capital mobility and about the roles that monetary (and exchange rate) policy ought to play in this endeavor. The research agenda on these crucial issues is far from complete.

My third comment is related to the problems I see in the delivery of the call for further reform in Latin America. I think that the cause of further policy reform in the region is not helped as much as it should be when a wide array of policies and initiatives are advocated together in a composite that has no clear priorities or timetable. Nobody can or will disagree that Latin American countries need to improve the provision of education and health services, revamp their financial and judicial systems, and clarify and enforce property rights. Latin Americans have known this for a long time; they may not have done much about it, but there is a difference between inaction and ignorance. After decades of reform, "reminding" Latin American governments that the region remains underdeveloped and that their countries still have a lot to do on many fronts without giving them at the same time a clear blueprint of how to tackle those pressing issues strikes me as disingenuous and a bit arrogant. The problem is, as the paper rightly notes, that the profession knows less about "best practices" in most of those areas than it would like. I am certain that part of the solution lies in doing more and better research in the "nontraditional" areas of efficient regulation and institution building. I am also convinced that another part of the solution consists of *not overselling* those reforms until we have a better understanding of the sequence and pace at which they should be implemented and of the horizon over which countries that adopt them may start reaping their benefits. In chapter 15 of this volume, Joseph Stiglitz tells us that one should set realistic targets for reform; I think this is a sound piece of advice and would just add that at least in Latin America, following it implies staying clear from all promises of instant gratification stemming from second-generation reforms.

Reference

Masson, P., M. Savastano, and S. Sharma. 1997. The scope for inflation targeting in developing countries. IMF Working Paper WP/97/130. Washington, D.C.: International Monetary Fund, October.

4
Economic Reforms in South Asia

T. N. Srinivasan

4.1 Introduction

South Asia comprises Bangledesh, Bhutan, India, Maldives, Nepal, Pakistan, and Sri Lanka and is home to nearly 1.5 billion people, two-fifths of them very poor, having less than one dollar (in purchasing power parity terms) a day to consume. Excluding the exceptional case of Sri Lanka, in the rest of South Asia indicators of social and human development, such as life expectancy, infant and child mortality, and educational attainment, show very slow progress in the past five decades.

The development strategies of the four large economies of the region, namely, Bangladesh, India, Pakistan, and Sri Lanka, have been similar. These countries emphasized import-substituting industrialization and assigned a dominant role to the state in the economy. The government owned and operated not only public utilities, railways, and other infrastructure but also manufacturing and service enterprises. The state also intervened in markets for many commodities, particularly those for inputs and outputs in agriculture. Banks, insurance companies, and other financial intermediaries were either publicly owned or tightly regulated so that the financial sector was heavily repressed. Controls on foreign trade and payments were extensive. Compared to their East Asian counterparts, the

T. N. Srinivasan is the Samuel C. Park, Jr., Professor of Economics and chairman of the Department of Economics at Yale University and a nonresident research fellow of the Center for Research on Economic Development and Policy Reform at Stanford University.

The author thanks two discussants, Arnold Harberger and Niraja Sivaramayya; Anne Krueger; and other conference participants for their comments. The author has drawn extensively on published country reports from the World Bank (1998a–1998c, 1998e, 1998f) in writing this paper, as well as on private communications with economists at the World Bank. Financial support from Ford Foundation Grant no. 950-1341 is gratefully acknowledged.

four large South Asian economies have been inward oriented, although the smaller economies of Bangladesh and Sri Lanka are more open than India and Pakistan.

Economic performance under this strategy was poor. The overall average annual rate of growth of GNP per capita of South Asia during the period 1965–73 (before the first oil shock) was only 1.2 percent. It increased marginally to 1.9 percent during 1973–80 and more than doubled to 2.9 percent during 1980–89 (World Bank 1991, table A2), when there was some hesitant liberalization of the economy and unsustainable fiscal expansion, particularly in India. These growth rates were lower, certainly in comparison with the spectacular growth rates achieved by East Asia, but also in comparison with low-income economies as a group.

Interestingly, the rapid growth of East Asia (other than China) since the midsixties was already evident by the late seventies. Yet in India, for example, analysts and policymakers tended either to dismiss the East Asian success as totally irrelevant for drawing any policy lessons applicable to India or to attribute it to idiosyncratic features of East Asia. However, East Asia's continued success in the eighties, particularly its being able to avoid the debt crisis of the period, could not be lightly dismissed or explained away as idiosyncratic. By the late eighties, the rapid growth of China, once it opened its economy and began its reform process in 1978, became evident. The rapid growth of East Asia and China, on one hand, and the collapse of the Soviet Union and Communist countries of Eastern Europe on the other, clearly indicated to South Asian policymakers that their development strategy had failed and economic reforms had to be undertaken. Latin American policymakers had come to the same conclusion somewhat earlier.

In India, in the mideighties, a hesitant and piecemeal attempt to liberalize the more irksome controls on the economy had begun. This modest liberalization, coupled with the abandonment of macroeconomic prudence in favor of fiscal expansionism financed by domestic and external borrowing (as well as monetization of part of the fiscal deficits), produced an average rate of growth of 5.5 percent per year in the eighties compared to the infamous "Hindu" rate of growth of 3.5 percent in the three decades earlier. However, both because most of the severe microeconomic distortions created by government controls and interventions in the economy largely remained and because the soaring overall public sector deficits were unsustainable, the higher rate of growth achieved in the eighties was also unsustainable. Thus, when a severe macroeconomic and balance-of-payments crisis hit in 1990–91 after the Gulf War broke out and domestic political uncertainty induced nonresident Indians to withdraw their deposits in India, the necessity for comprehensive and systemic reforms became very clear. Prime Minister Narasimha Rao, who had assumed power in June 1991, and Manmohan Singh, his finance minister, launched a broad-based systemic set of economic reforms in July 1991.

In some countries of South Asia the reform process had started earlier than in India. Sri Lanka began its reforms in 1977, although the commitment to the large Mahaveli irrigation project continued to create macroeconomic pressure for several years thereafter. However, economic liberalization in Bangladesh and Pakistan, as in India, gathered momentum only in the early nineties. The overall growth performance of South Asia since 1992 has shown significant improvements over the prereform period, although it would be unwise, and methodologically incorrect, to attribute the improvements entirely to reform. The annual growth rate of GDP during 1992–96 ranged from 5.4 percent in 1993 to 7.0 percent in 1994 (Asian Development Bank 1998, table A1). It has since slowed to 4.8 percent in 1997, in part because the reform process itself has slowed, if not altogether stalled, in India as well as Pakistan, and in part because of adverse external economic shocks consequent to the East Asian financial crisis.

In what follows I will review the current state of the reform process in the four large economies of South Asia with respect to policies relating to the macroeconomy, foreign trade, industry and infrastructure (including privatization), financial sector, social sectors, and last, governance. I will conclude with a brief discussion of the unfinished reform agenda and of aspects of the reform process on which existing knowledge seems inadequate and research is likely to pay rich dividends. I will also comment on the politico-economic environment, particularly in India and Pakistan after their nuclear explosions of May 1998, and note that in this environment it is unlikely that the remaining reforms will be undertaken any time soon.

4.2 Macroeconomic Policy Reform

Macroeconomic indicators are presented in table 4.1.

4.2.1 Bangladesh

The overall budget deficit has ranged between a relatively high 4.6 and 6.4 percent of GDP during 1992–96 (table 4.1).[1] It is estimated at 5.5 percent of GDP in 1997. More than three-quarters of the budget deficits during 1992–96 were covered by net foreign financing. Monetary accom-

---

1. The Bangladesh Bureau of Statistics, with the assistance of the Asian Development Bank and the World Bank, revised significantly upward data on macroeconomic indicators including GDP, savings, and investment. World Bank (1998a) was based on these revised data while the data for Bangladesh in Asian Development Bank (1998) were unrevised. I have no way of judging whether the revisions were appropriate. The World Bank, however, reported that "a panel of experts, both local and international, has reviewed the revised set of national accounts and concluded that although there still are deficiencies in the data, the revised numbers are a reasonably accurate reflection of economic activity" (1998a, 3 n. 3). Some analysts suggest that official macroeconomic data understate the true level and rate of growth of GDP in India.

Table 4.1   **Macroeconomic Indicators**

Indicator and Country	1992	1993	1994	1995	1996	1997	1998[a]	1999[a]	Per Capita GNP, 1996 (US$)
Growth rate in per capita GDP (% per year)									
Bangladesh	2.5	2.8	2.0	2.6	3.5	3.8	4.1	4.3	260
India	3.3	4.1	5.3	5.5	5.6	3.4	5.0	5.4	380
Pakistan	4.7	-1.0	0.9	2.4	1.3	0.6	2.3	2.5	480
Sri Lanka	3.3	5.6	4.2	4.0	2.6	5.2	4.5	4.9	740
Overall budget balance (% of GDP)									
Bangladesh	-6.4	-6.1	-4.6	-5.1	-5.9	-5.5			
India	-5.7	-7.4	-6.1	-7.1	-7.0	-6.7			
Pakistan	-7.4	-8.0	-5.9	-5.5	-6.3	-6.3			
Sri Lanka	-7.3	-8.4	-10.0	-9.6	-8.8	-4.9			
Current account balance (% of GDP)									
Bangladesh	-2.5	-2.6	-1.2	-2.7	-5.2	-2.6	-3.1	-2.7	
India	-1.4	-0.6	-1.2	-1.8	-1.0	-1.2	-1.5	-2.0	
Pakistan	-2.8	-7.1	-3.8	-4.1	-7.1	-6.5	-5.1	-5.2	
Sri Lanka	-6.3	-5.4	-7.9	-6.3	-5.3	-2.1	-4.2	-4.0	

Gross domestic investment (% of GDP)								
Bangladesh	12.1	14.3	18.1	19.1	17.0	17.4	17.2	18.0
India	24.0	21.7	24.0	26.2	27.1	26.6	27.1	29.0
Pakistan	19.9	20.5	19.4	18.3	18.7	18.4	20.0	22.0
Sri Lanka	24.3	25.6	27.0	25.7	24.2	25.8	26.7	27.6
Gross domestic savings (% of GDP)								
Bangladesh	5.8	7.0	13.4	12.8	7.5	9.0	8.6	8.8
India	22.5	21.1	23.0	24.4	25.6	25.5	25.6	27.1
Pakistan	16.9	13.5	15.6	14.2	11.6	11.4	12.5	13.5
Sri Lanka	15.0	16.0	15.2	15.3	15.5	16.5	17.5	18.0
Debt service (% of exports of goods and services)								
Bangladesh	9.0	10.2	11.6	10.3	12.1	11.4	10.7	10.5
India	28.6	26.9	27.5	37.3	41.9	31.8	29.9	28.9
Pakistan	24.9	27.4	33.4	34.9	33.9	37.0	35.0	34.0
Sri Lanka	14.6	11.8	11.2	11.6	12.9	11.4	11.2	11.0
Consumer price inflation (% per year)								
Bangladesh	5.1	1.3	1.8	5.2	4.0	3.9	5.5	5.0
India	9.6	3.8	11.8	10.0	9.2	6.5	7.0	7.2
Pakistan	9.8	9.8	11.2	13.0	10.8	11.6	10.0	10.2
Sri Lanka	11.4	11.7	8.4	7.7	15.9	9.6	10.0	9.0

Source: Asian Development Bank (1998, tables A2, A7, A8, A9, A16, A19, A23).
[a] Projections.

modation was the major source for the one-quarter that was domestically financed, though in the fiscal year 1998 the government has attempted to reduce monetary financing by resorting to weekly auctions of treasury bills, rather than borrowing from Bangladesh Bank. Whether this in fact means monetization has gone down depends on whether the Bangladesh Bank is directly or indirectly purchasing the bills.

In Bangladesh, as elsewhere in South Asia, reductions in fiscal deficits have been achieved by reducing capital expenditures, including expenditures on maintenance of infrastructure. To the extent that investment in low-priority projects is cut, such reductions are indeed desirable. But often growth-enhancing investments are reduced, and such reductions obviously are inappropriate from a long-run development perspective.

Bangladesh runs subsidized public food distribution programs, most of which are meant to provide a safety net for the poor, but few of which are well targeted. Deficits from the operations of the food distribution system, cash subsidies to exports, and losses of public sector enterprises (PSEs) contribute to the overall deficit of the public sector. Contingent liabilities arising from government guarantees of loans to PSEs have to be provided for as well.

As in the rest of South Asia, in Bangladesh the public sector, inclusive of government administration, is overstaffed and its employees are part of the small labor aristocracy that continues to enjoy wages, salaries, and perquisites that bear no relation to their productivity or to labor market realities. Recently pay increases have been awarded to this aristocracy. Reducing the size of the public sector bureaucracy and containing the growth of its emoluments seem politically infeasible.

Inflation in Bangladesh has been very moderate, with the consumer price index rising at an average annual rate of a little over 3 percent during 1980–96 (World Bank 1998f, table 4.15). Exports have grown at about 10 percent a year in value terms during 1990–96 and imports by about 11 percent (World Bank 1998f, table 6.2). The deficit in the current account of the balance of payments has been less than 4 percent (expected to be between 2 and 3 percent in 1998) of GDP at market prices, financed largely by external assistance. External debt, most of it concessional, was about 50 percent of GDP in 1997, and debt service was only about 11 percent of export earnings (World Bank 1998a, 7–10).

Bangladesh has been investing around 20.3 to 22.0 percent of GDP since 1991–92, with domestic savings financing around 14.3 to 16.3 percent of GDP. With net factor income and current transfers accounting for nearly 5 percent, the draft on foreign savings to finance domestic investment was negligible (World Bank 1998a, 4, table 2).

From a macroeconomic perspective, the reform agenda in Bangladesh has to address the fiscal deficit and the related issues of tax, expenditure, and public enterprise reforms including privatization and pricing of outputs of public enterprises.

4.2.2   India

Until the early eighties India's macroeconomic policies were in general conservative. Current revenues of the central government exceeded current expenditures so that a surplus was available to finance in part the deficit on capital finance. In the early eighties, fiscal prudence was abandoned—with the consequence that surpluses turned into deficits. This meant that the government had to borrow at home and abroad, to finance not only its investment as would normally be the case in a developing country, but also its current consumption.

Another aspect of the fiscal situation in the eighties was that the published figures of the fiscal deficit understated the real imbalances. The reason was that the government appropriated a large share of the loanable resources of the banking system through a statutory liquidity ratio (38.5 percent of the base at its maximum) and a cash reserve ratio (15 percent at its maximum) at administratively set interest rates below what would have been market-clearing levels. Also, at least in the early years, external borrowing was largely on concessional terms from multilateral lending institutions and from bilateral government-to-government external aid transactions. As the eighties wore on, while continuing to borrow at controlled interest rates in the domestic economy, the government resorted to borrowing from abroad on commercial terms both from the capital market and from nonresident Indians. In 1984–85, out of $24.3 billion of public and publicly guaranteed external debt, roughly 20 percent was owed to private creditors. By 1988–99, external debt had more than doubled to $50.2 billion, of which around 40 percent was owed to private creditors. Thus debt to private creditors quadrupled in less than five years. What was left of the gross fiscal deficit after financing through domestic and external borrowings, small saving provident funds, and so forth, was monetized through the sale of ad hoc treasury bills to the Reserve Bank of India (i.e., India's central bank).

Clearly the fiscal expansionism of the eighties was unsustainable. But while it lasted, it did generate faster growth because it was also accompanied by some liberalization of rigid controls on the economy. The average annual rates of growth of real GDP in the sixth and seventh five-year plans, which covered the eighties, were 5.5 and 5.8 percent, respectively, much higher than the "Hindu" rate of growth of 3.5 percent of the earlier three decades. When the macroeconomic crisis hit in 1990–91, the combined gross fiscal deficit of government at all levels had grown to about 10 percent of GDP at market prices. Including the losses of the nonfinancial PSEs, the consolidated public sector deficit stood at around 12.3 percent of GDP in 1990–91. More than a third of this deficit, nearly 4.8 percent of GDP, was for interest payments on domestic and external debt. An analysis by Willem Buiter and Urjit Patel (1992) showed that unless corrective steps were taken, India faced fiscal insolvency.

It is no surprise therefore that one of the major objectives of then finance minister Manmohan Singh's reforms of 1991 was to reduce the central government's fiscal deficit from 8.3 percent of GDP in 1990–91 to around 4 percent or lower in three years or so. In fact, he did achieve a significant reduction to 5.9 percent in his first full year as finance minister in 1991–92 and further to 5.7 percent in 1992–93; but then it ballooned to 7.4 percent in 1993–94 (World Bank 1998b, table A4.1). The deficits were 5.2, 6.3, and 6.5 percent of GDP in the three fiscal years ending with 1998–99. The level is projected to come down to 4.4 percent in 1999–2000—but this is very optimistic. What is more, the overall deficit of the nonfinancial public sector, which includes central public enterprises and state governments, has remained around 9 percent of GDP or more since 1992–93 (World Bank 1998b, annex table 2). Inflation, as measured by increases in the wholesale price index, has come down from 10.8 percent in 1993–94 to 5 percent in 1997–98. The fiscal consequences of the nuclear explosions in May 1998 are as yet unclear. Defense and atomic research expenditures have increased modestly (in real terms) in the 1998–99 budget. The effects of U.S. sanctions and Japanese actions have yet to manifest themselves.

Studies of the experience of a cross section of countries suggest that large public sector deficits reduce growth by crowding out productive private investment. Attempts to reduce the monetization of deficits through domestic borrowing naturally raise interest rates thereby increasing the cost of capital and reducing the profitability of investment. Some studies suggest that in India a rough one-to-one relation exists between the central government's fiscal deficit inclusive of the oil pool deficit and private investment. Although funds are largely fungible, and it would be inappropriate to attribute the deficit entirely to some categories of public expenditure and not to others, it is still fair to say that in India the public sector spends on activities that are better left to the private sector. If deficits are financed by increasing public debt, a potential debt trap can arise if the interest rate on debt exceeds the rate of growth of GDP. India is not there yet, but the possibility exists.

There have been several analyses of India's fiscal situation, notably by Joshi and Little (1994, 1996), by Buiter and Patel (1992, 1997), and, above all, by the Chelliah committee (India 1992b, 1993) on tax reforms. I cannot possibly add very much to these thorough-going analyses. What I propose to do instead is to highlight and update their insights on a few selected topics, including state finances, tax reform, disinvestment, and reduction of subsidies.

Without elaborating on the complex center-state fiscal setup in India, it suffices to recapitulate its main features. The constitution lays down the taxation powers of the center and states. Roughly, the states can tax land, agricultural income, and sales and impose excise taxes on alcohol while the center taxes personal and corporation income, wealth, and foreign trade and also imposes excise taxes. The constitution requires the center to share revenue from certain taxes in proportions recommended by the Finance Commission, which the president is constitutionally required to appoint every five years. In addition, the states also receive transfers recommended by the Planning Commission for financing part of their expenditure on annual development plans that are approved by the Planning Commission.

Undeniably the center has the responsibility to provide crucial public goods such as defense and a common currency. Also, given the diversity in levels of development among states, it could be argued that the center has a redistributive role in making transfers to poorer states. The states have been assigned large responsibilities in crucial sectors such as education, health, irrigation, and other investment in agricultural development. Naturally, they cannot discharge these responsibilities adequately if they cannot generate the required resources. Having said this, I must hasten to add that in practice the center-state tax-transfer system has had some disincentive and efficiency-reducing effects. Clearly the center's efforts to ensure tax compliance are likely to be less in the case of those taxes, such as the income tax, the revenues from which have to be shared with the states than in the case of taxes, such as customs, the proceeds of which accrue entirely to the center. By the same token, if transfers received from the center form a large part of its expenditure, and these transfers have no relation to its own efforts to raise resources, clearly a state is unlikely to be diligent in raising resources. The first eight Finance Commissions, which in effect recommended transfers that financed the gap between outlays and revenues of states, completely ignored this strong disincentive effect.

The states are constitutionally barred from borrowing in international financial markets and need the center's consent for any borrowing in the domestic market if they are indebted to the center or have an outstanding loan guaranteed by the center. Since all states are indebted to the center, this constraint is in principle binding on all of them. However, since there are few instances, if any, of a state being denied requested permission to enter the domestic capital market and the central government has repeatedly rescheduled debts of states to the center and even written them off, in a practical sense this constraint is largely nonoperational. The states share in the central government's borrowing from captive sources of finance such as banks, insurance companies, and nongovernment pension and provident funds, which are required to invest in designated government securities. Of course the states cannot directly monetize any part of their deficits.

Prima facie it would seem that these restrictions impose a hard budget constraint on states. But, in fact, the states have succeeded in getting around them; borrowing constraints on state governments are evaded by letting the enterprises owned by the states, on which there are no constraints, borrow; resources meant for investment are diverted to current expenditure; state PSEs have been, in effect, forced to lend to the government by letting the government buy their services on credit. In turn, these enterprises have run up arrears with their suppliers, which are themselves national PSEs—for example, state electricity boards (SEBs) have been tardy in paying their dues to Coal India and National Thermal Power (NTP) Corporation. This in turn has led the central government and PSEs to impose restrictions—Coal India now has a cash-and-carry policy, and the central government has chosen to retain up to 15 percent of the transfers due to the states to clear the SEBs' arrears with NTP.

The perverse incentives created by the Planning Commission in financing for five years the capital and operating costs of new state projects included in the current five-year plan should be noted. States are thus encouraged to initiate new projects that they do not, or cannot, operate once the center ceases to pay the operating costs. Also, since all states pay the same rate of interest on loans from the central government directly or indirectly, they feel no market pressure to maintain creditworthiness. The net result of all this is that gross fiscal deficits of the states have fluctuated between 2.6 and 3.4 percent of GDP since the eighties with no trend downward—indeed in the three fiscal years ending with 1997–98, the ratios have been between 3.1 and 3.5 percent (World Bank 1998b, fig. 1, annex table 4).

Under the present system, the states have created a large infrastructure and spent on social services, including many populist programs, without raising adequate resources to finance them through taxes or recovering costs from users of state-provided goods and services. They have recklessly expanded their payrolls to the point that a substantial part of their revenues are spent on wages and salaries alone. This compounds the problem created by the fact that the states have to match any largesse, such as the recent pay hikes, conferred by the center to its employees to prevent them from engaging in disruptive agitations.

The economic reforms of 1991 have radically altered the options open to states—they can now compete to attract foreign and domestic private capital to those infrastructural sectors earlier financed entirely by the government. But attracting private capital needs good-quality infrastructure, particularly power and roads, an educated labor force, and a business-friendly bureaucracy. Improvement in infrastructure depends on reforms of the operation, pricing, and regulation of the PSEs and additional investment that would call for substantial resources. Both to send appropriate signals to users and to raise resources for investment, states will have to address pricing issues with respect to electricity, irrigation, water, education, and other goods and services provided by the government. The fact that currently any private investor in electricity generation has to sell his output to SEBs that are virtually bankrupt means that such an investor cannot be sure of being paid. Since the state governments themselves are financially weak, their guarantees of payment by SEBs are not fully credible. For this reason the central government has had to offer "counterguarantees" insuring against default by state governments and SEBs in order to attract private foreign investment in the sector.

It is disquieting that as many as seven states decreased their spending during 1990–96 on both economic and social infrastructure. Only one state, Rajasthan, maintained or increased its spending on both. Some states, notably Andhra Pradesh, Gujarat, Haryana, Orissa, and Rajasthan, have initiated reforms in their power sectors. The reform process has to be expanded to include other states and other areas besides power, deepened, and accelerated to restore fiscal stability to the states.

Reforming the complex set of taxes, direct and indirect, at the center and states is a challenging and daunting task—the contours of needed reforms are well known and have been discussed in the several studies I mentioned earlier, as well as by the Chelliah committee. As a proportion of GDP, direct taxes hit a low of 2.3 percent in 1990–91, falling below the share of customs duties. The proportion of direct taxes in total taxes has fallen steeply from 40 percent in the fifties to less than 15 percent now. Some measures have been announced, most recently in the central budget for 1998–99, to expand the tax base by identifying potential taxpayers through several presumptive criteria. At the same time, the 1998–99 budget raised India's already high income tax exemption limits relative to per capita income. While there may be good administrative reasons for this step, it has nonetheless the undesirable consequence of reducing the tax base. Land taxes as a source of revenue have virtually disappeared, and agricultural incomes remain largely outside the tax net. Replacing the existing set of indirect taxes through a system of value-added taxes (VATs) has not made rapid progress. Issues such as whether, by amending the constitution if necessary, to allow the center to levy the VAT and share the revenues with the states or whether the VAT should be completely in state hands, with each state choosing its own rates, coverage, and exemptions, are yet to be discussed extensively, let alone resolved.

I have long felt that the center's roles should be confined to national defense, external relations, maintenance of national networks of communications and transport, a common currency, and maintenance of a single (i.e., national) common market for goods and factors, including labor. Thus freedom of movement of capital and labor across state boundaries has to be ensured by the center. To these responsibilities I would add a relatively circumscribed role of redistribution across states. All other activities should be left to the states. It is possible that such a scheme might accentuate existing interstate disparities; alternatively it might in fact encourage states to compete to provide an environment that is most conducive to economic and social development. I am optimistic that it would be the latter and that interstate competition in tax rates and provision and pricing of infrastructural services will in fact be a race to the top rather than a race to the bottom.

According to a recent government report (India 1997), explicit and implicit subsidies by the center and state governments were on the order of 14.4 percent of GDP in 1994–95, with 10.7 percent being for nonmerit goods. It is well known that these subsidies not only increase the fiscal deficit but also, in the case of infrastructure, reduce the quality and quantity of supply. Their distributional implications are opaque. Subsidies to electricity for agricultural use and to surface irrigation have led to adverse environmental consequences due to waterlogging and salinity arising from excessive use of water. Not much of a dent has yet been made in reducing these subsidies because political support is lacking.

Excessive overall public sector deficits also resulted in low public savings—gross savings of the public sector averaged 1.6 percent of GDP during 1992–97. Private savings have been rising slowly and accounted for 22.7 percent of GDP during 1992–97. Gross domestic investment averaged 25.7 percent of GDP during 1992–97 (India 1998, table 1.3). Current account deficits have been modest, at less than 2 percent of GDP in the nineties.

4.2.3 Pakistan

Until the early nineties Pakistan's growth record was the best among the four large economies of South Asia. During 1992–97 GDP growth averaged less than 5 percent a year, in contrast to averages of 5.2 and 6.4 percent, respectively, during 1965–80 and 1980–89 (World Bank 1991, table 2). Fiscal deficits averaged 7.4 percent of GDP and current account deficits 4.2 percent of GDP during 1983–95. Hasan (1998, tables 1.6, 1.8), reported fiscal deficits of 8.1 and 6.6 percent of GDP, respectively, during 1973–77 and 1978–83 and a current account deficit of 5.5 percent of GDP during 1974–83. Current account deficits increased to 6.8 and 6.0 percent of GDP, respectively, during 1995–96 and 1996–97, but fiscal deficits came down somewhat to 6.9 and 6.1 percent of GDP in the same two years (World Bank 1998c, table 1.1).[2] Clearly these deficits are unsustainable. Pakistan entered into two agreements with the International Monetary Fund (IMF) in October 1997 to draw over a period of three years from the Fund's Extended Fund Facility a sum of 455 million Special Drawing Rights (SDRs) and from the Enhanced Structural Adjustment Facility a sum of 682 million SDRs. The first review of these agreements was successfully concluded in March 1998. Consequent to the sanctions imposed by the United States after Pakistan's nuclear explosion in May 1998 the

2. Macroeconomic data for Pakistan in World Bank (1998c) differ somewhat from those in Asian Development Bank (1998) and reproduced in table 4.1 in this paper.

macroeconomic situation, particularly the balance-of-payments position, worsened considerably. However, with the United States choosing to abstain rather than oppose further IMF assistance, Pakistan is most likely to agree to yet another IMF program. According to the Asian Development Bank (1999, tables A16, A23) the current account deficit in 1998 was 3 percent of GDP while the fiscal deficit was 5.4 percent.

Pakistan's domestic saving rate has historically been low in comparison to other countries in South Asia. It averaged 12.8 percent of GDP during 1983–95, and it is projected to increase to 14.9 percent in 1997–98. The gross investment rate averaged 19.1 percent of GDP during 1983–95, and it is projected to *fall* to 17.8 percent in 1997–98 (World Bank 1998c, table 1.1).

Given the persistent macroeconomic instability it is not surprising that Pakistan's consumer inflation rate, averaging 8.4 percent during 1983–95, has been high. After increasing to 10.8 and 11.8 percent, respectively, in 1995–96 and 1996–97, it is projected to come down to 8.0 percent in 1997–98 (World Bank 1998c).

Clearly achieving macroeconomic stability has to be the first priority in the reform agenda. In this connection long-standing problems with the tax system, such as the facts that agricultural income is largely free of tax, the base of sales tax is narrow, tax evasion is rampant, and center-provincial tax-gathering and tax-sharing arrangements need to be reformed. As in India, a National Finance Commission determines how revenues are to be shared between central and provincial governments. Interestingly, and appropriately, the latest (1997) Finance Commission has proposed the sharing of all taxes in the same proportion and incentives for provinces to mobilize their own resources through matching grants from the federal government if a province succeeds in mobilizing resources beyond the target set by the commission. These are steps in the right direction.

4.2.4   Sri Lanka

In Sri Lanka too budget deficits have been high in the nineties, ranging between a low of 8 percent of GDP in 1992 and a high of 11.9 percent in the previous year (World Bank 1998e, table A.1).[3] Provisional figures for 1997 show a deficit of 7.9 percent of GDP. The share of tax revenues in GDP, at about 20 percent, is high for a country with Sri Lanka's per capita income. Prospects for increasing revenue, except recovery of the cost of publicly provided goods and services and elimination of tax exemptions and waivers, are not good. Privatization proceeds have been used to retire public debt. This together with improvements in government finances low-

---

3. These figures differ from those in table 4.1, for which Asian Development Bank (1998) was the source.

ered interest rates, which in turn led to a reduction in interest payments, which account for a sizable 30 percent of government current expenditures. A World Bank (1998e) report pointed out that given that defense expenditures account for 25 percent and civil service pensions account for a further 11 percent, only a small proportion of current expenditures are devoted to other spending, including outlays for education and health. Also capital expenditures have apparently reached their lowest levels in a long time. The report concluded that the fiscal situation, particularly the structure of public expenditures, is such that Sri Lanka would find it difficult to continue its enviable record of human resource development, let alone accelerate growth. The World Bank (1998e) assigned high priority to reducing the size of the government payroll and reforming the civil service pension system.

Foreign savings have financed a quarter to a third of Sri Lanka's gross domestic investment in the nineties, which has varied between 22.2 percent of GDP in 1990 to a maximum of 27 percent in 1994. It is estimated to be 24.4 percent in 1997 (World Bank 1998e, table A.4). Sri Lanka's inflation rate has been high—ranging from 7.7 percent in 1995 to 21.5 percent in 1990 (World Bank 1998e, table A.12).

4.3   Foreign Trade Reform

4.3.1   Bangladesh

A simple average tariff rate on all products was 114 percent in 1989; by 1993 it had been brought down to 4.1 percent (World Bank 1998f, table 6.7).[4] According to the World Bank (1993), 2,306 items covering 39.5 percent of all items at the eight-digit level of the harmonized system were subject to import restrictions (tariff and nontariff) in 1988. By 1993 only 584 items, or 10 percent of all items, were still restricted. Further reductions in tariff rates and removal of quantitative reductions were achieved during 1993–96. Since then there has apparently been no further trade liberalization. Commodity concentration of exports is high, with garments and knitwear accounting for three-fourths of export earnings in 1997–98. Bangladesh as well as other South Asian economies will face a competitive world market for textiles and apparel once the Multi-Fiber Arrangement is phased out in 2005. It is important to ensure that Bangladesh is internationally competitive in garment exports and its export basket becomes diversified.

4. The 4.1 percent figure is most likely an error. According to World Bank (1993, table 3.3), economywide unweighted average protection in 1988–89 was 94 percent, and it came down to only 72 percent by 1992–93. However, the 72 percent includes a consumption tax of 22 percent.

4.3.2   India

India's insulation from world markets until the reforms of 1991 stemmed from a long-standing distrust of markets and international trade in general and the fear that greater involvement in foreign trade would inevitably retard India's industrialization.

The consequences of misguided state-controlled, public-sector-dominated import-substituting industrialization with an emphasis on heavy industry are well known and well documented. As economic theory teaches us, restricting imports through tariffs and quotas, that is, explicit and implicit taxation of imports, is at the same time taxation of exports. In addition, India's exchange rate remained overvalued for long periods of time. To offset the negative effects of import taxes and exchange rate overvaluation on exports various measures of implicit and explicit subsidization of exports were put in place. But access to some of them, such as duty drawbacks and others, were cumbersome, time consuming, and corruption prone. The overall impact of export subsidization in offsetting the bias against exports was at best modest and incomplete, and at worst negligible. While world exports grew at a rapid pace until the first oil shock of 1973 and at more modest rates thereafter, India's share in this growing world market dwindled from about 2 percent in the fifties to 0.44 percent in 1981. It has climbed slowly since to about 0.62 percent in 1997. Interestingly, China, whose share in world exports also declined in its prereform period from about 2.5 percent or so to 0.8 percent, has now regained what had been lost and gained some more. In 1997 China's share was around 3 percent. The share of India's foreign trade (exports plus imports) in GDP remained virtually unchanged, around 12 to 14 percent of GDP during the four decades prior to the reforms of 1991.

Besides quantitative restrictions on imports, there were tariffs as well, though clearly with binding quotas tariffs were not effective constraints on imports. Nontariff barriers covered virtually *all* (95 percent) of imports in 1988–89 (World Bank 1998b, annex table 8). The import-weighted average of tariffs on all imports on the eve of reforms was 87 percent, with the average for consumer goods almost double, at 164 percent (World Bank 1998b, annex table 10). There was, of course, enormous variance in tariffs across commodities, with rates on some imports exceeding 300 percent. Given that tariffs on raw materials and capital goods were lower than on final goods, the rates of effective protection on some of the manufactured goods were extremely high. For example, imports of passenger automobiles were banned on the grounds they were luxury goods. But this gave unlimited protection to domestic manufactures. By controlling the price of this presumed luxury, and rationing its available domestic output, the policy in effect transferred high rents to those who got the allocations, such as politicians and bureaucrats. The rationale of this policy by an ostensibly socialist regime was inexplicable, unless the rent transfer was indeed intended.

With respect to agriculture as a whole, taking into account high tariffs on such purchased inputs as fertilizers and exchange rate overvaluation, the situation was one of disprotection on the average by about 18 percent between 1985–86 and 1990–91 (World Bank 1996, 73, table 4.1). Foreign trade in a number of agricultural commodities was canalized, and the operation of the canalizing agencies did not exactly promote agricultural trade. Taking quantitative restrictions and other nontariff barriers into account, the coverage of nontariff barriers was almost universal (99.96 percent on all primary commodities, including agricultural commodities; World Bank 1998b, annex table 8).

Given the harm that the control regime was doing to India's growth and foreign trade, it is not surprising that Manmohan Singh, who in his doctoral thesis at Oxford had called attention to the crippling effect of India's trade policy and unwarranted export pessimism, would tackle reform of the external trade regime as a priority. He abolished licensing and quantitative restrictions on most imports except consumer goods. However, external trade in agricultural commodities was largely left out of his reform. Tariffs were reduced. By the time Singh left office in 1995, the import-weighted average tariff on all imports had come down to 33 percent from its level of 57 percent in 1990–91. It has come down further to around 20 percent in 1997–98. The variance in tariffs has been reduced as well. Even consumer goods imports on average had an import-weighted tariff of 48 percent in 1995, only 50 percent higher than the overall average, as compared to 100 percent higher in 1990–91. In 1997–98 the rate was 31 percent, a third higher than the overall average. This downward drift in tariffs has been interrupted by an across-the-board 8 percent (later reduced to 4 percent) surcharge on all imports (except food and medicines) announced in the budget for 1998–99. This is an extremely unfortunate signal to send if the intended message is one of continuing trade liberalization.

The exchange rate is now by and large market determined, though it would be more accurate to say that we have a regime of managed, rather than clean, floating rates in place. The real effective exchange rate had depreciated by about 40 percent in 1995 relative to its value in 1990 but seems to have appreciated since then.

The exchange rate depreciation until 1995, together with reductions in import duties and restrictions, brought about a very modest increase in India's share of world exports, as I mentioned earlier, from about 0.53 percent in 1990 to about 0.60 percent in 1995. With the slowing of the reductions in tariffs since 1995, no change in nontariff barriers, and some appreciation of the real effective exchange rate since 1995, it is not surprising that our export share has gone up by only 0.02 to 0.62 percent between 1995 and 1997. In absolute terms, India's exports, at $33 billion in 1996, were less than Thailand's $52 billion. In the past two years export growth has slowed considerably. However, over the period as a whole, the share of total trade in GDP increased significantly, from 15.6 percent in 1990–91 to 23.2 percent.

Turning now to the present and future, I will concentrate on areas directly related to foreign trade, such as tariffs and nontariff barriers, consumer goods imports, integration of agriculture into world markets, and infrastructural bottlenecks to trade.

First, turning to consumer goods imports, India can no longer use the balance-of-payments provision of GATT-WTO (Article XVIII B) to continue its quantitative restrictions. Indeed, India has agreed to phase them out by 2003, although this has not been well publicized. Tentative steps have been taken by transferring around 350 items from a list of restricted imports to the open general license categories, but many of these items are of limited significance. An immediate conversion of remaining quantitative restrictions on consumer goods imports into tariffs and their phased reduction thereafter would be desirable.

The levels and variance of other tariffs have to be reduced. Compared to other developing countries in the region, India's average and maximum tariffs are still high. Announcing a phased reduction would create more certainty for investors, both domestic and foreign. Bureaucratic and procedural hurdles faced by exporters and others are still formidable. It is true that compared to the prereform era, the number of clearances needed are far fewer, and all of them can be obtained at a single window, so to speak. But this would not impress many, since in other countries no clearances have to be obtained.

Agricultural trade has yet to be freed from internal barriers, let alone be integrated with world markets. Nontariff barriers still exist on imports of rice and wheat, even though domestic prices are lower than world prices. There are quantitative restrictions on exports of most agricultural commodities except some traditional exports, basmati rice and durum wheat. Imports accounting for nearly three-fourths of the value of agricultural production are still subject to nontariff barriers.

India is still not a common market for a number of reasons. For example, many states levy pernicious interstate sales taxes. In the case of agricultural commodities, restrictions on interstate movement, and even interdistrict movement within a state, either exist or are frequently imposed. Also, since the prices of agricultural commodities, particularly those that enter the food basket, such as onions, are politically important, restrictions on their internal movement as well as exports (or liberalization of imports) have often been imposed in order to moderate domestic price fluctuations. For example, an unusually hot summer and delayed monsoon rains in 1998 contributed to a shortage of onions and drove the price to seven times its level a year earlier. With elections due in November 1998 in states governed by the dominant party of the ruling coalition at the center, the price of onions became a hot political issue. The central government responded by suspending onion exports temporarily and ordering 10,000 tons of imports (*New York Times,* 12 October 1998, A3). There is massive government intervention in the market for cotton, including monopoly procurement in the state of Maharashtra. The fact of the matter is that cotton export policy is driven by the goal of keeping prices low for the domestic textile industry. Pakistan follows a similar policy with respect to its cotton trade.

4.3.3   Pakistan

Pakistan like India laid great emphasis on import-substituting industrialization. Hasan pointed out: "In the 1950s, as greater emphasis was laid on import substitution and as agricultural output stagnated, exports actually tended to decline. Strong agricultural growth and spurt of manufactured goods exports resulted in a growth of nearly 8 per cent per annum over 1960–93, substantially higher than the growth in GDP of nearly 6 per cent over same the period. But in recent years exports have tended to stagnate. During the four trade years 1993–6, export volume growth was slightly negative" (1998, 44). According to him:

> There are three basic reasons why Pakistan did not make fuller use of the opportunities offered by the explosive growth in world trade in manufactured goods. First, the development strategy did not emphasize exports sufficiently. Second, the trade policy distortions with relatively high duties on intermediate products discouraged processing for exports. There has been a general anti-export bias resulting from the high cost of imports required for exports and the relative attraction of the domestic market. Third, in the industrial strategy, there has been an excessive emphasis on processing of domestic raw materials, notably cotton. Policy failures are a fundamental reason why major opportunities were missed in exports and why the structure of exports remains so dependent on cotton-based exports. (47–48)

Hasan also noted the heavy dependence of Pakistan's exports on raw cotton and cotton yarn. The World Bank (1998c) confirmed that nearly two-thirds of the value of exports in 1996–97 consisted of cotton and textiles and more than half of exports went to the United States and Europe.

Even as of the end of 1996 there were fourteen different tariff slabs, the maximum tariff rate was 65 percent, and a minimum tariff of 10 percent applied to all imports except for wheat, fertilizers, and life-saving drugs. The World Bank (1998c) reported that the tariff reforms in March 1997 reduced the maximum tariff to 45 percent and the number of slabs to six and abolished the minimum tariff. The report added:

> Despite this progress, the tariff structure is still characterized by substantial differentiation among rates and distinctions between goods competing with domestic products and others, providing excessive protection to some domestic industries. For instance, the import of plant and machinery is subject to a concessional rate of 10%, except for machinery competing with the domestic engineering industry which is taxed at 35%. Turning to non-tariff barriers, most quantitative restrictions were removed relatively early in the trade liberalization process. However, the remaining 68 items on the negative list still include several textile products which can compete with domestic production. At least 17 items are subject to procedural requirements which de facto restrict imports. (19)

Like other developing countries, including India, Pakistan tried to offset the antiexport bias of its tariff structure through duty drawbacks, concessional tariffs on imports used in export production, concessional export financing, and duty-free imports within export-processing zones. As elsewhere the offsets, even when fully utilized, were only partial, and in any case the bureaucratic hurdles and procedures to be cleared in order to obtain them were formidable. Given all this, the World Bank was stating the obvious in recommending that "further tariff rationalization and trade liberalization, as well as more effective export promotion policies, are essential to provide stronger incentives for reallocation of resources in accordance with Pakistan's comparative advantage, remove anti-export bias, enhance consumer welfare, and reduce the current account deficit to a sustainable level" (1998c, 19).

4.3.4 Sri Lanka

As is to be expected of a small open economy, Sri Lankan tariffs have always been lower than those of India and Pakistan. As of 1990 the weighted mean tariff on all products was only 24.1 percent and the difference in mean tariff between primary and manufactured product groups was also small (World Bank 1998f, table 6.7). In 1995 a tariff reform reduced the number of tariff slabs to just three (35, 20, and 10 percent) and removed quantitative restrictions. By 1997 the weighted mean tariff on all products had been reduced somewhat to 20.7 percent. However, the structure of tariffs and the cascading effects of turnover taxes and markups are such that the effective protection rates on several products continue to be high. Rationalizing the tariff and tax structures to reduce effective protection rates is a priority for trade reform.

4.4 Privatization

4.4.1 Bangladesh

After independence in 1971 a wave of nationalization resulted in the public sector share in assets of the modern manufacturing sector going up from 34 percent in 1970 to 92 percent in 1973. Besides power, railways and other infrastructure were also publicly owned. Realizing that it could not efficiently manage such a vast set of enterprises, the government began privatization programs as early as in 1973. There were several subsequent efforts (World Bank 1993, 72). Bangladesh has recently established a Privatization Board, but it appears that no official statement on privatization policy has been issued and no enabling legislation to provide an appropriate legal framework for the operation of the board has yet been enacted (World Bank 1998a). Operational autonomy and adequate professional and financial expertise are yet to be provided to the board. There is thus considerable uncertainty about the government's intentions regarding privatization. Since 1996 the board had initiated privatization of thirty-two public enterprises, but as of 1998 only five of these, all of them small, have actually been handed over to the private sector.

Clearly, given their rather privileged position relative to the rest of the employed labor force regarding wages, benefits, and job security, it is natural that employees of state-owned enterprises, particularly in a context of rather slow growth in employment opportunities relative to growth in the labor force, would resist privatization. It is therefore essential that they and their representative unions are not only consulted but also persuaded that privatization is in the larger interest of the country and that their own future will be protected through appropriate combinations of incentives for early retirement, adequate severance payments, and retraining and placement for those who do not wish to retire.

4.4.2 India

In the postindependence period, even prior to the establishment of the Planning Commission in 1950, the Industrial Policy Resolution of 1948 (amended and elaborated in 1956) set the broad outlines of India's industrial development strategy by dividing industries into three groups: those to be developed exclusively by the public sector, those reserved for the private sector, and those open to development by either or both sectors. Development of key industries, such as railways, telecommunications, and electricity generation, was assigned to the public sector. In addition, industries producing key industrial raw materials and equipment, such as steel, petroleum, and heavy machinery including electric generators, were also in the public sector. The resolution was motivated by the idea that infrastructure and industries supplying key raw materials constituted what

Lenin had described as the "commanding heights" on an industrial battle-field. By controlling these, the course of development of all industries, in the private and public sectors, could be made to flow in socially desirable directions.[5] Moreover, instead of using taxation to generate revenue (e.g., for investment in the public sector), the pricing of goods and services produced and supplied by the public sector could be used to generate surpluses. It was also believed that the choice of location of public sector projects could be used to promote development of backward regions. Finally, the wages and working conditions of workers in the public sector were supposed to be a model for the private sector to follow.

The actual performance of the public sector has not conformed to the roles envisaged. Far from promoting private sector development and channeling it in socially desirable directions, there has been poor performance in supplying key inputs at reasonable cost, in appropriate amounts, and at the time and place where demand arises. Thus the public sector has acted as a brake on private sector development. Choice of location, technology, employment, and pricing policies of the public sector have become so politicized that efficient development is an exception. Far from generating resources, the public sector has become a monumental waste and liability for taxpayers. It is true that the industrialization strategy did generate a diversified industrial base and capability in designing and fabricating industrial plants and machinery. But the strategy virtually ignored considerations of scale economies, vastly restricted domestic and import competition, constrained technological upgrading through licensing and purchase of foreign technologies, encouraged capital-intensive technologies, and discouraged employment generation because restrictive labor laws raised

5. The breathtakingly naive faith in controls is seen in the following statement in the first five-year plan:

> Control and regulation of exports and imports, and in the case of certain select commodities state trading, are necessary not only from the point of view of utilizing to the best advantage the limited foreign exchange resources available but also for securing an allocation of the productive resources of the country in line with the targets defined in the Plan. . . . To some extent, over-all controls through fiscal, monetary and commercial policy can influence the allocation of resources, but physical controls are also necessary. . . . The targets of production defined in a plan cannot also be achieved unless a structure of relative prices favouring the desired allocation of resources is maintained. . . . In the case of certain key commodities, it may be necessary to keep down their prices in order to obviate the need for price rises in several industries which use these commodities. To make this policy effective, controls on production and on movement and physical allocations to consumers become inescapable. . . . Controls in a word are the means by which Government maintains a balance between various sectional interests. . . . Viewed in the proper perspective, controls are but another aspect of the problem of incentives, for to the extent that controls limit the freedom of action on the part of certain classes, they provide correspondingly an incentive to certain others and the practical problem is always to balance the loss of satisfaction in one case against the gain in the other. *For one to ask for fuller employment and more rapid development and at the same time to object to controls is obviously to support two contradictory objectives.* (India, Planning Commission 1951, 42–43; emphasis added)

the costs of hiring and firing. The consequence was an industrial sector, including most importantly its state-owned component, that was high cost and globally uncompetitive and out of tune with India's capital scarcity and labor abundance. It is no surprise therefore that the agenda of reforms initiated in 1991 included removal of government shackles from the private sector but also privatization.

The enterprises to be privatized can be divided into three categories: (A) those producing internationally tradable goods and services, (B) nontradables, in particular those with the characteristics of natural monopolies, and (C) others.

The primary objective of privatization is to utilize competition to improve efficiency and ensure that the resources employed earn the maximum returns. As such, the most important consideration in privatizing an enterprise is to ensure that once privatized, it will face adequate competition from other domestic and foreign enterprises and there will be incentives for profit, and hence for cost reduction. In enterprises of category A, except for a few traded goods, such as fertilizers or wide-bodied passenger jet aircraft, where the global market structure is not competitive, competition is easily arranged. It is enough to allow unrestricted imports, initially with a moderate tariff, if necessary, to allow the newly privatized enterprise to adjust gradually to import competition. The tariff should be progressively reduced over time with the schedule of reduction announced in advance. Since enterprises of category C are not natural monopolies, in principle there should be no insurmountable problems in ensuring competition.

Enterprises of category B are the most difficult to privatize. This category includes the basic infrastructure services—electricity, water, and telecommunications. Clearly, even if privatization merely creates a private monopoly, some efficiency gains would be achieved in the sense that a privately owned monopoly, unlike a publicly owned monopoly, would have greater incentives for cost reduction. However, the distortion arising from monopoly pricing will remain.

Consideration should be given to unbundling of monopoly and potentially competitive elements in vertically integrated enterprises, for example, generation, transmission, and distribution of power. A number of issues arise in reforming these basic industries, which until recently were state monopolies in most developing countries including India. Paul Joskow (1998) described these issues at some length.[6] He rightly pointed out the obvious fact that reforms, such as restructuring or privatization of public enterprises, are not ends in themselves but are means toward achieving other policy goals. The first step of course is to define with some

6. Chapter 5, by Aaron Tornell, and chapter 6, by Roger Noll, in this volume also address issues relating to privatization.

clarity what these goals are. For example, in India divestment consists of sale to private investors of specified percentages of equity in public enterprises. But there has been no official pronouncement, as far as I know, as to what was intended to be achieved by the proposed percentages of equity to be sold, which vary across enterprises. It is true that not all public enterprises are of the same significance to national priorities and a one-size-fits-all approach need not be the most effective way to reform them. Yet there has to be some rationale for the choice of particular percentages, and none has been offered thus far. This apart, even the government's commitment to disinvestment appears doubtful. For example, having established the Disinvestment Commission, the government has chosen to reduce the commission's power by not letting it monitor the privatization process and has eroded its credibility by failing to act on its recommendations. These actions send the most unfortunate signals about the disinvestment process to foreign and domestic investors, who are potential purchasers of divested equity.

Joskow suggested several goals for restructuring: the first is to improve the ability of the sector that is being restructured to mobilize adequate resources to support sector investments to balance supply and demand efficiently. This goal seems to be implicit in the figures proposed for internal resource mobilization of the public sector in the Indian central government's budget of 1998–99. A second goal is to increase productivity by reducing operating costs and investing in more efficient plant and equipment. This goal is very relevant in the Indian context. For example, India's public sector fertilizer plants are of different capacities, were built at different times, and operate with different product mixes and technologies, particularly with respect to feedstocks. The capacities for urea production range from 0.132 million tons from a plant commissioned in 1951 to 8 million tons from a plant commissioned in 1975. In all, thirty-eight plants commissioned between 1951 and 1996 operate. The earliest nonurea unit was commissioned in 1901 and the latest in 1996, and in all there are fifty-one plants (India, Department of Fertilizers 1998, tables I-1, A-I-1), again of varying capacities. At one plant feedstocks included, until it converted to fuel oil, very costly electricity for electrolysis of water to produce hydrogen. This plant was built in the fifties, in part because of a colossal misperception that cheap electricity from a nearby hydroelectric plant would be forever in excess supply. Other plants have varied feedstocks, such as naphtha, fuel oil, and coal. A large part of the problem of India's fertilizer pricing and the related issue of fertilizer subsidies (accounting for about 0.5 percent of GDP in 1997–98) arose from the fact that the costs of fertilizers produced from these diverse plants varied substantially from each other and also from prevailing world prices, and the policy objective was to ensure full utilization of the capacity that had been created.

Joskow's third goal is to bring prices in line with costs (including non-priced environmental costs) to provide consumers with good price signals. Clearly this is an extremely important goal—needless to say, underpricing of electricity for agricultural use and the subsidization of nitrogenous fertilizers have resulted in extremely distorted use of both water and fertilizers. Coupled with underpricing, inefficient and inequitable allocation of surface water from public irrigation systems has encouraged excessive use of groundwater. Salinity and waterlogging and the loss of cultivable land as well as exploitation of aquifers beyond sustainable levels have been the outcomes of such excessive use.

The fourth and fifth goals involve, respectively, the need for the sector that is being restructured to generate enough surplus over costs to finance its own investment and the need to ensure that those parts of the sector remaining in the public sector charge prices compatible with the introduction of competition in privatized parts. Again the last objective is quite relevant in the Indian context. If one were to privatize electricity generation as well as distribution to make them competitive, while retaining transmission as a public sector (or as a regulated private sector) monopoly, the fees charged for the use of the transmission grid will be of great significance to the efficiency and viability of competition in generation and transmission. Given the natural ebbs and flows of demand during the course of a day, let alone across seasons, and seasonal variation in supply from hydroelectric plants, not to mention random shocks to supplies and demands, the structure of prices has to be sensitive to these factors if overall efficiency of generation and distribution is to be achieved.

Apart from clarifying the goals to be achieved through privatization and restructuring, two other needed steps are to define a reform model that, as Joskow rightly said has to go well beyond sloganeering and chanting the mantras of privatization, deregulation, and competition. The model has to define which segments of the industry will remain monopolies, albeit regulated ones, and which segments will be opened to competition. Even in the case of a regulated monopoly it is possible that future entry, and hence competition, is feasible and anticipated, in which case regulation has to take this into account in its functioning.

For the segments in which competition is to be introduced, the form of competition, the mechanisms, and the sequencing and pace of their introduction have to be thought through. Finally, given that the eventual structure of the industry will include competitive and regulated monopolies as segments, the extent of horizontal integration at each level of the production chain and vertical integration between levels of the production chain ought to be clarified. For example, if electricity generation and distribution are to be privatized while transmission is a monopoly, should generating companies be allowed to have distribution subsidiaries? Should there be a national transmission monopoly or should there be many regional monopolies? Even more important, should the transmission monopoly be allowed to own generating or distribution subsidiaries? In evaluating the recently introduced reforms in the electricity sectors of the states of Orissa, Rajasthan, and others, it is important that these issues be thought through in some depth. The same issues arise in the telecommunications sector as well.

Legislation for enabling a regulatory framework for electricity has recently been approved by the Indian Parliament. The Securities and Exchanges Board of India has been in operation for several years, and a Telecommunications Regulatory Authority of India has been established. The issues regarding the organization of each regulatory agency, such as its independence both from government and politics and from the industry it is to regulate, transparency of its procedures, and its accountability, expertise, and credibility have come to the fore.

I have not so far touched on the managerial autonomy, particularly the freedom to hire and fire, choose the wage and salary structure, and the like, that any enterprise needs to function in a competitive environment. As far as the private sector is concerned, India's labor laws, particularly the Industrial Disputes Act, severely constrain managerial autonomy. In the case of public sector enterprises, despite memoranda of understanding and whatnot, there has been little autonomy in practice for management. It remains to be seen whether the autonomy promised for the "navaratnas," or "nine gems," constituting the large and profitable public enterprises, will in fact materialize.

The reform of India's labor and bankruptcy laws are essential for successful privatization and rehabilitation of sick enterprises. As Mahalanobis pointed out long ago, "Certain welfare measures tend to be implemented in India ahead of economic growth, for example, labour laws which are probably the most highly protective of labour interests in the narrowest sense, in the whole world. There is practically no link between output and remuneration; hiring and firing are highly restricted. It is extremely difficult to maintain an economic level of productivity or improve productivity. . . . The present form of protection of organized labour, which constitutes, including their families, about five or six percent of the whole population, would operate as an obstacle to growth and would also increase inequalities" (1969, 442). He was surely right in suggesting that "it would seem better to try to attain the highest possible efficiency of labour and increasing productivity, and use the additional value obtained in this way to create more employment rather than lower the industrial efficiency by slack or restrictive practices through overstaffing" (Mahalanobis 1961, 157). Alas the labor aristocracy in the public sector as well as in organized industry continues to be pampered and the late professor's advice is yet to be heeded!

4.4.3 Pakistan

As in India, in Pakistan state-owned enterprises (SOEs) play a dominant role in infrastructure, energy, telecommunications, and financial services (World Bank 1998c). Pakistani SOEs, like their Indian counterparts, are overstaffed, operationally inefficient, and poorly managed. In 1996–97 the overall deficit of seven major SOEs amounted to 1.7 percent of GDP. Committees appointed by the government have made several recommendations to improve the performance of these seven SOEs, but these are yet to be effectively implemented and extended to other SOEs.

Pakistan has had greater success in privatizing small and medium-size industrial units and small banks. Also minority shareholdings in Pakistan Airlines and Pakistan Telecommunications have been sold to private investors.

In contrast to the cases of the Privatization Board in Bangladesh and the Disinvestment Commission in India, the powers of Pakistan's privatization commission have been enhanced. However, it needs adequate financial resources as well as professional staff. Like India, Pakistan has established some regulatory authorities for infrastructure but has not made sufficient headway in making them credible, autonomous, and effective. As in the other countries of the region, and for the same reasons, employees of SOEs in Pakistan resist privatization and have to be persuaded to abandon their resistance by providing appropriate incentives for retirement, separation, retraining, and placement.

4.4.4 Sri Lanka

Sri Lanka has been the most vigorous among the four large South Asian economies in pursuing privatization. According to the World Bank (1998e), since 1996 the government has leased out the last six of its tea estates, sold 35 percent of its equity and transferred management control to private hands of Sri Lanka Telecommunications, sold all of its equity in the National Development Bank, and reprivatized seven enterprises that had been renationalized in 1996. Privatization proceeds accounted for 2.5 percent of GDP in 1996, of which a little over two-fifths has been used to retire public debt. Sri Lanka has succeeded in encouraging the private sector to participate in several infrastructure projects, mainly telecommunications and ports, but also in the energy sector. Management of public enterprises has improved, and there are plans for restructuring other government bodies. In short, Sri Lankan privatization is the only success story in South Asia.

4.5   Financial Sector Reform

4.5.1   Bangladesh

Bangladesh's financial sector is weak, with nonperforming loans accounting for 33 percent of the combined portfolio of nationalized and private domestic commercial banks. Although the government recapitalized the nationalized commercial banks in 1990, they have again become capital deficient. As elsewhere in the region, the cost to the Bangladesh economy of a weak financial sector with a huge overhang of nonperforming loans is substantial. Actions needed to recover overdue loans, penalize defaulters, and restructure or close unviable institutions are slow in coming and do not go far enough because of political constraints. Bangladesh's capital markets are thin and perhaps the weakest in the region—the government is currently implementing a capital market development program to strengthen these markets.

4.5.2   India

Ronald McKinnon (1973) and Edward Shaw (1973) used the term "financial repression" to describe a system in developing countries in which the government determines who gets and gives credit and at what terms. Such control is exercised through one or more of the following: government regulations on which financial institutions will be permitted to do business, and how they will operate, government's ownership of banks and other financial intermediaries, and government controls over international capital movements.

India, until the recent reforms, had all of these. Most commercial banks (with the exception of a few foreign banks and some small banks) and insurance companies were owned by the government, and interest rates were controlled. There were selective credit controls and directed lending to priority sectors. Through the cash reserve requirement ratio (CRRR) and statutory liquidity requirement ratio (SLRR), the government ensured that more than 50 percent of the deposits of commercial banks was invested in government securities. Moreover, the government monetized part of its fiscal deficits through forced sale of ad hoc treasury bills to the Reserve Bank of India. The nationalized banks as well as the Reserve Bank had little autonomy in decision making. India was no exception in repressing the financial sector—such repression has been almost universal in developing countries until recently.

The broad contours of India's financial sector reforms are well known. First, interest rates for loans greater than 0.2 million rupees are no longer administratively set, although they continue to be administratively set with respect to savings deposits, small savings, nonresident Indian deposits, and loans under 0.2 million rupees. The CRRR and SLRR, which were as high as 25 and 38.5 percent, respectively, prior to 1991, are now 10 and 25 percent. Since April 1998, banks have been permitted to set interest rates, up to a maximum equal to the prime rate, on loans under 0.2 million rupees. Private (domestic and foreign) entrants have been allowed into the banking sector, and these now account for about 17 percent of bank assets. The Reserve Bank has enhanced its regulatory powers over nonbank financial institutions (NBFIs) and has set capital adequacy norms and prudential regulations for NBFIs. Above all, regulations on banks regarding income recognition, definition of nonperforming assets, and provisions have been strengthened. But a lot more remains to be done.

It would seem that India has by no means abandoned the political culture that has characterized lending by state-owned commercial banks, as well as the directed credit to priority sectors. Gross nonperforming assets of the banking system are about 17.8 percent of total loans (World Bank 1998b, 14). Several government committees have made recommendations on reforms of the financial sector, including two committees chaired by M. Narasimham. Also the Committee for Harmonizing the Role and Operations of Development Finance Institutions and Banks and the Committee on Rural Credit have reported recommendations. These committees have comprehensively examined the issues involved in arriving at their recommendations.

The recommendations of the second Narasimham committee include

Reduce the government's and Reserve Bank of India's share of equity in banks to 33 percent, by dilution

Separate the Reserve Bank from its role on bank boards

Raise bank capital to 9 percent of risk-weighted assets by 2000 and 10 percent by 2002; mark to market and give government securities a 5 percent "risk weight" to begin to deal with their interest rate risk; give foreign open positions a 100 percent risk weight (i.e., 8 percent of the open position would have to be matched by capital, up from the current, separate 5 percent requirement)

Reduce nonperforming assets sharply; tighten definitions; avoid further recapitalization by the government; any "hiving off" should involve major operational restructuring to prevent the problem's recurrence; closure of weak banks that cannot be revived, with safeguarding of depositor and employee interests

Give banks more autonomy in bank management and pay setting (for banks that have gone to the market); lengthen terms for top managers; restructure and develop voluntary retirement schemes as appropriate; upgrade staff and computerize faster; improve risk management; improve disclosure

Leave deposit insurance coverage as is, but move to risk based premiums (World Bank 1998b, 29, box 6)

I am glad that the committee has endorsed the view that others, including myself, have been advocating: namely, that capital adequacy norms have to be judged in relation to the riskiness of the loan portfolio. The committee rightly recommends India move toward a norm of 10 percent, rather than the average Basle norm of 8 percent. It points out that there are virtually no markets in India for hedging risks and rightly suggests that capital adequacy norms should therefore take into account market risks in addition to credit risks. The committee's proposal for risk weights of various components of bank portfolios—in particular, assigning a 5 percent weight for market risks of government and government-approved securities—is right on the mark. It has sensibly recommended tightening the criteria for classification of a loan as nonperforming and for income recognition and appraising. The committee is absolutely right in insisting that measures be put in place to ensure that nonperforming assets do not arise in the future before clearing the balance sheets of banks of their nonperforming assets through any of the suggested proposals.

I was disappointed that the committee gave in to government pressure and in the end did not recommend that the scope of directed credit to priority sectors be reduced from 40 to 10 percent, while correctly arguing for total elimination of interest rate subsidies on loans to priority sectors. The committee has rightly emphasized the urgency of reducing excess employment and ensuring longer tenures for chief executives of state-owned banks, as well as lateral recruitment and appropriate compensation for the chief executives. The scandalous quality of customer service delivered by public sector banks has to be addressed. Computerization of operations must be extended. There should be no further recourse to debt waivers in rural lending.

Let me turn briefly to inflows of foreign capital and convertibility of the rupee for capital transactions. It would be extremely unwise to rush to make the rupee fully convertible. Capital inflows need not necessarily be welfare enhancing. As was argued long ago by Brecher and Alejandro (1977), in a situation of continuing protection of capital-intensive import-competing sectors any foreign capital attracted to such protected sectors would be welfare reducing. Thus, until such protection is removed, increased capital inflows including foreign direct investment would not be beneficial if they went to heavily protected sectors. Unless India's macroeconomic framework is brought firmly under control and the banking sector in particular, as well as the financial sector more broadly, is brought into sound shape, augmented capital inflows triggered by full convertibility of the rupee might be invested inappropriately, thus increasing the probability of a financial crisis when such investments fail. The management capability of banks in their credit operations with the private sector has to be improved. This improvement should include better understanding of, and ability to, appraise the risk characteristics of advances to the private sector. Also capital requirements have to be increased progressively to 10 percent, as recommended by the second Narasimham committee.

It is virtually impossible to design a financial system that is at once free of controls and open to external capital inflows and outflows and at the same time completely immune to financial crises and panics. The recent Southeast Asian crisis and the others that preceded it suggest several factors that could make a financial crisis more probable: a weak domestic financial sector that has little or no capacity to appraise risks properly, expectations arising from past experience that the government will not allow any major bank or financial institution to fail, and mismatches in the maturity of borrowed funds relative to advances, that is, borrowing short and lending long, particularly with external borrowing. Ensuring that these factors are not present in a country is certainly not politically easy, particularly if it involves cutting off popular loans, shutting weak financial institutions, and taking action early enough.

The insurance sector is currently a public monopoly that controls a significant share of investible funds. It is known to be inefficient and overstaffed. It is essential that the sector be opened to competition. Reforms are yet to be undertaken even though several announcements of forthcoming actions have been made. A related issue is that of pensions and provident funds. Moving to a fully funded transferable system and involving some options for investing part of the funds in equities ought to be examined. State-supported provisions for retirement are available for only a small part of the labor force. Extending some form of social security to the entire labor force has to be part of the reform agenda. Also, as the Reserve Bank extends its control over nonbank financial intermediaries, it should ensure healthy competition between banks and nonbanks in order to provide the best set of financing options for the public. In India, mortgage finance for housing and other real estate is still underdeveloped. This is another area for immediate attention.

Reforms in the financial and real sectors are complementary. Access to funds for working capital as well as for long-term investment through an efficiently functioning set of financial intermediaries is undoubtedly essential if the reforms in the real sector are to succeed and if the real sector is to grow more rapidly. Financial sector reforms are thus essential to real sector growth. Equally, if the domestic real sector is not reformed, with an efficient financial sector savers and investors could look outside the home economy for the use of their funds. While investors would certainly benefit from higher returns on their investments, clearly domestic investment, and hence growth, would be lower than would be the case if there were no distortions in the domestic real sector. There is also the danger that signals for investment emerging from a distorted real sector could be so faulty that investible resources end up in the wrong sectors, even if these are invested at home. Thus real sector reform is essential if financial sector reform is to bear fruit in terms of more rapid growth.

India is a signatory of the General Agreement on Trade in Services and the Financial Services Agreement, both offshoots of the final agreement of the Uruguay Round of multilateral trade negotiations. As such, India needs to ensure that domestic financial sector reforms anticipate what is needed to compete in the emerging liberal world financial order.

4.5.3   Pakistan

According to the World Bank (1998c), nonperforming assets of banks and development finance institutions were estimated to be around 18.5 percent of their total loan portfolios and 5.1 percent of GDP as of June 1997. Nonperforming assets of nationalized commercial banks accounted for nearly 30 percent of their loan portfolios. Fortunately the government has initiated reforms with the World Bank's technical and financial assistance. The management of nationalized commercial banks is to be put in the hands of professional bank managers recruited from the private sector. A good beginning has been made in reducing overstaffing, recovering nonperforming loans, and closing unprofitable branches. The World Bank (1998c) rightly emphasized that while these reforms have helped to arrest deterioration in the financial position of the banking system, there is still a long way to go to achieve a strong and dynamic banking sector. It recommends that Pakistan further divest partially privatized commercial banks, prepare the three remaining commercial banks and two development finance institutions for privatization, phase out concessional credit except for exports, and reduce the statutory liquidity requirement ratio to 15 percent.

4.5.4   Sri Lanka

Inefficient state-owned banks dominate the banking sector. The World Bank pointed out that "despite two asset clean-up operations in 1993 and 1996 (costing a cumulative 5 percent of GDP), these banks continue to hold fragile portfolios, which remain a constant threat to achieving fiscal objectives. Since outright privatization does not seem possible under current political circumstances, the second-best solution is to grant them appropriate managerial autonomy, preferably by an Act of Parliament," coupled with performance-based rewards and punishments (1998e, 14). While commending Sri Lanka for liberalizing interest rates and improving the management of monetary policy, the World Bank advocated a "more forceful liberalization of the financial market, in particular investment opportunities for pension funds and insurance companies" (1998e, 14).

4.6   Infrastructure Reform

Inadequate and poorly performing infrastructure, consisting of energy, transport, and telecommunications, is a major constraint throughout the region to reaping the full potential of economic liberalization. However, many distinct features of infrastructural activities complicate the task of reforming the sector.

First, these activities involve relatively large and lumpy investment. Second, because of the lumpiness of investment and for other reasons, there are likely to be significant economies of scale in many infrastructural activities. Third, apart from scale economies, there are likely to be externalities of various kinds, such as network externalities in telecommunications and transport networks, environmental externalities in the case of power generation activities, externalities in the form of prevention of communicable diseases in the case of investment in water supply systems, sewage, and waste disposal, and so forth. Fourth, related to externalities is that some of the services are like public goods; that is, they are nonrival and nonexcludable in their use. Fifth, there are often distinguishable categories of users of infrastructural services. To cite a few examples: In rail and other transportation, passenger services can be distinguished from cargo or freight services; within each class of service, further distinctions, such as between suburban, local, and long-distance transportation, can be made as well. In telephone services, local calls are distinguished from national and international trunk calls, and so on. In the power sector of South Asia, household consumers, agriculturalists, and commercial and industrial users have been distinguished in pricing. Since the same basic plant and equipment are used to provide several categories of service, issues of cross-subsidization of one or more category of users by others arise.

These several aspects imply that a competitive market system is unlikely to provide socially optimal amounts and allocations of most of the infrastructural services. Indeed, because of extensive scale economies and the large size of investment required, some of these activities have the characteristics of natural monopolies. While market failure calls for corrective government action, there is a wide spectrum of choices in the type of action. For example, a service that is a natural monopoly can be produced by a state enterprise or by a private enterprise regulated by the state. In some cases production, transportation or transmission, and delivery to the ultimate user can all be vertically integrated into one state-run or state-regulated private monopoly. In other cases some segments, such as production and distribution, are the domain of competitive private enterprises, while transportation is a monopoly. There are also a number of choices of regulatory framework, if regulation is chosen: for a large economy, should there be a single regulatory agency for the economy as a whole or should there be several, possibly regional, regulatory agencies? A whole host of issues surround the mechanism of regulation. Different forms of organization for production, transportation, and distribution as well as regulation have efficiency and equity implications.

Paul Joskow (1998) pointed out that historically the performance of state enterprises in providing infrastructural services has been quite poor in developing countries. Much of the population does not have access to these services at all, as has long been the case of the rural population with respect to telecommunications and even electricity in South Asia. Some are lucky enough to gain access sometime, after not only waiting for many years in a queue, as used to be the case for telephone connections, but also more often than not paying bribes or using influence.

The quality of service is poor in many developing countries, with high rates of equipment outages, fluctuating voltages, and interruptions of supply as in the case of electricity in South Asia. The poor performance of public utilities has led private producers to install their own costly and often very polluting small captive power generators. The enterprises usually employ many more workers than needed for their functioning, so their productivity is low and those employed usually enjoy much higher wages and perquisites than similar workers elsewhere in the economy.

Again in South Asia, prices charged for infrastructural services do not even cover the variable costs of their supply, let alone contribute to fixed costs. Needless to say, they do not generate surpluses to finance investment in their expansion. Above all, staffing, particularly the appointment of the executive officers who are to manage these enterprises, is often highly politicized and frequently corrupt. The sad performance of enterprises providing infrastructural services has been a factor in the poor performance of many developing countries. Thus the case for reforming infrastructural sectors is very strong both from the perspective of improving their own performance and from the perspective that an unreformed and poorly performing infrastructure will severely limit the realization of potential benefits from reforms in other sectors.

The task of reforming infrastructural sectors is complex because of specific aspects of these sectors. For example, simply selling a public sector monopoly to the private sector, and thus turning it into a private monopoly, will not in general improve matters much, though because profit is his primary motive a private monopolist is more likely than the manager of a state monopoly to minimize costs and to ensure that he does not lose customers because of poor service quality relative to price. Since it is the efficiency gain arising from competition that is the primary objective of privatization, clearly segments of infrastructure that are potentially competitive ought to be privatized. For example, in power, these might be generation and distribution but not necessarily transmission.

As Joskow pointed out, as infrastructural sectors are privatized and restructured to promote competition in potentially competitive segments, the creation of supporting regulatory institutions is vital. What is more, he argued rightly, such creation has to be an integral part of the whole reform program and not an afterthought.

Let me turn to the situation in individual countries.

4.6.1   Bangladesh

Although, strictly speaking, the oil and natural gas industry is not part of economic infrastructure, because it supplies a major input to infrastructure proper, namely, electricity generation and transportation, its performance has a major impact on infrastructure. The recent discovery of sizable offshore reserves of gas has generated considerable interest among foreign investors in developing them. However, the bidding process and shifts in the government's position during the selection process have not been helpful. First of all, sending a clear message about Bangladesh's intentions regarding foreign direct investment is essential. Second, unless the issues relating to pricing of gas for different uses (such as power generation, feedstock in fertilizer production, and fuel in households) are sorted out prior to inviting bids, avoidable uncertainties will be created. The performance of the power sector in Bangladesh has been abysmal, with heavy systems losses (some of which can in fact be accounted for by theft of power, as in India). The World Bank was certainly on the mark in saying that "to ensure the orderly and effective participation of the private sector, it is important to quickly complete the establishment of the legal, regulatory and policy framework in the power, gas and telecommunications sectors and establish firmly the 'rules of the game'" (1998a, 15).

4.6.2   India

Indian policymakers have not devoted enough thought to the creation and design of regulatory institutions. Other than the Securities and Exchanges Board of India, which regulates the financial sector, only two—namely, the Telecom Regulatory Authority of India (TRAI) and the Tariff Authority for Major Ports—have been set up. Since a regulatory agency is a creation of the government, if there is not clarity in defining the power of the regulatory authority vis-à-vis the government, it would severely undermine the independence of the regulatory authority. For example, the Department of Telecommunications (DOT) is both a policymaker and a publicly owned supplier of telecommunications services. As result, TRAI and DOT have conflicted, most recently in the setting of tariffs for local and long-distance telephone calls. Clearly the two roles of DOT have to be vested in separate institutions so that TRAI as a regulator will have jurisdiction over all suppliers. In the power sector, the Parliament has enacted a law enabling the states to establish regulatory authorities, though none have as yet been established. With respect to roads, ports, and irrigation, only a beginning has been made.

According to the government's own economic survey (India 1998, table 9.4), the total gross subsidy on the sale of power in 1996–97 was a staggering 201,470 million rupees or 1.8 percent of GDP, of which 156,280 million rupees were due to subsidized sale to farmers. In two states, Punjab and Tamil Nadu, farmers are not charged at all for their use of electricity. As against a 3 percent rate of return on the net fixed assets in service stipulated in the Electricity Supply Act of 1948, the actual rate of return in 1997–98 was minus 17.6 percent! Starting with Orissa, five other states— Andhra Pradesh, Gujarat, Haryana, Uttar Pradesh, and Rajasthan—have begun the reform process in this vital sector. These states have endorsed the creation of an independent regulatory agency for power, approved the principle that tariffs should reflect costs, agreed to divest their shares in power-generating companies and to encourage competition among independent power producers, and finally agreed to privatize the distribution function of the SEBs. While these decisions by the five states are to be welcomed, and the substantial progress made by Orissa is encouraging, it is still too early to say whether all the steps in the reform process will be successfully implemented in these states, let alone other states embracing them.

In the past several decades, the telephone was viewed as a luxury consumer service that enabled private communication rather than an essential producer service needed to link markets, producers, and consumers. As such, the fact that one had to wait several years for a telephone connection was not viewed as having high social costs. Fortunately India has recently moved away from this unfortunate idea, so meeting anticipated demand through public and private provision of telephone services is now viewed as appropriate. The private sector is now a significant participant in telecommunications. The annual growth of new telephone connections in different parts of the country increases steadily every year, but there is still a long way to go before all Indian villages at least have access to a public call office.

According to Peters:

> India's ports were originally designed to handle specific categories of traffic which have declined over time while other types of traffic have gained importance. But the ports' berth configurations were not adjusted to the categories of cargo which grew most.
>
> In almost all ports productivity levels are extremely low by international standards.
>
> Documentary procedures related to cargo handling . . . are extremely complicated.
>
> Land-side port access facilities and arrangements for moving inbound and outbound cargo are unsatisfactory. (1997, 7–8)

The net result of all this is that some ports (e.g., Calcutta) handle much less cargo than they did fifty years ago. In the line trades, very few carriers serve India's ports through direct calls because doing so would mean unacceptably long waiting times: the average turnaround time for a ship in India's major ports exceeded a week in 1997 (India 1998, 132), compared to a few hours in Singapore and other ports in Asia. Most general cargo traffic to and out of India takes place through transshipment at more efficient ports such as Colombo. The added costs to India's exporters and importers are substantial.

Realizing the urgent need for reforms, the government has invited private interests to finance new port facilities on a "build, operate, and transfer" (BOT) basis. This is a welcome move away from the situation described by Peters: "the principal reasons for such inefficiencies lies in the fact that India's ports are still managed like bureaucracies burdened with rules for the employment and dispatch of labour which critically undermine any effort at improving productivity" (1997, 8). Indeed recalcitrant unionized labor is a serious bottleneck to any productivity-raising change at ports, as well as in other public sector entities. There is still a long way to go before India's ports can compete with more efficient ports in the region such as Colombo in Sri Lanka, let alone Singapore.

The inefficient functioning of publicly owned railways over a long period of time has resulted in a diversion of long-distance cargo traffic from railways to privately run road transport. But with investment in roads by the public sector lagging behind growth in traffic, the conditions of roads have deteriorated, with the consequence that the cost of cargo transportation has increased. Until recently there were no toll roads in India. With the amendment of the National Highways Act to enable a levy of toll on selected sections of national highways, private sector participation on a BOT basis has been facilitated. Agreement on a few projects has been reached, and one small project, the construction of a 24-kilometer bypass near Mumbai, has been completed. In road transport, again much remains to be done.

4.6.3 Pakistan

The World Bank drew attention to a complex set of interrelated problems faced by Pakistan's public sector power utilities, the Water and Power Development Authority (WAPDA) and Karachi Electric Supply Corporation. They have become so serious "that they threatened national fiscal stability in addition to bringing both institutions to the brink of financial insolvency—adversely affecting their operations, decimating their investments, and creating serious liquidity problems for other public enterprises through cross-areas" (World Bank 1998c, 22). The litany of problems, which are also prevalent in Bangladesh and India, include inefficient operations, high losses, and theft; overstaffing, poor management, and poor maintenance; failure (willful or otherwise) to collect bills from key consumers; and politically determined and inappropriate tariff structures, including heavy subsidization of agricultural uses. Above all, the government has initiated a comprehensive program to bring WAPDA back to financial health and improve the efficiency of the power sector. The World Bank rightly stressed that "given the dire circumstances faced by the power sector, this reform programme must be implemented fully and in a timely manner" (1998c, 24).

4.6.4   Sri Lanka

As noted earlier in the section on privatization, Sri Lanka has succeeded in attracting several private sector projects in energy production, in the telecommunications sector, and in the expansion of ports. The government is also divesting 40 percent of its equity in Air Lanka. It is setting up an independent regulator for the power sector and unbundling the vertically integrated Ceylon Electricity Board into separate companies for hydroproduction, thermal power generation, transmission, and generation, though privatization of these parts is not currently on the reform agenda.

4.7   Social Sectors

In 1993, 1.3 billion people in the developing world were deemed poor, that is, living on less than one dollar a day, of which nearly 40 percent lived in South Asia (Demery and Walton 1998, table 1). South Asia unsurprisingly lags behind other developing countries with respect to social indicators. But within Asia there are substantial differences in the outcomes of poverty alleviation policies and in social achievement. Sri Lanka's longstanding and impressive achievements in human development for a country with its level of per capita income are well known. So are similar achievements in the southern states of India, particularly Kerala, that are neighbors of Sri Lanka. At the other end are Pakistan and some of the northern states of India, where social indicators, particularly for women, are among the worst in South Asia and the world. Bangladesh is in the middle, with some notable achievements, such as in reduction of fertility, but only moderate success in improving other social indicators. Table 4.2 presents data on social indicators for South Asia.

It goes without saying that social development is of great intrinsic value. But its instrumental value, in improving productivity in all sectors including agriculture and manufacturing, both by enabling the adoption of new technology and by enhancing learning-by-doing effects, is important as well. The contrast between the East Asian and South Asian growth records has been attributed to the early emphasis given to education and health in East Asia. Given the importance of social sectors not only from the perspective of long-term growth and development but also from the perspective of poverty alleviation, both through faster growth and through improvements in the income-earning capacity of the poor, it would be a matter of concern if economic reform, particularly its component of fiscal stabilization, comes at the expense of resources devoted to human capital accumulation. However, if the reduction in resources is accompanied by significant improvements in their productivity in achieving

Table 4.2   **Social Indicators**

Indicator	Bangladesh	India	Pakistan	Sri Lanka
Life expectancy at birth, 1996 (years)	58	63	63	73
Infant mortality rate, 1996 (per 1,000 live births)	77	65	88	15
Child mortality rate, 1988–97 (per 1,000)				
Male	47	29	22	10
Female	62	42	37	9
Total fertility rate, 1996 (births per women)	3.4	3.1	5.1	1.2
Low-weight babies, 1989–95 (% of births)	34	14	25	17
Child malnutrition, 1990–91 (% of children under 5)	68	40	40	38
Gross enrollment, 1995 (% of relevant age group)				
Primary	92	100	74	113
Secondary	–	49	26	75
Tertiary	–	6	3	5

Source: World Bank (1998f, tables 2.10, 2.15, 2.17).

social development, as seems possible, such concern would be alleviated. Let me turn to the situation in each of the four countries.

4.7.1 Bangladesh

As the World Bank noted, Bangladesh has made progress in improving social conditions and reducing poverty (1998a, 17). Total fertility has declined to 3.3 during 1995–97 from 6.1 in 1980. Poverty as measured by the proportion of the population having resources inadequate to meet basic needs has declined from 42.7 percent in 1991–92 to 35.6 percent in 1995–96. However, improvements in reproductive health have been slow in coming, with maternal mortality at 44 per 100,000 live births during 1990–96 being one of the highest in the world and infant mortality at 77 per 1,000 live births 1996 being high (World Bank 1998f, tables 2.15, 2.17). Child malnutrition is also unacceptably high.

Progress in increasing enrollment in primary and secondary schools, and particularly in achieving parity in enrollment between boys and girls in primary education, has been significant. But quality of education at all levels is poor, and the productivity of public resources spent on education is low, with high dropout and low completion rates.

One distinctive characteristic of Bangladesh society is the large number of nongovernmental organizations engaged in poverty-alleviating activities, particularly in providing children of poor households with access to basic education. Replication of their success by the government in Bangladesh as well as in the rest of South Asia would dramatically improve educational attainments of all children.

Turning to resources spent, it would seem that as a proportion of GDP, expenditures on annual development programs (ADP) have declined to 7.4 percent in 1996 after rising from 6.2 percent in 1990 to 8.6 percent in 1995. What is more, in comparison to July–February 1997 ADP spending in July–February 1998 has fallen by 11.5 percent (World Bank 1998a, tables 13, 14). While recognizing that the reduction in fiscal deficits in 1996 and 1997 is likely to have been largely due to cuts in ADP spending, the World Bank suggested the possibility that some reduction in ADP spending would have been desirable anyway "if projects of questionable priority and quality . . . are dropped" (1998c, 11). Since such projects should be dropped, whether ADP spending is rising or falling, other than saying that the potential adverse effect of falling ADP spending is attenuated by their being dropped, one cannot view such falls as necessarily desirable.

4.7.2   India

Eradication of poverty has long been the stated overarching objective of Indian economic development. Yet after nearly fifty years of planning since independence, more than a third of India's population still has monthly consumption below an extremely modest national poverty line. Contrary to the assertion by Western economists and agencies such as the United Nations Development Program (UNDP) that developing countries were fixated on income growth and neglected poverty alleviation and human development, in India the objective has never been growth in and of itself but only as an instrument for poverty alleviation.

In the postindependence era, except for the modest first five-year plan, every other five-year plan envisaged more than 5 percent growth in national income per year. But the average rate of growth achieved in the forty-seven years since we began planning in 1950 has been about 4 percent. For the three decades until the beginning of the sixth plan in 1980–81, the average rate of growth was even lower, at 3.5 percent per annum, the infamous Hindu rate of growth.

It is this massive failure to achieve rapid growth that is at the root of the failure to eliminate poverty. Ravallion and Datt (1996) estimated roughly a unitary elasticity for the poverty headcount ratio with respect to growth in real per capita income. Had India's per capita income grown by 5 percent per year since 1950–51, it would have grown tenfold by 1998–99. Other things remaining the same, given a unitary elasticity the headcount poverty ratio would now be about 6 percent, or one-tenth its 1950–51 value of around 60 percent or so. Alternatively, if poverty is to be halved in ten years from its present value of, say, 36 percent, per capita income has to double, or grow by 7.1 percent a year. It is not my intention to suggest that these calculations be taken literally, only to argue the vital importance of considerably accelerating India's rate of growth if a serious dent is to be made in the appalling poverty in India. I must also add the obvious point that the quality or character of growth, and not simply its rate, matters for poverty alleviation: growth has to enhance the prospects of the poor.

Apart from the tried and tested policy of rapid and shared growth, other ostensibly poverty-alleviating policies include transfers of various kinds and policies that augment the earned income of poor households. The two main transfer programs in India are the Public Distribution System (PDS) and the provision of Integrated Child Development Services. The first provides a limited quantity of certain essential commodities, primarily foodgrains at subsidized prices. The second relates to a set of programs that provide nutritional supplements and health care to children at no out-of-pocket cost to parents. There are several income-augmenting programs: the Integrated Rural Development Programme, Development of Women and Children in Rural Areas, Training of Youth and Self-employment Programmes, and two public works programs for employment generation, namely, Jawahar Rozgar Yojana (JRY) and the Employment Assurance Scheme. Some of these programs overlap with each other.

The first important point to note is that taken together all these major poverty alleviation programs accounted for a measly 1.36 percent of GDP of expenditure by the center and states in 1993–94. The situation is unlikely to have changed much in the five years since. What is more, 50 percent of expenditure on all antipoverty programs is accounted for by the untargeted food subsidy of the PDS. Thus it would be a distortion to say that a lot has been spent on antipoverty programs. The central government alone spent 1.3 percent of GDP on explicit subsidies in 1996–97 (India 1998, table 2.1). Implicit subsidies by the center, and explicit and implicit subsidies by state governments, have to be added to this figure.

The second important point is that even the meager amount spent on antipoverty programs was largely misspent and cost-ineffective. It is like pouring a dribble of water into a leaky bucket—obviously not much would remain in the bucket. The study of Radhakrishna and Subbarao (1997) was very revealing. They found that in 1986–87 the PDS and other consumer subsidy programs accounted for less than 2.7 percent of the per capita expenditure of the poor in rural areas and 3.2 percent in urban areas. Their impact on poverty and nutritional status were minimal. Had the PDS not existed there would have been 2 percent more poor people in the country as a whole so that the poverty ratio would have been 40 percent instead of 38 percent in that year. Even more disturbing, the abolition of PDS would have had a negligible impact on the rural areas of the states.

The costs of the meager transfer through PDS and other subsidies were very high. The central government alone spent more than 4.25 rupees to transfer one rupee to the poor. Combining central and state government expenditures, in Andhra Pradesh it took 6.35 rupees to transfer one rupee to the poor. The most cost-effective scheme was the Integrated Child Development Services, which spent 1.80 rupees to transfer one rupee to the poor.

Employment generation programs, which are in principle self-targeting, have the potential to be most cost-effective. For example, according to the figures quoted by Radhakrishna and Subbarao (1997), in Bangladesh the leakage to the nonpoor under their analogue of the Indian PDS was as high as 70 percent, while in employment-oriented programs it ranged between zero and 36 percent. The cost per taka of transfer was as high as 6.55 in the former and between 1.32 and 1.49 in the latter. Unfortunately India's employment programs are far from realizing their potential. In 1993–94 JRY programs did generate nearly one billion person-days of employment, a third of the estimated underemployment in the country. Yet during 1992, a JRY worker got on average about four days of employment in a month, and the worker's family in all got a little over five days of employment. However, the average wage of the JRY worker was higher than the prevailing wage, thereby reducing its potential for self-targeting. In other words, a JRY worker was not necessarily poor—taking this mistargeting into account, it cost about 4.35 rupees to transfer one rupee to the poor through JRY.

The difficulty of targeting and its politicization are clearly seen in Madhya Pradesh. When bureaucrats did the targeting in the Integrated Rural Development Programme, they missed quite a few poor people and included many nonpoor people, but there was an upper limit on mistargeting, namely, the known proportion of poor in the area. Once the targeting was transferred to the locally elected Panchayats, however, the list of beneficiaries became grossly inflated—in the Sagar district of Madhya Pradesh *every* household was deemed poor enough to be a beneficiary of the development program! In some JRY programs in Bihar, village pathways and roads were constructed, but not by workers from the villages themselves. In one district, wells were repaired, and bridges built, but no respondent from the district reported being employed in these activities!

It is not surprising that compared to growth, redistributive policies contributed only modestly to the equally modest reduction in poverty alleviation over the past four decades. Accelerating growth and making it more "poor oriented" are the only efficacious long-term solutions to the problem of poverty. Turning to the issue of making growth poor oriented, it is useful to begin with the well-known correlates of poverty in India. If one is poor in India, one is more likely to live in a rural area, more likely to be a member of the scheduled caste tribe or other socially discriminated group, more likely to be malnourished, sick, and in poor health, more likely to be illiterate or poorly educated and low skilled, more likely to live in certain states rather than in others, more likely to be a landless agricultural worker, wage earner, or marginal farmer, and so on. Also inequalities in education and health, mortality, and morbidity between males and females, particularly children, are higher among the poor than among the nonpoor. What all this means is that a propoor growth strategy will create rapidly expanding job opportunities, in rural areas in particular, on farms and off farms. It will emphasize the accumulation of human capital by the poor by addressing the inefficiencies and inequities in the health and educational sectors. I would also argue that an effective strategy will involve the private sector, particularly nongovernmental organizations, in many activities where they can be more effective and will confine government involvement to those areas where there is no more effective and efficient private alternative. While decentralization of government and devolution of both power and resources to local bodies are very desirable, I am not certain whether socially discriminated groups will fare any better with local Panchayats, rather than the state or central administration, making decisions.

Reforms in other areas, such as completing trade liberalization by extending it to agriculture and consumer goods, repealing or amending labor and bankruptcy laws to allow managerial autonomy in employment decisions, and strengthening the financial sector by tackling the overhang of nonperforming loans of banks and reducing the extent of directed credit and of politicization of the credit allocation process, are important from the perspective of poverty alleviation as well. Of the several reasons for this, the most important is that such reforms will accelerate income growth, thereby alleviating poverty, and will also result in more rapid employment generation by reducing the costs of hiring. Trade liberalization, in particular, would increase incentives for the manufacture and export of labor-intensive products, in which India has (or should have in a nondistortionary environment) comparative advantages. Employment opportunities arising from such export growth will be poverty alleviating. It is an unfortunate fact that India has been losing its share of world markets in these products to its competitors, particularly China.

In rhetoric, though emphatically not in reality, the educational and health sectors have always been accorded very high priority in India. The reality—in contrast to the soaring rhetoric—is sobering. General living standards have certainly improved since independence: Life expectancy at birth has nearly doubled, the literacy rate of the population above age five has tripled, and the per capita availability of food and clothing have increased significantly. But these achievements have been modest, not only in comparison with the goals and aspirations of the people at the dawn of independence and earlier, but even more so in comparison with what has been achieved by many other developing countries in Asia and some in

Africa. That even within India the achievements of some states, such as Kerala in education, health, and life expectancy, compare favorably with those of countries with much higher levels of income is a sad commentary on the failure of other states and of the country as a whole.

The fact of India's failure is accepted by all, but much less consensus exists on assigning blame or identifying causes for this failure. For example, Drèze and Sen (1995), while conceding the considerable truth in the diagnosis that the blame lies with the insufficient development of market incentives in India, argued that this is not the only cause. They suggested that "there are many failures, particularly in the development of public educational facilities, health care provisions, social security arrangements, local democracy, environmental protection and so on, and stifling of market incentives is one part of that larger picture" (Drèze and Sen 1995, 8).

As Jagdish Bhagwati (1998) remarked in his review of the work of Drèze and Sen, these authors ignored the long-standing and informed debate in India of the failures they listed. He pointed out that had market incentives not been stifled, including access to international markets, India's growth in the past five decades not only would have been considerably faster but also would have benefited the poor significantly. This growth would have given the poor more resources of their own to spend on health and education, and the government would have had more resources to spend as well. The second point is that the stifling of market incentives and the several failures listed by Sen and Drèze have the same root cause—the pursuit of a development strategy that gave a central role to state-directed, state-controlled, import-substituting, capital-intensive industrialization in general and the development of heavy industries in particular. The "license-permit raj" that executed this development strategy became a cancerous growth on the economy and the body politic and failed to deliver growth and social justice.

The economic reforms initiated by Manmohan Singh in 1991 signaled a decisive move away from the dysfunctional development strategy. But they have not gone smoothly forward; indeed they have stalled. Two important sectors, namely, the agricultural and social sectors, have largely been left out of the reform process.

This is unfortunate for two reasons. First of all, a population and a labor force that are either largely illiterate or minimally educated, and that are subject to debilitating illnesses, invariably limit the potential benefits from economic reforms in other sectors. Second, as rightly stressed by Drèze and Sen, education and health are valuable achievements in themselves and are also instrumental in enhancing an individual's effective freedom.

It is well established that the allocation of resources, public and private, to primary and secondary education in India has been inadequate, even though private and social returns to these stages of education are high. More resources have been devoted to higher education in India than in other developing countries, for example, China. The consequences of this misallocation of resources have been extremely serious for the poor in general, and female children in particular, who depend on public spending to a larger extent than the nonpoor to become educated. This is particularly unfortunate because, without access to good schooling and health care facilities, their chances of escaping poverty in their lifetimes are considerably diminished.

It has been estimated that 35 million children between the ages of six and ten are out of school—denying them an education is to deny them and the nation the high returns from primary education, such as better family health, smaller family size, and healthier children for educated women.[7] Less than half of the children from poor households enroll, and only one in five of those who enroll completes eight years of basic education. This means that the poor, because they do not enroll or they drop out before completing eight years of school, do not benefit from public spending to the same extent as the nonpoor. The wealthy send their children of both sexes to school wherever they live, but there are enormous interstate disparities in enrollment and completion among the poor. Girls from poor households are only one-fifth as likely to complete eight years of education as their female counterparts from well-to-do households.

The proportion of six- to fourteen-year-olds in school from the bottom 40 percent of the distribution of households by economic status, varies from a low of 37.8 percent in Bihar to 88.7 percent in Kerala; in the top 20 percent of the distribution the variation is much less, from 84.6 percent in Assam to 96.1 percent in Kerala. Simulation exercises show that of a cohort of 100 children from the bottom 40 percent, only 14 complete eighth grade in Rajasthan and West Bengal, while 53 do so in Kerala. A staggering 64 either do not enter schooling or drop out before completing first grade in Bihar, and 62 drop out in Andhra Pradesh, while only 6 drop out in Kerala. Among the top 20 percent of rich households, there is considerably less variation in completion and dropouts—dropouts vary from 9 in West Bengal to one in Kerala—completion rates vary from 67 in Meghalaya to 92 in Kerala.

The differences between the sexes also narrow as incomes rise—in rural India the average *odds* of a girl in the poorest quintile being enrolled is 0.66 as opposed to 0.75 for a boy, while the odds are, respectively, 1.31 and 1.23 for the richest quintile. Interestingly, the marginal odds—that is, the probability of enrollment if the average enrollment in the population as a whole were to rise by a percentage point—is almost equal for girls

---

7. I have drawn the data and analysis of health and education in India from World Bank (1998d).

and boys in the poorest quintile at 1.08 and 1.09, respectively. This implies that subsidies to primary education that raise average enrollment rates not only are propoor but also have no bias against female children.

Analysis of the determinants of differences in enrollment and dropout rates across states and income groups suggests that state poverty alone does not explain those gaps—for example, Tamil Nadu and Himachal Pradesh have higher poverty rates than Andhra Pradesh, but Andhra Pradesh fares much worse than the other two in educational attainment. Of course, both demand factors, such as household characteristics and behaviors, and supply factors affect the outcomes. Interestingly, whether or not a primary or secondary school is present in a village has no significant effect on enrollment except in a few states. This is probably because school quality in terms of teacher absenteeism and availability of blackboards and teaching aids matters much more than school presence. Also, the distance of the village school from the location of the homesteads of the poor, particularly scheduled castes, matters. A survey of low-literacy districts in eight states found that schools with a high concentration of scheduled tribe students are of poorer quality—more of them are located in *kuccha* buildings, they have less furniture, they have fewer teachers with recent training, and so forth.

This sad story of the relative neglect of primary education and its disproportionately deleterious consequences for poor children, particularly girls, clearly suggests the urgent tasks ahead. First, access to schools, their quality, and their efficiency has to be improved: on one hand, by influencing demand factors such as household income and, on the other, by acting on supply factors, focusing on school quality. Reducing gaps in enrollment and improving teacher performance, quality of books, and management of schools are important. Local community participation in monitoring school management and performance has to be fostered—the experience of Madhya Pradesh in devolving primary schooling management to Panchayati Raj institutions and its innovative educational guarantee scheme is very encouraging in this regard. Above all, spending on primary education has to be increased, with the central government contributing a significant share.

Turning now to health, there is synergy between health, nutrition, and schooling. It should cause no surprise that the poor suffer disproportionately from illnesses, diseases, and their consequences. Their infant, child, and maternal mortality rates are much higher than those of the nonpoor. Rates of child malnutrition are higher as well. Although life expectancy has doubled since independence, and the infant mortality rate has halved, still child mortality in India is among the highest in the world. Communicable diseases and perinatal and maternal mortality account for 12.5 percent of the deaths of women aged fifteen to forty-five—these cause 470 deaths per 100,000 population, a rate 4 times that of China and 2.5 times that of the world as a whole. The incidence of tuberculosis among the poor is 4.5 times that among the rich, malaria 3.2 times, leprosy 2.8 times, and so on.

The rich-poor gap in the incidence of noncommunicable diseases is not as wide as the gap with respect to communicable diseases. In part this is because the poor die off at greater rates at younger ages through communicable diseases than the rich, and beyond this the rich have longer lifespans. Epidemics kill the poor at disproportionately high rates. Infectious diseases are the bane of the poor. Given the negative externalities of infectious and communicable diseases, public sector involvement in preventing them is in general appropriate. Public expenditures targeted at preventing and dealing with communicable diseases will benefit the poor disproportionately. Moreover, since the externalities from such diseases are significant, targeting them would be socially desirable from this perspective as well.

4.7.3 Pakistan

The World Bank (1998e) pointed out that economic growth and the flow of remittances from Pakistani emigrants, both of which contributed to the substantial reduction in poverty in 1970s and 1980s, declined in the 1990s. The rise in inflation to double digits, unemployment created by the shedding of surplus labor by privatized state-owned enterprises, and the withdrawal or reduction of subsidies, particularly for wheat could all have contributed to an increase in poverty since 1991. Whether they did in fact do so is not clear "because the data are ambiguous on this. The 1998 Census and an improved household expenditure survey should clarify the situation" (World Bank 1998e, 30). In any case, the optimism of the World Bank that the increase in poverty since 1991 would be temporary, assuming that it is borne out by better data, can be justified only if the reform process is intensified and completed rather than reversed. In the political and economic situation after the nuclear explosion, with $3 billion of external debt coming due for repayment soon, this cannot be taken for granted. Paula Newberg, who has written extensively on Pakistan, commented on the likely deal among international lenders that would rescue Pakistan from its payment crisis as they have done several times in the past: "Pakistan and its creditors are locked in this unfortunate self-defeating embrace. What appears to be convenient in the short term may be worse for the long term. This pattern of bailouts keeps getting repeated, and in the meantime Pakistan's structural problems are never solved" (*New York Times,* 30 August 1998, A12).

Pakistan's social indicators, as mentioned earlier, are abysmal, with only 35 percent of the population (20 percent of women) literate, a gross primary school enrollment rate of only 60 percent (49 percent for girls), and an infant mortality rate of 90 per 1,000 live births. According to the World

Bank, "These low levels of social indicators are manifestations of inability to address social sector issues in the past, due to (1) inadequate provision of budgetary resources to basic social sectors; (2) poor quality and inadequate coverage of basic social services; (3) weak institutional, management, and implementation capacity of line departments and agencies responsible for providing these services; and (4) absence of beneficiary participation in planning and delivery of services, leading to establishment of inappropriate delivery systems with little or no accountability to stakeholders" (1998e, 31).

The government, with the support of the World Bank, launched the Social Action Program in 1992 "to expand and improve the delivery of social services in elementary education, primary health, population welfare, and rural water supply and sanitation" (World Bank 1998e, 31). Even in the absence of any political and economic shocks, the successful implementation of the Social Action Program cannot be taken for granted. But with shocks, the prospects of implementation are sadly even dimmer.

4.7.4   Sri Lanka

The World Bank pointed out that "Sri Lanka continues to face serious problems: unemployment (and underemployment) is relatively high, 22 percent of the population is estimated to live below the poverty line, and education and health outcomes, long time successes in Sri Lanka, are eroding given the country's epidemiological transition and the rising expectation of its population" (1998e, 9). The World Bank was of course right in its assessment that "undeniably the civil conflict is the most difficult challenge for the country and there is no doubt that its resolution would be the greatest contribution to Sri Lanka's future economic success." The report identified several policy problems in the educational sector, such as constrained access to university education and restriction on the medium of instruction, nonpublic financing, and private sector participation. While recognizing that in the health sector the government has "consistently encouraged private investors . . . by providing market-based incentives," the report concluded: "Notwithstanding its overall good performance, however, steady increases in per capita income and the aging of the population have raised new challenges" and "whatever the options taken in reforming the [educational and health] sectors, the changes are likely to be costly and time consuming" (16). The one bright spot that the report highlighted is the set of measures taken in 1997 and 1998 to consolidate and better target social welfare programs. These included the consolidation into one program called Samurdhi of food and kerosene stamps and emergency assistance. The report found that "Samurdhi has now become the main delivery mechanism for social welfare [and] has undoubtedly helped in preserving some of the gains in poverty alleviation in Sri Lanka. However, it still remains costly (almost one percent of GDP), and there remains considerable scope for further consolidation without jeopardizing assistance to the poor" (11).

4.8 Governance

"Governance" is the most recent buzzword to gain currency in development policy discussions, particularly at multilateral agencies such as the World Bank, the IMF, the UNDP, and so on.[8] The word has come to be used to cover a broad spectrum of issues in the context of development from, at one end, the broad issue of democracy versus authoritarianism in development and, at the other, narrow issues of political and economic corruption. But the issue of corruption has drawn more attention, with indexes of corruption being put together and used by the practitioners, in what I would call mindless cross-country growth regressions, as one of the determinants of growth performance or lack thereof. Of course, corruption is not a new issue—what is new is the World Bank and IMF jumping on the bandwagon of corruption, perhaps motivated by the desire of their bureaucracies to find a role to play when, after fifty years of operation, many see no particular reason for their continued existence. Whether or not the issues of corruption and governance are simply self-serving reinventions by the Bretton Woods bureaucracies to sustain themselves, they are, and have been, extremely salient in South Asian development.

Ahluwalia noted that the "phrase good governance is used in widely different ways. . . . It is often used in a narrow sense to refer to problems of corruption, which is not only morally corrosive but is also viewed as a source of serious economic inefficiency. It is also used in a wider sense to refer to the effectiveness of government policies and systems in achieving declared objectives. Policies and programmes can be ineffective even in the absence of corruption because they are poorly designed to achieve their objectives, or there is a mismatch between the administrative requirements of a particular policy and the actual capability of the state machinery" (1997, 1). He pointed out that governance issues in all these senses have surfaced in India since comprehensive economic reforms were initiated in 1991. The abolition of discretionary government controls on economic activity since the reforms had an impact on corruption, though it is not easily quantified. Allowing the private sector to invest in sectors that

8. A workshop on governance issues in South Asia was held at the Economic Growth Center, Yale University, New Haven, Connecticut, on 19 November 1997. The featured speakers and discussants included the following policymakers from South Asia: Montek Singh Ahluwalia, member of the Planning Commission and former finance secretary of India; Javed Burki, vice-president of the World Bank; Tawfiq-e-Elahi Chowdhury, secretary of the Ministry of Energy and Mineral Resources of Bangladesh; and the late Sanjivi Guhan, professor emeritus at the Madras Institute of Development Studies and former finance secretary of the state of Tamil Nadu, India. This section draws on the papers of Ahluwalia, Burki, Chowdhury, and Guhan.

were state monopolies prior to reform (particularly infrastructure), as well as privatization in general, have brought governance issues to the fore. He concluded:

> Economic reforms will help to improve governance by reducing the scope for discretionary power and increasing the degree of transparency in policy and procedures. But economic reforms are no guarantee against malfeasance. Governance problems can arise in any system and improved governance is therefore only likely if the political and administrative system and civil society generally works jointly to achieve it. Whether it will do so goes beyond narrow issues of the design of economic reforms and into the realm of the functioning of political systems. One thing is certain. India's democratic politics and free press will ensure that these issues will remain in the forefront of public consciousness and therefore on the political agenda, and there will be continuous pressure for improvement. (Ahluwalia 1997, 27)

Burki (1997) first traced a number of developments in Pakistan that brought poor governance and corruption to the center of the political stage in 1996–97. His examples from Pakistan's history illustrated how poor governance and rampant corruption could inflict an enormous amount of damage on the economy and the society. He identified the reasons why corruption afflicted the Pakistani political and economic systems in the past several decades and why the people reacted with such vehemence to these developments in the fall and spring of 1996–97 and assessed the efforts being made by the government currently in power. He examined whether these efforts will succeed in reversing the deterioration in the quality of governance and prevalence of corruption. Interestingly, he located the roots of the culture of corruption in Pakistan in the feudal structure of land ownership and the assertion of power by large landholders soon after the creation of Pakistan. He found that, first, regimes in Pakistan fell because of the public's perception of deterioration in the quality of governance and increase in the incidence of corruption. Second, people demonstrated a willingness to move against regimes once they crossed some vaguely defined threshold with respect to poor governance and corruption. Third, even when leaders were made aware of the terrible consequences of bad governance and pervasive corruption and, consequently, were prepared to take steps to improve the situation, they responded with ad hoc measures that did not address the basic causes behind these phenomena. In conclusion he argued:

> An important way of dealing with the issues of poor governance and pervasive corruption is to change the culture that sanctions and supports these phenomena. To change the culture, the leaders must be prepared to reconstruct the institutions that were destroyed by successive governments in the country and to establish new ones needed by a modernizing economy. Institutional engineering needed to rectify the pres-

ent situation must cover a wide front. It must deal with the reform of
the civil service and the judicial system, institutionalize various kinds
of accountability systems, strengthen electoral laws and put limits on
campaign contributions, establish citizens' trust, promote the independence of the press. In other words, the agenda of reform in the areas
of governance and corruption is large and complicated. It can only be
implemented if there is the political will to introduce lasting structural
changes which would hurt—at least over the short term—a number of
deeply entrenched vested interests. If deep crisis provokes change then
this appears the right time in Pakistan to reform a system that has progressively decayed and become dysfunctional. Whether the present government is prepared to meet the challenge is something only time will
tell. (Burki 1997, 25)

Chowdhury (1997) analyzed the important issues of governance in Bangladesh at various levels from macro to micro. While examining the general framework and functioning of the government, he provided a few
illustrations of good versus bad and wasteful governance and attempts to
draw some general conclusions. After introducing the issue of governance
in the context of the history, political background, and contemporary situation in Bangladesh, the paper identified some serious weaknesses in the
overall framework of governance in the country and deals with macroeconomic and sectoral issues. Illustrative examples of successes and failures
of governance were provided, particularly the notable success of Grameen
Bank in extending credit to the very poor, particularly women. It has successfully diversified its lending to cover a wide array of activities, and a
special rural housing finance scheme has been introduced. Its social programs aimed at improving the quality of life of its members have been
expanded to cover health, family planning, hygiene, education, and the
environment. On balance, Chowdhury found:

> The initiatives in Bangladesh including the public sector to reform and
> restructure overall governance have had only limited sustained effects.
> Independent Commissions, Cabinet Committees, expert groups, secre-
> taries' committees, task forces—all forms of standard drills have been
> performed. Although much deliberation has taken place on how to im-
> prove governance, most of these have quickly been reduced to changes
> in the form and the structure (rather than the purpose) of government
> generating intense infighting among entrenched interest groups. Given
> the short experience with democratic governance after a long military
> rule, politicians have avoided a "clash" with the bureaucracy and "rock-
> ing the boat" in their initial years in power. Instead, most reforms in
> the public service have been achieved through the "backdoor"—either
> through deregulation and liberalization or by experimenting with new
> ideas, methods and practices. But in the fast changing world where bar-
> riers are falling apart, governments are equally in competition as much

as their private sector counterparts and there is no escape from meeting the challenges of governance face to face. Fortunately in Bangladesh there are some homegrown experiences which could give confidence that the big change is feasible and help usher it in. (1997, 36–37)

In a long and very thoughtful essay "Three Pieces on Governance," the late Sanjivi Guhan offered a trenchant critique of the World Bank's notions of governance then proceeded to explore the principles of good governance drawing on the insights of philosophers from Aristotle to John Rawls and finally to a discussion of concrete issues relating to governance in the contemporary context of India. Guhan distinguished three main elements in the World Bank's conception of governance. First is an economic role for the state; this has been conceived as including "five fundamental tasks": (a) establishing a legal foundation, (b) maintaining a nondistortionary policy environment with macroeconomic stability, (c) investing in basic social services and infrastructure, (d) protecting the vulnerable, and (e) protecting the environment. Second is a set of specific policies (or "policy reforms") required to move toward such a state: these include, as the principal ingredients, fiscal consolidation; reduction and redirection of public expenditures; reform and reduction of taxes; maintenance of competitive exchange rates; financial, trade, and investment liberalization; overall deregulation; and privatization of state enterprises. Third, essentially noneconomic aspects of governance include competitive, electoral democracy; transparency, accountability, participation, and responsiveness in the processes of government; assurance of safety and security to citizens; nonarbitrary rule of law; effective enforcement of contracts; protection of human rights; and even reduction of military expenditures.

Guhan faulted the World Bank for taking a purely instrumental view of political components (including democracy) of governance in that they are deemed desirable only insofar as they contribute to economic efficiency and that what matters for the Bank is not "governance" in any comprehensive sense but only "state-versus-market" issues in the realm of economic administration. He found that the Bank's policy advice in this context is much too general to be of use in formulating viable operational plans for reforms; but in any case, the empirical evidence on the efficacy of the advice is not conclusive. Guhan argued that in the ultimate analysis, for its advice to be accepted by its client governments, the Bank has to rely far more on its leverage as a provider of funds than on its propaganda about or the inherent persuasiveness of the virtues of its advice. However, such aid-related conditionalities are most often ineffective. Also, the Bank does not seem to realize the contradictions involved in its advising the state to retreat in favor of the market and yet asserting that only a strong state can resist the vested interests that have a stake in the status quo, for then such a strong state might be less willing to retreat. In Guhan's view, the Bank has been asking less developed countries to adjust to adverse changes in their external environment while ignoring the fact that some of these changes have been caused by actions of the developed countries themselves or of international institutions in which the developed countries are extremely powerful.

After discussing the philosophical underpinnings of a theory of state, Guhan identified six desiderata for the state from the perspective of good governance. These describe a state that (a) enables the full and free development of its citizens; (b) seeks to promote cohesion amid political and social pluralities; (c) exercises effective authority that is subject to responsibility; (d) maintains due separation and balance within the triad of basic institutions, the legislative, executive, and judiciary; (e) governs an economy that is pluralistic, technically efficient, socially just, and morally acceptable in terms of its relations with the market and in its handling of corruption and of interest and demand groups; and (f) seeks to promote these various objectives in practical action through optimal reform of institutional structures and the promotion of values and virtues required to sustain them.

Guhan then went on to examine the Indian state in light of the six desiderata. In the longest section of the paper, he analyzed aspects of India's constitution. In particular, he drew attention to its articulation of "positive" freedoms in the articles on directive principles of state policy and of "negative" freedoms in its articles on fundamental rights, the pluralities that characterize Indian society in terms of territory (the center and the states), language, religion, caste and ethnicity, and institutional and political approaches to containing conflict and promoting cooperation. His analysis led him to conclude: "Among all the threats to minimally good governance in India, caste is the most long-standing, serious, currently most critical and, in its nature, likely to be the most pervasive and persistent one" (Guhan 1997, 57). Recognizing that caste and other related factors contributing to the crisis cannot themselves be eliminated in an acceptable horizon, he proposed a set of radical—but politically not infeasible—electoral reforms. In his view these could go a long way in mitigating, though not in eliminating, the worst effects of caste on electoral policies.

4.9   Conclusion

I will be brief in concluding this already long paper. To begin with, the current domestic and external political situation in South Asia is not conducive to strengthening and completing the process of sorely needed economic reforms, particularly the long-delayed integration of South Asia with the world economy. The detonation in May 1998 of nuclear devices by India and Pakistan, the almost universal external condemnation of these actions, and the imposition of economic sanctions by the United States are the most recent adverse shocks.

In Bangladesh, the party in power enjoys an absolute majority in the legislature, although the threat of extraparliamentary agitation by the opposition is always present. And it cannot be taken for granted that the military will not be tempted to take over once again. However there are no insurgencies other than a relatively minor one by the non-Muslim tribes in the hill tracts of Chittagong.

India, although its democratic framework is deep-rooted and stable, has an unstable coalition holding power at the center whose real commitment to economic reform, particularly openness to import competition and foreign investment, is weak at best. The political uncertainty of the tenure of the government in power, further exacerbation of the long-standing conflict with Pakistan since the nuclear explosions, continuing but subdued conflict with China, insurgencies in Kashmir and in the northeast, all divert resources and the attention of policymakers away from the task of mobilizing political support for pushing the reform process forward. In India's federal setup the policies and performance of state governments matter a great deal to the success of reform. Here again barring a handful of states, the situation is not encouraging.

Pakistan, according to some analysts, has had a problem of national identity since its creation as a state on purely religious grounds. Ruled by military dictatorships for a substantial part of its postindependence history, and with continuing dominance of feudal landholders, the roots of democracy are not strong. The long-standing antagonism with India (which has virtually eliminated the potentially large benefits of trade with India) and sectarian violence, including the conflict in the Sindh province with descendants of refugees from India, do not provide a political environment conducive to economic reform. In Sri Lanka the ethnic conflict with the Tamil minority not only has taken a large toll in terms of loss of life and property but also continues to dominate the Sri Lankan political agenda.

Although the content of the needed reform agenda naturally varies across countries of the region, several common themes stand out. First, there is need for fiscal consolidation in all countries, but achieving it would require strong and sustained action on several fronts: (1) reforming the tax system by enlarging the tax base, increasing the use of direct taxes relative to indirect taxes, bringing agricultural incomes into the tax net, introducing some form of VAT to replace a whole host of excise and sales taxes, and reforming the system of tax raising and sharing between governments at the center and lower levels, and (2) reforming the expenditure side of the budget by containing growth in the size and cost of the bureaucracy, considerably reducing, if not completely eliminating, explicit and implicit subsidies that have no convincing economic or social rationale, and charging appropriate prices for publicly provided goods and services.

Second, the privatization process, which save in Sri Lanka has not gone as far as it could or should, has to be accelerated. Prior to privatizing state-owned enterprises in some key infrastructural sectors where effective competition is hard to arrange, a framework has to be established for regulating privatized enterprises.

Third, related to privatization is the need for investing and improving the performance of the infrastructure consisting of power, transport, and telecommunications. Without reasonably priced and efficiently supplied infrastructural services, which are largely nontraded, the potential benefits of reforms in other sectors will not be realized in full.

Fourth, also related to privatization are the issues of labor market reform and the easing of the exit of unviable enterprises from the market. Without radical rewriting of labor and bankruptcy laws, these issues cannot be addressed.

Fifth, the financial sector, particularly the banking system, is in poor shape with a large overhang of nonperforming assets. Directed credit, interest subsidies, and high reserve requirements continue. A large part of the banking system continues to be state owned. The capital base of banks is inadequate. Financial sector reforms are urgently needed both because efficient financial intermediation is essential for growth and because with a poorly performing financial sector, external capital flows induced by economic liberalization will be misused.

Sixth, except in Sri Lanka and to a significant extent in Bangladesh, foreign trade liberalization has a long way to go, particularly in integrating agriculture with world markets and reducing barriers to imports of consumer goods.

Seventh, except in Sri Lanka, expenditures on social sectors are inadequate and inefficiently used; sex disparities in access to health care and education are large; composition of expenditures among levels of education and between preventive and curative health care is inappropriate; expenditures on poverty alleviation programs are often not well targeted and are poorly executed. Since the only assets the poor have are their own labor, both the inadequacies of the system of education and health care and the inefficiency of poverty alleviation programs have disproportionate effects on them. Above all, only the rapid growth that the reform process is meant to bring about can eradicate poverty in South Asia. Demery and Walton (1998, table 5) compared the growth in per capita consumption required to reduce the proportion of population in poverty by half in twenty-five years with actual growth rates. They found that if poverty line consumption is a dollar a day, the required growth rate of 1.3 percent was below both the actual growth rate of 1.9 percent during 1991–95 and the World Bank's projected growth rate of 3.5 percent during 1997–2000. However, if the poverty line is raised to a still modest two dollars a day, the required growth rate of 4.5 percent is higher than both the actual and projected rates.

Eighth, and last though not least, governance issues, particularly endemic corruption, have to be addressed.

References

Ahluwalia, Montek K. 1997. Governance issues in India's economic reforms. Paper presented at the workshop on Governance Issues in South Asia, Yale University, 19 November.

Asian Development Bank. 1998. *Asian development outlook 1998.* Oxford: Oxford University Press.

———. 1999. *Asian development outlook 1999.* Oxford: Oxford University Press.

Bhagwati, J. 1998. Review of Joshi and Little (1996) and Dréze and Sen (1995). *Economic Journal* 107 (January): 196–200.

Brecher, R., and C. Alejandro. 1977. Tariffs, foreign capital and immiserizing growth. *Journal of International Economics* 7:317–22.

Buiter, W., and U. Patel. 1992. Debt, deficits and inflation: An application to the public finances of India. *Journal of Public Economics* 47:171–205.

———. 1997. Budgetary aspects of stabilization and structural adjustment. In *Macroeconomic dimensions of public finance: Essays in honour of Vito Tanzi,* ed. M. Blejer and T. Ter-Minassian, 363–412. London and New York: Routledge.

Burki, S. 1997. Governance, corruption and development: The case of Pakistan. Paper presented at the workshop on Governance Issues in South Asia, Yale University, 19 November.

Chowdhury, T. 1997. Governance in Bangladesh: The good, the bad and the ugly. Paper presented at the workshop on Governance Issues in South Asia, Yale University, 19 November.

Demery, L., and M. Walton. 1998. Are poverty and social goals for the 21st century attainable? Washington, D.C.: World Bank. Processed.

Drèze, J., and A. Sen. 1995. *India economic development and social opportunity.* Oxford: Clarendon.

Guhan, S. 1997. Three pieces on governance. Paper presented at the workshop on Governance Issues in South Asia, Yale University, 19 November.

Hasan, P. 1998. *Pakistan's economy at the crossroads: Past policies and present imperatives.* Oxford: Oxford University Press.

India. 1992a. *Economic survey 1991–92.* New Delhi: Government of India Press.

———. 1992b. *Tax Reform Committee: Final report,* part 1. New Delhi: Ministry of Finance.

———. 1993. *Tax Reform Committee: Final report,* part 2. New Delhi: Ministry of Finance.

———. 1997. *Government subsidies in India.* New Delhi: Ministry of Finance.

———. 1998. *Economic survey 1997–98.* New Delhi: Government of India Press.

———. Department of Fertilizers. 1998. *Fertilizer pricing policy: Report of the high powered review committee.* New Delhi: Ministry of Chemicals and Fertilizers.

———. Planning Commission. 1951. *The first five year plan.* New Delhi: Government of India Press.

Joshi, V., and I. Little. 1994. *India: Macroeconomics and political economy 1964–1991.* Washington, D.C.: World Bank.

———. 1996. *India's economic reforms 1991–2001.* Oxford: Clarendon.

Joskow, P. 1998. Regulatory priorities for reforming infrastructure sectors in developing countries. Paper presented at the annual conference on development economics, World Bank, Washington, D.C., 20–21 April.

Mahalanobis, P. C. 1961. *Talks on planning.* Indian Statistical Series, no. 14. Calcutta: Statistical Publishing Society.

———. 1969. The Asian drama: An Indian view. *Sankhya: The Indian Journal of Statistics,* ser. B, 31 (pts. 3, 4): 435–58.

McKinnon, R. 1973. *Money and capital in economic development.* Washington, D.C.: Brookings Institution.

Peters, H. 1997. Reforming India's port system: A position paper. Paper presented at the Japan Chamber of Commerce and the World Bank's follow-up workshop on the Power and Transportation Sectors, India, Tokyo, 14 May.

Radhakrishna, R., and K. Subbarao. 1997. India's public distribution system. Discussion Paper no. 380. Washington, D.C.: World Bank.

Ravallion, M., and G. Datt. 1996. India's checkered history in the fight against poverty: Are there lessons for the future? *Economic and Political Weekly* 31 (special no.): 2479–86.

Shaw, E. 1973. *Financial deepening in economic development.* New York: Oxford University Press.

World Bank. 1991. *World development report 1991.* New York: Oxford University Press.

———. 1993. Bangladesh: Implementing structural reform. Report no. 11569-BD. Washington, D.C.: World Bank, 24 March.

———. 1996. India: Country economic memorandum. Report no. 15882-IN. Washington, D.C.: World Bank, 8 August.

———. 1998a. *Bangladesh: Economic trends and the policy agenda.* Washington, D.C.: World Bank; Manila: Asian Development Bank, May.

———. 1998b. India: 1998 Macro economic update. Report no. 18089-IN. Washington, D.C.: World Bank, 30 June.

———. 1998c. *Pakistan economic update: Adjustment and reforms for a better future.* Washington, D.C.: World Bank, 22 April.

———. 1998d. Reducing poverty in India: Options for more effective public services. Country Studies Report no. 14345. Washington, D.C.: World Bank.

———. 1998e. Sri Lanka: Recent economic developments and prospects. Report no. 17761-CE. Washington, D.C.: World Bank, 1 May.

———. 1998f. *World development indicators 1998.* Washington, D.C.: World Bank.

II

Shifting to Reliance on Markets

5

Privatizing the Privatized

Aaron Tornell

5.1 Introduction

It has become part of accepted wisdom that privatizing state-owned enterprises and introducing competition is socially desirable because private owners will maximize profits instead of engaging in political patronage. As a result, productive efficiency and economic growth will increase. Consequently, consumers will enjoy a higher standard of living, better quality goods, and lower prices. During the past decade, however, we have learned that simply transferring the ownership of state-owned enterprises to private hands and breaking up state monopolies does not automatically lead to higher efficiency. It is also necessary to privatize the privatized.

Privatizing the privatized entails at least three reforms. First, property rights *within* each firm should be reestablished, so that new owners enjoy full residual rights of control in their firm. Second, *outside* the firm, new owners must face "hard budget constraints." That is, new owners should not have the power to either extract fiscal transfers or obtain bailouts. Third, a noncorruptible judicial system and transparent bankruptcy procedures that are free from political pressures should be established.

Policymakers can be assured that privatization will increase efficiency only if these three conditions are satisfied. Unfortunately, not all of these

Aaron Tornell is associate professor of economics at Harvard University and a research associate of the National Bureau of Economic Research.

Part of this paper was written during the author's visit to the Center for Research on Economic Development and Policy Reform at Stanford University. An earlier version of this paper was presented at the NBER conference China's Economic Reforms and Development, held in the summer of 1998 at Peking University. The author thanks Olivier Blanchard, Martin Feldstein, Nick Hope, Anne Krueger, Rafael La Porta, and Florencio Lopez-de-Silanes for helpful discussions. All errors are the author's.

conditions have been satisfied in many of the countries that have implemented privatization programs. The question arises as to what course of action should be undertaken in such cases. Should one wait until the government has the capacity to implement the required reforms? What if privatizers have only a small window of opportunity? Either they privatize hastily today, or not at all. Should they go ahead with privatization and hope that the newly privatized firms will create demand for good laws?

In order to address these issues it is convenient to classify state-owned enterprises into two groups: small shops and large behemoths. In the case of small shops, such as restaurants, the power of the state is not necessary to establish unitary control within the firm. Furthermore, small shops are not big enough to command a soft budget constraint. Accordingly, it is clear that the best strategy is to privatize the small shop sector as quickly as possible. This will promote the growth of the competitive private sector, increase the rate of economic growth, and reinforce demand for laws that protect private property.

In the case of behemoths, unfortunately, the answers to the above questions are not clear-cut. In this case privatization without prior implementation of the three reforms mentioned above will simply replace government bureaucrats with private mafias (i.e., private groups with the power to extract fiscal transfers). These private mafias might behave more voraciously than the bureaucrats they are replacing, reducing aggregate efficiency and further hindering the growth of the competitive private sector.

Once a decision has been made on whether to privatize before or after implementing the three reforms mentioned above, the more traditional issues of privatization must be tackled. In this respect, two major issues are of concern to policymakers. First, what criteria should be used to transfer state-owned enterprises to the private sector? Should distributive and social justice criteria enter into the objective function of privatizers? Or should the only objective be to transfer a state-owned enterprise to those agents who value it most and ensure that the price received is the highest possible? If so, what type of auction schemes are the most appropriate? The second set of issues of practical concern relates to state monopolies where network externalities are essential. What principles should guide their restructuring? How should regulation with regard to pricing and access be designed? What is the best entry policy?

In this paper we will discuss in more detail the issues we have raised, we will provide some examples that illustrate some of the trade-offs involved, and we will enumerate some unresolved questions. The objective is limited: we will neither propose definitive answers nor conduct empirical tests of the various hypothesis that have been proposed. Future empirical and theoretical research on these questions should help policymakers to make decisions that would facilitate the policy reform process.

Needless to say the list of issues we will consider is not exhaustive. In particular, we will consider neither transitional aspects of privatization in Eastern Europe and China nor aspects of the privatization of particular sectors such as social security and education.[1] Nonetheless, we would like to point out that the framework we propose applies to Eastern Europe and China.

The structure of the paper is as follows. In section 5.2 we will discuss the reestablishment of property rights within the firm. In section 5.3 we will analyze the elimination of soft budget constraints and bankruptcy reform. In sections 5.4 and 5.5 we will discuss restructuring and regulation issues as well as auction design. Finally, section 5.6 contains conclusions and an agenda for future research.

5.2   Property Rights within the Firm

In this section we will consider the first necessary condition for privatizing the privatized. Specifically, we will address the need to ensure that the new owners enjoy full control over their firms. One important case in which this condition might not hold is that of a large corporation in which managers do not own a significant share of the firm. The agency problems involved and their potential solutions are well known (see Hart 1995). In order to concentrate on other mechanisms at work in privatizing countries, we will disregard this case by identifying managers with shareholders.

In many state-owned enterprises control of the firm is divided among several "stakeholders." The stakeholders of a firm are groups whose payoff depends largely on the activities undertaken by the firm. These groups often have the power to interrupt the functioning of the firm. One such group of stakeholders is labor unions. They not only have the power to control the wage bill but also have the power to define what tasks must be performed by each worker. Other stakeholders include the networks of suppliers that sell inputs with excessively high markups. A typical example is the case of transport companies that systematically lose a significant share of the merchandise they transport. When a state-owned enterprise is located in a small city where it is the primary employer, there is a third class of stakeholders formed by local and state politicians and their allies in the central government. These political rings form patronage networks that help politicians stay in power.

An important implication, in the case of behemoths, is that new private owners typically do not have the ability to eliminate the power of other stakeholders and establish their control rights. Stakeholders have a vested interest in maintaining the patronage networks and the inefficiencies of the firm. Thus eliminating their power entails a severe political struggle that can only be undertaken by the state. Therefore, in practice, only two

1. On these issues, see Blanchard (1997) and Feldstein (1998).

outcomes are possible: either stakeholders are weakened and property rights within the firm reestablished prior to privatization, or the newly privatized firm will suffer from divided control. It is very rare to observe behemoths in which new owners have weakened other stakeholders.

It follows that if a large state-owned enterprise is privatized without reducing the power of major stakeholders, then the new owners will receive cash flow rights and, at most, some control rights. Why should this prevent the new owners from implementing efficient production and investment decisions? In other words, why is it that the Coase theorem cannot be implemented?

A firm with divided control among several stakeholders, who act noncooperatively, is equivalent to an economy where all agents have open access to the capital stock of others. In contrast to a private access economy, agents in a common access economy have the ability to appropriate a share from the capital stock of others. This appropriation can be accomplished by outright expropriation or through the fiscal process. That is, appropriation occurs by extracting fiscal subsidies, which in turn must be financed through higher taxes on the rest of the population or through higher inflation. In the case of a firm, the existence of open access means that each stakeholder has the power to set the quantities and the prices of the inputs it supplies.

Two points are worth noting. First, the existence of open access does not imply that stakeholders will appropriate the entire capital stock at once and drive it to zero. They will do so at inefficiently high rates, but aggregate capital may even still grow, though at an inefficiently low rate. That is, there is a "milking effect." Second, when there is open access, an increase in the physical return to capital does not induce more investment and a higher growth rate. This is because the equilibrium appropriation rate increases, and thus the rate of return faced by each agent (after appropriation by others) remains unchanged. This is the "voracity effect" (Tornell and Lane 1999).

To explain the milking and voracity effects, consider a firm that has only two stakeholders: the union and the owner. The union has the power to set the wage bill, whereas the owner decides what share of profits to reinvest. If the union were to increase wages excessively, the owner would reduce the reinvestment rate. Consequently, future capital and future wages would be smaller than they would have been had the union followed a less aggressive wage policy. This interplay between wage setting and the reinvestment decision determines an equilibrium, which is generally characterized by excessive wages and low investment relative to the unitary control case. Note that in this equilibrium there is a milking effect, but the firm is not destroyed by stakeholders. The stakeholders do not dismantle the firm and invest their booty outside the firm at the market rate of return because the firm has a higher rate of return and there are breakup costs.

However, each stakeholder drives the other stakeholder down to its reservation level, resulting in a milking effect. That is, at each point in time the union sets the wage bill at a level that is higher than what labor productivity would indicate. Nonetheless, this wage level is lower than what would induce the owner to shut the firm down. Why does the union not set the wage at a lower level? Given the appropriation policy of the other stakeholders, such a "sacrifice" would not pay off. Lower wages today will not lead to greater reinvestment; they will simply leave more resources for the other stakeholders to appropriate today. For instance, the owner will simply remove more resources in the form of profits, suppliers will increase their prices, and so forth.

Suppose the firm enjoys a windfall or its productivity increases exogenously. Will the owner increase the reinvestment rate to take advantage of the new opportunities? Not only is the answer no, but the reinvestment rate will actually fall! The reason for this is straightforward. Suppose the physical rate of return goes up by 10 percent. This implies that the union can afford to increase its appropriation rate (i.e., the wage bill) by 10 percent while still leaving the owner indifferent between shutting down and keeping the firm alive. Similarly, the owner will be able to increase his appropriation rate (i.e., reduce the reinvestment rate) by 10 percent while still leaving the union indifferent between devouring the firm with excessive wage demands and keeping it alive. Since the physical rate of return of the firm grows by 10 percent while the total appropriation rate goes up by 20 percent, it follows that the growth rate of the firm will experience a net decrease of 10 percent as a result of the windfall. This illustrates the voracity effect.

An important implication of the voracity effect is that the owner of the firm has no incentive to adopt new technologies that increase the profitability of the firm. This is because, ex post, the union would increase the wage bill so as to leave the firm with the same rate of return it receives without the innovation. This implies that the existence of divided control within a firm induces "rational atrophy." In such a manner, dominant firms in a given industry systematically fail to adopt technological innovations that have proved to reduce costs.

In summary, if a state-owned enterprise with control divided among several stakeholders is privatized without prior reestablishment of property rights, the new owner will find it optimal to milk the firm. Furthermore, since other stakeholders will appropriate any increases in the raw profitability of the firm, the new owners will not make efficiency-enhancing investments.

To illustrate that these points are not simply theoretical niceties, we will relate the experience of the integrated steel producers in the United States. This is a striking example of milking, voracity, and rational atrophy in action. Although the integrated steel producers in the United States are not state-owned enterprises, analyzing their evolution is relevant for the study of privatization for two reasons. First, as in many state-owned enterprises, control is divided within these firms. Second, U.S. integrated steel firms had sufficient political power to enjoy, at least for a while, soft budget constraints.

During the 1970s and 1980s, the integrated steel industry in the United States was successful in obtaining trade protection. Unfortunately, higher revenues were squandered in the form of higher wages and investments outside of the steel industry. The wage premium of steel over manufacturing increased from 24 percent in 1970 to 57 percent in 1982, despite the fact that the ratio of labor productivity in steel to that in manufacturing fell from 0.7 to 0.6 during this period. Furthermore, there was a concurrent fall in the share of profits that management of big integrated steel producers, such as U.S. Steel, invested in steel. Profits were increasingly invested in sectors outside of the steel industry (out of the reach of unions) or distributed as dividends. As a result, the ratio of steel-related assets to total assets in U.S. Steel fell from 56 percent in 1976 to 19 percent in 1990.

The existence of rational atrophy is evidenced by the failure of the integrated steel firms to adopt, on a timely basis, new technologies that were available and had been proved to increase productivity. The most important of those technological innovations were continuous casting and minimill technology. As a result, trade protection had the unintended effect of inducing the entry of new, small steel producers (minimills) that in recent years have managed to capture more than 40 percent of the U.S. steel market. It should be clear that divided control is at the root of this self-inflicted atrophy. That is, the failure of established firms to adopt new technologies, thus allowing small entrants to capture a significant share of the U.S. market.

Next, we will consider the actions taken by some governments to reestablish unitary control in state-owned enterprises. The most striking examples of the struggles involved in reestablishing property rights are the cases of British Steel and British Coal. Stakeholders in these sectors were so entrenched that even government ministers attempted to block the restructuring process. In order to restructure these firms, Prime Minister Thatcher hired a businessman, Sir Ian MacGregor, who had no links to the political establishment. It took seven years of restructuring before British Steel was privatized. The case of British Coal was more dramatic: when MacGregor decided to close some inefficient coal mines in 1984, the head of the miners' union, Arthur Scargill, launched a strike that lasted almost a year. This strike was nationwide, and it appeared that it would spread to other sectors, with the danger of toppling the government as a strike had done in 1974. After offering workers severance payments far in excess of those required by law and helping Scargill's rivals to create new unions and break the picket line, MacGregor was able to defeat Scargill.

It should be clear that no private agent would have had the power to do this. These episodes are amply described in MacGregor (1986) and Thatcher (1993).

Another well-known example of the reestablishment of property rights occurred in Mexico. Before privatization the steel and mining sectors were heavily unionized. Furthermore, since the state-owned enterprises were located in company towns, there was opposition to the privatization, not only from unions but also from politicians at the local and national levels. The government sought to replace the sole labor contract with five different contracts, one for each plant. Moreover, it wanted to include in the new contracts the right of new owners to reduce employment as needed. The union not only refused to consider these issues but also would not agree to a direct, secret ballot by the workers on these issues. After months of unwillingness on the part of the unions to make any concessions, the government used the threat of bankruptcy to induce the unions to accept a secret vote by the workers. To supplement this strategy, the army was called in to protect the plants and mines, and workers were offered a severance package similar to that given the British Coal miners. Throughout the process, there were several marches to Mexico City and street blockades. In order to neutralize high-ranking opponents of privatization, the ministry in charge of privatization hired as an advisor Sir Ian MacGregor to explain why those measures were necessary.

Similar measures were undertaken during the privatization of almost all other Mexican state-owned enterprises. The most dramatic example occurred at the Port of Veracruz. Although historically Veracruz had been the most important Mexican port, in the preceding decades it had become next to impossible to import or export any merchandise through the harbor due to heavy union entrenchment. As a remedy to this in the early 1990s, President Salinas called on the army to take the port by surprise and secure it from the unions.

As a result of these actions, almost all newly privatized firms in the United Kingdom and Mexico experienced an increase in productive efficiency and profitability. These improvements in efficiency have been documented by La Porta and Lopez-de-Silanes (1997) in the case of Mexico and Newbery (1997) and Vickers and Yarrow (1989) for the United Kingdom. Earlier papers that found that privatized firms are more efficient than state-owned enterprises are Boardman and Vining (1992) and Megginson, Nash, and Van Randenborgh (1994).

The privatization of two Mexican airlines illustrates the milking effect that occurs when a state-owned enterprise is privatized without reestablishing unitary control prior to privatization (Hanson 1994; Rogozinski 1997). Aeromexico and Mexicana were originally private airlines. However, the government had to take them over as a result of financial problems in 1959 and 1982, respectively.

The strongest stakeholders in each of these cases were the unions. In the midst of a labor contract dispute, the government decided to let Aeromexico go bankrupt in the late 1980s.[2] A new company was created with the assets and landing rights of Aeromexico, but it was free of stakeholders. In 1988 the government sold its 65 percent stake in Aeromexico for US$300 million. The other airline, Mexicana, represents the first important privatization of the administration of President Salinas. In contrast to Aeromexico, it was privatized without any prior labor restructuring despite the fact that it too had a very strong union and divided control. The government owned 51 percent of Mexicana's shares—the remaining shares were publicly held. In 1989 the government transferred 50 percent of its shares, plus the control of Mexicana, to a private group. The payment was not in cash but in the form of debt to the government. In addition, the controlling group committed $140 million to be injected as capital. In light of our previous discussion, the inability of the government to sell Mexicana for cash can be attributed to the fact that unitary control within the firm was not reestablished prior to privatization.

The events that ensued show that divided control leads to inefficient outcomes. While Aeromexico, which enjoyed unitary control, did quite well in the early 1990s, Mexicana's performance was dismal. Aeromexico reduced its workforce from 12,000 to 3,000 and succeeded in raising the on-time arrival rate from 75 percent in 1988 to 95 percent in 1991. In contrast, Mexicana was only able to reduce employment from 14,000 to 11,000 and increase its on-time arrival rate from 73 percent in 1989 to 86 percent in 1991. What is more astonishing, however, is that although Aeromexico was initially a much smaller airline than Mexicana, it became the dominant firm a few years later. Aeromexico increased its share of the domestic market from around 35 percent in 1989 to roughly 45 percent in 1993. In contrast, during the same period, Mexicana's share fell from 50 to 30 percent.

One important difference during this time is that Aeromexico leased airplanes to increase its fleet while Mexicana purchased new planes, dramatically increasing its debt. Some have pointed out that the prudent policy was definitely to lease planes instead of purchasing them. The result was that in 1993 Mexicana was on the brink of bankruptcy.

Seizing the opportunity, Aeromexico bought a controlling share in Mexicana. The controlling group of Aeromexico financed this purchase in part by borrowing. Ex post, this purchase was not a good idea because Aeromexico encountered financial difficulties. To make a long story short, the creditors took control of both airlines, and the debts of both companies were recently taken over by Fobaproa, the government's bailout agency.

---

2. Aeromexico and Fundidora Monterrey were the first cases in which a large firm was allowed to go bankrupt since the Partido Revolucionario Institucional (PRI) came to power in the 1930s.

5.3   Elimination of Soft Budget Constraints

The term "soft budget constraint" was coined by Janos Kornai to identify a situation that was prevalent in Communist Europe (see Kornai 1992). Under the Communist regime inefficiently run firms did not face the threat of bankruptcy. They simply received fiscal transfers to cover the difference between their revenues and costs. The existence of soft budget constraints meant that firms were able to induce the government to finance their deficits.

Several state-owned enterprises throughout the Western world have also enjoyed soft budget constraints. Clearly, strong political forces are at work behind this privilege. Thus it is far from true that a firm's soft budget constraint will vanish with the sole act of privatizing it, or by decree. The point we want to emphasize in this section is that if the privatization of a state-owned enterprise is not accompanied by decisive government action that eliminates the soft budget constraint enjoyed by a firm, it is not likely that efficiency in that firm will improve.

Here we describe ways in which soft budget constraints have manifested themselves in the aftermath of privatization. We will consider three situations: banks with low capitalization and implicit government guarantees, private mafias, and nontransparent bankruptcy procedures.

5.3.1   Banks

The existence of banks that are poorly capitalized and that enjoy implicit government guarantees has disastrous effects throughout the economy. First, not only does it exacerbate the milking effect in firms where there is divided control, but it can also induce inefficient decisions in firms with unitary control. Second, this banking condition restrains the growth of the competitive private sector.

In several countries, the privatization of banks has led to lending booms (i.e., abnormally high growth of loans during a span of a few years). These lending booms have been associated with deterioration in bank loan portfolios, as an increasing share of loans are allocated to very risky projects with negative expected present value. Another possibility is that lending booms reflect corruption. In both cases the result is that after a few years, a significant share of loans become nonperforming. Since it is politically very costly for governments to let banks go bankrupt, a bailout takes place.

It has not been the case that all countries that have privatized their banking systems have lacked an adequate prudential regulatory framework. For instance, in Mexico new regulations were adopted before the privatization was initiated, yet this was insufficient to promote prudent lending practices. Thus the solution cannot simply be "to improve the regulatory framework."

According to some observers, the problem has been caused by the confluence of two factors. First, the capital owned by the people who control a bank is small relative to capital of the bank that is at risk. Second, there is an implicit guarantee on the part of the government to bail out depositors and, in several cases, bank owners too. In these circumstances it becomes profitable for people who control a bank to allocate loans to projects with negative expected value. These projects are profitable from the perspective of bank owners either because (1) they have high-variance returns, (2) they generate personal benefits (perhaps they are loans to companies with which bank owners have links), or (3) bank owners are simply stealing the funds.

In the Mexican case, for instance, although at the time of privatization the capital of each bank was equal to 8 percent of total assets, as required by regulations, the owners' capital was quite small. The mechanism at work was the following. Bank A lent money to the owner of bank B so that she could meet the required capital adequacy ratio. Bank B in turn lent money to the owner of bank C, and so on. As a result, the net aggregate capital of the Mexican banking system was actually quite small.

If the privatization of state-owned enterprises occurs in a situation where owners do not enjoy full control rights and banks enjoy implicit bailout guarantees, all hell breaks loose. First, milking is no longer limited to the assets of the firm. Managers or owners may borrow using the firm's assets as collateral and appropriate such funds in diverse manners. As a case in point, an owner may buy inputs with a high markup relative to the market price and then have the difference deposited in a secret account. As a result, the firm accumulates debt, while the owner's private wealth increases. Banks are willing to lend to such a firm, despite knowing that resources will be used inefficiently, because they expect a government bailout.

A second mechanism that has been observed concerns lending by banks to buyers of state-owned enterprises that are being privatized. In some cases, bank owners have acquired the state-owned enterprises themselves. In this case the lending spree can continue virtually unchecked. This cycle was particularly pronounced in Chile during the second half of the 1970s—at the time, large private conglomerates formed around the big banks. The unfortunate end of this episode was the well-known Chilean renationalization of banks that took place in the early 1980s, costing nearly 15 percent of GDP (Hachette and Luders 1993).

A horror story that illustrates quite clearly the points made above is that of Mr. Cabal-Peniche, a successful banana grower in the south of Mexico. In 1991 he acquired a medium-size bank. At the time, this acquisition was heralded as one of the successes of the Mexican privatization program in promoting popular capitalism. The bank borrowed abroad and lent Cabal money to buy, among other things, Del Monte. Cabal continued to borrow money; a few years later he simply disappeared with more than US$500 million. He is still a fugitive. The Mexican government was forced to absorb all the liabilities and Del Monte, a costly bailout.

Another consequence of a hasty bank privatization is the formation of "evergreen accounts." When banks enjoy government guarantees and the stake of bank owners is very small, banks have incentives to make risky loans with high variance and low expected return. After a few years a significant share of these loans become nonperforming. Banks with low capitalization do not have incentives to officially recognize these bad loans. In this way they avoid having to inject new capital in order to make the appropriate provisions. This situation can persist for a long time if there is regulatory forbearance. When this occurs, banks lend to the nonperforming accounts the interest that had to be paid and the amount that had to be amortized. Given that these accounts never become performing, the bank is forced to capitalize unpaid interest indefinitely. That is why they are known as "evergreen accounts." Since these accounts grow exponentially, over time banks have less resources available to lend to new projects. This in turn restrains the growth of the private sector. The recent Mexican experience is a clear illustration of this mechanism (Krueger and Tornell 1998).

The question arises as to why authorities allow the schemes mentioned above to occur. One possible explanation is that at the time, authorities do not realize that buyers of banks are not using their own capital. Another explanation given is that privatizers face strong pressures to complete the privatization process quickly. Otherwise, the support for privatization will end, and the forces of the past will reorganize to block further progress.

5.3.2 Bankruptcy Procedures and Reform of the Judicial System

If inefficient investment decisions that lead to financial problems are not followed by bankruptcy, then firm controllers might have incentives to undertake inefficient actions. We have discussed the circumstances in which such processes will occur. In many countries judicial systems are heavily influenced by politicians. Furthermore, in some cases bankruptcy procedures are so convoluted that it is virtually impossible for creditors to seize the assets of nonperforming debtors. Even worse, bankruptcy cases are decided based on political criteria. It should be clear that in order for privatization to increase efficiency, it is necessary to implement judicial reform. Unfortunately, we have learned during the past decade that this is easier said than done.

The legal systems of many countries developed during the statist era. In fact, they were a useful tool for political control. Firms knew that political support to the regime would be translated into favorable future legal decisions in the event that the firm in question ran into trouble. Interestingly, this convoluted system proved to be very useful during the preprivatizing restructuring of state-owned enterprises and in negotiations with stakeholders, as described above.

Legal reform has proved much more difficult to achieve than theory would indicate. The drawback has been that in the postprivatization phase, this lack of legal reform has impeded quick sanctions against inefficient activities undertaken by owners of newly privatized firms. In almost every instance politicians have had sufficiently strong incentives to intervene in favor of firms that should have gone bankrupt.

An efficient bankruptcy procedure should lead to liquidation when the firm is not viable and should lead to restructuring when financial distress has been caused by transitory bad shocks. Furthermore, bankruptcy rules should be sufficiently simple, thus making it impossible for politicians to induce discretionary decisions.

It is not clear that countries undergoing reform should adopt the bankruptcy procedures used in developed countries, such as the United States. U.S. bankruptcy procedures are quite complicated and in some instances lead to inefficient decisions: Chapter 7 bankruptcy leads to unnecessary liquidation of viable firms, while Chapter 11 sometimes leads to inefficient reorganization under existing management. Recently, there have been proposals to reform bankruptcy procedures (see Aghion, Hart, and Moore 1994). Under these proposals all claims of a bankrupt firm would be canceled. The senior claimants would receive the equity of the new firm, and the other claimants would receive options to purchase equity. Shares would then be traded among claimants. Finally, the new shareholders would vote on whether to liquidate or restructure the firm.

Under this scheme, the only role of the judge is to coordinate the process. Accordingly, with this type of scheme the government has no room to defend incumbent management. It would be of practical importance to analyze how this type of procedure might be implemented in specific countries.

Policymakers (at least in Latin America and the United Kingdom) have been aware for some time of these alternative bankruptcy procedures. So why is it that these procedures have not been adopted yet? Or at a different level, why has there been no legal reform? Is it simply a lack of knowledge on the part of authorities? Or is legal reform something that cannot be imposed from the top, but rather, a slow process that must start from below? Perhaps as the private sector develops will it demand a better legal framework. I am not aware of any cross-country analysis of the evolution of legal systems. In the case of Mexico, the lack of bankruptcy reform can be explained by the huge stock of nonperforming loans. This implies that a coalition of debtors will veto such reform.

5.3.3   Privatization Decisions and Private Mafias

Suppose that the government does not, at present, have the capacity to reduce the power of stakeholders within state-owned enterprises, nor can it implement judicial reform in the short run. However, the political process has enabled the privatization of some state-owned enterprises. Is the optimal policy to gather a small team of noncorruptible privatizers, let them do the job as quickly as possible, and then hope for the best? Or is it more efficacious to wait until the government has the capacity to re-establish property rights in the state-owned enterprises and implement hard budget constraints? These issues have been at the core of the priva-tization decision in transition economies, as well as in market economies. Unfortunately, the answers to these questions are not obvious.

Suppose it is unlikely that the government will ever be able to eliminate the power of stakeholders in a given firm. Meanwhile, there is a chance that private agents might have the incentives and the resources to buy out stakeholders or neutralize their power. Furthermore, suppose that the firm in question is not powerful enough to enjoy a soft budget constraint. In this case it is clear that privatizing without prior restructuring is the right policy.

In contrast, if several stakeholders are deeply entrenched and no single stakeholder has the ability to establish unitary control, then it is not clear that a hasty privatization is socially desirable. Since it would take the full power of the state to reestablish private property rights, waiting until the government acquires the capacity to enforce property rights might be the correct strategy. However, suppose the government will never attain such power. Then what is socially preferable, to keep state-owned enterprises in government hands or privatize them?

If the private sector has not been privatized, what difference does it make if a firm is in the state's hands or in private hands? One viewpoint is that if a firm is in the state's hands, it is easier for politicians to induce the firm to undertake inefficient actions, such as having excess employment. Meanwhile, under private management it is more difficult for politicians to influence the firm; thus the firm's productive efficiency might increase (Shleifer and Vishny 1994). A second viewpoint is that since control is divided within the firm, the new owners will have incentives to milk it. Meanwhile, if the firm is kept under government control, the manager will ultimately have to respond to top government officials. To the extent that top officials internalize part of the future costs associated with firms' in-efficiency, they will restrain managers from undertaking inefficient actions. Note also that private owners have the capacity to milk a firm in "legal" ways, whereas bureaucrats are in some sense restrained by government regulations. We thus conclude that in the case of behemoths, it is not clear that transferring them to the private sector is socially efficient. This is because privatization might lead to the formation of "private mafias," that is, private groups with the power to extract fiscal transfers.

This last point is related to the political economy concept of encom-passing groups (see Olson 1982; Tornell and Lane 1999). Among econo-mies that suffer from the existence of rent-seeking groups, those with very few encompassing groups tend to experience less aggregate rent seeking than those with many powerful groups. This is the result of two mechanisms. Encompassing groups are de facto claimants to a significant share of national income. Furthermore, since there are very few encompassing groups in the economy, they are able to overcome the free-rider problem and not induce policies that will kill the goose that lays the golden egg. In contrast, when several groups have the power to extract fiscal transfers, it is unlikely that these parties will be able to coordinate in limiting their fiscal appropriations. Thus such an economy will experience overappropriation and decline.

A revealing example of how privatization might place state-owned enterprises in the hands of private mafias, who might behave more voraciously than bureaucrats, is the case of the postal service and airports in Argentina. In the early 1990s the administration of President Menem initiated the privatization of airports and the postal service. The stated objective was to create an efficient communications infrastructure in order to increase productivity in Argentina. In a recent book Domingo Cavallo, minister of the economy at the time, described how forces in the highest echelons of power, both in Parliament and in the executive branch, were trying to ensure that these government monopolies ended up in the hands of Mr. Yabran and his associates. Cavallo (1997) described the fights waged in order to impede this transfer of assets, and how this was connected to his dismissal as minister of the economy. Mr. Yabran has been associated with several crimes and political conflicts in Argentina. For mysterious reasons he has recently killed himself.

Now, we would like to elaborate on how the points we have made relate to transition economies. It will be useful to distinguish small shops, such as restaurants, from behemoths, such as oil companies. The former are not likely to enjoy soft budget constraints, nor will they suffer from acute divided control within the firm. For the latter, the opposite is true. Therefore, for the small shop sector it is clear that the correct policy is to privatize as fast as possible. Not only will productive efficiency increase but it will also promote the development of a new competitive private sector. However, for large enterprises privatizing as fast as possible may not be the best policy for the reasons described above.

In the early 1990s Russia engineered a massive transfer of state-owned enterprises to the private sector under the "voucher" privatization (Boycko, Shleifer, and Vishny 1995). Privatization vouchers were distributed among the entire population. Then auctions for almost all state-owned enterprises took place. The objective was to transfer as much state property to the private sector as possible while the window of opportunity remained open. In this manner, it would have been impossible for the Communists ever to recreate the status quo ante. The privatization was performed with neither any restructuring of the major state-owned enterprises nor the elimination of the stakeholders' power. It was believed that in the future the population would sell its shares and that some big investors would acquire a significant share of firms. These large groups would then force inefficient management out of firms and as a result, privatization would improve efficiency. In the case of large state-owned enterprises, this was not the outcome.[3] Instead, preexisting stakeholders and managers increased their ownership shares in these firms. As is well known, the result of the Russian privatization scheme has been the formation of the infamous "oligarchs' club" (Goldman 1998). These oligarchs have been quite efficient in extracting fiscal transfers. Of course, this need not mean that the alternative of not having privatized would have been superior. However, the answer is not unambiguous because the looting might generate popular discontent, bringing to power those phantoms feared by reformers in the first place.

Last, we would like to comment on the idea often expressed in policy circles that in less developed countries as well as in transition economies, through time a new competitive private sector will develop. Thus the problems posed by state-owned enterprises' stakeholders and soft budget constraints will disappear if left to themselves. The argument is that an increasing share of GDP will be produced by the new competitive private sector and the old state-owned enterprise sector will become minuscule and powerless. The policy implication of this view is that government efforts should concentrate on promoting new enterprises and not expend energy trying to eliminate the power of stakeholders.

The validity of this statement is far from obvious. If stakeholders are strong to begin with, it is not clear that the new private sector will be able to grow and render this oligarchic sector small relative to the economy. As the economy experiences incipient growth, stakeholders will demand more fiscal subsidies and also expand their ownership of fixed factors that confer political power. This in turn will be translated into a higher tax burden on the competitive new private sector. The result will be either an inhibition of the development of the private sector or, at best, a growth path along which the oligarchic sector grows at the same pace as the rest of the economy. As a result, this economy will be trapped in a low-growth trajectory. Tornell and Velasco (1992) presented a model in which the economy evolves along such a path.

Given that the government does not have the ability to eliminate the power of stakeholders, when is it more likely that the relative size and power of the state-owned enterprise sector will decline: under privatization or under no privatization? To address this issue, we must first note that in the case of large state-owned enterprises, the choice is between leaving firms and their stakeholders within the state or converting them into pri-

---

3. This scheme was criticized early on by the head privatizer in Mexico in a provocative article entitled "Too Much Vodka!" (Rogozinski 1993).

vate mafias. In both cases, stakeholders will have the power to extract fiscal subsidies. The question then becomes: under which regime will the stakeholders have less power to pillage the state? As we mentioned earlier, at present there is neither enough cross-country evidence nor enough theoretical work to answer the preceding questions.

In summary, it is not clear whether it is socially optimal to privatize state-owned enterprises before privatizing the privatized. On the one hand, the window of opportunity for privatizing might not reopen. On the other hand, a hasty privatization might leave state-owned enterprises assets in the hands of private mafias. It is possible that these mafias will grow in power and extract even more fiscal resources than what the alternative of waiting might have entailed. In other words, privatization should not be used as a pretext to avoid confronting the real problem facing the economy: the existence of strong stakeholders that face divided control within their firms and soft budget constraints.

5.4   Restructuring and Regulation

Large state-owned enterprises are typically conglomerates that encapsulate almost all firms in a given industry. During the privatization of these enterprises, the question arises as to the manner in which they should be broken up as well as into how many units they should be divided. There are two cases to consider. In one case, common networks are vital to the industry, such as in electricity, fixed-link telephony, gas, water, rail, and similar industries. In the other case, such networks are not vital.

In the case that networks are not vital, the general consensus is that state-owned enterprises should be broken up into as many independent firms as possible. This is constrained by the need to avoid a loss of efficiency due to the existence of economies of scale or scope. Monopolies are dealt with in such a manner. The case of Mexico Steel is a good example. Five plants made up the state steel monopoly in Mexico. Some argued that since steel is a commodity and Mexico an open market, a private conglomerate of the five would not enjoy monopoly power. They wanted the firm to be privatized as it was to exploit the synergies across the plants. They claimed that the plants would fail independent of each other. Others argued that even in the absence of monopoly power a conglomerate would still command huge political power at the national level. Since it would be the largest employer in each of the states where plants were located, a conglomerate would be able to influence national elections. This political power could then be used to extract fiscal concessions or even to induce the implementation of trade barriers (despite the North American Free Trade Agreement). In the end, the steel conglomerate was broken up and each of the five plants was sold to a different group. Eight years have passed since this breakup; only one of the newly created firms has had financial problems, and the controlling group has been replaced. Coincidentally, this firm is the only one that was not broken up.

By contrast, in industries where networks are essential, the issues involved are more complicated, and there is no consensus on the most appropriate policy. In fact different countries have followed diverse privatization strategies in specific sectors.

An important point is that when a network is essential, a state-owned enterprise does not differ much from a private regulated monopoly. This is because it is extremely difficult to regulate a big conglomerate, both for logistical and for political reasons. If privatization is to make a difference, it must first separate the network from the units that form the state-owned enterprise. Second, it must ensure the existence of competition in the newly created units. Finally, privatizers must create a clear framework to regulate the network company and to establish clear access rules and prices for the new units. These issues are discussed in more detail by Noll in chapter 6 in this volume.

Two observations are in order. First, the existence of competition among the new units eliminates the need for detailed regulation of those units, making the regulatory task an order of magnitude simpler. Second, there is no clear justification for privatizing the network company and converting it into a private monopoly, as the gains in efficiency derive from competition in the new units.

The privatization of the power industry in the United Kingdom clearly illustrates the points just mentioned (see Newbery 1997; Vickers and Yarrow 1989). This industry has three segments: generation, transmission (from plants to consumption centers), and distribution. The case for having several plants connected to the same network derives from the notion that if there were a reduction in energy generation in one plant, due to maintenance or accident, other plants could cover that shortage. However, once various plants are interconnected, some sort of coordination must ensure that at the margin, the cheapest energy is produced. For this reason, electricity generation-transmission has been traditionally considered a natural monopoly.

In the United Kingdom, as part of the privatization process, the three segments were separated into different companies. The transmission network was to be controlled in a centralized manner by one company, while distribution companies and generation plants would be owned by several firms. In order to allocate access rights to the generating plants, a sort of stock market for electricity was created. In this market, each generator submits bids every day, stipulating the quantity and price of electricity it is willing to supply the next day. Thus a clearing mechanism selects the cheapest energy for each hour of the day.

Another interesting example of the issues involved is the story of the privatization of the telephone companies in Mexico and Argentina (Rogozinski 1997). While both systems were privatized, the phone monopoly was not broken up in Mexico while it was divided into two companies in Argentina. In each country the options were hotly debated, and the rationales seemed sensible a priori. The phone systems in both countries needed significant investment in new fiberoptic lines and equipment. The Mexican government decided to grant a six-year monopoly in long-distance service to the newly privatized company. At the end of that period, however, the market would be opened to new entrants. It was argued that the threat of competition would induce Telmex to invest its profits in new lines and equipment during the monopoly period, so that it would have a dominant position once the six years had elapsed. It seems the strategy worked since Telmex complied with its original investment plan by the time the long-distance market was opened in 1997. At present, Telmex is the dominant firm in both local and long-distance telephone service. This has in turn led to complaints of anticompetitive behavior.

The argument made in Argentina was that splitting the phone company into two firms would induce competition. As a result, both firms would invest in new lines and equipment in order to gain a larger market share. Of course, it is not clear how collusion would be avoided. I am not aware of any study that compares the evolution of the privatized telephone companies in Mexico and Argentina. Furthermore, there is a lack of systematic cross-country comparisons of the behavior of prices and investment of state-owned enterprises in which networks are essential. Cross-country studies of the industries that have been privatized during the past decade would be very useful.

Postprivatization regulation is a very important issue in industries with network externalities. Regulation must cover pricing, access to the network, and entry into the industry. Fortunately, a large literature deals with these issues. See, for instance, in Armstrong, Cowan, and Vickers (1994), Bishop, Kay, and Mayer (1994), Noll (chap. 6 in this volume) and Viscusi et al. (1992). The evolution of regulation is also a very important issue. How do we ensure that once the privatized firm has made sunk investments, regulation will not be changed in order to reduce the ex post rate of return? How do we prevent a capture of the regulators by the regulated firms? These and related issues have been analyzed by Krueger (1993) and Noll (1989).

5.5   Auction Design

Suppose that the stakeholder question has been answered one way or the other. The next question then is how to transfer a given state-owned enterprise to the private sector. One possibility is to transfer ownership either to stakeholders or to the population at large (or to both, as most commonly occurs). The second possibility is to sell part or all of the state-owned enterprise to a strategic group and place the rest in the stock market. In any case, the objective should be to transfer a state-owned enterprise to those who can use it most efficiently and profitably and to ensure that the buyers pay as much as possible.

One difficulty with placing a state-owned enterprise in the stock market is that with few exceptions, state-owned enterprises are loss-making firms. As a result, it is unlikely that the stock market will place positive prices on these firms. A strategy that has been followed in some cases is for the government to restructure the state-owned enterprise, and after a few profitable years launch a public offering. Such was the case with British Steel.

An alternative is to sell the state-owned enterprise to a small group of strategic buyers. In this case, it is possible to price the state-owned enterprise based on counterfactuals. That is, it is possible to discuss with buyers what the expected income of the company would be were it managed under international best practices. Then by applying appropriate country and industry risk premiums, an appropriate reference price can be obtained. Technical advisors and investment banks play a useful role in this process.

Suppose the decision was made to sell part or all of a state-owned enterprise to a strategic buyer and that technical advisors calculated a reference price for the firm as an ongoing business. As our discussions in previous sections suggest, the government should aim at obtaining all-cash bids and terminating its direct involvement with the state-owned enterprise. Otherwise, it risks having to make transfers to this company in the future.

If the government limits offers to all-cash offers, it substantially reduces the number of potential bidders. This can be problematic because, as is well known from auction theory, when there are few buyers it is very difficult to elicit the reference price. The maximum price that can be obtained through an auction equals the second highest value.

Thus, if auction rules limit offers to all cash, the privatizer might attract only one or two buyers. As a result, the single bidder will offer only a pittance for the company; or if there are few bidders, they are likely to collude and will similarly pay, relatively, a few pennies.

Thus a question of practical relevance is how to design auctions in cases where all-cash bids are desired but where there are very few bidders able to make cash bids. As we shall explain below, one way to achieve this objective is to allow noncash bids. In this way the number of bidders will increase, and any of the standard auctions will elicit a price in the neighborhood of the reference price.

Permitting noncash bids opens Pandora's box. This is because an infinite number of offers, vectors of deferred payments, and guarantees are now possible. Once the privatizer moves away from the clear prerequisite of all-cash offers, it is not possible to prevent a bidder from offering any vector of deferred payments. Disqualifying that bidder ex post would provoke political pressures and allegations of corruption.

It is clear that in general, different discount rates must be applied to value each of the bids. When these transactions are performed in countries like the United States or the United Kingdom, valuations are done after the bids are handed in by a team of accountants, investment bankers, and lawyers. However, this procedure is politically very dangerous for a bureaucrat in charge of privatizing a state-owned enterprise because he might be accused of favoritism. To illustrate this, suppose that bidder 1 offers 100 million cash while bidder 2 offers 1 billion to be paid in five years. Who is the winner? It depends on the discount factor used. Of course, bid 2 is more risky, and probably the bidder will simply milk the firm and run away. However, if the bureaucrat sets the discount rate for bid 2 at a high enough rate that bidder 2 loses, then bidder 2 will most likely accuse the bureaucrat of favoring bidder 1. Although this example is a caricature, anyone familiar with some privatization experiences will see its validity.

The solution implemented in Mexico was to produce valuation rules that were made public in advance of the auctions. Basically, the discount rate applied to each payment increased exponentially as the offered payment for a given year converged to the projected cash flow of the given year.

Recall that the initial objective was to obtain all-cash bids. In order to effect this goal, discount rates were set at high enough levels that bidders would find it profitable to borrow funds in the capital market in order make all-cash bids.

Summing up, if the objective is to obtain all-cash bids, it is sometimes necessary to allow noncash bids in order to increase the number of potential bidders so as to escape the second highest bid principle. However, doing so may thwart the transparency of the privatization process. Thus mechanisms different from those used in typical mergers and acquisitions transactions must be devised. The best way to achieve this objective remains an open question.

The second set of questions has to do with the type of auction the privatizer should adopt. Should there be a sealed bid auction or an open auction? Should bidders be allowed to know the bids made by the other bidders? Should there be one or multiple rounds of bids? Should a minimum price be established? Under the standard assumptions in the auction design literature, there is a sense in which open and sealed bids are equivalent. However, when a state-owned enterprise is privatized, some elements do not accurately fit this framework. On one hand, buyers' values might be positively correlated, in which case the privatizer would like a bidder to learn what the bids of others are. On the other hand, there might be few bidders—this increases the danger of collusion. An open auction or a repeated auction in which information is shared, might ameliorate the first concern. However, these strategies might increase the likelihood of collusion.

We now consider the third question regarding auction design. Typically, state-owned enterprises are big conglomerates, and it is generally optimal to sell the different parts of the state-owned enterprise as independent firms. In this case the questions that arise are: Should all parts be auctioned simultaneously or sequentially? Should bids for combinations of parts be allowed? To address these questions, it is important to note that in many cases state-owned enterprises have very profitable units and, concurrently, other units that need some investment. So the question arises as to whether there should be a rule according to which: (1) profitable parts will be sold only in conjunction with one of the parts that needs investment and (2) the set of winning bids will be the one that maximizes the sum of the bids. The latter condition thus implies that a given plant might end up in the hands of someone who did not offer the highest bid for that plant.

The idea aired in policy circles is that offering all plants simultaneously in a big auction and using the rules just described is efficient in cases where there are few bidders; this approach increases competition and it allows efficient aggregation of plants. To see this, suppose that there are three bidders and three plants. Bidder 1 is interested in plant A, bidder 2 in A and B, while bidder 3 only wants C and B. In the absence of rules 1 and 2, bidder 3 will offer zero for plant C because zero is the second highest bid. However, if those rules were imposed, plant C could only be sold in conjunction with A or B. It then follows that bidder 1 might be willing to make a bid for C. This in turn will induce bidder 3 to offer a positive price for C, instead of zero.

It is interesting to compare the 1991 auction of the Mexican steel plants with the auction of the radio spectrum rights occurring in 1994 in the United States. In both cases, all units were auctioned simultaneously, not sequentially. In the Mexican case, however, bids for combinations of units were allowed, but not so in the United States. Multiple rounds of bids with sharing of information were used in the United States, whereas in Mexico there was a single highest bid, closed envelope auction (with no sharing of information). The reason for these differences is that the United States had many potential buyers and thousands of spectrum rights to be auctioned, while Mexico had less than ten plants and few bidders. Thus Mexican privatizers were more concerned with collusion, as the buyers knew quite well the plants and their potential. In contrast, United States privatizers were more concerned with efficient transmission of information across bidders. Furthermore, bids for combinations of licenses were not allowed in the United States because, with the high number of licenses to be auctioned, the complexity of the auction process would have increased immensely.

The issues that we have enumerated in this section are of interest to policymakers. A systematic analysis of the trade-offs involved in innovative auction design should help guide policy in countries that are initiating reform. The following references deal with the issues we have discussed in this section. Kikeri, Nellis, and Shirley (1992), Lopez-de-Silanes (1997), McMillan (1994), Milgrom (forthcoming), and Nankani and Vuylsteke (1988).

5.6 Concluding Remarks and Research Agenda

Traditionally, the analysis of privatization has dealt with two main issues. The first concerns the criteria that should be used to transfer a state-owned enterprise to the private sector. More specifically, should the only objective be to maximize the price of the firm? Also what are the most appropriate auction rules? The second issue deals with the principles that should guide the restructuring of a state monopoly and the appropriate accompanying regulatory framework.

Although these issues are indispensable in the design of any privatization program, other issues regarding the existence of well-established property rights must also be taken into consideration. We have identified three reforms that must be implemented if privatization is to increase efficiency. First, unitary control rights within the firm should be reestablished. Second, privatized firms should not face soft budget constraints. Third, a noncorruptible judicial system and transparent bankruptcy procedures should be established.

In this paper we have posed many questions while providing no answers. Further empirical research is necessary in order to better aid the policy-making process and to guide theoretical research. We have identified in this paper five areas in which future research would be useful. It has been nearly a decade since a large number of countries initiated privatization. Therefore, it should soon be possible to perform systematic cross-country empirical studies and produce the data needed to begin to answer the questions we have raised.

An initial area of research would involve a cross-country comparison of the evolution of privatized industries in which network externalities are essential, for instance, telephone and electrical power industries. It will be important to study under which circumstances the breaking up of monopolies has led to more efficient outcomes. This will involve comparing regulatory frameworks and measuring social benefits. The main question is under which regimes is there the least chance of the regulators being captured by those they are supposed to be regulating? A second important area that deserves research is auction design. It will be useful to have insight into what results have been obtained with different auction schemes over the past decade. Can we identify which auctions have worked best in specific circumstances? Third, a cross-country study of the evolution of privatized banking systems is needed. Why is it that in several countries, such as Chile and Mexico, privatization was followed by severe lending booms and crises? What lessons have we learned regarding the proper regulation of banks? Fourth, it would be beneficial to perform a cross-country study that identifies the stakeholders in a certain set of industries and analyzes the postprivatization performance of firms in which unitary control has been reestablished versus those in which it has not. Case studies describing the creation of private mafias in the aftermath of privatization would be illuminating. Finally, the construction of indexes of the prevalence of soft budget constraints would allow us to study, across time and across countries, the interrelations between privatization and the evolution of fiscal discipline.

References

Aghion, P., O. Hart, and J. Moore. 1994. Improving bankruptcy procedure. *Washington University Law Quarterly* 72 (3): 849–72.

Armstrong, M., S. Cowan, and J. Vickers. 1994. *Regulatory reform.* Cambridge, Mass.: MIT Press.

Aspe, P. 1993. *Economic transformation the Mexican way.* Cambridge, Mass.: MIT Press.

Barberis, N., M. Boycko, A. Shleifer, and N. Tsukanova. 1996. How does privatization work? Evidence from the Russian shops. *Journal of Political Economy* 104 (4): 764–90.

Bishop, M., J. Kay, and C. Mayer. 1994. *The regulatory challenge.* Oxford: Oxford University Press.

Blanchard, O. 1997. *The economics of post-communist transition.* Clarendon Lectures. Oxford: Oxford University Press.

Boardman, A., and A. Vining. 1992. Ownership versus competition: Efficiency in public enterprise. *Public Choice* 73:205–39.

Boycko, M., A. Shleifer, and R. Vishny. 1995. *Privatizing Russia.* Cambridge, Mass.: MIT Press.

Cavallo, D. 1997. *El peso de la verdad.* Buenos Aires: Editorial Planeta.

Feldstein, M., ed. 1998. *Privatizing social security.* Chicago: University of Chicago Press.

Goldman, M. 1998. Russian billionaire's club. *International Economy,* September/October, 11–15.

Hachette, D., and R. Luders. 1993. *Privatization in Chile.* San Francisco: ICS Press.

Hanson, G. 1994. Antitrust in post-privatization Latin America: An analysis of the Mexican airlines industry. *Quarterly Review of Economics and Finance* 34: 199–216.

Hart, O. 1995. *Firms, contracts and financial structure.* Oxford: Oxford University Press.

Kikeri, S., J. Nellis, and M. Shirley. 1992. Privatization: The lessons from experience. Washington, D.C.: World Bank.

Kornai, J. 1992. *The socialist system: The political economy of socialism.* Princeton, N.J.: Princeton University Press.

Krueger, A. 1993. *Political economy of policy reform in developing countries.* Cambridge, Mass.: MIT Press.

Krueger, A., and A. Tornell. 1998. The role of bank restructuring in recuperating from crises: Mexico, 1995–1998. Cambridge, Mass.: Harvard University. Mimeograph.

La Porta, R., and F. Lopez-de-Silanes. 1997. The benefits of privatization: Evidence from Mexico. NBER Working Paper no. 6215. Cambridge, Mass.: National Bureau of Economic Research.

Lopez-de-Silanes, F. 1997. Determinants of privatization prices. *Quarterly Journal of Economics* 112 (4): 965–1026.

MacGregor, I. 1986. *The enemies within.* London: Collins.

McMillan, J. 1994. Selling spectrum rights. *Journal of Economic Perspectives* 8 (3): 145–62.

Megginson, W., R. Nash, and M. Van Randenborgh. 1994. The financial and operating performance of newly privatized firms: An international empirical analysis. *Journal of Finance* 49 (2): 403–52.

Milgrom, P. Forthcoming. *Auction theory for privatization.* Cambridge: Cambridge University Press.

Nankani, H., and C. Vuylsteke. 1988. *Techniques of privatization of state owned enterprises.* Washington, D.C.: World Bank.

Newbery, D. 1997. Privatization, restructuring and regulation of network utilities. Walras-Pareto Lectures. Cambridge: University of Cambridge. Mimeograph.

Noll, R. 1989. Economic perspectives on the politics of regulation. In *Handbook of industrial organization,* ed. Richard Schmalensee and Robert Willig. Amsterdam: North-Holland.

Olson, M. 1982. *The rise and decline of nations.* New Haven, Conn.: Yale University Press.

Rogozinski, J. 1993. Too much vodka! *International Economy,* March/April, 52–64.

———. 1997. *La privatizacion en Mexico.* Mexico: Editorial Trillas.

Shleifer, A., and R. Vishny. 1994. Politicians and firms. *Quarterly Journal of Economics* 109 (4): 995–1025.

Thatcher, M. 1993. *The Downing Street years.* London: Harper Collins.

Tornell, A. 1997. Rational atrophy: The U.S. steel industry. Cambridge, Mass.: Harvard University. Mimeograph.

Tornell, A., and P. Lane. 1999. Voracity and growth. *American Economic Review* 89 (1): 22–46.

Tornell, A., and A. Velasco. 1992. The tragedy of the commons and economic growth. *Journal of Political Economy* 100 (6): 1208–31.

Vickers, J., and G. Yarrow. 1989. *Privatization.* Cambridge, Mass.: MIT Press.

Viscusi, W., et al. 1992. *Economics of regulation and antitrust.* Lexington, Mass.: Heath.

Comment on the Paper by Aaron Tornell   Nicholas C. Hope

Aaron Tornell's theme is that converting state-owned enterprises (SOEs) to private ownership does not guarantee enhanced efficiency. His conditions for successful privatization of a former SOE with professional management include that (1) internal property rights be assigned to the new

Nicholas C. Hope is deputy director of the Center for Research on Economic Development and Policy Reform at Stanford University.

owners in a manner that enables them fully to control their enterprise; (2) effective financial discipline be imposed from outside the firm, meaning that access to credit, equity, or fiscal support is justified by commercial prospects; (3) there be a fair, honest judiciary that enforces property rights and the commercial law (especially as regards exit procedures); and (4) an effective regulatory system be in place that curbs the market power of natural monopolies and effective competition performs the same function for other firms.

As he observes, in most developing and transition economies, and probably in some developed ones, these conditions are not often met. New owners are frequently obligated to old stakeholders. A "company town" often remains just that even after ownership is transferred, which allows the budget constraint to stay soft. And introducing effective financial, legal, and regulatory systems can be the work of a generation. Again paraphrasing, his pragmatic advice to policymakers is to privatize small firms boldly but to proceed warily for very large ones.

I agree with that advice. A noteworthy observation is that China came to the same practical conclusion for its industrial SOEs at least four years ago. Early in 1995, China already had decided that of more than 100,000 enterprises, the state needed to retain ownership of no more than a thousand, essentially those with considerable size and market share. The rights of potential private owners were unclear, but that now seems resolved. With an important decision of the National People's Congress in March 1999, China announced that private ownership is an integral feature of the market economy that it is establishing. China faces two important questions in implementing its own pragmatic policies. First, can it afford to cede property rights to private owners in a way that separates them from the influence of old stakeholders? Second, how can China improve the performance of the large enterprises it still controls?

Tornell's paper investigates aspects of the first question when it takes up the issue of valuation in an interesting section on auctions. Apart from any considerations of social equity, the cash value realized from the disposal of a firm is important because control can be delegated more effectively to new owners if old stakeholders can be bought off. In some transition economies, prospective new owners have been concerned about their responsibilities for the "three overhangs": their new firm's liabilities

to current workers, pensioners, municipal officials, and others who have claims on the cash flow of the firm;
to creditors, including banks, suppliers, and governments; and
relating to past operations of the firm, in particular, environmental damage that needs remediation.

The extent of new owners' obligations needs to be defined before ownership is transferred, if control is to be internalized and incentives to "milk" the firm weakened. Many governments face fiscal weaknesses that limit their ability to take over the financial obligations of their SOEs before divestiture. I support Tornell's call for more research on auction design and on the impact of unitary control on performance, by noting that an important, more general research issue is what methods of enterprise divestiture will minimize the fiscal burdens on governments while ensuring adequate internal control for the firm's new owners.

The second question raises many issues for developing economies with underdeveloped market-oriented institutions. The paper discusses institutional deficiencies without providing much by way of answer to the key question of how to improve performance in second-best, or worse, situations. The combination of weak banks, weak or incompetent regulators, weak internal governance systems, and inadequate competition might make privatization of large enterprises unattractive. Unfortunately, the same conditions obtain if large firms are retained in public ownership, and the issue for policymakers is how to make firms in these situations perform better. China has been experimenting with alternative options for state asset management that would clearly separate the ownership function of the state from the managers and regulators of the enterprise. Incentives to managers can be linked more closely to profitability, again subject to the problems that arise from the unresolved claims of old stakeholders. And more effective regulation of admittedly weak banks might go some way toward hardening the budget constraint for SOEs. Under suboptimal conditions, decisions on whether and when to privatize become more art than science. Research could help, but China's experience in essentially a real-life experiment might be equally valuable in learning what approaches work best.

Telecommunications Reform in Developing Countries

Roger G. Noll

During the late 1980s, telecommunications policy in developing countries entered a new era of neoliberal reform. This reform process achieved what some have called a watershed in early 1998, when the liberalization agreement of the World Trade Organization's (WTO's) Group on Basic Telecommunications came into force (Drake 1999). The WTO Basic Telecommunications Agreement commits the signatories to liberalizing basic telecommunications. Originally 69 countries signed the agreement, but by early 1999 the number was up to 80 of the 132 WTO members (Panda 1999). Twenty of these countries, including not only the advanced, industrialized nations but also Chile, Dominican Republic, El Salvador, and Guatemala, committed to complete openness to competition and foreign investment in what amounts to a single market (Tyler and Joy 1997). Many other developing and transition countries have embarked on less ambitious reforms. The developing and transition countries that have adopted reform commitments are so indicated in table 6.1 below.

Although the goals and process of reform differ among countries, the trend is unmistakable. In the early 1980s, the dominant institutional arrangement began moving from a state-owned monopoly run by a cabinet ministry toward a privatized and at least partially competitive industry subject to looser public control through either periodically renewed franchise contracts or American- or British-style continuous regulatory sur-

Roger G. Noll is the Morris M. Doyle Professor of Public Policy in the Department of Economics and a senior fellow of the Stanford Institute for Economic Policy Research at Stanford University, and a senior fellow of the Brookings Institution.

The author gratefully acknowledges financial support for the research reported herein from the Markle Foundation, research assistance from Kassra Nassiri, and helpful comments from Anne Krueger.

veillance.[1] The purpose of this essay is to review the history and origins of these reforms, the politics and economics of the new regime, and the lessons to be learned from the experiences of the pioneer countries that have now acquired several years of experience with a new, liberalized industry. This chapter focuses on telecommunications; however, most of the theoretical arguments about the economics and politics of policy reform apply to other infrastructural industries, such as electricity and transportation. Moreover, many apply to urban water systems as well, as is apparent in the following chapter of this volume.

The structure of this chapter is as follows. Section 6.1 describes the history and performance of telecommunications in developing countries. The main purpose is to explain the causes and consequences of reform. Section 6.2 discusses the types of reforms that are under way and identifies the structural choices available and the political factors that influence this choice. Section 6.3 examines the economics and politics of the governance institutions during and after reform. Section 6.4 offers conclusions from the lessons of the past and questions that remain unanswered.

The main conclusion is that liberalization has substantially improved the performance of the industry and that the more radical the reform, the greater the improvement. Nevertheless, liberalizing countries display considerable variance in postreform performance. To some degree, this variation can be explained by details of the governance institutions in the sector; however, because reform has been relatively recent in most countries, further empirical research is likely vastly to improve our understanding of the relation between performance and the details of the reform package.

6.1   Historical Roots of Reform

The neoliberal reform movement, which began in the 1980s, is the third era of telecommunications policy in developing countries.[2] In the first era, telephone companies in nearly all developing countries were foreign owned, some by colonial governments but most by multinational firms with headquarters in developed countries, such as AT&T, ITT, or Cable and Wireless. Typically these entities provided little or no service outside of the national capital and other large cities. Penetration of service was very low, being confined to wealthy individuals, large businesses, and government agencies and officials. For the most part, these companies, even

1. For an account of the beginnings of this reform in the advanced, industrialized democracies, see Snow (1986).
2. For an early history of the industry, see Kingsbury (1915). Many recent compendia of reform case studies contain essays with useful historical backgrounds for particular countries, including Levy and Spiller (1996), Ramamurti (1996), Roth (1987), Saunders, Warford, and Wellenius (1983), and Wellenius and Stern (1994).

the privately owned monopolies, were either unregulated or loosely controlled through franchise contracts. In some countries several companies operated, and competition sometimes emerged in the largest cities; however, near the end of this era, exit and acquisitions caused the number of firms and the extent of competition to fall.

The second era witnessed the acquisition of foreign-owned telephone companies by domestic national governments. Some companies were acquired in the 1930s (e.g., Mexico) and 1940s (e.g., Argentina and India); however, the main wave of nationalization took place in later decades. Whereas this movement was fueled in part by the transformation of developing countries from colonies into independent nations, many countries, especially in Latin America, that had gained independence much earlier did not absorb telephone service into the government until the 1960s. The process was completed by the early 1970s.

Some countries did not pursue nationalization to the extent of creating a single, nationwide company. One variation was to separate the local access company from the company that provided long-distance and international service. Another variant was that small companies in secondary cities or rural areas were not incorporated into the nationalized enterprise that provided service in the largest cities. This variant was especially common if the smaller companies were either public entities or cooperatives; however, in any case, these exceptions typically accounted for a small fraction of all telephone customers. The discussion in this section will ignore these variations and focus on the rise and consequences of nationalized monopolies.

6.1.1   A Diversion: The Theory of Policy Outcomes

Three aspects of the nationalization movement are worth bearing in mind because they shed light on how this era should be viewed in the spectrum between an anomaly reflecting the impetuousness of youth and a durable arrangement that is likely to return in the near future. A continuing theme in the contemporary development policy literature, and one discussed at length in section 6.3, is the issue of credible commitments to newly privatized entities not to renationalize them or indirectly to expropriate them through regulation.[3] The presumptions behind this argument are that public policies emanate from the underlying economic and political incentives facing political leaders and that the incentives behind the first wave of nationalization are still present. If so, the commitment problem is quite serious. Two other theoretical insights point to circumstances in which this rather pessimistic view of developing countries may not be true: path dependence and ideological shift.

The idea of path dependence has economic and political dimensions.

---

3. For a clear statement of the commitment issue, see Levy and Spiller (1996).

The economic version is a story about nonconvexities in production technology, such as economies of scale, economies of scope, joint products, switching costs, and externalities.[4] The core idea is that a change in the structure of an economy, whether intentional or accidental, can so change relative prices and marginal factor productivities that the incentives of private and government actors are fundamentally changed, thereby altering the path of development of an industry or an entire economy. Because an efficiently managed telecommunications sector is large (2 or 3 percent of GDP and as much as 10 percent of gross domestic investment), is linked to many other industries, has network characteristics in that it requires common standards among suppliers and users to be maximally valuable, and is an integral input to the production and dissemination of information, which is a public good, it is a good candidate to cause the kinds of changes in the evolution of an economy that are predicted by path dependence theory. If path dependence is to be taken seriously, an economic policy analysis of telecommunications should inquire whether policy reform in this sector will have the effects described in this theory.

The political version of path dependence is known as the theory of structure-induced equilibrium (Shepsle 1979; Shepsle and Weingast 1981), which in turn is derived from the Condorcet paradox and the Arrow (1951) impossibility theorem. The Condorcet-Arrow theory, sometimes called chaos theory (McKelvey 1979), concludes that liberal social decision processes (i.e., choice mechanisms based on aggregating individual preferences) are unstable under standard normative principles and assumptions about individual behavior. Specifically, majority-rule democracy does not have an equilibrium if individuals are rational optimizers, if no majority has identical preferences over all possible combinations of public policies, if no person or oligarchic elite has a veto over the policy alternatives that can be considered, and if rejected policy proposals can be reconsidered.[5] In the context of telecommunications, examples of assumptions that imply instability of policy are that citizen-users differ in the priority (or value weight) they accord to improved telephone service in comparison with other policy reforms, that neither a telephone company nor a specific user group can veto proposed changes in telecommuni-

---

4. The idea of path dependence can be traced to Marshall ([1879] 1935) and Arrow (1962), although its full implications have only recently been given great attention. Other important contributions to the economics of path dependence and the related concept of lock-in include Arthur (1989, 1994), David (1985, 1993), Farrell and Shapiro (1988, 1989), and Romer (1986, 1990).

5. A common misperception is that the instability of majority rule arises from the fact that voting mechanisms, unlike markets, do not allow people to express the intensity of their preferences. But Arrow's results apply to all social decision processes, not just to voting mechanisms. E.g., the Kaldor-Hicks debate over the indeterminacy of benefit-cost analysis as a social decision criterion, due to the relative price and real income effects of policy interventions, is another illustration of Arrow's theorem (Kaldor 1939; Hicks 1939).

cations policy, and that privatizing a company today does not rule out a proposal to renationalize it tomorrow. As is apparent from these illustrations, the conditions that lead to instability of majority rule are extremely plausible.

Chaos theory does not necessarily predict that social decision processes will be chaotic, but it does indicate where sources of stability can be found, namely, in design features of government decision processes that violate the assumptions that lead to chaos. For our purposes, the important point is that institutions, or the structure and process of decision making (McCubbins, Noll, and Weingast 1989), constrain the feasible set of policies and in some cases can make the outcome stable (equilibrium). The structure and process of government is complex and includes how citizens influence government officials (e.g., the representation system) and how these officials (including elected officials, their political appointees, civil servants, and judges) resolve their disagreements in making policy decisions.

Path dependence enters this theory through the way that structure and process affect policy. The feasible set of policy changes, or the "win set," is defined as policies that would defeat the status quo if they were considered. In general, if either the method of making decisions or the social outcome changes (due to change in either policy or underlying economic conditions), so does the win set, even if the distribution of preferences in the polity has not changed. In this sense, policy is path dependent: a planned or unplanned, intentional or accidental change in the status quo alters the win set. If this choice represents an endogenous resolution of policy uncertainty (the choice of one of many feasible outcomes) or an exogenous event (a colonial power decides to grant independence while nothing has changed in the colony), the likely evolution of future policy is altered.

In the case of telecommunications policy, nationalization may have been in the win set under the conditions of the 1950s and 1960s, but not in the win set of the conditions in the 1990s, because of intervening changes in either technology, exogenous economic circumstances (including preferences of citizens), or the design of the government. In examining the credibility of reform, one should inquire whether the events between nationalization and privatization have so altered the feasible set of policies that expropriation of the newly privatized companies is no longer plausible or even feasible.

Path dependence implies the existence of multiple feasible outcomes when preferences do not change. Economic models normally do not attempt to explain, or even to take into account, changes in preferences, but other social sciences do. Frequently the term that many other social scientists use to refer to preferences is "ideology," which is off-putting to many others (including economists and business executives) for two reasons. First, the common parlance use of ideology connotes a fixed commitment to a set of sociopolitical values, independent of rational argument and empirical evidence. Second, some scholars in the humanities and social sciences adopt the nihilistic view that any model of how the world works is a "social construct" that lacks an objective basis in reality, being no more than another mythical human belief system, none of which should be privileged over any other. As a result, policy analysts tend to ignore arguments based on ideology on the presumption that they are based on a denial of objective rationality.

In reality, some social scientists use the concept of ideology in a way that incorporates rationality and advances in knowledge. The core of this view of ideology is that preferences over policies and institutions are derived from combining personal valuations of social outcomes with theories about cause-effect relationships (how institutions and nature interact to produce social outcomes).[6] A person's political ideology is both a system for evaluating alternative social outcomes and a set of beliefs about how policy decisions (including the design of public institutions) affect outcomes. If ideology includes beliefs about the accuracy of theories of cause and effect as well as characterizations of values, acceptance of economic theory (as well as physical science) is an "ideology," even when the theory is accepted and applied on the basis of a rational evaluation of alternative theories. Thus progress in economics and improved economic education can cause the same person to make different (and better) decisions, based on the same set of facts, preferences over outcomes, and initial conditions, as time progresses.

A propitious example is Goldstein's (1986, 1993) theory of the emergence of increasingly free trade in the 1930s. Goldstein's argument has two parts. First, sparked by the events of the Great Depression, political leaders and influential citizens developed a more sophisticated economic view of the effects of international trade. Second, politicians reformed the structure and process of trade policy to reduce the influence of parochial protectionist interests and to increase the influence of the common interest in overall macroeconomic performance. Two changes in structure and process accomplished this objective. One shifted the locus of trade decisions from tax policy (deciding tariffs separately in each country on a product-by-product basis) to treaty negotiation (deciding the entire structure of tariffs between two or more countries in a comprehensive document that each government has to accept or reject in totality). The other created trade adjustment policies that operate as a safety valve to prevent isolated

6. For an example of this approach applied to regulation, see Derthick and Quirk (1985) on American deregulation in the 1970s. Similarly, Athreya (1996) noted that liberalization in India was facilitated by a generational change in leadership in the late 1970s because the new cohort had broader experiences with (and sympathies for) market economies. See also Noll and Weingast (1991) on the use of ideological appointments to regulatory agencies as a commitment strategy.

examples of economic disruption that citizens might attribute to free trade from causing protectionist policy to spread to all of trade policy.

A feature of Goldstein's theory is that it combines the ideological argument with the structure-induced equilibrium argument to predict that the new regime is stable. Political leaders, after an ideological shift that reflects adoption of a better economic theory, created a structure and process of decision making on trade policy that made liberalization of trade policy feasible but removed broad protectionist policies like the Smoot-Hawley tariff from the feasible set. Note that Goldstein explicitly took into account the fact that individuals—perhaps most individuals—have an incentive to protect their own interests by advocating high tariffs on products that they or their neighbors produce, that they are likely to react intensely to personal economic disruptions that plausibly can be attributed to free trade, and that this reaction will be passed on to their political representatives. Goldstein argued that political leaders, realizing the presence of protectionist incentives and the greater benefit to all from free trade, changed the structure and process of trade policy to reduce the influence of these incentives.[7]

The concept of commitment in neoliberal reform is a part of the broader model of neoinstitutionalist political economic theory. A credible commitment in the development literature refers to a set of institutional arrangements that creates powerful incentives for political leaders not to reverse a reform and that is transparent to an outsider who then will make a long-term investment on the basis of the perceived stability of reform. As such, commitment devices fall within the domain of structure-induced equilibrium. Neoliberal reformers create a structure and process of policy making that increases the durability of the new policy. Examples are a system of independent regulation with review by an independent judiciary, or a financial arrangement that imposes costs on the government if it reneges on its reform commitments.

The broader political economic model of policy stability incorporates the idea that the policy preferences of the relevant actors may have changed. They may have changed their views on how the world works (ideology). Changes in the economy may have shifted their incentives (economic path dependence). Institutional changes having no direct connection to the reform in question, such as how government officials are selected or interact to make policy decisions, may have altered the politically feasible set of policies (political path dependence).

---

7. The important institutional innovation in trade policy was to change tariff setting from a taxation process, in which each tariff was set independently of tariff decisions in other countries and separately by Congress where revenues to the government were a focal objective, to a subject of international treaties, in which the president negotiated with other countries for mutual simultaneous reductions in a large number of tariffs and Congress was forced to vote the agreement up or down without amendment.

6.1.2   Circumstances Surrounding Nationalization

The broader historical circumstances surrounding the nationalization era have three elements that may be consequential for understanding the nature and extent of the commitment problem.

State-Owned Infrastructure in Developed Countries

At the time that developing countries nationalized telecommunications, most developed countries also had state-owned infrastructural industries, a circumstance that survived into the 1980s (Snow 1986). Despite the well-known efficiency problems of state-owned enterprises, the state-owned monopolies did not perform horribly and certainly did not prevent economic growth in Europe (Joskow 1998). The unusual feature of developing countries was not that they nationalized telephones, electricity, water, railroads, and other core infrastructural industries but that for the first half of the twentieth century many European colonies and independent developing countries *did not* nationalize this sector. Moreover, the exceptions to the general pattern of state ownership, the United States and Canada, did not have extensive colonial empires, although the United States did exercise considerable economic influence, especially in Latin America. To the extent that colonial connections influenced policy choice, the models offered to nearly all developing countries were Britain, France, Portugal, and Spain, all of which had nationalized industries. As the first era became the second, the pertinent question would not seem to be why developing nations were nationalizing their telephone companies but why the industry was privately owned for so long in many developing countries.

Applied to the commitment problem, to the extent that advanced economies influence institutional choice in the developing world by virtue of their example, that example is changing. Unlike the period when developing countries were nationalizing telecommunications, during the third era most advanced industrialized economies are in the process of liberalizing their own systems. Indeed, if a legacy of nationalized enterprises is a reason to doubt commitment to liberalization, western European nations, too, should have a credibility problem.

Anticolonialism

During the nationalization era the most salient political fact in most developing countries was resentment over colonialism, even in countries that had gained their independence in the nineteenth century. The violent, repressive, and exploitative history of colonialism caused almost all domestic issues to be framed in terms of the lingering effects of colonial rule. Because infrastructural industries were important, visible, and foreign owned, they were natural targets for anticolonial resentment. In the case of newly independent countries, nationalization was part of the process of sweeping away the institutions of colonial influence, whether governmental or private. Indeed, an important barrier to liberalization in all developing countries, and one still present in Africa and South Asia, is the view that privatization amounts to loss of sovereignty (Mustafa, Laidlaw, and Brand 1997; Petrazzini 1995). Moreover, because anticolonial resentment did not make careful distinctions between direct political control and other means of exercising economic and political influence, anticolonialism was aimed not just at the particular colonial power that ruled a developing nation but at all large Western nations. Again, the more difficult question is not why independence brought nationalization but why long-independent nations, such as most of Latin America, took so long to nationalize.

Anti-Western attitudes arising from colonialism certainly have not disappeared. In parts of the world, notably some countries in Africa, the Middle East, and South Asia, anti-Western sentiment is as intense as it was in the period when these nations gained independence.[8] But to the extent that anticolonialism influenced prior nationalization, the intensity of this sentiment should have some predictive power in the era of liberalization: countries with the strongest anti-Western sentiments should be less prone to mimic Western institutions by privatizing and, if they do liberalize, should be least able to make a credible commitment to liberalization, especially if part of the liberalization program includes encouraging foreign investment. Put somewhat differently, part of the credibility of a threat to reexpropriate foreign investments is a domestic political environment that is prone to blame foreigners, especially Western governments and capitalists, for domestic problems.

Socialism

The peak of the nationalization movement corresponded to the period of maximum influence of the Soviet Union and the rise of China in international affairs. In the 1950s and 1960s, socialism appeared to offer a viable alternative to Western market capitalism as a means to achieve long-term economic growth. The Russians and later the Chinese were not shy about preaching their message to leaders of the developing world and gladly provided educational opportunities about the wisdom as well as the mechanics of Leninism and Maoism. Meanwhile, some Westerners who deplored the loss of personal freedoms in these systems nevertheless believed that a centralized, coercive national economic system might well outperform a largely decentralized, capitalist system. In the West both academics who studied developing areas and practitioners in institutions

---

8. Interestingly, countries in South Asia began to reform telecommunications only in the mid-1990s, and most countries in Africa and the Middle East have neither started the reform process nor signed the WTO Basic Telecommunications Agreement.

such as the World Bank emphasized a model of top-down, state-led economic development, featuring large capital projects undertaken by governments with financial assistance from developed nations, either directly through foreign aid or indirectly through international agencies.[9]

From the milieu of the nationalization era emerged a view of development that emphasized escape from colonial influence through strong domestic control over key institutions (including important businesses) and comprehensive central planning to guide the path of economic growth. A great deal of emphasis was placed on self-reliance and self-control, leading unfortunately to the pursuit of autarky (import substitution, strict currency controls, restrictions on foreign investment). Nationalization was part of a broader strategy to wrest power and influence from Western foreigners and to create centralized institutions that were strong enough to take control of the development process, undertaken by a new generation of political leaders who were patterning their policies on economic models of development dominant among intellectual elites and practiced in other nations that were or appeared to be very successful economically.

The influence of the Soviet and Maoist models of development is disappearing, with parts of Africa being the last stronghold. The approach to development that has become dominant in the West places less emphasis on top-down planning and more on decentralization and internationalization. To the extent that leaders in developing countries are influenced by theory and experience and pick domestic institutions at least in part on the basis of their likely performance, these developments support the credibility of the present commitment to liberalization. Thus the state-centered system in which important industries were nationalized was not a strange choice for a newly independent nation in the 1950s and 1960s but had become idiosyncratic by the 1990s outside of Africa, the Middle East, and the Asian states that were created in the wake of the demise of the Soviet Union.

6.1.3   Practical Lessons from the Second Era

In many countries, nationalization was followed by a short-lived improvement in performance.[10] Before nationalization, one complaint about foreign-dominated companies was that they focused excessively on serving elites and, in particular, foreigners and the companies that did business with them. Some countries thought that telecommunications would remain a toy for elites and foreigners and nationalized it to guarantee that

9. Athreya (1996), Chowdary (1998), and Sinha (1996) all argue that reform in India was delayed and slowed by the early commitment to socialism and state-led development immediately after independence in 1947.
10. This section distills the information contained in the national and regional case studies listed in the bibliography and the extensive performance data from 1960 through 1996 in International Telecommunication Union (1998).

its customers would be heavily taxed for other, more legitimate purposes or simply to generate patronage jobs for political allies. In other countries, a broader future for the sector was foreseen, and one objective of nationalization was to expand service so that it would provide greater benefits to the domestic economy. To expand service required capital investment, and so frequently nationalization was followed by increased investment and service improvements.

These improvements did not last long. The ubiquitous, depressing fact about telecommunications during the nationalized era was its deterioration. One performance indicator of the telecommunications industry available for almost all nations is penetration of telephones, as measured by the number of main lines per 100 population. Table 6.1 contains the penetration levels of a large number of developing and transition countries from 1981, before reform began, through 1996, when many countries were well launched into reform. As a baseline, penetration levels in advanced, industrialized countries in Western Europe, North America, the Far East, and Australia and New Zealand (table 6.2) for the most part fell in the range of 25 to 45 per 100 population in the 1981–86 period. As is apparent from table 6.1, penetration rates in the developing countries were generally highest in Latin America and lowest in Africa and Asia, but in all cases they were extremely low. The transition economies had higher penetration rates than all but a few developing countries, but substantially lower than the industrialized countries.

Another performance indicator is the length of the waiting list for both repairs and new service. In many developing countries, restoring service to a line that was not functioning properly could take months, rather than the hours or days required in developed countries. Because developing countries are relatively poor, one would expect lower penetration rates than in richer countries; however, the length of the waiting list for new service indicates large unsatisfied demand at current prices. Galal and Nauriyal (1995) provided data on the waiting time *in years* for service in several countries just prior to reforms launched between 1986 and 1991: Argentina (4.1), Chile (5.7), Jamaica (9.0), Malaysia (1.6), Mexico (4.9), Philippines (14.7), and Venezuela (2.5). By contrast, in most developed countries, service is installed within days after it is ordered.

Still another performance indicator is the likelihood that the telephone will work: if a customer tries to make a call, what is the probability of success, and if a customer's line is dead, how long does it take to repair it? In many developing countries, the probability of receiving a dial tone was 80 percent or less, and the probability of successfully completing a call after a dial tone was received also was 80 percent or less, and even lower for a long-distance or international call. For example, long-distance call completion rates were under 50 percent in Argentina (Hill and Abdala 1996) and Venezuela (Galal and Nauriyal 1995).

Table 6.1 Telephone Lines per 100 Inhabitants: Developing Countries

Country	1981	1986	1991	1996
Latin America				
Argentina[a]	7.7	9.3	9.7	17.0
Belize[a]	2.6	4.7	11.0	13.3
Bolivia[a]	2.6	2.6	2.7	4.3
Brazil[a]	4.3	5.5	6.9	9.6
Chile[a]	3.4	4.5	7.9	15.6
Colombia[a]	4.2	5.9	7.7	11.8
Costa Rica	7.3	7.9	9.9	15.5
Cuba	2.4	2.8	3.2	3.2
Ecuador[a]	3.0	3.1	4.7	7.3
El Salvador[a]	1.6	1.9	2.5	5.6
Guatemala[a]	1.2	1.6	2.1	3.1
Guyana	2.1	2.5	2.0	6.0
Haiti	0.4	0.5	0.7	–
Honduras	0.9	1.2	1.9	3.1
Jamaica[a]	2.6	3.5	5.4	14.2
Mexico[a]	4.3	5.2	7.2	9.5
Nicaragua[a]	1.1	1.3	1.3	2.6
Panama	6.9	8.0	9.4	12.2
Paraguay	1.7	2.1	2.7	3.6
Peru[a]	1.8	2.2	2.5	6.0
Uruguay	7.7	10.1	14.5	20.9
Venezuela[a]	5.6	7.5	8.0	11.7
Middle East				
Afghanistan	0.2	0.2	0.2	0.1
Algeria	1.9	2.6	3.5	4.4
Egypt	1.0	2.2	3.4	5.0
Iran	2.5	2.9	4.1	9.5
Iraq	2.0	3.5	3.6	3.3
Jordan	3.2	5.7	7.2	6.0
Lebanon	–	9.5	8.5	14.9
Libya	2.8	3.9	5.0	6.8
Morocco[a]	0.9	1.1	2.0	4.6
Oman	1.5	3.4	6.4	8.6
Syria	3.4	4.2	3.9	8.2
Tunisia	1.9	2.9	4.0	6.4
Turkey[a]	2.8	5.4	14.2	22.4
Yemen	0.3	0.8	1.1	1.3
Africa				
Angola	0.5	0.6	0.8	0.5
Botswana	0.8	1.1	2.5	4.8
Burkina-Faso	0.1	0.1	0.2	0.3
Burundi	0.0	0.1	0.2	0.2
Cameroon	0.2	0.3	0.4	0.5
Central African Republic	0.1	0.1	0.2	0.3
Chad	0.0	0.0	0.1	0.1
Congo	0.5	0.5	0.7	0.8

Table 6.1   (continued)

Country	1981	1986	1991	1996
Côte d'Ivoire[a]	0.5	0.6	0.7	0.9
Equatorial Guinea	0.2	0.3	0.4	0.9
Ethiopia	0.2	0.2	0.3	0.3
Gabon	1.3	1.5	2.7	3.2
Gambia[a]	0.3	0.4	1.0	1.9
Ghana[a]	0.3	0.2	0.3	0.4
Guinea	0.2	0.3	0.2	0.2
Guinea-Bissau	0.2	0.6	0.6	0.7
Kenya	0.5	0.6	0.8	0.8
Lesotho	0.3	0.6	0.7	–
Liberia	0.4	0.4	0.1	0.2
Madagascar	0.2	0.2	0.3	0.3
Malawi	0.2	0.3	0.3	0.4
Mali	0.1	0.1	0.1	0.2
Mauritania	0.2	0.2	0.3	0.4
Mozambique	0.3	0.3	0.4	0.3
Namibia	3.1	3.8	4.1	5.4
Niger	0.1	0.1	0.1	0.2
Nigeria[a]	0.2	0.3	0.3	–
Rwanda	0.1	0.1	0.2	0.3
Senegal[a]	0.3	0.3	0.6	1.1
Sierra Leone	0.3	0.4	0.3	0.4
Somalia	0.1	0.2	0.2	0.2
Sudan	0.2	0.3	0.3	0.4
Swaziland	1.0	1.4	1.7	2.2
Tanzania	0.2	0.2	0.3	0.3
Togo	0.2	0.3	0.3	0.6
Uganda	0.2	0.2	0.2	0.2
Zaire[a]	0.1	0.1	0.1	0.1
Zambia	0.6	0.6	0.8	0.9
Zimbabwe[a]	1.3	1.2	1.2	1.5
Asia				
Bangladesh[a]	–	0.2	0.2	0.3
Bhutan	0.1	0.1	0.5	1.0
China	0.2	0.3	0.7	4.5
India[a]	0.3	0.4	0.7	1.5
Indonesia[a]	0.3	0.4	0.7	2.1
Laos	0.2	0.2	0.2	0.6
Malaysia[a]	3.5	6.5	10.0	18.3
Mongolia	–	2.6	3.1	3.9
Myanmar	–	0.1	0.2	0.4
Nepal	–	0.1	0.3	0.5
North Korea	–	3.2	3.6	4.9
Papua New Guinea[a]	0.8	0.8	0.9	1.1
Philippines[a]	0.9	1.0	1.0	2.5
Seychelles	5.5	10.2	13.2	19.6
Sri Lanka[a]	0.4	0.6	0.7	1.4
Thailand[a]	0.8	1.5	2.8	7.0

(continued)

Table 6.1   (continued)

Country	1981	1986	1991	1996
Transition				
Belarus	7.8	11.1	16.4	20.8
Czech Republic[a]	11.7	13.4	16.6	27.3
Estonia	15.4	18.1	21.2	29.9
Georgia	6.7	8.3	10.3	10.5
Hungary[a]	6.0	7.3	10.9	26.1
Latvia	18.4	21.0	24.3	29.8
Lithuania	12.1	16.4	21.9	26.8
Macedonia	n.a.	12.5	14.3	17.0
Poland[a]	5.6	7.0	9.3	16.9
Romania[a]	7.6	9.3	10.8	14.0
Russia	7.9	10.9	15.2	17.5
Slovak Republic	9.6	10.9	14.4	23.2
Tajikistan	3.4	4.0	4.7	4.2
Turkmenistan	4.1	5.1	6.3	7.4
Ukraine	8.0	10.8	14.2	18.1
Uzbekistan	4.0	5.4	7.0	6.7
Yugoslavia	8.1	12.8	17.1	19.7

Sources: Panda (1999) and International Telecommunication Union (1998).
[a]Indicates submitted commitment to WTO Basic Telecommunications Agreement.

The underlying cause of the poor performance of nationalized telephone companies was their unbelievable inefficiency. The number of employees per telephone line often was extremely high compared to both developed countries and the "best practice" developing nations. In addition, nationalized telephone entities generally were starved for investment funds, which led to inadequate replacement and expansion of capital facilities.

One source of this poor performance was scarce and expensive capital. The marginal capital cost of a new line in nearly all developing countries is two or three times the cost in developed nations, and sometimes even higher. In some developing countries, such as Argentina, Brazil, and India, a major source of the problem was import substitution: the attempt to develop a domestic telecommunications equipment industry, including switch manufacturing, which has a very large minimum efficient scale and involves an extremely complex product that has never yet been efficiently produced in a developing country. In most countries, telecommunications equipment is not manufactured domestically and so must be imported. Protectionist tariffs, currency controls, and regional trade preferences for neighboring high-cost producers made imported capital equipment expensive.

Capital scarcity also arose from the way investment funds were made available. Because telephone companies were part of the government, rev-

Table 6.2   Telephone Lines per 100 Population: Industrialized Economies

Country	1981	1986	1991	1996
Europe and offshoots				
Australia	30.7	37.3	42.9	46.9
Austria	34.0	40.6	46.6	51.9
Belgium	26.3	32.7	41.0	46.5
Canada	41.3	49.4	56.2	60.2
Denmark	44.7	51.3	57.2	61.8
Finland	38.3	46.2	54.0	54.9
France	32.7	43.0	51.0	56.4
Germany	35.1	42.9	42.1	53.8
Greece	24.7	33.0	40.8	50.9
Iceland	38.0	46.4	52.2	57.6
Ireland	15.6	21.2	29.7	39.5
Israel	23.4	29.7	34.1	44.1
Italy	24.5	31.9	39.9	44.0
Netherlands	35.8	41.4	47.6	54.3
New Zealand	37.2	40.5	43.8	49.9
Norway	31.7	44.6	51.4	55.5
Portugal	11.3	15.6	27.4	37.5
Sweden	58.8	64.2	69.1	68.2
Switzerland	45.5	51.4	59.3	64.0
United Kingdom	33.4	38.3	44.9	52.8
United States	46.7	50.6	55.3	64.0
Asia				
Hong Kong	27.0	34.1	45.9	54.7
Japan	34.2	38.5	45.4	48.9
Korea	8.4	18.2	33.7	43.0
Singapore	24.1	32.5	40.3	51.3
Taiwan	15.5	23.3	33.3	46.6

Sources: See table 6.1 sources.

Note: All of these countries have at least partially liberalized telecommunications, and all but Taiwan, which is not a WTO member, have signed the WTO Basic Telecommunications Agreement.

enues accrued to the treasury as if they were taxes, and expenditures were appropriated as part of the annual government budget. Moreover, in many cases government companies made no attempt to collect bills for either residential service for government officials or office service for government agencies. In addition, poor fiscal and monetary management cumulated to erode all investment funds in the budget, including those for telecommunications. Because long-term capital investments make up a large fraction (usually two-thirds to three-quarters) of the costs of a telecommunications company, the costs of keeping a system running in the short run were much lower than the costs of making investments to sustain the company in the long run as facilities became obsolete and demand grew. Hence, in the short run a nationalized telephone company can be operated as a very large cash cow, even if prices are actually too low to make the enterprise viable in the long run.

In many developing countries, the policy response to this circumstance was to use the short-term cash flow from operations to finance other parts of the government. Then, in the face of deteriorating service, governments mollified customers by cutting real prices (in most cases, by refraining from raising nominal prices as inflation eroded the value of the domestic currency). The political attraction of this policy was enhanced in countries in which, for reasons unrelated to telecommunications policy, governments were unstable. If expected terms of office are short, the deterioration in service during the tenure of an administration will be small, and the problem of coping with them will be faced by subsequent officeholders.

Another source of inefficiency was employment practices. Although service was poor (including slow installation and repair), nationalized telephone companies typically employed far more workers than were necessary. Employment per unit of output was extremely high, even after adjusting for the lower productivity of workers in poor countries. One cause was the use of nationalized enterprises for patronage, but another cause was the perverse incentive structure that the budget process created for managers of nationalized entities. Whereas the budgetary process could starve capital investment funds without much short-term consequence, it could not starve operating funds to pay salaries without creating an immediate political backlash. Hence, the budget process gave managers an incentive to substitute labor for capital, which in a capital-intensive industry like telecommunications is extremely inefficient.

6.1.4 · Dawn of the Third Era

The neoliberal reform era had two fundamental causes. The first has little to do with telecommunications and most to do with the economic crises that swept over many developing countries in the 1970s and 1980s. The second is the poor performance of the telecommunications sector, irrespective of the larger economic conditions of developing countries. Of course, these two factors are not all that matters. Some of the worst performing state-owned telephone companies are in nations that show no sign of reforming. Thus poor performance can be said to provide a good argument for reform, maybe increasing its probability, but not to cause it. One poorly understood issue that cries out for more research is the cause and timing of reform.

To discuss in detail the more general economic problems of developing countries at the dawn of the neoliberal reform period is beyond the scope of this chapter. The important point here is that periodic economic crises in developing countries caused a reevaluation of all economic policies, not just those in telecommunications. The centerpiece of neoliberal reform was domestic macroeconomic and international economic policies. The crises of the 1970s and 1980s occurred as the belief in state-led, semiautarkic development gradually was supplanted by a belief in fiscal balance, monetary restraint, openness to trade and foreign investment, and flexible exchange rates. Partly because of external pressures from those who could provide a short-term rescue for collapsing economies and partly because of domestic political changes, developing countries were persuaded to adopt these changes. But the international and domestic macroeconomic reforms threatened significant additional short-term domestic economic disruption at a time when these nations were especially strapped for funds to pay for policies that would ease the transition. Neoliberal reform of state-owned enterprises could help in this regard by cutting state subsidies, creating a new tax base, and generating revenues from privatization sales. Thus part of the impetus for neoliberal reform in telecommunications and other infrastructural industries had nothing to do with their performance, but instead with the possibility of using their reform as a means to ease the pain of the larger neoliberal reform agenda.

Nevertheless, the beginning of neoliberal reform also reflects the fact that the experience with nationalized entities during the second era was not a happy one. In any nation where the political structure makes the government even slightly responsive to the interests of its citizens, part of the motivation for policy reform is simply extremely poor performance. The stark difference between idealistic expectations prior to nationalization and harsh reality a decade or two later plausibly could have led the most dedicated proponent of socialism and state-led development to learn something during this unhappy interregnum.

Fixing these performance problems within the structure of nationalized enterprise was very difficult because it would incur two big political costs. First, it meant increasing investment by an amount measured in percents of GDP and 10 percents of government investment through either a price increase or budget reallocation far from marginal for a government trying to please the International Monetary Fund (IMF) and other international investors with its parallel macroeconomic reforms. Second, it required reducing the serious overemployment problem and preferences for high-cost, low-quality equipment from domestic or regional manufacturers.

Privatization to foreign investors is a natural solution to both problems. Privatization allows a net infusion of capital investment from abroad while partially depoliticizing the solution to the overemployment and procurement problems. Indeed, if new investment is great enough, the employment problem can be solved at least in part by expanding output rather than reducing jobs.

6.1.5   Performance after Reform

The performance of telecommunications entities has improved almost everywhere, regardless of whether reforms were undertaken. For example, table 6.1 reveals that telephone penetration has risen in most, though far from all, developing countries. Hence, one cannot baldly assert that neoliberal reform is a necessary condition for improved performance. Indeed, as yet no research has focused on why some state-owned enterprises have improved their performance in the 1990s, and how these cases differ from the larger number of state-owned utilities that still perform poorly in Africa and, to a lesser extent, Asia, Latin America, and the Middle East.

Quite a bit of research has focused on the average effects of reform on performance and has found that improvements have been greater for reformed companies. Case studies reveal that after reform, investment rates of telephone utilities increase by 50 percent or more and labor productivity, measured as main lines per employee, typically increases by 25 to 50 percent, and sometimes more.[11] More systematic research using a large sample of countries concludes that reform improved performance in four ways: a privatized firm usually operates with lower average cost (measured appropriately as opportunity cost—one needs to correct for factor price differences that reflect political rather than market influences), has a more efficient price structure, has a higher rate of investment, and is less successful in acquiring protection against competition (Boubakri and Cosset 1998; D'Souza and Megginson 1998; Galal et al. 1994; Megginson, Nash, and Van Randenborgh 1994; Ramamurti 1996; Vickers and Yarrow 1988).

This research indicates that telecommunications reform has been broadly successful. This success provides motivation for examining in some detail exactly what reform measures have been tried, and whether the details of reform actually affect future performance.

6.2 Basic Features of Neoliberal Reform

In the context of telecommunications policy, neoliberal reform is a movement away from a ministerial, state-owned enterprise toward greater reliance on private organizations and market incentives to shape the evolution and performance of the industry. No single model of neoliberal reform describes the new institutional arrangements in most, let alone all, developing countries. Hence, attempts to characterize the neoliberal reform model are certain to contain more error than accuracy when applied to any particular country. Thus a more useful approach is to describe neoliberal reform as a movement away from one ideal-type (ministerial state-owned enterprise) toward another ideal-type (unregulated competitive private enterprise), with many feasible intermediate steps.

11. There are some exceptions. The reforms in the Philippines do not appear to have had much of an effect, and in Jamaica labor productivity actually fell after reform (Esfahani 1996; Galal and Nauriyal 1995).

Neoliberalism is distinct from libertarianism. The latter implies unfettered private property rights and individual economic behavior, including the absence of policies to promote competition or to regulate monopoly. Neoliberal reform assumes that government can have a legitimate role correcting market imperfections, such as regulating the prices and service quality of a natural monopoly or using regulation and antitrust law actively to promote competition if an incumbent monopoly is not natural.

In designing a neoliberal reform program, the government has two tasks. The first is to identify the best feasible ownership structure for the incumbent carrier, and to implement a transition to that ownership. The second is to adopt a policy with respect to the market structure of the industry, including governance arrangements for telecommunications policy. Because decisions about ownership and market structure have a range of outcomes, I will not attempt to describe every plausible neoliberal reform. Instead, I will describe the most important issues surrounding the choice of ownership and market structure and identify what might be called the ideal or prototypical neoliberal structural reform of the industry. Section 6.3 will deal with the problem of designing governance institutions.

6.2.1   Ownership

In nearly every country, the starting place for reform is a state-owned enterprise that is part of a cabinet ministry. The important features of ministerial operation are that high-level managerial appointments are maximally political and that detailed, day-to-day decision making about prices, investments, wages, and the like, are directly controlled by the chief executive (president or prime minister) and, sometimes, the legislature.

The prototypical neoliberal ownership reform is to convert a ministerial telephone entity into a joint stock company that is privately owned and, therefore, controlled by private investors. In principle, the government could decide not to influence the structure of ownership by simply converting the state-owned enterprise into a joint stock company and selling the stock wherever and to whomever it could. In practice, because successful privatization usually entails providing investors with considerable information and assurances about the future governance structure, in most developing countries atomized ownership neither maximizes revenues, nor assures a smooth management transition, nor provides for an adequate infusion of funds for private investment. Hence, the best available path usually is to sell a large portion of ownership to one or a few large investors.

An ideal-type neoliberal reform would not place restrictions on the identities of these owners; however, in most countries the structure that is likely to result from unrestricted privatization is predictable and involves extensive participation by foreign firms. Three factors influence the likely outcome of unconstrained privatization: technical requirements, capital requirements, and political requirements.

First, a modern telecommunications system requires managers who are sophisticated in both technological and business aspects of the industry. In all but the largest, economically most diverse developing economies, no potential domestic investor is likely to be as skilled in operating a telecommunications carrier as foreign companies from developed countries. Moreover, foreign ownership can be an effective way to transfer skills to a developing country. Hence, this factor favors foreign ownership.

Second, telephone companies are huge and require enormous amounts of financial capital to improve their performance. Consequently, potential investors need to have access to large sources of financial capital both to acquire and then to renovate and expand the company. Domestic investors are not likely to be willing and able to provide adequate financial capital at something approximating the competitive rate of return, and maybe not even if privatization is structured in such a way that the firm is likely to earn substantially more than the competitive return. Thus, as with the first factor, capital requirements favor foreign investors.

Third, because of the importance of the industry, a privatized telephone company is likely to be subject to public scrutiny and governmental intervention. Indeed, no country in the world has a telephone industry that is not subject to considerable public control and periodic political controversy. Unlike the other two factors, the political salience of the industry favors domestic ownership. The cause lies in the principle of representation and political responsiveness. National governments (even undemocratic ones) are likely to favor domestic over foreign economic interests, all else equal, because the latter have greater domestic political importance and influence. Domestic ownership creates an interest group that is better positioned to influence domestic politics.

From these observations, the practically relevant neoliberal ideal is to sell controlling interest in the company to a consortium of foreign and domestic investors in which the former are financially more significant but the latter have a stake large enough to insulate the company from attacks that characterize it as a neocolonial institution and to make the company a credible political influence on matters affecting it. Knowing this, the government can minimize the transactions costs of privatization by deciding in advance to auction ownership to the highest bidder, without restricting the composition of the entities that will bid. In practice, if the government includes a restriction that the bidders be consortia that include experienced foreign firms plus some domestic investors, the result is not likely to differ much from the unrestricted outcome.

The neoliberal ideal faces problems of political feasibility. In most cases, compromises must be made with political forces that fear privatization in general and foreign ownership in particular. Thus countries are likely to pick a variation on the neoliberal ideal that has one or more of the following features. First, the fraction of the company that is foreign owned, either in total or within the controlling consortium, is frequently limited to less than half to assure domestic majority ownership. Second, the government itself may retain a significant ownership share. Third, ownership may be given or sold at a reduced price to the domestic political interests that most fear privatization, such as labor unions or equipment suppliers. Fourth, to increase popular support for reform, some ownership may be sold in atomized quantities to small domestic investors, even though the realized price of these shares is less than the price of shares sold to the controlling consortium because atomized sales have greater transactions costs and because the domestic capital market is underdeveloped.

Argentina provides a useful illustration of this overall political strategy (Petrazzini 1995; Hill and Abdala 1996). Argentina sold 60 percent of its two main telephone companies to large, mainly foreign investors for $5.7 billion.[12] Thirty percent of each company was sold to small domestic investors for $2.1 billion, and 10 percent was sold to employees of the firms for $17 million. Thus 1 percent of the equity cost foreigners and large domestic investors $900 million, small domestic investors $700 million, and employees $2 million.

While these measures may increase the political feasibility of neoliberal reform, they come with a cost. These restrictions dilute the control and financial returns of foreign investors, who must be the primary source of financial capital and expertise if the newly privatized entity is to succeed. The government's dilemma in considering the extent to which it will restrict the allocation of ownership is that enhancements to short-term political feasibility must be purchased at the expense of long-term performance. Thus these restrictions have both positive and negative effects on the long-term political sustainability of reform.

If domestic politics proves to create impossibly high barriers to even these restrictive variants of the neoliberal ideal, the least drastic reform that can still be called neoliberal is public corporatization that grants to the public corporation the power to control its expenditures, to incur debt, and to make capital investments without formal government approval. In this case, the ministerial public enterprise is converted into a formally independent joint stock company in which the government owns all or most of the stock. The most important feature of public corporatization is that it transfers day-to-day managerial control from political leaders (ministers and legislators) to corporate executives. Likewise, the revenues

---

12. This figure includes cash, debt, accumulated unpaid interest, and the portion of the mandatory investment commitment of these investors that would become an equity interest of the other investors. Each consortium had to commit $600 million in investment expenditures within two years, 40 percent of which would be part of the equity of the other investors. Details of the transaction are found in Gillary (1999).

of the company are primarily, if not fully, under the control of the company and constitute a hard budget constraint for expenditures. In principle, corporatization can solve the problem of inadequate financial capital if the company is allowed to incur foreign debt.

Of course, public corporatization has shortcomings. Government ownership allows political leaders to appoint all or most of the company's directors, and usually these will be the same types of people who ran the ministerial state-owned enterprise: cabinet ministers (finance, commerce, trade, labor) and recipients of political patronage. In addition, future reversal of reform (removal back to a ministry) is easier if the government owns the company and so does not have to buy its stock to renationalize it. These problems can be mitigated by partial privatization, in which private investors buy a minority interest in the company; however, because of the issue of control, the share price that private investors are willing to pay for minority ownership is likely to be low compared to the price if private investors are given majority control.

Some scholars who believe that private enterprise is more efficient are willing to live with public corporatization if by so doing they can achieve better outcomes on other issues (especially market structure; see, e.g., Petrazzini 1996). For example, many observers contend that creating a truly competitive environment is easier if the government retains control of the incumbent monopolist, because of the greater tractability of the problem of nondiscriminatory interconnection (see, e.g., Galal 1996; Manzetti 1997; Petrazzini 1996). The assumption underpinning this argument is that the durability of the government's commitment to competition is independent of the ownership structure of the company, which is almost surely false. Competition will lower profits, and most likely employment and wages, of the incumbent monopolist. Under corporatization, the government retains its financial stake in the flow of monopoly profits and its political responsibility for the welfare of the employees of the company it controls. Thus the government's greater ability to implement competition must be weighed against the inevitable political pressures that will arise to undermine its commitment to competition. This argument does not necessarily mean that the net effect of corporatization on the prospects for competition will be negative, but competition has generally been slow to emerge everywhere, and the few countries where it has emerged tend to have privatized telephone companies.

6.2.2 Market Structure

Ideally, neoliberal reform involves a commitment to a competitive market structure if it is economically and politically feasible. In practice, with the exception of Chile, no developing country has fully implemented competition in all segments of the telecommunications industry. A number of reasons have been advanced to defend the decision to rely on monopoly.

This section explores these reasons and concludes that a commitment to long-term monopoly is indefensible and that even temporary protection of incumbent monopolists is dubious.

In the ideal-type neoliberal reform, decision makers must ascertain whether production technology dictates that the most efficient industry structure is a monopoly. For nearly all of the history of the telephone, conventional wisdom held that the industry is a natural monopoly. Originally, the main basis for this belief was the presence of economies of scale in switches and transmission links—that is, the connection between customer equipment and the first switch in the network and connections between switches for carrying interexchange, long-distance, and international calls. This belief probably never was accurate, but technology has made it increasingly unlikely.

The natural monopoly argument was most plausible early in the history of the telephone industry. At that time, the industry produced a single, homogeneous product—a voice-grade telephone circuit—and almost all service was local access and local calls. The technology to supply these services made use of copper wire pairs, which connected each customer to the nearest local switch, and switches in which connections initially were made manually by operators but eventually were completed by electromechanical devices. The optimal capacity of an operator-controlled or electromechanical switching system is related to peak usage. Because of the statistical uncertainty of calling activity, the ratio of optimal switching capacity to number of customers declines as the number of customers increases, thereby creating economies of scale in the old switching technologies. Likewise, whereas the number of copper wires in a local network was strictly proportional to the number of customers, constructing a traditional local telephone network had fixed costs (telephone poles and underground conduits), which were another source of scale economies.

A more recent argument in support of the natural monopoly idea is the "network" feature of telecommunications. A network technology has the characteristic that its value to one user depends on the number of others who also use it. In the case of telecommunications, the value of access depends on whether one user can reach others. Thus, for the telecommunications industry to supply maximum value to customers, it must be interconnected. Regardless of the pattern of ownership, each customer must be able to reach every other customer for the usage value of the system to be maximized.

In principle, the requirement to interconnect does not imply a single, monopoly owner. Instead, separate companies can arrange to connect. Analytically, one can anthropomorphize each network of customers as a single actor seeking service to connect to other networks, which is exactly what national monopoly telephone carriers arrange to do to make international telecommunications feasible. All that is required to complete a ubiquitous network is common technical standards for the information to be transmitted from one network to another (the counterpart to railroad gauges and electrical current specifications) and an agreement among the networks about sharing the costs of their interconnection. Of course, as is discussed in detail elsewhere in this chapter, the theoretical simplicity of this requirement masks what has proved to be the very large and as yet unsolved practical problem of arranging procompetitive interconnection agreements between incumbent monopolists and entrants.

Regardless of the merits of the natural monopoly argument, in countries where policy did not encourage or require monopoly, competition emerged soon after the invention of the telephone. In the United States, competition blossomed as soon as the original telephone patents expired before 1900 and was common in cities during the early history of the telephone industry (Brock 1981). Within ten years of the expiration of the Bell patents, the market share of the old Bell monopoly slipped below half. A virtual Bell monopoly was not reestablished until the decade between 1910 and 1920, after a new patent monopoly emerged for long-distance transmission. Both the federal and state governments responded by allowing local mergers and regulating the industry rather than requiring nondiscriminatory access to AT&T's long-distance system for all local access companies. The policy challenges presented then by the need for procompetitive interconnection rules, and the failure to solve the problem, presaged the interconnection debates that have emerged at the end of the twentieth century, and in the United States after the passage of the Telecommunications Act of 1996, when once again the policy environment has become favorable to competition.

Even in some developing countries, competition emerged before 1900. For example, in Buenos Aires, where entrepreneurs were not constrained by the Bell patents, "ferocious competition" among four firms, one domestic and three foreign, broke out in 1881 (Petrazzini 1996, 109). When these firms agreed to merge to monopoly in 1882, predictably prices rose and service quality fell. Then, in 1887, competition emerged again, persisting for forty years until ITT bought the competitors and once again merged them to monopoly. This time, the government responded by imposing regulation, followed a decade later by nationalization, rather than using competition policy to attack the monopoly.

The presence of competition, despite economies of scale in some components of production, should not have been surprising. As the number of telephone customers in a locality grew, scale economies in network components became less significant in the overall cost structure of telephone companies. Other factors, such as diseconomies of scale in management and less than fully efficient operation by firms that were not subject to the discipline of competition, could offset scale economies. Eventually, when competition came to an end through merger, the motive of the company was not necessarily to improve operating efficiency but instead to eliminate competition. Moreover, a durable merger to monopoly was aided by government policies that created entry barriers and substituted regulation or nationalization as the means for improving the performance of the incumbent monopolist.

The modern telecommunications industry is less likely than the early one to be a natural monopoly because of intervening technological progress combined with enormous growth in demand.[13] Whereas technological progress has reduced scale economies for most components of a telephone network, another effect that probably is even more important is that technological progress has vastly reduced the real cost per unit of output of all components of the network. The latter effect has reduced the economic significance of scale economies in comparison to managerial efficiency, technical capabilities, and service quality as determinants of the cost structure of a telephone network.

Digital microelectronic technology allows many messages to be transmitted over the same physical connection (whether by wire or over the air) and, more recently, over the same electromagnetic frequency on the same transmission medium, which in turn has reduced the physical resources necessary for connections in both local loops and interexchange transmission. The replacement of mechanical switches by digital switches based on microelectronic technology vastly reduces the cost of switching capacity (which is now analogous to computer memory) and eliminates scale economies in switches except at very small scale. Finally, radio technologies for customer connections and long-distance transmission do not have significant economies of scale. Fiberoptic cables do exhibit scale economies, but their cost per circuit is so low that given the demand for transmission, this technology has not undermined the feasibility of multifirm competition.

The implications of these developments are as follows. First, relatively small digital fixed wireless service for local access without mobility reaches minimum efficient scale at a few thousand customers in a local calling area at a cost and performance comparable to wireline service in all areas except where the spatial density of telephone customers is the highest. Second, in areas of high customer density, wireline competition is likely to be economically feasible. Third, transmission has become so inexpensive and such a low proportion of long-distance costs that it is unlikely to create important scale economies in long-distance service between major population centers.

Technological progress in the use of telecommunications also has created heterogeneous demand among customers. Examples of features that have created heterogeneous demand for technical characteristics in the

---

13. For a good review of cost studies of telephone systems, see Crandall and Waverman (1995).

network are mobility (cellular telephones provide high-quality mobility at low cost), speedy transmission of large data files (inexpensive networked personal computers and workstations create demand for transmitting many kinds of information other than voice communication), and high-speed digital transmission (Internet and other services require rapid transmission of complex information for interactive computer use). These developments favor entry by specialized firms that fill a particular qualitative niche in terms of the capabilities they offer to users. Whereas a single network can offer all qualitative features to all customers, the practical reality is that many uses, especially for large businesses, are most efficiently provided over a separate network designed to satisfy specialized demands but also connected to other networks to permit simpler forms of communication (especially voice-grade and low-end computer transmissions) between them.

For these reasons, technological progress has favored competition over monopoly in telecommunications services. Policy decisions early in the twentieth century that were based on the idea that telephony is a natural monopoly were probably incorrect then, but they are certainly incorrect now for all types of interexchange connections and local access in cities. In smaller urbanized communities and rural areas, wireline technology may still be a natural monopoly. But off-air technologies for providing access, such as fixed-base digital radio and low-earth satellites, are not natural monopolies, and technological progress favors them as the most cost-effective means for providing service in remote areas where demand for service is low. Perhaps already, but certainly in the near future, the only remaining natural monopolies are likely to be in communities so small and poor that demand is insufficient to justify more service than a single pay telephone.

If modern telecommunications is not a natural monopoly in almost all circumstances, the structural reality is that access service is a monopoly almost everywhere, and even long-distance service is monopolized in most of the world. Some analysts recognize that the industry probably is not a natural monopoly but question the significance of this point because they suspect that monopoly is a durable reality (especially in basic access service) that policymakers must accept, focusing their attention instead on how best to liberalize telecommunications policy in a durably monopolized circumstance (Joskow 1998). Thus a practically relevant policy question is how fast, and even whether, competition can be successful in the presence of a powerful, entrenched monopoly.

The presence of entrenched monopoly is not necessarily hopeless. Working in favor of potential competitors are two factors: the inefficiency of incumbents and the presence of heterogeneous demand. In countries where service is very poor and penetration is low, entrants can take advantage of excess demand to build a network of equal scale and superior performance that is especially attractive to the best customers. Thus the worse is the performance of the incumbent, the better is the prospect for effective competition.

Working against competitive entry is the availability to incumbents of effective strategies that make entry difficult. Examples are denial of adequate interconnection, refusal to sell some services without purchasing others so that an entrant must enter all parts of the industry simultaneously, and predatory pricing. These problems are essentially regulatory challenges in managing the transition to competition. How these problems can be solved, and whether their solution is plausibly within the competence of regulators, is addressed in section 6.3.

Another defense of monopoly, especially in developing nations, is that it can be used to promote more rapid improvements in capacity and quality of service, even if the monopoly is not natural. The basic idea is that a monopoly can be granted subject to a condition that it meet aggressive service goals, and that this agreement will lead to more rapid improvements than competition. In reality, this argument is bad economics. To illustrate why requires decomposing the argument into several separate elements.

One argument is that a protected monopoly reduces the risk facing a firm, which in turn increases the firm's willingness to invest. By itself, this argument is false. With one exception, monopolists and competitive firms face exactly the same investment risks concerning costs, demand, and the political environment. Thus, for any given investment, the cost of capital facing a firm is affected in the same way by risk factors, and hence the effect of risk on the revenue from a marginal investment that is sufficient to justify it are the same.

Market structure does have two additional effects on the financial attractiveness of investment to a firm, both of which work in favor of competition. First, the greater market power of a monopolist provides an incentive to undertake less investment than justified by cost and risk considerations. Absent an explicit policy to engage in internal cross-subsidization within the monopoly firm, the best that regulators can do is to impose investment requirements that duplicate the investments that would be made under competition. Neither a monopolist nor a competitor will make investments unless expected revenues justify the expense. Second, the one source of risk that is present under competition but not monopoly is the possibility that competitors will be more efficient and so win customers by offering better combinations of price and quality of service. The presence of monopoly does not eliminate this risk but instead transfers the risk to consumers as a hidden cost of monopoly. The fact that the risk of inferior service can be passed on but not avoided is an argument in favor of competition, not monopoly.

Given these advantages of competition, advocates of monopoly as a means to improve performance usually also advocate cross-subsidization. The idea is to let the monopoly earn from some customers excess profits that can be used to finance money-losing investments for other customers. The most basic attack on cross-subsidy is the questionable wisdom of making economically unremunerative investments in a capital-starved developing country. Moreover, as is apparent from table 6.1, the extent of service in most developing countries is so small that significant subsidies to low-income customers cannot possibly be taking place. Instead, the cross-subsidies run from long-distance (especially international) service to basic access service for wealthy and middle-class customers. But even if the political attractiveness of subsidized service is irresistible, cross-subsidization is a poor way to achieve it.

Cross-subsidies cannot possibly beat the alternative of opening all markets to competition, imposing a tax on all telecommunications services, and using the revenues to finance direct subsidies for users who require them. The most efficient mechanism for providing a subsidy is through a competitive bidding system in which the bids are the amount of subsidy a firm would require to provide the desired service. In the absence of natural monopoly, the monopoly provider of self-financing services can at best be as efficient as a competitive supplier, so the best that can be expected from cross-subsidization is to replicate the outcome of an explicit tax-subsidy system.

Equal performance from monopolists and competitors is a theoretical ideal, not a practical reality. Like all private firms, a monopolist prefers not to make investments that lose money and so will drag its feet in making them. Unless enforcement of the franchise agreement is perfect, the firm will invest less than the maximum that could be financed by the cross-subsidy in the price structure. Moreover, because monopolists have weaker incentives to be efficient and because regulation of monopoly further weakens these incentives, monopoly will be less efficient than competition. Consequently, to pay for the same amount of subsidized investment, the after-tax price faced by customers who pay the subsidy will be higher under a monopoly cross-subsidy regime than with an explicit tax-subsidy system.

The last gasp of the advocate of cross-subsidy is to claim that explicit tax-subsidy systems are politically infeasible for two reasons. First, they are inconsistent with neoliberal reform, which on the fiscal policy front seeks to shrink the size of the budget. Neither domestic fiscal conservatives nor international bankers (including the IMF and the World Bank) will accept solutions involving a bigger public sector. Second, telecommunications firms and their customers who would pay the tax will resist it, causing political support for neoliberal reform to dissipate. The problem with these arguments is that they assume selective rationality and even stupidity on the part of all relevant parties. Somehow all relevant political actors will prefer a more costly, less efficient reform with hidden taxes to a more efficient system in which the tax, though lower, is explicit. In principle, one cannot disprove this argument on theoretical grounds, but its plausibility seems questionable.

As a practical matter, the most likely explanation for the decision to embrace monopoly is the desire to maximize the revenues or political advantages that accrue to the government from neoliberal reform.[14] Two especially important features of neoliberal reform in telecommunications are that the market value and potential cash flow of a telecommunications monopoly is extremely high and that telecommunications reform is usually part of a much larger package of policies, including more disciplined fiscal and monetary policies.

Recall that in most cases the most important element of a neoliberal reform package is not to reform infrastructure industries but to eliminate large fiscal deficits and the lax monetary policy (and resulting inflation) that is used to finance them. Fiscal and monetary reform can complicate telecommunications reform. As explained in section 6.1, nationalized telecommunications firms can be a source of substantial net cash flows for the government, especially if they are not properly maintained and expanded, which explains why they are starved for investment and perform poorly. As a result, reformers, especially those in the finance ministry, are likely to seek ways to make the fiscal impact of telecommunications reform positive in order to offset the short-term cash flow loss from the state-owned enterprise. Preserving monopoly while improving its efficiency maximizes the fiscal benefit to the government. If the company is corporatized, the government as the primary or only stockholder can collect the monopoly profits—those that are not used for increased investment—as dividends. If the company is privatized, buyers will pay the discounted present value of the monopoly profits. In both cases, the financial returns to the government are higher than if the reformed company must face competition.

The validity of this argument for continuing a protected monopoly in telecommunications depends on a further argument about the domestic politics of a comprehensive neoliberal reform, and in any case it is at best a defense of temporary monopoly. The political argument is that an implicit tax through monopoly pricing in telecommunications generates less opposition than other taxes or expenditure reductions that could deliver the same fiscal benefit. Unlike the comparison between cross-subsidies and tax-subsidies, where both tax the same people, this argument is not irrational on its face. Other taxes may have imperfect compliance and greater distortions, and both other taxes and expenditure reductions are likely to have a much different incidence, which may cause either to provoke more political resistance.

At best, the political argument justifies a temporary commitment to

---

14. Chowdary (1998, 17) argued that revenue maximization was the sole objective of the system selected for licensing entrants in local telephony in India.

monopoly. If the government privatizes the monopoly, the effect of potential monopoly profits several years into the future on the sales price of the company will be of little importance, due to discounting.[15] Hence, committing to promote competition in the future will have a modest depressing effect on the government's sales revenues. Because the optimal public sector discount rate typically is much lower than the private rate and because presumably the government counts consumer satisfaction as well as profits, the value to the government of avoiding long-term monopoly is much higher than the value of monopoly to private investors. Consequently, the government ought to be willing to make a modest sacrifice in purchase price in order to limit the term of the monopoly.

Likewise, if the government corporatizes the firm with a commitment to privatize it after competition is introduced, it can convert the cash flow from its ownership into an immediate cash infusion by selling a revenue bond for the years of monopoly plus the sales price of the firm after competition is introduced. This maneuver exactly replicates the effect of selling the firm today, including the modest financial sacrifice that arises from granting a temporary rather than a permanent monopoly. Hence, the financial incentive to create a permanent monopoly is not materially different in the two regimes.

The preceding critical tour of the arguments for monopoly leads to the conclusion that competition is likely to be a superior alternative. In addition to its efficiency advantages, competition holds another political attraction as well. Given that developing countries are likely to find foreign investment very attractive for increasing capital flows into the industry, competition offers the possibility of defusing future anticolonial reactions to foreign control. The presence of several competitors eliminates both the appearance and the reality of exploitative foreign control of the industry, thereby reducing the chance of subsequent counterreform.

6.3   Regulation and Neoliberal Reform

Section 6.2 argues that the goal of neoliberal reform in telecommunications as well as electricity, transportation, and even in some cases water (see chapter 7 in this volume) should be a privatized, at least partially competitive industry, although for political reasons, some defensible and some not, countries usually pursue far less ambitious objectives. Indeed, one wireline carrier and two radio telephone companies in the same area is the norm around the world for the market structure of local service. In any case, the goal of competition cannot be achieved instantaneously

---

15. Private investors in foreign companies typically demand rates of return that would enable them to recover their investment in four or five years. Thus the sales price of a temporary ten-year monopoly will be roughly 75 to 80 percent of the price of a permanent monopoly.

because the status quo is monopoly. Even in countries with several telephone companies, some of which are private, service is monopolized locally by exclusive franchises, and long-distance and international services are provided by either a separate nationalized entity or, more commonly, the largest state-owned local access provider.

Consequently, as noted by Joskow (1998), in embarking on neoliberal reform programs, countries face a twofold problem: to prevent the incumbent monopolist from extracting monopoly profits from its customers (the price regulation problem) and to create market conditions that foster competition (the entry problem). In addition, governments must convince potential investors that regulatory institutions will not be used to expropriate their investments and that regulatory arrangements, if fair and reasonable, are enforceable and politically durable (the commitment problem).

This section examines the problem of establishing an effective and efficient mechanism for dealing with the incumbent monopolist and, if competition is the goal, for managing the transition. This problem raises three types of questions that can be characterized as designing the leaves, trees, and forests of regulatory institutions. The leaves are the details of regulatory decision-making processes: how regulators collect information, promulgate decisions, and enforce rules, and what specific conceptual approaches agencies take to making decisions. The trees are the structure and authority of the regulatory agency: the formal power and scope of the agency's legal mandate, the relationship of the agency to the rest of the government (ministers, legislators, courts), the procedures for appointing and removing the agency's leaders, and the budget and staff of the agency. The forest is the overall institutional environment of the nation: the representativeness of its leaders, the stability of its policies and institutions, its system of commercial law, and the nature of the system for enforcing law—are contracts enforced, does the legal system obey the rule of law, and are economic rights and the rights of minorities protected? Although the discussion in this section will use illustrations from telecommunications, it also applies more generally to all infrastructural industries.

6.3.1   Background Economics

Recall the historical tendency for governments to use nationalized telecommunications firms as cash cows to support the government. This policy is feasible for a reasonably long period because a large proportion of the cost of a telecommunications firm is sunk in durable capital investments. The failure to use the cash flow from the operation of the company to maintain, replace, and expand capital facilities accounts for the deteriorating performance of state-owned firms. With privatization, investors must expect to be able to retain sufficient revenues to cover these capital costs plus a competitive return on their investments or they will not invest in the enterprise.

Because the incumbent is a monopoly that can expect to enjoy substantial market power for a considerable period after it is privatized, the economic feasibility of establishing a price structure that enables the firm to satisfy this cash flow requirement is not really in doubt as long as the firm is reasonably well managed. Thus, from the perspective of investors, the main financial risk associated with acquiring the privatized firm is whether the government will allow prices that make the investment worthwhile. Because telecommunications investments are so durable, the primary determinant of financial risk is not the adequacy of the initial price structure but the firm's expectations about the policies of the government for controlling prices in the future.

In the literature of regulatory economics the commitment problem refers to whether government can take actions today to convince investors that future regulatory decisions will not cause expected earnings from their investments to fall below the competitive return. This subsection deals with one part of the commitment problem: establishing pricing rules that enable a well-managed firm to earn a reasonable return on investment. The next subsection deals with another aspect of the problem, which is assuring that a reasonable system of regulation will be enforced fairly and will endure. In reality, the former problem is far easier to solve than the latter.

A core problem in designing regulatory institutions is how to deal with the fact that regulators are not likely to know as much as the firm about demand, cost, technology, and, as a result, the true efficiency and profitability of the firm.[16] If regulators possess perfect information, they can set prices equal to the prices that would emerge in a competitive industry, and the firm would then have to operate with maximal feasible efficiency in order to earn a competitive return on its investments. In this case, the only advantage of competition over monopoly would be that the former avoids the direct costs of the regulatory process.

The selection of a pricing method is primarily a problem of regulatory design (the leaves problem), but it is also related to the trees problem (what powers and resources to give to the regulators) and the forest problem (what legal rules regarding economic rights the agency must follow).

6.3.2   Cost-of-Service Regulation

Until the 1980s, the standard approach to solving this regulatory problem was cost-of-service regulation. In this system, regulators periodically audit the books of the regulated firm for some recent historical period (usually a year), estimate the total costs of the firm for that period, and

---

16. For a comprehensive treatment of this issue, see Laffont and Tirole (1998). For interesting discussions of how these concepts apply to developing countries, see Galal and Nauriyal (1995) and Joskow (1998).

insist that the firm set prices such that had those prices been charged in that historical period, the total revenues of the firm would have equaled its total costs. In addition, regulators also concern themselves with some aspects of the price structure to assure that no politically salient customer group is charged an unreasonably high price.[17] Aside from simple errors in calculations, a virtual certainty due to the complexity of telecommunications firms, uncertainty creeps into this process for three reasons.

First, because capital investments are durable, regulators must pick a depreciation rate, which then determines how much of a firm's investment cost should be recovered in a year. This decision is fundamentally arbitrary because the regulator cannot know when in the future, through obsolescence or physical deterioration, a capital facility should be replaced, or how optimally to allocate the responsibility for paying for the facility between current and future customers.

Second, whereas the concept of a competitive return on investment is clear, the actual competitive rate of return is impossible to calculate with precision. The cost of capital is affected by random, short-term volatility in markets for financial assets and depends on investor expectations about future conditions in all of the input and output markets in which the firm operates as well as the future political climate for regulated firms. Consequently, regulators can only crudely estimate the minimum return necessary to induce adequate financial investment by the firm.

Third, regulators do not know whether the costs incurred by the firm actually were reasonable. Regulators cannot know precisely the best combination of inputs for producing the services sold in the historical period. Even if they could, the proper standard for evaluating the efficiency of the firm is whether it made good decisions based on the information available to it at the time. These decisions must be based on expected demand, which is uncertain, and on the optimal choice of technology and investments over the life of durable capital assets, not just on conditions in a single historical period.

Thus the fundamental problem with cost-of-service regulation is that regulators cannot know the firm's true costs and demand and cannot know whether the firm is efficient. The most common response to this problem is to use the periodic cost audit for a second purpose, which is to adjust future revenues to account for errors in the previous regulatory constraint. Thus, if the revenues of a firm did not cover its estimated costs

---

17. Telecommunications regulators frequently set the price for certain core services, such as new service installation, the basic monthly access charge, and usage charges for local, long-distance, and international calls. Typically, regulators do not attempt to base these prices on estimates of service-specific costs, instead adjusting them periodically to take into account overall trends in total costs. Firms are then given a great deal of latitude, sometimes complete freedom; to set other prices, subject to the requirement that total revenues equal total costs. For more details, see Noll (1985).

in the historical audit period, the shortfall will be added to the revenues that can be recovered in the next period. Likewise, subtractions from future revenues (or customer rebates) will be required if the firm earned excess profits.[18]

This system of regulation has three significant costs. The first is that it requires an elaborate regulatory process that employs many skilled professionals in order to produce reasonably accurate estimates of the firm's costs and, even more demanding, to reach reasonable conclusions about the efficiency of the firm's operations. Moreover, regulatory agencies are likely to exhibit significant economies of scale since the problem of assessing the reasonableness of costs is not closely related to the size of the regulated firm. Thus the cost of regulation is higher in relation to the welfare at stake in the regulatory process in a small developing country, where professional accountants, economists, and engineers are likely to be scarce and the size of the regulated industry is likely to be relatively small.

The second cost of this form of regulation is that it is likely to distort the input choices of the regulated firm. Given the uncertainties surrounding the regulator's estimate of the competitive return on investment, the optimal strategy for the regulator is to err on the side of generosity to the firm. The reason is the asymmetry of the costs of an error. If the regulator slightly overestimates the competitive return to capital, prices will be slightly higher, but the firm has an adequate incentive to make capital investments so that service quality (and customer satisfaction) is maintained. If the regulator slightly underestimates the cost of financial capital, the incentive to invest disappears entirely. Even if the firm expects the error to be corrected in the future, in the short run the firm will have difficulty maintaining its interest and dividend payments to investors if it also maintains an adequate investment program. Thus slightly lower prices will be accompanied by deteriorating performance.

The tendency to be slightly generous in calculating the financial cost of capital gives firms the opportunity to earn excess profits on capital investments, but not on other inputs. Thus firms, in seeking to maximize profits, have an incentive to overinvest in capital facilities. At some point, regulators will detect this overinvestment and disallow their recovery; however, because regulators lack perfect information about production technology, they will not be able to prevent overinvestment to some degree. Consequently, the regulated firm will not be efficient in its capital investment decisions.

Third, cost-of-service regulation blunts the incentive of the firm to operate efficiently. Somewhat higher costs than are necessary are not likely to

18. Rebates and negative adjustments were used by the U.S. Federal Communications Commission (FCC) until the 1980s, when the Supreme Court ruled that the FCC lacked the authority to order them. This decision made the FCC's regulatory system asymmetric: firms were entitled to recover losses but did not have to return excess profits.

be detected by the regulator and so lead to higher prices. Because monopolists do not face the discipline of competition, their incentive to minimize cost is blunted; however, unregulated monopolists can charge monopoly prices, so that inefficiency cannot be compensated for by further price increases. If regulation causes prices to be below the monopoly level, inefficiency is less costly to the firm because the regulator will allow it to raise prices in the direction that the firm prefers.

The second and third problems interact in the following way. If a firm has already engaged in as much profit-enhancing overinvestment as it can get away with, the incentive to operate efficiently (notwithstanding excess investment) is essentially eliminated. No profit-enhancing investments or price increases are available to the firm; however, other unnecessary costs will be passed through in price increases.

The underlying economic conditions in a developing country may keep the inefficiencies of cost-of-service regulation from being very important, and indeed, as Joskow (1998) reminds us, the U.S. telephone system performed very well for nearly a century under this system. The most important feature of newly privatized telephone companies is that they require enormous capital investment to improve service and meet unsatisfied demand. Moreover, these firms generally have excess labor relative to capital. Hence, the incentive to be excessively capital intensive plausibly is of dubious significance for many years. Moreover, because these firms face extensive opportunities for profitable capital investments, they seem less likely to fall prey to the generally weak incentives to control costs that affect regulated monopolies operating in more stagnant market conditions. Thus it is not clear that concerns about the inefficiencies that arose in developed countries after well-functioning networks were constructed are transferrable to the context of a developing country in which the main problem is building a network of adequate capacity and reliability.

6.3.3 Alternative Pricing Mechanisms

The inefficiencies of cost-of-service regulation have led economists and some regulators to propose alternative methods that do not depend so heavily on cost audits of the regulated firm. The three primary alternatives are price-cap regulation, benchmark competition regulation, and negotiated franchise contracts.

The basic idea of these alternatives is to break the connection between prices and costs so that a profit-maximizing firm can increase its profits only by cutting costs. If prices are set at something approximating costs and then frozen, the firm has a high-powered incentive to cut costs and improve efficiency. The resulting excess profits of the firm do not harm consumers because, in the absence of the sharper incentives to cut costs, the initial price decision would be sustained by the inefficiencies created by cost-of-service regulation.

Price-cap regulation represents the maximal disconnection of prices from costs.[19] When price caps are initiated, the regulator begins with the existing price structure. If these prices were adequate to cover costs (which would apply to firms subject to cost-of-service regulation), the regulator first creates a price index using current prices and outputs. If the regulator believes that prices were too low (a frequent problem with nationalized firms) or that the firm did not minimize costs in the past, the initial price index can be adjusted up or down to initialize the system appropriately.

After determining the initial price index, the regulator then estimates the extent to which the industry can be expected to have future increases in productivity that exceed the average for the economy and cuts the real price index in future years by this estimated excess productivity growth. This adjusted index becomes the firm's price cap. The regulatory rule, then, is that the firm must not change prices in a way that causes the actual real price index to exceed the cap. The shorthand for this system is "PI-X," where average annual price changes, weighted by historical quantities, cannot exceed the rate of increase in a standard price index (PI) minus excess expected productivity growth (X). As with cost-of-service regulation, the regulator may also impose further ceilings on particular, politically salient prices.

If the regulator can promise never to change this formula and not otherwise to interfere with future prices, this system creates a powerful incentive to minimize costs. Furthermore, if the regulator does not place additional restrictions on specific prices, the firm's profit-maximizing price structure also will be efficient. Hence, looking to the future, price-cap regulation has the property that if regulators make the best use of the information they have about demand, costs, and technology, the price-cap formula will produce a future path of prices and costs that is at least as good as, and probably better than, the outcome from cost-of-service regulation.

Pure price-cap regulation is impossible to implement for two fundamental reasons. First, because the regulator cannot perfectly estimate future excess productivity growth in the industry, the price adjustment formula is certain to cause the profits of the regulated firm either to rise or to fall as actual productivity diverges from estimated productivity. Eventually, the firm will find itself in the position of either the nationalized firm, with revenues insufficient to cover its costs (including a competitive return on investment), or a de facto unregulated monopolist, earning monopoly profits and finding that the price cap no longer constrains its pricing behavior. Both outcomes are inefficient and, most likely, politically unstable, or else privatization with regulation would not have been the original political choice.

19. For excellent discussions of price-cap regulation, see Baron (1989) and Laffont and Tirole (1998).

The second reason that pure price caps cannot be implemented is that technological progress causes the bundle of products to change. Entirely new products may be created, or technology may cause an increase in the optimal quality (and the cost) of an established product. Price-cap regulation has no provision for adjusting the original price index to account for changes in technology because there is neither a base price nor a base quantity for new or altered products.

These two problems naturally lead to periodic adjustments of price caps. In telecommunications, the planned duration of price caps typically has been in the range of five years; however, in both the United States and the United Kingdom, where price caps have been in use since the late 1980s, regulators have readjusted price indexes before their planned readjustment dates. Usually the primary reason has been to increase the stringency of the index (by increasing X) because the firm has cut costs and increased profits by more than the regulators expected.

If price caps are frequently readjusted, price-cap regulation becomes very close to cost-of-service regulation. As a practical matter, cost-of-service regulation does not require that the regulator examine costs and readjust the ceiling on total revenues every year. In the United States, many regulatory bodies that practiced cost-of-service regulation reviewed costs and reset prices only if someone, either the regulated firm or a customer group, complained (Joskow 1974). For example, the U.S. FCC once went thirty-four years between formal investigations to determine the costs of long-distance service. This practice is called "regulatory lag," or a period during which, if the firm cuts costs, it can keep the savings as long as the regulator chooses not to audit its costs. The most important lesson from the theory of price caps and the practice of cost-of-service regulation is that in the long run, prices and costs will be lower if regulators do not continuously audit costs and scrutinize the operations of regulated firms.

Benchmark regulation sets the prices of a regulated firm on the basis of information about other firms. One approach is to use the costs of another firm to establish a price-cap index or total revenue ceiling. This cost basis can be created by randomly selecting firms to audit or relying on the audit of another firm by another regulator. An even simpler approach is to set prices on the basis of the prices set by other regulators without even considering costs.

Most developing countries are unlikely to have a large number of regulated monopoly telephone companies, so randomly auditing the costs of some domestic companies as a basis for regulating the others is not likely to be a feasible strategy. Hence, the realistic choice is for one country to rely on the cost audits and price decisions in another country, which may create problems of reliability and domestic political feasibility. In any case, telephone companies are likely to have significant cost differences for legitimate reasons having to do with subscriber density, the pattern of demand among different services, domestic factor prices, international trade policies, and the nature and extent of sunk capital costs. Thus, even under the simplest benchmark system, regulators are likely to be called upon to consider adjusting price regulations to take account of these differences. The basis for these adjustments will be the same kind of information that regulators must collect and evaluate to update either a price-cap index or a cost-of-service revenue requirement, although the regulator may not be required to evaluate as much information under benchmark competition.

Whether benchmark competition is an attractive alternative to the other approaches depends on the extent to which the regulator will need to adjust the benchmark to accommodate special local conditions. If other regulatory processes are sufficiently reliable and the conditions of the regulated industry sufficiently similar that another regulatory body can trust their results, regulators can achieve comparably effective regulation at much lower cost. But a conscious decision to rely on the benchmark and, as a result, to create a bare-bones regulatory structure leads to other problems. First, investors in the regulated firm may regard the system as imposing additional risks if they believe that benchmark costs and prices are likely not to be good indicators of their own costs, or if they believe that in the future regulators in benchmark countries may be inclined to expropriate the capital of their telephone companies. Second, the domestic company has a strong incentive to take advantage of the minimal capabilities of the regulator by demanding extensive exceptions to the benchmark, supported by extensive information that the regulator cannot evaluate.

Negotiated franchise agreements set prices for the term of a contract. The franchise agreement indirectly reflects expectations about costs in that the firm's negotiating position will be based on its cost estimates. In the pure form, the contract specifies the services it covers and the prices the firm will charge (perhaps with some adjustment formula over time to reflect inflation and productivity changes). In this sense, the product of the negotiation is much like the product of other forms of regulation: a pricing formula that will be in force until some future date when it will be adjusted.

The reputed advantage of a franchise agreement is that it avoids the need for a formal regulatory authority. In reality, this is not the case, for several reasons.

First, during the initial negotiations, the government needs to have information about costs, demand, and technical possibilities in order to establish a rational negotiating position. The single most powerful lesson of recent research on regulatory mechanisms is that the government will be able to extract a better deal from the regulated firm if it can reduce the firm's informational advantage. The government can generate better information for itself by deciding to use competitive bidding to determine prices and service obligations as well as the amount it will receive for the privatized entity; however, to evaluate these bids, the government also must have some basis for comparing the price and service commitments in bids for the company, which requires information about costs and demand. In the absence of such information, government is in danger of awarding the franchise to a "lowball" bidder that knows full well its bid is unrealistic but relies on the fact that once it is entrenched, the government will face significant costs if it seeks either to enforce the performance agreement or to dislodge the winning bidder.

Second, if a firm acquires a company with a franchise agreement that is good for only a few years, it legitimately has a concern about the outcome of future negotiations for renewing the agreement. A firm can easily walk away from the initial negotiations, but once it has bought the company, it has substantial sunk costs that can be recovered only through multiple renewals of the agreement. To avoid being placed in a weak bargaining position at the time of renewal, the firm will require either that first-period prices be very high (or the purchase price of the company be very low) or that future agreements be guaranteed to allow the firm to cover a reasonable estimate of costs. Because the second alternative almost certainly is more efficient, both parties will prefer it, but to implement it the government must be capable of gathering and evaluating the same information that it needs to undertake other forms of regulation.

One way out of the renegotiation problem is for the government not to sell the company but instead to sign an operating contract with the franchisee. In this case, the franchisee does not have sunk costs that can be recovered only through multiple renewals of the agreement, and in negotiating prices it is concerned only about recovering its actual operating costs during the period of the franchise. Unfortunately, this form of agreement creates another major problem that largely vitiates the neoliberal reform. The franchisee no longer is responsible for capital investments; the decision about how much to invest still resides with the government. Moreover, the franchisee also has no incentive to undertake repair and maintenance that will keep capital investments in optimal operating condition. In essence, in this system the government has retained responsibility for capital investments while distancing itself from their operation. This arrangement is likely to be very inefficient.

Third, a long-term contract cannot fully anticipate all the significant changes in market conditions that will arise over its term. Just as in the case of price-cap regulation, unexpected events can cause either party to seek to renegotiate the contract. Consequently, both parties are likely to want to incorporate provisions for reopening negotiations and protections concerning the relation between prices and costs should the other party exercise these provisions to change the price agreement. The result is likely to be a process that looks very much like cost-of-service regulation.

The upshot of the preceding analysis is that a nation is not likely to be able to avoid investing in a regulatory process, regardless of the details of the formal arrangements between the firm and the government. On the basis of either their effects on the efficiency of the firm or the cost of the process, these alternatives are not likely to differ very much, especially in a developing country. The most important implication is that every approach other than cost-of-service regulation with continuous monitoring, which is dominated by a system that has regulatory lag, creates intermittent demand for the services of regulators. Consequently, a specialized regulator with authority over a small number of companies will be essential to rational policy making on occasion but will not be useful much of the time. Whereas intermittent excess capacity is worth avoiding in any context, in developing countries, where the skills needed for effective regulation can be extremely scarce, opportunities for avoiding this excess capacity are especially attractive.

The preceding observation argues for one of two approaches. One is to create a general regulator with responsibility for all newly privatized monopoly utilities, which is the model followed in implementing state regulation in the United States. This approach is not fully satisfactory, for even in the developed context of the United States, assigning multiple responsibilities to an agency still does not enable agencies in smaller states to be large enough and to possess sufficient specialized expertise to be effective. The other approach is to for several nations to collaborate in establishing an international authority to regulate telephone companies in all participating countries, which is the approach taken to resolving international trade disputes under the WTO, the European Union, and the North American Free Trade Agreement.

The latter alternative has never been attempted in any form of utility regulation, for each nation seems to want to retain full autonomy in these industries. Nevertheless, it has crept in indirectly through trade disputes about the use of regulation as an indirect trade barrier (Noll 1997). Internationalization of regulation has many attractive features (Noll 2000). First, it allows the development of specialized expertise in telephones at a scale that a small developing country cannot afford. Second, it captures economies of scale in regulation by applying the lessons learned when a new problem is raised in one proceeding to the same problem as it arises in subsequent cases. Third, it permits the regulator to use information about technology, costs, and demand in one country to assist it in detecting inefficiencies in other countries, much as in the theory of benchmark competition. Thus a promising agenda for developing nations is to consider creating joint regulatory authorities, perhaps through existing regional trade alliances.

6.3.4   Political Factors Influencing Regulation

The discussion to this point has focused on the mechanics of price regulation, specifically what method will be used to set prices. In practice, this choice is likely to be less important than the broader issues of the structure and process of the regulatory authority. All regulatory processes are inherently conflictual, and participants in the regulatory process will seek to influence that process to their own advantage in any way available to them. Submitting information to regulators that supports a favorable decision is only one way of exercising influence. Another is to seek intervention by political allies. Moreover, because every group expects that others will try to exercise the same political influence, collectively they are likely to seek some mechanism for protecting themselves against highly unfavorable outcomes that reflect effective political intervention on behalf of others.

Commitment is one aspect of this problem. Restated for the present discussion, the commitment problem refers to the desire on the part of a privatized utility to be permanently protected against other interests that might seek low output prices, high input prices, financially unrealistic service requirements, or confiscatory taxes that, effectively, would expropriate the firm's investments for the benefit of others. In addition to the commitment problem, which is one of price-cost margins that are too low, regulation presents another danger that actually has proved to be more common: regulatory capture. Here the problem is that regulators are especially solicitous to the regulated firm, allowing it to charge high prices, earn high profits, and provide low-quality service.

To understand both expropriation and capture requires identifying their political and bureaucratic causes.[20] In general, all policy making, including regulation, is subject to inefficiencies and unfairness that stem from representation bias. Representation bias arises because those who organize themselves to participate in the policy process are more likely to have their interests taken into account in policy decisions.

One source of representation bias is incomplete information. Because information is imperfect, policymakers seek data from more expert sources. For information pertaining to the details of technology, demand, and costs in an industry, those who supply service frequently have extensive private information that is necessary for making efficient policy. Because all parties can be expected to submit information that is beneficial to their interests, on balance the effect of the information they do submit is to bias policy outcomes in their favor.

A second reason for representation bias is that not all interests are likely to apply pressure on political officials to intervene on their behalf. Political

20. The following discussion summarizes the extensive literature on the politics of regulation that is surveyed in Noll (1989).

pressure here refers to a credible threat to withhold support from an official whose policy preferences and actions are unsatisfactory. If some groups with a stake in the regulatory process are organized to make such a threat but others are not, political intervention will be biased in favor of organized groups.

The third mechanism that can bias regulatory decisions relates to the interests and biases of the regulators. These biases can arise because agencies may be staffed by political actors who are not fully representative of even all the organized groups, let alone the groups that are not organized. For example, in a parliamentary system with strong, ideologically based parties, each important interest may be represented by only one party, so that swings in the partisan control of government cause significant swings in the identity of the interests that regulators favor. In addition, regulatory officials may be inclined to favor some interests for other than political reasons. For example, regulators may expect to have short government careers and so may seek to enhance their postregulation employment by favoring a likely future employer. Or some specialized skills of regulators may be obtained or usefully applied only in organizations that actively participate in the regulatory process, so that regulators naturally are inclined to think like those who are represented before their agency.

These problems are intensified because not all interests are likely to participate in the regulatory process. Participation is motivated by the prospect of economic gains and so is determined by the stakes of a group in regulatory outcomes and the costs they must incur to become effectively represented. In general, groups that are already organized, that are small and homogeneous in their interests, and that have high per capita stakes are more likely to be represented. In particular, the regulated firm and perhaps a few very large users and input suppliers are likely to participate actively, while most user groups are not.

With this background, we can identify how both expropriation and capture can emerge. Expropriation can arise for two reasons, one internal and one external to the agency. First, user groups may be well organized in the regulatory process and cause service to be provided below cost. Second, an election may cause political pressure to be placed on regulators to favor users against suppliers. Capture can arise for parallel reasons. The firm, and perhaps some but not most users, may be effectively represented in the regulatory process, causing regulators to allow the firm to earn excess profits, perhaps as a reward for cross-subsidizing select users (such as government officials). Or electoral politics may bring to power a party that favors the regulated firm at the expense of user interests.

6.3.5   Regulatory Design Implications

The solution to both capture and expropriation is the same: to construct a regulatory agency that is unlikely to be unduly influenced by any particular interests. Basically, the design of the agency must assure that as much relevant information is presented to the regulators as is reasonably feasible, that the decision makers are neither homogeneous in their biases nor subject to unbalanced external pressure, and that neutral arbiters can intervene should the agency make an unreasonable decision. These requirements raise both the tree and forest issues: the design of the agency, its connections to the larger system of government, and the principles for deciding whether the agency or the government as a whole has acted unreasonably or unfairly. The specific arrangements that contribute to this objective are as follows.

First, the personnel of regulatory agencies should be heterogeneous and stable. Short-term changes in the political control of government should not cause dramatic short-term swings in the composition of the agency, and the careers of regulatory officials should be secure through political change as well as long enough and remunerative enough that regulators are not constantly seeking interesting future employment possibilities. The personnel requirement implies that civil service procedures should govern influential regulatory positions and that political appointments to agencies should not be purely partisan. The U.S. independent regulatory commission, in which political appointments to a multiheaded body are for several years and are subject to partisan diversity rules, represents the extreme form of insulation from political pressures. The British and Japanese systems, in which heads of regulatory authorities and their lieutenants are professionals but policy authority rests in a cabinet ministry run by a partisan appointment, seek to achieve independence by giving more authority to civil servants.

Second, the agency can be given independent authority to generate information and even resources to represent interests that otherwise are not organized to participate in its processes. For example, regulators can undertake their own investigations and research on technologies, the performance of firms that they do not regulate, and cost and demand. In some cases, separate bureaus within the agency can be established to advocate for unrepresented interests.

Third, the agency can be subject to openness requirements. The agency can be required to conduct all business in public, to refrain from secret contacts with either interested parties or political officials, and to release all relevant information pertaining to a decision as well as a preliminary indication of the decision it is likely to make before the actual decision is made. Openness requirements are beneficial because they give advance warning to those who are affected by a decision, enabling them to intervene if the decision is unfavorable, but simultaneously guaranteeing that both the existence and the content of their intervention will be public. Openness forces regulators to reveal the informational basis for their decisions and is therefore useful for revealing whether the agency's decision is biased and unsupported by facts (McCubbins, Noll, and Weingast 1987, 1989).

Fourth, a nation can adopt a form of "high law" (such as a constitution) that constrains ordinary laws (such as legislation, decrees, or administrative rules). An example is a prohibition against expropriating property without compensation if the property owner is not using the property in a manner that is negligent, monopolistic, or criminal.

Fifth, the decisions of the agency can be subject to review by another body that is freer of representation biases, especially biases affecting participation in the agency's processes, at the instigation of anyone who is dissatisfied with a decision. The most common reviewing body is a general purpose court that itself is politically independent and diverse in composition (see Levy and Spiller 1996). The advantage of a general purpose court is that it is less likely to favor a particular industrial interest and less likely to regard itself as possessing sufficient specialized expertise that it can substitute its own technical analysis for that of the regulator. The issues to be decided through judicial review are whether the decision is supported by the evidence, is authorized by the regulator's formal policy objectives, as stated in its formal legal mandate, and respects limitations that are imposed by high law. The use of judicial review, by implication, requires that the agency's authority and decision-making processes be clearly specified in some form of legal document, such as legislation or decree, that predates the decision under review.

The unfortunate part of this litany of procedural and structural safeguards is that they are costly to implement and assume the presence of a highly developed legal system not yet present in many developing countries (Kerf and Smith 1996; Wellenius 1998). For some large developing countries with a substantial middle class, such as Brazil, India, or Mexico, these safeguards plausibly are present and affordable, so that a recommendation to implement Western-style regulatory agencies is not out of the question. In a small, poor country, the domestic supply of professionals to implement this kind of regulatory system is low and inelastic. Hence, the realistic choice facing a small country is either a system with elaborate safeguards that is operated primarily by foreigners (perhaps in a regional regulatory authority as described above) or a far less elaborate system. Moreover, the cost of protecting against confiscation of property is lower than the cost of protecting against capture. Reasonable protection against expropriation involves little more than an enforceable high law against expropriation that is enforced by an independent judicial system where regulated businesses have standing. Protection against capture requires creating a structure and process that gives regulators enough relevant information to do a reasonably good job and that enfranchises otherwise unrepresented interests, which implies a large bureaucracy. The more plausible scenario in a small, poor country that retains regulatory autonomy is that the regulator will be too small and weak to avoid capture rather than that the system will lead to expropriation.

The preceding conclusion does not imply that neoliberal reform is not desirable in small, poor countries. Private monopolies that are not tightly regulated may earn high profits but have a powerful incentive to provide service to anyone who can pay their prices, and thereby to eliminate multiyear waiting lists for obtaining a connection. If these firms can profit from usage, they also have an incentive to avoid service quality problems such as failure to obtain a dial tone, failure to reach a called number, and interruption of service.

Other than high prices to those who subscribe, the unsatisfactory feature of the performance of loosely regulated monopoly is in providing "universal service"—that is, extending the penetration of phone service to anyone who will not or cannot pay the supercompetitive prices that may emerge under weak regulation. But decades of experience with nationalized telephone companies teaches that they also do not serve the universal service objective. History teaches that the stronger political influence affecting nationalized entities is more likely to be used to provide a cash flow to the government and to support excessive employment at the expense of both universal service and efficient operation.

The political issues surrounding the creation of effective regulators also make both benchmark regulation and international collaborative regulation more attractive. By pooling resources, a regional association of small nations can produce a regulator that is more expert, more independent, and freer from representation bias than any could create on its own. Of course, for either the soft (benchmark) or strong (international agency) forms of collaboration to work, the political institutions and values of the collaborators must be broadly similar.

6.3.6 Facilitating Competition

The inherent difficulty of implementing effective regulation is a powerful argument in favor of policies to encourage competition. Moreover, the universal service problem arises in part because monopolies have an incentive to provide less service than the market can support, so that in a nation likely to have weak regulation the universal service goal is a reason for permitting competition. But creating a competitive telecommunications industry is far from easy. The first step is to eliminate regulatory entry barriers. This task is easier said then done, because in almost all countries regulation typically requires that all firms obtain a license or franchise, and then the entrant, like the incumbent, must satisfy requirements about filing tariffs and sometimes cost information. The fundamental reason for this practice is that regulation frequently creates massive cross-subsidies in the price structure, which encourages entry to serve customers who pay high prices. If entrants are not required to participate in the cross-subsidy system, the cross-subsidies are unstable. To protect the pricing structure regulators simply prevent competition that might attack the source of the subsidies. Preventing entry is an expensive way to protect cross-subsidies and is still another reason to adopt explicit industry-wide taxes as a means to implement subsidies. But in any case, extensive cross-subsidization within the price structure of a regulated firm is fundamentally at odds with the objective of promoting competition. Regulators can have one or the other, but not both.

Abstracting from the dubious purpose of sustaining cross-subsidies, if several firms enter a market, anything more than perfunctory notification requirements are unnecessary and can be pernicious because notification facilitates collusion. Entrants, because they are competing with a dominant firm that is subject to price regulation, need not themselves be subject to price regulation because they lack market power: their combination of price and service must equal or beat the incumbent's offerings for them to succeed. Whereas relieving entrants of regulation seems simple and obvious, few countries have been able to do so.

Assuming that regulatory entry barriers can be avoided, the fundamental problem in promoting competition in telecommunications is overcoming the economic and technical advantages of an incumbent monopolist that arise from the network aspect of the industry: telecommunications services derive their value from connecting the originator of a message to the recipient. Whereas some customers may be content to reach few other customers, in general the demand for telecommunications by one customer is increasing in the number of other parties who can be reached. Because an entrant cannot immediately enter at a scale that gives it a large fraction of access customers, initially at least almost all connections must make use of the facilities of the incumbent. Unlike nearly all other industries, competitors in telecommunications must accommodate joint use of their facilities in order for the industry to operate efficiently in a competitive environment.

In all infrastructural industries including telecommunications, by far the most difficult regulatory problem has been to force an incumbent to provide efficient interconnection arrangements for its competitors (Armstrong, Cowan, and Vickers 1994; Joskow and Noll 1999). Interconnection pricing must cope with two fundamental problems: the inevitable market power of local access carriers in termination charges and the incentive of the incumbent monopolist not to offer interconnection to entrants.

A basic principle of telephone pricing is that the calling party pays. This policy protects consumers against facing the equivalent of an automatic, unauthorized collect call every time the telephone rings, but it also creates a big economic distinction between origination (use of the customer's access provider) and termination (use of the recipient's access provider). If the industry is competitive, access firms will compete over the service prices they offer customers, including the origination fee. However, a customer cannot choose how a call will be terminated, so companies will not compete over termination charges unless the principle of "caller pays" is abandoned. Hence, even in a competitive environment, an access firm is likely to have substantial market power in termination charges.

Incumbent monopolists have the additional advantage that they can use termination charges to create a barrier to entry. The incumbent will seek to retain all customers who are profitably served by the existing network. If entrants cannot offer their customers the opportunity to connect to customers of the incumbent, the entrant will win few customers because the object of telecommunications is to reach other parties. The sole exception is that a large company or group of customers may still have an incentive to create a private network, allowing communications within the group that is served by the entrant, and then to rely on separate service from the incumbent for contacting others. But the vast majority of customers are not likely to want to subscribe to two separate telephone systems, and even if they were so inclined, requiring them to do so is inefficient because interconnection of two systems is far cheaper than extending the reach of each to all customers who want to reach users of both networks.

Given an entrant's need for interconnection, an incumbent monopolist has two strategies that enable it to create barriers to entry. One is to charge high prices for completing connections that make use of the entrant's facilities. The other is to provide technically inferior connections between its facilities and the facilities of a competitor. Together these strategies create the "interconnection problem" for entrants. High prices for most connections can force the entrant to suffer financial losses every time one of its customers connects with a customer of the incumbent, and poor interconnection prevents the entrant from competing effectively for customers who care about service quality. If the incumbent adopts interconnection policies that create an entry barrier, successful entry requires offering services (access and long distance) at sufficient scale that entrants can avoid the facilities of the incumbent for a large fraction of their service and can impose costs on the incumbent that are comparable to the costs the latter imposes on the former for the remaining services that use the facilities of both. If such is the case, extensive regulatory intervention is unnecessary, for parties with the power to impose costs on each other have a strong incentive to negotiate efficient interconnection agreements. This argument constitutes the main reason for breaking up a nationalized telecommunications entity into several components when it is privatized.

The interconnection issue has given rise to many different approaches to policies for encouraging competition. Denial of efficient interconnection is a ubiquitous problem in telecommunications, and no nation has yet fully solved the problem of facilitating competition among local access providers (Armstrong et al. 1994; Joskow and Noll 1999).

One approach is simply to ignore the problem and to require that competitors negotiate interconnection agreements privately. Whereas this policy can work if the firms are roughly equally well established, it is not likely to generate entry by firms that initially lack a significant customer base. Negotiations, without further rules and requirements, cannot solve the problem if only one negotiator has an incentive to make a deal. When entry is first permitted entrants have few customers, so the customers of the incumbent are not likely to place a high value on reaching the entrant's network. Consequently, the incumbent has no good reason to negotiate an agreement that does anything less than preserve all of its existing net revenues.

As a supplement to private negotiation, one can rely on competition (antitrust) policy to detect and punish anticompetitive pricing. This approach was tried in New Zealand. Unfortunately, antitrust action, because it is a slow process, imposes additional costs on entrants. Moreover, the tests for anticompetitive pricing also all involve comparing prices and costs and so have informational requirements that are like those of regulation. In New Zealand, this approach failed for another reason. The British Privy Council, which serves as New Zealand's supreme court, overturned a lower court decision that the incumbent monopolist behaved anticompetitively when it insisted on interconnection prices that were based on the "efficient component pricing rule" (ECPR), which had the effect of ending competition for most services.

For long-distance and value-added services, another relatively easy solution to the problem is to require vertical separation of these services from local access. Vertical segmentation of the industry removes the incentive of an incumbent local access monopolist to favor one provider of the other services over any other. A similar but somewhat less effective strategy is to require the incumbent to operate competitive services through a separate subsidiary and to offer service to its affiliates under the same terms that are offered to competitors. This policy does not eliminate the incumbent's incentive to discriminate against an entrant but makes such discrimination easier to detect; however, the incumbent still may operate the competitive subsidiary at a loss by charging extremely high prices for access to the monopoly components of the network and obtain further advantages if it provides better technical capabilities or more complete and up-to-date information about the technical features of the network to its affiliate.

The last mechanism for coping with the interconnection issue is to attempt to formulate procompetitive rules for interconnection arrangements between the incumbent and its competitors. Interconnection regulation is an alternative to vertical segmentation for promoting long-distance competition and is at least temporarily a necessary means for promoting local access competition. Interconnection regulation has two components, one dealing with prices and the other dealing with technical interconnection arrangements.

With respect to pricing, the absence of effective practice has led to a three-way debate over the best theoretical approach. One proposal is to make use of price-cap regulation, another is to set interconnection prices equal to long-run average incremental cost, and the last is the ECPR. None is fully satisfactory because each has a significant potential loophole that could lead to inefficiencies.

If strategic considerations are ignored, price-cap regulation has the property that a firm will not offer a service if it is inefficient in doing so and will adopt Ramsey pricing—prices that exceed marginal cost by an amount inversely proportional to the elasticity of demand—for every service that it does offer. Unfortunately, strategic considerations may prevent price caps from assuring that efficient entry will occur.

First, the incumbent may wish to punish small-scale entry in one market as a means of foreclosing it in other markets, either to preserve monopoly elsewhere or to prevent the entrant from growing in a manner that would enable it to capture economies of scale, scope, or experience (learning by doing).

Second, the incumbent may enjoy opportunities for price discrimination in one market that are not available in another, which would be destroyed if the first market became competitive. By setting a high price for inputs for the potentially competitive market, the incumbent can create a price squeeze on competitors that permits the incumbent to practice price discrimination.

Third, price caps have the unfortunate property that they increase the attractiveness of predatory pricing strategies. In the absence of price-cap regulation, a firm will charge profit-maximizing prices in each market, but under binding price-cap regulation, profit-enhancing price increases are available (but unattainable) in each market. In the latter case, if a firm cuts its price predatorily, part of the financial losses during the predation period can be recovered by profit-enhancing price increases elsewhere.

The strategic possibilities under price caps are ameliorated if the services offered by a firm are separated into distinct groups, with a separate price cap for a bundle that contains only competitive services. This policy prevents offsetting anticompetitive prices in competitive markets with price changes in monopoly markets, which is the key to several of the strategies described above. But if regulators hope that all prices are potentially competitive but do not know the sequence and intensity of entry across services, they must either have a large number of small bundles or be prepared to redefine the bundles whenever a firm enters a new market or a new product is introduced. The former amounts to freezing the price of an incumbent monopolist when it faces entry (and so is anticompetitive), and in any case its implementation requires estimating costs. The latter amounts to something like cost-of-service regulation if entry is frequent and so bundles must be redefined frequently.

Another approach to pricing policy is simply to have regulators set interconnection prices equal to long-run average incremental cost. Specifically, this pricing rule requires charging an entrant only for the costs of creating a connection to the incumbent's network and then using that network. Aside from the problems of cost-of-service regulation, this system creates other problems as well. Suppose, for example, that the incumbent local access monopolist faces significantly different costs of service in different areas. If the regulator sets a single price equal to systemwide average cost, the entrant has a financial incentive to enter in places where the costs of local access are below average but to purchase interconnection service in areas where costs are high. If regulators set a separate price for each area, allowing prices to reflect differences in costs, they are required to devote far more resources to measuring the costs of the incumbent firm.

The approach followed in the United States is to establish elaborate regulatory rules regarding the interconnection services each carrier must offer and the prices they can charge.[21] In the United States, local access carriers are required to sell customer connections at wholesale (to be resold by their competitors), to "unbundle" and sell separately the components of local service so that their competitors can construct hybrid networks (partly their own facilities, partly the resold facilities of the incumbent), and to interconnect their networks to the networks of their competitors with service that is technically equivalent in quality and capability with the interconnection they provide to themselves. Moreover, all of these services are to be priced at the forward-looking long-run incremental cost of an efficiently designed network, regardless of the actual cost of the incumbent. Theoretically, this system is designed to generate exactly the scope and nature of entry that is most efficient; however, the informational requirements that this scheme places on regulators is truly awesome and probably beyond the capability of U.S. regulators, let alone regulators in much smaller countries.

In the process of setting interconnection prices, regulators also have faced another issue: whether the incumbent will be guaranteed that competition will not prevent it from recovering the costs of its investments (commonly called its "stranded costs"). The premise of such a guarantee is that regulation is a contract between the government and the incumbent monopolist in which the latter agrees to have its business decisions controlled by the government in return for the government's promise not to expropriate its capital. Thus the decision to permit competition is made equivalent to the decision to nationalize, with the government bearing the responsibility to compensate the incumbent for financial losses that it suffers due to competitive entry. The method for compensating the entrant

21. For a detailed exposition of this approach and its implementation problems, see Joskow and Noll (1999).

is not simply to appropriate the funds as part of the government's budget but to set interconnection prices in a manner that fully compensates the monopolist for its lost business, essentially making the monopolist indifferent between maintaining and losing its customers as long as its investments for serving them are in place. This argument was the basis for the Privy Council's decision regarding interconnection pricing by the incumbent monopolist in New Zealand.

If this view is accepted and if entry causes customers to switch to competitive service providers, entrants somehow must be taxed to pay the incumbent for the excess capacity that is left after customers migrate. Out of this requirement has emerged the ECPR (Willig 1979; Baumol and Sidak 1994). This approach to pricing was designed to be the least distorting method for pricing interconnection that insures the incumbent against financial loss. In essence, interconnection prices are set so that the incumbent recovers all the costs it did not save when its customers switched to its competitors. Thus suppose the incumbent's price, P, equals average cost, C, which can be decomposed as follows: $C = C_1 + C_2$, where C_1 is the component of cost that can be saved if a customer switches to an entrant and C_2 is the "stranded cost" component that remains after the customer switches. Under ECPR, the entrant must pay C_2 to the incumbent, so the entrant's financial cost of serving the customer is $C_2 + C_e$, where C_e is the entrant's average cost.[22] To compete effectively with the incumbent, the entrant must be able to offer service at the same or lower price as the incumbent charges, $P = C$. Thus the entrant can be profitable and compete effectively only if its average total cost, C_e is below the cost savings of the incumbent when the customer switches, C_1.

ECPR tracks the expected pricing behavior of a competitive firm facing either efficient entry or a fall in demand relative to supply in a competitive market. A firm will stay in the market as long as price exceeds variable cost. Hence, ECPR is efficient in the sense that entry occurs only if the entrant offers society a cost saving.

The policy issue raised by ECPR is the extent to which the effect of entry on prices in a competitive market sheds useful light on regulatory policy in a market that is making the transition from regulated or state-owned monopoly to competition that is very likely to be substantially less than perfect, and perhaps no more than duopoly. The conceptual foundation of ECPR is that the incumbent is operating efficiently with zero excess profits. In this milieu, entry can accomplish very little, even if the incumbent monopoly is not a natural. If one buys this assumption, then the ECPR framework makes sense—its main concern is protecting against

22. When entrants pay incumbents for several types of services, ECPR becomes a Ramsey pricing formula (the departure of each component price from long-run marginal cost is inversely proportional to the component's elasticity of demand), but the basic principles and effects are the same as in the simple example.

entrants who are not efficient but who, instead, are responding to distortions in pricing that arise in regulated markets.

The criticism of ECPR from both academic economists (Economides and White 1995; Joskow 1998; Laffont and Tirole 1998) and regulators arises primarily from a fundamentally different conceptual model of regulation. The critics start with the position that regulated or state-owned monopolies are inefficient, in particular, that they sit on a stock of costly and poorly performing investment, and that entry will lower costs (including investment costs). Under this assumption, the philosophical principle that the inefficient incumbent is entitled to continue to earn returns on its bad investments is not as compelling. To the critics, ECPR enshrines the inefficiencies of the incumbent carrier not only as social obligations that must be repaid but as obligations on competitors and their customers. By so doing, it reduces the benefits of allowing competition, which is to punish inefficient operation by the incumbent monopoly. Consequently, the critics tend to come down in favor of either price caps or forward-looking, cost-based methods for pricing unbundled network elements, and either this approach or no charge at all ("bill and keep") for call completion services between competing local carriers.

From the perspective of developing countries, the debate about interconnection pricing among economists in advanced, industrialized democracies has a certain otherworldly character. All of the cost-based pricing proposals for wholesale of network elements and all interconnection proposals other than bill-and-keep require a lot of information and a resource-rich regulator. Obviously, one cannot just take the word of the incumbent or a competitor concerning either the incumbent's historical incremental capital cost or the forward-looking average incremental cost of various services. To be effective, regulation must have sufficient sophistication to reduce the informational advantage of carriers, and in a complex, dynamic industry like telecommunications, satisfying this requirement is far from trivial. Moreover, even in the best of circumstances, the regulated prices that one competitor charges another are virtually certain to be "wrong" (not perfectly efficient) and hence to cause distortions in both entry and consumer prices. Thus, in developing countries, it probably is not worthwhile to pursue hybrid entry through regulating unbundled wholesale pricing of access elements except as a short-run strategy while entrants build their own networks, and it is probably quite attractive to consider bill-and-keep rather than completion charges among competitors.

The research literature does not support a very firm conclusion on which regulatory approach a nation should adopt for encouraging access entry, partly because the experience to date with any approach to interconnection pricing is too limited to support robust empirical analysis. Nevertheless, three policies are likely to be reasonably effective and easy to implement: to eliminate artificial barriers to entry that arise from imposing on entrants the same licensing requirements imposed on the incumbent monopolist; to separate local access from long distance, thereby eliminating the incentive of a local access supplier to discriminate in favor of its affiliate; and either to eliminate usage-based interconnection tariffs or to place a ceiling on interconnection prices that is closer to actual costs than the ECPR price, whether through cost-of-service regulation or a more arbitrarily selected price ceiling in a form of price-cap regulation that does not bundle monopoly and competitive services.

A useful side requirement is that originating and terminating access usage charges be equal both to each other and for local and long-distance carriers. The logic of this requirement rests mainly on the fact that origination and termination access costs are virtually identical and do not differ according to the distance of the call. Because long-distance calling has quite elastic demand, an incumbent monopolist faces a disincentive to raise long-distance prices through high usage-based access charges, which can dampen its ardor for high interconnection prices for local access if these interconnection prices must be equal. Likewise, if an incumbent is encouraged to exercise its market power in terminating access charges, a rule that requires a parallel increase in the incumbent's originating access charges will undermine its ability to compete for access customers.

Finally, the presence of regulation in telecommunications should not cause the industry to be ignored by competition policy agencies. Competition policy is not a panacea because it also requires substantial information. But ongoing independent scrutiny by competition policy agencies is useful because it provides an independent source of information and pressure in the regulatory process to encourage competition and thereby helps to protect against regulatory capture. Moreover, competition policy agencies are more expert in anticompetitive business strategies and so can assist regulators in implementing a policy to encourage entry.

In one important sense, some developing countries may face better prospects for significant competition in local access than the developed countries that are attempting to introduce it. The obvious disadvantage of developing countries is that their smaller markets may prevent competitors from achieving sufficient scale to be successful; however, as discussed above, the scale barriers to competition probably always were overstated and in any case are disappearing due to technological change. The advantage of developing economies is the poor performance of incumbent monopolists. Multiyear waiting lines and vast areas where no service is offered at all offer entrants the possibility of gaining a large number of new subscribers very quickly without having to win them from the incumbent. And poor service quality is likely to make customers less attached to the incumbent than is the case in developed countries, where service is generally much better. Of course, soon after neoliberal reform of an incumbent monopolist, these favorable conditions will erode because even a profit-maximizing monopolist will perform better on all these counts than a state-owned ministerial monopolist. Hence, nations that postpone opening their markets to competition risk forgoing the benefits of competition for a much longer time than the duration of the formal postponement.

6.4   Conclusions

Two areas of conclusions are suggested by the preceding analysis. One pertains to the policy advice that can be deduced from both theory and empirical analysis of the performance of the industry to date, and the other pertains to the areas where more knowledge might be very useful.

6.4.1   What We Know

Economic theory teaches that the first job of policymakers is to create institutions that convey the right incentives to buyers and sellers in a market. In the context of telecommunications, this task is made more difficult by the technical characteristics of the industry and its historical structure. The most important technical characteristic is its network character, which makes monopoly difficult to overcome even if the monopoly is not natural. History matters because of the inheritance of a nationalized structure that is highly politicized and highly inefficient. This history leads to bad news and good news: the bad is that some powerful political forces have a stake in preserving their private benefits that arise from the inefficiency, but the good news is that modest changes can create dramatic improvements in performance. There is nothing like a poorly performing nationalized incumbent to set the stage for a highly successful introduction of privatization and competition.

Getting more to the details, we know that governments have a powerful incentive to privatize in a manner that creates a monopoly, partly because this maximizes their revenues from privatization and partly because it threatens less disruption of employment by the incumbent. And simple privatization with weak regulation certainly solves the problem of the visible commitment to let the firm operate without expropriation for long enough to recover its investment. But this approach creates another problem, regulatory capture. If historical path dependence implies that the commitment problem is really not too severe while the window for relatively easy introduction of competition is short, the commitment to loosely regulated temporary monopoly is a mistake.

In any event, at least temporary monopoly is likely to be a reality regardless of how the industry is liberalized. Hence, for some period a country is well advised to attempt to control monopolistic behavior. To do so will benefit consumers and the national economy by providing lower prices, and because monopoly profits are not necessary to induce investment, lower prices do not come at the expense of slower improvements in service and expansion of capacity. Indeed, a plausible threat of competition is an inducement to improve service and increase capacity.

Economics is less clear about exactly what form regulation should take. In practice, all forms of regulation are distortionary and create incentives for anticompetitive behavior. Even though price-cap regulation as it appears in the theoretical literature cannot be implemented, the fundamental insight of price-cap regulation is useful and applicable: less intensive and more intermittent scrutiny of a firm's costs and profits actually produces, on average, lower costs and prices in the long run. Nevertheless, regardless of the name attached to the particular regulatory system, all realistic alternatives require that regulators periodically audit the firm and check not only for the reasonableness of the overall price structure in relation to costs but also for the reasonableness of specific prices that can have a significant effect on the viability of competition.

Of course, good regulation is expensive and may not be feasible in some countries. In these cases, the desirability of an early commitment to competition, when the incumbent is more vulnerable to successful entry, is especially important, for it can minimize the extent to which costly regulation will be needed. In addition, developing countries, especially smaller ones, might capture significant benefits from pooling their resources to form regional regulatory entities, which may be necessary to generate sufficient regulatory firepower to give competition even a fighting chance.

6.4.2   What We Don't Know

The main hole in research about neoliberal reform of telephone service in developing countries is empirical knowledge. Serious reforms only began in the mid- to late 1980s, and sufficient data to evaluate the many differences in details across countries is only now emerging. The comparative performance of different methods for reorganizing the incumbent and different regulatory systems, and their dependence on the history and circumstances of a country, in some cases have not been identified convincingly by theory and in other cases have not been quantified. As in much of applied microeconomics, the theory-to-fact ratio is far too high in this area.

Research to date has quite naturally focused on case studies of reforms. The best studies describe the reform (with varying degrees of detail), use basic principles of economics to make predictions about the incentive structure that was created by the reform, compare the pre- and postreform performance of the industry, and reach conclusions about its strengths and weaknesses. Sometimes these are gathered together in a multiauthor compendium that tries to make generalizations about the cases. Examples that exhibit considerable variation in the sophistication with which they pursue this approach are Levy and Spiller (1996), Galal et al. (1994), Kikeri, Nellis, and Shirley (1992), Petrazzini (1995), Ramamurti (1996), Roth (1987), and Wellenius and Stern (1994).

Whereas much of this work is extremely useful, its contribution has two important limits. First, the cases are not thoroughly integrated: they do not contain the same information and are not based on the same conceptual model because they have different authors who take somewhat different approaches. Any attempt to integrate them is limited by the absence of full comparability. Second, the number of cases is too small to support general conclusions. The books listed at the end of the preceding paragraph cover mostly the same cases and collectively provide reasonably complete information on only about ten developing countries. In short, the number of policy decisions in a reform process is so large that a summary of case studies that attempts to draw inferences about the independent contribution of each part of the reform has negative degrees of freedom. Of course, one cannot fault the authors and editors of comparative case studies for this shortcoming, for a book of case studies that could support an econometric test of the effects of differences in the details would be encyclopedic in length.

A few authors have tried to construct larger samples in order to sustain statistical analyses of the effects of reform. Examples are Boubakri and Cosset (1998), D'Souza and Megginson (1998), and Megginson et al. (1994). The strength of these papers is that they provide interesting information about the overall effect of reform on several measures of performance, including profits, prices, productivity, and investment. But to date, this work has not adopted a very comprehensive approach to characterizing the institutional and policy differences among reforming countries. Instead, reform is represented by simple indicators, such as whether a state-owned enterprise was privatized. As with the case studies, one cannot fault these authors for the simplicity with which they characterize reform, for the task of developing good quantitative indicators of the institutional details would require something like a case study for each country in the sample.

The main research agenda, then, is to combine the richness of institutional detail that one finds in the best case studies with a large enough statistical sample to support stronger conclusions about the direct links between distinct policy decisions and ultimate performance. This task is not a small one.

References

Armstrong, Mark, Simon Cowan, and John Vickers. 1994. *Regulatory reform: Economic analysis and British experience.* Cambridge, Mass.: MIT Press.

Arrow, Kenneth A. 1951. *Social choice and individual values.* New York: Wiley.

———. 1962. The economics of learning by doing. *Review of Economic Studies* 29:155–73.

Arthur, Brian. 1989. Competing technologies, increasing returns, and lock-in by historical events. *Economic Journal* 99:116–31.

————. 1994. *Increasing returns and path dependence.* Ann Arbor: University of Michigan Press.

Athreya, M. B. 1996. India's telecommunications policy. *Telecommunications Policy* 20:11–22.

Baron, David P. 1989. Design of regulatory mechanisms and institutions. In *Handbook of industrial organization,* vol. 2, ed. Richard Schmalensee and Robert Willig, 1347–1448. New York: North-Holland.

Baumol, William J., and J. Gregory Sidak. 1994. *Toward competition in local telephony.* Cambridge, Mass.: MIT Press.

Boubakri, Narjess, and Jean-Claude Cosset. 1998. The financial and operating performance of newly privatized firms. *Journal of Finance* 53:1081–1110.

Brock, Gerald W. 1981. *The telecommunications industry: The dynamics of market structure.* Cambridge, Mass.: Harvard University Press.

Chowdary, T. H. 1998. Politics and economics of telecom liberalization in India. *Telecommunications Policy* 22:9–22.

Crandall, Robert W., and Leonard Waverman. 1995. *Talk is cheap.* Washington, D.C.: Brookings Institution.

David, Paul A. 1985. Clio and the economics of QWERTY. *American Economic Review Papers and Proceedings* 75:332–37.

————. 1993. Path-dependence and predictability in dynamical systems with local network externalities: A paradigm for economic history. In *Technology and the wealth of nations,* ed. Dominique Foray and Christopher Freeman. London: Pinter.

Derthick, Martha, and Paul Quirk. 1985. *The politics of deregulation.* Washington, D.C.: Brookings Institution.

Drake, William J., rapporteur. 1999. *Toward sustainable competition in global telecommunications: From principle to practice.* Washington, D.C.: Aspen Institute.

D'Souza, Juliet, and William L. Megginson. 1998. Sources of performance improvement in privatized firms: A clinical study of the telecommunication industry. Athens: University of Georgia. Manuscript.

Economides, Nicholas, and Lawrence White. 1995. Access and interconnection pricing: How efficient is the "efficient component pricing rule"? *Antitrust Bulletin,* fall, 557–79.

Esfahani, Hadi Salehi. 1996. The political economy of the telecommunications sector in the Philippines. In *Regulations, institutions, and commitment: Comparative studies of telecommunications,* ed. Brian Levy and Pablo T. Spiller, 145–201. New York: Oxford University Press.

Farrell, Joseph, and Carl Shapiro. 1988. Dynamic competition and switching costs. *Rand Journal of Economics* 19:123–37.

————. 1989. Optimal contracts with lock-in. *American Economic Review* 79: 51–68.

Galal, Ahmed. 1996. Chile: Regulatory specificity, credibility of commitment, and distributional demands. In *Regulations, institutions, and commitment: Comparative studies of telecommunications,* ed. Brian Levy and Pablo T. Spiller, 121–44. New York: Cambridge University Press.

Galal, Ahmed, Leroy Jones, Pankaj Tandon, and Ingo Vogelsang. 1994. *The welfare consequences of selling public enterprises: An empirical analysis.* New York: Oxford University Press.

Galal, Ahmed, and Bharat Nauriyal. 1995. Regulating telecommunications in developing countries. Policy Research Working Paper no. 1520. Washington, D.C.: World Bank.

Gillary, Carin Lisa. 1999. *The effect of political stability on the outcome of telecommunications privatization in developing countries.* Senior thesis, Stanford University, Stanford, Calif.

Goldstein, Judith. 1986. The political economy of trade: Institutions of protection. *American Political Science Review* 80:161–84.

———. 1993. *Ideas, interest, and American trade policy.* Ithaca, N.Y.: Cornell University Press.

Hicks, John R. 1939. The foundations of welfare economics. *Economic Journal* 49:696–712.

Hill, Alice, and Manuel Angel Abdala. 1996. Argentina: The sequencing of privatization and regulation. In *Regulations, institutions, and commitment: Comparative studies of telecommunications,* ed. Brian Levy and Pablo T. Spiller, 202–50. New York: Cambridge University Press.

International Telecommunication Union. 1998. *World telecommunications indicators: Chronological time series, 1960–1996.* Geneva: International Telecommunication Union. Diskettes.

Joskow, Paul L. 1974. Inflation and environmental concern: Structural change in the process of public utility price regulation. *Journal of Law and Economics* 17:291–328.

———. 1998. Regulatory priorities for reforming infrastructure sectors in developing countries. Washington, D.C.: World Bank. Manuscript.

Joskow, Paul L., and Roger G. Noll. 1999. The Bell doctrine. *Stanford Law Review* 51:1249–1315.

Kaldor, Nicholas. 1939. Welfare propositions in economics. *Economic Journal* 49:549–52.

Kerf, Michel, and Warrick Smith. 1996. Privatizing Africa's infrastructure: Promise and challenge. Africa Region Series, Technical Paper no. 337. Washington, D.C.: World Bank.

Kikeri, Sunita, John Nellis, and Mary Shirley. 1992. *Privatization: The lessons of experience.* Washington, D.C.: World Bank.

Kingsbury, John E. 1915. *The telephone and telegraphy exchange: Their invention and development.* London: Longman Green.

Laffont, Jean-Jacques, and Jean Tirole. 1998. *Competition in telecommunications: Munich lectures.* Toulouse: Univeriste Sciences Sociales. Manuscript.

Levy, Brian, and Pablo T. Spiller. 1996. A framework for resolving the regulatory problem. In *Regulations, institutions, and commitment: Comparative studies of telecommunications,* ed. Brian Levy and Pablo T. Spiller, 1–35. New York: Cambridge University Press.

Manzetti, Luigi. 1997. Privatization and regulation: Lessons from Argentina and Chile. *North-South Agenda,* no. 24.

Marshall, Alfred. (1879) 1935. *The pure theory of foreign trade; The pure theory of domestic values.* London: London School of Economics Press.

McCubbins, Mathew D., Roger G. Noll, and Barry R. Weingast. 1987. Administrative procedures as instruments of political control. *Journal of Law, Economics, and Organization* 3:243–77.

———. 1989. Structure and process, politics and policy: Administrative arrangements and the political control of agencies. *Virginia Law Review* 78:431–82.

McKelvey, Richard D. 1979. General conditions for global intransitivities in formal voting models. *Econometrica* 47:1085–1111.

Megginson, William L., Robert C. Nash, and Matthias Van Randenborgh. 1994. The financial and operating performance of newly privatized firms: An international empirical analysis. *Journal of Finance* 49:847–59.

Mustafa, Mohammad A., Bruce Laidlaw, and Mark Brand. 1997. Telecommunications policies in sub-Saharan Africa. Discussion Paper no. 353. Washington, D.C.: World Bank.

Noll, Roger G. 1985. "Let them make toll calls": A state regulator's lament. *American Economic Review Papers and Proceedings* 75:52–56.

———. 1989. Economic perspectives on the politics of regulation. In *Handbook of industrial organization,* vol. 2, ed. Richard Schmalensee and Robert Willig, 1253–88. New York: North-Holland.

———. 1997. Internationalizing regulatory reform. In *Comparative disadvantages?* ed. Pietro Nivola. Washington, D.C.: Brookings Institution.

———. 2000. Regulatory reform and international trade policy. In *Deregulation and interdependence in the Asia-Pacific region,* ed. Takatoshi Ito and Anne O. Krueger. Chicago: University of Chicago Press.

Noll, Roger G., and Barry R. Weingast. 1991. Rational actor theory, social norms, and policy implementation: Applications to administrative processes and bureaucratic culture. In *The economic approach to politics: A critical reassessment of the theory of rational action,* ed. Kristen Renwick Monroe. New York: Harper Collins.

Panda, Sonal Sharadkumar. 1999. *For whom the bell tolls: Domestic institutions and the political economy of telecommunications reform in developing countries.* Senior thesis, Stanford University, Stanford, Calif.

Petrazzini, Ben A. 1995. *The political economy of telecommunications reform in developing countries: Privatization and liberalization in comparative perspective.* Westport, Conn.: Greenwood.

———. 1996. Telecommunications policy in India: The political underpinnings of reform. *Telecommunications Policy* 20:39–51.

Ramamurti, Rava, ed. 1996. *Privatizing monopolies: Lessons from the telecommunications and transport sectors in Latin America.* Baltimore: Johns Hopkins University Press.

Romer, Paul. 1986. Increasing returns and long-run growth. *Journal of Political Economy* 94:1002–37.

———. 1990. Endogenous technological change. *Journal of Political Economy* 98 (pt. 2): S71–S102.

Roth, Gabriel. 1987. *The private provision of public services in developing countries.* New York: Oxford University Press.

Saunders, Robert, Jeremy J. Warford, and Bjorn Wellenius. 1983. *Telecommunications and economic development.* Baltimore: Johns Hopkins University Press.

Shepsle, Kenneth A. 1979. Institutional arrangements and equilibrium in multidimensional voting models. *American Journal of Political Science* 23:27–59.

Shepsle, Kenneth A., and Barry R. Weingast. 1981. Structure-induced equilibrium and legislative choice. *Public Choice* 37:503–20.

Sinha, Nikhil. 1996. The political economy of India's telecommunications reforms. *Telecommunications Policy* 20:23–38.

Snow, Marcellus S., ed. 1986. *Marketplace for telecommunications.* New York: Longman.

Tyler, Michael, and Carol Joy. 1997. *1.1.98—Telecommunications in the new era: Competing in the single market.* London: Multiplex.

Vickers, John, and George Yarrow. 1988. *Privatization: An economic analysis.* Cambridge, Mass.: MIT Press.

Wellenius, Bjorn. 1998. Regulating the telecommunications sector: The experience in Latin America. Washington, D.C.: World Bank. Manuscript.

Wellenius, Bjorn, and Peter A. Stern, eds. 1994. *Implementing reforms in the telecommunications sector: Lessons from experience.* Washington, D.C.: World Bank.

Willig, Robert D. 1979. The theory of network access pricing. In *Issues in public utility regulation,* ed. Henry M. Trebing. East Lansing: Michigan State University Public Utilities Papers.

Comment on the Paper by Roger G. Noll   Takatoshi Ito

In the past two decades, industries traditionally considered to be producing "public goods"—airlines, railroads, telecommunications, and electricity—have been successfully deregulated and privatized in many countries. Three factors seem to have motivated this change. First, government management of these utilities has been plagued by corruption, overstaffing, inefficient pricing, and cross-subsidies. Second, technological changes have reduced fixed costs, thus facilitating more competition. Third, demand for these utilities has gone beyond the "civil minimum," necessitating innovative management, which is more likely under privatization.

Roger Noll describes why telecommunications reform is necessary in developing countries. Specifically, competition is now possible in large measure because of technological change. First, technological advances in microwaves and fiberoptics have made it possible for more companies to break into long-distance telephone services. Second, mobile phones are now competing with fixed phones. The former may well be a more efficient way of providing telecommunications in developing countries given the high fixed costs of extending telephone lines. Third, the introduction of satellite phones in the near future will make barriers between local and international services irrelevant. Finally, a strong source of competition to local phones may well come from cable TV.

Pricing reform is an important issue in this industry. Will elaborate price-cap regulation be needed? Will enhanced competition due to technological changes make price regulation unnecessary? Will universal service and quality be assured under reform?

Finally, it is important to consider whether telecommunications policies in developing countries should differ from those in advanced countries. It would be useful to differentiate appropriate telecommunications strategies for countries with different income levels. Why have some developing countries made progress and others not? In terms of ownership structure, should developing countries move to the AT&T atomized model? Or the partial privatization of the NTT model? The paper emphasizes that getting the institutions right in the beginning is important. But if the first step is wrong, the dynamic path may not lead to the right endpoint. These are important issues to consider in the future.

Takatoshi Ito is deputy vice minister for international affairs in the Ministry of Finance, Japan, and former professor of economics at Hitotsubashi University.

7

Reforming Urban Water Systems in Developing Countries

Roger G. Noll, Mary M. Shirley, and Simon Cowan

Political, technological, and institutional changes have spurred many developing countries to adopt reforms in order to improve the performance of their infrastructural industries by setting prices that are more in line with costs, creating independent regulatory agencies, involving the private sector in formerly nationalized industries, and allowing more competition. The earliest reforms were in telecommunications (see chap. 6 in this volume) and transportation, and quite a bit of economics research has focused on these sectors. More recently, electricity and urban water systems have been included in the reform process. While some research has examined electricity reform, very little has dealt with water.

This chapter analyzes reforms of urban water systems. The chapter first summarizes and extends the basic economic conceptual model of water systems and then applies this model to organize and to compare the results of World Bank case studies of reforms in the capital cities of six developing countries.[1] The main theme is that water supply, though conceptu-

Roger G. Noll is the Morris M. Doyle Professor of Public Policy in the Department of Economics and a senior fellow of the Stanford Institute for Economic Policy Research at Stanford University, and a senior fellow of the Brookings Institution. Mary M. Shirley is the research manager for competition policy and regulation in the Development Research Group at the World Bank. Simon Cowan is a Wigmore Fellow and tutor in economics at Worcester College, Oxford.

The views expressed are the authors' own and do not necessarily reflect those of the World Bank, its Board of Directors, or the countries they represent. The authors thank Penelope Brook-Cowen, George Clarke, Luke Haggarty, Takatoshi Ito, Anne Krueger, Mathew Mc-Cubbins, Scott Wallsten, Ana Maria Zuluaga, and conference participants for their very useful suggestions. Roger Noll gratefully acknowledges research support from the Markle Foundation.

1. The six studies are Alcazar et al. (1999) for Buenos Aires, Argentina; Alcazar, Xu, and Zuluaga (1999) for Lima, Peru; Haggarty, Brook-Cowen, and Zuluaga (1999) for Mexico

ally rather simple and seemingly straightforward to reform, is sufficiently different from other infrastructural industries that appropriate reform is more variable across countries and is frequently very difficult.

Water supply has four key features that strongly affect the choice of the best performing organization of the market. First, the costs, availability, and quality of water resources vary substantially according to locality, leading to major differences in appropriate market structure, regulatory institutions, and price rules. Second, direct competition is possible in some aspects of water supply, but in others it frequently is neither feasible nor socially desirable, and the appropriate scope of competition also depends on local conditions. Third, average asset lives are very long in water supply, so governments face considerable obstacles in trying to convince private companies that economically reasonable depreciation rules will stay in place long enough to allow capital costs eventually to be recovered. Fourth, water use causes important health and environmental externalities that frequently are very difficult to internalize or to regulate efficiently.

Despite these problems, many countries have begun to experiment with reforms that involve some degree of private participation. The World Bank utility database lists fifty-three cases in which private operators manage urban water or sewage systems in twenty-seven developing countries. Of these, only three are sales of equity to private operators. Differences between water and other utilities and local differences in water resources and institutions are reflected in the variety of governance institutions and forms of private participation. A majority (29) are concessions in which the operator is responsible for investment in expansion as well as operations; the rest are management contracts (11) and leases (10).[2]

The difficulty in approximating optimal management of a water system in practice is illustrated by recent water reforms in Abidjan, Côte d'Ivoire; Buenos Aires, Argentina; Conakry, Guinea; Lima, Peru; Mexico City, Mexico; and Santiago, Chile.[3] The two systems in this group with the highest costs are Lima and Mexico City. Because of their locations and water endowments, water consumption in these two cities produces costly externalities: water-borne diseases from pollution in Lima and damage to buildings from ground subsidence as the aquifer is depleted in Mexico City. In both cities, the reform process was terminated before an efficient

---

City, Mexico; Shirley, Xu, and Zuluaga (1999) for Santiago, Chile; and Menard and Clarke (1999a, 1999b) for Conakry, Guinea, and Abidjan, Côte d'Ivoire.

2. Data on private participation in infrastructure are assembled by the Private Sector Development Department. We exclude private participation in the construction and operation of single greenfield plants or facilities (most of which are "BOT" schemes, in which a private entity builds a facility, operates it for a while, and then transfers ownership of it to a governmental entity).

3. The lease contracts in Côte d'Ivoire and Guinea cover all major urban areas in the country. Our numbers cover only the capital cities unless otherwise indicated; however, the nature of the leases distorts some of the indicators.

policy and institutional structure was in place because the political costs of change were too great. In contrast, Abidjan, Buenos Aires, Conakry, and Santiago have sustainable water systems with lower opportunity and externality costs. In three of these cities, reform has worked reasonably well, but in the fourth, Conakry, weak governance institutions have caused the benefits of reforms to be less than was realistically feasible, despite enormous possibilities for delivering greater net social benefits.

The experience with reforms in these cases illustrates the effects of water's unique characteristics. Because competition has not been part of any reform plan and, in any event, is likely to have more limited efficient scope than in other infrastructure, reformers have faced greater regulatory challenges. The presence of important externalities in some locales further complicates regulation and creates political problems. Nevertheless, water's distinguishing characteristics do not imply that private participation is undesirable. Even in very weak institutional environments, such as Guinea, private participation plausibly is more efficient than a system of public management.

The next section summarizes the economic theory of water policy. Following that we consider supply, demand, and policy in our case studies and then assess their recent reform efforts. We conclude with some pressing issues for further research.

7.1 Economic Theory of Water System Policy

The economic theory of water supply yields several important implications for policy and the political feasibility of reform. The economics of urban water systems has four main components: (1) the private supply cost of water delivery, (2) the demand for water by major customer groups, (3) the externalities associated with water delivery and use, and (4) the market and political institutions that allocate water among competing uses. We first consider supply costs and their implications for policy and political feasibility, distinguishing between renewable and nonrenewable water resources. Next we consider demand, externalities, and regulatory instruments.

7.1.1 Water Costs

The cost of exploiting a water resource depends on whether current extraction rates are sustainable. Water usage is sustainable if the net usage of water (including the maintenance of the quality of the water that remains and is returned to the environment) is now, and in the future will be, less than the inflow. If usage is sustainable, the opportunity cost of incremental water use today is zero. In this case, the only relevant costs of the resource are the private costs of water treatment and distribution plus the external costs of exploitation and use. If water use at prices reflecting these costs exceeds inflow, either temporarily or permanently, then usage in one period has an opportunity cost equal to the net value of forgone use in the future. We first consider the costs of sustainable resource systems then extend the analysis to unsustainable systems.

Private Costs of Sustainable Resource Systems

Water delivery systems have four components: (1) capturing the basic natural resource (diversions, reservoirs, and wells), (2) transporting the water to areas where it will have an economic use (aqueducts, penstocks, and mains), (3) treating the water to raise its quality, and (4) delivering water to users (ditches, pipes, and taps). All components require very long term investments in fixed capital assets. Although operating costs can be substantial for treatment facilities and for wells and transport options that involve extensive pumping, the fixed costs of a water system usually are very high compared to the variable costs. For example, fixed costs account for over 80 percent of the costs of supplying water in the United Kingdom (Armstrong, Cowan, and Vickers 1994).[4]

The private costs of water systems depend on the short-term variability in the flow of water into the resource. If water usage always is less than inflow throughout the year, water system design is greatly simplified. Water need not be stored, so that capture simply means diverting water into the transportation system. Pumps and diversion canals provide a steady flow of water to satisfy all demand at all times.[5]

In most water systems, some components exhibit engineering economies of scale and so appear to be a natural monopoly. Of course, engineering scale economies do not necessarily translate into organizational scale economies that cause the most efficient market structure to be a monopoly. Three factors can offset engineering scale economies: diseconomies of scale in organizational management, quality-differentiated demand that cannot be satisfied efficiently in a single network, and productive inefficiencies arising from lack of competition. The consensus view is that the simplicity and generally low cost of water systems causes water to be the most likely infrastructural industry to be a natural monopoly; however, this conclusion has not been the subject of extensive empirical testing, and some analysts believe that considerable competition could be introduced

4. Storage systems typically are extremely durable, long-term capital investments with negligible variable costs. The classic example is a large reservoir, but another common storage method is simply to flood the surface above a large underground aquifer to increase the water table for later well extraction.

5. Seasonal and annual variability in the flow of water into the resource introduces another source of costs. Intermittent flows can cause temporary circumstances in which usage exceeds inflow, even though over a longer period usage is less than total inflow. For subsurface aquifers, pumping that exceeds inflow causes the water table to drop, thereby increasing pumping costs. For all types of water sources, storage systems can be used to transfer water from periods of excessive supply to periods of excess demand.

into at least some aspects of water supply (London Economics 1998). For reasons explored below, this conclusion probably is not accurate for all aspects of urban water systems in all locations, but it is probably true for some components of many systems.

Water transportation and distribution systems typically exhibit engineering scale economies for two reasons. First, the capacity of a canal or pipe is governed by its cross-sectional area, which increases in proportion to the square of the external dimensions of the conduit. While larger conduits must withstand more weight, within the relevant scale range strength requirements do not offset the volumetric gain from expanded circumference. Second, larger canals and pipes have less turbulence, so that effective capacity expands more rapidly than in proportion to the expansion of the cross-sectional area of the conduit.

Likewise, water capture from a particular resource also is likely to have natural monopoly characteristics. A reservoir typically exhibits substantial economies of scale up to an upper bound that is determined by the geology of the site and the intertemporal variation in water flow. For example, a dam to impound a river with a highly variable seasonal flow at the bottom of a deep canyon typically will have huge economies of scale up to a storage capacity that is many times annual flow. A large minimum efficient scale of a single reservoir, however, does not imply a natural monopoly in either the entire system or even in the part of the system that requires these facilities. In multireservoir water systems, a single reservoir is like a single electrical generation facility in a large electrical grid. Analogously to electrical utilities, in a multireservoir system one can imagine a decentralized, competitive wholesale water market in which competing reservoirs bid to deliver water to either long-distance transportation systems or user communities.

Pumping from an underground aquifer is not a natural monopoly; however, efficient pumping may require some form of centralized management. Pumping from many wells, whether from a fully renewable underground aquifer or an aquifer that serves as a reservoir through injections in periods of excess flow, can be organized into multiple, independent sources. However, because pumping from one well can cause a drop in the water table such that pumping at other wells is more expensive, efficient exploitation of a single aquifer from many wells may require some form of centralized regulation of pumping. Whether managing the externality is more efficiently accomplished through owning all the wells or coordinating their outputs (perhaps by production taxes) is an empirical question. In the petroleum industry, where the pumping externality also is important, decentralized ownership of wells combined with centralized, cooperative field management is widespread, indicating that a similar structure might be most efficient in water systems.

Finally, water treatment is mildly a natural monopoly. Whereas treatment plants in themselves may not exhibit scale economies, treating water that is delivered from a single transportation system is likely to be most efficiently accomplished at a single site at or near the end of the transportation conduit, as opposed to diverting the water through separate conduits to several different treatment plants.

Two significant conclusions follow from this discussion of the direct costs of water systems. First, even though capture, transportation, and treatment from each water resource may be a natural monopoly, for urban systems that rely on multiple water sources, decentralization and competition among vertically integrated entities that operate a single capture-transportation system still may be feasible. Second, distribution is most likely to be a natural monopoly bottleneck to an urban water system.

Whereas competition in any component of the piped water system has not been considered in any of the water systems in our sample, it is not entirely unknown (Roth 1987). In many urban areas in poor countries where the piped distribution system is sparsely developed or delivers water of poor quality, private water vendors, using trucks or carrying large water bottles, sell potable water on the streets. In addition, some residents dig private wells or construct catchment facilities for rainwater as an alternative to obtaining piped water. Finally, parallel piped water systems can be found in some arid areas, where one system delivers pure water for direct human consumption and the other delivers lower quality or reclaimed water for such uses as flushing toilets and watering gardens. Thus some competition even in delivery, based on quality differentiation and price, can be found, indicating that reformers ought to consider whether their water system really is a ubiquitous natural monopoly.

Policy Implications of the Cost Structure

A water system's high ratio of fixed to variable costs has important implications for pricing. As long as average water flow exceeds average use in the long run, the optimal pricing structure is a two-part tariff. The first part is a capacity charge that determines a user's maximum usage during periods of excess demand plus any other costs that are not recovered from the second part. The second part is a usage price equal to marginal cost.

Two alternatives to the optimal two-part tariff are theoretically less efficient but may be practically attractive because they are easier to implement. One is a two-part tariff in which the first part is a fixed hook-up charge that does not imply a limit on usage. The second is a variant of peak-load pricing, in which usage prices include capital costs and, during the low-flow period, are higher to reflect the marginal cost of storage capacity. These price structures are less efficient than the capacity charge approach because they do not permit consumers to determine their maximal claim on capacity in low-flow periods, but they are easier to implement because they do not require that utilities have the technical capability to cap individual usage during low-flow periods.

Because the marginal cost of water usage frequently is very low except in periods of temporary shortage, the implied usage charge in a two-part tariff also is very low. Indeed, in many systems, especially ones that tap nearby abundant resources, the costs of metering and usage-based billing are high compared to the cost of water, in which case the question arises whether metering is actually worth the cost. The principles guiding the decision to meter, however, extend beyond whether charging for usage vastly increases the system's marginal cost of delivering water to customers. For metering to be justified, the efficiency gains from giving customers an incentive to curtail usage that has a high variable cost or a high opportunity cost due to variability of flow must offset the transactions costs of metering. A third consideration is whether usage-based prices are an efficient means to internalize the costs of externalities from water use. This issue is discussed at length below. The important point here is that if externalities are a substantial part of the cost of urban water systems, the benefits from charging for usage can tip the scales in favor of metering even in cases in which the direct private costs of supply (delivery and storage) are very low.

Costs, Rents, and the Political Economy of Water

Regardless of the details of the price structure, a high ratio of fixed to variable costs in a self-financing water utility implies that a large proportion of revenue is quasi rents. By definition these quasi rents do not need to be collected in the short run to induce continued supply. Because capital investments in water systems are extremely durable, a water utility may be able to operate for many years, even decades, without recovering its fixed costs. But if quasi rents are not paid, investors will not recover their investments, and private funds for new investments are not likely to be forthcoming. If the urban area is experiencing economic development or population growth, underinvestment soon leads to shortages even if the system is operating well, but even in a static community, eventually elements of the system will need to be replaced. Hence, if a society decides to rely on private water distribution, optimal future investment requires that the government be able to make a credible promise that it will not expropriate these quasi rents from investors by imposing low prices. We will return to the problem of commitments after discussing other issues that can give rise to regulatory supervision of water utilities.

Quasi rents are not the only rents arising in water systems. Two others are monopoly rents and Ricardian rents. Monopoly rents arise when a water utility can set price above average cost because effective competition is absent. Ricardian rents do not arise from market power but from the superior productivity of better resources. Ricardian rents can occur under optimal pricing in a water system with multiple sources or storage sites. For example, a water system in a region with a large river and an underground aquifer may be optimally served by one large reservoir and some wells. In this case, the first-best usage price will include the pumping cost of the wells, causing the usage price of water from the reservoir to be above its marginal cost.

Whereas payments of quasi rents have important implications for efficiency, these other forms of rents do not contribute to efficiency, and in most societies they carry little, no, or even negative normative weight as distributional entitlements.[6] On the contrary, policy intervention to limit monopoly profits can improve efficiency as well as distribution. Whereas monopolists theoretically can extract excess profits through an efficient system of price discrimination, the more common circumstance is for some prices to exceed corresponding marginal costs and hence inefficiently to exclude some users whose valuation of output exceeds the cost of supplying it.

The Regulatory Design Problem: Commitment without Capture

Monopoly rents, high fixed costs, and different costs from different resources create a potential problem for government to commit to allow efficient prices and full cost recovery in water systems, a problem that is certainly important in other infrastructural industries but may be most important in water. The presence of substantial rents can give rise to two types of political demands to extract these rents.

First, consumer groups may organize to force down prices to average total cost (to extract Ricardian rents) or even average variable cost (to extract quasi rents). The effect of this policy is to encourage consumption while discouraging investment, thereby creating excess demand. Second, water utilities may be able to siphon substantial cash from the system. If this cash flow is siphoned by operators (whether private or public) rather than used to pay off investors or to make necessary repairs and replacement investments, the water system eventually will deteriorate, again causing excess demand but in this case at high, rather than low, prices.

The possibility of monopoly rents is especially important not just because of allocative and productive inefficiencies but also because they give

---

6. Unlike quasi rents but like monopoly rents, investors do not need to receive Ricardian rents to induce future investments; however, if the productivity of a resource is uncertain until an attempt is made to exploit it, the recovery of at least some Ricardian rents ex post is necessary to induce optimal exploration for new resources ex ante. Exploration incentives are unlikely to be very important in the case of water supply, so that the recovery of Ricardian rents is unlikely to have significant efficiency consequences. The main problem arising from an attempt to extract Ricardian rents is that the method employed frequently is to set prices equal to the average cost of water. These prices are below the marginal cost of supply, forcing utilities to satisfy demand by exploiting expensive resources for which the cost of water is below its value to consumers. For example, British Gas, the distributor of natural gas in the United Kingdom, used to relate its retail price to the average price paid to gas suppliers at the beachhead. In the 1980s the retail price was below marginal costs because marginal fields were more expensive to develop. Improved extraction technology, however, has meant that price has been above marginal cost in the 1990s. See Armstrong et al. (1994).

rise to pressure for regulation or other government intervention to reduce prices and improve service. Thus the presence of a natural monopoly in some aspects of water delivery increases the credibility problem. Given that political pressures to control monopoly are widely regarded as normatively valid and so are probably impossible and certainly difficult to resist, how can government commit to limit monopoly rents, while not expropriating quasi rents and inefficiently extracting Ricardian rents as well?

Governments have no perfect way to make these commitments, but they can increase the likelihood that a commitment will be honored by increasing the difficulty of abrogating it.[7] The likely durability of a commitment can be increased in four ways:

1. Insulate governance institutions from short-term political forces that influence elected officials and civil servants who serve at their pleasure. Examples are regulatory authorities and judicial overseers with long-term appointments and decision-making autonomy.
2. Create "high law" (like the U.S. Constitution) that is difficult to amend to protect the rights of investors. One example is a rule stipulating that the government cannot unilaterally abrogate contracts with private entities, and another is constitutional protection against expropriation of property without reasonable compensation (in this case, the value of utility assets in a hypothetical competitive regime).
3. Adopt a system of representation that reduces the likelihood that advocates of expropriation will gain power. Examples are proportional representation and separation of powers, that is, governments in which policy change requires unanimous consent among several political bodies, each having a different base in the electorate.
4. Commit financial resources to large projects, such as by making loans, guaranteeing debt, or issuing contingent liabilities that mature only if assets are expropriated. The government also can maintain a large but not controlling equity stake so that it bears part of the financial cost of low prices.

Commitment mechanisms can give rise to regulatory capture. If regulation is too distant from broadly based political pressures or too vigilantly protects the government's financial stake, it can become a mechanism for serving the interests of the regulated entity. Excessively protective regulation has been as much a problem as expropriation, as reflected by the fact that most of the research literature on the politics of regulation focuses on capture, not expropriation.

The risk of capture is increased when the design of regulatory agencies makes them responsive to the regulated utility or some other organized interest among its customers and suppliers. Regulation is inherently anti-

7. See Lupia and McCubbins (1998) for a formal treatment of these mechanisms.

competitive because it causes price and entry decisions to be the result of a nonmarket interaction among interested groups that participate in the regulatory process.[8] Because participation is expensive, the information and political pressures that an agency receives are likely to be biased in favor of groups with large stakes in its decisions. Design instruments for ameliorating excessive influence by well-organized interests are open information, procedural transparency, standing for anyone affected by a regulatory decision and competition policy advocates, and a broad scope for judicial review.

Vertical separation of a water system that has multiple sources can provide additional protection against regulatory capture and also can reduce expropriation and commitment problems. If a local retail utility buys water at market prices from multiple sources, the distribution system is likely to be the only significant source of monopoly rents and so can be directly regulated for this purpose. The remainder of the system can be freed by statute from the authority of the regulator and instead governed solely by competition policy. Whereas a distribution utility will have high sunk costs and so will need to collect quasi rents to maintain efficient investment, most of the quasi rents and most likely all of the Ricardian rents will be spread over many independent actors rather than in a single, vertically integrated entity.

Extensions to Unsustainable Resources with Externalities

The preceding analysis deals with a water system in which exploitation does not cause the quality of the resource to decline for either urban customers or others who are not part of the water system. Some water resources, for example, a large lake or underground aquifer, can be regarded as essentially nonrenewable. Using part of that resource today has the opportunity cost of using the same quantity of water in the future. In addition, extracting more water now can raise the cost of extracting a given quantity tomorrow as a lake becomes smaller or an underground water table sinks. Likewise, greater exploitation today can lower water quality for other uses either now or in the future.[9] First-best usage prices must take into account all of these effects so that each user faces the marginal direct cost plus the opportunity cost of water usage.

In principle, regardless of whether water use is sustainable in the long run, users who suffer temporarily from deteriorating quality, higher costs, or lower availability can outbid other immediate users to retain the size and quality of the resource. The same principle applies to allocating water usage through time if usage is not sustainable. Variation in the market

---

8. For a summary of the literature on how imperfect information and the economics of organization bias regulatory outcomes, see Noll (1989).

9. See, e.g., Gisser (1983) on the economics of nonrenewable water.

value of usage typically can be dealt with efficiently if permanent, transferable property rights in the resource are well defined. Under such circumstances the holder of the resource can balance the financial benefits of short-term exploitation against the return from postponing exploitation to a period when the market price is higher. As long as water prices fully reflect all of the social costs of water exploitation and usage, including the opportunity cost of future use, there is no reason to believe that markets for a finite and diminishing stock of water will work any less well than markets for other nonrenewable resources.

In practice, Coasian transactions costs may be sufficiently different among categories of users that the market on its own does not adequately deal with these problems. In addition, collective action problems may mean that some users are not organized to participate effectively in a market for water supplies, so that their valuations of water will not affect water allocation. Whereas these problems can prevent some efficient uses of a renewable resource, the problem is worse as well as more complicated if effective demand is not sustainable because in this case excessive use by one group imposes harm on another group. For example, people who live on a river or lake may have their welfare adversely affected by a drop in the water's edge, but if they are not part of the market for the affected water source, they cannot bid to retain an adequate water level. Or as is the case in Mexico City, property owners are adversely affected if the depletion of an aquifer causes ground subsidence, cracking buildings and making some structures unsafe. If for some reason components of a full-blown water market fail to emerge because of externalities, incompletely defined property rights, and transactions costs, market allocations will be inefficient.

In principle, the government can compensate for this form of market failure by either taxing usage or directly allocating quantities independently of the price system. In practice, efficiently intervening in either way is itself subject to distorting influences because the political influence of the various groups (such as urban dwellers, farmers, and fishermen) will not necessarily accurately reflect the opportunity cost of water to each. Indeed, organizational and institutional factors that distort the market are likely to distort political influence as well. For these reasons, the best policy response to water market distortions may be no policy at all, or it may be to facilitate the creation of an organization to aggregate the demands of the excluded users.

7.1.2   Water Demand

The significance of water, as distinct from other infrastructural industries, derives from the fact that human survival depends on access to water that is free of unhealthy pollutants. Hence, at some level, the demand for healthful water must be perfectly inelastic. As a practical matter, water demand for many uses is likely to exhibit some elasticity, with estimates for developing countries in the range of -0.25 and -0.7. Even in the poorest urban areas many uses of water are not purely for subsistence. Moreover, humans pick areas for urban settlement on the basis of the economic value of the location, including whether water supply is sufficient to make human life sustainable. Consequently, even where water is relatively expensive, the price is still low enough that marginal uses among low-income households are far more prosaic than sustaining human life, such as washing, cleaning, and gardening.

For essentially all uses, water consumption can be varied substantially by small changes in usage methods. Water is usually one input into a household production process, with opportunities for changes in input proportions in response to movements in relative prices. Moreover, part of demand is euphemistically called "waste," that is, failure to fix leaking pipes or to turn off taps after use. The price of water strongly influences these so-called water losses. An aspect of waste that is not widely recognized is that if water is very inexpensive, "wasting" water is perfectly rational. If the price of inexpensive water simply reflects the fact that it is plentiful and its delivery costs are very low, then wasting water is inefficient only if creates a significant external diseconomy, an issue that is explored in the next subsection.

This conclusion applies to both consumers and water utilities. A frequently used indicator of the efficiency of a water utility is its proportion of "unaccounted-for water." One source of unaccounted-for water is a leaky distribution system. Fixing these leaks is a substitute for expanding diversion, storage, transportation, treatment, and distribution capacity. Repairing leaks is worthwhile only if the value of the water saved justifies the investment in new pipes, which may not be the case if plentiful, high-quality water is available nearby.

The other important implication of demand that exhibits some price elasticity is that a mistake in pricing can have large consequences for water use. Prices that are too low create a demand to expand water delivery beyond the efficient point. If the costs of the water system are not primarily financed by water revenues, but by general taxes or revenue from another utility (such as electricity), underpricing water can be very expensive to society by leading to massive, uneconomic expansion of the water delivery system. Alternatively, if water prices must cover all costs and if costs are high due to inefficient or corrupt management, much economically warranted water usage can be cut off, and a small improvement in the efficiency of the operation of the water utility can yield large economic benefits.

Another problem with water prices is that consumers may not value water quality highly enough because of informational imperfections. Some users may not understand the relation between water quality and health. Others may understand this relation in principle, but they cannot costlessly observe aspects of quality such as the presence of microorganisms or trace chemicals that are health hazards. If the effective demand for quality is too low because of informational imperfections, consumers may respond to higher prices for piped water by consuming too much low-quality water from contaminated alternative sources. This market failure can be corrected by subsidizing some minimum amount for human consumption. Subsidies may introduce other distortions, however, and their costs must be weighed against the benefits of the health effects from consumption of safe water.

7.1.3   Usage Externalities

The preceding discussion deals with one form of externality: the costs of extracting water resources that are imposed on other users. This subsection deals with two additional externalities associated with usage: pollution and spillage.

Pollution and Sewage Treatment

The purpose of urban water systems is to increase the availability of water at relatively low cost, thereby expanding the uses of water. This expanded usage inevitably increases the amount of polluted water that a community produces. Water that is polluted through use often is simply returned to the natural environment by dumping it into a nearby stream, lake, ocean, dry canyon, cesspool, or vacant plot of land. The external costs imposed by water pollution depend on the circumstances surrounding its disposal. Whereas all pollution will have some effect on the natural environment, the cost depends on the value of the environment for other uses (including preserving the original state of nature).

The most important source of variability in the costs of pollution arises from the exposure of human populations to unhealthy pollutants, either by polluting the environment in which they live or by polluting their food and water sources. Research on the effects of improved water systems demonstrates that simply increasing the quality of water at the point of consumption is not very effective in improving the health of the population. For example, a careful study of water and sanitation systems in eight developing countries found that improved wastewater and sanitation policies significantly improved the health and bodyweight of children, especially in urban areas, and that improvements in the quality of delivered water improved health only if accompanied by improvements in sanitation (Esrey 1996). One family cannot capture the benefits of sanitation by installing sewage disposal if all around it are dumping their wastes in the neighborhood; hence, even with perfect information, private incentives to install sewage are less than its social value.

If either users or water utilities are not held accountable for the costs that they impose on others, they will overproduce pollution and use an inefficiently large amount of water for polluting purposes. The economist's stock solution to this problem is to impose a tax on pollution that fully reflects the marginal cost of pollution on others (see Baumol and Oates 1988; Cropper and Oates 1992). Taxes create a financial penalty for water pollution and so provide a financial reason to invest in either sewers or water treatment facilities. These investments, in turn, will raise the price of water use and so curtail consumption and the pollution that it creates. Users and water utilities will then have an incentive to cut back on polluting uses of water, and to treat wastewater to remove pollutants, until the marginal cost of abatement equals the marginal cost of pollution. If instead of using taxes the government issues regulations that require these investments, the utility has a financial incentive to delay taking actions (to postpone costs) and to undertake the minimum actions that are consistent with the law.

The decision about the level of tax to impose (or, more generally, how much abatement to require) is subject to distortions in the political process. Of course, distortions in the political process may cause the government to demand too much rather than too little abatement. In addition, political distortions may misallocate the burdens of pollution and pollution abatement for the same reason that they can distort the price structure.

The pollution issue raises a problem of institutional design: how can the government commit to a long-term pollution policy that reduces the harms from pollution while avoiding overzealous pursuit of environmental policy that indirectly expropriates the investments of the water utility? The optimal design of environmental policy institutions and instruments is beyond the scope of this paper; however, an essential part of the assessment of the performance of an urban water system is whether this problem has been addressed in a reasonable way.

Water Spillage

Another externality arises when water is priced so low that there is little economic incentive to repair a leaky tap, or even to turn off a tap in the garden before water floods the street. In a society with an extensive and mandatory sewage system, or with good natural drainage due to topography or soil conditions, uncontrolled release of water is not likely to create much of an externality. But in some communities water spillage neither runs off, percolates into the soil, nor evaporates quickly but instead remains in standing puddles or slow-moving open waterways. In these circumstances, water spillage creates a serious external cost by serving as a breeding ground for disease-carrying insects and disease-causing microorganisms.

The implication of this externality is that in some conditions water usage should be priced even if delivery costs are low compared to metering costs and consumers have very limited incomes. Failing to price water usage gives consumers insufficient incentive to prevent spills that create community health problems. Fortunately, because water demand has some elasticity while the cost of epidemics of infectious diseases is high, very large benefits sometimes can be obtained with relatively small price increases. But in other cases the effect of pricing water usage is to cause users to switch from relatively high quality piped water to dangerously polluted natural water sources, in which case the usage price makes matters worse.

7.1.4   Regulatory Instruments

Many of the significant implications for regulatory policy have already been raised in the discussions of costs, demand, and externalities. These discussions have focused on optimal pricing theory, in which the price system is based on social costs, and on avoiding both expropriation and capture. This implies cost-based price regulation of water utilities. But cost-based price regulation is at variance with the recent emphasis in the policy literature on price-cap regulation. Price caps decouple prices from costs, so future price adjustments are not based on any measurable item, such as costs, that the firm can influence. The main reason for implementing price-cap regulation is that otherwise, if firms possess more information about their operations than regulators and if regulators base prices on indicators that a firm controls, firms can increase their profits by distorting the performance indicator. The firm thereby achieves higher profits (and prices) but does not produce at maximum production efficiency.

Price regulation that adjusts price index ceilings without considering costs can solve several problems.[10] First, it assures future price performance at least as good as expected prices under cost-based regulation. Second, it leads to a second-best optimal price structure, given the firm's overall price index requirement, because a firm facing a price index constraint maximizes profits by setting second-best optimal prices in relation to its privately known costs. Third, it eliminates the incentive of the firm to distort its production behavior and generates an unconstrained incentive to minimize costs, given its quality decision. Fourth, by eliminating the requirement to measure costs, it avoids an expensive regulatory system that employs large numbers of professional accountants, engineers, and economists, an especially important attribute in small, poor countries where individuals with these skills are few in number.

In reality, a pure price index regulatory system cannot be implemented. Regulators do not have sufficient information to pick a price adjustment formula that neither expropriates the firm's capital nor, eventually, allows the firm to earn monopoly profits as if it were not regulated. Moreover,

10. For comprehensive reviews of the price-cap literature, see Baron (1989) and Laffont and Tirole (1998).

this form of regulation faces problems when technology changes the optimal product mix and quality offerings of a firm. In practice, price-cap regulation usually is implemented with periodic cost and quality reviews to adjust the pricing formula.

Other factors particular to water systems and other industries that generate large externalities can affect the efficacy of a price index system. For example, if price ceilings are updated by cost audits only infrequently, the firm can influence the magnitude of externality costs through decisions about investments in capacity and water treatment, and usage through its pricing and investment decisions. The firm's general incentive to minimize cost after the price index is adopted will lead it to reduce costly efforts to diminish external costs. Taxes are often imposed to encourage the firm to internalize externalities, but the incentive effects of a tax based on the external costs of the water system are not as sharp if the firm is subject to price caps. If the cap is a binding constraint, the tax will be part of the initial and subsequent cost basis for the price cap and so will be recovered completely by raising the after-tax retail price of water. Hence, the incidence of the tax will fall more on consumers and less on the water utility than would be the case if the utility were an unconstrained profit-maximizing firm. The higher retail price will reduce usage and so give the firm some incentive to make investments to reduce pollution, but the incentive is weaker than if the cap did not exist. The alternative policy of putting the full incidence of the tax on the water utility is also inefficient because it does not discourage use as a means to curtail pollution.

The theoretical solution to this problem is to have part but not all of the tax enter the price constraint, based on the elasticity of demand and the marginal cost of both water supply and externalities. Practically speaking, even if this formula is based on historical costs and takes the form of an automatic adjustment formula, it imposes a substantially greater informational burden on the regulators each time the price formula is adjusted. Under cost-based regulation or standard price-cap regulation, regulators typically do not need to know the details of the components of marginal and total costs or demand elasticity to know how to set an overall revenue requirement or price-cap formula. In general, a greater informational asymmetry between regulators and the regulated firm advantages the firm at the expense of its customers, so an attempt to deal optimally with externality problems through the system of price regulation can be expected to reduce the effectiveness of regulation.

The upshot of this discussion is that the likely outcome of well-intentioned attempts to control externalities of water systems is likely to include performance standards as well as economic incentives through the price structure. Efficient regulation of prices makes efficient use of tax incentives in environmental regulation more difficult and so increases the attraction of performance standards over pollution taxes. In addition, the difficulty of efficiently dealing with externalities through the regulatory system constitutes an argument in favor of integrating sewers into the water supply system.

7.2 Water Reforms in Six Capital Cities

The preceding discussion suggests that optimal design of water systems will vary with the nature of water resources, but certain general principles are universal. To summarize, in systems where a large proportion of the cost is opportunity cost of depletion of the resource or externalities, regulation should charge consumers the marginal social cost. To attract private investors, governments will need to provide credible commitment that quasi rents can be recovered for future investment. Mechanisms that limit monopoly rents and reduce the risk of capture will enhance credibility as well as efficiency.

This section summarizes and compares studies that were commissioned by the World Bank of reforms in six cities within the preceding theoretical framework.[11] In the late 1980s or early 1990s all six cities planned reforms that included eventual private participation through sale of assets (Santiago), concessions (Buenos Aires and Lima), leases (Abidjan and Conakry), and service or management contracts (Mexico City).[12] In Abidjan, a private contractor managed the secondary network and maintained the primary network under a lease contract starting in 1959, before independence. The operator's responsibilities were increased in 1987, which is the date of the reform examined here.

In Santiago and Lima a number of preparatory steps toward private participation were taken, including negotiations with potential bidders, but the privatization process was never completed. Santiago proceeded to introduce all of the planned regulatory changes in 1990 but kept the utility under public ownership. Lima introduced only a few of the regulatory changes that were planned under the proposed concession before stopping the reform.

In Mexico City service contracts with four private companies were introduced in 1993–94 to expand metering and regularize billing. The plan also contained provisions to contract out operation and maintenance of the network, but this stage of the contract is already three years behind

---

11. Information in this section is taken from Alcazar et al. (1999), Alcazar, Xu, and Zuluaga (1999), Haggarty et al. (1999), Shirley et al. (1999), and Menard and Clarke (1999a, 1999b).

12. A sale is defined as private ownership of a controlling stake. A concession is a contract where the operator manages all aspects of the system, including financing and implementing all investment, but the government retains ownership. A lease is a contract where the operator manages the system, raises working capital, and makes maintenance investment but is not responsible for other investments. A service contract is one where the contractor performs specific tasks for a fee and takes no capital risk.

schedule with no clear sign of when, if ever, it will be fully implemented. In Buenos Aires and Conakry private involvement was implemented as planned: in Buenos Aires with the signing of a concession contract in 1992 and in Conakry with a lease in 1989. Finally, Abidjan introduced changes in tariffs and the leaseholder's investment responsibilities in 1987.

7.2.1   Prereform Conditions

As argued in the theoretical discussion, location-specific aspects of water resources as well as the surrounding institutional environment strongly influence the performance of a water utility. This subsection analyzes how private supply costs, externalities, price policy, demand conditions, and the prereform political environment shaped performance and the demand for reform.

Private Costs of Supply

By private costs, we mean the long-run direct economic costs of an efficient water supply system, ignoring externalities arising from resource exploitation, usage, and disposal. As discussed above, private costs are strongly influenced by whether the water resource is sustainable at current extraction rates. Short-term variability in supply is also an important determinant of costs.

Water resources can be considered sustainable with low variability in four of the cities in our sample: Abidjan, Conakry, Buenos Aires, and Santiago (table 7.1). In all four, relatively clean water from rivers or an aquifer is in ample supply with the rate of extraction well below the rate of replenishment.[13] Transport costs are negligible in Buenos Aires because it is located on the supplying river and in Abidjan, Conakry, and Santiago because their systems are largely gravity fed. Although comparable numbers are not available, Abidjan probably has higher costs than the other three because it relies the most on pumping.

Lima and Mexico City are in very different circumstances (table 7.1). Lima is in a desert and two-thirds of its water comes from a badly polluted river where extraction needs exceed available supply during the dry season. The rest is from an aquifer that becomes contaminated by saltwater when extraction during the dry season causes the water table near the ocean to drop. Water is rationed during the dry season, and interruptions are frequent. Mexico City relies for nearly two-thirds of its raw water on wells from 70 to 200 meters deep in the city's rapidly depleting aquifer, while the rest is pumped uphill from distant rivers. One source is 127 kilometers distant and 1,200 meters below the city. The extraction rate from the aqui-

13. Buenos Aires suffered seasonal shortages before reform, but these were caused by inadequate maintenance of storage facilities rather than by shortages of raw water. Similarly, Conakry had chronic shortages until the construction of a new transmission canal and treatment plant in the early 1990s.

Table 7.1   Nature of Water Resources

	Buenos Aires	Lima	Mexico City	Santiago	Abidjan	Conakry
Principal source	River (92%)	River (2/3); wells (1/3)	Wells (82% in 1987; 64% in 1993)	River (89%)	Wells (100%)	River (90%); wells (10%)
Variability	Low	High	Low	Low	Low	Low
Sustainable?[a]	Yes	No	No	Yes	Yes	Yes

[a] At current rates of extraction

fer is currently 37 percent higher than the replenishment rate. Hence, the opportunity cost of water consumption is much higher in Lima and Mexico City than in the rest of our sample.

Another cost consideration is whether the present capacity for shipping and transporting water can meet current demand and provide reliable service or whether substantial investment is required to serve all potential customers or to raise service standards. All of these cities are growing, some quite rapidly, mostly through migration of poor rural populations to the outer edges of the metropolitan areas. An influx of foreign migrants accounts for substantial growth in Buenos Aires and Abidjan, while Conakry has gained a large number of refugees. Santiago and Mexico City were able to keep pace with this expansion and connect most of their potential customers (table 7.2). By the time of reform, Abidjan, Buenos Aires, and Lima had connected only 60 to 75 percent of potential clients, and Conakry only 38 percent.[14] Sewage connection rates lag behind water, especially in the two African cases, while sewage treatment was minimal in all of the cities.

The cost of expansion is high in Buenos Aires, Lima, and Conakry because the scale of the new investments that are required is so large. In these cities, expansion of service requires not only laying more connection pipes in the existing network but substantially increasing the capacity of the backbone water system. According to the concession agreement for Buenos Aires, some US$1.2 billion would need to be invested to bring coverage to about 80 percent in five years. The cost to expand service to 100 percent of the population of Lima in thirty years was estimated in 1994 at $3 billion. The cost to expand and upgrade the water system in Conakry to meet all potential demand at a reasonable price is about $105 million, which is large in relation to Guinea's GDP. In contrast, investment costs to keep pace with growing demand in Abidjan and Santiago were much lower because no large facilities were needed. Future expansion in Abidjan will require major investments since the system is now at 90 percent capacity. Mexico City was providing water to most people in the service area at the time of reform. Future expansion will be costly because of the need to develop water sources outside and below the basin and to pump water up to the city as the aquifer diminishes. Current plans are to develop a source 140 kilometers from the city with an investment cost of $500 million.

---

14. These numbers understate the amount of the population that was not connected because they exclude squatters and poor suburban areas that are outside the utility's water district. The meaning of a connection varies. In the Latin American cases it generally refers to a hook-up to internal pipes within the house, while in the African cities a connection is usually a standpipe in the yard close to the house. As a result a connection typically serves a much larger number of people in Africa than in Latin America; e.g., a connection in Abidjan serves an average of fifteen people versus five in Santiago.

Table 7.2   Conditions in Water Systems before Reform

	Buenos Aires 1992	Lima 1991	Mexico City 1990	Santiago 1988	Abidjan 1987	Conakry 1984
Population in service area (millions)	8.5	6.1	8.3	4.4	2.0	1.0
Growth rate, 1980–95 (%)	1.5[a]	2.3[b]	3.1[c]	1.8	5.1	9.0
Connection rate (% of population)						
Water[d]	70	75	95	99	60	38[e]
Sewage	58	70	86	88	35	10[e]
Principal externalities	Water-borne diseases; pollution of aquifer	Cholera epidemic in 1989; pollution; contamination of aquifer	Water-borne diseases; depletion of aquifer; pollution	Water-borne diseases; pollution; risk to crop exports	Water-borne diseases; pollution	No sewage collection; high incidence of water-borne diseases

[a] 1980–91.
[b] 1993–96.
[c] 1990–95.
[d] Includes private taps in yards.
[e] 1989.

Before reform, service quality—pressure, interruptions, and water quality—ranged from very good in Abidjan, good in Santiago, and fair in Buenos Aires to poor in Mexico City and very poor in Lima and Conakry. Underinvestment in maintenance and replacement of aging systems led to leakage, low pressure, and occasional interruptions in Buenos Aires and Santiago. In Mexico City neighborhoods in the southeast, which were at the periphery of a poorly maintained system, had serious problems of pressure, outages, and leaks. Even today, 172 out of a total of 499 *colonias* (districts) have no service at least six hours a week. In Lima about 48 percent of the connected population received water service for an average of less than twelve hours a day, 28 percent for less than six hours a day. This was partly because of seasonal variation in supply and inadequate storage facilities but also because of breaks in the lines and pressure problems. The system in Conakry was on the verge of collapse, delivering poor-quality water (in some cases through lead pipes) for only a few hours a day.

Externalities

An important external benefit of easy access to safe water for drinking and bathing is the reduction of contagious diseases. Before reform, the social benefits from expanding water connections and improving reliability and quality were highest in Lima and Conakry. Unconnected households in Lima spent as much as seven hours per day collecting water from public standpipes (Sheila Webb and Associates 1992), which reduces time for childrearing. Moreover, residents of Lima's slums suffer from an average of eight cases of diarrhea a year, a significant proportion of which is caused by polluted water. Before reform, connected users in Conakry drank very poor quality piped water, while unconnected consumers used either well water that was contaminated by latrines or water from venders or standpipes that was stored in unsanitary conditions.[15] The lack of safe water for drinking and hygiene and improper sewage disposal accounted for high rates of infant deaths from gastroenteric diseases and periodic epidemics of cholera.

The other two cities with low rates of connection, Buenos Aires and Abidjan, suffered smaller but still important external effects as well. Most of the 30 percent of the population without connections in Buenos Aires relied on well water. They suffered higher rates of water-borne disease than the rest of the city because of contamination of groundwater by untreated industrial waste and raw sewage seeping from the cesspools of households that were not connected to the sewer system. Some unconnected areas in

---

15. Most unconnected households in Conakry rely on shallow, hand-dug wells (as little as fifteen feet below the surface). People report in interviews that they know the water to be unsafe but sometimes use it. Less than 1 percent of the population gets water from vendors and less than 5 percent from public standpipes. The amount of theft of water from the piped system is unknown but is believed to be high.

Abidjan used wells that were contaminated by ocean water, leading to higher rates of water-borne diseases than the rest of the city. Storage of water in unsafe conditions was also a source of disease.

Santiago's main social costs stem from dumping raw sewage into rivers that surrounding farms use to irrigate food crops. The main external costs of this practice were a higher rate of water-borne diseases than for the rest of Chile and a risk to food exports. In Mexico City, although rates of connection were high, people at the periphery, where service interruptions are frequent, also suffered higher rates of water-borne diseases. Nevertheless, Mexico City's incidence of cholera is believed to be lower than the national rate.

Among the social costs of water reform are the external effects of increased water usage on others. These costs were low in Buenos Aires and the two African cities. The main usage externality in Buenos Aires arises from dumping untreated wastewater into two rivers that flow through the city, which affects people who live along their banks. These rivers discharge into the River Plate, which is large enough that dilution and natural self-purification are sufficient that downstream communities do not suffer significant pollution. The main usage externality in Abidjan is the eventual threat to its aquifer from latrines as the city expands toward the hilly, northern area that is the source of its raw water. In Conakry, as we have seen, wastewater contaminates the aquifer that is the source of water for users not connected to the system.

The externalities of resource exploitation probably were higher in Lima and Mexico City than for the other cases because these systems are unsustainable. Scarcity of water in Lima led to rationing and unsafe storage, along with pollution of ocean fishing grounds and irrigation water by untreated waste, which have been blamed for a cholera epidemic that started in Lima and killed almost 3,000 people in Peru in 1991. The most important usage externality in Mexico City stems from the fact that the city is built on a dry lake. Because of the nature of the soil, pumping from the aquifer has caused the city to sink. The downtown area has sunk by an average of 7.5 meters since the beginning of the twentieth century, causing cracks in buildings and making some structures unsafe. Some sections have fallen even faster; parts of the city center have sunk by over 2 meters in the past decade alone. Besides the damage to structures, the sinking has also caused increased water leakage as pipes buckle and break.

Prices and Demand

Although the private and social costs of water usage are highest in Lima and Mexico City, this was not reflected in higher prices. Table 7.3 presents two approximations of price, reflecting the troublesome problem of dealing with bills that are not paid. The first is the average price that is billed, calculated by dividing total billings by estimated total consumption. The second approximation is the average revenue collected per unit of output:

Table 7.3   Average Revenues Collected per Volume Distributed (U.S. dollars per cubic meter)

Average Price[a]	Buenos Aires	Lima[b]	Mexico City[b]	Santiago	Abidjan	Conakr
Based on bills						
Prereform	.21	.21	n.a.	.09	.85	.30
Postreform	.18	.20	.37	.14	.87	1.00[c]
Based on revenues						
Prereform	.18	.15	.22	.08	.81	.13
Postreform	.16	.18	.18	.14	.87	.62[c]

Note: Prereform and postreform dates are as follows: Buenos Aires, 1992 and 1993; Lima, 1991 and 1992; Mexico City, 1992 and 1995; Santiago, 1988 and 1990; Abidjan, 1987 and 1990; and Conakr 1984 and 1995.
[a]Revenues net of indirect taxes and adjusted for collection rates per cubic meter produced adjusted fc unaccounted-for water.
[b]Includes sewage.
[c]The World Bank subsidized these prices. The amounts that customers were actually billed was $.3 and the amount actually paid was $.19.

the ratio of total revenues collected to total cubic meters distributed. These average prices reflect very different systems of revenue collection: the extent of metering varied greatly, nonmetered charges were estimated differently, the number of unregistered connections differed, and the extent and success of trying to collect bills varied enormously. In addition, a hook-up to pipes within a building could be considered a different good than a private standpipe outside the structure. Nevertheless, when compared with average costs, these average prices give some sense of how far Lima and Mexico City's water tariffs were from reflecting the marginal social costs of water consumption when compared to similar tariffs in cities with much lower costs.[16] They also help to explain why Buenos Aires was the only city able to bid a concession on the basis of a tariff reduction, which is plausibly part of the reason it was able to proceed with its planned private contract.[17] (Recall that Abidjan's system was already privately operated.)

Although the high opportunity and external costs of water in Lima and

16. Good recent estimates of marginal costs are not available for these cities. The estimates available also suggest that prereform prices were too low. World Bank (1994a) estimated the marginal cost of water and sewage in Lima at US$.45. The average incremental cost (AIC) of groundwater and water from the Rimac River in Lima was estimated at $.25/m³, while water from the next available source (the Atlantic watershed) was estimated to cost $.53/m³ (Alcazar, Xu, and Zuluaga 1999). Groundwater in Mexico City was estimated to have an AIC of $.41 and water from the next available source, the Cutzamala River, of $.82 (Haggarty et al. 1999). The rate-setting agency in Mexico City charged private, nonresidential users $1.00/m³ to extract water from private bore holes in 1997 (field interviews). In contrast, Nasser (1997) estimated the marginal cost of water in Buenos Aires to be as little as $.15.

17. One reason tariffs in Buenos Aires were so high was that they were increased in anticipation of continued inflation in the two years before privatization, but since inflation was falling rapidly, the result was an increase in real terms.

Table 7.4   **Metering, Billing, Losses, and Consumption**

	Buenos Aires 1992	Lima 1991	Mexico City 1992	Santiago 1988	Abidjan 1987	Conakry 1984
Connections metered (%)	2	9[a]	n.a.	99	96	5
Billed amounts collected (%)	90	43[b]	n.a.	93	64	12
Unaccounted-for water (%)	44	42	37–47	34	13	54
Water consumption per capita (average liters per day)	352	217	237	190	63	37
Water production per capita (average liters per day)	628	372	368	285	70	59

Metered and read; about 30 percent are metered.
1985.

Mexico City suggest that the return to installing meters would be positive, the rate of metering was lower than in Buenos Aires, Santiago, and Abidjan (table 7.4). In Lima only 30 percent of connections were metered, and only 9 percent of the meters were read. Although we do not know the extent of metering before reform in Mexico City, about a third of all connections were not registered, and many that were registered either did not receive or did not pay the bill. Fifty-three percent of revenues were from large industrial or commercial users, representing only about 2 percent of the customer base and 20 percent of total water usage.

Conakry, the other city in our sample with virtually free water and almost no metering, was in very different circumstances than Lima and Mexico City. Unlike the other two, Conakry's source of raw water was renewable and reliable. Its main usage externality was contamination of the aquifer under the city, which unconnected households then consume from wells. This externality could be eliminated by connecting existing consumers to sewers or unconnected households to water. But either of these strategies was financially impossible because prices in Conakry were insufficient to cover the private costs of operating the water system, let alone the capital costs of expansion of sewer installation.

Unaccounted-for water (UFW), the difference between water delivered to the distribution system and water sold, was high in Buenos Aires, Lima, Mexico City, and Conakry (table 7.4). High UFW was partly due to commercial losses (failure to register, meter, and bill connections) and partly due to physical losses (pipe breaks and overflows).[18] As argued above, reducing UFW might not be worth the cost when water is plentiful, as in Abidjan, Conakry, Buenos Aires, and Santiago. Yet even in these cities, with the exception of Abidjan, the rates of UFW before reform in table 7.4 seem very high. By way of comparison the average for the United States is 12, for Tokyo is 15, and for Singapore is 6. Where water extraction exceeds replenishment and losses have high social costs, as in Mexico City and Lima, reductions in the rates of UFW seem unambiguously worthwhile. UFW that arises from failure to collect revenues that are needed to keep the system operating at reasonable quality is unlikely to be justified anywhere.

Another sign of incorrect incentives was the relatively high rates of per capita production and consumption of water in Lima and Mexico City. Production per capita was 368 liters per day in Mexico City and 628 liters per day in Buenos Aires. Both numbers are very high in comparison with Europe, where the average rate is 150 to 200 liters per day. Consumption in Mexico City is especially excessive, considering that costs are also very high. Lima's consumption per capita was lower only because of rationing. The low rates of consumption and production per capita in the African cities partly reflect their higher prices and lower purchasing power, but it is also partly a result of carrying water from an outside standpipe rather than having it pumped into the home.

The performance of these systems indicates that water policy provided little incentive for the utilities in Lima and Mexico City to consider the high private and social costs of water in making decisions about meters, bill collection, maintenance, or investment, or for consumers to consider costs in making decisions about usage. Pricing policy in Conakry left little incentive or wherewithal for the utility to attempt to capture the high social benefits to be gained from expanding and upgrading the system.

Prereform Institutions and Operations

Before reform quasi rents were being captured for consumers by pricing below fixed costs in all our sample cities except Abidjan and Buenos Aires. After 1959, Abidjan's water system was run under a lease with a private firm.[19] Prices were high enough to cover operations, capital costs, and investment in expansion of the system. In Buenos Aires, tariffs before reform barely covered the costs of the inefficient utility running the system but were high enough to permit an efficient operator to improve service, expand the system, and earn a reasonable return on capital. Evidence for

18. A district-by-district study of the water system in Lima found that two-thirds of the losses were due to leakage (World Bank 1994a).

19. The firm, Société de Distribution des Eaux de Côte d'Ivoire, is owned by a French water company, Société d'Aménagement Urbain et Rural (48 percent), private Ivoreans (48 percent), and National Financing Bank (4 percent).

this is the fact that the subsequent concession attracted three bidders who offered a lower tariff and promised annual investments of US$240 million over the first five years; average annual investment in water over the previous decade had been only $10 million.

None of the other water systems earned enough revenues to cover total costs. They varied in the extent to which their costs were high because of inefficient operation. Santiago's water utility was relatively efficient with prices set below fixed cost by the government for political reasons. It lost money during the 1980s until the government raised prices to breakeven levels shortly before the 1990 reforms. Lima's state-owned utility was at the other extreme and highly inefficient. Its tariffs were below its operating costs but probably would not have covered the fixed costs of an efficient operator and certainly would have been below the fixed costs of a system providing reasonable service to the entire client base.

Conakry's utility was even less efficient than Lima's, with the highest rate of staffing (42 per 1,000 customers) for an almost inoperative system. Tariffs did not cover operating costs, much less capital costs; the water company owed US$4 million in interest arrears on its external debt alone in 1983. As in Lima, tariffs were too low to cover the fixed costs of an efficient operator.

Mexico City's circumstances are not strictly comparable because the system is not operated by a single corporate entity. Different types of costs and revenues were the responsibility of different organizations. One municipal entity was responsible for building new infrastructure, another was responsible for administration, and sixteen political subunits of the municipal government (*delegaciones*) were responsible for the operation and maintenance of the secondary distribution network. The *delegaciones* and the other distribution and investment units operated as government departments, and their costs were covered by government transfers. The federal government paid a significant share of the investment costs for the large projects that bring water from outside the Mexico City basin. Responsibility for billing, collecting, and funding operational and local investment costs rests with the government of Mexico City (the Distrito Federal). Tariffs were raised only five times between 1970 and 1990 and covered less than half of the system's operating costs.

Politics Leading to Reform

The political benefits of water reform are often low, which means that political costs must also be low for net political gains to be positive. The major political hurdle to reform arises from the fact that governments can take advantage of the durable fixed assets in water systems to divert quasi rents for politically useful purposes, such as low prices for political supporters. Governments also derive political benefits from making patronage appointments, locating new connections in areas chosen to secure political support, or awarding lucrative contracts to political allies. Reform, especially if it involves private participation, requires governments to raise prices to cover the private and social costs of water and to give up political command of employment and investment.

In contrast, the political benefits from water reform are often small. Water supply is local in character and so has political saliency only in some urban areas, whereas economic reform in developing countries is usually a national decision. Revenues from private participation are small or nil because water assets have relatively low value compared to many other industries that are candidates for privatization, so that even most governments that are committed to reform still may take a long time to get around to water. Finally, water reform frequently means raising prices. While excluded users or users whose service is frequently interrupted or of low quality may welcome high prices and regular, high-quality service, others may resist a reform that has very attractive overall economic benefits. In the six cases, the political desirability and feasibility of reform depended heavily on how much prices would have to increase to permit cost recovery and the extent to which the regime's supporters would be harmed.

The political economy of water reform is illustrated by contrasting Santiago, Lima, and Buenos Aires. All three governments announced plans to sell or concession their water companies and embarked on sweeping programs of privatization of other state assets. Both Chile and Peru gave low priority to water privatization, delayed the transaction, and, after initially contacting bidders, ultimately failed to privatize. In contrast, Argentina treated the Buenos Aires concession as a priority and moved promptly to auction the system. This difference in outcomes was not due to the situation in the sector, for the water system in Lima was in much worse shape than in Buenos Aires.

The Buenos Aires concession went forward because the net political benefits to President Menem were larger than the benefits to President Fujimori in Peru or to General Pinochet in Chile from taking similar actions. Menem received solid support from the poorer suburban areas of Buenos Aires in the 1989 election, but mixed support from the middle- and high-income central district. Yet a coalition of political factions representing middle-income voters formed the core support base for Menem's reform program in Congress. The water system concession was designed to benefit voters who were already connected to the system. The tender was awarded on the basis of the lowest water tariff and was designed to bring substantial improvements in service. The poor also were expected to benefit from increased access but were required to pay much of the cost of the expansion of the secondary network through a so-called infrastructure charge.

In contrast, both Santiago and Lima would have had to raise prices substantially to attract private investment. The bidding documents for Lima's concession, for example, would have permitted an increase in tariffs of up to 40 percent, and some observers thought even that increase was inadequate to attract enough investment to meet the government's target of 98 percent of potential clients connected in ten years with twenty-four-hour continuous service. Many slum dwellers in Lima, who were President Fujimori's core constituents, would not be able to afford the cost of a new connection and a higher water bill, so the president's political benefits from the concession were small. The net political benefits were further reduced by a US$600 million loan in 1994 that made a number of short-run improvements in the system, thereby reducing the immediate benefits of proceeding with reform.

Net political benefits were small in Chile, but for different reasons. Full cost recovery required doubling prices in real terms, but this was not why privatization did not proceed.[20] The political costs of raising water prices were low because, judging by the 1988 referendum, Santiago was not a strong base of support for Pinochet and, in any event, an explicit subsidy was planned to reduce the immediate impact of reform on consumers. But the prospective political benefits to Pinochet of completing the reform were also low. Views on the Pinochet administration were highly polarized, and General Pinochet had little expectation of changing his support base in Santiago, for good or ill, because of water privatization. Thus, even though the government was ideologically committed to privatizing the water system and passed all the necessary enabling legislation, it delayed the transaction until after all other major infrastructure was privatized. This delay proved fatal. The 1989 elections, which took the Pinochet administration by surprise (Constable and Valenzuela 1989), brought in a coalition that was ideologically opposed to selling water assets and so stopped the process.[21] Hence, the utility was not privatized as planned, although privatization is again on the agenda.

As in Lima, the net political gain from water reform in Mexico City was low or negative. At the time of the decision to auction service contracts, the ruling party, Partido Revolucionario Institucional (PRI), had lost support in the capital. In the 1988 presidential elections, the PRI won only 27 percent of the city's vote. The new Salinas administration designed water reform to minimize political costs. The new service contracts did not raise prices anywhere close to costs, did not create incentives to lay off supporters in the myriad water agencies, and did not cede control over water investments to the operators. Furthermore, responsibility for revenues and maintenance was to be extended to the private operators in the

20. Chile phased in price regulation based on the marginal costs of an efficient benchmark company adjusted to assure at least a 7 percent return on assets by 1995. That price is twice the 1989 average price in 1996 dollars.

21. Constable and Valenzuela (1989) further argued that the general regarded the polls suggesting his defeat as biased and ignored them.

third and final phase of the contracts. Since the third contractual phase coincided with a growing threat that the opposition party would capture the Mexico City government (as indeed it did), the final phase of the contracts was put on indefinite hold.

Conakry's move from the lowest to the highest water tariffs in our sample resulted from a combination of internal and external political factors. Guinea was another case where prices would have had to rise considerably to make private operation feasible. Conakry's water system was in a state of collapse by the mid-1980s, with almost no households connected, only 5 percent of connections with a working meter, less than 12 percent of users actually charged for their connection, and almost two-thirds of water lost through leaky pipes and illegal connections. Water was available only a few hours a day and was of poor quality when available, while government price controls made bottled water scarce. The utility had little incentive to reduce losses or increase billing because prices were well below operating costs and, in any case, it could not cut off nonpayers. The water utility depended on government transfers and was in a state of continuous financial crisis. Guinea had been ruled by a dictator (Sekou Toure) whose main concern was providing water to the military and government elite. The death of Sekou Toure in 1984 led to a new military dictatorship, which was uninterested in protecting the government elite because its support base was military and rural. Still, the government might not have agreed to a private lease had not the World Bank and the French government, which were expected to fund the large new investments needed, insisted on private participation as the price of their support.

Finally, although Abidjan's system was well run, a crisis in public finances in the mid-1980s made it hard for the government of Côte d'Ivoire to implement the investment required to meet the rapidly expanding demand for water in Abidjan. The World Bank and French government pushed Côte d'Ivoire to shift more responsibility for implementation of investments to the lessor, who also agreed to reduce tariffs for a number of users.

7.2.2   Assessment of the Reforms

How well did reform approximate the optimal policy principles described earlier? We first consider pricing policy. We then assess how well regulatory design provided commitment to durable policies and prevented capture or reneging.

Pricing and Operating Efficiency

Among the six cities, Santiago's pricing formula is best in terms of both efficiency and equity (table 7.5). The fixed part of the tariff covers the maintenance and operation of the system and such administrative costs

Table 7.5   Pricing Formulas after Reform

	Buenos Aires	Lima	Mexico City	Santiago	Abidjan	Conakry
Adjustments in tariffs	Adjusted to cost index when increase is more than 7%. Review every 5 years.	Arbitrary cost-plus based on company request.	Commission proposes, municipal assembly must approve.	Adjusted to cover marginal costs and average costs of efficient company every 5 years. Inflation adjusted yearly.	Cost-plus revision every 5 years.	Cost-plus revision every 4 years.
Metered tariff	50% of unmetered charge for similar consumer usage fee plus consumption fee for consumption over 30 m^3. Metering = 8% of connections in 1995.	Usage fee by type of consumer. Read meters = 8% of connections in 1996.	Different usage fees based on volume blocks. Metering = 64% of connections in 1998.	Usage fee same for all customers plus flat fee. Peak/off-peak rates. Metering = 100% of connections since 1985.	Different usage fees based on volume blocks. Metering = 98% of connections in 1996.	Different usage fees based on volume blocks. Metering = 99% of connections in 1997.
Unmetered tariff	Location, size, and type of property; size of built area; age and type of house adjusted by K factor.	Flat charge based on estimated minimum monthly consumption level for type of consumer.	Flat fee based on location and type of property, except in areas 70% metered, then charged average metered charge.	No unmetered connections.	Almost no unmetered connections.	Almost no unmetered connections.

(*continued*)

Table 7.5 (continued)

	Buenos Aires	Lima	Mexico City	Santiago	Abidjan	Conakry
Subsidy policy	Unmetered price based on property attributes; nonresidential pays approximately double residential.	Cross-subsidy business to residential; connected to group taps and standpipes.	Cross-subsidy business to residential, metered to unmetered.	Means-targeted subsidy for an average 60% of bill for first 20 m^3 consumed.	Cross-subsidy for low-volume consumption.	First years of lease, government subsidized all consumers. Now cross-subsidy for low-volume consumption.
1996 Tariff[a] (U.S. dollars per cubic meter)	.23[b]	.32 (includes sewage)	.22 (includes sewage)	.29	.51	.74

[a] Average revenue collected per cubic meter distributed, calculated as in table 7.3.
[b] 1995.

as billing and collections. All connections are metered, and the variable cost per cubic meter is set according to the long-run marginal costs of a hypothetical best practice, efficient company, adjusted to cover average costs and assure at least a 7 percent return on assets. Instead of cross-subsidies, financial assistance is provided through a direct, means-tested discount. Tariffs are indexed annually to inflation and readjusted every five years to account for changes in real costs.

One weakness of Santiago's price system is that the externalities from dumping untreated sewage are not internalized through either a tax or imposed treatment costs. Although the law prohibits unhealthful pollution, the utility's performance standards are not enforced. The price formula allows full passthrough of the cost of sewage treatment. This provision eliminates the economic disincentive to invest in sewage treatment, but it does not eliminate the political disincentive if water consumers perceive that the tariff saving exceeds the value to them of reduced risk of epidemics. This circumstance is plausible, for society at large, not just Santiago water customers, bears the cost of polluted discharges. In particular, farmers have been forced to bear part of the cost of water pollution since 1991 when the Chilean government responded to Peru's cholera epidemic by prohibiting the use of untreated sewage to irrigate food crops that grow close to the ground and destroyed all such crops in the field.

Prices in Buenos Aires have many more distortions than in Santiago. Only 14 percent of connections in 1998 are metered. Unmetered customers pay a fixed charge based on the size, location, characteristics (low income, luxury), and age of buildings; size of the property; and type of service. Metered customers pay a fixed charge equal to half the bill for an equivalent unmetered customer plus a variable charge for use above 30 m³. Cross-subsidies are large. In 1995, for example, the ratio of tariffs for properties of similar size but different characteristics was 7:1. Tariffs are adjusted every five years, based on investment plans. Tariffs are not indexed to inflation but instead are adjusted whenever a composite cost index (K) increases by over 7 percent. The social cost of reducing pollution of the aquifer in Buenos Aires by cesspools was initially internalized for those who had wells and cesspools by charging new consumers a connection fee that included part of the capital charges for expanding the system. When this proved uncollectible, the concessionaire negotiated its replacement with a fee for all customers.

Lima raised tariffs despite the decision to delay planned privatization, which paradoxically may have had perverse effects on further reforms. Most of Lima's customers are still unmetered and pay a flat tariff based on hypothetical consumption estimates for the customer's type.[22] The estimated consumption used for billing may be higher than the amount actu-

---

22. E.g., consumers in low-income neighborhoods are assumed to consume 22 m³.

ally consumed since the company often makes no allowance for periods when water is cut off. Cross-subsidies abound in the price structure. Non-residential consumers pay two to six times the rates charged residences, giving large-volume consumers an incentive to drill private bore holes, further depleting the aquifer. Tariff increases are ad hoc, occurring when the company's request coincides with the government's desire to reduce the budgetary burden of its subsidy. Currently, the social cost of depletion and contamination of the aquifer is borne by people who fall ill and customers who invest in wells, cisterns, and other off-system facilities that are motivated by the desire to avoid shortages or unreasonably high prices for the services provided.

Tariff rates in Mexico City continue to be very low. Since 1995, prices can be changed only by vote of the municipal assembly. The increase in average tariffs in table 7.5 has come from metering, better collection, and reductions in unregistered connections, not from price increases. Cross-subsidies also are common. In 1998, residential consumers paid between 20 and 80 percent of the nonresidential tariff, and residents of larger dwellings paid prices that were two to four times as high as the prices charged for small dwellings. The cost of aquifer depletion is borne by property owners and the federal government, which continues to pay most of the cost of pumping water from outside the Mexico City basin.

Abidjan's reform did not change its cost-plus pricing regime, which passes all costs on to consumers. Metering, billing, and collecting from private consumers are almost universal; the main exception has been large accounts receivable run up by the government. Large-volume consumers, who are almost all industrial, cross-subsidize all other users, including the government, while small consumers (less than 18 m³) pay least, about a third of the tariff on large volumes (over 300 m³).[23] Consumers in rural areas within the district also are cross-subsidized. Even taking into account the possibility that exchange rate valuation may overstate water tariffs, consumers in Abidjan pay much higher prices than those in the Latin American cities. Affordability does not seem to be a problem, perhaps because of cross-subsidization and lower consumption patterns motivated by yard taps, as well as the absence of a fixed charge.

The signing of a lease in Conakry introduced a cost-plus pricing regime similar to Abidjan's. Prices were initially subsidized by the government with funds from international and bilateral aid agencies, but they nevertheless increased sharply from about US$.13/m³ in 1988 to $.90/m³ by 1994.[24] Small-volume consumers are subsidized, although by far less than

23. In 1996 the tariffs were US$.36 for up to 18 m³, $.55 for 18 to 90 m³, $.91 for 90 to 300 m³, $1.04 for over 300 m³, and $.76 for the government.

24. The price has since dropped in dollar terms to about $.80/m³ in 1997 because of devaluation; the tariff in local currency has not fallen. As in Côte d'Ivoire, tariffs are uniform across the lease, which cross-subsidizes other urban areas; however, these users are a much smaller part of the customer base in Guinea.

in Abidjan.[25] Affordability is a serious problem: an average monthly residential bill in Conakry in 1996 was about $22 for a connection that serves, on average, twenty-seven people, compared to an average annual per capita income of $560, or the monthly salary of a top civil servant of $150.[26] In contrast, an average bill was $12 in Abidjan, serving fifteen people with higher per capita income ($660 in 1996). The net effect of higher per capita consumption and fewer people per connection is that total water consumption per connection is about 6 percent higher in Conakry, compared to prices that are over 50 percent higher. Moreover, according to household surveys the owner of the connection customarily does not charge other users in Conakry, while selling water to neighbors is accepted in Abidjan, which explains why households are less likely to acquire a connection in Conakry.

Many people in Conakry get water for free. Even though metering went from virtually nil to almost universal, only about 60 percent of billed charges are collected from private customers because Guinea's laws make it hard to disconnect nonpayers permanently or penalize persons for illegal connections, while lack of good information on the city's population makes it hard for the company to keep track of customers. But the worst source of accounts receivable has been the government, which paid only 10 percent of its bill in 1993. The operator has been keeping the revenues it collected for the government water investment fund to cover these arrears.[27]

One reason tariffs are so high in Conakry is that the costs of a system sized for a larger customer base are spread over so few paying connections. Conakry, with a 1.7 million population, had only 17,338 legal connections in 1996, many of which were delinquent. Another 3,500 illegal connections are believed to exist. In addition, the system has only 130 standpipes, serving an estimated 975 persons each. In comparison, Abidjan has close to 180,000 connections for 2.8 million people. In addition, Conakry's tariff was set to cover the cost of servicing the debt contracted prior to the lease, even though much of this was inefficiently invested.[28] Thus Conakry has a system with abundant, low-cost water that is priced beyond the means of many citizens.[29] Only about 748,000 people, or less than half of Conakry's population, have access to water from a legal connection or a public standpipe.

25. In 1996 the tariffs were $.60 for up to 20 m³, $.75 for 20 to 60 m³, and $.81 for over 60 m³. Thus the lowest tariff in Conakry is 70 percent of the highest, compared to 35 percent in Abidjan.

26. The bill is estimated based on average daily consumption of 37 liters per capita in Conakry compared to Abidjan's per capita consumption was 63 liters per day.

27. The introduction of meters drastically reduced government consumption, and the intervention of the French aid agency in 1996 helped the government and the company settle their cross-debts and keep down arrears.

28. In Buenos Aires and Lima the government absorbed past debts before moving tariffs closer to cost recovery.

29. The volume of water distributed in 1997 was only about one-fourth the system's potential production (9.3 million m³ compared to 36.5 million m³ production capacity).

Price policies also have had an effect on UFW in all cities except Abidjan, where it was already in the range of European cities before reform. UFW fell from 44 to 34 percent in Buenos Aires and from 34 to 19 percent in Santiago (comparing 1992 and 1996). UFW in Mexico City and Lima fell by about 5 percentage points but continued high at 37 and 36 percent, respectively, in 1996, a sign that their reforms were less effective in providing efficient incentives. In Conakry, UFW was not accurately measured before reform and remained very high at 50 percent in 1996 because of the inability to collect bills and prevent illegal connections.

Contractual and Regulatory Institutions

How well do the contractual and regulatory institutions in our sample rank against what theory would suggest? The governance institutions vary widely in some respects (table 7.6), but they are universally weak in dealing with wastewater and sewage treatment or the allocation of use among competing demands. None of the cities tax pollution, and where wastewater is controlled the costs have largely fallen on farmers and food consumers. Usage rights are allocated by government command. Chile has private, tradable water rights, but the market is so thin as to be nonexistent because property rights in water generally are not recorded.

Santiago's institutions are the best designed to provide commitment against expropriation, resist capture, and provide incentives to overcome market failures and reduce externalities, despite the fact that the utility is state owned.[30] The regulator's independence and discretion, the price formulas and processes, and commercial autonomy of the utility are spelled out in detailed regulations. Because Chile's constitutional, electoral, and legislative institutions make it very difficult to change laws, water regulation is protected from politically motivated expropriation of quasi rents.[31] Another safeguard is a means-tested subsidy for water bills, which is calculated in a way that benefits many middle- as well as low-income consumers and hence has reduced the incentive of water consumers to seek inefficient price reductions.[32] The company can appeal the regulator's decisions to a neutral arbitration committee or an independent court system.

Santiago has fewer safeguards against capture or reneging by the operator. Tariffs are set secretly, with little scope for consumer input or judicial review. Although performance requirements are spelled out in the laws and injured parties have the right to sue the company for noncompliance,

---

30. The institutions were created when privatization seemed imminent. Note too that the institutions rule all urban water systems in Chile, some of which are private, including a small private operator in Santiago (serving 5 percent of the city's population).

31. An absolute majority is required to change laws, and the constitutional provision for nonelected senators plus an electoral system that tends to split the legislature make the water legislation very hard to change. For details, see Baldez and Carey (1997).

32. See Gelbach and Pritchett (1997) for a discussion of politically sustainable subsidies.

Table 7.6   **Contractual and Regulatory Provisions after Reform**

	Buenos Aires	Lima[a]	Mexico City	Santiago	Abidjan	Conakry
Protection against expropriation	Reputation Courts (not independent) International arbitrage	Reputation	None	Independent regulator with limited discretion Election rules make laws hard to reverse Independent court Reputation Arbitration	Donor pressures Operator control of revenues International arbitration	Donor pressures Operator control of revenues International arbitration
Representation of consumer and other interests in regulatory procedures	Local government reps on board No consumer reps	None	Local government control No consumer reps	None Tariff setting secret	None	None
Coverage; universal service requirements	80% water, 64% sewage in 5 years, yearly targets Regulator must approve 5-year investment plan	95% water and sewage in 10 years	Not part of service contract	100% coverage required by law Regulator must approve 5-year investment plan	Not part of lease contract	Not part of lease contract
UFW; standing water requirements	UFW from 45% to 25% by year 30 45% water network renovated by year 30 Nonresidential must be metered[b]	95% metering, 25% UFW in 10 years	100% metering target UFW part of stage 3, on indefinite hold	100% metering required by law	None	Maintenance targets (not enforced)

(continued)

Table 7.6 (continued)

	Buenos Aires	Lima[a]	Mexico City	Santiago	Abidjan	Conakry
Wastewater use; sewage treatment requirements	100% secondary treatment of effluents of those connected to sewers, year 13	None	Not part of service contract Farm use of untreated wastewater controlled	Farm use of untreated wastewater controlled Sewage treatment required by law, not enforced	Not part of lease contract	Not part of lease contract
Enforcement of water contract requirements	Performance bond ($150 million) Fines Can revoke concession	Fines US$50 million security deposit Can revoke concession	Fines Payment made against work	Fines Can revoke concession Consumers can sue operator	Fines Can revoke lease	Performance bond ($400,000) Fines Can revoke lease
Allocation among users	Not an issue	Upstream use by farms, mines not controlled	Federal government allocates arbitrarily	Tradable water rights; existing rights grandfathered	Not an issue	Not an issue

[a]Refers to draft concession contract and actual regulatory arrangements.
[b]This requirement was later reduced.

no suit has occurred. Fines for nonperformance are set by law and were quite low until recently. Thus far the regulator has been reluctant to sanction companies and has never revoked a concession. Even when the small private operator in Santiago failed to meet its required investment plan and this contributed to its inability to supply consumers during the 1996 drought, the regulator never considered revoking the concession.

Institutional protections against both expropriation and capture seem weaker in Buenos Aires than in Santiago. The regulator answers to a board of political appointees, two each from the federal, provincial, and municipal governments. Increasing political divisions between these administrations have made the regulator's decisions more partisan.[33] Thus in 1998 the municipal representatives blocked the cost-adjusted price increase required under the concession, and eventually 1.6 percent was granted instead of the 11.7 percent requested. The company can appeal regulatory decisions to the ministry or the judiciary, but the courts are not regarded as independent. The company has protected itself by going directly to the executive branch, where reputation effects work in its favor. For example, after the dispute over price adjustments in 1998, the ministry added 3 percent to the 1.6 percent price increase approved by the regulatory board. Concern about Argentina's reputation with investors is an important incentive for the federal government since it must safeguard the credibility of the country's fixed parity with the dollar.

The government also has experienced problems in forcing the company to adhere to the original agreement. In 1997, the company forced renegotiation of the contract, dealing directly with the government rather than going through the regulator. The company claimed that the original privatization agreement ought to be voided because the government did not reveal all the facts about the utility, even though the tender disclaimed the accuracy of the information it contained. Among other things, the renegotiation overturned several fines levied by the regulator for failure to meet performance goals and reduced the concession's coverage requirements for the first five years.

Regulatory and contractual designs in Lima and Mexico City offer less protection against confiscation of quasi rents than in either Santiago or Buenos Aires. Power in Peru is centralized in the executive branch, and both the legislature and judiciary are very weak. Despite legal and budget autonomy, Lima's regulator has in practice been subservient to the central government.[34] The regulator answers to the same ministry as the water

33. Since 1994 the municipal government has been popularly elected and has been controlled by the opposition party. The province was controlled by President Menem's main rival within his party.

34. In addition, the Law of Sanitary Services has an article stating that "tariffs can be modified in the event that the population's interests are affected by the privatization process" (Alcazar, Xu, and Zuluaga 1999, 25).

utility, has no legal standing to protest interference, and unlike other regulatory bodies in Peru does not have a board or council representing nongovernment interests. While the regulatory institutions might have been strengthened had the concession been tendered as planned, curbing the power of the executive to act arbitrarily is likely to prove difficult, although in the short run executive dominance does not necessarily imply a poorly performing utility. Peru has a relatively open economy, which could induce a presidential concern about reputation that would work in favor of a private, partly foreign-owned water operator. Nevertheless, Peru's strong executive system does not help to build the credibility of all long-term commitments, including the one to an open economy. This problem will need to be addressed if Peru's new plan to carry out privatization is to succeed.

Political interests dominate Mexico City's water regulation. Mexico has no independent regulator and no safeguards against expropriation through underpricing. Mexico reduced the financial exposure of private operators by dividing the city into zones and paying fee-for-service in the first two phases of the contracts. The phasing-in of operating risk under the contract was expected to build credibility and contain political opposition to private operation. Ultimately, direct election of the mayor and assembly made political circumstances even less favorable for reform, while Mexico City's handling of contractors (including persistent late payments of fees to operators) reduced government credibility as a partner.

Mexico City lacks mechanisms to mediate competing interests for the use of its scarce and costly water. The federal government finances a large part of the investment and decides how to share raw water between agriculture and the municipal system. The municipality tries to control extraction from the aquifer by charging high prices (US$1/m^3 in 1997) for well water for nonresidential uses. The exceptions to this charge are many, and some are made for political reasons.

The Abidjan contract is a lease, so the operator bears no investment risk. Operating risks also are low, even though courts are not independent and the provisions for international dispute arbitration have not proved practical. The company is protected in part because the French government and the World Bank have been willing to assist in clearing up problems between the operator and the Côte d'Ivoire government. For example, in 1997 the French aid agency, Caisse Française de Dévelopement, loaned the Côte d'Ivoire CFA Fr 12 billion conditional on tariff adjustments and payment of its water bills. Furthermore, the operator collects all revenues, including funds for the government to use for investment, and it has withheld the funds when the government has failed to pay its bills.

Institutions to ensure that the operator complies with its obligations under the contract are weak. Four different government bodies, all lacking clear lines of responsibility or political insulation, monitor the private operator. The leaseholder manages the system, collects all revenues, and undertakes most investments, despite the fact that larger projects are supposed to be competitively bid.

Finally, the lease in Conakry did not overcome an extraordinarily weak institutional setting. The leaseholder's main risk has been from confiscation of quasi rents by the government and consumers through nonpayment of water bills in a legal system where cutoffs are hard to enforce.[35] As in Côte d'Ivoire, the operator has been able to reduce its risk because it collects revenues and can simply keep the funds due the government to cover arrears. It can also use the backing of international actors like the World Bank and the French government in its negotiations with the government and the regulator.

Enforcement of the contract's performance requirements also is weak. No credible regulatory body exists. Instead, a state enterprise is responsible for both investment and regulation and has been in constant conflict with the operator. The staff of the state enterprise is weak and poorly paid, information about operations is almost nonexistent, and the fact that the lease covers urban areas in the entire country has made it almost impossible to sort out activities in Conakry. The operator routinely violates its obligations to submit information under the contract or to maintain the assets.

Public versus Private Operation

Given these institutional weaknesses and the ubiquitous presence of monopoly, the case for private over public operation is not as clear as it would be if competition were present. To gain some further insight on this issue, four of the six cases had sufficient information to allow a crude cost-benefit calculation for the reform. (Too little information was available to support this calculation for Mexico City and Abidjan.) Using the approach developed by Galal et al. (1994), we have worked with the authors of these four cases to calculate the net consumer surplus and net changes in the welfare of workers (largely wage and shares in the private operator minus any net costs to laid-off workers), the government (mostly taxes minus lost quasi rents, conversion of debt to equity, etc.), and buyers during the postreform period. These components were then projected to create a calculation that was based on ten postreform years for each case. The net changes in welfare were then compared to a counterfactual for the same period based on prereform trends, accounting for any changes that would have occurred regardless of ownership. The results of these calculations are as follows.

---

35. Although the operator can and does cut off nonpayers, it cannot prosecute them for their arrears. Nor are there penalties for connecting illegally. Often nonpayers reconnect under another name or illegally tap into a pipe outside their houses.

The Buenos Aires concession resulted in net domestic gains for the ten-year postreform period equal to US$150 per capita in 1996 dollars, almost all of which went to consumers. The average annual gain in the ten postreform years was 51 percent of system revenues in the last prereform year. The increase in consumer surplus is due to the 27 percent drop in tariffs, which was only partly offset by subsequent increases, and the rapid expansion of the system. Coverage of water rose from 70 to 81 percent and sewage from 58 to 62 percent in the first three years of the concession.

Santiago's domestic welfare gains under state ownership were also large: US$64 per capita in 1996 dollars for the ten-year period. The average annual gain in the postreform period is 52 percent of system revenues in the last prereform year. About 85 percent of these gains accrue to the government from increasing prices to bring them more in line with cost, and most of the rest went to workers.[36]

Lima's ten-year gain from reforms under state ownership was US$7 per capita in 1996 dollars, about 40 percent of which went to the government and the rest to consumers. The average annual gain amounts to only 7 percent of the revenues in the last year before reform. Had the concession been signed and all of the requirements been fulfilled, the domestic welfare gains would have been eleven times larger at $85 per capita in 1996 dollars (annual gains equal to 61 percent of revenues), split between consumers and domestic buyers. While new connections increased under state ownership, the rate just kept pace with the growth of the city. Under the concession, coverage was planned to rise from 75 to 85 percent for water and 70 to 83 percent for sewage by 1996. While assuming that all of the concession targets would have been met is unrealistic, the size of the projected gain indicates that there would have been considerable room for reneging under privatization before the city would be worse off.

In Conakry, the ten-year gains from the reform are higher than in Lima at US$12 per capita in 1996 dollars, despite the problems of the reformed utility. The average annual gains equal 112 percent of sales in the last prereform year. The percentage gain is enormous because the moribund state enterprise that preceded the reform was incapable of reaching most consumers or supplying reliable, safe water to the few it did reach. Under private operation, capacity more than doubled, water quality and service improved dramatically, the population served almost doubled, and coverage expanded from 38 to 45 percent. Although over half of the city's population is unable to afford piped water under private operation, one cannot assume that they would have had access to piped water under any realistic counterfactual. Guinea's weak institutions made it hard for the government to negotiate and commit to an affordable water tariff with the private

---

36. Although Santiago only increased coverage from 99 to 100 percent, it incorporated peripheral communities into the service zone and reduced shared housing.

operator. These same weaknesses paralyzed operation under public own-ership. Since the city's consumers who cannot afford connections have no safe alternative, water-borne diseases continue to be a problem. In 1994, for example, 330 people died of cholera in Conakry.

These cost-benefit calculations suggest that net changes in welfare from private participation are positive and large. Although Santiago had large gains under state ownership, its strong public institutions make it an out-lier. We could not quantify the external benefits from the reforms, but these also seem generally positive. If we assume that any increase in water and sewage connections had positive health effects where people were con-suming unsafe alternatives and practicing poor hygiene, then there were health benefits even in Guinea. The gains are reduced by some associated costs. Although the amount of sewage is not necessarily increased because of increased access to water, the amount of wastewater is. Although trans-porting waste away from human contact has health benefits, these are re-duced if untreated wastewater or spillage creates other costs. As we have seen, externalities from pollution or spillage were probably high in Lima and Conakry and low in Buenos Aires and Santiago.

7.3   Conclusion

Among the six cases, if water reform more closely approximates optimal policy, the system performs more effectively. Thus Santiago's water institu-tions are closest to what theory would recommend, which explains why it has the most efficient system.

None of the six reforms was designed to cope with water's distinguish-ing characteristics. First, all reforms failed to maximize benefits from health and external effects. Only two of the contracts (plus the failed Lima concession) addressed coverage and UFW, none of them had effective pro-visions to control pollution or wastewater use, and enforcement of the requirements that were present was weak in all cases. Even two institution-ally strong, low-cost cities—Buenos Aires and Santiago—have not been able to charge polluters the marginal cost of pollution. To the contrary, the possibility that the cost of sewage treatment would substantially in-crease water bills in Santiago may be one reason why the treatment facility has not yet been built.

Second, only Santiago provided formal, institutionalized protection against expropriation of quasi rents, and none is effective in protecting against capture. To protect against expropriation, the other reforms relied on reputation effects, outside intervention, and hostage revenues. These informal mechanisms have drawbacks. The diversion of revenues to pay government arrears in Abidjan and Conakry, for example, reduced the funds available for new investment. Informal mechanisms also seem to be less durable and to make capture more likely. As to protection against capture, no reform gave opposing interests such as consumers standing in the regulatory process. In most cases decisions are made by a national water regulator for all urban centers, which has reduced the influence of local interests in the process. In the two cases where the regulator must respond to local government representatives, Buenos Aires and Mexico City, decisions have been politicized, making commitments against expropriation of returns through low prices less credible.

Third, local water conditions have profound effects on the political economy of reform. The two cases with the highest opportunity cost of usage, Lima and Mexico City, also made the least progress in internalizing their externalities. The political system simply was unwilling to raise prices to the extent that was required to reflect the high social marginal cost of water. In contrast, the Buenos Aires concession illustrates the political advantages of a low-cost, renewable water system. There it was feasible to reduce water prices and still generate enough return to attract private investment.

Fourth, despite serious failings, the privately operated systems produced gains over a reasonable counterfactual. For example, the lease in Conakry brought safer water and a 40 percent increase in number of connections, something all knowledgeable observers agreed would not have occurred under state ownership. Nevertheless, Conakry's experience, and to a lesser extent Abidjan's, illustrates the cost of private operation where institutions are very weak. These cities have low-cost sustainable systems, but their prices appear to be much higher than in Buenos Aires or Santiago. These high prices are partly due to the African governments' weak ability to overcome informational asymmetries with private operators and partly due to their inability to offer commitment against expropriation of rents. Interestingly, rents are not expropriated in Abidjan or Conakry though low consumer prices but by forcing the operator to supply nonpayers, especially the government.

Conakry would be far better off with realistic prices, effective enforcement of rules against illegal connections and nonpayment, and a subsidy to assure low-income consumers access to safe water. How this would work in practice in such a weak institutional environment is questionable. The government is already free-riding on the rest of the bill-paying populace in Conakry, and efforts by outside aid agencies such as the World Bank to settle arrears and raise the capacity of the judiciary to enforce payment have had limited success. Recent efforts by the World Bank to reduce costs in Africa by allowing private self-supply, community participation in service delivery, greater innovation and variation in technology, and the like, may be more practical than a subsidy.

Our analysis is based on a small sample, and our survey of the sparse literature leaves many questions about water system reform in developing countries unanswered. Once recent experiments in water reform have more of a history, future research should be able to draw on a larger sample and analyze how well the many different contractual options being used perform in different institutional settings.

An important issue for further research is the cost, practicality, and effectiveness of competition in water supply. None of the cities opted for competition in any aspect of the system, which is still relatively rare in water supply. Although Chile's legislation allows competitive bidding for new concessions or for old ones that are revoked for noncompliance with regulations, even this limited form of competition seldom is used. Comparative competition, often touted for water systems, is not used by any of the cities in our sample, even Mexico City, which relies on numerous wells supplemented by distant sources and which divided the city into zones in each of which distribution was contracted out to a separate operator. How do water and sewers differ from other networks where competition has been introduced? Would it be possible to increase competition in institutionally weak settings such as Abidjan and Conakry to reduce the risk of capture? Why is yardstick competition not more widely practiced?

More systematic and theory-driven data collection also is needed to support the development of better performance measures. Comparing the performance of water systems would be easier and more accurate with better disaggregated data. Metered and unmetered water are different products, as are water taps in the house, taps in the yard, and public standpipes, yet coverage and pricing statistics often do not distinguish among them. Information on costs, including direct, opportunity, and social costs, is very poor, as is information on quality, such as potability, pressure, continuity, and the like. UFW is widely used as a measure of efficiency without considering whether supply is plentiful and sustainable or scarce and nonrenewable. Judgments are made about the appropriateness of prices based solely on the principle of cost recovery without always considering whether operational costs are high because of inefficiency or whether significant opportunity costs and externalities are present. Researchers cannot adequately correct these mistakes in the absence of a better standard for data collection, such as exists in telecommunications and energy.

References

Alcazar, Lorena, Manuel Angel Abdala, Mary M. Shirley, and Ana Maria Zuluaga. 1999. The case of the Aguas Argentinas concession. Washington, D.C.: World Bank. Draft.

Alcazar, Lorena, and Penelope Brook-Cowen. 1996. Institutions, politics and contracts: Private sector participation in urban water supply. Washington, D.C.: World Bank. Research proposal, processed.

Alcazar, Lorena, Colin Xu, and Ana Maria Zuluaga. 1999. Reforming urban water supply: The case of Peru. Washington, D.C.: World Bank. Draft.

Armstrong, Mark, Simon Cowan, and John Vickers. 1994. *Regulatory reform: Economic analysis and British experience.* Cambridge, Mass.: MIT Press.

Artana, Daniel, Fernando Navajas, and Santiago Urbiztondo. 1997. La regulaciòn econòmica en las concesiones de agua potable y desagues cloacales in Buenos Aires y Corrientes, Argentina. IDB Working Paper no. R-312. Washington, D.C.: Inter-American Development Bank.

Baldez, Lisa, and John Carey. 1997. Budget procedure and fiscal restraint in posttransition Chile. In *Political institutions and the determinants of public policy: When do institutions matter?* ed. Stephan Haggard and Mathew D. McCubbins. San Diego: University of California. Processed.

Baron, David P. 1989. Design of regulatory mechanisms and institutions. In *Handbook of industrial organization,* vol. 2, ed. Richard Schmalensee and Robert Willig. New York: North-Holland.

Baumol, William, and W. E. Oates. 1988. *The theory of environmental policy,* 2d ed. Cambridge: Cambridge University Press.

Constable, Pamela, and Arturo Valenzuela. 1989. Chile's return to democracy. *Foreign Affairs* 68:169–86.

Cowan, Simon. 1997. Price-cap regulation and inefficiency in relative pricing. *Journal of Regulatory Economics* 12 (1): 53–70.

Cropper, M. L., and W. E. Oates. 1992. Environmental economics: A survey. *Journal of Economic Literature* 30:675–740.

Esrey, Steven A. 1996. Water, waste, and well-being: A multicountry study. *American Journal of Epidemiology* 143 (6): 608–23.

Galal, Ahmed, Leroy Jones, Pankaj Tandon, and Ingo Vogelsang. 1994. *Welfare consequences of selling public enterprises: An empirical analysis.* New York: Oxford University Press.

Gelbach, Jonath B., and Lant H. Pritchett. 1997. More for the poor is less for the poor: The politics of targeting. Policy Research Working Paper no. 1799. Washington, D.C.: World Bank, Development Research Group.

Gisser, M. 1983. Groundwater: Focusing on the real issue. *Journal of Political Economy* 91:1001–27.

Haggarty, Luke, Penelope Brook-Cowen, and Ana Maria Zuluaga. 1999. Institutions, politics and contracts: Private sector participation in urban water supply systems: The case of Mexico City water sector service contracts. Washington, D.C.: World Bank. Draft.

Laffont, Jean-Jacques, and Jean Tirole. 1998. *Competition in telecommunications.* Manuscript.

London Economics. 1998. Competition in water. Report to the Department of International Development, London.

Lupia, Arthur, and Mathew McCubbins. 1998. Political credibility and economic reform. June. Draft.

Menard, Claude, and George Clarke. 1999a. Reforming urban water supply: The case of Abidjan, Côte d'Ivoire. Washington, D.C.: World Bank. Draft.

———. 1999b. A transitory regime: Water supply in Conakry, Guinea. Washington, D.C.: World Bank. Draft.

Munasinghe, Mohan. 1992. *Water supply and environmental management: Developing world applications.* Boulder, Colo.: Westview.

Nasser, Thomas-Olivier. 1997. Water concession in Buenos Aires: Issues and propositions. Processed.

Noll, Roger G. 1989. Economic perspectives on the politics of regulation. In *Hand-*

book of industrial organization, vol. 2, ed. Richard Schmalensee and Robert Willig. New York: North-Holland.

Roth, Gabriel. 1987. *The private provision of public services in developing countries.* New York: Oxford University Press.

Sheila Webb and Associates. 1992. Waterborne diseases in Peru. World Bank Policy Research Working Paper no. 969. Washington, D.C.: World Bank.

Shirley, Mary, Colin Xu, and Ana Maria Zuluaga. 1999. Institutions, politics and contracts: Private sector participation in urban water supply systems: The case of Chile. Washington, D.C.: World Bank. Draft.

World Bank. 1994a. Peru: Lima Rehabilitation and Management Project staff appraisal report. Washington, D.C.: World Bank. Processed.

———. 1994b. *World development report: Infrastructure for development.* New York: Oxford University Press.

———. 1995. *Bureaucrats in business: The economics and politics of government ownership.* New York: Oxford University Press.

Comment on the Paper by Roger G. Noll, Mary M. Shirley, and Simon Cowan   Takatoshi Ito

Noll, Shirley, and Cowan's paper starts with the notion that "political, technological, and institutional changes have spurred many developing countries to adopt reforms in order to improve the performance of their infrastructural industries by setting prices that are more in line with costs, creating independent regulatory agencies, involving the private sector in formerly nationalized industries, and allowing more competition." However, these "political, technological, and institutional changes" are not fully explicated in the subsequent discussion. Why did it become politically incorrect to run the water system? What technological progress was there in metering the usage of water? My basic question is: What's wrong with the government providing a basic utility like water?

The 1980s and 1990s witnessed the privatization of some industries that had traditionally been run by the government. Airlines, railroads, and telephones, for example, were once thought to be textbook examples of "public goods" best provided by the government in response to market failure. However, advances in theory (such as contestable market theory) coupled with technological progress (lowering fixed costs) and government failure have provided the motivation for these sectors to be privatized. In contrast, water supply is still in public hands in many industrialized countries. As such, what are the technological changes and government failures in this sector that would justify privatization? In the case of the poorest developing countries, does lack of funds on the part of the public sector justify privatization?

Takatoshi Ito is deputy vice minister for international affairs in the Ministry of Finance, Japan, and former professor of economics at Hitotsubashi University.

Unlike the airline and telecommunications sectors, water supply is a much more homogeneous service. There is little scope for competition once pipelines are laid. Hence, the scope for innovation—which may entail private sector participation—is limited.

Government-run utilities are often inefficient for a variety of reasons: unduly low and unsophisticated pricing, cost overruns, and bloated bureaucracies. But if the government simply privatizes the water supply company, it risks letting loose a natural monopoly. The challenge, therefore, is to put in place some sort of price controls that, on one hand, ensure that monopoly profits are not earned but, on the other hand, permit quasi rents so that owners recover their operational costs. The authors discuss the difficulties faced by the government in committing itself to a future pricing policy after privatization. Additionally, governments may find it difficult to obtain accurate cost data once the utility has been privatized. Finally, it is important to note that sophisticated pricing policies—two-part tariffs, peak-load pricing, or add-on sewage charges—may well be possible even in public corporations if managers are given the right incentives.

There seems to be both governmental failure and market failure in the provision of utilities. It has been shown that the former outweighed the latter in the case of airlines. But it does not seem absolutely clear whether the same holds true in the provision of water supply. Some aspects of governmental failure may well be corrected once governments are convinced to engage in reforms. It must be admitted, though, that the ability and willingness to conduct reform varies from country to country. In sum, the decision to privatize must be a function of the "cleanliness" of the bureaucracy as well as the managerial skills in the public and private sectors. The conditions under which it is prudent to privatize a natural monopoly like water supply poses an interesting research question.

Lack of funds in the poorest developing countries is cited as another justification for privatizing infrastructure. Some argue that the need for infrastructural investment in these countries far outweighs the availability of funds. However, to the extent that the water supply connection ratio is relatively high (70 percent in Buenos Aires and 99 percent in Santiago), lack of funds does not seem to be a major concern.

A number of important issues still need to be examined: First, to make the supply of water more efficient, would it be better to separate construction and operation? The government could build the system (with the help of international development institutions), while the private sector could operate it. Efficient pricing regulation by the government in this scenario could eliminate inefficiencies caused by unsophisticated pricing. Conversely, one could argue that the private sector should undertake the building too, if cost overruns inherent in governmental involvement are a major concern.

Second, not many cities in advanced countries have fully privatized their water supply systems. But to the extent they have, it is important to gather evidence on the effects of privatization on efficiency so as to better guide the efforts of developing countries.

Third, since water is considered part of the "civil minimum," any costs of disruption in service or deterioration in quality are higher than those of corresponding problems in the telephone and railroad sectors. As such, the role of regulation should be tighter in the case of this utility.

All in all, in the case of the water supply system, I am not convinced that privatization with enhanced supervision is any better or easier than reform within the government.

III

The Human Dimensions of Economic Policy Reform

8

Labor Market Reforms
Issues, Evidence, and Prospects

T. Paul Schultz

8.1 Introduction

The general objectives of labor market reforms are notably conflicting in terms of short-run and long-run efficiency and equity. Few policy reforms focus only on the labor market, while many deal with foreign exchange and trade systems, domestic tax-subsidy regimes, and industrial organizations, markets, and property rights. One might conclude that economic problems in labor markets are not today salient or central to progress. Alternatively, the magnitude of the problems in trade, taxation, and industrial organization may directly increase the leeway for misallocations of workers and human capital investments in the economy that seriously retard development.

These conditions that contribute to the severity of labor market distortions may, therefore, have to be resolved first if labor market reforms are expected to succeed. Perhaps the political economy also constrains direct reform of labor markets by precluding legislation that makes appropriate changes in labor codes or worker benefits transparently to the disadvantage of powerful and concentrated interest groups. If this impression is valid, it may explain why the historical and even analytical literature on labor market reforms is so sparse. This explanation may also prepare the reader for not expecting here a synthesis of a well-developed literature but only an impressionistic menu of issues, some indications of relevant empirical patterns, and prospects.

Labor markets can be inefficient in allocating labor for many reasons,

T. Paul Schultz is the Malcolm K. Brachman Professor of Economics at Yale University.
The author has benefited from the comments of Mario Blejer, Jenny Hunt, Anne Krueger, Germano Mwabu, John Pencavel, Julie Schaffner, T. N. Srinivasan, and Takatoshi Ito.

but I could find few salient empirical studies that estimate the magnitude of the deadweight loss caused by one or another market failure, distortion, segmentation, or regulatory intervention. Applying current microeconometric standards of public finance, the conventional estimates of wage distortions are potentially subject to a variety of biases that may be difficult to correct. Moreover, these Harberger wage "triangles," or approximations of how much wages of observationally equivalent workers differ in different "segments" of the labor market, are but the first step toward evaluating the lost social output caused by these market failures, or the gains that could be recovered by suitable policy reforms.

Section 8.2 reviews a number of economic issues that are intertwined in labor market institutions and regulations and considers the benefits and costs that are hypothetically tied to reforms. Programs and policies that are commonly linked to labor market distortions and segmentation are considered in section 8.3, which ends with an overview of the studies I have seen on the changing wage structures in the transition economies. It would be myopic to regard these changes in the value of different types of labor in this period of transition from centrally planned to market-oriented economies as due to the removal of some specific labor market "distortion." Rather these changes in the relative values of labor between systems reflect more fundamental tasks of establishing property rights and markets for capital, finding mechanisms to stimulate competitive markets, and creating incentives to adopt and develop efficient modern technologies.

8.2   Objectives in the Labor Market and Reforms

Evaluating the performance of the labor market can be approached, first, in terms of static efficiency of utilizing fully the productive contribution of the adult population and, second, in terms of dynamic efficiency of investing optimally in the human capital of workers and redeploying them over time to jobs where their present discounted productivity is maximized. A third objective is fairness in wage differences and ultimately equality in consumption opportunities after taxes and transfers. Combining these three objectives to arrive at a single criterion of macroeconomic performance of the labor market is not straightforward. There is little agreement on even the rough empirical magnitudes of the losses associated with the least complicated static forms of distortions or segmentation of the labor market that have attracted the most attention.

8.2.1   Static Efficiency

Minimizing unemployment and achieving a high rate of utilization of the adult population in economically productive activity is one definition of an efficient labor market. In order for the labor market to clear efficiently, wages adjust sufficiently to achieve full (e.g., noninflationary) employment, workers respond to changes in wages across jobs in different firms, sectors, and regions, and workers optimally search for and accept improved alternative employment opportunities as they arise.

But labor contracts typically have a duration and specify many contingencies, more explicitly in the formally contracted or covered sector than in the informal or uncovered sector, where only customary practices discipline the employment relationship. Governments often legislate highly complex regulations on acceptable forms of labor contract so as to achieve their goals, among which is sometimes a stated objective, as in Latin America, of strengthening labor to deal on "equal terms" with the concentrated power of large capitalistic firms, or in other situations governments seek to weaken union power to achieve another balance. Restrictions may be specified on firing and hiring, on unemployment and social insurance (e.g., job-related accidents, medical care, retirement) financed typically by payroll taxes on the worker and firm, on occupational safety standards and mandated fringe benefits (e.g., holidays, vacations, sick pay, maternity leave), and finally on minimum wages.

Governments typically establish intricate rules under which workers can (freely?) organize themselves to participate in the collective bargaining process that determines their wage and employment conditions and thereby may affect the relative strength of the two sides, as noted above. These contracts are then negotiated by labor, management, and perhaps government representatives, balancing objectives at the level of a plant or firm, or at the level of an industry, or at the level of a national confederation of workers and employers.

Disagreements in the practice of labor relations may then be adjudicated by conventional courts or resolved by special government tribunals that introduce additional uncertainties and lags in outcomes and provide further room for politics to modify economic outcomes in the labor market (mainly for the covered sector). Public sector employees are often provided with distinct institutions to resolve their wage and employment conditions, with further appeal processes that protect civil service workers from arbitrary (or any) disciplinary incentives, as protection from politicians filling public jobs as patronage. In section 8.3 of this paper some of these public regulations of the labor market are examined to assess their social costs and potential for policy reform. These institutional and legislative variations in the labor market can be exceedingly complex and legally convoluted, making it hard to construct empirical measures that can be qualitatively compared across countries to proxy "flexibility," "distortion," "segmentation," "regulatory burden," "equity," or "efficiency." More specific institutional comparisons can help in this regard but do not eliminate the frustratingly unquantifiable dimensions of the conflicting objectives and achievements of labor markets (Pencavel 1991, 1995).

Much of the current debate on labor market reforms in low-income countries is shaped by the contrasting achievements of the high-income OECD countries after 1973 as their total factor productivity growth slowed. In the subsequent twenty-five years real wages in the United States have stagnated, but employment has grown briskly, and the unemployment rate has fallen from 9 to less than 5 percent. In Western Europe unemployment (and early retirement) has increased and real wages have continued to advance modestly, with the exception of the United Kingdom, which reformed its labor market under the Thatcher administrations and has followed the U.S. approach. The Delors report for the European Union reached the conclusion that in continental Western Europe excessive job security, generous unemployment benefits, high minimum wages, liberal eligibility rules for and generous levels of welfare benefits, and finally restrictions on part-time work were major causes of the persistently high, long-duration unemployment found recently in Europe. Some labor economists in the United States subscribe to this view that the inflexibility of the labor market in Europe and the generosity of the European safety net of welfare programs were the cause of the differential growth in employment and resulting unemployment between Western Europe and the United States after 1980 (e.g., Haveman 1996). But this European arrangement of labor market and welfare programs also claims some offsetting gains: wage and consumption inequality are lower in Europe (Blank 1994), and firms and workers have longer tenure matches, which could provide stronger incentives to invest in firm-specific training that may be responsible for labor productivity gains and aggregate growth.

What remains clear, however, is that unemployment is higher in continental Europe, and other indicators of underutilization of labor are evident including more rapid declines in participation rates for men in Europe than in the United States and legal segmentation of the labor force into part-time and full-time workers, which can widen compensation and training gaps between these segments of the labor force (OCED 1997).

Japan illustrates how institutionalizing the temporary work category creates a potentially inefficient segmentation of the labor force. Female workers are a large and rapidly growing share of the Japanese labor force, but they are predominantly categorized as "untenured" or temporary workers. When employment is cut in Japan, women are more likely than men to be fired from the larger firms that hired permanent (predominantly male) workers with the expectation of lifetime employment. The special contractual status of the untenured workers also provides firms with less incentive to train them and explains why they are less costly to fire and rehire when economic conditions of the firm improve. This feature of the Japanese labor code provides the labor market with more flexibility, or a buffer stock of temporary workers. But to achieve flexibility in this manner, the code introduces a form of segmentation. The dualism in the Japanese labor market erodes the motivation of women workers and their employers to invest in their training. These labor market institutions undoubtedly are part of the reason that Japanese women have very flat earnings-age profiles over their life cycles compared with the profiles in other high-income, well-educated countries and that the wages of women relative to men are the lowest in OECD comparisons (Schultz 1997).

In low-income countries, the static inefficiency of the labor market is not as clearly reflected in the unemployment rate as it is in the OECD countries. This is partly because most low-income countries do not have the welfare programs of the high-income countries that support from public revenues the unemployed, poor, disabled, and sick. Measurement of unemployment is also more uncertain outside of the formal sector, and often half or more of the labor force works in what is called the informal or uncovered (by government regulations) sector, defined generally to include the self-employed and those who work in an unpaid capacity in their families or in an uncovered wage sector of the economy. Not only is there often no unemployment insurance for those working in the informal sector, there is more ambiguity in defining unemployment when hours are flexible and work in the market and home become mixed (OECD 1994, 1995; Atkinson and Micklewright 1991).

The major source of inefficiency in low-income country labor markets is therefore summarized by the dualism between the formal and informal sectors of the labor force. The general welfare consequences of such dualism in the labor force is graphically described by Johnson and Mieszkowski (1970) in the case of labor unions and generalized to minimum wages by Mincer (1976), and other forms of segmentation by Cain (1986). Segmentation is a source of inefficiency because the formal or covered sector limits wages, imposes taxes on labor, or restricts the flexibility of the labor contract in other ways, while it is typically assumed that the informal or uncovered sector efficiently allocates its labor and other resources (Brown, Gilroy, and Kohen 1982).

In many Latin American countries the combination of payroll taxes and labor contract regulations on firing creates a wide wedge between the wage received by the worker and the cost of labor to the formal sector employer. For example, in 1992 the average Brazilian worker in the formal sector received a take-home wage that was about 53 percent of the wage and payroll taxes paid by the worker and employer (Marquez 1995). Estimates vary but suggest that workers value the additional medical care and social insurance at perhaps 20 to 30 percent of their tax value. This suggests that comparable workers cost an employer in the formal sector 30 to 40 percent more than they cost an employer in the informal sector.[1]

Such segmented parts of the labor force imply an inefficiency in allocat-

---

1. Informal sector employers also have difficulty gaining access to an export market for their output because government regulation of foreign exchange markets can require them to submit to the labor market regulation regime.

ing labor that depends not only on the intersector wage gap for comparably productive workers but also on the elasticity of demand and supply of labor in the two sectors (Mincer 1976). This form of labor market segmentation is also likely to displace workers from the labor force entirely, as the wage is depressed in the informal competitive sector, and some individuals then allocate all of their productive time to home production. To quantify the deadweight loss from such a distortion in the labor market one therefore also wants to know the productive possibilities in home production or how much labor productivity declines in the home production sector as it absorbs more of the population's labor supply.

The figures provided above on payroll taxes for Brazil would also be of a similar magnitude for many other countries in Latin America, such as Colombia, Peru, Bolivia, Ecuador, and perhaps Mexico and much of Central America, where the informal sector employs half or more of the labor force (Marquez 1995). When the formal sector firm has no legal way to discharge workers, even in bankruptcy, as in India (see chap. 4 in this volume), another form of labor market segmentation arises that raises substantially the expected cost of labor for the formal compared with the informal sector, but these issues may be better formulated in an intertemporal context.

8.2.2 Dynamic Efficiency

Flexibility is most concretely defined as the ability to hire and fire without excessive costs and the mobility of workers to change jobs, sectors, and regions of employment without legal or social restrictions. As noted later in section 8.3, some schemes of job severance pay or firing penalties provide incentives to employers to dismiss workers before they can accumulate sufficient tenure or be reclassified from temporary to permanent worker. These provisions of the labor code would seem intended to provide the worker with job security and thereby encourage more efficient levels of investment in firm-specific training. But the response of employers may be to hire more workers on short-term contracts and thereby avoid the severance penalties and legal challenges to termination of long-term employees (Marquez 1995). As changes are introduced in these provisions of the labor code in a specific country, it is possible with annual labor force surveys to estimate the consequences of these reforms on job turnover, the growth of wages with respect to tenure on the job, wage levels, and employment growth by tenure category. But in reality the policy evaluation task is empirically daunting, and labor code reform evaluations are rarely undertaken even though the required labor force surveys are available from a growing number of countries (Schaffner 1997).

In addition to public policies that encourage or discourage job turnover, which seems to be substantially higher in some low-income than in high-income countries (Schaffner 1997; Kim and Topel 1995), there are cultural and institutional variations in labor market arrangements. The hypothesis was advanced in the 1980s that part of the reason for Japan's strikingly rapid growth in labor productivity, steep wage-age profiles, and heavy investment in worker training was that it was traditional in Japan to hire workers into the larger firms directly out of school and retain them for their entire lifetimes. This implicit lifetime employment contract could, it was hypothesized, explain the other productivity-related aspects of the Japanese economy noted earlier, including the need for a mandatory early retirement provision (Hashimoto and Raisian 1985; Mincer and Higuchi 1988).[2] Clearly, the slowdown in the Japanese economy in the 1990s has provided another perspective on some of the costs of the rigidities that this system entails.

Evolving pressures on the Japanese economy for shifting workers from lower to higher productivity sectors may have been more difficult to satisfy within the traditional consensus-oriented institutions of the Japanese labor market, because such shifts require redistribution of personal incomes. This reallocation problem in Japan may be compared with the efficient reduction in real wages for all workers that was implemented to accommodate the oil shocks of the 1970s. Although worker-employer bargaining occurs on a decentralized basis, wages in those sectors of the Japanese economy that have failed to increase their labor productivity at the pace achieved elsewhere in the world have continued to grow with national wages. The redeployment of labor out of the stagnant and low-productivity sectors of agriculture, retail sales, distribution, and so forth, has not occurred smoothly. Just as insolvent financial institutions have not been allowed to fail, workers in industries that have failed to increase their productivity are given insufficient wage incentives to change their sector of employment.

The existence of a large informal sector in which wages are determined competitively and turnover is not regulated provides a buffer to absorb unemployment. Fluctuations in the Brazilian economy from 1970 to 1990 did not greatly affect the quantity of jobs, but it did shift them between the formal (inflexible) and informal (competitive) sector, without causing unemployment rates to change systematically (Amadeo et al. 1994). This apparent flexibility of the overall Brazilian labor market is of course purchased at the cost of dualism, which has the inefficient features of a

---

2. Counterexamples are also to be found. Korea in the 1970s and 1980s increased its employment in manufacturing, invested heavily in training of its workforce, and achieved remarkable growth in labor productivity. Nonetheless, high levels of turnover of workers were evident, where the typical worker in manufacturing was hired directly out of school but had job duration of only four years, on average, compared with nine in the United States and higher in Japan (Kim and Topel 1995). The rapid turnover of workers in the Korean case did not appear to reduce the motivation of Korean firms to make a heavy commitment to training (World Bank 1995). This highly educated and mobile labor force was a strength of the Korean economy in helping it to deal with structural changes.

segmented labor market where wages for the same type of labor differ between the covered (formal, regulated, unionized) segment and the uncovered (informal, unregulated, nonunionized) segment of the labor market (Johnson and Mieszkowski 1970; Vijverberg and van der Gaag 1990). Should the low unemployment achieved by Brazil in the 1970s and 1980s be viewed as an indicator of satisfactory flexibility in the labor market, or does the adjustment to external shocks by only the informal labor market suggest this is an inefficient arrangement putting the entire burden of structural adjustment on workers in the informal sector?

This raises a second concept of flexibility: do wage differences across sectors, regions, and skill levels adjust readily to facilitate the redeployment of labor in an efficient manner following a change in the relative prices of inputs and outputs or technology? In the Brazilian case, foreign exchange deficits in the 1980s led the government to restrict imports, which however failed to achieve a reallocation of labor from import-competing to export industries (Marquez 1995). Employment grew in services and trade, which are predominantly informal sectors, along with government services. Manufacturing employment associated with Brazil's export industries tended to grow only at the rate achieved by the overall economy in this period.

Government regulations that encourage the growth of the informal sector also tend to make it difficult for the smaller scale informal firms to export their output, however productive they may be or tradable their products. Another consequence of putting the burden of structural adjustment on the informal sector is that recessions tend to cause greater variation in wages and unemployment among less skilled workers, whose employment is concentrated in the informal sector. Female and younger inexperienced workers may also be displaced from formal sector jobs if the formal sector contracts, as minimum wage floors increase in real terms and payroll taxes rise, discouraging employment of less productive demographic groups. But few studies make a compelling case for how large the resource gains would be if this form of formal-informal dualism were eliminated or payroll taxes reduced and these revenues obtained from a tax with a wider base, such as a value-added tax (Schaffner 1998).

Few studies posit a framework within which to evaluate the flexibility of the labor market to redeploy workers efficiently across a national economy as it experiences structural change. Kim and Topel (1995) offered a methodology for gauging how efficient or integrated a labor market is and applied it to a study of Korea from 1970 to 1990. First, they showed that employment has grown across industry in parallel with growth in labor productivity by industry, as one would expect if the demand for outputs of those industries were elastic because of their access to international markets. They regressed employment and labor productivity measured by output per worker by manufacturing industries and over time on dummies for year and industry. The employment and productivity residuals from these regressions are strongly positively correlated, leading them to conclude that the growth in industry-specific employment is being driven by growth in that industry's labor productivity, though they might also have included controls for international price (productivity) trends by industry that might capture industry-specific technological changes that would be relevant to export-oriented firms.

Second, they demonstrated that the growth in real wages across industries in this two-decade period is not correlated significantly with growth in employment for that industry and year, using the same regression residual method. They concluded from this lack of pattern between employment growth and wage growth that the Korean labor market is unified across these manufacturing sectors. Average labor productivity tripled in Korea in this twenty-year period but differed markedly by industry. Korea appears to have redeployed workers fast enough to keep wages growing at about the same rate across the economy. Interindustry mobility of workers was high, but the entry of new workers into the entire manufacturing sector occurred mostly by hiring urban-schooled youth, while the out-migration of workers from agriculture found employment in urban services. High turnover within manufacturing may have contributed to the absence of growing gaps between the wage levels in rapidly growing and in stagnating manufacturing industries. A major limitation of their Korean analysis is that it is restricted to male workers in urban manufacturing employment and is thus unable to capture the informal sector or clarify the inefficient dualism that lies outside of manufacturing for males. Their approach provides a quantitative methodology for evaluating the flexibility and integration of the labor market within at least this dominant and growing segment of the Korean labor force and could be applied to the entire labor force in other countries where nationally representative surveys are available.

8.2.3 Inequality

The ratio of wages between more and less educated workers has increased in a growing number of countries after about 1980, though the magnitude and timing of this trend appears to have been affected by a variety of domestic policies, some of which may be classified as long-term human capital investment strategies rather than labor market or welfare policies. The standard analysis of changes in U.S. wage differentials during the 1960s and 1970s assigned substantial explanatory weight to the changing relative size of the baby boom cohort entering the labor force in the 1970s and the changing relative proportion of recent cohorts with different amounts of education (e.g., Welch 1979). But starting in about 1980, the ratio of wages of college graduates to those of high school graduates began to increase, nearly doubling in a decade (Katz and Murphy 1992; Murphy and Welch 1992). The associated growth in wage inequality was less readily explained by changes in the size of birth cohorts or the relative size of educational strata. Nor did the change in industrial composition of employment or the opening of the U.S. economy to international trade appear to account for these changes in wage structure (Topel 1997). One was left with the "residual hypothesis" that technical change had developed a skill bias, creating greater derived demand for more educated labor, which was responsible for the added wage inequality in the United States, United Kingdom, and Australia. These trends were less extreme in Canada, where educational inequalities grew less pronounced, and were more muted in many European countries and in Japan (Davis 1992; Gottschalk and Smeeding 1997; Schultz 1998b).

These trends in inequality might be more dramatic if those who are unemployed (or no longer participating in the labor force) could somehow be included at the bottom of the wage distribution. There have been substantial declines in participation rates of males belonging to the lowest education and wage groups in the United States from 1967 to 1987 (Juhn 1992), and the pattern of declining participation among those groups experiencing wage declines has continued (Welch 1997). The generosity of welfare programs and of unemployment insurance in excess of competitive wages has contributed to this disemployment effect of the least productive or the least motivated to work. It appears likely that offsetting the gains in continental Europe of more equal consumption opportunities achieved by the safety net of welfare programs is the lost productive contribution of those retiring prematurely from market employment. As taxes on market earnings increase to support the expanding services of the welfare state system, more workers are dissuaded from working by the declines in their after-tax wages (Rosen 1996). There are clearly differences in objectives between the United States and much of northwestern Europe in terms of these contrasting labor market and welfare policies.

Aside from the United Kingdom, measures to reduce the inflexibility of the labor market have not been broadly pursued in Europe, and thus labor market reforms cannot be evaluated to determine how they might affect employment, unemployment, labor productivity, and wage and income inequality. As in the United States, when the duration of unemployment benefits has been changed, these policy changes have had the expected effect on the probability that a worker with a specific duration of unemployment will find employment (Meyer 1989; Anderson and Meyer 1993). When Germany or Austria changed its age limits for early retirement or the duration of unemployment benefits for the elderly, transitions to retirement and hazards of reemployment in the treatment group responded in much the same way as they did in U.S. studies (Hunt 1995; Winter-Ebmer 1996). When Spain created a special category of short-term employment for which employers would not be penalized if the new workers were subsequently laid off, aggregate employment began to rise and unemployment to fall in the 1990s. But these modifications in minor features of labor legislation are not comprehensive enough to affect clearly aggregate trends in unemployment or employment growth. For example, changes in eligibility rules for unemployment benefits are still subject to the interpretation of local labor management committees in Germany and may not follow the letter of the law in reducing the generosity of federal labor legislation. Thus there is little evidence that tentative and small efforts to make European labor markets more flexible have yet made much of a difference.

It is useful to compare these wage changes with the evolution of wage structures in low- and middle-income market economies, and later the patterns in the transition economies. A growing number of these developing countries have collected comparable cross-sectional labor market surveys for several decades. It is common to find that the wage returns to schooling first increase, at the onset of sustained rapid economic growth, and then decrease, as the relative supply of educated workers increases sharply and apparently catches up to the rate of growth of demand for these more skilled workers.

Studies suggest this pattern occurred in Taiwan, Korea, Brazil, and Colombia, for example. In Taiwan wage returns to schooling are reported to have increased from 1964 to 1975, and then from 1976 to 1995, the average wage returns to an additional year of schooling gradually fell from 9 to 7 percent for full-time wage earners (Schultz 1998a; Grindling et al. 1995). In Korea the returns to secondary and higher education increase until 1976 and slowly decline until 1987, when the returns to college education begin to diminish more rapidly. The decline in the log variance in wages by one-third during the 1980s is attributed to this narrowing of wage inequality related to schooling (Kim and Topel 1995; Choi 1993). Brazil, despite its unusually high level of income inequality, experienced an increase in rates of return to secondary and higher education in the 1960s, followed by a sustained decline in the 1980s. The decline in returns to education in Brazil is steeper in states where the supplies of educated workers are relatively larger and the growth in wages and development has been more rapid, such as in São Paulo and Rio de Janeiro (Reis, Guilherme, and Barros 1991). Colombia also experienced a widening of ratios between the earnings of education groups before the mid-1960s, whereas these wage ratios have declined as has wage inequality after the 1970s, when the supply of better educated workers increased more rapidly (Londoño 1995). Cross-country and time-series differences in income inequality derived from World Bank data sources assembled by Deininger and Squire (1996) suggest that income inequality has tended to decline slowly, on average, with economic development since the mid-1960s, particularly in those low- and middle-income countries that have expanded their educational systems more rapidly. Only in the high-income group of countries (i.e., OECD) is there a clear tendency after 1980 for income inequality to increase, and to this group should probably now be added the transition economies that are discussed later, in subsection 8.3.8 (Schultz 1998b). In some middle-income countries there is also evidence that education-based wage differentials have recently risen with trade liberalization (Robbins 1995; Harrison and Hanson 1999).

The tendency for wage ratios by schooling groups to increase, at least initially, serves the purpose of motivating individuals and families to sacrifice current output and consumption to increase the schooling of youth. These rising private wage returns to schooling also signal the public sector to coordinate the expansion of the appropriate levels of training for which the labor market is willing to pay an increasing proportional premium. Wage differentials between regions may also serve a similar purpose by fostering economically productive levels of migration, if the political system can accommodate the strains of adjustment on urban (or possibly also rural) infrastructure, such as housing, schooling, health, and sanitation. Changes in age-earnings profiles are a more complicated development and may be due to a combination of pressures: the obsolescence of skills acquired under an earlier but now reformed regime, the technological obsolescence of past schooling in a technologically dynamic economy, and the slowing of population growth of younger cohorts due to the demographic transition.

The primary policy implication of these development-induced changes in wage structures is that those countries that have expanded their educational systems in advance of the requirements of their economy have tended to perform well and eventually achieved a reduction in wage inequality. The question remains whether the educational, mobility, and training policies that these countries adopted were directed at labor market reform or human capital social investments. Although increasing the supply of educated labor to the economy can reduce substantially inequality while enhancing the prospects for growth, it is more speculative whether generous welfare programs à la the European model narrow inequality without sacrificing labor market efficiency.

8.3 Public Policies and Programs Affecting the Labor Market

Segmentation, dualism, or discrimination can arise from a variety of distortions in the labor market, and the inefficiency it imposes on the economy depends on the magnitude of the distortion, or the difference in wages or labor costs in different sectors for workers of the same productivity, how the distortion is caused and corrected, and the elasticity of the supply of and demand for labor in the various segments of the labor market (Cain 1986; Schultz 1993). The most discussed form of dualism is between the contractual labor sector subject to government regulations and the remaining unregulated sector, as typically illustrated by Latin America (de Soto 1989). This difference in the cost of labor in the two sectors arises because of a host of government measures, not typically due to a single intervention. The combination of payroll taxes is the most visible, but it is augmented by more difficult to quantify restrictions on the conditions of employment, penalties and justification for firing, minimum wage and mandated fringe benefits, institutional protection for public sector employees, industrial interest groups, unions, and so forth.

8.3.1 Firing Costs and Worker Turnover

A troubling aspect of labor market flexibility is its downside for discouraging investment in worker skills that cannot be transferred to another job. Becker (1964) emphasized that to the extent that on-the-job training (OJT) enhanced the productivity of the worker only on the current job, this form of firm-specific training might be undervalued by worker and employer and hence subject to underinvestment. Without a binding long-term employment contract, the employer (through terminating the worker) or worker (through quitting and job turnover) can reduce the expected return on OJT to the other party. As noted earlier, the U.S. and Japanese labor markets from 1960 to 1980 have been contrasted in terms of how the lifetime employment relationships honored by larger Japanese firms provided stronger incentives to invest in OJT and might explain faster Japanese labor productivity growth. But I know of no empirical evidence on the magnitude of the underinvestment in firm-specific training that is associated with a more "flexible" labor market or an estimate of the social costs that should be borne to reduce inefficient turnover. One justification for penalizing employers for firing workers is that these measures encourage firm-specific training, and yet this approach can backfire, at least according to Latin American evidence (Schaffner 1997).

For example, in Brazil, the accumulated value of a worker's personal insurance account (FGTS) is paid to the worker when he or she leaves the job. This scheme encourages the employer to lay off younger workers to reduce his payments out of the firm's FGTS and may encourage workers who are credit constrained to change jobs to draw down their accumulated balances (Amadeo et al. 1994). This form of "unemployment insurance" is credited with contributing to Brazil's high turnover rates in the formal sector and for discouraging OJT. Because the payment is a lump sum, it does not require the worker to be unemployed or to search for a job. Indeed taking a job in the informal sector while drawing down FGTS benefits is like collecting a pension or vacation paycheck. A similar feature of the labor code in Colombia was modified to reduce its incentives to lay off workers with shorter tenure, and an increase in job durations was observed (Schaffner 1997). The combination of very high payroll taxes on labor and heavy severance payments for employers in the formal sector of Latin

America contributes to the formal-informal labor market dualism that characterizes this continent (de Soto 1989).

8.3.2   Unemployment Insurance, Public Work, and Training Programs

Other social programs and policies can help to redistribute across persons the unequal burden of unemployment. Unemployment insurance (UI) is the most direct mechanism by which the public sector provides eligible workers with a benefit replacing some fraction of lost wages, for a specified duration of unemployment. A large and sophisticated literature deals with designing UI schemes to minimize bad incentive effects: to reduce adverse selection bias (workers becoming unemployed who want to work less, or firms laying off workers who are only temporarily redundant) and to reduce moral hazard (not searching for a new job until UI is exhausted, unless the wage offer is sufficiently above the UI benefit; Meyer 1989). The United States was the first, to my knowledge, to opt (from 1937) for varying the UI tax on employers in response to their past layoff experience and to diminish the incentive for firms to use cyclical layoffs (unemployment) as a cost-saving device when confronted with cyclical demand for their output. Nonetheless, the United States is singled out as the high-income country with the greatest volatility in unemployment over the business cycle, suggesting that U.S. employers are less able to adjust wages over the business cycle or prefer for other reasons to adjust employment rather than wages.

Public work programs such as were introduced in Chile in its recession after 1975 (PEM and POJH) recategorized the unemployed and assigned some of these persons to relief jobs in the public sector. The Netherlands reduced its unemployment by introducing welfare legislation that assigned many of the unemployed to disability programs and then sought to cut back these expanded programs. Various European countries liberalized their retirement pensions available for older unemployed workers, and they were thus able to reduce the rate of long-term unemployment. Clearly, the magnitude of unemployment is affected by the scale of the (after tax) UI replacement rate, the duration of coverage, eligibility, and the variety of other disability and welfare programs that may offer competitive benefits. When unemployment benefits are based on the monetary value of prior wages, periods of rapid inflation as in Russia can reduce benefits to the point where there is no incentive to even register as unemployed (Foley 1997).

UI schemes make unemployment more attractive to the individual and thereby increase its frequency, other things equal. Adjusting UI premiums for the firm according to the unemployment experience of the firm's past employees (i.e., experience rating) is one means to encourage firms to reduce their cyclical variation in employment and thereby reduce unemployment. But experience rating of UI taxes by firm has not been widely adopted by countries other than the United States (Baicker, Goldin, and Katz 1997). Other forms of social welfare legislation, as they have evolved in most high-income countries, change further the costs and benefits of unemployment of different durations, with likely consequences on unemployment and labor force participation levels. In addition, the very concept of unemployment as a calibrating measure of labor market flexibility or efficiency of labor utilization is more problematic in a low- or middle-income country. When as in Brazil, Peru, Ecuador, Bolivia, or Colombia informal sector activities still occupy as much as half of the labor force, the comparability of unemployment rates across countries is complicated.[3]

Can the public sector help workers to find new jobs after they become displaced from others or raise the productivity of the unemployed to foster their reemployment after they have lost wage benefits associated with firm-specific training capital? Public programs to accomplish these goals are rationalized on at least three different grounds: strictly in terms of an efficient human capital investment that raises the worker's lifetime productivity; as a subsidy to encourage firm-specific OJT, which may otherwise be subject to underinvestment; and as an equitable compensation for the unfair incidence of personal burdens related to the structural adjustment process. In the United States, sophisticated efforts to evaluate the internal rates of return from job retraining programs do not find robust evidence that these undertakings have yielded competitive payoffs, and certainly not of the same magnitude as for regular schooling, and perhaps not even equal to the more modest returns associated with vocational education (Heckman, LaLonde, and Smith 1999). Training programs in Latin America, in addition, tend to be oriented toward workers already employed in the formal sector. They can thus be most readily justified on the basis of the second argument listed above, and even on that basis they do not get high marks for efficiency (Paredes and Riveros 1994).

Chile provides an exceptional case study of how these large public training programs can be reformed. In 1976 Chile terminated its inflexible and costly INACAP public training program, which provided vocational training for relatively well educated youth who were generally already employed in the formal sector. This program in Chile was similar to those in Brazil (SENAI) and Colombia (SENA), whereas in Mexico CIMO concentrated on small enterprises. In its place Chile created a National Training and Employment Service (SENCE) that removed the state from implementing the program. Instead the agency auctioned training contracts off

---

3. Unemployment becomes more difficult to quantify and validate in a survey among the self-employed, those working in family unpaid jobs, or even those working in casual work that is not specified by a contract or subject to the withholding of taxes or social insurance payments. Self-employed farmers, e.g., may be underemployed in a particular season of the year, as in the north of Thailand, but then substitute to that time of year other activities that are not tied to season, such as maintenance investments or temporary migration.

to groups in the private sector, who were then responsible for instituting cost recovery tuition fees and monitoring how successful those enrolled in their programs were in qualifying for better paying jobs after their training (Paredes and Riveros 1994). Private firms in Chile were also given tax incentives to encourage more training of low-wage workers, entitling them to deduct from taxable profits these training costs up to a per worker ceiling. Although these programs continue to be designed to serve the needs of employed workers and firms, rather than to facilitate retraining of the unemployed who lost their jobs due to structural adjustment, the reforms in Chile are reportedly flexible in responding to the current needs of the economy and in expanding resources invested in the training of the least skilled workers.

8.3.3   Mandated Fringe Benefits and Minimum Wages

Studies of mandated fringe benefits for specific groups of workers in the United States and Canada suggest that most of such benefits are "passed through" to workers in the form of reduced take-home pay. For example, Gruber (1994) found in the United States that as states legislate maternity benefits for workers, according to congressional guidelines, the wage rates of younger women (i.e., of childbearing age) decrease relative to those in previous years in the same state, relative to neighboring states in the same year without such benefits, and relative to men and older women in the same state and year. Employment effects are insignificant, perhaps because the costs of the benefits are largely deducted from the wages of the beneficiaries. Across OECD countries, Ruhm (1998) reported that short (three month) parental leave has no effect on women's wages, but longer leave is associated with lower female wages and increased female employment. In other less flexible markets that are unable to reduce wages to the beneficiary group, one might expect there would be a decline in employment from the employer's side, even as there could be a greater supply of labor offered to fill the remaining jobs that are now more highly compensated. This literature suggests that mandated benefits for women, and specifically maternity leave, may reduce employment opportunities for young women in a highly regulated labor market. Regardless, these benefits are not likely to achieve their stated objective of uniformly improving women's welfare. In a more regulated labor market, as one finds in many low-income countries in the formal sector, this same policy intervention to provide women with maternity benefits would probably reduce the fraction of women of childbearing ages employed.

In one of the oldest cases of labor market regulation, minimum wages have been viewed as helping one group of workers to remain employed and benefit from their wages being pulled up to the minimum wage, and hurting another group whose productivity does not warrant a job at the minimum wage and who thus are displaced from low-wage jobs into unemployment or out of the covered labor force. The ratio of minimum wages to national GNP per capita tends to be lower in high-income countries than in low-income countries.[4] Thus the marginal worker who is helped or hurt by the minimum wage tends to be among the relatively poor in industrially advanced, high-income countries but is often in the urban middle class in low-income countries. With UI and other welfare programs available to support those who lose their jobs in high-income countries, the magnitude of minimum wage gains and losses are debated conditional on the existence of this safety net for those who lose their jobs. There is currently no agreement among economists on the welfare balance of these program effects even in high-income countries (Card and Krueger 1995; Deere, Murphy, and Welch 1996).

In low-income countries those who benefit from a minimum wage tend to be among the relatively high income groups, and the burden of downward adjustment in wages and employment is imposed on the many poorer workers who generally lack public welfare systems and can rely only on private family transfers (Schultz and Mwabu 1998). In a middle-income country, Chile, the minimum wage remains controversial. In June 1989 an exception was granted for youths aged 14 to 18, for whom the minimum wage was reduced by 16 percent, with the expectation that it would increase employment among this group who sustain high unemployment rates (Bravo and Contreras 1998). Comparisons of employment between 1989 and 1990 and between the age groups 14–18 and 19–23 were not able to identify a significant employment effect for the difference between the two age groups. Thus, even when suitable data and well-designed policy reforms are observed, the magnitude of the regulatory effects in the labor market may still be difficult to measure, possibly obscured by noncompliance or nonenforcement. The nonparametric (kernel) distribution of wages in the two age groups in Chile indicates a surprisingly large fraction of workers report their wages are below the legal minimum, although this could be attributed to errors in measurement (Bravo and Contreras 1998, fig. 1). Enforcement of minimum wages adds an uncertainty to the evaluation of their impact for which no solution has been proposed (Schultz 1988).

The relative size of the informal sector tends to increase with many forms of government regulation of the labor market, including high social insurance taxes on labor, effectively enforced minimum wage legislation, lifetime job security provisions, and mandated fringe benefits, such as in

---

4. E.g., in countries with PPP income per capita of about $2,000 in 1995 the unit ratio of minimum wages to GNP per capita is 1.0, whereas this ratio falls to 0.5 for countries with an average income per capita of $8,000 (World Bank 1995).

health care and, especially in the transition countries, firm-provided housing for workers. The consequences of creating this dichotomy between formal and informal sectors and jobs are sufficiently complex and interdependent with other distortions in the economy that few generalizations stand out from the existing empirical literature. Nonetheless, a predominant view emerges from studies in Latin America and Eastern Europe that the inefficiencies introduced by labor market regulations are a substantial impediment to growth, as was concluded from the initial appraisal of the problem of labor market inflexibility in Western Europe.

8.3.4   Public-Private Wage Differentials and Employment Conditions

One plausible distortion in the labor market is between the public and private sectors, given the lack of competitive pressures on the public sector and its capacity to draw subsidies and create its own protection. With public access to large household surveys or censuses that collect information on wages and worker characteristics, it has become a routine task to analyze public-private wage structures, conditional on such worker characteristics as years of schooling completed, years of postschooling experience (or age), and sex (e.g., Lindauer and Sabot 1983; Hartog and Oosterbeek 1993).

Although exercises of this type can be informative, they may not accurately portray an inefficient distortion in wages between the private and public sector because unobserved differences in the productivity of workers may vary between the two sectors. For example, women are sometimes observed to receive higher wages relative to men in the public sector than they do in the private sector, and this might be interpreted as discrimination against women in the private sector. But because entry into the two sectors is selective on the part of workers, and hiring may also be selective on the part of employers, there is reason to expect some sample selection bias in estimating the wage function for either sector. Comparisons across sectors of the uncorrected parameter estimates of wage functions within sectors, using standard methods to decompose the sources of group (i.e., gender) differences in wages between sectors (or groups), can be misleading (Schultz 1993). Women entering public sector employment are often pursuing different career objectives from those working in the private sector and are less likely to interrupt their time in the labor force for other family tasks. The age or postschool years of experience of women may thus represent more accurately the relevant job experiences of women in the public sector than will postschool years of experience of women in the private sector. Estimates of age-wage profiles will then tend to be steeper for women in the public sector than the private sector. One reason could be that the age or experience variable measures relevant labor market experience with more measurement error for women in the private sector than in the public sector, biasing down the experience profile parameters in the private sector. The same reasoning explains why the average age-wage profiles for women will tend to be flatter than for men: age measures the conceptually relevant labor market experience variable with greater error for women than for men, or in other words, the discrepancy between actual and potential postschooling experience increases more rapidly with age for women than for men.

More comprehensive analyses have sought to explain both the wage structures in the public and private sectors as well as the process of allocating workers between the sectors. These sample selection models generally depend on identifying information in the form of observed variables that are hypothesized to influence the selection decision rule by sector but theoretically do not play a part in the determination of worker productivity or wages (van der Gaag and Vijverberg 1988; Gjourko and Tracy 1988; Stelcner, van der Gaag, and Vijverberg 1989; Schultz 1993; Terrel 1993; Assad 1997; Tansel 1998). As improved methods are brought to bear on this issue, public sector administration wages are sometimes found to be slightly lower than private sector wages.[5] These findings might still be accounted for by the greater security of public employment due to bureaucratic rigidities that limit the firing of civil servants, even in Chile after its labor market reforms (Romaguera, Eschevarria, and Gonzalez 1995).

It is important to distinguish between public administrative employment, for which it is typically difficult to assess the productivity of bureaucracies or even the output of professors and medical personnel, and employment in state-owned enterprises, where outputs may be competitively marketed and the productivity of workers compared more readily with workers in the private sector. It is, however, more likely for state-owned enterprises to exist in a protected niche and receive a variety of hidden subsidies. I have not found public-private wage and employment studies of this type conducted *over time* during a period when the labor market was reformed or privatization was implemented. Such investigations over time might provide a more satisfactory basis for evaluating the effects of these public labor market reforms.

Studies based on a single cross section of the labor force that finds specific public-private wage differentials cannot confidently attribute the differentials to a particular feature of the case study, such as the greater security of employment in the civil service that was postulated in the previous paragraph. There are of course anecdotal accounts of public sector wages collapsing in periods of public crisis and structural reform, in Africa for example in the 1980s. But these casual observations are complemented by plausible stories suggesting that teachers with little pay work few hours

---

5. Few survey data sources obtain good data on the value of fringe benefits, perhaps because workers do not know their cost or have a clear idea of their monetary value. Most studies are of wages plus income in kind, but not total compensation.

and eventually turn to local parents to make up the difference in their below-market public paychecks.

8.3.5 Interindustry Wage Differences

Differences in wages between industries have intrigued economists for a long time. Even with improving survey and census data on workers and their wages, and with more satisfactory panels that follow workers as they change jobs and sectors, differences often remain between industry average wages (by education, age, and sex) for which there is no consensus explanation—for example, expected risks of unemployment, accident and morbidity risks, nonmonetized compensation such as income in kind (e.g., housing), or fringe benefits such as health insurance and the like.

One relatively neglected factor behind labor market distortions by industry is the effective protection provided industries by trade regimes and domestic taxes and subsidies. Given protection in product markets, firms with such monopolistic power may be forced to share their rents with organized (or potentially organized) labor (Pencavel 1995). This would seem to be a plausible explanation for why industry wage differentials in Colombia in 1973 were strongly positively correlated with the industry's level of effective protection (Schultz 1982). The political economy of trade and domestic policy regimes should have much to say about sectoral distortions of labor markets (Krueger 1974, 1983, 1992). But this link between the microeconometric study of wage structures and the sectoral analysis of protection has not attracted much interest in developing countries where protection could be a major source of labor market distortion and rent-seeking activity (Krueger 1983). The liberalization of the world trading system since the Second World War, which should continue according to the 1994 Uruguay Round multilateral trade agreement, has reduced and will reduce further interindustry distortions that should affect labor markets. Documentation of the importance of this development must await future research.

8.3.6 Labor Unions as a Source of Factor Market Distortion

Unions represent a classic case of labor market dualism, where the monopolistic power of a firm or industry allows a collective bargaining agent for workers to restrict employment and raise wages in a firm or in a union-represented industrial sector. Johnson and Mieszkowski (1970) emphasized the general equilibrium effects of such a union-induced wage differential, which would displace employment into the uncovered sector and lower that sector's competitively determined wage. Thus the full reallocation effects of labor due to the union-induced wage distortion would depend on labor supply and demand elasticities in both the covered and uncovered sectors and in home production (Pencavel 1995). Unions can also improve labor productivity among their members, reducing the distortion associated with a given union-nonunion wage differential.

It is also often empirically observed that wage structures in union firms are less unequal than in nonunion firms, providing less incentive to invest in schooling and OJT in a unionized firm (Freeman 1980). Analyses of the United States and Canada confirm that perhaps a fifth of the increased inequality in wages since 1980 can be associated with the decreasing share of union workers (Lemieux 1993).

As with minimum wages, union wage gains are likely to be concentrated among the middle- and upper-income workers in most low-income countries, though union members are more widely dispersed across the spectrum of wages in high-income countries. Consequently, in a low-income economy the power of unions to raise wages for their members may be associated with raising wages at the top of the national distribution of wages, thereby adding to overall wage and income inequalities, as illustrated in South Africa in 1993 (Schultz and Mwabu 1998). Conversely, unions appear to be reducing wage inequality in the United States and Canada (Lemieux 1993).

I have not seen evidence on whether labor market distortions due to unions are increasing or decreasing in the world as a whole. Their relative numerical strength has been declining in the United States and United Kingdom, although the percentage union-nonunion wage differential does not appear to have diminished in recent decades (Blanchflower 1997). If protective trade regimes were a major source of union wage power, labor market distortions attributable to unions should be widely diminishing, most notably in countries liberalizing their trade regimes.

However, the capacity of state-owned enterprises and their "union" constituencies to resist liberalization in such countries as India, China, and Russia suggests that this form of political collusion may represent the largest remaining inefficiency in world labor markets.[6] Russian agricultural state enterprises are a vast sector with labor productivity well below the national average and yet endowed with some of the world's richest farmland. The Russian Sovhoz and Kolhoz show little tendency to be displaced by private entrants or restructured to respond more efficiently to international price incentives and to new high-return technologies. Agricultural labor market reforms in Russia have been undermined and delayed by the failure to create a market for land and to separate workers' rights to

6. Many examples can be found where state-owned enterprises lobby as unions and management to maintain the wage growth of workers despite meager gains in productivity and declining international prices of the sector's output. The Indian coal industry is an example often cited, where disciplining the sector has not proved effective and privatization might therefore appear to be a promising strategy for policy reform (Banerji and Sabot 1993; Horton, Kanbur, and Mazumdar 1994; Rama 1994; World Bank 1995).

ownership claims on the land from their expectations of being paid to work that land regardless of their productivity. In China the lack of marketable ownership of land and its periodic redistribution at the village level weaken incentives for the farmer to invest in improving the fertility of the land and to consolidate it into more efficient-sized production units.

8.3.7   Centralization of Wage Setting

There is conflicting evidence on the consequences of centralized collective bargaining for macroeconomic performance (OECD 1997). Bruno and Sachs (1985) found what they call corporatist institutional structures, which typically include centralized wage setting, were associated in the 1960s and 1970s with the ability of a country to reduce inflation with less of a reduction in its rate of economic growth. But their corporatist state involvement in wage setting typically combines centralization in union-management wage negotiations and national consensus to promote greater wage equality, as in Scandinavia and the Netherlands, and to share widely the burdens of adjustment to clearly perceived macroeconomic shocks. Calmfors and Driffill (1988) reported a U-shaped relationship between economic performance and centralization of a country's bargaining system, for which they hypothesized that highly decentralized bargaining allowed efficient competitive pressures to operate and highly centralized systems allowed the inflationary externalities of wage setting to be internalized within the corporatist coalition. But extending this approach to the more recent period (through 1996) and allowing other dimensions of the labor market to differ, such as union density, collective bargaining coverage, and coordination of negotiations across sectors, fails to find statistically significant robust performance effects of centralization per se (OECD 1997). However, a robust inverse relation does remain between earnings inequality and degree of centralization in wage setting. But even this intercountry correlation leaves interpretations of causality in doubt, for many institutional factors, policy instruments, and changes in the relative supplies of skilled or educated workers are determinants of earnings inequality.

The example of Japan in the 1970s that is used by Bruno and Sachs (1985) to illustrate their overall thesis is not similar to the centralized wage-setting process in many OECD countries. Japan was able to reduce real wages promptly in response to the two increases in international oil prices so as to curb domestic demand and foster export growth needed to pay for the more costly energy imports and thereby maintain its current account balance and resume smoothly its growth. Of course, the United States and Europe experienced cycles of recession and unemployment, of different durations, to achieve their realignment of relative prices and structural adjustment to balance their international payments in this same period. But the Japanese achievement of coordinated adjustment in real wages cannot be attributed to a centralized union-management wage negotiation process but rather to different attitudes toward sharing responsibility and a social consensus that encouraged groups to accept short-run losses to achieve widely recognized long-run gains.

8.3.8   Transition from Planned to Market Economies

Many of the transition economies are in the process of constructing political, legal, and economic systems that protect property rights of not only land but also natural resources and industrial capital, while creating tax systems that withdraw government revenues from private income streams without unduly distorting production incentives. Providing freer markets for labor is an important ingredient in this process, which appears to have occurred more readily in Eastern Europe than it has in Russia. Despite the great success of China in doubling output from agriculture in the 1980s by decentralizing management to the household responsibility system, it has proved more difficult for China to create a free flow of labor out of agriculture as labor productivity in agriculture has increased and regional differentials in wages grown wider. Workers born in rural areas are limited in their ability to respond to urban wage opportunities, except as temporary workers without the right to reside permanently in the city. What costs these rigidities impose on the overall labor market remain unassessed but are probably large and discourage firm-specific training of these temporary workers.

Given the complexity of the various changes occurring in the transition countries, do these reforms have common consequences for wage structures or the productivity of certain types of labor? In the Czech Republic, Slovakia, Slovenia, and perhaps East Germany, it is possible to compare in similar labor market surveys the wage structures that prevailed before and after the end of Communism, although housing and services in kind are inadequately accounted for (Chase 1997; Orazem and Vodopivec 1994; Krueger and Pischke 1995; Hunt 1999b). A few changes in wage patterns emerge that seem to be a consequence of the change in economic regimes.

The percentage premium in wages for an additional year of schooling has tended to increase, particularly among younger workers with more recent secondary and higher educations. The informal private small enterprise sector is dominated by services, which were relatively neglected under central planning and have grown, whereas employment in heavy industrial sectors has declined. The skills associated with services have gained ground relatively, and most employment in services is female, whereas skills in the declining heavy industries are more frequently provided by male workers. These sectoral shifts may explain small increases often noted in the wages of women workers relative to men in Eastern Europe. Despite subsidies for the poor and pensioners, who are concentrated in rural areas, wages in urban-based areas have advanced relative to rural levels, in accord with the relative productivity of urban industries compared with agriculture and rural natural-resource-based industries. The upward slope of wage profiles with age or postschooling experience has become flatter overall, as the experience of older workers is less relevant to the new economic opportunities and consequently less rewarded in the more competitive labor market.

In Communist Russia there appear to have been no national labor force surveys from which to benchmark changes that occurred after the onset of economic reforms. The starting point for comparisons of wage structures in Russia is therefore 1992, when the first monitoring survey was collected. However, the first surveys are drawn by the Russian state statistical agency for the World Bank and may not be sampled representatively. Job turnover in 1992 is comparable in Russia to that measured in industrially advanced market economies, but the shift from state-owned enterprises to private employment started at a very slow pace (Foley 1997). Changes in the Russian wage structure are less notable than in Eastern Europe, with women's wages possibly declining relative to men's. Women are more likely than men to experience unemployment, and when women are unemployed they are more likely to exit the labor force than men (Foley 1997). As in Eastern Europe, returns to secondary and perhaps higher education appear to have increased, but unemployment is moderately high among workers with university education, at least initially. In Russia age-wage profiles have also become flatter, providing less of a wage premium for older workers, and this development may partly explain the greater propensity for older workers to experience unemployment and then exit the labor force, as observed in East Germany. The gender gap in wages became more favorable to women in East Germany after reunification, but women lost their share of employment in the wake of these reforms (Hunt 1999), as if the evolution of the wage structure reduced the derived demands for more costly female labor. In general, the transition reforms in Eastern Europe and Russia have increased the returns to schooling and decreased the relative wages of the old, with the relative wage status of women varying from country to country. In most of these countries birthrates have plunged, reducing a competing demand on women's time for child care, and yet their very high rates of labor force participation have tended to decline toward the levels observed in industrially advanced market economies.

China has only recently begun collecting systematically and sharing with social scientists large surveys of its population that include information on wages and worker characteristics. Most rural workers within China were employed within their family farms after the agricultural reforms starting in the late 1970s. Farm management and production surveys have been used to estimate agricultural production functions for a few local areas from which it should be possible to derive estimates of the marginal product of labor. But these production function studies have not disaggregated labor inputs sufficiently by education, age, and sex to allow one to infer the wage structure in agriculture. Consequently, the available information on wage structures for China relates predominantly to workers in urban areas, and these urban surveys are consistently available only for about the past decade. Surveys also tend to be collected for only a few provinces in China at a time, raising the possibility that those provinces for which data are available are somehow unrepresentative of the total country.

With these caveats in mind regarding the information base on which to generalize about such a large and varied country as China, three recent surveys have been used to examine the structure of wages. Based on a 1989–91 panel from the Economic Health and Nutrition Survey in eight provinces, wage returns to schooling appear to be moderate but tend to be greater for women than for men, 4 versus 2 percent per year of schooling completed, and rising over time. Women employed in urban areas in state-owned enterprises receive lower wages than they do in the private sector, controlling for schooling, experience, and province. The wage gap between men and women with comparable productive characteristics is on the order of 15 percent (Subramaniam 1997).

The Survey of Income Distribution in 1995 conducted in eleven provinces supported by the Asian Development Bank showed somewhat larger returns to schooling, also favoring women, with a similar 15 to 20 percent gender-based wage difference after holding the standard worker characteristic variables constant (Asian Development Bank 1998). Finally, a sample survey of urban households collected by the State Statistical Bureau from three provinces in 1986–87 and 1993–94 provides a third view of changes in wage structure (Yu 1998). Returns to primary education decreased over this seven-year period, whereas secondary and higher and vocational schooling returns were initially higher than primary returns and increased for both men and women. The differences in wages between provinces also increased, with the advantage in Guangdong over Hunan and Sichuan province growing from 30 to 70 percent. Returns to education increase in general, but they are higher in the interior, poorer provinces where the relative supply of educated workers is lower. The gender difference in wages not explained by a regression decomposition of the conventional wage function increases from 16 to 24 percent. There are indications that the age profiles of wages have become flatter, suggesting that the wage premiums received by older workers is falling. These three studies of China confirm that regional differences are growing, educational returns are moderate but growing larger, and gender differences are relatively moderate and increasing.

These indicators of change in wage structure from the labor markets of countries moving from central planning to market orientation have several common features: they indicate growing rewards for schooling, diminishing differentials favoring the old, and possibly higher premiums to the young for their first years of labor market experience in the new market environment. Also, most studies indicate that wage inequality measured by the variance of the log of wages is increasing not only because of the increase in educational differentials in wages but also because of an increase in the unexplained wage inequality within age, education, sex, and region groups. This latter development is also notable in some industrially advanced countries such as the United States and has been interpreted as the returns to unobserved skills. In Eastern Europe, Russia, and China these within-group wage inequalities are also increasing over the time period observed. Wage differentials set by the bureaucratic centrally planned regimes appear to have been smaller than those arising in the more market-oriented regimes that have begun to take their place.

8.4   Data Requirements for the Evaluation of Labor Market Reforms

The data required to evaluate labor market reforms would ideally include a series of household surveys with comprehensive labor force information, including all forms of compensation. They would span the period of the reform and continue for a sufficient time to capture lags in adjustment to the reforms, which may involve several years, given the persistence of individual wages in many settings. In repeated independent cross sections, however, there may still be unobserved differences among workers with the same observed productive characteristics before and after the reform, and these unobserved changing characteristics could account for the outcomes of interest. Therefore, it is valuable to have information collected from the same individuals over time in the form of a *panel* survey, which allows one to control for persistent heterogeneity across persons (Freeman 1984). The problems of correcting for attrition bias in such panels appears to be less serious than the heterogeneity bias arising from unobserved differences related to reforms (Manski and Altonji 1998). Only a few high-income industrially advanced countries have such panel survey programs, the noted examples being the Panel Study of Income Dynamics and the National Labor Force Surveys of Youth in the United States and the German Socio-Economic Panel. Brazil has a new labor force panel survey, which may in the future allow economists to evaluate the labor market impact of short-run changes in Brazil's labor legislation and economic changes.

In addition, for confident attribution of the effect of labor market reform, other simultaneous changes in policies or programs should not be occurring that might affect directly or indirectly the labor force. Multiple simultaneous policy interventions complicate greatly the evaluation task, as in the transition economies. The most convincing cases of policy evaluation arise when reform legislation varies the definition of the population eligible for some program, and a seemingly arbitrary difference in age, or residential location, defines the moving boundary for those who can receive the benefits of a specific program.[7]

Another approach is for the subnational administrative units in a country to introduce labor market reforms according to their own timetables or with distinctive legislated features that allow the researcher to identify who should be affected by the program across subregions within a population. Governments organized along federal lines may provide subnational administrative regions with flexibility to pursue different reforms at different times, and yet national data gathering occurs at frequent intervals for the entire population. The United States has provided its states with some independence in legislating major changes in welfare and labor force regulations. Thus the duration of unemployment benefits and their size have often been a state prerogative, providing the researcher with some cross-sectional and time-series variation in program design and change. Similarly, minimum wage legislation is set by the federal government but can be and is augmented by states. The problem remains, however, that the states taking the lead in adopting more generous (or less generous) policies may not be random but correlated with other factors that also influence labor market outcomes.

It is unlikely that fundamental reforms of the labor market will be pursued in isolation, and this independence of policy is only assumed to justify the evaluation methods. Nor is it likely that subnational administrative units will randomly adopt reforms of basic labor market policies to help economists evaluate their independent consequences (Heckman et al. 1998). The prospects are thus not bright for obtaining the perfect data to evaluate how labor market reforms contribute to economic development. But as evaluation of localized and relatively isolated labor market reforms become more commonplace, our body of knowledge should accumulate on how best to assess the magnitude of the distortions caused by specific labor policies and programs. What has been costly in the past, and can be predictably reformed, will become a top target for future reform.

8.5 Trends and Policy Options in the Labor Market

Looking forward, several trends are likely to continue. The nature of these trends may suggest ways in which labor market reforms could be better designed or more precisely evaluated. Trade liberalization has prob-

---

7. E.g., mothers with children born after a specific year are eligible for a free medical care program in the United States, whereas they are not if their children were born in previous years; or eligibility for Medicaid increases in a particular year from only mothers below the poverty line to mothers below 1.33 times the poverty line. Thus change in the legislative limits on eligibility for a program is one method for extracting from a series of cross-sectional surveys or a panel survey estimates of how economic behavior has changed as a result of program expansion (or contraction) and what the welfare consequences of this change in eligibility are (e.g., Currie 1995).

ably been the most pervasive force changing the world's economies and perhaps also the most critical constraint on the performance of the labor market. Growth in international trade should continue to outstrip growth in world GNP, and national economies will become, in some sense, more open to international prices and the relative values of different types of labor. The decline in the relative wages of less educated workers in the industrially advanced countries, noted from about 1980, is widely attributed to technological change, or more precisely these relative wage changes are a residual that cannot otherwise be accounted for by the relative supplies of educated workers, or the industrial composition of output, or demands in national economies. However, in some low-income countries such as China, and perhaps India, returns to schooling among workers are also on the rise. This could be due to the increasing international market orientation in these economies and an opening to foreign investment that has bid up the wage for more educated workers in export manufacturing industries. Eastern Europe, Russia, Chile, and Mexico are also undergoing a widening in educational differentials in wages, at least in manufacturing (Robbins 1995).[8] Thus the consequences of growing trade liberalization and transition and the disequilibrium they introduce may raise returns to education, as workers and entrepreneurs with more schooling demonstrate they are better equipped at adapting to the new opportunities opened up by this disequilibrium (Schultz 1975).

In response to this trend in returns to schooling the public sector will be called on to coordinate the expansion of the national educational system and assign resources to those segments where the social returns to schooling are greatest. Regulations on the private educational sector should also be relaxed so it too can contribute in a complementary fashion to the appropriate expansion in and diversification of the supply of educated workers.

A second trend that has become well established in the past several decades is the increase in women's participation in the labor force outside of their own families or businesses. This trend of increasing women's participation in the wage labor force should, by itself, contribute to reducing women's wages relative to men's, at least initially. But instead, women's wages have in many countries increased relative to those received by men, and fragmentary evidence suggests this pattern is spreading. This change in wages may be explained either by a shift in demand toward those products and services that women have a comparative advantage in producing, or it may be explained by women upgrading their labor market skills more rapidly than men. The latter appears to be the case with regard to schooling, where the ratio of the years of schooling of women to that of men

8. These patterns of increased relative wages of skilled labor in countries with both an abundance and shortage of skilled labor should not be interpreted as a contradiction of Heckscher-Ohlin-Samuelson model, for many other conditions are changing.

has been increasing in all regions since early UNESCO estimates became available in the 1960s (Schultz 1987, 1995), and the absolute difference in years of schooling between men and women started to decrease in the world after about 1980, at least according to Barro and Lee's (1994) estimates. However, these gender differences in years of schooling are still not closing as of 1985 in south and west Asia and Africa (Schultz 1998b). If these world trends in schooling continue, women's wages relative to men's should follow in the future. The rising educational attainment of young women is also closely linked to their later age at marriage and decline in lifetime fertility, which will contribute to further growth in the supply of female labor to the market labor force.

Accommodating the growth in female labor force participation and labor supply may call for some public efforts to reduce labor market dualism that discourages the hiring and training of women and to open specific occupational and industrial segments of the labor force that have been traditionally sex segregated. With increasing incomes, demand for services tends to grow as a fraction of income. Some of these services may prove to be surprisingly tradable, such as certain financial services and programming, and may gravitate to low-wage better educated countries. Much of the growth in female labor supply is likely to be in rural areas. In South Asian cultures it may be difficult for young women to leave rural areas without their menfolk, whereas industries could locate in rural areas with improved infrastructure and employ the low-cost local supply of female labor. Imagination and caution will be required to design legislation to realize these social gains.

Investment in the education of women and men is a high priority, with private rates of return being substantial at the primary education level, until nearly all youth complete this rudimentary education. Secondary education is then likely to be the highest social return activity. On average, private and social returns are higher for women than for men, especially in societies where women receive much less than half of the schooling (Schultz 1995). Since rural education will facilitate migration to take urban jobs, much of the social gains to this education accrue in the urban sector. The rural population may not be expected to finance all of the public costs of rural education under these conditions. The central government should therefore subsidize the availability and quality of rural schools both on grounds of efficiency and equity, because rural areas are poorer and more likely to be credit constrained in their investment in human capital. Out-migration from agriculture should also be encouraged as labor productivity in agriculture increases and urban employment growth progresses, to prevent income inequalities between regions from growing wider.

Large and sometimes growing regional inequalities are a serious challenge for world development. When they are contained within a country there is a clear reason to promote interregional mobility, to help raise the income opportunities of migrants, and for society to raise the income opportunities of those who remain behind in the lower income sending regions. Democracy and the federal political process give administrative and financial power to the states in proportion to their populations, which provides politicians in low-income states with an incentive to attract resources to the state but to resist out-migration. Yet the lesson of numerous public programs that have sought to encourage migration to the poor frontiers of a nation, such as Brazil and Indonesia, or to subsidize private investment in low-wage states is clear: few such programs work in the sense of reducing wage differentials between high- and low-income states. Few low-income states have taken the reverse and economically promising approach of facilitating out-migration by job matching, information dissemination, and credits to finance out-migration. The initiative for such programs will have to come from a federal government. With the reported success of joint group liability lending programs to poor women with little collateral, for example, Grameen Bank of Bangladesh, there should be an opportunity in the case of interregional migration to devise a way to provide small loans to invest in out-migration and secure repayment, perhaps by making the repayment of an individual's loan a requirement before the next member of the origin village community (or family) can qualify for a subsequent rotating loan.

UI and severance payments could be designed to increase labor market flexibility by moderating firing costs for employers, moving more of these insurance costs from the payroll tax to a broader based centralized tax, leaving only a fraction of the firm's past excess turnover as a penalty tax (experience rating) for cyclically varying its employment level and presumably underinvesting in the firm's (temporary) workers.

Minimum wages could also be designed not to discriminate against the employment of demographic groups with lower than average wages. The young and women are particularly harmed by minimum wages that are likely to exclude them from formal sector jobs where training might help to raise their skills and productivity. The levels of minimum wages should be legislated at a low enough level not to affect the great majority of workers in both the formal and informal sectors, and coverage should legally apply to both sectors, even if enforcement would be problematic in some settings.

Can medical care insurance be funded by the central government so as not to discriminate between the formal sector, which receives this higher quality care, and the informal sector, which must rely on poorer quality public clinics? Moving the costs of medical care and UI from firm-based payroll taxes to central government taxes on value added, income, or sales should reduce the distortion currently existing between the formal and informal sectors of many economies and should improve the allocative efficiency of the labor market. Shifting some fraction of pensions to the private sector, as Chile and now Argentina and Mexico have done, could go further to diminish the wedge between the formal and informal sectors. Clearly, the decision to provide medical and pension programs to all workers is a major but very costly step toward the welfare state that was implicated in the inflexibility noted in Western European economies of late. Yet to eliminate the distortion represented by the formal and informal sectors of the labor market, the 50 to 75 percent payroll taxes of the formal sector must be somehow reduced, and this can be achieved only by substituting a less distorting taxation system for the current tax on labor in the covered sector.

Segmentation in the labor force by ethnic minority should be dealt with, as in the case of women and the poorer segments of the rural population, by designing ways for the central government to subsidize educational facilities in the regions where poor ethnic groups are concentrated. Helping these groups through human capital credit programs for out-migration and investment in schooling could be economically advantageous and prevent the gap between the incomes of ethnic minorities and the rest of society from widening further.

Finally, I have hypothesized that trade liberalization has been a powerful force reducing distortions that favor one industry or group of producers vis-à-vis another. Reducing these rents at the source, through trade liberalization, should reduce the power of unions and other coalitions to raise wages inefficiently for one group as opposed to another. Segmentation in the labor market promises to be eroded by equalizing the margin of effective protection across an economy and lowering the average level of such protection. There may be a good case to compensate, through temporary credits for training investment or relocation costs, those most directly hurt by trade liberalization and structural adjustment. Redistributing these benefits and costs should be beneficial, but quantifying who bears the costs and setting limits on the duration of benefits will be a challenge.

The lack of literature evaluating the costs and benefits of labor market reforms does not indicate that reforms have not occurred or that they have not made a major contribution to output and growth. Casual evidence indicates that labor markets have been exceedingly flexible and important for the growth achieved in such countries as Taiwan and Korea (Kim and Topel 1995), for the agricultural productivity growth in China during the 1980s, and in Chile after 1982, for example. Why is research in this field so sparse, and what would improve it?

8.6   What Research Would Inform Policy

Household records from representative labor force surveys are the foundation for most labor market policy research. Only a few countries and regions, such as the Arab Middle East, India, parts of Africa, and Japan, continue to restrict the public's access to these surveys or simply fail to collect them as a routine matter. A high priority is to encourage those countries without regular household surveys to establish them and to make these data available in all countries to the public, with information on the region where each household is interviewed to link to local policy conditions, while taking the necessary precautions to preserve individual respondent confidentiality. Governments should be convinced to place their surveys in the public domain. To inform policy about labor markets requires first that the research community consult such data.

Where this tradition of routinized randomly sampled household surveys has become established, research can proceed in many directions to analyze the sources of segmentation in the labor force and to quantify the magnitude of the distortions that result from public policies and misguided institutions. As in most research, quantification will proceed in steps, dealing sequentially first with the major sources of heterogeneity among workers and then developing approaches for dealing with more minor sources of statistical bias, that is, sample selection and measurement error. Although heterogeneity of workers remains a source of uncertainty, comparisons of wage structures in different sectors of the economy can begin to inform policy by assigning an approximate magnitude to the differences between the wages of workers in the two sectors who otherwise appear comparable in terms of observable (exogenous) characteristics.

When these group differences in wages are very large, as when a male unionized worker receives an hourly wage that is 145 percent larger than a male nonunion worker in South Africa, matched by years of education and age, a prima facie conclusion is that these two sectors in South Africa are not jointly efficiently allocating labor (Schultz and Mwabu 1998). Perhaps intersectoral wage differences of 10 or 15 percent might be explained in terms of the unionized firms hiring only the more productive workers or paying efficiency (higher) wages to create incentives to reduce shirking or the like. Thus simple analyses of labor market surveys can focus attention on sectors where policy reforms have the greatest likelihood of raising productivity. How such reforms can be accomplished involves much more complex institutional and political issues.

Similarly, comparisons of wages of workers in state-owned firms and private firms should help in setting priorities for where privatization should be explored or other competitive pressures introduced. Marked wage differences between industries also should alert policymakers to the possibility that high-wage industries may not be competitive, may receive a disproportionate level of protection from imports, or may receive disproportionate subsidies from the state, and so on. Once labor force surveys are readily available to researchers outside of the government, these wage differentials should begin to inform policy—not only in the labor market but in determining trade regulations, taxes, subsidies, and how to organize industries to operate competitively. It is not surprising that the countries that have continued to restrict the release of their labor force surveys, except possibly to publish government cross-tabulations of the data, tend to have more distorted and segmented labor markets and probably rank among the least competitive economies. Thus these are the very countries that have the most to gain socially from reforming their labor markets and also the strongest vested interests in resisting such reforms.

Many policy questions can be addressed with a single cross-sectional survey of modest size, of about five thousand households. But with the establishment of such surveys, it is possible to evaluate the consequences of change in public policies on changes in wage structures, employment composition, and the personal distribution of consumption that emerge after a policy reform. Evidence from this form of before-and-after comparison is more compelling than single static comparisons of intersectoral differences in wage structures, for there are always many other things that differ between sectors and cannot be held constant that could explain a group difference in wages. Changes in official policy take time to erode long-established wage differences between groups of workers. The policy evaluation process can draw its final conclusions on the consequences of reform only after time has elapsed.

Surveys that try to follow the same persons over time, as public policies evolve, have great appeal because these panel data permit the researcher to hold constant all the unobserved persistent characteristics of the individual, while comparing her or his evolution in the labor market. But these panel surveys are costly and are likely to remain luxuries of the high-income countries, except where they are absolutely necessary for obtaining a critical policy parameter.

In the past thirty years, the annual number of professionally collected household labor force and income-expenditure surveys in the low-income world has probably increased ten- or twentyfold. But the number of economists and statisticians trained to analyze these microsurvey data to inform government policymakers would seem to have increased more slowly. The social value of their potential policy analyses should now be large. However, there is a chicken-egg problem of attributing causal effects. More widely accessible data of this form may increase the usefulness and precision of such research on labor markets, while the dearth of policy-oriented labor market research leads governments to conclude that extensive household survey programs are expensive for their policy payoff. Without such data available to researchers, young economists from these developing countries may reasonably opt to concentrate on theory, whereas with assured access to these data, more young economists might specialize in a balanced portfolio of economic theory and empirical economics. Developing a better understanding of this dynamic problem of data generation and policy analysis, and implementing a remedy, could contribute to development in many poor parts of the world.

References

Amadeo, E., R. P. Barros, J. M. Camargo, R. P. Mendoza, V. Pero, and A. Urani. 1994. Brazil. In *Human resources and the adjustment process,* ed. R. Paredes and L. A. Riveros. Washington, D.C.: Inter-American Development Bank.

Anderson, P., and B. Meyer. 1993. Unemployment insurance in the United States. *Journal of Labor Economics* 11 (1, pt. 2): S70–S95.

Asian Development Bank. 1998. Women in development: The People's Republic of China. Country Briefing Paper. Manila: Asian Development Bank.

Assad, R. 1997. The effect of public sector hiring and compensation policies on the Egyptian labor market. *World Bank Economic Review* 11 (1): 85–118.

Atkinson, A. B., and J. Micklewright. 1991. Unemployment compensation and labor market transition. *Journal of Economic Literature* 29 (4): 1679–1727.

Baicker, K., C. Goldin, and L. F. Katz. 1997. A distinctive system: Origins and impact of U.S. unemployment compensation. NBER Working Paper no. 5889. Cambridge, Mass.: National Bureau of Economic Research.

Banerji, A., and R. H. Sabot. 1993. Wage distortions, over-manning, and reform in developing country public enterprises. Washington, D.C.: World Bank, Policy Research Department.

Barro, R. J., and J. W. Lee. 1994. International comparison of educational attainment. *Journal of Monetary Economics* 32 (3): 363–94.

Becker, G. S. 1964. *Human capital.* New York: Columbia University Press.

Blanchflower, D. G. 1997. Changes over time in union relative wage effects in Great Britain and the United States. NBER Working Paper no. 6100. Cambridge, Mass.: National Bureau of Economic Research.

Blank, R. 1994. *Social protection versus economic flexibility.* Chicago: University of Chicago Press.

Bravo, D., and D. Contreras. 1998. Is there any relationship between minimum wage and employment? Santiago: University of Chile. Processed.

Brown, C., C. Gilroy, and A. Kohen. 1982. The effect of the minimum wage on employment and unemployment. *Journal of Economic Literature* 20 (2): 487–528.

Bruno, M., and J. Sachs. 1985. *Economics of worldwide stagflation.* Oxford: Blackwell.

Cain, G. G. 1986. The economic analysis of labor market discrimination. In *Handbook of labor economics,* vol. 1, ed. O. C. Ashenfelter and R. Layard, 693–785. Amsterdam: North-Holland.

Calmfors, L., and J. Driffill. 1988. Bargaining structure, corporatism, and macroeconomic performance. *Economic Policy,* April, 14–61.

Card, D., A. B. Krueger. 1995. *Myth and measurement: The new economics of minimum wage.* Princeton, N.J.: Princeton University Press.

Chase, R. S. 1997. Markets for human capital. Economic Growth Center Discussion Paper no. 770. New Haven, Conn.: Yale University.

Choi, K. S. 1993. Technological change and educational wage differentials in Korea. Economic Growth Center Discussion Paper no. 698. New Haven, Conn.: Yale University.

Currie, J. 1995. *Welfare and the well being of children.* Chur, Switzerland: Harwood.

Davis, S. J. 1992. Cross country patterns of changes in relative wages. In *NBER macroeconomics annual 1992,* ed. Olivier Blanchard and Stanley Fischer. Cambridge, Mass.: MIT Press.

Deere, D., K. Murphy, and F. Welch. 1996. Reexamining methods of estimating minimum wage effects. *American Economic Review* 85 (2): 232–37.

Deininger, K., and L. Squire. 1996. A new data set measuring income inequality. *World Bank Economic Review* 10 (3): 562–91.

de Soto, H. 1989. *The other path: The invisible revolution in the Third World.* New York: Harper and Row.

Foley, M. 1997. Labor market dynamics, unemployment duration, and multiple job holding in Russia: The economic transition. Ph.D. diss., Yale University, New Haven, Conn.

Freeman, R. B. 1980. Unionism and the dispersion of wages. *Industrial and Labor Relations Review* 33 (1): 3–23.

———. 1984. Longitudinal analysis of the effects of trade unions. *Journal of Labor Economics* 2 (1): 1–26

Gjourko, J., and J. Tracy. 1988. Analysis of public and private wages allowing for endogenous choices of both government and union state. *Journal of Labor Economics* 6 (2): 229–53.

Gottschalk, P., and T. M. Smeeding. 1997. Cross national comparisons of earnings and income equality. *Journal of Economic Literature* 35 (2): 633–87.

Grindling, T. H., M. Goldfarb, and C. C. Chang. 1995. Changing returns to education in Taiwan, 1978–1991. *World Development* 16:343–56.

Gruber, J. 1994. The incidence of mandated maternity benefits. *American Economic Review* 84 (3): 622–41.

Harrison, Ann, and G. Hanson. 1999. Who gains from trade reforms? Some remaining puzzles. NBER Working Paper no. 6915. Cambridge, Mass.: National Bureau of Economic Research.

Hartog, J., and H. Oosterbeek. 1993. Public and private sector wages in Netherlands. *European Economic Review* 37 (1): 97–114.

Hashimoto, M., and J. Raisian. 1985. Employment tenure and earnings profiles in Japan and the United States. *American Economic Review* 75 (3): 721–35.

Haveman, R. 1996. Reducing poverty while increasing employment. *OECD Economic Studies* 26 (1): 7–42.

Heckman, J. J., R. J. LaLonde, and J. A. Smith. 1999. The economics and econometrics of active labor market programs. In *Handbook of labor economics,* vol. 3, ed. O. Ashenfelter and D. Card. Amsterdam: North-Holland.

Horton, S., R. Kanbur, and D. Mazundar, eds. 1994. *Labor markets in era of adjustment.* Vols. 1 and 2, *Case studies.* EDI Development Studies. Washington, D.C.: World Bank.

Hunt, J. 1995. The effect of unemployment compensation on unemployment duration in Germany. *Journal of Labor Economics* 13 (1): 88–120

———. 1999. Post unification wage growth in East Germany. NBER Working Paper no. 6879. Cambridge, Mass.: National Bureau of Economic Research.

Johnson, H. G., and P. Mieszkowski. 1970. The effect of unionization on the distribution of income. *Quarterly Journal of Economics* 84 (4): 539–61.

Juhn, C. 1992. Decline of male labor market participation. *Quarterly Journal of Economics* 107 (1): 79–121.

Katz, L. F., and K. M. Murphy. 1992. Changes in relative wages, 1963–1987: Supply and demand factors. *Quarterly Journal of Economics* 107 (1): 35–78.

Kim, D. I., and R. H. Topel. 1995. Labor markets and economic growth: Lessons from Korea's industrialization, 1970–1990. In *Differences and changes in wage structures,* ed. R. B. Freeman and L. B. Katz, 227–64. Chicago: University of Chicago Press.

Krueger, A. B., and J. S. Pischke. 1995. A comparative analysis of East and West German labor markets. In *Differences and changes in wage structures.* ed. R. B. Freeman and L. F. Katz, 405–45. Chicago: University of Chicago Press.

Krueger, A. O. 1974. The political economy of the rent seeking society. *American Economic Review* 64 (1): 291–303.

———. 1983. *Trade and employment in developing countries.* Chicago: University of Chicago Press.

———. 1992. *The political economy of agricultural pricing policy.* Vol. 5, *A synthesis.* World Bank Comparative Study. Baltimore: John Hopkins University Press.

Lemieux, T. 1993. Unions and wage inequality in Canada and the United States. In *Small differences that matter,* ed. D. Card and R. B. Freeman. Chicago: University of Chicago Press.

Lindauer, D. L., and R. Sabot. 1983. The public/private wage differential in a poor urban economy. *Journal of Development Economics* 12 (3): 137–52.

Londoño, J. L. 1995. *Distribucion del ingreso v desarrollo economico.* Bogota: Tercer Mundo.

Manski, C. F., and J. G. Altonji, eds. 1998. Attrition in longitudinal surveys. *Journal of Human Resources* 33 (2): 251–574.

Marquez, G., ed. 1995. *Reforming the labor market in a liberalized economy.* Washington, D.C.: Inter-American Development Bank.

Meyer, B. 1989. A quasi-experimental approach to the effect of unemployment insurance. NBER Working Paper no. 3159. Cambridge, Mass.: National Bureau of Economic Research.

Mincer, J. 1976. Unemployment effects of minimum wage changes. *Journal of Political Economy* 84 (4, pt. 2): S87–S105.

Mincer, J., and Y. Higuchi. 1988. Wage structures and labor turnover in the United States and Japan. *Japanese and International Economics* 2 (6): 99–133.

Murphy, K. M., and F. Welch. 1992. The structure of wages. *Quarterly Journal of Economics* 107 (1): 285–326.

OECD (Organization for Economic Cooperation and Development). 1994. *The OECD Job Study: Evidence and explanations.* Paris: Organization for Economic Cooperation and Development.

———. 1995. *The OECD Job Study: Evidence and explanations, taxation, employment and unemployment.* Paris: Organization for Economic Cooperation and Development.

———. 1997. *Employment outlook.* Paris: Organization for Economic Cooperation and Development, July.

Orazem, P. F., and M. Vodopivec. 1994. Winners and losers in transition. *World Bank Economic Review* 9 (2): 201–30.

Paredes, R., and L. A. Riveros. 1994. *Human resources and the adjustment process.* Washington, D.C.: Inter-American Development Bank.

Pencavel, J. 1991. *Labor markets under trade unionism.* Cambridge, Mass.: Blackwell.

———. 1995. The role of labor unions in fostering economic development. Stanford, Calif.: Stanford University. Processed.

Rama, Martin. 1994. Flexibility in Sri Lanka labor market. Policy Review in Working Paper no. 1262. Washington, D.C.: World Bank.

Reis, A., J. Guilherme, and R. P. Barros. 1991. Wage inequality and the distribution of education. *Journal of Development Economics* 36 (1): 117–43.

Robbins, D. 1995. Schematic summary of findings for country wage and employment structure studies. Cambridge, Mass.: Harvard Institute of International Development. Processed.

Romaguera, P., C. Eschevarria, and P. Gonzalez. 1995. Chile. In *Reforming the labor market in a liberalized economy*, ed. G. Marquez. Washington, D.C.: Inter-American Development Bank.

Rosen, S. 1996. Public employment and the welfare state in Sweden. *Journal of Economic Literature* 34 (2): 729–40.

Ruhm, C. J. 1998. The economic consequences of parental leave mandates: Lessons from Europe. *Quarterly Journal of Economics* 113 (1): 285–317.

Schaffner, J. A. 1997. Job stability in developing and developed countries. Working Paper no. 18. Stanford, Calif.: Center for Research on Economic Development and Policy Reform.

———. 1998. Premiums to employment in larger establishments: Evidence from Peru. *Journal of Development Economics* 55 (1): 81–114.

Schultz, T. P. 1982. Effective protection and the distribution of personal income by sector in Colombia. In *Trade and employment in developing countries*, ed. A. O. Krueger. Chicago: University of Chicago Press.

———. 1987. School expenditures and enrollments, 1960–1980. In *Population growth and economic development*, ed. D. G. Johnson and R. Lee. National Academy of Sciences Background Paper. Madison: University of Wisconsin Press.

———. 1988. Firm and family employment, development and minimum wages (in Spanish). *Estudios de Economia* 51 (1): 85–125.

———. 1993. Labor market discrimination: Measurement and interpretation. In *Unfair advantage: Labor market discrimination in developing countries*, ed. N. Birdsall and R. Sabot. World Bank Regional and Sectoral Studies. Washington, D.C.: World Bank.

———, ed. 1995. *Investment in women's human capital.* Chicago: University of Chicago Press.

———. 1997. Aging, immigration and women in the labor force: Japan compared to other OECD countries. In *Japan and the U.S. in the developing world*, ed. G. Ranis. San Francisco: International Center for Economic Growth.

———. 1998a. Income inequality in Taiwan, 1976–1995. *Political economy of Taiwan's development in the 21st century: Two volumes in memory of John Fei*, ed. G. Ranis, Sheng-Cheng Hu, and Yun-Peng Chu. Cheltenham, England: Elgar.

———. 1998b. Inequality in the distribution of personal income in the world. *Journal of Population Economics* 11 (3): 307–44.

Schultz, T. P., and G. Mwabu. 1998. Labor unions and the distribution of wages and employment in South Africa. *Industrial and Labor Relations Review* 51 (4): 680–703.

Schultz, T. W. 1975. The value of the ability to deal with disequilibria. *Journal of Economic Literature* 13 (3): 827–46.

Stelcner, M., J. van der Gaag, and W. Vijverberg. 1989. A switching regression model of public private sector wage differentials in Peru. *Journal of Human Resources* 24 (3): 545–59.

Subramaniam, R. 1997. Wage structures in China. New Haven, Conn.: Yale University, Economic Growth Center. Unpublished paper.

Tansel, A. 1998. Public private employment choice, wage differential, and gender in Turkey. Ankara: Middle East Technical University.

Terrel, K. 1993. Public-private wage differential in Haiti. *Journal of Development Economics* 42:293–314.

Topel, R. 1990. Specific capital and unemployment: Measurement of the costs and consequences of job loss. *Carnegie-Rochester Conference Series on Public Policy*, autumn, 181–214.

———. 1997. Factor proportions and relative wages: The supply side determinants of wage inequality. *Journal of Economic Perspectives* 11 (2): 55–74.

van der Gaag, J., and W. Vijverberg. 1988. A switching regression model for wage determination in the public and private sectors of a developing country. *Review of Economics and Statistics* 70 (2): 244–52.

Vijverberg, W., and J. van der Gaag. 1990. Testing for labor market duality. Living Standard Measurement Survey, Working Paper no. 66. Washington, D.C.: World Bank.

Welch, F. 1979. The baby boom babies' financial bust. *Journal of Political Economy* 87 (5, pt. 2): 568–98.

———. 1997. Wages and participation. *Journal of Labor Economics* 15 (1, pt. 2): S77–S103.

Winter-Ebmer R. 1996. Potential unemployment benefit duration and spell length: Lessons from a quasi experiment in Austria. Discussion Paper no. 1534. London: Centre for Economic Policy Research.

World Bank. 1995. *World development report 1995: Workers in an integrating world.* New York: Oxford University Press.

Yu, X. 1998. Earning and returns to education during the economic transition in urban China. New Haven, Conn.: Yale University, Economic Growth Center. Processed.

Comment on the Paper by T. Paul Schultz   Mario I. Blejer

Paul Schultz's paper contains a very comprehensive review of the most salient questions related to labor market reforms and raises a number of important issues, some of which are still widely open since no real consensus has emerged from the existing literature or from the observations of actual developments. One of the most significant among such issues relates to the question of why labor market reforms are, apparently, much more difficult to implement than reforms in other economic areas. In fact, it is quite evident that labor market reforms are frequently delayed and, in many cases, left to the end of the reform process. And even then, in the last stages of the process, they are only half executed and, in many instances, are actually reversed.

Schultz provides some explanations for this observation. In his opinion, there is some merit to the view that conditions in other areas actually contribute to labor market distortions in a direct manner and, therefore, it is necessary to first resolve these problems before labor market difficulties can be properly addressed. Thus it is difficult to confront labor market issues before reforms in trade, taxes, and industrial organization are implemented or before there is enough progress regarding privatization. In addition, Schultz highlights the fact that it is likely to be more difficult, from the political point of view, to carry out labor market reforms because their

Mario I. Blejer is senior advisor in the Asia and Pacific Department at the International Monetary Fund.

The views expressed are those solely of the author.

effects for those who are directly affected are much more transparent and, in some cases, more immediate.

While these factors are indeed important in explaining the protracted nature of labor market reforms, it is also possible to make the opposite argument and claim that without labor market reforms it is much more difficult to proceed on other fronts. Privatization, trade liberalization, rationalization of the tax system, and other structural reforms may be blocked or slowed by lack of progress in the labor market. In addition, while the political economy of labor market reform would certainly tend to be more complicated, it is important to dwell in more detail on the dynamic aspects of such interactions.

In order to provide some insight on this question, it may be useful to illustrate the problem by looking at some related aspects of the Argentine experience. Argentina started a far-reaching liberalization effort in the early 1990s and has implemented an impressive and comprehensive set of structural reforms since then. The structural reforms in Argentina were part and parcel of a comprehensive effort to stabilize and modernize the economy after years of *dirigisme* and hyperinflation. The effort on the stabilization front was largely based on the introduction of a currency board to eliminate inflationary financing of chronic budget deficits and led to the achievement of substantive macroeconomic balances that resulted in the total obliteration of inflation and the virtual eradication of fiscal deficits. The Mexican crisis of 1994–95 caused, however, a short but severe recession and resulted in a substantial jump in unemployment, which reached more than 18 percent of the labor force (in a country where traditionally levels of unemployment were extremely low).[1]

While labor market reforms were considered, from the beginning of the process, an integral component of the transformation package, very little progress if any has been achieved on this front over the years. Attempts to make the labor market more flexible in order to improve employment opportunities and to reduce the negotiating power of labor unions were at the forefront of the rhetoric of reform, but in practice, it proved extremely difficult to legislate labor market changes and, if approved by Parliament, to actually implement these changes. In 1998, as part of an agreement with the International Monetary Fund, the Argentine government submitted to Parliament a comprehensive package of labor market reforms. It included a number of measures traditionally utilized to increase market flexibility, such as the introduction of temporary contracts, a cutback in severance payments, a reduction in labor taxes, and some other proposals geared to reduce the scope of collective bargaining. After a prolonged and acrimonious debate, the Argentine Parliament approved, in September 1998, a very

1. Unemployment was subsequently reduced to the range of 13 percent, although it rose again in the aftermath of the devaluation of the Brazilian real in the winter of 1999.

different version of the bill that in practice eliminated most of the key changes sought by the government and, in most opinions, reduced rather than increased the flexibility of the labor market.

In view of this turn of events, it is indeed important to try to understand the reasons for such developments. While the standard explanation, namely, that the vested interests of the trade unions are biased in favor of the currently employed and against the unemployed, could have some merit, it is more likely that the actual reasons for the difficulties in implementing labor market reforms are rooted in public perceptions about their effects. In particular, it is apparent that the public is highly ambivalent regarding the relation between increased labor market flexibility and lower levels of unemployment. Indeed, it has proved difficult to convince a skeptical public that reducing labor security and facilitating the firing process is bound to improve labor market conditions. This perception arises to a large extent from the type and the history of unemployment in Argentina.

As mentioned above, Argentina has had a history of low unemployment despite the marked influence of trade unions (the backbone of the Peronist movement) and the low level of labor market flexibility. Unemployment increased rapidly and suddenly following the "tequila" effect emanating from the 1994–95 Mexican crisis. The immediate reason was the wave of bankruptcies caused by the "credit crunch"—that is, the rapid contraction in available credit and the consequent increase in real interest rates. While in fact most of the bankruptcies took place in firms and sectors that were not fit to compete in the new, liberal environment created by the overall reform process and they therefore reflected a delayed consequence of the modernization strategy initiated a few years before, in the public's mind the increase in unemployment was rooted in macroeconomic factors and not in the structure of the labor market. This created demand for expansionary macroeconomic policies rather than support for reforms in labor relations.

Moreover, the type of unemployment that affected Argentina after 1995 was strongly connected with the rapid technological change facilitated by trade liberalization policies that provided an incentive for importing modern capital equipment and for adopting other labor-saving technologies. While it was widely accepted that this process, as well as the displacement of labor arising from privatizations and from public sector consolidation, cannot and should not be reversed, the widespread perception has been that rather than reforming the labor market, the appropriate response should be an effort to retrain displaced workers. In other words, increased unemployment gave rise to demand for educational reform rather than for labor market reform.

Strengthening these public perceptions is the fact that, objectively, the empirical evidence linking labor market rigidities and unemployment is indeed weak. As pointed out recently by Nickel (1997), employment protection, labor standards, and labor taxes do not seem to be correlated with unemployment in Europe.[2] And while flexibility would indeed improve efficiency and competitiveness, and therefore employment possibilities, these indirect links are too tenuous to be easily incorporated in the public perception. "Selling" labor market reforms, therefore, turns out to be a much more complicated, costly, and difficult process, and this can explain the tendency to delay its implementation.

Reference

Nickel, Stephen. 1997. Unemployment and labor market rigidities: Europe versus North America. *Journal of Economic Perspectives* 11, no. 3 (summer): 55–74.

Comment on the Paper by T. Paul Schultz   Julie Schaffner

Labor market reform is very much on the frontiers of both policy and research. We are fortunate that Paul Schultz was willing to write a paper on this important, but highly unwieldy subject. He draws on his knowledge of the wide array of empirical literatures that contribute to "what (little) we know" about the subject, raising many important points, most of which are hard to argue with. My comments will focus on "what we need to know" in this area.

A natural place to start in sketching out the research agenda is to list all the specific policies included under the heading of "labor market policies" and then to develop a systematic way of identifying the empirical questions to which policymakers would like answers when determining the best structure for each policy. At the very least the list of policies includes firing restrictions, unemployment insurance schemes, minimum wage regulations, fringe benefit mandates, regulation of workers' organizations, training policies, policies affecting geographic and occupational mobility (migration prohibitions, migration credits, provision of job-matching services), and public works. This is a long and diverse list.

In setting out the research agenda, it is furthermore useful to describe in detail the parameters that shape each policy's effects on the economy. For example, for a complete description of firing restrictions one must

---

2. Nickel found, however, that unionization, the length of unemployment benefits, the lack of active government measures to push the unemployed back into work, and, to some extent, minimum wages were correlated with levels of unemployment.

Julie Schaffner is affiliated with the Fletcher School of Law and Diplomacy at Tufts University and the Boston University Department of Economics. She was assistant professor of economics and deputy director of the Center for Research on Economic Development and Policy Reform at Stanford University when this comment was written.

specify: What requirements are there for advance notice for, or bureaucratic approval of, dismissals? What rights do workers have to severance pay or reinstatement in the cases of just and unjust dismissal? What constitute grounds for just dismissal? How long must the worker be on the job before severance pay is required? How are severance payments calculated (usually as a function of job tenure)? What provisions are made for the use of temporary or fixed-term contracts that circumvent these requirements? In the case of restrictions on workers' organizations, one must specify: Are unions restricted to organizing at the plant level, or may they organize at the industry level? What is the scope for collective action? Are workers legally entitled to pay for strike days? Are employers allowed to hire replacement workers? What benefits may unions offer their members? Do union agreements apply to nonmembers? In the case of unemployment insurance, one must specify: How high are unemployment insurance benefits and how long do they last? Who is eligible to receive them? Are they financed by payroll or other taxes? If employers are taxed, to what extent are their payments experience rated?

Surprisingly little research to date pays attention to the details of labor market policies. Even studies of labor market regulation tend to make only broad-brush comparisons across countries. Policymakers undertaking labor market reforms, on the other hand, cannot write legislation that makes only vague references to liberalizing labor markets. They write legislation that changes many specific policy parameters, often leaving the complex, inherited structure of the laws intact. Thus, if research is going to become more useful to policymakers, it must start paying more attention to detail. Paying more attention to detail may have an additional benefit: exciting research advances in this area are likely to be made by researchers who find clever ways of exploiting policy idiosyncrasies (e.g., oddities in eligibility requirements that cause policy treatments to differ greatly for similar groups) for the development of empirical identification strategies.

In preparing for research on labor market regulation, it is also useful to invest in careful study of the institutions that shape the regulations' effects. Even if one memorized the large volumes describing the details of labor market policy, one would not understand what the law really means for employers and workers in a country until one studied institutions like labor courts and tribunals and ministries of labor. For example, the effects of severance pay policies may be shaped in important ways by labor court precedents regarding what constitutes just dismissal. They may also be affected by rules regarding who pays court costs, and how long it typically takes for a case to come to court, which might affect workers' and employers' willingness to bring cases to court. The effects of minimum wage legislation may be shaped by the enforcement activities of budget-constrained ministries of labor.

Again, very little research has paid attention to such institutions, which are poorly understood, especially by economists. In some areas, changes in the rules shaping these institutions might have larger effects on the economy than changes in labor market regulations themselves. Attention to institutional details (e.g., differences across provinces in labor court precedents) might also pay off in the development of empirical identification strategies.

After identifying the legal and institutional details of each policy whose economic effects one would like to estimate, the next step in setting out the research agenda is to take a reasonably rich model of labor markets and use it to generate a comprehensive list of potential costs and benefits that might follow from changes in particular policy parameters. This yields a very long list of questions on which we would like to have empirical evidence. By a "rich model" of the labor market, I mean a conceptual framework that acknowledges the possible importance of such labor market complexities as efficiency wage considerations, long-term contracting and incentives for training, and the heterogeneity of individual workers' productivity across jobs that underlies search and matching concerns.

The use of such a model to generate policy-relevant empirical questions might help researchers avoid focusing on such ill-defined concepts as labor market "flexibility." It would also make clear the great difficulty of the empirical problem. It suggests that one would want to measure not only the effects of policy changes on employment, unemployment, hours, training, and level and distribution of wages but also on the magnitude of much more difficult to measure labor use inefficiencies that might be labeled "disguised unemployment" (short-term employment in low-productivity jobs while searching for jobs that make better use of workers' skills and abilities) and "underemployment" (longer term employment in low-productivity jobs in segmented labor markets).

Failure to frame empirical work on labor market policy within a rich conceptual framework has led to several weaknesses in the literature to date. Some studies jump to conclusions that do not necessarily follow. For example, it is often assumed that incentives for employers and workers to invest in training are stronger where job security laws cause jobs to last longer. Deeper thought about how job security laws affect contractual incentives, however, renders their effect on training ambiguous. If laws make jobs last longer by making it difficult to fire workers, they may deprive employers of a tool (dismissal threats) used for giving workers an incentive to apply themselves in on-the-job training. Another example pertains to the analysis of minimum wage and trade union policies that affect private sector wage setting. If one thinks of labor markets as simple spot markets, then one is likely to think that the withdrawal of minimum wage legislation and the weakening of unions would go a long way toward eliminating the perceived dualism in developing country labor markets, thereby greatly reducing inefficiency and inequity. Once one acknowledges the possibility of efficiency wage considerations, however, this need not follow. Indeed, a number of recent studies (e.g., Schaffner 1998; Velenchik 1997) have suggested that to a great extent large, modern enterprises in developing countries pay higher wages for profit-maximizing reasons (e.g., to economize on turnover costs) rather than because they are forced into it by minimum wage legislation or unions. It thus appears likely that the elimination of minimum wages and the weakening of unions would have only small effects on labor market segmentation.

Priorities for future research must be set after comparing the long list of questions on which we would like empirical evidence to the empirical studies completed to date. A first group of studies, which might be labeled "macro" studies, includes cross-country studies and studies of changes over a period of policy reform in specific countries. Their advantage is that they involve real variation in policies. Their disadvantage is that the variation is usually of many policies at once, which renders it difficult to assess the effects of detailed policy changes, and thus difficult to produce the detailed recommendations of use to policymakers. The second group, which might be labeled "micro" studies, uses data from just one country, whether a single cross section, repeated cross sections, or a panel. Rather than looking at the effects of an actual reform, they attempt to learn something about the structure of labor markets, in order to improve economic models used for predicting policy effects. They have the potential advantage of linking up more precisely to more specific policy questions, but this potential advantage is seldom realized. As Paul Schultz's paper makes clear, macro- and microstudies together have touched on only a very small fraction of the questions regarding costs and benefits of policy parameter changes that would be useful to inform policy making. Thus the research agenda is wide open.

In setting out priorities for future research, Paul Schultz discusses the data he considers essential: household panel data over a fairly long period during which a particular country experienced labor market policy reform. I question these priorities for several reasons. At the most technical level, I am not convinced that panel data are superior to repeated cross-sectional data for studying policy reform episodes. I am especially concerned about sample attrition problems, which render panel data samples less and less representative over time. One type of attrition that seems especially difficult to deal with is that associated with migration. Migrant households are very difficult to follow in a survey, but if they are not retained in the panel, researchers lose information on a segment of the population that plays an important role in helping the economy adjust to policy reform. I also would emphasize somewhat different benefits of panel data than are mentioned in Schultz's paper. He emphasizes their usefulness for controlling for unobserved heterogeneity, and thus for answering questions that can be asked with repeated cross-sectional data, only better. I would probably emphasize their usefulness for answering questions that simply cannot be asked with repeated cross sections, fundamentally dynamic questions like: Who are the winners and losers? What movements across the income distribution are going on? These can be important for understanding the political economy of the problem.

I also question the exclusive focus on household survey data. An important and challenging piece of the research frontier might involve development of employer surveys, perhaps linked to surveys of samples of their workers, that shed greater light on the impact of labor market regulations.

Finally, I question what seems to me to be an emphasis on macro- rather than microstudies of policy questions. I worry that such emphasis might push researchers toward studies that consider the effects of "labor market reform" defined only vaguely and thus that simply cannot produce sufficiently specific guidance to policymakers.

References

Schaffner, Julie A. 1998. Premiums to employment in larger establishments: Evidence from Peru. *Journal of Development Economics* 55:81–113.
Velenchik, Ann D. 1997. Government intervention, efficiency wages, and the employer size wage effect in Zimbabwe. *Journal of Development Economics* 53: 305–38.

9

Improving School Quality
in Developing Countries

Michael Kremer

Economists who do not specialize in education often describe investment in human capital as essential for development and recommend that countries invest in education. They are typically less specific about how developing countries can do this effectively. This essay will selectively discuss what we know about how to improve school quality in developing countries, and what directions for future research I believe are likely to be promising. It does not review the literature on returns to education, which has been addressed elsewhere (Schultz 1988).

Section 9.1 discusses evidence on the impact of various educational inputs. It first examines the evidence from retrospective studies, which Hanushek (1995) summarized as indicating little or no effect of additional spending on school quality. I argue that it is difficult to draw strong conclusions from this literature, in part because many of the existing studies are subject to omitted variable bias. One strategy to overcome omitted variable bias is to use an instrumental variables approach that takes advantage of sources of variation in school inputs that are plausibly uncorrelated with other factors influencing educational outcomes. Angrist and Lavy (1999) found that class size reductions improve test scores in Israel using this approach, and Duflo (1998) found that expansion of the Indonesian educational system in the 1970s increased wages. Another approach to overcoming omitted variable bias is to conduct randomized trials on school inputs. Work along these lines in Kenya suggests that dropout rates are sensitive to the cost of education but does not suggest large effects of textbooks on test scores. Instrumental variables techniques and prospec-

Michael Kremer is professor of economics at Harvard University and a senior fellow of the Brookings Institution.

tive studies hold promise, and current evidence suggests that expanding access to education increases wages, but at this stage we are far from having found ways that reliably turn school expenditure into improved educational outcomes.

Given that the evidence on effects of increased expenditures is mixed, many people believe that school quality could be improved more by reform of school governance than by additional spending. Section 9.2 discusses reform of governance structures for education. It first notes that the high rates of teacher absenteeism in many developing countries suggest that current school governance is inadequate. It then discusses teacher incentives. Finally, it discusses empirical work on school vouchers in Colombia that I am conducting in collaboration with Josh Angrist, Elizabeth King, Erik Bloom, and Eric Bettinger, and theoretical work on the political and cultural effects of school choice that I am conducting with Andrei Sarychev. Based on the scant existing evidence, it seems plausible that school choice could improve pedagogy, but it also seems possible that it could increase the scope for schools to teach disparate, conflicting values and that over several generations this could lead to increasing polarization of society.

9.1   Evidence on Inputs

An extensive literature attempts to estimate the effect of various educational inputs by comparing educational outcomes between areas with different levels of inputs. Hanushek (1995) surveyed this literature. He reported that there is no consistent finding across the studies that test scores were improved by smaller class size, improved teacher qualifications, or more overall per capita spending. He did see some evidence that particular inputs, such as textbooks, are useful. At least on some of these issues, a meta-analysis might find more favorable results, since many of the studies Hanushek cited found insignificant positive effects and aggregating these might yield a significant positive impact (Kremer 1995). One important issue is whether test scores are economically meaningful. Knight and Sabot (1990) found evidence that such scores were correlated with wages in Kenya, even after controlling for IQ. Card and Krueger (1992) argued that educational spending in the United States affects long-run wages, although others have challenged their results. A weakness of retrospective studies is that variation in input levels may be correlated with unobserved characteristics that directly affect educational outcomes. For example, areas with more educational spending may also have parents who are more committed to education. If the parents directly assist their children in other ways, for example with homework, the studies Hanushek surveyed may overestimate the impact of inputs on educational outputs. Alternatively, if areas with poor educational performance receive compensatory assistance, then there may be a negative correlation between inputs and unobserved factors that positively influence achievement. In this case, retrospective studies will underestimate the impact of inputs on achievement. In the context of developing countries, it seems more plausible that retrospective studies will overestimate, rather than underestimate, the effect of inputs. However, it seems difficult to draw inferences from retrospective studies given these problems.

A second strategy for estimating the impact of various inputs on education is to search for some plausibly exogenous source of variation. For example, Angrist and Lavy (1999) took advantage of a rule with origins dating back to Maimonides that determines class size in Israel. According to the rule, maximum class size is forty, so that if forty-one pupils are enrolled in a grade, a second teacher is added. If eighty-one pupils are enrolled, a third teacher must be added, and so on. This produces a non-monotonic pattern of class size as a function of enrollment, with class size increasing one for one with enrollment up to an enrollment of forty, dropping to twenty as enrollment reaches forty-one, and then gradually increasing with enrollment until enrollment reaches eighty-one, at which point class size falls from forty to twenty-seven. Angrist and Lavy showed that if one uses standard methods to estimate the effect of class size on test scores in Israel, one finds no evidence that lower class size raises test scores, and perhaps even some slight evidence in the opposite direction. They then showed that instrumenting for actual class size with predicted class size given by Maimonides' rule yields evidence that lower class sizes increase math and reading scores among fourth and fifth graders, although not among third graders. The discrepancy between the ordinary least squares and instrumental variables estimates is apparently due to the fact that class sizes are systematically larger in large cities, and smaller in new development towns where immigrants and poor people predominate.

Similar positive results on the effect of educational inputs were found by Esther Duflo (1998), who examined the impact of a huge Indonesian school construction program financed with oil revenues in the 1970s. There was a mechanical rule linking the number of schools built in each region to the preexisting enrollment rate. Duflo examined educational attainment and earnings of children born in various regions in cohorts that reached school age at the time the schools were constructed and as a control used other cohorts that were born too early to take advantage of the new schools. Duflo found that the program increased years of schooling by 0.25 to 0.35 years and wages by 4 to 6 percent.

A third strategy is to conduct prospective, randomized evaluations. For example, Jamison et al. (1981) found that provision of mathematics education by radio in Nicaragua increased test scores by a phenomenal 1.2 standard deviations, and provision of mathematic workbooks increased test scores by a still impressive one-third of a standard deviation. In the study by Jamison et al., schools were randomized into three groups. One group received textbooks, another group received radio mathematics education, and a third group received no assistance. That study led to the widespread adoption of radio mathematics education programs in other Latin American countries as well as other developing countries. Unfortunately, however, radio education programs were often abandoned quickly. It would be interesting to find out more about why the programs were abandoned.

Recent work in Kenya by Paul Glewwe, Sylvie Moulin, and myself suggests that increasing class size and using the funds to reduce school fees and purchase textbooks would reduce dropout rates without measurably reducing test scores. We have been conducting a series of randomized evaluations of educational interventions in Kenya. School enrollments are dropping in Africa, and some argue that this is because governments are passing on more of the cost of education to parents through school fees. The elasticity of enrollment with respect to school fees is therefore of particular policy importance. A Dutch nonprofit organization, International Christelijk Steunfonds (ICS), randomly selected seven rural Kenyan primary schools from a group of fourteen schools for a program that provided textbooks and paid for the uniforms required of all Kenyan primary school students. This dramatically reduced the cost of attending school. The dropout rates were 6.8 percent at program schools and 16.5 percent in comparison schools. The program also attracted many students from neighboring schools, so overall enrollment was approximately 40 percent greater in program schools. There was no appreciable difference in test scores between program and comparison schools, suggesting that the joint impact on test scores of textbooks and of the enrollment increase was close to zero. Since the reduction in per pupil expenditure on teachers would have been sufficient to pay for both textbooks and uniforms, the Kenyan government could implement a similar policy without receiving outside funding or changing its other budgetary allocations.

Although there is intense debate about the effect of educational expenditure in developed countries, there is widespread consensus that provision of textbooks can substantially increase test scores in developing countries. Glewwe, Kremer, and Moulin (1998) evaluated a program through which the same Dutch nonprofit organization provided textbooks to twenty-five rural Kenyan primary schools that were chosen randomly from a group of one hundred candidate schools. After one school year, there was no measurable difference in average test scores between program and comparison schools. However, the program did improve test scores for those students who started out in the top quintile of initial academic achievement. Preliminary results suggest similar findings after the second and third years. Retrospective studies of textbooks in the same part of Kenya would have suggested large effects of textbooks on test scores, and to the extent that the prospective randomized study is more believable, this suggests that retrospective techniques would have been misleading.

In January 1997, wall charts in math, science, and geography were given to eighty-nine schools in rural Kenya while another eighty-nine schools served as a comparison group. After one year, a series of estimators provide little evidence that the program significantly increased test scores. An estimator based on comparing test scores in subjects for which wall charts were provided between schools that did and did not receive wall charts yields negative point estimates in most subjects, although the coefficients are close to zero and statistically insignificant. Controlling for average test scores in the school prior to the introduction of the program suggests a point estimate of the effect of wall charts that is almost exactly zero. An estimator based on comparing the relative performance of students in wall-chart and non-wall-chart subjects across the two groups of schools yields a positive but small and statistically insignificant point estimate: wall charts increased test scores by 1.8 percent of a standard deviation with a standard error of 3.6 percent of a standard deviation.

9.2 School Reform

In part out of frustration with the results of research on school inputs, educational researchers and policymakers have turned to issues of school governance, including teacher incentives and vouchers.[1]

One indication that governance in many schools is currently inadequate lies in the abysmal teacher attendance rates in many developing countries. The Public Report on Basic Education (PROBE) in India found that on an average working day, an average teacher spends approximately four hours in school (PROBE Team 1999). As part of our research in Kenya, we visited schools randomly and found that teachers were absent from the school 28.4 percent of the time and that they were in the school but out of class (despite the presence of someone from the organization visiting their classes!) an additional 12.4 percent of the time. Overall, teachers were absent from their classes 41 percent of the time.

The following subsections examine two strategies that might improve teacher effort: incentive pay and school choice.

9.2.1 Teacher Incentives

A natural response to evidence of low teacher effort is to introduce stronger teacher incentives, perhaps steep explicit incentives. Theoretically, incentives could be counterproductive. In fact, Holmstrom and Milgrom (1991) used the example of teaching to illustrate the perils of providing steep incentives when some dimensions of effort are observable and others are not. They argued that incentives may cause teachers to teach

---

1. These two areas of research should not be seen as substitutes for each other. Research on inputs will be needed by whoever makes decisions about school inputs, whether this is a national ministry of education, local school districts, or entrepreneurs running private schools.

to the test and spend less time encouraging creativity. This particular problem is of secondary importance in an environment where teacher absenteeism is pervasive and few teachers encourage creativity in any case. Still, schools may exert effort to raise test scores through a variety of other means that are even more socially undesirable than teaching to the test. Schools could try to improve average test scores by forcing weak students to drop out or denying admission to weak students. Appropriately designed incentives might be able to reduce these problems.

Another problem with explicit performance incentives is that teachers would have incentives to move to schools where students are performing well, and this might increase disparities among schools and regions. Basing incentives in improvements in performance eliminates this problem but creates a ratchet effect that weakens incentives. Basing incentives on performance relative to a one-time historical benchmark may work for a few years, but eventually the benchmark would become outdated. One possibility would be to base incentives on the change in performance of the school between the time the teacher arrived at the school and the current year.

Another alternative would be to base teacher incentives not on outcomes but rather on inputs, such as teacher attendance. This is less attractive to the extent that society cares about outputs rather than inputs. However, it requires teachers to bear somewhat less risk and may seem more fair. A World Bank program in Nicaragua incorporates incentives based on teacher attendance. However, it is not clear that teacher attendance can easily be monitored, since monitors and teachers would have incentives to collude. No studies on the effects of this program have been published.

Since output is difficult to measure and depends on many factors other than effort, incentives in most jobs are provided through discretionary merit pay and promotion decisions by a superior. A difficulty with this in a public school system is that the superior may not have strong incentives to improve school performance.

Together with Paul Glewwe and Sylvie Moulin, I am investigating a program of teacher incentives in Kenya conducted by ICS. ICS provided teachers in fifty Kenyan schools with an incentive program. Another fifty schools served as a comparison group. The treatment group was selected randomly. Teachers in schools with good test performance will receive prizes based on school performance. Incentives were set at the school level, rather than the teacher level, primarily because this is more politically acceptable in the international educational community. (Interestingly, there did not appear to be much resistance to teacher-level incentives in Kenya.) Students who dropped out during the year will be assigned the test scores they would have received if they had taken the test and randomly guessed the answers. This offers an incentive to create an environment geared toward preventing students from dropping out. The program began this year, so it is too early to report on outcomes.

9.2.2 School Choice

School choice has long been promoted by economists and now seems to be getting more political support, especially in the United States. Since 1991, thirty-two U.S. states have enacted laws allowing charter schools to compete for pupils with regular public schools. Advocates argue that public schools have weak incentives to perform and that school choice makes schools more competitive and more responsive to parents. The attractiveness of school vouchers is enhanced by the difficulty of providing effective teacher incentives within a state-run educational system, as discussed above. Moreover, schools that get vouchers have an incentive to keep students motivated and attending school. Among developing countries, Bangladesh, Colombia, and Tanzania have recently established voucher programs targeted at the poor.

Data

To date, evidence on school choice is limited. A lottery was used to allocate vouchers in a Milwaukee school choice program. In this program, students applied for the opportunity to attend a specific "choice" school in a specific year. Choice schools with more applicants than openings were required to admit students by lottery. Greene, Peterson, and Du (1996) compared lottery winners and losers and estimated that students who won the vouchers had higher mathematics and reading scores than students who did not win vouchers. Rouse (1998) extended the Greene et al. analysis, paying particular attention to statistical problems in the original study. She found similar results for mathematics scores but was unable to find a significant increase in reading scores.

I am working with Josh Angrist, Elizabeth King, Erik Bloom, and Eric Bettinger to evaluate Colombia's Programa de Amplicación de Cobertura de Educación Secundaria (PACES), a program to increase the coverage of secondary school. This program provided approximately 100,000 poor students with vouchers to attend private secondary schools between 1991 and 1997. Although 88 percent of Colombia's primary-school-age children (6 to 11 years old) were enrolled in primary schools in 1993, only half of the eligible population was enrolled in secondary schools. Sixty-four percent of secondary school students were in public schools, with this share being much lower for the richest quintile (39 percent) than for the poorest (81 percent).

Neighborhoods in Colombia are divided into six strata on the basis of socioeconomic characteristics. Only students residing in neighborhoods in the lowest two strata were eligible for the voucher program. The vouchers were also restricted to students who had attended public, rather than private, primary schools. This restriction helped exclude upper income households.

Once a PACES voucher is awarded it can be renewed yearly until eleventh grade, assuming the recipient attains a satisfactory level of academic performance. Seventy-seven percent of vouchers were renewed.

The maximum cash value of the voucher was initially set to correspond to the average tuition of a low- to middle-cost private school in Colombia's three largest cities. The purchasing power of the voucher has fallen over time, but it still covers about 50 percent of the cost of private schooling in the larger cities and about 70 percent of the cost in smaller municipalities. Parents are allowed to supplement the voucher if it does not cover the full cost of tuition. It is interesting to note that per pupil expenditure on public schools in Colombia is 140 percent of the cost of the voucher (Calderon 1996).

If more students in a particular municipality wish to participate than there are vouchers available, a lottery is held in that municipality to allocate the available vouchers.[2]

We are still collecting and coding data from a survey. However, based on our current data, the average applicant is now a 15-year-old ninth grader with two siblings. The applicants' parents have slightly more than five years of formal education. Boys and girls are equally represented in our sample. Most of the sample (87 percent) is still enrolled in school.

The data we have collected so far are consistent with the view that the lotteries were random. For example, we found no systematic differences between winners and losers by parental educational levels.

Preliminary evidence suggests that voucher winners had completed one-tenth of a year more of school than voucher losers three years into the program, as can be seen in table 9.1. However, they were no more likely to be currently in school. The difference in grade completion was due to a difference in repetition rates between voucher winners and losers. There are several possible interpretations of the declining grade repetition. It may be that students are going to better schools or working harder so that they can keep up their grades in order to retain their vouchers. Alternatively, schools may be loosening their promotion standards to allow students to pass and thus retain their vouchers. We hope to administer an academic test to distinguish these possibilities.

A few intriguing nonacademic outcomes suggest that behavior may have changed for voucher winners. As shown in table 9.2, voucher winners were less likely to be living with a companion or married than voucher losers. They were also less likely to work.

Vouchers and the Distribution of Values

Around the world, education is overwhelmingly publicly provided. James (1993) found that across a sample of twelve industrialized societies,

---

2. In a few cities, the local ICETEX office decided to assign vouchers based on primary school performance instead of randomly. (ICETEX is the Colombian Institute for Education, Credit, and Training Abroad.)

Table 9.1 **Educational Outcomes and Voucher Status**

| Dependent Variable | Control Group Means (1) | Coefficient on Voucher Status — Combined Sample | | | Bogata 1995: All Controls (5) |
		No Controls (2)	Basic Controls (3)	All Controls (4)	
Highest grade completed	7.3 (1.1)	.106** (.055)	.103** (.041)	.096** (.041)	.138** (.051)
Currently in school	.846 (.361)	.023 (.018)	.007 (.017)	.007 (.016)	.017 (.020)
Finished 6th grade	.942 (.234)	.020* (.011)	.017 (.011)	.015 (.011)	.022* (.012)
Finished 7th grade	.859 (.348)	.043** (.018)	.032* (.018)	.030* (.018)	.032 (.020)
Finished 8th grade	.657 (.475)	.098** (.025)	.092** (.025)	.087** (.025)	.105** (.028)
Started 6th grade in private school	.850 (.357)	.066** (.016)	.066* (.016)	.065** (.016)	.051** (.016)
Started 7th grade in private school	.687 (.464)	.149** (.022)	.149** (.021)	.149** (.021)	.152** (.024)
Currently in private school	.546 (.498)	.166** (.024)	.157** (.024)	.158** (.024)	.160** (.028)
Number of times 6th grade attended	1.2 (.432)	−.060** (.020)	−.055** (.020)	−.054** (.020)	−.068** (.025)
Repeated after 6th grade (including 6th)	.202 (.402)	−.058** (.019)	−.058** (.019)	−.054** (.019)	−.056** (.023)
Repetitions since 6th grade (including 6th)	.223 (.467)	−.061** (.023)	−.059** (.022)	−.056** (.022)	−.068** (.028)
Years in school since 6th grade	3.6 (1.2)	.044 (.062)	.031 (.044)	.028 (.044)	.047 (.051)
N	722	1,530	1,529	1,529	1,121

Note: The data come from applicant lists and surveys of students who applied for the PACES voucher program in Bogota 1995, Bogota 1997, and Jamundi 1993. Students applied immediately following fifth grade. Data were collected in mid-1998.

Col. (2) contains no controls. Col. (3) includes controls for city, year of application, whether applicant has phone, age, gender, type of survey and instrument, and month of interview. Col. (4) is similar to col. (3) except that it also includes controls for Bogota neighborhoods. Col. (5) uses only the Bogota 1995 subsample and includes all controls except city-year controls. The combined sample for completion of seventh and eighth grade excludes Bogota 1997.

Numbers in parentheses are standard deviations in col. (1) and robust standard errors in cols. (2) through (5).

*Significant at the 10 percent level.
**Significant at the 5 percent level.

Table 9.2   Noneducational Outcomes and Voucher Status

Dependent Variable	Control Group Means (1)	Combined Sample			Bogata 1995: All Controls (5)
		No Controls (2)	Basic Controls (3)	All Controls (4)	
Applicant is	.177	−.048**	−.041**	−.039**	−.056**
working	(.382)	(.020)	(.020)	(.020)	(.023)
Pregnant or	.037	−.012	−.012	−.012	−.016
has child	(.188)	(.010)	(.010)	(.010)	(.010)
Married or	.023	−.014**	−.015**	−.016**	−.015**
living with	(.151)	(.007)	(.007)	(.007)	(.007)
companion					
Victim of	.095	−.018	−.018	−.017	−.024
violence	(.293)	(.016)	(.016)	(.017)	(.019)
Mother	.546	.044	.031	.028	.045
works	(.498)	(.026)	(.043)	(.044)	(.032)
Father works	.852	.019	.049	.058	.021
	(.355)	(.020)	(.034)	(.035)	(.027)
N	600	1,235	1,235	1,235	1,016

Note: See table 9.1 note.
**Significant at the 5 percent level.

the median proportion of students attending private primary schools was 10 percent and the median proportion of students attending private secondary schools was 13.5 percent.[3] Moreover, choice of school within the public sector is often limited. Lott (1987) found that across ten countries, citizens have more choice in selecting public doctors or hospitals than in choosing public schools.

Given that the a priori case for vouchers is strong, at least to economists, and that the limited available evidence tends to suggest that vouchers are effective at improving school performance, the preponderance of public education is a mystery for economic theory.

Standard rationales for public support of education—positive externalities from education and credit constraints that prevent human capital investment—do not explain why the state operates schools rather than simply financing schools through vouchers. Other explanations of the preponderance of public schools are not fully convincing. Some conservatives

3. Across thirty-eight developing countries, the median proportion attending private primary schools was 11 percent, and the median proportion attending private secondary schools was 27.5 percent. The mean proportion attending private schools is higher than the median proportion, but this is due in large part to small-country outliers, such as the Netherlands and Belgium among industrial countries and Lesotho among developing countries.

argue that public schools predominate because of the power of teachers' unions. However, it is not clear why teachers, rather than other occupations, have been so successful in obtaining state support. After all, autoworkers also have powerful unions, but they have not been able to ensure that automobiles are overwhelmingly produced by the state.

Liberal opponents of vouchers argue that vouchers would lead to rich and poor children attending separate schools. Some liberal voucher opponents argue that children are influenced by their peers, so this segregation will exacerbate inequality. This argument is not fully satisfactory either. If parents are not credit constrained, school assignment will generally be efficient under vouchers and inefficient under a public school system without choice. Public policy could address credit constraints directly, rather than by eliminating school choice.

Nor is it clear that segregation by race or income need be greater under vouchers than under many existing public school systems. Segregation could be limited by prohibiting parents from adding to vouchers with their own funds and requiring schools to accept students by lottery, as in most existing U.S. school choice programs. Public education does not seem to be designed with much weight on reducing segregation. Historically, many U.S. public schools were legally segregated by race, and today public schools in the United States are segregated by neighborhood, often a close proxy for income and race. Until recently, many European students were tested to determine what type of secondary school they would attend. Outcomes on the tests were highly correlated with socioeconomic status.

Even if publicly provided education redistributes income to the poor, this would not explain its near universality, since the poor typically do not have much political power. Did the government of Indonesia create a nationwide public school system rather than a voucher system because it cared about the welfare of the poor? A more likely explanation is that the leaders of Indonesia wanted to control separatist tendencies, build nationhood, and strengthen their political support through a single national educational system. Moreover, outside the United States, preferences between public and private schools do not seem correlated with distributional views. The Netherlands, which has an extensive voucher system, is fairly egalitarian. Public support of private schools in Australia was introduced by a Labor government (James 1990).

Lott (1987) argued that politicians impose public education in order to indoctrinate children with the belief that transferring income through taxes is justified. However, Lott did not explain how politicians impose this indoctrination in a democratic country. I am working with Andrei Sarychev on a model in which parents would choose schools with an ideology similar to their own under a voucher system but prefer a system in which all children are educated in public schools teaching the ideology of the median voter.

Schools teach both cognitive skills and ideology. Externalities may be associated with both activities, creating a potential rationale for public financing of education. It is likely to be much easier to regulate teaching of cognitive skills within a voucher system than to regulate ideology. Controlling the ideology taught in schools may require public ownership of schools, limits on school choice by parents, and centralized hiring of teachers.

Externalities associated with learning cognitive skills could conceivably create inefficiencies under a voucher system, but these inefficiencies could be limited by appropriate regulation. Parents will prefer to obtain only the privately optimal amount of education, and in some cases this may be much less than is socially optimal. Under a voucher system, therefore, some parents might send their children to schools that pay kickbacks to the parents instead of spending the voucher funds on education.[4]

While kickbacks may be a serious problem in some countries with weak administrative systems and many parents who feel they face much more pressing needs than their children's education, kickbacks could probably be kept under control in many countries. The state could require institutions to be licensed in order to accept vouchers. Typically, in countries with voucher systems, inputs such as teacher-pupil ratios and teacher salaries and qualifications are regulated. Licenses could also be made conditional on outcomes such as test scores. For example, schools in which less than half the students pass a physics test could be decertified and barred from accepting vouchers.

There are also likely to be externalities leading people to prefer different ideological instruction for other people's children than for their own. To take a trivial but expositionally useful example, parents might prefer that other people's children be taught not to litter but that their own children spend more time learning physics and less time learning not to litter. In fact, public schools in the United States spend considerable time teaching children to take care of the environment. Under a voucher system, parents might prefer schools that spent more time on physics and less time on environmentalism. In the many developing countries with great ethnic diversity, members of each ethnic group may prefer that other ethnic groups be taught as much as possible in the national language and taught history

---

4. In response to a voucher program established by the Michigan legislature, the Romulus public school system opened a voucher school within the neighboring Detroit school district and offered a $50 signing bonus to students. Twenty-two hundred students enrolled, but these included many dropouts, and only a fifth of the students continued to attend the school. The following year, the Michigan legislature outlawed this practice, and the school closed (Toch 1998). More subtly, schools may supply consumption or entertainment to children instead of providing education that creates positive externalities. In fact, American schools, which share some characteristics of voucher schools, since they are locally operated, seem to reflect the preferences of children. American students have more freedom and are entertained with more spectator sports than students in many other countries.

that glorifies the nation as a whole. However, they may prefer an education for their children that preserves the local culture.

It is likely to be far more difficult for governments to regulate ideology than teaching of cognitive skills. The government can mandate textbooks but not the expression on a teacher's face. Testing children's ideology is likely to be much more difficult than testing their cognitive achievement. A child who does not know that force equals mass times acceleration will find it difficult to pretend that she does, but a child who does not actually identify with the nation may be able to successfully mislead a school inspector.

The experience of school choice in the Netherlands is illustrative. In the Netherlands, groups of as few as fifty parents can set up a school and demand that the state provide them with a building and pay teacher salaries.

Historically, a major source of cleavage in Dutch society has been religious. The fight for independence in the Netherlands was intertwined with the Protestant-Catholic antagonism of the period. Until the nineteenth century, Catholics were not allowed to set up their own schools.

The majority of students in the Netherlands attend religiously affiliated schools. The three dominant groups are Catholic, Calvinist, and Dutch Reformed. Table 9.3, taken from an anthropological study of a Dutch town by Gadourek (1956), shows that history texts differ sharply between Catholic, Calvinist, and Dutch Reformed schools, in ways that may well deepen divisions between the groups.

James noted that "the extensive reliance on private schools in Holland has reinforced the religious segmentation within society" (1989, 55). Dutch society is heavily influenced by the Protestant-Catholic split, with political parties organized by religion, television stations allocated to religious groups, and even soccer clubs organized on a religious basis. However, while school choice may have deepened religious segmentation, this does not seem to have led to great intolerance or violent social conflict in the Netherlands.

At least some of the recently established charter schools in the United States seem to be teaching nonmainstream ideology. For example, Toch (1998) reported that at Sankofa Shule, an African-centered charter school in Michigan, instead of observing Labor Day, Memorial Day, and Presidents' Day, students observe holidays such as African Independence Day and Malcolm X Remembrance Day. According to the school newsletter, "The traditional concept of Thanksgiving, like the Fourth of July, really has nothing to do with us." A daily affirmation by the entire school begins, "I pledge to my African nation . . ." Contrast this with the Pledge of Allegiance traditionally made in public schools, which stresses the "indivisibility" of the nation.

Many developing countries have considerable ethnic or religious division. Discussions of school vouchers in these countries should consider

Table 9.3   History Texts in the Netherlands

A. The Roman Catholic textbook *Rood, Wit en Blauw,* by J. A. Nillessen ('s-Hertogenbosch)	B. The Calvinist (Gereformeerd) reading book *Toen en Nu,* by W. G. Van der Hulst and R. Huizenga (Groningen, 12th ed. 1951)	C. The textbook *Van Hunebed tot Heden,* by S. B. D. Werff and S. H. Woudsma (Groningen, 3d ed. 1954), in use in the School of the Dutch Reformed church in Sassenheim

The paragraphs selected refer to one of the most important periods in the history of the territory, the origin of the independent state of the Netherlands.

Philip II

Philip II was a religious sovereign. To him the Catholic cause was beyond anything else. In those days, the apostasy was generally considered as a crime and had to be punished. Very many sovereigns did not bother about it too much. But Philip did. He was not too popular in the Netherlands. He was a proud Spaniard, and did not feel quite at home in the Netherlands.	Philip did not like the Dutchmen and the Dutchmen did not like him. He was a typical Spaniard: proud, ambitious, unfriendly, and a merciless persecutor of heretics. People understood quite well why the Spanish soldiers received orders to stay here. It was to wipe out heresy from the country, to rob the Dutchmen of their freedom, in the long run.	Philip II was by far not such a clever sovereign as his father. He was a typical Spaniard, and had nothing in common with the Dutchmen. He could not even understand their language. The purpose of his rule was as follows: the extirpation of the reformed religion in the Netherlands. Everybody had to be a Catholic!

The Inquisition

This was a tribunal of the Church. Its members were wise and pious bishops and priests.	Each day, now here then there, especially in the Southern Netherlands, innocent people were tortured and murdered. The inquisition was merciless . . .	Everybody hated the Inquisition. William of Orange, while still being a Catholic, hated it too, together with many other Catholics . . .

not only the effect on teaching of cognitive skills but also the effect on long-run social cohesion.

9.3   Conclusion

Many economists believe that human capital is essential to long-run growth. The importance of the topic calls out for further empirical research using randomized evaluations and plausible instruments for variation in school inputs, as well as for theoretical and empirical work on school governance.

References

Angrist, J. D., and V. Lavy, 1999. Using Maimonides' rule to estimate the effect of class size on scholastic achievement. *Quarterly Journal of Economics* 14 (2): 533–75.

Calderon, Alberto. 1996. Voucher program for secondary schools: The Colombian experience. Human Capital Development Working Paper no. 66. Washington, D.C.: World Bank.

Card, David, and Alan B. Krueger. 1992. Does school quality matter? Returns to education and the characteristics of public schools in the United States. *Journal of Political Economy* 100 (February): 1–40.

Duflo, Esther. 1998. Evaluating the schooling and labor market consequences of a school construction program: An analysis of the Indonesian experience. Cambridge: Massachusetts Institute of Technology. Photocopy.

Gadourek, I. 1956. *A Dutch community: Social and cultural structural process in a bulb-growing region in the Netherlands.* Leiden: Steinfert Kroese.

Glewwe, Paul, Michael Kremer, and Sylvie Moulin. 1998. Textbooks and test scores: Evidence from a prospective evaluation in Kenya. Harvard University. Photocopy.

Greene, Jay P., Paul E. Peterson, and Jiangtao Du. 1996. The effectiveness of school choice in Milwaukee: A secondary analysis of data from the program's evaluation. Paper presented at the annual meeting of the American Political Science Association, San Francisco, 30 August.

Hanushek, Eric A. 1995. Interpreting recent research on schooling in developing countries. *World Bank Research Observer* 10, no. 2 (August): 227–46.

Holmstrom, Bengt, and Paul Milgrom. 1991. Multitask principal—Agent analyses: Incentive contracts, asset ownership, and job design. *Journal of Law, Economics, and Organization* 7 (spring): 24–52.

James, Estelle. 1989. The private nonprofit provision of education: A comparison of Sweden and Holland. In *The nonprofit sector in international perspective: Studies in comparative culture and policy,* ed. E. James, 31–60. New York: Oxford University Press.

———. 1990. Private education and redistributive subsidies in Australia. In *Privatization and its alternatives,* ed. W. Dormle. Madison: University of Wisconsin Press.

———. 1993. Why do different countries choose a different public-private mix of educational services? *Journal of Human Resources* 28 (3): 571–92.

Jamison, Dean, Klaus Galda, Stephen Heyneman, and Barbara Searle. 1981. Improving elementary mathematics education in Nicaragua: An experimental study of the impact of textbooks and radio on achievement. *Journal of Educational Psychology* 73 (4): 556–67.

Knight, John B., and Richard Sabot. 1990. *Education, productivity, and inequality: The East African natural experiment.* New York: Oxford University Press.

Kremer, Michael. 1995. Research on schooling: What we know and what we don't: A comment on Hanushek. *World Bank Research Observer* 10, no. 2 (August): 247–54.

Lott, John. 1987. Why is education publicly provided? A critical survey. *Cato Journal* 7, no. 2 (fall): 475–502.

PROBE Team. 1999. *Public report on basic education in India.* New Delhi: Oxford University Press.

Rouse, Cecilia E. 1998. Private school vouchers and student achievement: An evaluation of the Milwaukee Parental Choice Program. *Quarterly Journal of Economics* 118:553–601.

Schultz, Paul T. 1988. Education investments and returns. In *Handbook of development economics,* vol. 1, ed. H. Chenery and T. N. Srinivasan, 543–630. Amsterdam: North-Holland.

Toch, Thomas. 1998. The new education bazaar. *U.S. News and World Report,* 27 April, 46.

Comment on the Paper by Michael Kremer   Anjini Kochar

Other authors in this volume have repeatedly made the point that academic research either fails to provide concrete policy recommendations or else provides an all-inclusive list of suggestions so long as to be uninformative. Michael Kremer's paper does not fall in this category of research. He focuses, instead, squarely on the policy question of *how* to improve education, or the nature of the investments that must be undertaken. Within this heading, he examines two forms of investment: first, the provision of instructional material such as textbooks and, second, methods to improve teacher attendance, such as pay incentives and school choice.

This focus on just one component of the body of research on educational issues in developing economies requires me to briefly raise some of the other issues in this literature. I therefore start my comments by discussing what we have learned from this broader literature, and what is yet to be known. I then address the issues Kremer has raised. The importance of the points he emphasizes will, however, vary across economies. Correspondingly, any discussion of these points must be country specific. Since my research has been primarily on the South Asian economies, I will evaluate his recommendations on the basis of the educational problems of these economies. I emphasize, however, that just as the recommendations advocated by Kremer need not apply to all economies, similarly, what may be true of the South Asian economies need not be true of other developing economies.

Research on Education

Research on education can broadly be classified into two groups. The first group takes education as an *input* and analyzes its effect both on "macro" outcomes such as national income and the growth rate of such income and on "micro" outcomes such as the income, health, and welfare of households and individuals within households. The second broad group of studies takes education as an *outcome* and analyzes the determinants

Anjini Kochar is assistant professor of economics and faculty fellow at the Center for Research on Economic Development and Policy Reform at Stanford University.

of two important dimensions of education, educational quantity (enrollments, completed years of education) and educational quality as generally reflected in test scores.

One of the robust findings that has emerged from research on education as an input is that it is one of the major determinants of both national income levels and growth. There is far less consensus, however, on *how* education affects growth. There is a similar debate on both the magnitude of private returns to education and how education affects individual and household outcomes. Thus, for example, Heckman and Hotz (1986) showed that wage earnings equations for Panama show a rate of return to education of about 12 percent, but this falls to 8 percent when the education of parents is included. Much more research is necessary on how one should interpret such results, and on whether they reflect the importance of the home environment or other factors.

Similarly, there is little agreement among economists about the relative importance of the many factors that determine the economic returns and costs associated with different levels of schooling, and hence the level of education chosen by any household. Some of the latest evidence from India shows that returns are lower than expected, with the rate of return on primary education being about 5 to 8 percent in rural areas. Rates of return from middle, secondary, and higher levels of education are generally estimated to be even lower. It is widely believed that the returns are significantly lower for girls than for boys and that this explains the gender gap in education in economies such as those of South Asia. It is, perhaps, surprising that few studies have documented this empirically. The seminal work on the topic thus remains Rosenzweig and Schultz's 1982 paper, which provided empirical evidence in support of the hypothesis that gender differences in survival rates among boys and girls are partly explained by differences in labor market employment rates among men and women.

The quantity of education is also affected by the costs of education, which include both direct and opportunity costs. Indeed, many of the policies implemented by governments of developing economies to improve enrollment rates for girls are premised on the assumption that low enrollments are primarily a consequence of the high opportunity costs associated with withdrawing girls from domestic work. Examples of such policies include "nonformal" schooling programs in economies such as India's, programs primarily targeted toward girls. There is, however, scant empirical research that convincingly demonstrates the importance of such opportunity costs in enrollment decisions.

Direct costs of education arise as a consequence of the cost of textbooks, uniforms, and any transportation involved in getting to schools. Kremer's paper speaks directly to the importance of such costs in affecting not just educational quantity but also educational quality.

At the onset of any discussion of educational quality, it is necessary to recognize that educational outcomes reflect not just the school environment but also the home environment. Policy initiatives have, however, focused on factors that affect the school environment, such as teacher attendance and the availability of inputs, rather than on factors that affect the home environment, such as the quantity and quality of parental inputs, primarily because improvements in the home environment are harder to effect. If, however, educational choices primarily reflect the nature of the home environment, policies that focus on the school environment may have very little impact. There is little research on the importance of the home environment relative to the school environment in developing economies, though this subject is receiving considerable attention in the research on educational outcomes in more developed economies.

It is hard to exaggerate the magnitude of the "quality" problem. A 1991 study conducted in twenty-three states by India's National Council of Educational Research and Training found that for a sample of 65,000 urban and rural fourth grade students, the average achievement on basic skills tests of arithmetic, reading comprehension, and spelling was only 46 percent. Other studies find that 70 percent of fourth grade students and 60 percent of fifth grade students were not able to achieve competency standards suggested for second grade students.[1]

What are the determinants of such low schooling quality? Kremer emphasizes teaching materials and teaching time, as reflected in teacher attendance. Other factors, which may be equally or even more important, however, are teaching methods and teacher quality. In one study conducted in the state of Madhya Pradesh in India, teachers were administered the same reading and mathematics tests as their students. About half the teachers could not identify the central idea in a paragraph they read or answer math questions on multiple factors. Only half of fourth grade teachers tested could correctly answer 80 percent of the questions on a fourth grade mathematics test (World Bank 1997). Given this, it is not at all surprising that the students in the same grade were unable to answer such questions!

Policy Reforms

Which policies, then, would most effectively address the many factors that determine educational quantity and quality, such as teacher absenteeism, teacher quality, and inadequate teaching methods? There is, in fact, scant research about the relative importance of each of these factors in explaining educational outcomes, or their underlying determinants. Thus we do not know whether teacher absenteeism constitutes deliberate "shirking" or whether it is a response to some exogenous factors (discussed below). Nor do we know whether any shirking that may occur can be ex-

---

1. These and other studies are cited in World Bank (1997).

plained by the absence of pecuniary or nonpecuniary rewards to effort put in by teachers. Designing solutions to the problem of teacher absenteeism requires addressing these issues.

Kremer outlines two solutions. The first is offering students a choice between schools, particularly between private and public sector schools. There is, however, little empirical evidence on the effect of school choice on educational outcomes. Kremer's ongoing research on this very important area will thus fill a significant void in the literature. In those economies where schooling infrastructure is so poor, particularly in the private sector, school choice hardly seems an issue. In India, for example, private sector investment is overwhelmingly biased in favor of secondary or tertiary education and urban areas. Thus 54 percent of all secondary schools are private, but private schools account for only 7 percent of primary schools and only 3 percent of primary schools in rural areas (Drèze and Sen 1995).

The second suggestion offered by Kremer to improve teacher incentives is to alter pay scales and salaries. This suggestion is premised on the belief that low attendance by teachers is a consequence of their relatively low pay. Data from India, however, reveal that salaries paid to teachers are comparable to those paid to public sector employees in other sectors, sectors that do not suffer from the same attendance problems experienced by the educational sector. Looking across economies, primary teachers' salaries in India, at about 3.6 times the average per capita income level, are better than those in some middle-income countries but worse than those in other low-income countries (World Bank 1997).

A far more important determinant of school quality in such environments appears to be the lack of availability of schooling infrastructure, as reflected in large classes and few teachers. In India, average classroom size is large and increasing, from forty-five students per room in 1986 to forty-nine students in 1993. Commonly, just one teacher and one classroom is available for students enrolled in the entire primary school. Such single-teacher schools, in which just one teacher is available for *all* students in grades one through five, account for almost one-third of all primary schools. As many as 60 percent of primary schools have two or fewer teachers. Such a school environment is hardly conducive to the use of good instructional techniques. Nor does it provide teachers with any incentives to improve educational outcomes.

Poor performance and attendance by teachers may also be the consequence of other factors outside their command. For example, many teachers explain their poor attendance by the fact that they are commonly assigned to schools at some distance from their residences. Others state that they are forced to miss school days because local government officials require them to participate in a variety of other tasks such as family planning drives, elections, and census operations.

It is in this context that we must evaluate whether improving instructional materials can improve educational outcomes. What needs to be recognized is that such materials can only improve educational levels if they are used. And providing teachers with "appropriate" grade-specific textbooks is no guarantee that they will be used, in an environment where a teacher is coping with large multigrade classrooms of students.

As stated earlier, the policies to address these issues will necessarily vary across economies. In many cases, however, the fundamental need appears to be to increase public expenditures on the educational sector and to ensure that these additional funds are used to increase the number of teachers. Where research can be helpful is in identifying precisely which factors explain the poor record of many governments in expanding the supply of teachers at a rate that at least keeps pace with the increase in enrollments. Further, given the importance of the home environment, another equally important priority is understanding how one can improve this environment, particularly to address such issues as gender differences in educational outcomes.

References

Drèze, Jean, and Amartya Sen. 1995. *India: Economic development and social opportunity.* Oxford: Clarendon.
Heckman, James J., and V. Joseph Hotz. 1986. An investigation of the labor market earnings of Panamanian males: Evaluating the sources of inequality. *Journal of Human Resources* 21 (4): 507–42.
Rosenzweig, Mark R., and T. Paul Schultz. 1982. Market opportunities, genetic endowments, and intrafamily resource distribution: Child survival in rural India. *American Economic Review* 72:803–15.
World Bank. 1997. *Primary education in India.* Washington, D.C.: World Bank.

Comment on the Paper by Michael Kremer   T. Paul Schultz

Michael Kremer's paper reports on an important and neglected social experimental approach to estimating the marginal product of school inputs on student test achievements. This is a significant achievement that has the potential to correct for many grave difficulties of traditional estimates of educational production functions from nonexperimental data. The paper does not, however, survey the full field of educational studies that might assist in the design of educational reforms. This note tries to fill this gap, at least partially.

There are basically two ways to employ evaluation methods to guide

T. Paul Schultz is the Malcolm K. Brachman Professor of Economics at Yale University.

reform of the educational sector. First, one can estimate an educational production function from which to infer how to improve the mix of inputs to achieve greater production efficiency at a specific level in the school system. Second, the mix of education by levels and types can be varied to increase the aggregate value of output for a given budget constraint for the educational sector. The two routes to evaluating reforms of the educational system require quite different data and analyses. In the former case, unit costs are reduced, perhaps by administratively supplying a particularly effective but neglected input, such as textbooks, as in one of the studies Kremer has coordinated in Kenya. On the other hand, the organizational form of the educational sector might also be changed to improve incentives to agents to motivate them to allocate resources and effort within schools and bureaucracies more efficiently. Examples could include monitoring school outputs (e.g., implementing and disseminating test scores) and decentralizing the allocation of educational budgets, perhaps to involve parents in rewarding those responsible for producing better schools. Evaluation of policy reforms in the pursuit of greater efficiency is typically based on the assumption that the output of educational production is measured adequately, perhaps by a test score. Consequently, maximizing this single output for a given outlay of public (and private) expenditures is the accepted social objective of the educational sector.

Other analysts would prefer to approximate the value of educational outputs in terms of the increased labor productivity of workers trained by a school system. To pursue this labor market evaluation approach requires that one return to the second way to evaluate educational returns to different levels and types of educational processes.

The second type of reform of the educational system starts by evaluating the payoff to modifying the mix of outputs, which might be illustrated by the number of students graduating from various levels of the school system, for example, primary, secondary, and more specialized forms of postsecondary schooling that are imperfect substitutes for each other in the economy. In this case, the evaluation depends critically on estimating the comparative market value of the different educational outputs as well as their social costs of production. Most economic studies of education in the past forty years have been devoted to estimating the wage differentials between workers with different levels of schooling, holding constant other productive characteristics of workers, such as age, sex, and race, that can be strictly interpreted as exogenous from the worker's preferences and adult worker's life cycle choices related to work and time allocation (Mincer 1974). There are many discussions of how these human capital estimates of the wage returns to education may be distorted or biased by the limitations of available data and statistical methods including variables omitted from the wage function, error in measuring schooling output, bias due to sample selection of those who are schooled and who work for wages, and individual heterogeneity of effects of school attendance (e.g., Griliches 1977; Schultz 1988; Card 1999). A large literature has grown up exploring these problems of evaluating the wage returns to different types of schooling. Substantial differences by school level in the private and social returns to resources invested in extending the schooling of students are often found within a single country. This suggests inefficiency in resource allocations among levels of the school system. For example, school systems are frequently observed in which the social returns to public expenditures on higher education have a lower expected payoff than if these resources were used to increase the number of primary or secondary school graduates. This pattern of "excess" supply of graduates of higher education relative to secondary schooling is documented in countries as diverse as India, Egypt, Thailand, and many countries of sub-Saharan Africa. Moreover, in most of these countries the benefits of the large public subsidies for higher education are disproportionately collected by the top quintile of the income distribution of households or families, which can be contrasted with the more equal distribution of benefits between rich and poor households due to expanding primary and secondary education (Schultz 1999). Thus the guidelines for efficient equalization of the social returns to marginal changes in the mix of outputs of students in the educational system may be reinforced, as in this case of higher education, by criteria of equity or assigning greater social weights to beneficiaries from disadvantaged socioeconomic strata of the society. There are also a handful of countries where returns to higher education remain relatively high despite rapid expansion of tertiary levels of schooling in the population, as in Korea.

The introduction of randomly sampled household surveys in most countries since the Second World War has provided governments with timely information on price levels, unemployment rates, and income distributions. These household surveys also provide the essential data for human capital studies of wage structures and primary information needed to evaluate the labor productivity returns to different forms of education. For whatever reason, there are still many regions in the world where these types of periodic household surveys are not analyzed with the objective of reforming public educational subsidies to relieve those bottlenecks in the educational system where the private and social wage returns are exceptionally high or could be more equitably distributed. As I note in chapter 8 in this volume, one reason for this failure is that the data are either not even collected by the government on a regular basis or not openly shared with the public for fear they will reveal an inadequacy in the government's policy or the poor quality of the data. Yet straightforward examination of the wage structure, or wage differentials by schooling for recent graduates, is an essential starting point for designing educational reforms. It remains a puzzle why wage structures are insufficiently emphasized by policymakers, particularly by those whose specialty is the training of teachers, the design of curriculums, and the organization of educational administrations.

Kremer's reservations about school evaluation methods based on conventional estimates of educational production functions is well founded. Because inputs are allocated within schools among students by teachers and school administrators for systematic reasons that reflect their own goals and private information, it is not generally possible to infer from naturally occurring variation in inputs across school districts or across families how those inputs would independently affect a randomly selected, or average, student's performance. In such settings, where the school production function has inputs endogenously allocated and where the inputs are also probably measured with error, the direct estimation of the production function is likely to be biased and potentially misleading. One solution to this problem that is widely neglected is to plan and analyze random experiments in the mix of inputs used by different schools or classes or students, and this approach is admirably described by Kremer.

Another approach that has received increasing attention in public finance is the use of instrumental variables methods, where instruments are sought that have good reason to affect the differential use of inputs across schools, families, and students but not to be otherwise correlated with the unexplained variation in educational outcomes. The choice of instruments is usually subject to criticism by other economists because empirical work often turns on a choice of compromises to correct what the researcher thinks are the more important problems while unavoidably neglecting other problems. In the design of experiments in the biological sciences to discriminate between competing hypotheses, creative talents are essential that reach far beyond routine science. Similarly, the specification and measurement of good "instruments" to estimate properly educational production functions or estimate individual returns to schooling involve a similarly complex craft, combining keen intuition with good science.

References

Card, David. 1999. The causal effect of education on earnings. In *Handbook of labor economics,* vol. 3, ed. O. Ashenfelter and D. Card. Amsterdam: North-Holland.

Griliches, Zvi. 1977. Estimating the returns to schooling. *Econometrica* 45 (1): 1–22.

Mincer, Jacob. 1974. *Schooling, experience and earnings.* New York: Columbia University Press.

Schultz, T. Paul. 1988. Education investment and returns. In *Handbook of development economics,* vol. 1, ed. H. Chenery and T. N. Srinivasan. Amsterdam: North-Holland.

———. 1999. Schooling and health investments in Africa. *Journal of Economic Perspectives* 13 (3): 67–88.

10

Adjusting to Trade Policy Reform

Steven Matusz and David Tarr

10.1 Introduction

Economic research has rather well documented the long-term benefits from improved resource allocation and efficiency that follow from trade reform. And although causation remains an issue, research has shown strong and consistent correlation between trade reform and growth. Despite this evidence of improved incomes from trade reform, some policymakers are reluctant to implement trade reform for fear of excessive adjustment costs. Policymakers' fears may in part be based on the political dynamics of reform (politicians in power fear they will incur the anger of the owners of displaced resources while the benefits may accrue in later years) but may also in part reflect how little has been written and is known about the nature, magnitude, and duration of adjustment costs. In this paper we attempt to fill this void in the literature by surveying the evidence on the adjustment costs of trade liberalization and placing those estimates of adjustment costs in perspective relative to gains from trade liberalization.

The paper is organized as follows: In section 10.2 we first define adjustment costs, distinguishing social and private costs of adjustment, and then develop a model for thinking about adjustment costs. We survey estimates of adjustment costs, both social and private, as well as studies of the em-

Steven Matusz is professor of economics in the Eli Broad College of Business at Michigan State University. David Tarr is a lead economist at the International Trade Division of the World Bank Development Research Group.

The authors thank Milan Brahmbhatt, Uri Dadush, Anne Krueger, Costas Michalopoulos, Martin Rama, Julie Schaffner, L. Alan Winters, and conference participants for thoughtful comments on earlier versions of this paper, and Maria Kasilag for logistical support. The views expressed in this paper are the authors' and do not necessarily reflect those of the World Bank.

ployment effects of trade liberalization in section 10.3. In section 10.4, we examine the impact of trade liberalization on macrostability. In section 10.5 we provide suggestions for future research, focusing on means of addressing opposition to reform as well as reducing adjustment costs. Our detailed summary and policy conclusions are given in section 10.6.

Briefly, our results are as follows: While we find that it is necessary to apply caveats to most of the more than fifty studies we survey, virtually all the studies found that adjustment costs are very small in relation to the benefits of trade liberalization. And those studies that focused on manufacturing employment in developing countries found that it had typically increased within one year after liberalization. Collectively, the weight of so many studies of various types, all pointing in more or less the same direction, makes it difficult to avoid the conclusion that adjustment costs are very small relative to the benefits of trade liberalization and that after the economy has one year to adjust to the trade liberalization, we should expect to see an increase in manufacturing employment.

The reasons adjustment costs are low in relation to the benefits are as follows: (1) Most important, adjustment costs are typically short term and terminate when workers find jobs, while benefits of trade reform can be expected to grow with the economy. (2) Estimates of the duration of unemployment for workers in most industries are not high, especially where workers were not earning substantial rents in their original jobs. (3) In many industries normal labor turnover exceeds dislocation from trade liberalization so that downsizing where necessary can be accomplished without much forced unemployment. (4) It has been observed that a significant portion of the resource reallocation after trade liberalization is accomplished through interindustry shifts, which minimize the dislocation of factors of production. In addition, developing countries would be expected to have comparative advantages in labor-intensive industries, so trade liberalization should favor labor. This may explain why manufacturing employment has typically increased after trade liberalization.

10.2   Defining and Modeling Adjustment Costs

10.2.1   Defining Adjustment Costs

One of the basic tenets of economics is that a regime of liberal international trade leads to a more efficient allocation of resources and a higher level of economic well-being than does a regime involving artificial distortions of trade. A voluminous amount of empirical research now exists supporting this claim.[1] Although we survey a number of studies in this

---

1. Thomas and Nash (1991) summarized a number of studies that indicate the direct (efficiency) gains from trade reform range from 1 or 2 percent of GDP per year up to as much

paper, researchers have by comparison spent little time identifying and quantifying the potential adjustment costs that may be associated with a movement away from a regime of distorted trade (the status quo) to a more liberal regime.

For the purposes of this paper, we define adjustment costs as encompassing a wide variety of potentially disadvantageous short-run outcomes that might result from trade liberalization. These outcomes may include reduction in employment and output, loss of industry-specific and firm-specific human capital, and macroeconomic instability resulting from balance-of-payments difficulties or reductions in government revenue. In analyzing these costs, it is important to distinguish between social and private costs. While the social costs of adjustment are relevant for considering the aggregate welfare effects of trade reform, it is the distribution of private costs within society that forms the basis of political opposition to reform.[2]

Even when the social benefits of trade liberalization outweigh the social costs, the existence of private costs can easily generate enough political opposition to block any reforms. The problem is especially evident when protection or liberalization in a particular industry is considered. Representatives of the industry in question will lobby for protection because the gains are concentrated in their industry. On the other hand, the consumers of the product, who lose from protection, are dispersed throughout the economy. Consumers would like to see lobbying against the protection, but there is a free-rider problem. Individual consumers do not lose enough from the protection to induce them to expend resources to lobby against the protection—rather they would like other consumers to lobby against the protection. A succession of particular industries lobbying for protection may then result in a protected overall trade regime. See Stigler (1971) for an elaboration.

Fernandez and Rodrik (1991) extended this argument by noting that even those who will gain from trade reform may be unwilling to support reform or may even oppose it. The problem is that it is not possible to identify with certainty all of the potential beneficiaries of reform. For example, some workers currently employed in import-competing industries

---

as 10 percent of GDP per year if production is characterized by increasing returns to scale. By eliminating incentives to smuggle, lobby, evade tariffs, and so on, trade reform can generate an additional (indirect) benefit. Thomas and Nash (1991) cited evidence that this indirect benefit may be larger than 6 percent of GDP in such countries as India and Turkey. In addition, some evidence exists that trade liberalization may improve long-run growth rates by improving incentives to invest and save and by exposing the economy to more advanced technologies. See Thomas and Nash (1991) for a brief survey of empirical evidence linking trade reforms to growth.

2. We describe private adjustment costs more fully in subsection 10.3.4, where we show that such costs can be quite large. We also explain in that subsection that private costs, even in the aggregate, need not coincide with the social costs identified in this paper.

may be able to make a smooth transition to employment in export industries once trade is liberalized. Those workers who do possess the skills to make this transition are likely to earn higher wages. While it may be possible to argue that a certain percentage of the labor force will make this transition, it is impossible to precisely identify the actual individuals who would benefit. Therefore, workers in import-competing industries may rationally see some chance that they will be better off under reform but also some chance that they will be worse off. It is not difficult to imagine many situations where the downside risk for these workers outweighs the upside potential.

Knowledge of the distribution of private costs and benefits associated with trade reform is relevant because such knowledge might guide the implementation of contemporaneous policies to diffuse some of the political opposition that may arise. One such policy is a uniform tariff, long favored by the International Monetary Fund and the World Bank as a means of diffusing political support for protection. Panagariya and Rodrik (1993) formalized the argument. A key advantage of a uniform tariff structure, they noted, is that it will minimize lobbying by special interests for protection because if diffuses the benefits of protection. If protection can be increased only by increasing protection for all industries, lobbying for protection then yields only dispersed benefits as well as costs. A uniform tariff thus creates a free-rider problem for the interests seeking protection.

Knowledge of the distribution of private costs is also useful because of genuine concern for an equitable distribution of income. On the other hand, social costs and benefits are the relevant measures to use when contemplating the aggregate welfare effect of trade reform. Obviously, reforms should not be undertaken if the costs outweigh the benefits. Even in situations where the benefits of reform are a little larger than the costs, it may not be beneficial to liberalize since policies designed to spread the burden of adjustment by redistributing income are likely to be distortionary and entail a social cost of their own. This is true whether these policies are motivated by political expediency or by concern for equity. The probability of being able to implement redistributive policies in a fashion that generates political support for reform and minimizes the adverse impact on the distribution of income grows as the ratio of social benefits to social costs increases.

Typically policy discussions focus on how to minimize adjustment costs. But during a period of unemployment, temporarily unemployed workers acquire information about their best job prospects. As numerous "search" models have formalized, in any period each worker should continue to search for a job rather than take an existing offer if his or her expectation of an improved job offer results in sufficiently increased lifetime earnings to compensate for the lost income of being unemployed during that period

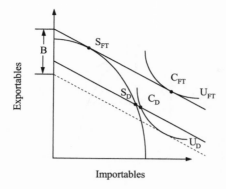

Fig. 10.1   Benefits of reform

(see Morgan and Manning 1985). Zero unemployment implies that vacancies are immediately filled and that workers spend no time searching. The lack of time spent searching will result in lost lifetime earnings and workers choosing jobs where the value of their marginal product is lower than in alternative positions. A situation of zero unemployment or zero adjustment costs is not likely to be socially optimal.

10.2.2   Employment and Output Loss: A Microtheoretic Framework

The general equilibrium measurement of the short-run output loss resulting from trade liberalization can be visualized by using the simple diagrammatic methods generally used to demonstrate the general equilibrium benefits of trade liberalization.[3] Consider a small country that produces exportables and importables. Assume that all consumers have the same preferences so that social welfare can be represented by a single set of indifference curves. The production possibilities curve for this economy is shown in figure 10.1. At the initial (distorted) equilibrium, production takes place at point S_D, consumption at point C_D. Moving to free trade causes the economy to slide up along its production possibilities curve to point S_{FT}. Consumption now occurs at point C_{FT}. This distance B represents the welfare gain, measured in terms of exportables. This is the amount of income that could be taken away from consumers who are faced with free trade prices and still leave them just as well off as they were in the distorted equilibrium.

To measure the costs of adjustment, Neary (1982) suggested looking at the difference along the adjustment path between the actual level of income and the level of income that would be attained once all adjustments have been undertaken. Consider figure 10.2, where it is assumed for simplicity that liberalization first causes all resources released from the im-

3. The diagrammatic treatment in this section is based on Neary (1982).

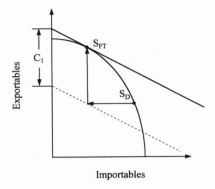

Fig. 10.2   Costs of reform

portable sector to become unemployed during the first period after liberalization, and then fully employed thereafter. In this case, the adjustment cost is measured as distance C_1. It is possible for C_1 to exceed B. However, the correct comparison is between a benefit *stream* of B continuing into the infinite future and a one-time adjustment cost of C_1. More specifically, the discounted benefits of liberalization exceed the discounted costs if and only if $B/r > C_1$, where r is the social rate of discount.

The time profile of adjustment used in this example is extreme. Data on adjustment costs indicate that adjustment occurs over several periods, with adjustment costs progressively declining; that is, $C_{t+1} < C_t$, where C_t is the adjustment cost during period t. This follows since resources are likely to be gradually reemployed. On the other hand, the benefits of liberalization do not decline and are likely to grow over time as the economy grows. Letting B_t represent the benefits during period t, the discounted benefits of trade reform exceed the discounted adjustment costs if and only if

$$\sum_{t=1}^{\infty} \frac{B_t}{(1 + r)^{t-1}} > \sum_{t=1}^{\infty} \frac{C_t}{(1 + r)^{t-1}}.$$

Those who have attempted empirical measurement of the costs and benefits of trade liberalization have generally taken into account both discounting and the time-dependent nature of the costs and benefits.

It is necessary to understand the dynamics of the labor market in order to gain deeper insight into the short-run employment effects of trade reform. Figure 10.3, which schematically illustrates the various labor market flows, provides the basis for such understanding.

The labor market illustrated in figure 10.3 is greatly simplified by assuming that at any point in time a worker can be either employed in the export sector, employed in the import-competing sector, unemployed, or not in

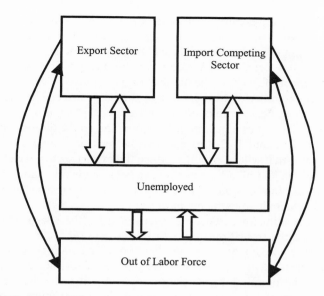

Fig. 10.3   Labor market

the labor force. The arrows in figure 10.3 represent flows between sectors. For example, the arrow pointing downward between the boxes labeled "export sector" and "unemployment" represents the flow of workers who are laid off from firms in the export sector and become unemployed. The corresponding arrow pointing upward represents the flow of workers who leave unemployment to take jobs in the export sector.

Assuming no change in the size of the labor force, a steady state equilibrium will be characterized by a situation where each flow between any two states (e.g., the flow of workers from the export sector into unemployment) is just matched by a flow of equal magnitude but in the opposite direction (a flow of workers out of unemployment into the export sector). In this sort of equilibrium, the size of each sector remains unchanged, as does the size of the workforce that is unemployed.

Trade reform results in an increased demand for workers by firms in the export sector combined with a decrease in demand for workers in the import-competing sector. It is known (see Roberts and Tybout 1997) that fixed costs in entering export markets create a kind of inertia, since firms in the export sector may be slow to respond to trade reforms until they are convinced they will stick or until the incentives to export change by more than a marginal amount, resulting in a slow response to trade reforms in the export sector. As the import-competing sector contracts, the arrows originating from the box labeled "import-competing sector" and pointing outward swell with workers who are laid off. Some of these workers may elect to retire, exiting the labor force entirely. Others will become unemployed while searching for new employment. At the same time, all arrows pointing toward the box labeled "import-competing sector" shrink in size since few firms in this sector will be hiring.[4] This will have the temporary effect of swelling the number of unemployed workers and possibly also the number of workers out of the labor force. This temporary reduction in aggregate employment (and the corresponding output loss) is the true social cost of adjustment.[5] Relating this to the discussion underlying figures 10.1 and 10.2, this cost can be measured by evaluating the level of output that will be produced once the export sector expands to its steady state size and all adjustments have been made and subtracting the value of output that is produced subsequent to the liberalization but prior to the time when all adjustments have been made.

The size of adjustment costs is determined by the speed with which workers make the transition from one state to another (e.g., from unemployment to employment in the import-competing sector). In principle, transition rates are functions of a variety of variables such as the demographics of the population, the distribution of skills, the degree of governmental support for unemployed workers, laws restricting involuntary separations, the degree of unionization, the share of economic activity undertaken by state-owned enterprises, and so on.

10.3 Employment and Output Loss: The Evidence

10.3.1 Trade Reform and Employment in Developing Countries

Unskilled labor is relatively abundant in developing countries. In the context of the Heckscher-Ohlin model, trade reform can be expected to increase the overall demand for such labor in the long run. This follows since such countries have a comparative advantage in goods that use unskilled labor intensively. Removing policies that favor import-competing sectors at the expense of (labor intensive) export sectors ultimately results in an expansion of the latter and contraction of the former. Any increase in the demand for unskilled labor results in a combination of higher wages and employment for this segment of the population.[6]

4. There will still be some hiring due to natural attrition (retirements, workers voluntarily quitting to relocate geographically or to take better jobs).

5. Surprisingly, there is little agreement among economists regarding the determinants of the steady state level of unemployment. Most models of international trade assume no unemployment in the steady state. Theoretical studies that explicitly allow for the existence of long-run unemployment have concluded that trade liberalization can either reduce (Matusz 1996) or increase (Matusz 1994) the steady state level of unemployment. In any event, it is not the mere existence of unemployment that poses the adjustment cost; rather it is the change in unemployment that matters.

6. Factor market distortions could conceivably invalidate the predictions of the Heckscher-Ohlin model of trade. E.g., government subsidies to capital combined with legislation that artificially inflates the cost of hiring workers could reduce relative production costs for

Table 10.1   **Employment in Manufacturing during Episodes of Liberalization
                    (thousands of persons)**

Episode[a]	Year before Liberalization	Average for Liberalization Period	Year after Liberalization
Argentina 1, 1967–70	1,836	1,847	1,914
Argentina 2, 1976–80	1,863	2,099	2,132
Brazil, 1965–73	1,780	2,182	3,397
Chile 2, 1974–81	515	487	351
Korea 2, 1978–79	2,000	2,196	2,099
Peru, 1979–80	675	717	736
Philippines 1, 1960–65	1,456	1,647	1,825
Philippines 2, 1970–74	2,056	2,313	2,596
Singapore, 1968–73	61	139	210
Sri Lanka 1, 1968–70	74	108	97
Sri Lanka 2, 1977–79	112	134	155
Turkey 1, 1970–73	485	551	651
Turkey 2, 1980–84	799	829	n.a.

Source: Papageorgiou, Choksi, and Michaely (1990, table 10).
[a]Range of years is period of liberalization.

Little hard evidence relates trade reform to overall labor demand. However, three recent studies suggest that trade reform has had the expected positive impact on employment in a variety of countries. First, a retrospective study of trade reform in nineteen countries by Papageorgiou, Choksi, and Michaely (1990) concluded that trade liberalization did not generally result in decreased employment even in the short run. The evidence they presented is reproduced here as table 10.1. They reported employment data prior to liberalization, during liberalization, and one year after liberalization. Compared with the preliberalization period, manufacturing employment was larger one year subsequent to the completion of liberalization in all but one of the twelve countries for which data are reported. In

capital-intensive industries compared with labor-intensive industries. In turn, this shift in relative production costs could reverse the pattern of trade predicated on the basis of factor endowments, and an expansion of the export sector could actually reduce employment. This possibility was recognized in Krueger (1983). However, her review of ten case studies (covering Argentina, Brazil, Chile, Indonesia, Ivory Coast, Pakistan, South Korea, Thailand, Tunisia, and Uruguay) indicates substantial scope for employment growth resulting from a switch toward export-oriented policies even when factor markets are characterized by substantial distortions.

The empirical relevance of the Heckscher-Ohlin model of trade has been questioned for more than forty years, ever since Leontief's celebrated finding that U.S. exports were labor intensive relative to its imports. Recent research has shown that a narrowly defined version of the model is a poor reflection of reality (see, e.g., Trefler 1995). On the other hand, when the assumption of identical technologies across countries is dropped and a home bias in consumption is allowed, the model does remarkably well in predicting such things as relative wages and the allocation of resources across sectors. It is these latter, more resilient implications that we focus on in this paper.

Table 10.2   **Annual Labor Growth among Existing Firms under Liberalization (percent per annum)**

Number of Employees	All Countries	Ghana	Malawi	Mali	Senegal	Tanzania
1–5	+18	+10	+19	+24	+7	+20
6–20	+11	+6	−3	+20	+12	+10
21–49	+3	+3	+2	+2	0	+3
50+	+1	−9	n.a.	+10	0	+17
All firms	+5	−1	+5	+13	+2	+9

Source: Parker, Riopelle, and Steel (1995, table 6.2).
Note: Size categories are based on total employment of the firm at the time of reforms.

fact, manufacturing employment was higher in twelve of thirteen cases during the liberalization period compared with the levels registered prior to liberalization.

Two caveats to the Papageorgiou et al. data are that they only provided information for manufacturing employment and they did not measure underemployment. This may mask changes in employment (either positive or negative) that may have occurred elsewhere in the economy or in underemployment. On the other hand, policymakers are often concerned about the possibility that liberalization may lead to "deindustrialization." The employment trends reported in table 10.1 do not support this hypothesis. Moreover, we note that in the case of Chile, the one reported case where manufacturing employment fell, employment in agriculture increased.

In a separate study, Parker, Riopelle, and Steel (1995) examined employment growth in micro- and small-scale enterprises (MSEs) subsequent to episodes of reform in Ghana, Malawi, Mali, Senegal, and Tanzania.[7] Their findings, reported in table 10.2, indicate that annual employment growth among existing MSEs was strong subsequent to reform implementation.[8] Harrison and Revenga (1995) studied sixteen countries that underwent significant liberalization in the past decade and a half. They were able to track total employment growth for six of these countries. Their data are reproduced in table 10.3. Employment continued to grow throughout the period prior to, during, and after reform in Costa Rica, Peru, and Uruguay. The same cannot be said for the transition economies of Eastern

7. The authors of this study define microenterprises as those with five or fewer workers and small-scale enterprises as those with six to forty-nine workers.
8. The reforms undertaken by these countries went beyond trade liberalization to include regulatory and financial reforms, as well as reforms in public enterprises and the tax structure. According to Parker et al., the reforms were most extensive and thorough in Ghana, followed closely by Mali. They ranked Malawi third in terms of the extensiveness of reforms, with Tanzania and Senegal having the least extensive reforms. The results for Ghana are confirmed by a survey of eighty-two small firms following the trade reforms of 1983 (see Steel and Webster 1992).

Table 10.3   **Total Employment (thousands of persons)**

Year	Costa Rica	Czechoslovakia	Peru	Poland	Romania	Uruguay
1982	759.9	8,184	n.a.	18,208.5	10,428.1	n.a.
1983	767.6	8,200	n.a.	18,374.7	10,457.8	n.a.
1984	839.7	8,251	n.a.	18,383.5	10,499.9	932.6
1985	826.7	8,317	n.a.	18,531.4	10,586.1	n.a.
1986	854.2	8,379	1,988.3	18,594.5	10,669.5	1,021.2
1987	923.3	8,409	2,061.1	18,596.2	10,718.6	1,090.7
1988	951.2	8,449	n.a.	18,474.1	10,805.4	1,103.1
1989	986.8	8,431	2,169.5	18,438.0	10,945.7	1,134.4
1990	1,017.2	8,249	n.a.	17,552.1	10,839.5	1,136.2
1991	1,006.6	7,710	2,337.0	n.a.	n.a.	n.a.

Source: Harrison and Revenga (1995), data underlying their figure 1.

Europe. As Harrison and Revenga noted, however, Czechoslovakia, Poland, and Romania were undergoing significant reforms that went well beyond trade liberalization, and the problem for many of the transition economies was to devise policies to halt the steep decline in output. In fact, the World Bank's *World Development Report* (1996) showed that output losses have been the smallest for those countries where broad liberalization has been the greatest.

Given the difficulty of controlling for all factors, the data in tables 10.1 through 10.3 do not suggest what the level of employment (or rate of growth of employment, as in the case of table 10.2) would have been had there been no liberalization, nor is it possible to infer from these data alone what the level of output would have been immediately following liberalization compared with the level of output obtained subsequent to all adjustments. That is, it is conceivable that employment would have grown at an even faster pace had trade not been liberalized. It is also conceivable that employment would have stagnated in the absence of reforms. It is impossible to say what might have been without properly controlling for other factors that may have affected employment. Since there is no reason to believe that the data are biased, however, the data are consistent with the expectation that reform leads to greater employment in the long run.

10.3.2 Formal Studies of Adjustment Costs

A number of researchers have attempted to measure explicitly the adjustment costs that can be expected to result from trade liberalization. Virtually all of these studies pertain to developed countries, but they may provide some insight regarding the costs borne by developing countries as well. On the one hand, formal labor markets in developing countries may be less flexible than in industrial countries, suggesting adjustment costs would be higher. On the other hand, a higher percentage of employment in developing countries is in agriculture and in informal labor markets that are very flexible—implying lower adjustment costs. Thus there is no clear bias in extrapolating developed country results to developing countries. Moreover, work by Hoddinott (1996) on labor markets in Côte d'Ivoire found the existence of an inverse relationship between wages and unemployment that is remarkably similar to relationships found by Blanchflower and Oswald (1995) for a large sample of developed countries. This similarity suggests that labor markets in at least one developing country behave in roughly the same way as labor markets in developed countries, and therefore, studies of adjustment costs for developed countries may have relevance for developing country experience.[9]

In the first study of its kind, Magee (1972) considered the costs and benefits that one could expect if the United States completely liberalized its trade with the rest of the world. In conducting his study, Magee explicitly accounted for the fact that the benefits of liberalization are permanent while the adjustment costs are temporary. In computing adjustment costs, Magee forecast the number of workers who would become unemployed due to reductions in import barriers and then multiplied by their average wage. He adjusted for the expected duration of unemployment and assumed that all adjustments would be completed within five years. Using alternative discount rates, he was then able to estimate the present discounted value of adjustment costs and compare them with the standard efficiency gains due to liberalization. The benefit-cost ratios calculated from Magee's work are reported in table 10.4.

Based on the figures reported in table 10.4, after only one year U.S. trade reform would create $5.7 worth of benefits measured in terms of efficiency gains for every dollar of adjustment cost. By the end of five years, trade reform would result in more than $8 of benefit for every dollar of adjustment cost. Even when the future is heavily discounted, by the end of the fifteenth year the reforms generate more than $19 of benefit for every dollar of adjustment cost. The final line of table 10.4 reports benefit-cost ratios where benefits are summed over the infinite future.

Magee's estimates are very rough and do not account for the costs of capital equipment that may be idled as a result of reduced import barriers.

---

9. Flexible labor market policies would be expected to lower adjustment costs. While nominally designed to protect workers, regulations that make it costly to fire employees may result in lower labor demand, employment, and wages and hold back growth in expanding sectors, thereby increasing adjustment costs. E.g., in Peru rising import penetration ratios across industrial sectors were found to be strongly associated with falling output value but to have only a weak association with employment. The weak adjustment of employment in the face of falling output could have been due to strict enforcement of Peru's Labor Stability Law and may have contributed significantly to the reversal of Peruvian reforms in the 1980s (Nogues 1991).

Table 10.4   **Estimated Benefit-Cost Ratios Associated with U.S. Import Liberalization**

Number of Years after Liberalization	Discount Rate (%)		
	4	7	10
1	5.7	5.7	5.7
2	6.3	6.3	6.3
3	7.0	7.0	7.0
4	7.7	7.6	7.6
5	8.3	8.2	8.2
15	25.0	21.8	19.5
Total	60.2	36.1	26.5

Source: Calculated from Magee (1972, tables 7, 8).

In an attempt to obtain more precise measures of adjustment costs that include the costs of idle capital, Baldwin, Mutti, and Richardson (1980) estimated the potential impact on the U.S. economy of a 50 percent multilateral tariff reduction. While Magee aggregated all trade into a few small categories, Baldwin et al. studied 367 distinct sectors. Like Magee, Baldwin et al. estimated the changes in employment that would result from the tariff reduction and valued this change in employment at an appropriate wage.[10] In addition, Baldwin et al. assumed that every 1 percent contraction in industry output is accompanied by a 1 percent contraction in capital utilization.[11] They noted that if capital equipment in general has a useful life of ten years, then 1 percent of the capital stock wears out every 1.2 months. The authors of this study then went on to assume that any capital idled by trade reform would be the oldest capital equipment. Therefore, if 1 percent of the capital stock was idled by trade reform, the maximum income loss would be equivalent to what that capital could have produced in 1.2 months.

In total, the authors estimated that every dollar of adjustment cost brings with it approximately $2.4 of benefits in the form of efficiency gains after just one year. Using a 10 percent discount rate and assuming that all adjustments are completed within one year of policy implementation, they calculated that benefits outweigh costs by a ratio of more than 24:1. The authors concluded that even though their study was imperfect, the esti-

10. While Magee used an average wage rate for all workers, Baldwin et al. assumed that the wage rate of a dislocated worker in a given industry was related to the demographic characteristics of the average worker in that industry. E.g., if workers in one industry have more education on average than workers in another, it would be logical to assume that the wage paid to the average worker in the former is higher than in the latter.

11. To date, no other studies have attempted to quantify the costs of capital idled by trade reform.

mated benefits of liberalization are so much larger than the estimated adjustment costs that it would be implausible for any reasonable variations on their analysis to yield opposite results.[12]

While Baldwin et al. found a very large ratio of benefits to costs, they also found that the costs are concentrated among a few industries. Specifically, industries with the largest declines in employment include food utensils and pottery (20.6 percent), rubber footwear (13.1 percent), artificial flowers (11.3 percent), and pottery products (9.7 percent).[13] More generally, the authors calculated that a 50 percent multilateral tariff reduction would reduce employment by 1 percent or more in fewer than 10 percent of the industries studied.[14]

A number of authors have attempted to quantify the potential economywide employment effects resulting from trade reform for countries other than the United States. One such study by Dixon, Parmenter, and Powell (1984) explored the consequences of a 25 percent reduction in Australia's level of protection. In particular, the authors of this study asked how trade reform could be expected to alter the occupational makeup of the economy. They explored several different scenarios and concluded that a 25 percent liberalization might force anywhere from 2 percent to as much as 14 percent of the labor force to change occupations within two years after the implementation of the policy.[15] By way of comparison, the authors of this study estimated that between 1961 and 1976, anywhere from 32 to 142 percent of the labor force changed occupations during a given two-year period.

Unlike Magee (1972) and Baldwin et al. (1980), the authors of this study made no attempt to quantify the potential efficiency gains from liberaliza-

---

12. Since Baldwin et al. were concerned with evaluating the impact of the Tokyo Round, they assumed a multilateral tariff reduction. This poses some difficulties, however, in applying their results to the effects of a unilateral tariff reduction, which is the more common question of interest to many policymakers. Another problem is that they assume that expansion of export sectors leads to a reduction in the duration of unemployment. While this may be true, it is also possible that such an assumption understates the true adjustment costs since export sectors may not expand as fast as import sectors contract.

13. These are generally very labor-intensive industries where comparative advantage would presumably lie with developing countries. Presumably, liberalization in labor-abundant countries could lead to concentrated employment reductions in relatively capital-intensive industries.

14. More recently, Cooper (1994) observed that U.S. employment in the textile, apparel, and leather sectors declined by approximately 20 percent between 1980 and 1990. Similar declines occurred in France, Germany, Italy, the Netherlands, Spain, and the United Kingdom. Cooper conjectured that these shifts were due to increased competition from developing countries. Even if true, this decline in employment amounts to roughly 2 percent per year in these industries, a magnitude dwarfed by annual turnover due to retirements and other voluntary quits.

15. Their four scenarios were a 25 percent across-the-board cut in protection; a reduction in the highest tariff rates to 31.17 percent; exempting textiles, footwear, and motor vehicles while cutting all other rates of protection by 75.85 percent; and exempting these sectors while cutting the remaining highest tariffs to 3.17 percent.

tion, nor did they attempt to quantify the value of lost output experienced when workers who are forced to switch occupations find themselves temporarily unemployed. Rather they implied that the labor market disruption associated with trade reform is no larger in magnitude than the disruptions that occur with the natural ebb and flow of the economy.

De Melo and Roland-Holst (1994) carried out one of the only studies relating trade reform to potential employment changes in a developing country. This study of the Uruguayan economy differs from the studies of the U.S. and Australian economies discussed above because of the recognition that much of the protection afforded domestic industries in developing countries is in the form of administered protection. This form of protection generates strong incentives for rent-seeking activities leading to welfare costs of protection that are larger than the standard efficiency losses. Based on their analysis, the authors concluded that elimination of tariffs and administered protection along with the elimination of all rent-seeking activity would likely result in the need for approximately 5 percent of the labor force to relocate. Since the authors did not estimate the time that relocating workers would spend unemployed nor did they estimate the value of production that would be lost during this transition period, it is not possible to obtain a direct measure of adjustment costs to weigh against their measure of the benefits of reform.[16] The difficulty of quantifying the costs of this labor shift is further compounded by the fact that the authors failed to compare this figure with the normal amount of job turnover.

All of the authors of the studies mentioned to this point have attempted to quantify the adjustments resulting from economywide trade reform. By contrast, a few authors have focused their attention on individual industries. For example, de Melo and Tarr (1990) investigated the efficiency gains and employment adjustments that would follow from a removal of quantitative restrictions on U.S. imports of textiles, steel, and automobiles.[17] According to their analysis, these reforms would generate the need for fewer than one-quarter of 1 percent of the labor force to relocate. To measure the costs borne by the relocating workers, the authors of this study used evidence from Jacobson (1978) to argue that these workers would experience some loss of earnings for approximately six years after displacement. They used this information to calculate the ratio of the present discounted value of the benefits of liberalization to the costs of worker

16. For the situation of complete trade reform, including elimination of rent-seeking activities, the authors estimated that the welfare gain for Uruguay would be equivalent to more than 8 percent of GDP.

17. While the focus of this study was on the removal of trade barriers in these three industries, the authors did account for the complex linkages of these industries with the rest of the economy. E.g., they allowed for the fact that automobile production uses steel as an input, and they allowed for the fact that other sectors of the economy (such as agriculture, other manufacturing, and services) compete for labor with the industries under study.

displacement. They estimated that gains to the U.S. economy from liberalization are approximately $28 for every dollar of cost.[18]

In a series of nine partial equilibrium case studies, Morkre and Tarr (1980) and Tarr and Morkre (1984) examined many of the important cases of U.S. protection applied to specific industries. In general, these studies found that the benefits of trade liberalization vastly exceed the adjustment costs. For example, Morkre and Tarr (1980) estimated the benefits and costs of removal of sugar quotas, footwear quotas, and tariffs on textile and apparel products by the United States. They estimated that removal of sugar quotas by the United States would result in about $16 of benefits for every dollar of unemployment costs. Liberalization of footwear quotas and textiles and apparel tariffs would produce benefit-cost ratios of about 68 and 57, respectively. Tarr and Morkre (1984) estimated that depending on elasticities, the removal of quotas in textiles and apparel would result in between $7 and $19 of benefits for every dollar of unemployment costs.

Takacs and Winters (1991) carefully studied the British footwear industry with the intent of projecting the effects of eliminating quantitative restrictions on imports. They made use of the fact that there exists a natural turnover of employment within the industry. The authors assumed that those workers who are displaced by trade liberalization become reemployed in the shoe industry when other workers voluntarily leave employment. For example, almost 17 percent of the employees at two large shoe manufacturers voluntarily left employment each year between 1984 and 1986. The authors estimated that if workers displaced due to trade liberalization are the first claimants on new job openings, workers displaced due to trade liberalization would become reemployed within seven weeks.[19] The authors went on to calculate the standard efficiency gain from liberalization for purposes of comparing this gain with the value of lost employment, where the value of lost employment was calculated at the workers' preunemployment wage.[20] Doing so, they calculated a benefit-cost ratio of

18. It should be noted that the benefits are true social benefits resulting from efficiency gains and quota rent capture by the U.S. economy, whereas the costs as measured by de Melo and Tarr may be private but not social costs. E.g., a worker who experiences a reduction in his wage because his skills are no longer in demand bears a private cost. However, this is not a social loss if his wage is a true reflection of how society values his skills. Therefore, the ratio 28:1 may be an understatement of the ratio of social benefits to social costs. An additional reason for believing this figure to be understated stems from the fact that the authors did not account for the growth of the benefits of liberalization over time, nor did they account for the fact that the benefits persist indefinitely.

19. This figure contrasts with the work of Bale (1976), who interviewed American workers displaced by trade liberalization between 1969 and 1970. Based on his interviews, Bale calculated an average duration of unemployment of thirty-one weeks for this group of trade-impacted workers.

20. As Takacs and Winters suggested, this wage may overstate or understate the true social cost of unemployment. E.g., the true value of a worker's skills should be measured by the wage that he could earn in his next best alternative employment. The social cost of unemployment is then overestimated to the extent that this next best alternative is lower than his

153 after just one year.[21] Even if the natural turnover rate is as low as 8 percent, the adjustment period is only fourteen weeks and abolition of quantitative restrictions can still be expected to generate more than $80 of benefit for every dollar of cost after just one year.[22]

Using data on industry-specific durations of unemployment reported by Bale (1973), Mutti (1978) compared the benefits of trade liberalization for five U.S. industries with adjustment costs. In order of increasing benefit-cost ratios (indicated in parentheses), the industries studied were iron and steel (1.3), machine tools (2.8), industrial chemicals (5.2), motor vehicles (5.2), and electrical machinery (24.4). In calculating these figures, Mutti used a discount rate of 10 percent and accounted for the persistence and growth of benefits over time.[23] By comparison with the studies mentioned earlier, these benefit-cost ratios are quite small. This can be attributed to the rather lengthy durations of unemployment that Mutti assumed in his analysis.

In summary, a variety of industry and country studies have been undertaken to try to quantify the magnitude of the adjustments that could be expected to accompany trade reform. In virtually every instance the estimated degree of adjustment is relatively small compared with the natural dynamics of the labor force. In studies where such comparisons are possible, it seems to be the case that each dollar of adjustment cost is associated with several dollars worth of efficiency gains. It is worth bearing in mind that adjustment costs are the largest in the period immediately after the implementation of reforms, disappearing after a period of one to five years. By contrast, the efficiency gains of liberalization grow over time and continue indefinitely.

10.3.3   Labor Market Dynamics in Developing Countries

The costs of adjusting to trade reform are clearly minimized when labor and capital markets are highly flexible so that the transition probabilities

---

wage prior to becoming unemployed. On the other hand, their measure may understate the social cost of unemployment since aggregate turnover rates may mask important differences among groups of workers. E.g., men tend to perform very specific tasks in the shoe industry, while women tend to perform others. Suppose that the turnover rate for women is much higher than for men. In reality, any men displaced due to liberalization could be expected to be unemployed for a much longer duration than women.

21. Once again the authors remind us that the benefits of liberalization persist indefinitely, while the adjustment costs terminate once all adjustments have been made. Assuming a discount rate of 7 percent for consistency with Magee (1972) and de Melo and Tarr (1990), the benefit-cost ratio would rise to 2,193!

22. One weakness of this study is that it ignored new entrants into the labor market. I.e., in a steady state, new entrants replace workers exiting the industry. These new entrants must then have longer spells of unemployment if trade-displaced workers now replace exiting workers.

23. The numbers reported here compare the standard efficiency gains with the direct costs of labor adjustment. I.e., they ignore the possibility that a decline in the motor vehicle sector might initiate a further decline in the iron and steel sector.

out of unemployment are relatively high. Most of the studies described thus far have explicitly accounted for the speed of adjustment by incorporating data on unemployment duration or rates of job turnover. Unfortunately, these measures are not typically available for most developing countries. The evidence that is available seems to indicate a wide variety of country-specific rates. For example, Haltiwanger and Singh (1996) reported on the labor market experiences of 60,000 civil service workers who were retrenched by the government of Ghana between 1987 and 1992. A survey of these workers revealed that 10 percent had quit the labor force with 97 percent of the remaining workers finding new employment within two years.[24] At the other end of the spectrum, the average duration of unemployment was fifty months for the 1.7 million workers (nearly 9 percent of the labor force) dismissed from Hungarian state enterprises between 1990 and 1992.[25]

In the absence of readily available data on labor markets, it may be possible to obtain some sense of the speed with which adjustment can take place in developing countries by again looking at the dynamic role played by MSEs. According to Liedholm and Mead (1995), MSEs account for a significant portion of employment in developing countries. While the majority of such enterprises consist of a single employee or are family owned and operated, MSEs hire a significant number of paid employees. Some characteristics of these enterprises are reproduced in table 10.5.

According to Liedholm and Mead, MSEs are highly dynamic. In particular, they reported that the annual rate at which new MSEs were created in the sample of countries they examined was generally in excess of 20 percent. This is a substantially higher start-up rate than found in industrialized countries.[26] Their data are reproduced in table 10.6. The very high start-up rates suggest that entrepreneurs in these countries are quick to respond to new opportunities, making speedy adjustment to trade reform quite likely. Looked at another way, the magnitude of dislocation caused by liberalization is unlikely to be significantly larger than dislocations associated with the everyday working of the economy.

10.3.4   Private Adjustment Costs

As mentioned earlier, research seems to suggest that significant trade liberalization is likely to result in a relatively small dislocation of workers

24. Of those finding employment, 20 percent obtained jobs in the formal sector, with the remainder becoming self-employed or taking jobs in the informal sector.

25. This figure, measured as of November 1992, was derived by extrapolating from the rate at which unemployed workers were finding jobs. The projected duration of unemployment was only seven months when measured in February 1991.

26. Liedholm and Mead suggested that the typical start-up rate for MSEs in industrialized countries is approximately 10 percent. They also reported that the failure rate for MSEs is also very high. In particular, the rate of closure in the Dominican Republic (the only country for which accurate data exist) was in excess of 20 percent during the early 1990s.

Table 10.5   **Characteristics of Micro- and Small-Scale Enterprises (MSEs)**

Characteristic	Botswana	Kenya	Lesotho	Malawi	Swaziland	Zimbabwe	Dominican Republic
MSE employment as percentage of population aged 15–64	17	18	17	23	26	27	19
Percentage of MSEs that are one-person enterprises	65	47	79	61	69	69	22
Percentage of all MSEs with 10–50 workers	3	2	1	1	2	2	18
Percentage of hired workers[a] in MSE labor force	39	24	10	18	15	16	36

Source: Liedholm and Mead (1995, table 2.1).

[a]Percentage of hired workers refers to percentage of salaried, out-of-family workers.

Table 10.6   **Annual MSE New Start Rate**

		Enterprise Size (number of workers)			
Country	Year	1	2–9	10+	Overall Average
Botswana	1991	32.9	11.5	4.2	25.2
Kenya	1992	33.7	10.3	1.6	21.2
Malawi	1991	26.9	14.1	13.1	21.7
Swaziland	1990	26.3	10.8	2.4	21.7
Zimbabwe	1990	22.8	10.6	18.7	19.3
Dominican Republic	1993	n.a.	n.a.	n.a.	20.6

Source: Liedholm and Mead (1995, table 3.1).

Note: Numbers in the table reflect percentage of all enterprises in that category created in the specified year.

and a correspondingly small cost for society. The private cost borne by a dislocated worker, however, may be a significant fraction of his lifetime earnings. Available research tends to show that the private losses borne by individual workers depend heavily on worker characteristics. On the one hand, there are workers who have substantial specific human capital accumulated in the industry or firm, or workers who are earning substantial wage premiums (possibly due to union power or high government wage scales or efficiency wages). These workers tend to lose a lot as a result of displacement. On the other hand, workers with little specific human capital or who are not earning wage premiums lose little or nothing from displacement, depending on the industry.

For example, Jacobson, LaLonde, and Sullivan (1993a, 1993b) studied a sample of American workers who were displaced from their jobs between 1980 and 1986.[27] They found that even as long as five years after the dislocation, workers who had long job tenure with their previous employers were earning on average 25 percent less than they earned in 1979.[28] In a similar study, Rama and MacIsaac (1996) found that after fifteen months, employees displaced from their jobs at the Ecuadorian Central Bank (BCE) in 1994 were on average earning only 55 percent of their predisplacement income. Rama and MacIsaac argued that the earnings loss is unlikely to shrink to the 25 percent figure reported by Jacobson et al. because there was no indication in the data of any recovery of income even after fifteen months despite a low overall unemployment rate. In addition, they asserted that pay at the BCE was out of line with salaries in the private sector, making it difficult for displaced employees to find simi-

27. They defined a displaced worker as one "whose job loss results from the plant closings and mass layoffs associated with economic restructuring" (Jacobson et al. 1993b).

28. These wage differences refer to the actual wage at a point in time compared with the wage the worker would have been expected to have earned had he or she not been displaced.

lar salaries in the private sector. In a separate study, Tansel (1996) found that Turkish workers laid off from privatized cement firms experienced earnings losses of 61 percent. Earnings losses for workers laid off from the state-owned petrochemical firm amounted to 57 percent.

By contrast, Jacobson (1978) found that two years after displacement, workers in low-wage industries actually earned more income than their nondisplaced counterparts in the original industry. Moreover, he found that six years after displacement, earnings losses had vanished for all industries, not just for low-wage industries. The difference in the results between the Jacobson studies is explained by the fact that the 1993 studies restrict the sample to workers with long job tenure and who are therefore likely to have accumulated specific human capital or earn wage premiums. His 1978 study, however, is a broad sample of short-, medium-, and long-tenure workers who have on average much less specific human capital. Similarly, Orazem, Vodopivec, and Wu (1995) found that more than two-thirds of displaced Slovenian workers who found new jobs actually earned wages higher than their predisplacement wages.[29] Mills and Sahn (1995) found that of the public sector workers retrenched in Guinea who were able to find new jobs, more than half had increased earnings. However, the average duration of unemployment for this group was approximately two and one half years,[30] and 30 percent of public sector workers who were retrenched between 1985 and 1988 were still unemployed as of 1992.

It is important to recognize that the private costs borne by dislocated workers and entrepreneurs need not coincide, even in the aggregate, with the social costs identified earlier in this paper. For example, some workers may enjoy a high wage due to distortions in the labor market. These distortions may include the presence of excessive union power or the existence of inflexible government wage scales. In such instances, there is a substantial private cost but no social cost (except perhaps that associated with a transitional period of unemployment) as competitive pressures from trade reform force a reduction in the size of distorted sectors. Similarly, liberalization of the trading regime might induce changes in the values that an economy places on various forms of human capital. Workers who have accumulated significant amounts of firm-specific or sector-specific human capital may suffer a substantial (private) loss as the demand for their skills declines.[31] In any event, this is no more a social cost than is the change in *any* price that is induced by changing market conditions.

29. Only one-third of displaced workers found reemployment during the period.
30. The average duration of unemployment can be calculated from the data that Mills and Sahn (1995) presented in their table 9.
31. E.g., during macroeconomic crises, real wages in Argentina, Bolivia, Chile, and Mexico fell by 33 percent or more before recovering (World Bank 1995b). It is unclear how much if any of these wage reductions were due to trade reform.

10.3.5   Retraining Programs to Reduce Adjustment Costs

Programs designed to retrain workers to make them more employable generate additional social costs to the extent that they require the use of resources that could have been used in other productive activities. However, such programs may reduce the social (and private) costs associated with adjustment if they have the desired effect of shortening spells of unemployment. A recent study of retraining programs in Hungary found that workers who participated had a slightly higher chance of becoming reemployed than those who did not participate (O'Leary 1997). Furthermore, the wages of participants on reemployment were slightly higher than those of nonparticipants who became reemployed. Perhaps the biggest difference between participants and nonparticipants was that the former obtained jobs with longer durations than the latter, indicating the potential for the retraining program to have a significantly positive effect on lifetime income of participants. However, it is not clear that the benefits of the program were sufficient to justify the costs.

Another program that provides government-sponsored training can be found in Mexico. The PROBECAT program provides short-term skills training to unemployed workers. An evaluation of this program found that it was effective in reducing the duration of unemployment for participants who had prior work experience and helped to raise the earnings of adult males who participated. The program, however, had no effect on the fate of trainees with no prior work experience or women who were reentering the workforce (see World Bank 1995b, box 17.1).

The United States has been providing trade adjustment assistance (TAA) to workers displaced by international trade since 1962. The U.S. program provides both monetary compensation (called trade readjustment allowances, TRAs) and retraining. In the early years of the program, it was found that income support was typically provided to workers who were not permanently separated from their employers; that is, the program was not well targeted (Corson and Nicholson 1981). However, changes in the design and monitoring of the program in 1982 and 1988 have resulted in targeting the payments to the intended recipients. U.S. recipients of TAA now are typically permanently separated from their employers and also experience greater difficulty in gaining reemployment than do typical recipients of unemployment compensation (Decker and Corson 1995). Following the changes of 1988, participation in an approved retraining program is a requirement to receive monetary compensation (TRA), unless a waiver is obtained. Evaluation of the experience of trade-displaced workers has revealed that participation in retraining programs did not have a positive impact on the earnings of trainees, at least in the first three years after the initial claim for unemployment compensation (Decker and Corson 1995).

Thus the results of retraining programs appear to be mixed. When retraining is required, as in the United States, it may be ineffective. More generally, the effectiveness of retraining programs tends to increase if they are demand driven, so, for example, subsidized apprenticeships in the private sector may work better than government-provided training programs.[32] An alternative approach to requiring retraining is to require participation in a job search program. This appears to increase the likelihood of employment and reduce unemployment benefits among recipients (Johnson and Klepinger 1991; Decker and Corson 1995).

10.3.6   Impact on Poverty

What is the impact of trade liberalization on poverty? First, experience suggests that rapid economic growth translates into sustainable reductions in poverty. Evidence also shows a significant association between trade liberalization and long-run improvements in economic growth. Thus there is likely to be a positive link between liberalization and eradication of poverty in the long run. Second, since trade reform reduces antiexport bias and to the extent that exports are intensive in the use of unskilled or rural labor (which may be expected but not guaranteed in developing countries), trade reform is expected to increase the real wage and reduce both poverty and inequality.

Third, the circumstances and causes of poverty vary greatly. The major resource of the poor is their own labor. Trade liberalization affects a poor family in two ways. First, it affects the wages they earn and (if there are labor market imperfections) whether they remain employed. If they are farmers, it affects the income they earn from the sale of products. Second, it affects the prices of the goods and services they consume. If trade liberalization raises staple food prices, producers (often poor farmers) will gain, while subsistence farmers will be unaffected and consumers (often the urban poor) will suffer. For example, in Peru, poor farmers produce little sorghum but much coffee. As a first pass, then, the liberalization of the coffee trade will raise coffee prices (and relieve poverty) while action on sorghum prices will not. A converse case is maize farmers in Mexico, who will probably be harmed as the North American Free Trade Agreement drives down prices (see Levy and Wijnbergen 1992).

Unfortunately, there are very few empirical studies of the impact of trade liberalization on the poor. One study of Mauritius, however, found evidence of such a trend. Trade and macrostabilization reforms during 1980s led to increased income and a sharp reduction of unemployment, poverty, and inequality (see English 1997).[33]

---

32. O'Leary (1995) discussed the measurement of the effectiveness of labor market programs in Hungary and Poland.

33. The macroreforms reduced inflation and resulted in a real exchange rate that was not overvalued, which helped to encourage foreign direct investment. These factors combined with encouragement of export-processing zones resulted in an increase of the number of firms in these zones from 115 in 1982 to 591 in 1988. Although comprehensive trade reform

One excellent and instructive study was based on the nationally representative Living Standards Measurement Survey of Panama (World Bank 1999). Panama has a distribution of income that is among the most unequal in the world: it has a Gini consumption (income) coefficient of 49 (60); 37 percent of the population lives in poverty and 19 percent lives in extreme poverty. Wage income represents 77 percent of the income of the poor, but unemployment (20 percent in 1989) and underemployment were very high. Moreover, close to three-fourths of the poor work in the informal sector, where workers earn 60 and 43 percent of what workers in the private and public formal sectors earn.

Prior to the 1990s, Panama was one of the most protected economies in Latin America. Combined with price controls and rigid labor market rules (which prevented termination and imposed minimum wages), this resulted in highly inefficient manufacturing and agricultural sectors that stifled growth and generated rents for certain groups (including workers who obtained jobs in the formal sector). But protection raised the price of the basic consumption basket and depressed wages of workers in the informal sector, where three-quarters of the poor work; that is, it was highly regressive, implicitly taxing the poor and increasing poverty. In late 1996 and 1997 the government introduced widespread trade reform to accompany previously implemented labor market reform, competition law reform, and privatization that had begun in 1994. Growth jumped in 1997, and crucially for the poor, unemployment fell to 13.2 percent from 16.2 percent in 1994.

Since agriculture represents 59 percent of the consumption expenditure and 41 percent of the income source of poor Panamanians, the study also went beyond an assessment of the empirical data and employed a model to simulate the complete elimination of agricultural protection. The authors estimated that this further trade liberalization would reduce the Gini coefficient by 0.6 percentage points, the poverty rate would fall by 1.7 percentage points, and extreme poverty would fall by 1.1 percentage points. Despite the reduction in the cost of the consumption basket for the average poor person, some farmers would lose. Net losers would represent only 2 percent of the population, of whom one-third are poor. The authors suggested programs for targeting the minority of poor farmers who would be adversely affected.

Trade liberalization is likely to be associated with reduced poverty in the long run. For the short to medium run, trade liberalization will reduce

---

was not implemented in the 1980s in Mauritius, value added and employment in the export-processing zones dramatically expanded following the reforms. Unemployment, which had been about 15 percent in the early 1980s, disappeared, and investors began worrying about a labor shortage in the early 1990s. The percentage of households below the poverty line fell from 40 percent in 1975 to 11 percent in 1992, and the Gini coefficient fell from 42 to 35 in the same period (World Bank 1995a, 70–71). This was primarily due to a reduction in unemployment but partly due to an increase in real wages.

the cost of the consumption basket of the poor, which by itself will have an impact on the reduction of poverty. The two studies cited also found a positive impact of trade liberalization on wages or employment of the poor since the poor tended to be located in unprotected sectors. But even when there is a general reduction in poverty, we must recognize that some of the poor may be made worse off. Some poor farmers, for example, may be made worse off by agricultural reform, especially in the short to medium run when adjustment costs remain.

10.4   Trade Reform and Macroeconomic Stability

A broad definition of adjustment costs would include the possible short-term loss of government revenue, balance-of-payments difficulties, and macroeconomic instability resulting from reform. These are particularly important concerns for developing countries since many tend to rely heavily on trade taxes as a source of government revenue. Data from the 1988 *World Development Report* reveal that in 1985 explicit trade taxes accounted for 38 percent of total tax revenues in low-income developing countries and 19 percent of total tax revenues in middle-income developing countries. In 1990, collected trade taxes as a percentage of GDP averaged 0.6 percent among OECD countries and 4.4 percent among non-OECD countries.[34] Policymakers in low-income countries are concerned that one of the costs of trade reform might be a substantial decline in government revenue, yielding larger fiscal deficits and inducing inflation.

While these concerns have some merit, trade reform need not entail diminished revenues. A number of countries have implemented successful trade reform programs without significant loss of revenue. For example, in the 1990s, Ghana, Kenya, Senegal, and Malawi implemented trade reforms without significant losses in revenue as a percentage of GDP (Ebrill et al. 1999).

Perhaps the foremost reason why trade reform need not lead to a loss of revenue is that developing countries have traditionally relied heavily on quantitative restrictions of imports. Government revenue actually increases when quantitative restrictions are converted into their tariff equivalents. If tariff rates are very high initially, they will generate little or no revenue; reductions of the tariffs to more moderate levels will increase the quantity of imports, and the increased quantity effect will increase revenues. For example, by reducing extremely high tariff rates, the incentive to smuggle is reduced, thus increasing the share of official transactions in imports. Low tariffs may be placed on previously exempted goods, thereby increasing revenue. Finally, an exchange rate depreciation, which should accompany tariff reduction, will also provide additional tariff revenue to

---

34. See Ebrill, Strotsky, and Gropp (1999). Trade taxes as percentages of GDP were 5.3 percent in Africa, 4.4 percent in Asia, and 3.5 percent in the Middle East.

partially offset reduced tariff rates. When tariffs rates are already uniform and in the moderate to low range, then further tariff reduction is much more likely to result in revenue loss.[35]

One World Bank study of nine countries that undertook thirty-five trade-oriented adjustment programs during the 1980s examined the impact of adjustment on tariff revenues. Of these nine countries, Côte d'Ivoire, Ghana, Jamaica, Pakistan, and Turkey actually increased their ratios of trade taxes relative to GDP while Indonesia, Mexico, and Morocco experienced declines in this measure.[36] Colombia's foreign trade taxes were 2.3 percent of GDP both before and after implementation of reforms. As a group, trade taxes as a percentage of GDP increased from 3.6 percent prior to reform to 4.5 percent subsequent to reform.

In a separate study, Thomas and Nash (1991) examined import tax revenues for fifteen countries that underwent moderate to substantial trade reforms during the period 1980–97. For Bangladesh, Colombia, Ghana, Jamaica, Madagascar, Mauritius, and Pakistan, trade reform consisted primarily of a switch from quantitative restrictions to tariff restrictions along with reductions in the number of duty exemptions. These countries were labeled *quota reformers*. The remaining eight countries pursued reductions in tariff rates more aggressively and were therefore called *tariff reformers*. Tariff reformers were Chile, Korea, Mexico, Morocco, Panama, the Philippines, Thailand, and Turkey. Figure 10.4 illustrates that import tax revenues measured as a percentage of GDP declined for tariff reformers but increased for quota reformers.

Evidence of the effects of reform on inflation, fiscal balance, and trade balance is quite encouraging. Thomas and Nash (1991) classified a group of twenty-four reforming countries according to whether the implemented reforms were substantial, moderate, or mild.[37] The substantial reformers

35. See Tanzi (1988) for further elaboration. The experience of Latin America after 1985 indicates that trade reform can be expected to lead to revenue loss (unless compensated by geographically neutral taxes) when trade reform starts from a position of already low tariffs (Ebrill et al. 1999).

36. The comparison is between the average annual value of foreign trade taxes as a percentage of GDP during the years 1986–89 with the same measure for the years 1978–82. See World Bank (1992, table 3.6).

37. A country was considered to have implemented substantial reform if there was any real depreciation of the exchange rate combined with substantial reduction in the antiexport bias of commercial policy, or a minimum 20 percent real depreciation of the exchange rate accompanied by moderate reduction in the antiexport bias of commercial policy. Moderate reformers had real exchange rate depreciation of less than 20 percent and moderate reduction in the antiexport bias of commercial policies, or mild reduction in the antiexport bias of commercial policy combined with depreciation of at least 20 percent, or real exchange rate depreciation of less than 20 percent combined with substantial reduction in the antiexport bias of commercial policies. All other combinations of changes in commercial policy and exchange rate (including cases of policy reversal) were considered to be cases of mild reform. It should be recognized that there is a certain degree of subjectivity in this classification system.

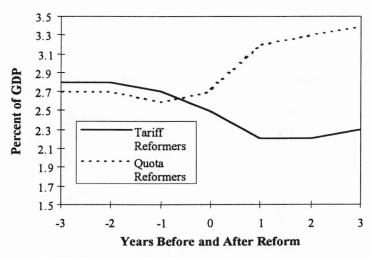

Fig. 10.4   Import taxes as a percentage of GDP
Source: Thomas and Nash (1991).

were Chile, Colombia, Ghana, Jamaica, Korea, Mauritius, Mexico, and
Turkey. The moderate reformers were Bangladesh, Madagascar, Morocco,
Pakistan, Panama, the Philippines, and Thailand. The mild reformers
were Côte d'Ivoire, Guyana, Kenya, Malawi, Senegal, Togo, Yugoslavia,
Zambia, and Zimbabwe. Table 10.7 shows that the substantial and moderate reformers were generally able to reduce inflation, fiscal deficits, and
trade deficits.[38] By contrast, the mild reformers had somewhat larger fiscal
deficits and somewhat higher inflation after reforms were implemented.
However, the trade deficits for this group did shrink after reform.

In general the data support the theory that removal of quantitative restraints typically leads to an increase in revenue and that trade reform
does not typically lead to macroeconomic instability. In economies where
protection is already low, further tariff reform can be expected to lower
government revenue. In these cases, it is important to develop taxes that
do not discriminate against imports in order to reap the benefits of trade
liberalization.

10.5   Directions for Future Research

Existing research gives us reason to be cautiously optimistic that a wide
range of economies are quite resilient and can adjust to trade liberalization swiftly and at minimal cost. However, although there have been many

---

38. The term "resource balance" is defined as the net exports of goods and nonfactor services.

Table 10.7   **Macroeconomic Indicators before and after Reform for 24 Countries**

Indicator and Country Group	3 Years before Reform	2 Years before Reform	1 Year before Reform	Year of Reform	1 Year after Reform	2 Years after Reform	3 Years after Reform
Inflation rate							
Substantial reform	31.5	34.3	30.6	55.5	25.9	22.9	22.6
Excluding Mexico	30.6	33.0	26.6	48.9	20.3	17.4	17.0
Moderate reform	12.4	11.8	12.3	9.3	8.9	8.1	7.6
Mild reform	15.5	15.7	15.3	17.4	14.8	16.9	19.3
Fiscal deficit/GDP							
Substantial reform	−4.8	−6.4	−7.8	−7.2	−6.1	−4.4	−4.6
Excluding Mexico	−5.1	−6.4	−6.5	−7.1	−5.9	−3.6	−2.6
Moderate reform	−7.2	−7.8	−6.0	−5.8	−5.4	−5.1	−4.7
Mild reform	−8.0	−6.8	−8.6	−8.9	−8.4	−8.0	−13.8
Trade deficit/GDP							
Substantial reform	−5.2	−3.4	−2.5	−1.5	0.4	−0.7	−1.1
Excluding Mexico	−5.6	−3.5	−3.6	−3.1	−0.7	−1.5	−1.9
Moderate reform	−8.8	−8.6	−7.1	−6.4	−7.1	−6.0	−4.4
Mild reform	−6.2	−9.9	−7.5	−7.8	−6.4	−6.4	−3.2

Source: Thomas and Nash (1991, table 5-1).

studies of the impact of trade liberalization on manufacturing employment in both developing and developed countries, attempts to quantify adjustment costs have been confined, for the most part, to industrial economies in general, and the United States in particular. On one hand, formal labor markets in developing countries may be less flexible than in industrial countries, suggesting adjustment costs would be higher. On the other hand, a higher percentage of employment in developing countries is in agriculture and in informal labor markets that are very flexible—implying lower adjustment costs. Although data limitations may make the task difficult, it would be extremely useful to try to rigorously measure adjustment costs for a range of developing countries. As we elaborate below, however, there are households living at the subsistence level in some developing countries who can ill afford an extended period of unemployment. Knowledge of the impacts on these households could allow appropriate provisions for them during adjustment. Such research should be careful to model, both theoretically and empirically, the relation between transition rates between states (as illustrated by the flows in fig. 10.3) and institutional features, such as a large number of state-owned enterprises, that are prominent in many developing countries.

Additional research should focus on identifying barriers that slow resource reallocation, thus creating excessive adjustment costs. For example, it is typically argued that legal restrictions that limit the ability of firms to lay off employees can result in generally inflexible labor markets. Similarly, overly generous unemployment benefits may reduce the incentives for newly laid-off workers to search for employment and therefore extend the time required for adjustment. Such policies may have beneficial aspects (e.g., in providing a social safety net) but may in fact be welfare reducing when their effects on adjustment are considered. Both theoretical and empirical work could shed light on the proper balance between policies designed to be a social safety net and those designed to speed adjustment. (See chap. 8, by Schultz, in this volume.)

Research to date on adjustment costs has, for the most part, not incorporated the heterogeneity of labor and households. It would be very useful to have studies of the impact of trade liberalization on the poorest households and on workers of different skill levels or incomes. The evidence indicates that economic growth reduces poverty and that trade liberalization increases economic growth, so trade liberalization should reduce poverty in the long run. But given our earlier discussion about the diverse nature of the poor, an adjustment process could conceivably adversely affect the poorest households. It would appear necessary to provide for the neediest in these situations, and further research could improve identification. In addition, both economic theory and the evidence cited above from the studies by Jacobsen and his coauthors suggest that earnings losses of workers depend on their characteristics, such as specific human capital and wage premiums due to union power or efficiency wages. It would be useful, however, to preselect a sample of workers by their characteristics to determine more clearly the impact of these phenomena on the social and private costs of adjustment.

Additional research should be undertaken to examine the most effective means of distributing the burden of adjustment more evenly across society and of reducing the costs of adjustment where they appear to be excessive. For example, providing unemployment compensation or other adjustment assistance to those who become unemployed due to trade reforms reduces the private costs borne by those individuals. But this is unlikely to be an optimally designed compensation scheme for several reasons. First, workers are displaced for a variety of reasons in a market economy, and it is difficult to rationalize adjustment assistance for trade-displaced workers and not, for example, for technology-displaced workers. Moreover, it is difficult to distinguish workers who are displaced due to trade liberalization from those who are displaced for other reasons. If programs are available only for trade-displaced workers, displaced workers will claim they were displaced for trade-related reasons. Second, generally the workers who suffer the largest adjustment costs are the ones who were earning substantial rents in their original jobs due to protection. In effect, they had received indirect transfers from workers in unprotected industries. Thus it is difficult to rationalize transfers that would compensate for all earnings losses since this implies continuing transfers from workers in unprotected industries, workers who in some cases may be less wealthy. Third, the incentive effects of compensation schemes on extending the duration of unemployment must be taken into account.[39]

Finally, additional research that would allow us to better identify the types of retraining programs that are most cost-effective in reducing adjustment costs would be also useful.

10.6   Summary and Conclusion

In this paper we have summarized the empirical research on the adjustment costs of trade liberalization. We began with three studies that empirically examined employment effects from thirty separate economywide episodes of trade liberalization in developing countries. In these studies it is difficult to disentangle the effects of trade liberalization from other events occurring simultaneously, but generally, manufacturing employment increased subsequent to the trade liberalization. Transition economies are a special case where manufacturing employment declined after liberaliza-

---

39. A program of very generous unemployment benefits could reduce the incentives for unemployed workers to search for new jobs, thereby extending the period of unemployment and increasing the social costs of adjustment.

tion, but employment decline was faster in transition economies that did not liberalize. We next surveyed studies that quantified the costs of adjustment from trade liberalization. These included economywide studies of Australia and Uruguay and two of the United States, as well as studies by several authors of trade liberalization in twenty-two industries in the United States and the United Kingdom. In general, these studies found that the benefits of trade liberalization are vastly greater than the costs— typically each dollar of adjustment cost is accompanied by more than $20 of benefits from trade liberalization.

We next reported on two studies of micro- and small-scale enterprises in eight African economies. It was found that MSEs in these countries are highly dynamic (even when compared to industrialized countries), making speedy adjustment to trade reform more likely. Then we examined studies of the private costs of adjustment in eight countries. These costs can be quite substantial in cases where the workers were earning substantial rents in their original jobs but tend to be small otherwise.

In the last empirical section, we discussed the impact of trade reform on macroeconomic stability drawing on two studies that examined the impact on the fiscal deficit in fifteen and nine countries, respectively. These studies concluded that countries eliminating quotas typically reduced their fiscal deficits and inflation, while those reducing tariffs had at first slightly larger fiscal deficits and inflation, which eventually shrank.

We find it necessary to apply caveats to most of the studies we surveyed regarding conclusions with respect to adjustment costs; thus it is necessary to be cautious regarding conclusions based on any few of them. Most notably, while there are numerous studies on the effects of trade liberalization on aggregate employment in developing countries, virtually all studies that quantified adjustment costs were done in industrialized countries. Collectively, however, the weight of so many studies of various types, all pointing in more or less the same direction, makes it difficult to avoid the conclusion that adjustment costs are very small in relation to the benefits of trade liberalization.

Why then have these studies found that adjustment costs are so small and that there is little decline (usually an increase) in manufacturing employment in developing countries one year after trade liberalization? Regarding manufacturing employment, these results are explained by a number of considerations: (1) Developing countries would be expected to have comparative advantage in labor-intensive industries, so trade liberalization should favor labor. (2) It has been observed that a great deal of interindustry shifts occur after trade liberalization, which minimizes the dislocation of factors of production. (3) In many industries normal labor turnover exceeds dislocation from trade liberalization, so downsizing where necessary can be accomplished without much forced unemployment.

The explanations for low adjustment costs in relation to benefits are as follows: (1) Most important, adjustment costs are typically short term and terminate when workers find jobs, while the benefits of trade reform can be expected to grow with the economy. (2) Estimates of the duration of unemployment for most industries are not high, especially where workers were not earning substantial rents in their original jobs. (3) As noted above, normal labor turnover often exceeds job displacement from trade liberalization.

Given these results we devoted some attention in this paper to an assessment of the private costs of trade liberalization. Knowledge of the distribution of the private costs and benefits associated with trade reform is useful because of concerns for equitable distribution of income and because such knowledge might guide the implementation of contemporaneous policies to diffuse some of the political opposition that may arise.

One policy we recommended is a uniform tariff; a uniform tariff will minimize lobbying by special interests for protection because it diffuses the benefits of protection. If the only way protection can be increased is by increasing protection for all industries, lobbying for protection then yields only dispersed benefits as well as costs to the lobbyists.

Finally, we briefly discussed policies to minimize adjustment costs where it appears that adjustment costs might be excessive and suggested areas where additional research would be useful. We noted that zero adjustment costs are socially suboptimal in a dynamic economy, since it would imply insufficient search time by temporarily unemployed workers. Moreover, given sound complementary policies, adjustment costs associated with trade liberalization are unlikely to provide an adequate reason for delays in opening to the outside world. Nonetheless, it is likely that policymakers can reduce such costs. Perhaps the most important complementary policies are ensuring macroeconomic stability and the credibility of policies so as to foster a quick, sustained private investment response in newly competitive sectors of the economy. Structural policy reforms to improve labor market flexibility and reform of the state enterprise sector may provide important complementary support. Of course, each of these policies is likely to be of great economic value on its own. The mutually supportive relations between trade, macroeconomic, labor market, and other policies may then serve to increase the credibility and payoffs to each.

References

Baldwin, Robert E., John H. Mutti, and J. David Richardson. 1980. Welfare effects on the United States of a significant multilateral tariff reduction. *Journal of International Economics* 10:405–23.

Bale, Malcom D. 1976. Estimates of trade displacement costs for U.S. workers. *Journal of International Economics* 6:245–50.

Blanchflower, David, and Andrew Oswald. 1995. *The wage curve.* Cambridge, Mass.: MIT Press.

Cooper, Richard N. 1994. Foreign trade, wages, and unemployment. Discussion Paper no. 1701. Cambridge, Mass.: Harvard University, Harvard Institute of Economic Research.

Corson, Walter, and Walter Nicholson. 1981. Trade adjustment assistance for workers: Results of a survey of recipients under the Trade Adjustment Assistance Act of 1974. *Research in Labor Economics* 4:417–69.

Decker, Paul, and Walter Corson. 1995. International trade and worker displacement: Evaluation of the Trade Adjustment Assistance Program. *Industrial and Labor Relations Review* 48 (4): 758–74.

de Melo, Jaime, and David Roland-Holst. 1994. Economywide costs of protection and labor market rigidities. In *The effects of protectionism on a small country: The case of Uruguay,* ed. Michael Connolly and Jaime de Melo. Washington, D.C.: World Bank.

de Melo, Jaime, and David Tarr. 1990. Welfare costs of U.S. quotas in textiles, steel and autos. *Review of Economics and Statistics* 72:489–97.

Dixon, Peter B., B. R. Parmenter, and Alan A. Powell. 1984. Trade liberalization and labor market disruption. *Journal of Policy Modeling* 6:431–54.

Ebrill, Liam, Janet Strotsky, and Reint Gropp. 1999. Revenue implications of trade liberalization. IMF Occasional Paper no. 180. Washington, D.C.: International Monetary Fund.

English, Phillip. 1997. *Mauritius: Re-igniting the engines of growth.* Washington, D.C.: World Bank, Economic Development Institute.

Fernandez, Raquel, and Dani Rodrik. 1991. Resistance to reform: Status quo bias in the presence of individual-specific uncertainty. *American Economic Review* 81:1146–55.

Haltiwanger, John, and Manisha Singh. 1996. Cross-country evidence on public sector retrenchment. Paper prepared for World Bank conference on Public Sector Retrenchment and Efficient Compensation Schemes.

Harrison, Ann, and Ana Revenga. 1995. Factor markets and trade policy reform. Washington, D.C.: World Bank. Manuscript.

Hoddinott, John. 1996. Wages and unemployment in an urban African labour market. *Economic Journal* 106:1610–26.

Jacobson, Louis S. 1978. Earnings losses of workers from manufacturing industries. In *The impact of international trade on investment and employment,* ed. William DeWald et al. Washington, D.C.: Government Printing Office.

Jacobson, Louis S., Robert J. LaLonde, and Daniel G. Sullivan. 1993a. Earnings losses of displaced workers. *American Economic Review* 83:685–709.

———. 1993b. Long-term earnings losses of high-seniority displaced workers. *Economic Perspectives* 17:2–20.

Johnson, Terry, and Daniel Klepinger. 1991. Evaluation of the impacts of the Washington Alternative Work Search Experiment. Unemployment Insurance Occasional Paper no. 91–4. Washington, D.C.: Department of Labor, Employment and Training Administration.

Krueger, Anne. 1983. *Trade and employment in developing countries: Synthesis and conclusions.* Chicago: University of Chicago Press.

Levy, Santiago, and Sweder van Wijnbergen. 1992. Mexican agriculture in the free trade agreement: Transition problems in economic reform. OECD Development Centre Technical Paper no. 63 1–92. Paris: Organization for Economic Cooperation and Development.

Liedholm, Carl, and Donald C. Mead. 1999. *Small enterprises and economic development: The dynamics of micro and small enterprises.* Studies in Development Economics, vol. 15. London and New York: Routledge.

Magee, Stephen P. 1972. The welfare effects of restrictions on U.S. trade. *Brookings Papers on Economic Activity,* no. 3:645–701.

Matusz, Steven J. 1994. International trade policy in a model of unemployment and wage differentials. *Canadian Journal of Economics* 27:939–49.

———. 1996. International trade, the division of labor, and unemployment. *International Economic Review* 37:71–84.

Mills, Bradford F., and David E. Sahn. 1995. Reducing the size of the public sector workforce: Institutional constraints and human consequences in Guinea. *Journal of Development Studies* 31:505–28.

Morgan, Peter, and Richard Manning. 1985. Optimal search. *Econometrica* 53:923–44.

Morkre, Morris, and David Tarr. 1980. *Effects of United States restrictions on imports: Five case studies and theory.* Bureau of Economics Report to the Federal Trade Commission. Washington, D.C.: Government Printing Office.

Mutti, John. 1978. Aspects of unilateral trade policy and factor adjustment costs. *Review of Economics and Statistics* 6 (1): 102–10.

Neary, J. Peter. 1982. Intersectoral capital mobility, wage stickiness, and the case for adjustment assistance. In *Import competition and response,* ed. Jagdish N. Bhagwati. Chicago: University of Chicago Press.

Nogues, Julio. 1991. Trade, employment, and growth in Peru since WWII. In *Liberalizing foreign trade,* ed. Demetris Papageorgiou, Michael Michaely, and Armeane Choski. Cambridge, Mass., and Oxford: Blackwell.

O'Leary, Christopher J. 1995. Performance indicators: A management tool for active labour programmes in Hungary and Poland. *International Labour Review* 134:729–51.

———. 1997. A net impact analysis of active labour programmes in Hungary. *Economics of Transition* 5 (2): 453–84.

Orazem, Peter, Milan Vodopivec, and Ruth Wu. 1995. Worker displacement during the transition: Experience from Slovenia. Policy Research Working Paper no. 1449. Washington, D.C.: World Bank, Policy Research Department, Transition Economics Division.

Panagariya, Arvind, and Dani Rodrik. 1993. Political economy arguments for a uniform tariff. *International Economic Review* 34:687–703.

Papageorgiou, Demetrios, Armeane M. Choksi, and Michael Michaely. 1990. *Liberalizing foreign trade in developing countries: The lessons of experience.* Washington, D.C.: World Bank.

Parker, Ronald L., Randall Riopelle, and William F. Steel. 1995. Small enterprises adjusting to liberalization in five African countries. World Bank Discussion Paper no. 271. Washington, D.C.: World Bank.

Rama, Martin, and Donna MacIsaac. 1996. Activity, earnings and welfare after retrenchment: Central bank employees in Ecuador. Paper prepared for World Bank conference on Public Sector Retrenchment and Efficient Compensation Schemes.

Roberts, Mark, and James Tybout. 1997. The decision to export in Colombia: An empirical model of entry with sunk costs. *American Economic Review* 87:545–63.

Steel, William F., and Leila M. Webster. 1992. How small enterprises in Ghana have responded to adjustment. *World Bank Economic Review* 6:423–38.

Stigler, George. 1971. The theory of regulation. *Bell Journal of Economics* 2 (1): 3–21.

Takacs, Wendy E., and L. Alan Winters. 1991. Labour adjustment costs and British footwear protection. *Oxford Economic Papers* 43:479–501.

Tansel, Aysit. 1996. Workers displaced due to privatization in Turkey: Before versus after displacement. Paper prepared for World Bank conference on Public Sector Retrenchment and Efficient Compensation Schemes.

Tanzi, Vito. 1988. The impact of macroeconomic policies on the level of taxation (and on the fiscal balance) in developing countries. IMF Working Paper no. 88/95. Washington, D.C.: International Monetary Fund.

Tarr, David, and Morris Morkre. 1984. *Aggregate costs to the United States of tariffs and quotas on imports.* Bureau of Economics Report to the Federal Trade Commission. Washington, D.C.: Government Printing Office.

Thomas, Vinod, and John Nash. 1991. *Best practices in trade policy reform.* Oxford: Oxford University Press.

Trefler, Daniel. 1995. The case of the missing trade and other mysteries. *American Economic Review* 85:1029–64.

World Bank. 1992. Trade policy reforms under adjustment programs. Washington, D.C.: World Bank, Operations Evaluation Department.

———. 1995a. *Mauritius—Country economic memorandum: Sharpening the competitive edge.* Washington, D.C.: World Bank, April.

———. 1995b. *World development report.* New York: Oxford University Press.

———. 1996. *World development report.* New York: Oxford University Press.

———. 1999. *Panama poverty assessment: Priorities and strategies for poverty reduction.* Washington, D.C.: World Bank, Human Development Department, Latin American and the Caribbean Region.

Comment on the Paper by Steven Matusz and David Tarr
Julie Schaffner

Matusz and Tarr have performed the useful service of reviewing a large number of studies regarding the costs of adjustment to trade policy reform, making clear that almost all studies to date find the costs of trade liberalization to be very small relative to the benefits. In my discussion I will focus on two sets of concerns: first, the reasons (as highlighted by the authors) for the finding that the costs are small relative to the benefits and, second, directions for future research.

Few economists would doubt the basic conclusion that in the aggregate, the costs of trade liberalization are small relative to the benefits. I suspect, however, that few policymakers who are reluctant to undertake trade liberalization would be convinced to move forward by this paper, or by the studies it reviews. Even if policymakers' only reason for hesitation were concerns about the possible magnitude of the costs, the studies are likely to have little effect. By defining research questions narrowly and by using models that are not rich enough, the studies "stack the deck" in favor of finding small costs and thus render themselves less compelling. Indeed,

Julie Schaffner is affiliated with the Fletcher School of Law and Diplomacy at Tufts University and the Boston University Department of Economics. She was assistant professor of economics and deputy director of the Center for Research on Economic Development and Policy Reform at Stanford University when this paper was written.

such weaknesses affect each of the explanations the authors highlight for the frequent finding that the costs of trade liberalization are small relative to the benefits.

The first explanation noted by the authors is simply that all the costs are short term while the benefits are permanent. This is true, but only because of the way the authors have defined terms and focused the research question. They have chosen to compare the benefits of trade reforms not to *all* costs but to *adjustment* costs, which by definition are short term and likely to be swamped by benefits that extend into the infinite future. This focus is reasonable within their framework of social cost-benefit analysis because they use the terms "social costs" and "social benefits" as synonyms for reductions and increases in discounted aggregate output. The only losses in aggregate output we can think of are temporary; thus in their framework all costs are adjustment costs.

When I think of social costs and benefits, however, I think of social welfare functions that allow society to care about the distribution as well as the magnitude of income. With this broader view of social costs in mind, it is possible for trade liberalization to bring a cost that lasts into the infinite future: an increase in income inequality. A complete review of the costs of adjustment to trade policy reform, then, should include discussion of the large recent literature on the role of trade expansion in explaining the rise of income inequality in the United States, United Kingdom, and various middle-income countries in recent decades (see, e.g., Johnson 1997; Robbins 1996). Increasing trade probably plays at most a small role in explaining rising inequality the United States. Skill-biased technical change is thought to be the more important culprit. Trade's role might be somewhat larger in the middle-income countries, both because trade is more important in those economies and because trade and technical change are more intimately related there. A careful weighing of the effects of trade on income distribution is unlikely to reverse the conclusion that trade liberalization is desirable. But it would lead to a research synthesis that is more balanced, and thus somewhat more likely to influence skeptics.

The second explanation highlighted by the authors is that typical unemployment durations in the countries studied are brief, an observation that leads researchers to build models in which displaced workers find their way quickly into new, productive employment, and in which short-term inefficiencies in labor utilization are small. The problem with this reliance on unemployment data is that it is possible for the incidence and duration of open unemployment to be low even when labor is greatly underutilized, especially in developing countries, where workers have no access to unemployment insurance. Workers may be underutilized even when not officially unemployed not only because they might exit the labor force but also because they might take low-productivity jobs, which make poor use of their skills and abilities. The authors acknowledge this, but only as a brief afterthought, rather than as a glaring deficiency that more convincing research would need to tackle.

The authors argue further that the inefficiency associated with unemployment is likely to be small in developing countries because the micro- and small enterprise sectors there appear to be so "dynamic." The evidence they provide to support this assessment is that micro- and small enterprise growth rates are high. This evidence falls far short of establishing their point. Growth rates of micro- and small enterprises may be high (and indeed they tend to be especially high in periods of structural adjustment), but labor may have low productivity in many of these enterprises. Thus the high growth rates may reflect high rates of inflow into "disguised unemployment."

The authors' third observation about why the costs are found to be small relative to the benefits of trade reform is that the numbers of workers leaving jobs in normal times tend to be greater than the numbers of workers that researchers estimate must leave declining industries as a result of trade reform. This leads researchers to conclude that the downsizing necessitated by trade reforms can be accomplished largely through attrition. The main difficulty with this comparison is that it assumes workers are homogeneous. They are not (and policymakers know this). Workers who leave jobs in normal times include many who are quitting and have good reemployment prospects. Dislocations associated with trade reform are likely to hit a broader set of workers, many of whom do not have good reemployment prospects and who must be displaced involuntarily.

The fourth reason the authors highlight is that employment seems to increase quickly in sectors favored by trade liberalization. It is certainly a great sign to see manufacturing employment growth only one year after reforms in developing countries (assuming that the studies control for the effects of changes in other policies and in world market conditions). But again, the evidence falls short of convincing us that short-term labor use is highly efficient. We do not know whether some of that manufacturing employment is in small, unproductive establishments. Even if the new employment is in productive establishments, it remains possible that the employment growth represents the inflow of young workers entering the labor market for the first time, while the middle-aged workers who were displaced from declining sectors have become unemployed or have left the labor force.

In amplifying this last explanation, the authors argue that employment should be expected to increase after trade liberalization in developing countries because they have comparative advantages in labor-intensive industries. That may follow obviously in a two-factor, two-good, two-region model of world trade, but it does not follow necessarily for all developing countries in a richer, more appropriate model of the world. Policymakers in Latin America, who are concerned with income distribution and who fear competition from India, China, and other lower income countries, might find analysis based on such simple models uncompelling. If we differentiate skilled from unskilled labor and differentiate between middle- and low-income countries, then it becomes possible that while all developing (i.e., middle and low income) countries are labor abundant relative to the developed countries, low-income countries might be unskilled labor abundant relative to middle-income countries. Opening to trade might then favor the skilled labor elite in middle-income developing countries, leaving the aggregate effects on unemployment and (unskilled) wages much less clear.

The authors emphasize three directions for future research: extension of adjustment cost studies from developed to developing countries, assessment of the effect of cross-country differences in labor market policies and institutions on the costs of adjustment, and study of policies that might be used to reduce or redistribute the costs of adjustment. I have three comments. First, the paper gives the impression that one can derive satisfactory estimates of adjustment costs in developing countries by simply plugging new empirical magnitudes into existing models. As my previous comments suggest, one might want to improve the models and methods (e.g., by explicitly acknowledging worker heterogeneity and potential differences in productivity across jobs available to the same individual) even to produce more satisfactory estimates for developed countries. Significant modifications are even more necessary if the results are to impress developing country policymakers, who simply cannot ignore concerns about possible disguised unemployment and underemployment in their large "informal" sectors.

Second, I would like to amplify the authors' call for study of the effects of labor market policies on adjustment. The authors emphasize study of the effects of policies and institutions on the *speed* of adjustment. I would stress the importance of studying their effects on the distribution of adjustment costs as well. Seniority-based firing rules, or severance pay policies structured to have similar effects, may slow adjustment, but they might also protect some of the most vulnerable workers (e.g., middle-aged workers with poor reemployment prospects). Policymakers and society would benefit from better information about both sides of this story.

Finally, I would place much greater emphasis on research relating to adjustment policies and much less emphasis on research designed to measure the costs of adjustment in developing countries. Additional studies yielding the unsurprising result that aggregate costs are small relative to the benefits of trade liberalization—even if they define costs more broadly and use richer models—are unlikely to convince policymakers to undertake trade liberalization. Research yielding practical advice about retraining, reemployment services, and other policies that might reduce or redistribute the costs of adjustment, on the other hand, might help policymakers to design policy packages that benefit more groups and thus help them to find politically more acceptable (and socially more desirable) ways of liberalizing trade.

References

Johnson, George E. 1997. Changes in earnings inequality: The role of demand shifts. *Journal of Economic Perspectives* 11 (2): 41–54.
Robbins, Donald J. 1996. HOS hits facts: Facts win. Cambridge, Mass.: Harvard Institute for International Development, October. Processed.

11

Reforming Poverty Alleviation Policies

Jonathan Morduch

In the world today, about one billion people live on less than one dollar per day, and about two to three billion live on less than two dollars per day (World Bank 1997). Thirty years ago, the numbers looked very different. Broad-based economic growth in populous countries like China and Indonesia has substantially reduced rates of absolute poverty. In Indonesia, for example, the fraction of the population below the poverty line fell from 58 to 17 percent between 1972 and 1982, and in Brazil the fraction fell from 50 to 21 percent between 1960 and 1980 (World Bank 1993a). Similarly, China boasts a reduction in rural poverty from 31 to 7 percent between 1978 and 1995, a decrease by 185 million people.[1] These changes have left a growing concentration of world poverty in slow-growth areas of South Asia and Africa.

A generation ago, approaches to poverty alleviation were also considerably different. While an active macroeconomic agenda had focused on "redistribution with growth," much of it represented in the studies in Chenery et al. (1974), approaches through the 1970s and mid-1980s tended to focus on poverty alleviation as a static problem. The prospect that economic

Jonathan Morduch is a MacArthur Foundation Research Fellow at Princeton University. The initial draft of this chapter was written while Morduch was a National Fellow at the Hoover Institution, Stanford University.

The initial draft of this paper was completed while the author was visiting the Center for Research on Economic Development and Policy Reform in the summer of 1998, and he appreciates their hospitality, as well as comments from Anjini Kochar, Anne Krueger, Costas Michalopoulos, Paul Schultz, T. N. Srinivasan, and conference participants.

1. But see the qualifications noted by Park, Wang, and Wu (1997) and Chen and Ravallion (1996). They argued that current poverty measures should be adjusted upward since the official numbers fail to account for regional price differences. The poverty reductions remain dramatic, however, in terms of absolute numbers.

growth would play an important role in poverty alleviation appeared dim, at least in the medium term, and the ascendant priority was the direct provision of "basic needs" like food, shelter, education, and health care. Strikingly, in the influential Streeten et al. (1981) volume *First Things First,* the chapter on basic needs and economic growth is devoted almost entirely to how basic needs provision affects prospects for growth, with little heed to how economic growth can improve the fulfillment of basic needs. The optimism of Robert McNamara's 1973 Nairobi speech, setting forth the imperatives of the basic needs approach from the vantage of the World Bank presidency, echoed the kind of optimism that surrounded the formulation of Lyndon Johnson's War on Poverty. Twenty-five years later, however, the promise of those early plans remains unfulfilled, both in the United States and in low-income countries.

As a result, the attitudes of many have almost completely flipped. First, the limits to government action have now been forcefully documented (e.g., Krueger 1990). Administrative capacity and tax bases are often limited, and despite rhetoric to the contrary, political commitment to poverty alleviation is often limited too, especially since concern with poverty alleviation must compete against other government objectives such as investing in long-term growth and implementing fiscal reforms. At the implementation stage, policies are often reshaped and bogged down by bureaucracies, further diminishing help for the poor.

Second, the potential benefits of economic growth are now better understood. The fall of the Soviet empire has played its part, pointedly demonstrating the power of compounding growth rates. While in any given year, for example, sacrificing 2 percent of expected GDP via a lower growth rate might appear to be a small cost if it buys social benefits, after thirty years the cumulative cost is levels of GDP that are 44 percent lower than they otherwise would have been—with correspondingly fewer resources for health, education, and other social services.

The World Bank's new policy lines tend to fall in with these changes, featuring "market friendly" policies, the search for "win-win" policy options (i.e., policies that appear to be politically costless), and the assertion that the long-term efficiency-equity trade-off is a fiction when it comes to investments in human capital and infrastructure.[2] In the end, this mainstream position is not very far from where it was in the early 1970s: the aim is to help poor households take advantage of broader processes of growth by removing economic barriers and building bridges that facilitate widespread gains. The broad policy prescriptions of *Redistribution with Growth* hardly seem dated a quarter-century later.

2. The lack of an efficiency-equity trade-off is misleading when considering optimal policies. It may be true that investing in basic human capital is likely to improve both equity and efficiency, but it is unlikely that the first-best level of investment in the cause of equity is generally free of opportunity costs.

Still, approaches are changing, and below I describe two examples that illustrate shifting perspectives. The discussion points to limits of the win-win vision and to places where recent research can help to sharpen policy dialogues.

The first is international health policy, in which the leading analytical framework of the 1990s, the application of "cost-effectiveness" principles, is a throwback to old-style planning exercises. The cost-effectiveness approach centers on identifying priorities for public health care and provides a structure for organizing a wide variety of health statistics. The strong language and scientific imprimatur helps to reinforce arguments against funneling large fractions of government budgets into expensive teaching hospitals that will improve a poor population's health far less than immunizing children against common diseases like measles. The technocratic approach, however, pays little heed to political incentives. And concerns with the basic principles of public finance tend to be tacked on, rather than fully integrated into the approach (the concerns include issues surrounding risk, externalities, informational asymmetries, cost recovery, and provision of health services by the private sector).

If international health policy discussion reflects older traditions, the second case represents new departures. This is microfinance, the expansion of financial services to low-income households—surely the most discussed new poverty alleviation strategy of the past decade. In sharp contrast to the vision from public health, advocates of microfinance are pushing a set of "best practices" that entail eschewing all ongoing government intervention and enthusiastically embracing market principles (Otero and Rhyne 1994; Morduch 2000). The best practices message has driven home the argument that heavily subsidized public credit programs are destined for failure, to be inevitably hobbled by booming default rates and weak targeting to poor households. By June 1986, for example, India's flagship Integrated Rural Development Programme was facing repayment rates of just 41 percent on loans to poor households (Pulley 1989, 33, table 5.20). By privileging full cost recovery at the expense of depth of outreach, however, best practices can be far off target for nonprofit programs whose bottom line is social impact.

Both improving health conditions and broadening access to financial services can offer critical ways to help households "hook" into growth processes. The focus is on these particular cases because they provide a telling contrast in policy approaches and because discussion of other linkages, notably labor market reform and educational policy, are the focus of other chapters in this volume.

While the two approaches start from opposite positions with respect to the efficacy of public action, both unite in a reluctance to explore effective public-private relations. The international health policy discussion does so by downplaying the role of the private sector and cost recovery, and the microfinance discussion does so by highlighting little else. Lessons from the vast body of microlevel theoretical and empirical work completed over the past two decades suggest, however, that poverty alleviation efforts can benefit substantially from public-private partnerships. Limits to government action have been described above, and limits to markets are also now better understood. Research has made progress in detailing these limits and in showing how families and community institutions help to mediate the problems. With respect to poverty alleviation, opening new markets and improving existing institutions can be an enormous benefit, but just improving markets will seldom ensure optimal redistribution. Inevitably, there are still loose ends in the research to date, but the broad sweep points to places where a private-public orientation can be most useful and examples are provided below.

Section 11.1 reviews new evidence on broad relations between economic growth and poverty. Sections 11.2 and 11.3 focus on health and finance. Section 11.4 describes possibilities for adding to how we conceptualize and measure poverty, and section 11.5 returns to the political incentives that constrain poverty alleviation policy.[3]

11.1   Redistribution with Growth Revisited

That poverty alleviation must go hand in hand with measures to increase national income was a central tenet of the work of the National Planning Committee of the Indian National Congress, formed in 1938 with Jawaharlal Nehru at its head. Nehru wrote that to "insure an irreducible minimum standard for everybody, national income had to be greatly increased . . . and we aimed at a 200 to 300 per cent increase in ten years" (Nehru 1946). The work of Indian planners after independence followed this line, with four main principles: (1) "The central concern of our planning has to be the removal of poverty as early as possible." (2) Without economic growth, income redistribution would lead to an average income that would still be "pitifully low." (3) Some degree of income inequality is needed in order to generate savings and incentives for investment. (4) Much of "rural activity is but loosely integrated with the growing sectors of the economy" so that "economic development is not likely to automatically lift the income of the entire population," leaving a fifth of the population in need of redistributive measures in order to benefit from the changing economy.[4]

---

3. The focus of the present paper is on long-term dynamic issues. Poverty alleviation policy is also concerned with addressing short-term emergencies such as those caused by drought, flooding, and dislocation brought on by economic and political upheaval. Drèze and Sen (1989) provided arguments on policy responses. The contributions in van de Walle and Nead (1995) offered perspectives on targeted redistribution.

4. The arguments are articulated in a paper circulated in August 1962 under the direction of Shri Pitambar Pant of the Planning Commission. The paper is reprinted as "Implications

Very similar ideas formed the basis of the World Bank's influential study, *Redistribution with Growth:* a strong belief in the importance of economic growth for poverty alleviation, but a pessimism that most poor households would benefit directly from such growth. The volume started with a concession: "It is now clear that more than a decade of rapid growth in underdeveloped countries has been of little or no benefit to perhaps a third of their population" (Chenery et al. 1974, xiii). Montek Ahluwalia, part of the Chenery team, subsequently presented cross-sectional evidence showing that inequality tended to worsen with growth before getting better, and this "Kuznets inverted-U" relationship was taken as a given.

This is no longer so. Evidence from the intervening decades yields no sharp evidence of an inverted U (see, e.g., Bruno, Ravallion, and Squire 1998, and the references therein), and the given is now that the growth-inequality relationship can go any which way.

Evidence on the growth-poverty relationship is much sharper and more encouraging. In analyzing eighty-eight recent periods of real growth in a cross section of countries, Deininger and Squire (1996) found, for example, that nearly 90 percent were associated with absolute improvements in income of the poorest quintile. Correspondingly, during seven periods of income decline, five led to worsening of the absolute position of the bottom quintile.[5]

Similarly, Bruno et al. (1998) considered the experiences of twenty countries between 1984 and 1993. Strikingly, they found that a 10 percent increase in mean income would, on average, lead to a 20 percent reduction in the fraction of the population living on less than one dollar per day, with gains felt by households considerably below the poverty line as well as those close to it.

The great bulk of the world's poor population turns out to be quite close to poverty lines. This can be seen by the relatively small size of the poverty gap measured across low-income countries. Using India's poverty line of $23 per capita per month (in 1985 U.S. dollars), Lipton and Ravallion (1995) reported that in 1985 the poverty gap (the cumulative amount of money that would be needed to completely eliminate poverty through perfectly targeted transfers) came to about 1 percent of total consumption in the developing world. Taking just the poorest one-third of countries, this

---

of Planning for a Minimum Level of Living" in Bardhan and Srinivasan (1974), and the quotes are from pages 13 and 14 of that volume. I thank T. N. Srinivasan for pointing me to relevant primary source materials.

5. In further investigating the thirteen anomalous cases, Deininger and Squire (1996) found only one robust anomaly: Colombia between 1970 and 1980, when income grew at slightly more than 2 percent while the income of the bottom quintile fell by just under 1 percent. Recent experiences in India are also consistent with these patterns. Between 1977–78 and 1988, the percentage of the population below the poverty line fell from 47 to 37 percent in urban areas of India and from 53 to 39 percent in rural areas. These changes have been attributed in largest part to growth (Datt and Ravallion 1992).

came to about 3 percent. Sustained broad-based growth can thus substantially reduce poverty rates—sooner rather than later. The emphasis on economic growth thus remains strong, while the urgency accorded to widespread income redistribution has withered.

This is not entirely uncontroversial, however. While the strongly redistributive push of the basic needs approach has few adherents today, echoes can be heard in recent arguments like those of Jean Drèze and Amartya Sen (1989). They argued that waiting for the fruit of economic growth can take years and that public action can (and should) be directed at helping poor households do better today. The argument underlies the approach to health policy described in the next section.

A striking example is given by the concerted malaria eradication campaign in Sri Lanka, which was followed by a drop in the mortality rate from malaria from 187 per 100,000 in 1946 to 66 in 1947 to 21 by 1953. Similarly, the Sri Lankan campaign against tuberculosis was associated with a drop in the morbidity level from 62 per 100,000 in 1940 to 16 per 100,000 by 1960. The crude death rate fell accordingly, from 22 per 1,000 in 1936 to below 10 by the 1950s. (The evidence here is from Rasaputra 1986, cited by Anand and Kanbur 1990.) Economic growth alone could not have delivered these results so quickly.

Drèze and Sen (1989) used country case studies and simple cross-country econometric regressions to buttress their argument. For example, they described a regression of the logarithm of the mortality rate for children under five on the logarithm of per capita GNP. (Child mortality rates provide a useful proxy for the basic welfare of poor households by reflecting the interaction of maternal health, education, child nutrition, and environmental conditions.) The same specification run for data on 122 countries (with populations over one million) in 1995 yields

$$\text{logarithm of child mortality} = \underset{(0.24)}{8.48} - \underset{(0.03)}{0.66}$$
$$* \text{ logarithm of GNP per capita,}$$

with standard errors in parentheses below and an R^2 of 0.77. The equation yields a strong negative correlation between income and mortality and a good fit (although the correlation is heightened by a long list of omitted variables).[6] The results are even stronger when estimating with GDP data adjusted to ensure purchasing power parity:

$$\text{logarithm of child mortality} = \underset{(0.34)}{10.82} - \underset{(0.04)}{0.89}$$
$$* \text{ logarithm of GDP per capita,}$$

---

6. The data are from World Bank (1998).

with an R^2 again of 0.77 (and 131 observations). The evidence shows that a 10 percent increase in average GDP is associated with a 9 percent drop in infant mortality.

The results suggest the efficacy of income-based strategies, but Drèze and Sen (1989) used the approach to point to countries that are doing much better than expected based on average income. They thus instead highlighted the efficacy of alternative strategies.

Analysis of the regression residuals shows that the child mortality rate in Sri Lanka, for example, is 26 percent of that predicted on the basis of its average income, a result due to earlier direct health interventions (as well as to geographic and institutional factors omitted from the specification). If income in Sri Lanka grew at a steady 3 percent per year, it would take forty-five years to reach the level of income associated with its current level of child mortality. Other countries with large residuals include countries with strong commitments to public health interventions like Jamaica (with mortality equal to 31 percent of predicted mortality) and former Soviet republics like Georgia (21 percent), Moldova (26), Azerbaijan (29), Armenia (29), Ukraine (30), Tajikistan (33), Estonia (39), Latvia (40), and Lithuania (45).[7] On the other end of the scale are countries with high levels of social and economic inequality: oil-rich countries like Saudi Arabia (155 percent) and Kuwait (172); Latin American countries with relatively high inequality like Peru (156 percent), Bolivia (163), Mexico (164), and Brazil (184); and a series of countries from sub-Saharan Africa (Gambia, Mauritania, Namibia, Guinea, Angola, South Africa, Botswana, and Gabon).

Without more careful analysis, the results are only suggestive. But they underscore the understandings put forward by Nehru and the National Planning Committee in considering poverty alleviation in the late 1930s. First, having more income is strongly associated with higher welfare. The strength of this relation is not all due to the causal link from income to welfare, however. But even if the true elasticity of health with respect to national income is a half (or a quarter) of the parameter estimate above, the responsiveness is still large and important. Second, without deliberate interventions, poor and socially isolated segments of populations are not guaranteed progress equal to that seen by others. The questions then become: How can policies encourage *broad-based* economic growth? How can interventions improve basic living standards for those for whom national economic growth is not sufficient in the medium term? How can political constraints be overcome? This mixed picture of the role of governments and markets provides the backdrop for viewing the two approaches considered below.

---

7. China is emphasized for being exceptional in Drèze and Sen's 1987 data, but once data adjusted for purchasing power parity are used, it turns out to be under five years of income growth (at just 3 percent per year) away from their predicted value for mortality.

11.2 Health Policy and Poverty Alleviation

Increasing human capital is thought to be one of the most critical ways for poor households to hook into growth processes. Although formal empirical work remains scant, improving health conditions is considered central to this aim: good health can enhance productivity (Strauss and Thomas 1995), and bad health can trigger and lengthen spells of poverty. While work on household behavior under risk in low-income countries has tended to focus on impacts of crop losses, health shocks are often even more devastating and deserve more attention (Kochar 1997).

Health inequalities remain large. Life expectancy in sub-Saharan Africa is just fifty years, while rates in East Asia exceed seventy years. Little over half of the sub-Saharan African population has access to health services and safe drinking water. There would appear to be little room for debate about the basic priorities for health policy in Africa and similar low-income regions. The life expectancy figures reflect the deaths of millions of children each year for lack of inexpensive inoculations or simple treatments for diarrhea. At the same time, modern hospitals are constructed in capital cities, equipped with cardiac units and cancer wards that serve mainly the urban rich at subsidized rates. In the 1980s, for example, Brazil, Jordan, and Venezuela were each spending over 70 percent of health budgets on large hospitals, while public health programs and community health centers went underfunded (World Bank 1993b). Few observers can avoid being frustrated at the imbalance.

This was the starting point of the ambitious and influential agenda on priorities for health care provision in low-income countries underwritten by the World Health Organization and implemented partly by faculty at Harvard's School of Public Health (Jamison et al. 1993). The World Bank's *World Development Report 1993: Investing in Health* partly represented the agenda, and the work still carries weight in some sectors of the Bank.

Faced with a web of problems in the health sector, the studies build around the aim of saving the greatest number of lives at the least expense. The approach begins with the calculation of the disability-adjusted life years (DALYs) that are saved through every intervention considered.[8] The framework provides a simple way to summarize health conditions. For example, calculation of DALYs shows that 45 percent of DALYs lost in

---

8. A DALY is a form of QALY (quality-adjusted life year). See Broome's (1993) discussion of QALYs and their limitations. By incorporating disabilities, the measure goes beyond life expectancy as a metric of health status and serves as a useful descriptive tool, allowing comparisons over different populations and diseases. In order to make comprehensive comparisons, the great bulk of the data on illness-specific mortality rates were of necessity estimated, extrapolated, or otherwise constructed, but unfortunately, standard errors were not provided for the estimates.

sub-Saharan Africa were due to "largely preventable or inexpensively curable diseases of children" like diarrhea, measles, respiratory infections, worm infections, and malaria (World Bank 1993b, 113), whereas in Asia the percentage was 25 to 30 percent.

The principle is put into practice in calculations of cost-effectiveness ratios that determine a package of "essential clinical services" that, it is argued, should be given priority in public spending since they save the greatest number of DALYs per dollar. The World Bank estimates that investing $100,000 in chemotherapy for tuberculosis, for example, would save the lives of about five hundred patients and reduce infection to others, gaining around 35,000 DALYs. The same investment in diabetes management, for example, would save only about 400 DALYs since the expected gain is less than a year of healthy life and again about five hundred patients could be treated. Treating tuberculosis thus gets high priority (World Bank 1993b, chap. 3, 61).

How much does the cost-effectiveness approach add to what we already know? In general, the policy priorities that emerge are not surprising: improve education, combat virulently communicable diseases, and encourage preventive care and the improvement of infrastructure like housing and sanitation. Even without cost-effectiveness calculations, a very similar list of priorities would likely have been drawn up since many of the top priorities can also be justified with reference to public goods (sanitation), externalities (disease control, education), and myopia (preventive care).

These basic public finance elements, however, are not well integrated into the cost-effectiveness approach. The tuberculosis-versus-diabetes case, for example, gives priority to addressing tuberculosis because of the threat of contagion, but it does so in a purely mechanistic way. The logic of priority setting in the cost-effectiveness approach does not arise because the presence of externalities associated with tuberculosis leads to a market failure (and thus yields a potentially beneficial role for state intervention). Instead, the priorities emerge from an accounting exercise that is not fundamentally rooted in the basic economic, social, and political circumstances of the given countries.

Does the logic really matter if most of the final rankings seem sensible? An affirmative answer springs from two main arguments. First, some key rankings can (and do) change depending on the approach taken. Second, the cost-effectiveness approach yields little guidance on the critical next steps in implementing policies.

A first fundamental tension is that the framework centers on priorities for public action, but many of the same governments that we see today were the ones that created misallocations yesterday. Cost-effectiveness advocates suggest that with better information (and growing public awareness), governments will start to rectify past mistakes. It is hard to believe, however, that all of the misguided priorities of the past arose from limited information about the cost-effectiveness of interventions. It seems reasonable to assume instead that governments make choices in part to acquire prestige, seek rents, and accommodate interest groups, in addition to trying to maximize some notion of welfare. These factors are often at odds with improving health conditions and are unlikely to change on their own, and I return to them briefly in the conclusion.

Second, the most relevant question for health planners is not what the government should do if it were the primary health provider for its population. Instead, the key question typically concerns what the government should do given the existing mix of health providers, markets, and local institutions. In most countries, the private health sector is large and important. In India, for example, nearly 80 percent of health spending goes through the private sector. In Asia, outside of India and China, roughly 60 percent is private, and even in China, 40 percent is provided outside of state mechanisms. Private markets account for 44 percent of spending on health in sub-Saharan Africa, 65 percent in Indonesia, 40 percent in Latin America and the Caribbean, and 29 percent in the former socialist countries. Among richer countries, private markets account for 25 percent of spending on health in Japan, 57 percent in the United States, and roughly 40 percent in the "established market economies" as a whole (basically the OECD). (Calculations are based on World Bank 1993b, appendix table A.9.)

Third, looking beyond the cost-effectiveness approach can highlight a broader set of socially valuable interventions (as well as places where public interventions will be of limited benefit). It also leads to new questions, such as, How can incentives be maintained in government health institutions? How do failures in markets for health services compare to market failures elsewhere? When can costs be recovered through user fees? How can improvements be best attained when governments are weak? These are the sorts of questions that are actively debated in the United States and in other OECD countries. They are no less relevant in less developed countries, but the new cost-effectiveness framework gives no direction. It is easy to imagine, though, that the answers to these questions will reshape priorities that emerge from simple cost-effectiveness orderings, and new research shows ways that this can happen.

A related set of inquiries concerns the simultaneous public and private provision of health services. While cost-effectiveness calculations tend to point to the efficacy of primary care, Hammer, Nabid, and Cercone (1995), for example, found that the net marginal impact of government spending on doctors in Malaysia was not significant with respect to infant mortality reductions (while immunizations mattered). Alderman and Lavy (1996) found similar sorts of crowding out of private health service provision. Ranking state interventions ought to take into account institutions that are already in place. For example, the private sector in low-income countries tends to focus on ambulatory care—that is, not inpatient hospital care and not preventive medicine. Private household spending in India, for example, constitutes 92 percent of primary curative care expenses, which itself is nearly half of total national spending on health. Governments only account for 24 percent of inpatient treatment expenditures, with households paying out of pocket for drugs and supplies (Berman 1998).

Of course, not all private care is high quality. Rohde and Vishwanath (1995), for example, considered a series of large Indian surveys and found that 80 percent of rural private "doctors" were in fact not certified at all, with only half having received formal health care training. Government clinics, on the other hand, while free, also tend to be low quality. Although many private practitioners are "less than fully qualified," they can handle many basic problems, and government clinics in no sense operate in a vacuum. Cost-effectiveness studies focus on the benefits of direct provision, but allocating part of government budgets to instead maintaining quality in the private sector (and encouraging expansion) may do more to improve health conditions than providing services directly.

Turning to poverty alleviation more specifically, another set of questions involves priorities that emerge when maximizing a broad notion of social welfare (or minimizing poverty), rather than maximizing a narrow gauge of health. For example, consider market failures due to asymmetric information. Welfare losses associated with the failure of markets to insure against high-cost but low-probability diseases can be higher than losses associated with failures to insure against low-cost, common health problems (which are already largely handled by private health providers). Thus optimal policy prescriptions will favor interventions that might otherwise appear to among the *least* cost-effective interventions (where "cost-effectiveness" is measured along the narrow dimension of health improvements only). Gertler and Gruber (1997), for example, found that Indonesian families can insure adequately against about 70 percent of common, moderate-size health shocks, but they are only able to deflect 30 percent of the negative impacts on consumption levels when health problems are major. This kind of evidence provides a compelling reason to consider public provision of insurance against catastrophic illness, despite a low cost-effectiveness rating.[9]

9. See Hammer (1993) for a specific treatment and Drèze and Stern (1987) for a general treatment. Benefits (lives saved) should properly be viewed in a general equilibrium framework. The calculation of DALYs is done so that sparing a child from death from measles is accorded the value of a lifetime saved. But if that child has a high likelihood of dying later from tuberculosis, many fewer years have been saved. This has implications for using the cost-effectiveness criterion. E.g., imagine that one disease, call it A, affects infants and another disease B affects older children. A proportion a of infants die from disease A, and a proportion b of the survivors die from disease B. To simplify matters, assume that if we reduce the incidence of disease B by one person, that person will live a long and healthy life

From a broader perspective, health issues cannot be disconnected from a household's general ability to protect welfare levels. A key element that makes health risks very different from other concerns is that illness often calls for immediate attention. If the condition is severe, it could require drawing down or reallocating assets substantially (Kochar 1997). Thus, when an earner becomes sick, the whole family suffers and may never recover financially.[10] The health problem thus can link closely to issues of insurance and finance. Viewing the problem in an integrated way can help show where improvements in insurance mechanisms can improve household welfare more than direct health interventions—or vice versa. But much more needs to be known about the relation among illness, uncertainly, and earning power.

In sum, the cost-effectiveness approach to health reform is most useful when addressed to well-intentioned bureaucracies that are the central providers of medical services but that lack comprehensive information on the mapping of medical inputs to medical outcomes. This is hardly the norm. Real progress in health sector reform and poverty alleviation will not come without paying closer attention to political incentives and the interrelations of government action, markets, and household behavior. Much will be gained by more fully integrating lessons from household economics and studies of markets and contracts into the conversation.

11.3 Finance and Poverty Alleviation

If leading health sector analysts have too readily ignored the private sector, leading microfinance advocates have too quickly dismissed ongoing private-public partnerships. Microfinance best practices focus strongly on the goal of becoming fully profit-making institutions, fueled by a strong suspicion of government involvement.

The microfinance movement has led the way in privileging the role of nongovernmental organizations, focusing on gender, and paying keen attention to incentives and delivery mechanisms. It has strongly argued that much poverty can be alleviated by providing small loans to poor house-

---

thereafter. If we reduce the incidence of A by one person, that person might live a long life or, with probability b, die from disease B. Thus, even if curing a child of disease A is less expensive than curing a child of disease B, if b is large enough, it will turn out that curing B *ultimately* saves more DALYs per dollar. (For simplicity, I have not valued the years between infancy and childhood. The point is just to illustrate the principle.) Dow et al. (1997), e.g., showed how these spillovers matter in practice. Expanding vaccination coverage in sub-Saharan Africa led to actions by mothers to improve neonatal care, increasing the average birthweight of children and thus lowering the incidence of infant mortality more broadly. Simple cost-effectiveness measures miss these kinds of spillovers.

10. Partly because of this, DALYs are calculated with weights on prime-age earners that are three to four times that of a year of life of young children or the elderly. However, this practice is ad hoc and not sufficient to capture the essence of the problem. See Anand and Hanson (1997) for a broader critique of issues in weighting DALYs.

holds—and that this can be done efficiently, despite a very mixed history of previous credit programs. All of this has put microfinance in the vanguard of new efforts to alleviate poverty.[11]

In the past two decades, a diverse assortment of new programs have been set up worldwide, and globally there are now about eight to ten million households served by microfinance programs, with continuing efforts to rapidly expand. Most of these programs lend small amounts, starting at around $75, to would-be entrepreneurs, and they employ a variety of innovative contractual forms in lieu of collateral, most notably group lending with joint liability (Morduch 1999a).

A slowly expanding minority of programs function well as banks and make modest profits. The leading two examples are Bolivia's BancoSol and the unit *desa* program of Indonesia's Bank Rakyat Indonesia (BRI). In 1995, for example, BRI made profits of $175 million through its unit *desa* operations, and it would have covered costs while charging its clients a real rate of just 7 percent per year for loans (Yaron, Benjamin, and Charitonenko 1998).

But these programs mainly cater to the "richest of the poor" and to nonpoor households (and BRI requires collateral), and unit costs are substantially lower than for programs focused on poor clients. At the end of 1998, the average loan balance at BancoSol was above $900 and that for BRI (at the end of 1996) was above $1,000. In contrast, average loan balances at Bangladesh's Grameen Bank, a subsidized bank with a strong commitment to depth of outreach, were $134 (August 1998). No carefully documented case shows that any of the few existing profit-making microfinance institutions are appreciably reducing poverty. (They may be making contributions in other ways, however, and once an appropriate regulatory framework is set up, experience suggests that it makes sense to get governments out of the way. These programs can then expand, contract, and innovate with market opportunities.)[12]

Leaders of the microfinance movement have been slow to accept the tension between profitability and poverty alleviation. For the most part, profit-seeking banks fail to penetrate further in low-income areas because

---

11. Adams and von Pischke (1992) described failures of subsidized credit programs. The greatest emphasis of the movement has been on credit, but encouraging saving is gaining in importance. Early microfinance programs were not effective in mobilizing savings and showed little interest in doing so. Partly, it was thought that poor households were too poor to save. One of the lessons from the recent microfinance experience, however, is that even poor households are eager to save if given appealing interest rates and flexible accounts. Providing appealing savings vehicles may be more valuable than production credit for poor households, since it also offers a tool for consumption smoothing.

12. One possible exception may be the Badan Kredit Desa (BKD) program, also from Indonesia. The BKD gives loans that average about $70 with three-month terms and real interest rates just under 50 percent per year. But there is no documentation of its client profiles or studies of its social impacts or evidence of its replicability. For best practices to be most convincing, priority should be given to better documenting cases like this.

transactions costs per unit for $100 loans can easily be over five times higher than for $500 loans, and making ends meet is a continual challenge. A recent survey shows that those programs that do maintain a focus on poverty cover only about 70 percent of their full costs (despite a stated "commitment" to achieving financial sustainability; *MicroBanking Bulletin* 1998). Loan officers fear that raising interest rates to breakeven levels will deter too many target clients, but the conversation is stalemated for lack of hard evidence (see Morduch 2000).

Lack of evidence has also hindered studies of the costs and benefits of subsidization. Most important, only a handful of social impact evaluations have had convincing control-treatment comparisons, and the evidence from those yields a mixed picture. Using data from 1991–92, for example, I found that Bangladeshi households with access to the Grameen Bank have no higher average consumption levels than comparable households without access, nor are their children substantially more likely to be in school. Pitt and Khandker (1998) found some net increases for the consumption of borrowers from Grameen (especially when the borrower is a woman: consumption rises by eighteen cents for every dollar borrowed) and some impacts on schooling. But their econometric approach required strong identifying assumptions, and the results are not evident when using simpler methods. Studies collected in Hulme and Mosley (1996) showed that households participating in eleven programs in a range of countries had income increases that were 117 to 544 percent of the increases seen by control groups. The control groups often started out much poorer than the treated groups, and sample sizes were small, however, so these results are suggestive at best.

It may be, though, that the greatest impacts for poor households lie elsewhere. Like Pitt and Khandker, I found evidence that households with access to Grameen have far less variable consumption patterns across seasons than households without access. And Hashemi, Schuler, and Riley (1996) pointed to improvements in the social status of women and in measures of "empowerment." Discussions of poverty alleviation are only now beginning to place a strong emphasis on reducing consumption variability and improving social status as ends in themselves, and it may be that financial approaches can help. With a client base that is 95 percent female, the Grameen Bank and institutions like it have proved able to serve women in ways that have eluded other approaches.

If these initial results prove to be robust, are the benefits greater than the costs of subsidization? Having a constructive conversation will require a frank assessment of institutional progress to date. The Grameen Bank has been a true leader in the movement, providing hope and opportunity to its two million clients, and its model has now been replicated on four continents. But a close look at the accounting data from 1985 to 1996 shows that the Grameen Bank's repayment rates appeared to be around

92 percent, rather than the 98 percent it reported, a difference large enough to critically undermine prospects for financial self-sufficiency.[13] And while the bank reported $1.5 million in profits between 1985 and 1996, my calculations suggest that it would have posted losses of $26 to $30 million in 1996 alone had it made timely provisions for overdue loans, not counted funds from grants as income, and not received cheap credit. Grameen paid an average of 3.7 percent on borrowed capital (a −1.7 percent real rate), and the total value of access to these soft loans was $79.2 million between 1985 and 1996. An additional implicit subsidy of $47.3 million was received by Grameen through access to equity that was used to generate returns below opportunity costs.[14] Pulling the evidence together indicates that for 1985–96, Grameen would have faced a deficit summing to about $150 million if it had had to pay "market" interest rates, make timely provisions for loan losses, and eschew direct grants. The deficit could have been eliminated by increasing nominal interest rates on its general loan product from 20 to 33 percent (and similarly raising charges elsewhere).[15] But the bank is reluctant to do so for fear of undermining social impacts.

Even if the bank and programs like it are not the economic miracles that many have claimed, they may still do much good.[16] So why have there not been cost-benefit studies of subsidization? Part of the answer is that they can be costly and difficult to do well. But the problem also lies partly with the narrow set of best practices. In failing to acknowledge the trade-off between profitability and poverty alleviation, best practices view profitability as sufficient evidence of success (e.g., Consultative Group to Assist the Poorest 1996). Studies of social impacts have thus been seen as immaterial. Subsidies are most often seen as the root of problems, not as a possible part of the answer.

13. The financial calculations in this section are from Morduch (1998b). The reported rates of loans overdue take the amount of loans overdue over one year (or two years) as the numerator. The denominator is the size of the current portfolio. The recalculation instead uses the size of the portfolio at the time that the loans were made.

14. Although subsidies have increased over time in absolute quantities, the bank's scale has grown even more quickly. As a result, the subsidy per dollar outstanding has fallen substantially, leveling off at about eight cents on the dollar.

15. Inflation has been about 5 percent recently. Alternatively, radically stripping down administrative costs would provide breathing room—the path taken by the Association for Social Advancement, another large competitor. In the early 1990s salary and personnel costs accounted for half of Grameen's total costs, while interest costs were held below 25 percent. Lowering wages has been impossible since they are linked to government wage scales, so the emphasis has had to be on increasing efficiency. By 1996, salary and personnel costs were roughly equal to interest costs (Morduch 1999b).

16. It should be noted, however, that their official rhetoric stays with the pursuit of financial sustainability. The Grameen Bank's current path, pursuing cross-subsidization and alternative income generation projects (including an Internet provision service and other for-profit spinoffs), is appealing in the medium term, but it has its own perils: the bank's mission risks getting diluted and profitable sectors are vulnerable to competition over time.

The antisubsidy stance springs from three worries. First, donors can be fickle, and programs that aim to exist into the future need independence. Second, donor budgets are limited, restricting the scale of operations to the size of the dole. Self-sufficient programs, on the other hand, can expand to meet demand. Third, subsidized programs run the risk of becoming inefficient without hard bottom lines.

It is not obvious, though, that the three worries are founded. It is true that donors can be fickle, but governments may find value in subsidizing microfinance well after international agencies have moved on. If subsidized microfinance proves to deliver more bang for the buck than other social investments, should subsidies be turned down? Second, scale certainly matters, but small, well-targeted programs can also play critical roles in broader poverty alleviation strategies.

The third issue, the danger of slipping into inefficiency, has been demonstrated many times over by large public banks. Heavy, direct government involvement in credit programs has almost uniformly been a disaster in the past. But the key to efficiency is the maintenance of hard budget constraints, not necessarily profits. Several donors already use strict and explicit performance targets when lending to microfinance institutions, conditioning future tranches on performance to date. The lessons can be applied more widely. The kind of relationship that is needed would, for example, entail clear and credible guidelines for letting subsidized programs fail when they fall below their given targets. Ongoing independent evaluations will be critical to this success.

Where does this leave the research agenda? The central issue is whether subsidized microfinance is better or worse than alternative antipoverty programs, and cost-benefit studies are a priority. Those studies will need to treat counterfactual scenarios carefully. Those who argue against subsidies assert that approaching full profitability is unlikely to make a major dent in the depth of outreach. If true, subsidization can have large opportunity costs, and more poverty can be reduced without subsidies than with.

Much comes down to a debate about a parameter: the elasticity of credit demand with respect to the interest rate. And no one has much more than anecdotes to support their claims. Practitioners in Bangladesh tend to believe that the elasticity is high, and accordingly they keep interest rates relatively low (below 25 percent real). Practitioners in Latin America tend to believe that the elasticity is low, and they set interest rates as high as needed (BancoSol's real rate approaches 40 percent). Both could be correct in their contexts, but since comparisons are meaningless without controlling for client profiles by occupation and income, much more work needs to be done here. Until then, discussants are likely to continue talking at cross-purposes.

As with health policy, greater emphasis is also needed on issues of industrial organization. To what degree will subsidized programs crowd out private providers, both formal and informal? How can incentives in non-profits be maintained? To what degree will achieving financial sustainability ensure that microfinance institutions gain substantially greater access to capital markets (especially when their main assets remain portfolios not backed by collateral)?

Finally, in viewing the promise of microfinance broadly, it is helpful to assess prospects in places where microfinance has not yet taken root. Programs have done best in reasonably stable, densely populated areas. Experience so far shows that microfinance faces its greatest challenges in places where the problem of poverty is deepest: in areas of low population density and areas with highly seasonal income patterns (e.g., in rural sub-Saharan Africa). Even in the best of circumstances, credit from microfinance programs helps to fund self-employment activities that most often supplement income for borrowers rather than drive fundamental shifts in employment patterns. It has not proved able to generate substantial numbers of new jobs for others. Making a real dent in poverty rates will require increasing overall levels of economic growth and employment generation, and microfinance cannot substitute for these processes.

Still, microfinance has made great headway in the face of widespread doubt, and it has opened up exciting possibilities. While hopes that microfinance institutions can effectively and widely serve core groups of poor households and also make a profit have yet to be realized, recent research suggests ways that incentives and efficiency can be maintained in nonprofit programs. With creativity, the interests of both public and private sectors can be brought together in new approaches built on understandings of markets and informal institutions, backed by ongoing cost-benefit studies.

11.4   The Concept and Measurement of Poverty

Until here, the specific definition of "poverty" has largely been left open. But the way that we think about poverty and its alleviation is conditioned by how we measure it. We most often measure poverty in a very narrow way, focusing on current deprivations in consumption or income. Measures like the United Nations Development Program's Human Development Index (HDI; and, more satisfactorily, Morris's Physical Quality of Life Index) attempt to broaden the concept. But by tossing measures of national income and social indicators into a single index with no theoretical rationale, the HDI offers little help in policy formulation (Ravallion 1997). If we are to move beyond traditional measures, it would be useful instead to gauge the condition of poor households along the dimensions of growth, vulnerability, mobility, and other features linked to policy issues—treating these aspects specifically and separately.

Refining traditional income-based approaches is also critical, whether one views income as a means to achieving broader aspects of welfare or as an end in itself. Academic work on poverty measurement has yielded a broad array of measures from which to choose. Strikingly, it is the simplest measures, the headcount index (the fraction of the population living below a given poverty line) and the poverty gap, that continue to see most use. Their popularity remains despite cogent criticisms from academics—notably that both measures are invariant under regressive transfers from poor households to less poor households (Watts 1968).[17]

The academic agenda has followed Sen (1976) to develop indexes that are instead rooted in axioms with broader appeal (the satisfaction of the Pigou-Dalton transfer principle, e.g.) or followed Atkinson (1987) to use notions of stochastic dominance to make rankings of poverty levels in income distributions without having to invoke particular poverty measures or, in some cases, even poverty lines (see the surveys in Deaton 1997 and Lipton and Ravallion 1995). Both approaches can yield robust information on whether there was an overall improvement or a setback, or whether the results are indeterminate—which is sometimes all a policymaker needs to know.

So why do the methods not find greater use? The answer, I suspect, is that policymakers typically desire to know much more than just simple rankings. Understandably, policymakers often want to be able to compare specific costs against specific benefits in order to weigh alternative policies. Debating these issues requires cardinal information, not just rankings of distributions. Increasingly, the compromise solution has been to measure poverty at varying poverty lines, so that observers can gauge the extent of "hardcore" poverty as well as overall poverty levels. Although not elegant, it is a simple step in the right direction.

The greatest payoff will be in developing other indexes like the headcount that are less ad hoc but still "meaningful"—that is, that yield cardinal information that can, in principle, map into (and expand) policy discussion (Foster 1994). Morduch (1998b) provided one example of the way existing information can be aggregated to broaden perspectives on the poverty problem, and there are many other possibilities.

While the headcount index counts people and the poverty gaps adds up money, the average exit time proposed in Morduch (1998b) maps the income distribution to the space of time. Specifically, it answers the hypothetical question: how long will it take, on average, for the population to reach a given poverty line if the income of all individuals grows at a given annual rate? The index thus provides a simple metric of the potential for economic growth to reduce poverty. Formally, if the income of household

17. The distributional sensitivity implied by the transfer axiom can be important. Consider, e.g., the effects of rice price increases in Java, Indonesia, in 1981. Headcount measures of poverty fell because most poor households were farmers (net rice producers). However, distributionally sensitive measures rose because the very poorest households were landless (net rice consumers) and were made much worse off (World Bank 1990, box 2.2).

i grows at a constant positive rate g per year, the number of years that it would take to reach the poverty line, z, via growth is $t_i = (\ln z - \ln y_i)/g$ for households below the poverty line and $t_i = 0$ for those above.

In Bangladesh, for example, the median poor rural household in the 1988–89 Household Expenditure Survey spent Tk. 284 per month per capita relative to the poverty line of Tk. 370 (in 1989, Tk. 32.1 = $1). So if their expenditure grew at 3 percent per year, it would take 8.8 years to reduce half of rural poverty through growth alone. While rough, this sort of calculation identifies the contribution that growth can make to poverty alleviation, and it can be a useful input to policy discussions.

The average exit time is then simply t_i averaged over the entire population. The index turns out to be a simple ordinal transformation of the index proposed by Watts (1968) and thus has its appealing ordinal properties.[18] Like the poverty gap, the measure describes an important "if-then" relationship and is based on "best case" assumptions. Even though growth is unlikely to be constant or uniform across households, by using best case assumptions rather than context-specific assumptions, the average exit time is clear, simple, and comparable across regions and time periods.

Expanding frameworks like this can bring into relief the next steps in understanding the dynamics of poverty—for example, better understanding why the income of some households grows faster than others, and why some are better able to take advantage of the fruit of broad-based development. As a starting point, measures of households' poverty over time will provide policymakers with a sense of the degree of poor households' mobility and vulnerability to adverse events. The inquiries should also highlight gender dimensions of poverty. Do women and girls bear disproportionate costs of coping with risk? Are they more vulnerable to downturns? How do gender roles and attitudes change through time?

Shaffer (1998) provided a comparison of a traditional poverty analysis focused on describing patterns of income versus a participatory poverty assessment that allows qualitative inputs from interviewees living in the same poor regions of Guinea. He found that traditional metrics show little evidence of gender biases in poverty rates. But in the participatory assessment there was consensus that women were considerably worse off than men: first, women worked harder and, second, they had less say in family choices.

Using "nontraditional" approaches like participatory poverty assessments will help to bring these kinds of tensions to light, but they are time intensive and typically based on small samples. The continuing challenge is to broaden the focus of large, high-quality household surveys.

---

18. The measure satisfies the monotonicity transfer and transfer sensitivity axioms. As a result of its additively separable form, the measure is also decomposable into the population-weighted measures of subpopulations of the poor.

11.5   Concluding Thoughts: Political Incentives

The potential role for public-private partnerships has been raised above, but improving poverty alleviation policy will require far more than workable ideas: it will also depend on political commitment. Much of the discussion of international health policy assumes the benevolence of bureaucracies. In contrast, one of the critical steps for the microfinance movement has been to try to avoid governments entirely.

For the most part, the leading players in microfinance are nongovernmental organizations, backed mainly by private foundations and international donors. But this backing will inevitably weaken, and with most programs running at losses, the near-exclusive focus on externally funded nongovernmental organizations will have to soften. Limits arising from turning to a full-market orientation have been described above, so alternatively, governments will have to be viewed as viable partners. This is already happening in China (with mixed results). These public-private partnerships will require a new and careful engagement between programs and governments.

Creating effective private-public relationships has to at least begin by taking government objectives seriously. The tension between political incentives and antipoverty policy is made concrete by the recent backlash against targeted poverty alleviation programs.[19] If political viability is a concern, targeted programs may be inferior to universal programs in which everyone, rich and poor, receives transfers. First, as it is sometimes said, "programs for the poor are poor programs." Their political constituency is often weak, and they are often administered poorly. Second, poor households may do better by getting a smaller share of a larger pie rather than a larger share of a smaller one. One example is given by the fiscal reforms in Sri Lanka in the 1970s. The switch from universal food subsidies to targeted food stamps was followed by reductions in the budget, and the real value of the transfers was allowed to be cut in half through inflation. Anand and Kanbur (1990) argued that this was due to indifference on the part of the middle class and a weak voice on the part of the poor. As a result, poor households suffered absolutely despite better targeting (Lipton and Ravallion 1995). Another example is given by social security in the United States, which is the most important "antipoverty" program by far, although it is designed as a universal pension program.

All the same, universal programs can be expensive; when budgets are tight and fiscal instruments are limited, some form of targeting is imperative. Cheap preventive health measures have successfully been provided universally. But universally subsidized clinical services or subsidized credit

19. See, e.g., van de Walle (1998) and the comments by Lawrence Summers in Tanzi and Chu (1998).

would surely be too costly and difficult to work. Where possible, one way forward is to ease tensions and build political commitments through working with the private sector to help provide the relevant public goods.

Another is to push to better understand the genesis of political constraints. New analytical tools developed under the banner of "positive political economy" are helping researchers to understand voting patterns and bureaucratic decisions in contexts with a clear set of constituencies. When it comes to poverty alleviation, constituencies in support of aggressive policies are often weak, although the beneficiaries of the policies are often numerous. Understanding the lack of political resolve on poverty alleviation will be helped by taking a step backward from the basic positive political economy framework to better understand why poor households often mobilize along ethnic, religious, or regional lines (if at all), rather than along class lines. The inquiry may also yield an important by-product: through better understanding the genesis of political consciousness and the determination of allegiances, researchers may find a deeper appreciation of the condition of poverty itself.

References

Adams, Dale, and J. D. von Pischke. 1992. Microenterprise credit programs: Deja vu. *World Development* 20 (10): 1463–70.

Alderman, Harold, and Victor Lavy. 1996. Household response to public health services: Cost and quality trade-offs. *World Bank Research Observer* 11, no. 1 (February).

Anand, Sudhir, and Kara Hanson. 1997. Disability-adjusted life years: A critical review. *Journal of Health Economics* 16:685–702.

Anand, Sudhir, and Ravi Kanbur. 1990. Public policy and basic need provision: Intervention and achievement in Sri Lanka. In *The political economy of hunger,* vol. 3, ed. Jean Drèze, Amartya Sen, and Athar Hussain. Oxford: Clarendon.

Atkinson, A. B. 1987. On the measurement of poverty. *Econometrica* 55, no. 4 (July): 749–64.

Bardhan, Pranab, and T. N. Srinivasan, eds. 1974. *Poverty and income distribution in India.* Calcutta: Statistical Publishing Society.

Berman, Peter. 1998. Rethinking health care systems: Private health care provision in India. *World Development* 26, no. 8 (August): 1463–79.

Broome, John. 1993. QALYs. *Journal of Public Economics* 50 (2): 149–67.

Bruno, Michael, Martin Ravallion, and Lyn Squire. 1998. Equity and growth in developing countries: Old and new perspectives on the policy issues. In *Income distribution and high-quality growth,* ed. Vito Tanzi and Ke-young Chu. Cambridge, Mass.: MIT Press.

Chen, Shaohua, and Martin Ravallion. 1996. Data in transition: Assessing rural living standards in southern China. *China Economic Review* 7:23–56.

Chenery, Hollis, Montek S. Ahluwalia, C. L. G. Bell, John H. Dulloy, and Richard Jolly. 1974. *Redistribution with growth.* London: Oxford University Press.

Consultative Group to Assist the Poorest. 1996. Microcredit interest rates. Occasional Paper no. 1. Washington, D.C.: Consultative Group to Assist the Poorest, August.

Datt, Gaurav, and Martin Ravallion. 1992. Growth and redistribution components of changes in poverty measures: A decomposition with applications to Brazil and India in the 1980s. *Journal of Development Economics* 38:275–95.

Deaton, Angus. 1997. *The analysis of household surveys.* Baltimore: Johns Hopkins University Press.

Deininger, Klaus, and Lyn Squire. 1996. A new data set measuring income inequality. *World Bank Economic Review* 10, no. 3 (September): 565–91.

Dow, William H., Thoams Philipson, Xavier Sala-i-Martin, and Jessica Holmes. 1997. Health investment complementarities under competing risks. Santa Monica, Calif.: RAND. Draft.

Drèze, Jean, and Amartya Sen. 1989. *Hunger and public action.* Oxford: Clarendon.

Drèze, Jean, and Nicholas Stern. 1987. The theory of cost-benefit analysis. In *Handbook of public economics,* ed. Alan Auerbach and Martin Feldstein, 909–89. Amsterdam: North-Holland.

Foster, James. 1994. Normative measurement: Is theory relevant? *American Economic Review Papers and Proceedings* 84, no. 2 (May): 365–70.

Gertler, Paul, and Jonathan Gruber. 1997. Insuring consumption against illness. NBER Working Paper no. 6035. Cambridge, Mass.: National Bureau of Economic Research, May.

Hammer, Jeffrey S. 1993. Prices and protocols in public health care. *World Bank Economic Review* 11 (3): 409–32.

Hammer, Jeffrey S., Ijez Nabid, and James Cercone. 1995. The incidence of public spending in health in Malaysia. In *Public spending and the poor,* ed. Dominique van de Walle and Kimberly Nead. Baltimore: Johns Hopkins University Press.

Hashemi, Syed M., Sidney Ruth Schuler, and Ann P. Riley. 1996. Rural credit programs and women's empowerment in Bangladesh. *World Development* 24 (4): 635–53.

Hulme, David, and Paul Mosley, eds. 1996. *Finance against poverty.* London: Routledge.

Jamison, Dean T., W. Henry Mosley, Anthony R. Measham, and José-Luis Bobadilla, eds. 1993. *Disease control priorities in developing countries.* New York: Oxford University Press.

Kochar, Anjini. 1997. Household savings and portfolio choices in developing countries: The impact of ill-health, income uncertainty and credit constraints. Stanford, Calif.: Stanford University, Department of Economics. Draft.

Krueger, Anne. 1990. Government failures in development. *Journal of Economic Perspectives* 4, no. 3 (summer): 9–23.

Lipton, Michael, and Martin Ravallion. 1995. Poverty and policy. In *Handbook of development economics,* vol. 3, ed. Jere Behrman and T. N. Srinivasan. Amsterdam: North-Holland.

MicroBanking Bulletin. 1998. Boulder, Colo.: Economics Institute, July.

Morduch, Jonathan. 1998a. Does microfinance really help the poor? New evidence from flagship programs in Bangladesh. Princeton, N.J.: Princeton University, Research Program in Development Studies. Draft.

———. 1998b. Growth, poverty, and average exit time. *Economics Letters* 58:385–90.

———. 1999a. The microfinance promise. *Journal of Economic Literature* 37, no. 4 (December): 1569–1614.

———. 1999b. The role of subsidies in microfinance: Evidence from the Grameen Bank. *Journal of Development Economics* 60 (October): 229–48.

————. 2000. The microfinance schism. *World Development* 28, no. 4 (April): 617–30.

Nehru, Jawaharlal. 1946. *Discovery of India.* New York: Jay.

Otero, Maria, and Elisabeth Rhyne. 1994. *The new world of microenterprise finance.* West Hartford, Conn.: Kumarian.

Park, Albert, Sangui Wang, and Guobao Wu. 1997. Assessing China's war on poverty. Ann Arbor: University of Michigan, Department of Economics. Draft.

Pitt, Mark, and Shahidur Khandker. 1998. The impact of group-based credit programs on poor households in Bangladesh: Does the gender of participants matter? *Journal of Political Economy* 106, no. 5 (October): 958–96.

Pulley, Robert. 1989. *Making the poor creditworthy: A case study of the integrated rural development program in India.* World Bank Discussion Paper no. 58. Washington, D.C.: World Bank.

Rasaputra, W. 1986. Public policy: An assessment of the Sri Lanka experience. Helsinki: Central Bank of Ceylon and World Institute for Development Economics Research. Draft.

Ravallion, Martin. 1997. Good and bad growth: The human development reports. *World Development* 25 (5): 631–38.

Rohde, J. E., and H. Vishwanath. 1995. *The rural private practitioner.* New Delhi: Oxford University Press.

Sen, Amartya. 1976. Poverty: An ordinal approach to measurement. *Econometrica* 44:219–31.

Shaffer, Paul. 1998. Who's "Poor"? Comparing household survey and participatory poverty assessment results from the Republic of Guinea. *World Development* 26 (12): 2119–35.

Strauss, John, and Duncan Thomas. 1995. Human resources: Empirical modeling of household and family decisions. In *Handbook of development economics,* vol. 3a, ed. Jere Behrman and T. N. Srinivasan. Amsterdam: North-Holland.

Streeten, Paul, with Shahid Javed Burki, Mahbub Ul Haq, Norman Hicks, and Frances Stewart. 1981. *First things first: Meeting basic human needs in developing countries.* New York: Oxford University Press.

Tanzi, Vito, and Ke-young Chu, eds. 1998. *Income distribution and high-quality growth.* Cambridge, Mass.: MIT Press.

van de Walle, Dominique. 1998. Targeting revisited. *World Bank Research Observer* 13, no. 2 (August): 231–48.

van de Walle, Dominique, and Kimberly Nead, eds. 1995. *Public spending and the poor.* Baltimore: Johns Hopkins University Press.

Watts, Harold. 1968. An economic definition of poverty. In *On understanding poverty,* ed. Daniel Patrick Moynihan. New York: Basic Books.

World Bank. 1990. *World development report 1990.* New York: Oxford University Press.

————. 1993a. *The East Asian miracle.* Washington, D.C.: World Bank.

————. 1993b. *World development report 1993.* New York: Oxford University Press.

————. 1997. *Poverty reduction and the World Bank: Progress in fiscal 1996 and 1997.* Washington, D.C.: World Bank.

————. 1998. World development indicators. Washington, D.C.: World Bank. CD-ROM.

Yaron, Jacob, McDonald Benjamin, and Stephanie Charitonenko. 1998. Promoting efficient rural financial intermediation. *World Bank Research Observer* 13, no. 2 (August): 147–70.

Comment on the Paper by Jonathan Morduch
Anjini Kochar

Jonathan Morduch makes two major points in this paper, points that are later substantiated with reference to research on the health sector and on microfinance. The first point is that reductions in poverty appear to be largely the consequence of broad-based economic growth. The second point is that the basic empirical approaches that inform policy on poverty are flawed in two respects. First, empirical work on poverty is primarily static and does not incorporate dynamic issues such as the ability of households to benefit from economic growth or their ability to cope with adverse economic shocks. Second, not enough is known about how households can "hook into" growth processes. Thus, even though there *is* research on dynamic issues and on issues relevant to poverty, this research does not benefit policymakers to any substantial degree. The result is a very weak link between the academic debate and the policy discussions of the topic.

While I agree that there is a lack of connection between academic research on poverty issues and policy, I do not believe that this is because of the nature of empirical work in the area. Instead, I believe that the primary reason is the lack of consensus among researchers on the root causes of poverty and hence on methods to alleviate poverty. Correspondingly, there is little that academic researchers can convincingly communicate to policymakers on this topic. Following Morduch's lead, I will also illustrate this point with reference to health policy and microfinance.

Health Policy

Morduch devotes much of his discussion of health policy to a criticism of policies that emphasize cost-effectiveness and that hence calculate the cost of illness on the basis of DALYs. The claim is that such policies are flawed in that they do not build on knowledge of institutions, markets, or the availability of alternative sources of insurance against health risks. In short, little attention is paid to the environment households face and the factors that determine household choices regarding responses to illness.

Morduch identifies two drawbacks of such policy. First, it may yield a set of priorities that is not the best from a poverty viewpoint precisely because it ignores such issues as the differential ability of the household to cope with different kinds of risks, spillovers across households, and so forth. As an example, Morduch cites the emphasis placed by such policy on preventible or inexpensively curable diseases such as childhood diseases and child health. This emphasis disregards research that shows that

Anjini Kochar is assistant professor of economics and faculty fellow at the Center for Research on Economic Development and Policy Reform at Stanford University.

families can handle small medical events on their own quite well but are only able to deflect a small portion of the negative impacts of major health problems (Gertler and Gruber 1997). Morduch thus suggests that greater attention needs to be paid to insuring households against catastrophic illnesses. A second identified drawback of such policy is that it may under-emphasize the importance of the health of primary earners. Morduch accordingly advocates greater attention to the health problems of primary earners, taking into account existing institutions and issues of implementation.

That both areas identified by Morduch are potentially more important areas for policy focus is, however, open to question. Research on the illnesses to which households are most vulnerable is still in its infancy, and there are certainly no clear guidelines that researchers can offer to policy-makers.

For example, minor illnesses may still contribute to *poverty,* even if households appear to be well insured against such illnesses. Tests of the extent to which households are insured against any specific income shock are generally based on an analysis of the sensitivity of the *change* in consumption across two time periods to the shock in question. Issues regarding poverty, however, relate to the effect of any given variable on the *level* of consumption. Thus any given factor can have a substantial effect on poverty, even if household consumption appears well insured against such factors. Households that are exposed to frequent bouts of minor illnesses may very well have factored such illnesses into their income choices, choosing low-return occupations that accommodate periodic absences from work. Pitt, Rosenzweig, and Hassan (1990) provided some evidence that individuals with poor "endowments" of health do indeed choose less physically demanding jobs at lower wages.

Similarly, a policy that focuses on primary earners ignores the fact that illness is rarely an exogenous income or preference shock. Instead, households can frequently choose the magnitude of the shock by choosing the level of medical expenditure. It may thus be the case that the illness of a primary earner has a greater effect on consumption mainly because households are willing to incur medical expenditures for such members but not for others.

A focus on primary earners also ignores research that argues that income elasticities may be relatively low for consumption goods such as nutrition and the welfare of children (as reflected in their health and education), goods that are particularly important from a poverty perspective. Almost all we know about the determinants of expenditures on such goods suggests that such expenditures respond more to the income of mothers than that of fathers. If so, a health policy that focuses on primary earners may end up having a *negative* impact on poverty.

A final point that Morduch makes with regard to the health sector is the need to seek collaborations between the public and the private sector. Before we seek such collaborations, however, we need to learn much more about the functioning of the private health sector. Thus there are important issues of incentives, even in the private sector, reflected in the poor growth of this sector, particularly in rural areas. In India, for example, the growth in the numbers of doctors, nurses, and beds has not kept pace with the growth of population.

While Morduch's general point about the need to understand the "industrial organization" of the health sector is an important one, I would place greater emphasis on other research areas. The first of these is the effect of illness on poverty. Does improved health help households benefit from economic growth? If so, is this through occupational choice? Is it the health of men or women that is more important? How does adult health affect outcomes other than consumption, particularly as they relate to children? The second area for research relates to coping mechanisms and the efficiency of private safety nets. The household appears to be the major source of insurance in most developing economies against a wide range of income and preference shocks. But how effective is the household in providing insurance? Are all members equally well protected? What is the cost of such insurance?

The last issue, related to the second, concerns the "dynamics" of existing institutions. Morduch has emphasized the need for dynamic research that takes into account the ability of households to benefit from economic growth and their ability to cope with adverse economic shocks. In doing so, however, we should recognize that the very institutions households rely on are themselves in a state of flux and that such institutional changes need to be kept in mind when analyzing policy choices. Thus research on factors that affect coresidence and the sharing of income within the household suggests that inter- and intragenerational coresidence, and, correspondingly, the insurance value of the household, is only likely to diminish over time. If so, policymakers should be wary of designing policies based on the premise that the household does provide good insurance against a variety of adverse outcomes, including declines in income with age.

Microfinance and Poverty Alleviation

Morduch offers the field of microfinance as another example of a policy area that is not grounded in good research. He notes the generally poor record of microfinance institutions (MFIs) in catering to the poor or to the agricultural sector, and their dependence on subsidies. The relevant question then raised is whether they have a role to play in poverty alleviation. Morduch suggests that they do but asserts that research is required on areas such as the elasticity of credit demand with respect to interest rates, the financial profitability of MFIs that cater to the poor, and industrial organization issues such as private-public sector linkages and whether subsidized programs will crowd out "sustainable" programs.

The prior research question that must be addressed, however, is the role of financial institutions in alleviating poverty relative to other markets and institutions. Financial institutions may help reduce poverty in two ways. The first is by helping households accumulate productive assets that in turn increase income. The second is by reducing the vulnerability of households to income shocks through the provision of credit, thereby reducing the effect of such shocks on income and saving choices.

There are two reasons to doubt whether the relatively small investments in physical capital financed by MFIs can have any significant impact on poverty. The first is the failure of earlier credit programs, such as the Integrated Rural Development Programme. These programs, initiated in the late 1960s and 1970s, had a goal similar to that of some MFIs, namely, to reduce poverty through the creation of assets. They failed, however, both as institutions and in their impact on poverty. The innovations of MFIs, such as closer monitoring, group lending, and so forth, are likely to improve their institutional performance relative to earlier credit institutions. But few innovations, other than the focus on women, are specifically geared to correct the earlier failures of credit institutions to have any impact on poverty. And while research has shown that outcomes such as the health and education of children are more sensitive to the income of women than of men, much more research is necessary to interpret this result. In particular, it is not at all clear that providing credit to women has a larger impact than direct investments in the health and education of women.

The second reason to doubt whether MFIs can have a substantial impact on poverty comes from the observation made by Morduch and others that "success" in poverty alleviation in countries such as China, Indonesia, and Brazil has generally been associated with broad-based economic growth. While research on the link between poverty and growth in these cases is still scant, it is far more plausible that poverty reduction has occurred because of an increase in wage employment and because of increasing returns to education and health than because of an increase in income from self-employment or the assets financed by MFIs. Similarly, even should poverty be primarily attributable to the vulnerability of households to risk, increased wage employment in the "organized" sector, which provides health insurance and pensions, is far more likely to have reduced such vulnerability than any credit provided through MFIs.

Rather than the research agenda proposed by Morduch, then, I would encourage far greater research on the basic question of the determinants of poverty and the link, if any, between credit and poverty.

References

Gertler, Paul, and Jonathan Gruber. 1997. Insuring consumption against illness. NBER Working Paper no. 6035. Cambridge, Mass.: National Bureau of Economic Research.
Pitt, Mark M., Mark R. Rosenzweig, and M. N. Hassan. 1990. Productivity, health and inequality in the intrahousehold distribution of food in low-income countries. *American Economic Review* 80:723–46.

IV

Second-Stage
Macroeconomic Reforms

12

Rationalizing the Government Budget
Or Why Fiscal Policy Is So Difficult

Vito Tanzi

Many policy actions go under the name of fiscal policy. Broadly defined, fiscal policy is the manipulation of fiscal tools to achieve desirable economic objectives. The achievement of these objectives is assumed to promote the maximization of a country's welfare. The budget is the key instrument of fiscal policy.

It is not generally recognized that the way we think about fiscal policy was much influenced by the formal framework developed in the 1950s and 1960s mostly by northern European economists such as Jan Tinbergen, Bent Hansen, Leif Johansen, and a few others. Some economists operating in the United States, such as Alvin Hansen, Richard Musgrave, Robert Solow, Laurence Klein, and others, also contributed to this development.

Building on Keynes's seminal work, these economists developed a way of thinking about economic policy in general and, more specifically, about fiscal policy that came to influence, or even dominate, both the theory and, to some extent, the practice of fiscal policy (see esp. Tinbergen 1952; Hansen 1958; Johansen 1965; Musgrave 1959). This way of thinking, and the technical framework that accompanied it, incorporated strong but unstated assumptions about (1) the organization of the public sector and the inclusiveness of the budget, (2) the existence of essential and efficient fiscal institutions, (3) the availability of good information, (4) the goals of the policymakers, and (5) the quality and honesty of the bureaucracy. These assumptions may have been realistic for the countries of origin of the

Vito Tanzi is director of the Fiscal Affairs Department of the International Monetary Fund.

The views expressed in this paper are those of the author and do not reflect official IMF positions.

above-mentioned economists—countries such as the Netherlands, Norway, Sweden, and, to a lesser extent, the United States. However, they could be highly unrealistic for other countries and especially for developing countries and, since the early 1990s, for economies in transition. We shall argue that when the above assumptions are not realistic, the rationalization of the government budget and the pursuit of sound fiscal policy can become very difficult. We shall also suggest ways to make the budget more rational.

12.1   A Brief Review of the Theory of Fiscal Policy

In the theory of fiscal policy, as developed by the authors mentioned above, the policymakers, who constitute the government of a country, are charged with the task of promoting general economic welfare through the use of policy instruments.

Let W represent the national welfare. W depends on the value of *intermediate* objectives such as $y_1, y_2, \ldots, y_n$. Thus

$$(1) \qquad\qquad W = f(y_1, y_2, \ldots, y_n).$$

Examples of these policy objectives might be household consumption, economic growth, income distribution, the rate of inflation, the unemployment rate, the current account balance, public debt, and so on. The value of each intermediate objective, y_i, can be changed by the use of policy instruments. In some cases a specific policy instrument may be especially effective in bringing about a change in the value of a particular objective. For example, a change in a tax, say a value-added tax, may change the rate of saving of households. The instruments of *fiscal* policies are taxes and various categories of public spending. These instruments make up the budget of a country.

A policy instrument is *efficient* in shaping a given objective when a realistic, or feasible, change in its value can bring about a significant change in the value of the objective. Let the policy instruments be represented by $x_1, x_2, \ldots, x_k$. These may refer to various taxes, or even to particular features of a given tax, to the budgetary allocation to each functional or economic expenditure category, and so on. These policy instruments are assumed to be under the full control of the policymakers: they can change these instruments at their discretion. A given change in x_i is expected to generate a precise change in y_i. In our discussion we will be dealing with the fiscal instruments that make up a government budget.[1]

A set of equations ties the intermediate objectives to the policy instruments. Another equation ties the national welfare, W, to the objectives as

---

1. However, I have argued elsewhere that fiscal policy goals can be and are often pursued through nonfiscal instruments (see Tanzi 1998b). We shall come back to this issue below.

shown in equation (1). In theory, these equations could be solved to generate the level of welfare associated with a given set of policies, that is, with specific values for $x_1, x_2, \ldots, x_k$. By changing policy instruments, the policymakers can move policy objectives in the desirable direction, thus maximizing welfare.

Over the years, econometric models were developed empirically linking changes in policy instruments to changes in economic objectives.[2] Some of these models became very large, complex, and popular. However, in more recent years, they lost much of their popularity, and economists became more humble about their ability to link policy instruments to objectives. Still, even in the absence of econometric models, policymakers and economists have continued to assume the existence of direct and quantifiable relations between changes in instruments and changes in objectives. Economic textbooks continue to present modern analytical versions of this normative approach to policy.

In the rest of this paper we will identify problems that often make the theory as outlined above a much too simplistic version of reality. In the process we will show why in many countries the rationalization of the budget deficit and the pursuit of optimal fiscal policy are such difficult tasks.

12.2   The Importance of the Institutional Setup

The theory of fiscal policy outlined above is highly dependent on several crucial assumptions. When in the context of a specific country's situation these assumptions prove to be unrealistic, the usefulness of the theory is much reduced and fiscal policy becomes messy and difficult. In particular the theory is silent on two key questions: the institutional setup and the objectives and behavior of policymakers and bureaucrats.[3] Each of these questions involves several aspects. We deal with these aspects in this and in the next section of this paper.

12.2.1   Inclusiveness of the Budget

A first aspect concerns the inclusiveness of the budget or the organization of the public sector. Optimal fiscal policy would need to be based on a rational budget, and a rational budget should include *all* the fiscal activities of the public sector. However, in many countries, three major omissions limit the scope of the budget: (1) subnational governments, (2) extra-

---

2. It is much more difficult to link objectives to national welfare because of difficulties in assigning weights to objectives and because of other difficulties. E.g., it is difficult to assign trade-offs between unemployment and inflation or between the welfare of different individuals.

3. The theory is also silent about the technical competence of the policymakers. We shall largely ignore this important aspect in this paper, but see Tanzi (1994).

budgetary accounts and institutions, and (3) quasi-fiscal activities and quasi-fiscal regulations.

Subnational Governments

In most countries the national budget, that is, the budget approved by parliament and controlled by the national government, represents only part of the implicit budget of the whole public sector. In several countries it represents a small part. For example, in federal countries, such as the United States, Argentina, Australia, Canada, Brazil, Switzerland, India, Russia, and some others, the *sub*national governments (states or provinces and municipalities) account for a substantial share of public spending. In some cases they account for more than half of total public spending. These subnational governments, which can be in the thousands, are not under the control of the national authorities and thus act independently from them. As a consequence, their fiscal actions and their spending are difficult to control or even monitor. It is thus difficult to coordinate the fiscal actions of these subnational governments with those of the national government.[4] In particular cases the actions of the national government are neutralized by those of the subnational governments. Assuming that the national government is pursuing a rational policy for the whole country, these actions obviously make its task more difficult.

Lack of coordination has been a concern and a problem in most federal countries, including the United States. It has been a concern even in countries that in a strict sense are not federal countries if de facto or administrative decentralization has taken place. It is a major obstacle to the achievement of a rational budget policy especially in countries (Russia, Brazil) where arm's-length relations do not fully prevail between national and subnational governments.[5] The difficulties created by a decentralized fiscal structure were recognized by some of the originators of the theory of fiscal policy, but not enough attention was paid to them.[6] Musgrave, for example, wrote that "the function of the Stabilization Branch . . . must be performed largely at the central level" (1959, 181). This, however, is very difficult to do when local governments are powerful and act independently and in a not predictable way (see Tanzi 1966). As a consequence, the more decentralized the fiscal structure of a country, and the less predictable and controllable the actions of subnational governments, the

4. In many cases, the outcomes of fiscal activities at the subnational government level are only known with much delay.

5. In Argentina over the 1980s and part of the 1990s, while the national government was cutting spending and its labor force, local governments were expanding theirs, thus largely neutralizing the fiscal action of the national government. This expansion was in part based on the assumption by the authorities of the subnational governments that, ex post, the national government would pay bills left unpaid by local governments.

6. See Johansen (1965, 14–16) and Musgrave (1959, 179–82). For a recent survey of problems created by decentralized governments, see Ter-Minassian (1997).

more difficult it will be to rationalize the government budget and to pursue an optimal fiscal policy.

Extrabudgetary Institutions

Decentralization of fiscal activity is not only the result of the existence of subnational governments.[7] It can also be the result of administrative, legal, or political arrangements whereby some public institutions have the power to act independently from the national government.[8] Examples of such institutions are public pension funds, public enterprises, stabilization funds, and so on. These institutions may have their own resources, may be able to borrow from the capital market or from their suppliers, at times through the buildup of arrears vis-à-vis the latter, and, in some cases, may be able to use their political power to pressure the national government to finance, ex ante or ex post, parts of their activities. The more important these extrabudgetary institutions, and the greater their political power, the more difficult it will be for the national government to pursue its vision of the national interest based on a rational budget representative of the whole public sector activity. Of course, if one assumes that the national objective pursued by the national government, an objective that ought to be the outcome of the political process, is not the right one, then the whole theory of fiscal policy collapses.[9]

In both of the cases mentioned above the policymakers de facto control only partially the instruments of fiscal policy. Decentralization implies a fragmentation of the budget and of budgetary or fiscal policy. This fragmentation of the budget is particularly damaging in the pursuit of macroeconomic stabilization.

Fiscal policy becomes even more difficult when the executive branch and the legislators pursue substantially different objectives. In fact, in extreme cases they may see the role of the state in totally different lights. Then the national government may not even control the instruments that are supposed to be within its own sphere of direct influence. This clearly has been the case in Russia in recent years and, to a much lesser extent, in several other countries including Brazil and, perhaps, even the United States. In Russia the government has had great difficulty in convincing the legislature (the Duma) to approve measures (such as the tax code) that would improve fiscal policy at least at the national level.[10]

---

7. The existence and independence of subnational governments is often recognized in the constitution of a country and is thus difficult to change.

8. At least, in principle, this kind of decentralization should be easier to eliminate or to deal with.

9. When the national government does not pursue the national interest, extrabudgetary accounts tend to proliferate.

10. In Russia lack of coordination with extrabudgetary institutions and subnational governments has also made the pursuit of good fiscal policy very difficult.

Quasi-Fiscal Activities and Regulations

Rational fiscal policy must be pursued through the use of fiscal instruments such as taxes and public spending.[11] This is mostly the case in several advanced countries and especially in the northern European countries. In Sweden, for example, the fiscal role of the government, which is very large, is pursued almost exclusively through taxes and public spending. In many countries, however, especially when their ability to raise taxes is limited, fiscal policy is often pursued through nonfiscal instruments.[12] The latter replaces the more traditional fiscal instruments in the pursuit of similar goals (see Tanzi 1998b). These other instruments are largely *quasi-fiscal activities* and *quasi-fiscal regulations*. Because these other instruments are not part of the budget and because they are under the control of other ministries or institutions, and not under the control of the fiscal authorities, often they are not seen as part of fiscal policy. Their existence contributes to the fragmentation of the budgetary process and makes the official budget a much less useful tool than it would be if only fiscal tools were used. A few examples of such instruments are mentioned below. However, these examples cover only the tip of the iceberg. In all cases the government tries to achieve through regulations and other means objectives that could have been achieved through public spending and taxing.

"Directed" or "policy" loans are good examples of quasi-fiscal activities.[13] These loans are given by financial institutions to particular borrowers under the direction of some minister or some other high-level government official. Industrial policy is often promoted through their use. These loans promote particular activities.[14] They have been very popular in the countries of Southeast Asia. Observers who have commented that before the 1997 financial crisis the countries of Southeast Asia had sound fiscal policies (because they had balanced budgets or even small surpluses) have forgotten that many loans that enterprises, and to a lesser extent some individuals, were receiving from banks were directed loans. These loans may have provided large subsidies to those who received them. If the governments that had wanted to encourage the activities undertaken by those receiving the loans had provided equivalently valued subsidies through the

---

11. This does not imply that taxes are always efficient and public spending is always productive.

12. This, e.g., is the case in China, which has a tax burden less than a fourth that of Sweden but a very large public sector role in the economy.

13. These loans have attracted a lot of attention recently because of their role in the economic crises of the countries of Southeast Asia.

14. In some cases the borrower is the government. E.g., until the mid-1980s, Italian commercial banks were required to allocate portions of their deposits to the purchase of government debt instruments. These implicit taxes on banks did not appear in the budget and reduced considerably the interest cost of the public debt. See Bruni, Penati, and Porta (1989).

budget, higher public spending would have resulted and the fiscal accounts would have looked less sound.

Another important example of fiscal policy goals pursued outside the budget through quasi-fiscal activities is social spending that the state enterprises of Russia and of other economies in transition finance through their own budgets. In earlier years this social spending had been particularly high. That spending was not reflected in the national budget. Thus the fiscal accounts did not fully reflect the countries' fiscal policy.

Central banks have often been forced to lend at highly subsidized rates, thus, once again, replacing the government budget in the promotion of particular activities (see Fry 1997; Mackenzie and Stella 1996). There are many examples of countries where the fiscal deficit was largely shifted from the budget to the central bank, thus creating an impression of a sounder fiscal policy. For example, rescue operations for banking systems in difficulty are often undertaken by central banks. Thus the resulting expenditure does not show up, at least not immediately, in the budget. Reporting this as a budgetary expenditure, as it should be, would of course change a country's reporting of its fiscal outcome (see Daniel and Saal 1997).

The pursuit of a rational government budget would require that all actions with a clearly fiscal objective be promoted through a unified and comprehensive budget. This would lead to the replacement of most quasi-fiscal activities and quasi-fiscal regulations with taxes and budgetary spending. This change would bring more transparency to fiscal policy and would reveal the absurdity or the costs of many policies. It would thus, likely, reduce the scope of governmental action. However, by replacing regulations with taxes and spending, the net result would be a rational budget but with a higher share of tax revenue and public spending in GDP. One could of course visualize exceptions when, for example, taxes have such high welfare costs while a certain objective is so important that other instruments might become preferable. In other words, it is likely that in some situations the choice of regulations may be preferable on welfare grounds. These situations, however, are likely to be rare.

12.2.2   Fiscal Institutions

It is much more difficult to rationalize the government budget in the absence of efficient fiscal institutions. These institutions facilitate the making of sound budgetary decisions and allow the implementation of these decisions without excessive distortions. Macroeconomists, even those with a strong interest in fiscal policy, have paid little attention to these institutional aspects and have generally attributed poor fiscal policy results to poor decisions made at the top, that is, by ministers. Yet the institutional setup of a country is a major contributor to the quality of fiscal policy. There is a lot of endogeneity in budgetary decisions in the sense that the information that policymakers receive on current budgetary developments influences the decisions that they make. Good information promotes good policy decisions, and good institutions tend to provide good information. Thus more policy mistakes are likely to be made when essential fiscal institutions are not well developed.

Several institutions are essential to good fiscal policy and to the formulation of rational budgets. We briefly survey the most important.

Macroeconomic Unit

Rational budgetary decisions must be based on a realistic assessment of likely macroeconomic developments over the fiscal year. Thus a first essential institution is a macroeconomic unit (within the ministry of finance) capable of making realistic forecasts of economic development, including inflation, of expected revenue, and of public spending on the assumption of unchanged policies.[15] In our work at the International Monetary Fund (IMF) we have been surprised to find that many countries do not have such a unit so that budgetary decisions are often made in a macroeconomic vacuum or, even worse, on the basis of highly unrealistic forecasts. Forecasts must be transparent and must be based on realistic assumptions. Transparency and competence in this area are very important attributes.

Budget Office

The input from the macroeconomic unit must be used by the budget office to coordinate the budgetary requests of the various spending units and ensure that they remain within a given total. Normally a top-down approach is preferable, whereby total spending is decided first by the full government and then the spending units are instructed that their combined requests cannot exceed the overall ceiling and will thus be evaluated within the established macroeconomic parameters.[16]

The budget office will need to have a lot of information on the working of the various ministries and must have the skills to be able to evaluate the relative merits of the spending requests submitted by the spending units. Many budget offices do not have these skills so that, often, the more politically powerful ministers end up getting the biggest budgetary increases for their ministries, regardless of merit. Attempts are being made to develop efficiency indicators, that is, quantitative evaluations of the output expected from particular spending (say, ratios of students to teachers, doctors to patients, etc.) to help the budget office in its task of evaluating the merit of spending requests.

---

15. The definition of unchanged policies may not be as simple as it may sound.

16. This top-down approach works better than the alternative whereby total spending is determined ex post, i.e., after individual requests from the spending units have been received.

Important tasks of the budget office are the classification of expenditures, according to clear principles and categories, and the presentation of the budget in an easily understood manner. These tasks are important to allow legislators to understand the decisions they will have to make at the time when the budget is approved. In many countries the budgetary presentation is so complex and confused that few members of parliament fully understand what they are voting for.[17] The budget classification is also very important after the budget has been approved to help to monitor actual expenditure. Without proper classification, spending units may use budgetary appropriations for purposes different from the ones intended in the approved budget. This is, once again, a common problem in many countries.

Treasury

As approved by the legislature, the budget document authorizes, for the fiscal year, a given level of government spending and the way that spending must be allocated among spending units (ministries, etc.) and among uses (wages, etc.). However, the actual execution of the budget is a complex matter. During the fiscal year there will be need to

Allocate public revenue to spending units,
Disburse money to each spending unit at a pace that parallels spending,
Make sure that at any one time enough funds are available to match the flow of spending in order to avoid building up unpaid bills,[18]
Make sure that the actual use of money does not diverge from the legislated one,
Prevent the buildup of arrears by spending units,
Economize on the use of cash balances,[19]
Ensure that "value for money" is obtained by maximizing benefits from spending, and
Keep good accounts and provide needed information to policymakers on a regular and frequent basis and in the format most useful to them. This is especially difficult when the existence of multiple accounts complicates the consolidation of what is happening. In some countries thousands of accounts may exist. These accounts make the process much less transparent and the fight against corruption more difficult.

The above may sound like pedestrian tasks not worthy of economists' attention but they are fundamental in determining the quality of the fiscal

---

17. In these cases lobbies have an easier time because they can influence particular legislators to push especially for particular programs.
18. Because the flow of tax revenue is likely to differ from the flow of spending, it is important to have a good financial program and a good cash management system.
19. The management of cash is very important. In too many cases parts of the government are flush with cash, while the government must borrow to finance other parts.

policy that a country will experience. At each step, the process may fail and in fact it often fails so that the *effective* execution of the budget is different from the *legislated* one. Also, because the information conveyed upward to policymakers is poor or dated, the policy decisions that the latter make are themselves of poorer quality.

These problems are especially important in transition economies and in developing countries. But developed countries including the United States are not immune from them. The Fiscal Affairs Department of the IMF has been very active over the years in helping countries to improve the functions of the budget office and the treasury.

Tax Administration and Customs

Although most think of the budget as concerning only the spending side of the government's activity, revenue is obviously an important part of it. The role of the tax administration (and of customs in developing countries) is fundamental. If these institutions fail, the theoretically best tax system will give poor results. And if revenue is not forthcoming, fiscal difficulties will follow.

Current (1999) discussion of a new architecture for the international financial system to prevent financial crises has recognized the need for transparency in the way fiscal policy decisions are made and are presented to legislators and the public, in the working of fiscal institutions, in the quality and availability of fiscal data, and in the assumptions incorporated in the making of the budget. The IMF has developed a Code of Conduct on Fiscal Transparency, and member countries have been invited to adopt such a code. Transparency reports have started to be prepared.

12.3   Rational Budgets and Principal-Agent Problems

The theory of fiscal policy as outlined earlier makes several crucial but implicit assumptions about the behavior of individuals. In this section we discuss the importance of some of them.

The first assumption is that the same fundamental goals that would be pursued by an ideal government are also pursued by the actual government and, subsequently, by the ministers and other high public officials who make up the government of a country at a given moment in time. It is assumed that these policymakers, honestly and competently, attempt to implement economic policies aimed at maximizing the national interest. Thus they behave in the same way as the ministers in an ideal government would behave.

The second is that the instructions given by the ministers to the heads of the institutions and departments, which will be responsible for implementing the policies, are clear, are not challenged, and are carried out faithfully and competently by those who receive them. Thus, for example, the heads of the tax and customs administrations will instruct their subordinates to follow faithfully and efficiently the instructions they receive from the relevant government official, who, in this case, is often the minister of finance.

The third is that the instructions given by the heads of institutions and departments to their subordinates (public servants) are also carried out faithfully and competently. Nobody challenges them. Nobody puts sand in the mechanism. Nobody tries to take advantage of public position for personal benefit.

The basic chain of command and the crucial links can be schematized:

Ideal government → Actual government → Ministers →

Heads of institutions and departments → Civil servants.

The basic idea is that ideal policies are created at the top and are transmitted all the way down to the civil servants without resistance, distortion, or contamination. Between their creation and their final implementation, fiscal decisions go through many stages at which mistakes, indifference, passive resistance, implicit opposition, and various forms of principal-agent problems may distort the final outcome. The theory of fiscal policy simply ignores these potential problems. A good analogy is that of the production and consumption of electricity. If there is a lot of resistance in the transmission lines, the electricity received will be much less than the electricity produced.

One could argue that at least in some mature democracies, with well-functioning market economies, with efficient public institutions, with well-paid, well-trained, and proud bureaucracies, and with public officials and policymakers dedicated to improving the lives of citizens, the ideal framework of public policy may not be a caricature of the actual policy-making process. In these democracies, when economic difficulties appear, they are often caused by external events (wars, natural catastrophes, etc.), by over-ambitious expectations of what government policy can do, or simply by honest policy mistakes. For example, mistaken policies led to excessive public spending by the government in Sweden and eventually to an economic crisis (see Lindbeck 1997). Therefore, economic difficulties are not caused only by principal-agent problems, that is, by distortions of economic policies and economic instruments. In these societies, discussions of public policies can focus on the policies themselves and not worry much about how these policies will be carried out or implemented.

However, we should not overemphasize the distinction. Even mature democracies have not been immune to some of the problems discussed in this paper. For example, the problems of corruption and lobbying are not limited to poorer countries or less mature democracies. And problems of implementation have also appeared in advanced countries. For example, the U.S. Internal Revenue Service has occasionally argued that some changes in tax legislation would be difficult to implement, but it was ignored by the U.S. Congress.

Unfortunately, in most countries, the policy-making process is neither as smooth nor as rational as outlined above. In these countries, in addition to the random difficulties originating from honest mistakes, external shocks, natural catastrophes, and wars, economic difficulties may be caused by problems that arise in formulating, transmitting, and implementing policies. Some of these problems can be broadly thought of as principal-agent problems. In this section a preliminary discussion of this issue is outlined.[20]

12.3.1 Problems in Formulating Policies

The government running a country should be the faithful executor of policies that will maximize the welfare of the citizens of that country. In other words, its goals should be the same as those of an ideal government with only the public interest as its objective. This is the "normative" role of the state as, for example, outlined in Musgrave's *Theory of Public Finance* (1959). The government should correct for market failures, should redistribute income to implement society's prevalent view of fairness, and should stabilize the economy. This fundamental role should aim, within feasible resources and administrative limits, at protecting citizens from particular economic risks. The possibility of "government failure" is not contemplated by this normative theory.

When we observe real-life economic policy in many countries, we soon realize that the role played by the government often diverges substantially from the welfare-enhancing, normative role in economics textbooks. In extreme cases (Uganda under Idi Amin, Zaire under Mobutu, Haiti under Duvalier), the divergence is so great that it can be attributed to the perverted personality of the leader. In other cases, the divergence may be due to the ignorance of policymakers, ignorance that leads them to pursue misguided policies in spite of good intentions. In many other cases, however, the divergence is not accidental but is due to more subtle and complex reasons.

Over the past three decades there has been a great expansion in the literature on public choice in general and rent seeking in particular (see Mueller 1989; Krueger 1974). Its basic message is that attempts at solving problems of market failure through governmental intervention may not be successful because they may create problems of government failure. When government failure is greater than market failure, economic policy is less likely to contribute to an improvement in welfare. The public choice

---

20. For an earlier discussion of some of these problems, see Tanzi (1994).

literature developed an approach that in some way had been anticipated by the Italian public finance writing of the early part of this century (*scienza delle finanze*). The Italian school had explicitly recognized the weaknesses of human nature and of institutions and had maintained that these weaknesses cannot be ignored when policies are prescribed. The public choice literature has also attempted to bring some realism to the pristine view of policy making that came from the north of Europe and from the theoretical literature on public finance.[21]

This is not the place to review the work on public choice. However, in its application to the behavior of top policymakers, that is, those who make up the government in the narrow sense, it points to the existence of possible principal-agent problems. We assume here that the principals are the citizens of the countries. They would demand welfare-maximizing policies consistent with the role of an ideal state. The agent is the actual government that at times pursues policies that are not welfare maximizing. These two roles may diverge considerably, essentially because the behavior prescribed by the ideal role of the state may not be in the interest of the individuals who constitute the government. The reasons for this divergence are many.

In the real world, policymakers assign more weight to their own welfare and that of individuals close to them than to the general population. Governments are often elected by voters who expect them to promote policies that benefit the latter even at the cost of the public interest. Some of these voters contribute financially to election campaigns. Thus at times policies are pursued to provide special benefits to individuals belonging to particular political parties, regions, ethnic groups, and so on. Nontransparent policies and fiscal illusion are often used by the government to hide its biases.

At other times policies are greatly influenced by those who can be called the "keepers of the gate," that is, the small group of individuals who, in their privileged positions as relatives, close friends, or political associates, have easy and frequent access to top policymakers so that they are able to influence them. The power of these keepers of the gate can be extraordinary, and as the experience of many countries indicates, this power can distort policies in directions that are far removed from the ideal. In some countries it would be difficult to understand why certain policies are enacted unless one understood the private economic interests of the wives, children, or other close relatives and friends of presidents, prime ministers, or top ministers. This is especially the case when, because of age, poor

---

21. Unfortunately, the public choice literature, though an important field, has remained somewhat isolated from the mainstream. It has created its own grounds and has its own followers but at times continues to be ignored by others.

health, or lack of sophistication in economic matters, policymakers come to rely heavily on these individuals for advice and guidance; or when they are themselves confused about which policies are best suited to maximize economic welfare.[22] Keepers of the gate will often be able to influence policy making in a way that benefits them or occasionally those who pay for their services. The role of keepers of the gate has not been analyzed in the literature. There is no question that in many countries it is very important.

Keepers of the gate may not influence so much general policies but rather how these policies are carried out. For example, they may not affect whether a value-added tax is levied or an import duty is applied or even the rates at which these taxes are imposed. Rather they may have an impact on who is exempt from them.[23] Equally, they may not determine whether banks give policy loans but who gets the loans.

12.3.2   Problems between the Government (as Principal) and Top Bureaucrats (as Agent)

Through its ministers, the government formulates its policies and then, once these policies have been approved by the relevant legislative bodies, it instructs top bureaucrats—the heads of the institutions or departments charged with carrying out the policies—to implement them. For example, once the government has proposed and parliament has legislated changes in tax policy, these changes must be implemented by the tax administration.[24] In order to do this, the latter must supplement the legislated changes with detailed regulations and instructions to administrative personnel and must reallocate the needed personnel and resources to deal with the new policies. This process often gives a lot of discretion to the head of the tax administration or to other top managers. To some extent the heads of the tax administration and other top managers have the power to apply the law forcefully or half-heartedly.[25] For example, they have the power to decide how many administrative resources will go to the new activity. It has been said that tax administration *is* tax policy because of the discretion mentioned above. In other words, the administration of the law can, de facto, change the original intent of the law, and the director of taxation has much power in deciding how a law will be applied. Similar considerations apply to other areas of policy. Another example is

22. The role of economic sophistication in policy making is an aspect that has not been studied.

23. Sometimes these exemptions are not in the law but are given in a discretionary way.

24. Of course, principal-agent problems can also develop between the government and individual ministers.

25. For an interesting discussion of this issue by a former French minister of finance and economics, see Arthuis (1998).

that of wage reductions in the public sector. In many countries, attempts at reducing spending through constraints on real wages have been defeated by a process of levitation whereby the heads of administrative units have granted faster promotions to compensate for cuts in real wages.

Examples from many countries indicate that the heads of departments responsible for the implementation of laws or directives received from the government often have the power to change the intent of the laws in significant ways.[26] They may use this power to undermine changes when they do not like them or when they can extract some personal benefit from this behavior. Economic policy is full of examples of countries where major policy changes generate no visible changes in the economy. One reason is that economic policies can be emasculated in the process of transmission or implementation. This emasculation may be intentional for the reasons mentioned above, or it may be the consequence of total inefficiency in the implementation stage of the policies.

12.3.3   Problems between Top Bureaucrats (as Principal) and Employees (as Agent)

Civil servants working in public institutions such as customs, treasuries, tax administrations, health or educational agencies, and so on do not have the power to change the laws or even the directives they receive from above. However, they have, in many cases, the power to apply them in ways that effectively change their character. A growing literature deals with the extent to which public employees can use public power for private ends. This is a common definition of corruption. Corruption can be considered a classic example of a principal-agent problem because the use of public power for personal ends can interfere with the goals of economic policy and can bring policy results that are at odds with the intended ones (see Tanzi 1998a).

Bureaucratic corruption is an example of the privatization of policy instruments. Tools that should be used to promote public or social goals are diverted into the generation of private gains. When widespread corruption is present, mechanical relations between instruments, $x_1, x_2, \ldots, x_k$, and objectives, $y_1, y_2, \ldots, y_n$, no longer exist. In this case a change in a policy instrument can result in a whole range of outcomes in terms of changes in objectives.

12.4   Concluding Remarks

In this paper we have surveyed some of the obstacles that make fiscal policy difficult and, probably, much more difficult than policies in other

---

26. They can also use their power for their own benefit.

areas. We have focused particularly on problems of implementation rather than on problems of conceptualization. The latter have attracted most of the attention of economists.

Problems of conceptualization can be difficult and can lead to mistakes. These problems appear under many circumstances, and some are easier to deal with than others. For example, major changes in economic activity can have significant effects on revenue and expenditure. Inflation, especially in the presence of high public debt, can greatly distort the accounts, thus reducing the informational value of the conventionally measured deficit. The proper treatment of privatization proceeds and of foreign grants remains a controversial issue. Should they be treated as financing of the deficit or ordinary revenue that reduces the deficit? The proper way to take account of the cost of rescue operations for banking crises remains unsettled. The proper treatment of investment expenditure on the part of public enterprises that operate at arm's length from the government is still another unsettled issue. These problems affect the comparability of fiscal policy over time or across countries. These issues should be resolved by good analytical work.

However, in my view, it is time to pay more attention to problems of implementation. Research that deals with issues of transparency of fiscal policy is very important. We need to understand better and account for the incentives that influence the behavior of ministers, heads of departments, and general civil servants. The ongoing literature on corruption is a beginning in an area that could prove very fertile.

The rationalization of the budget is not an easy enterprise. Constitutional, legal, political, administrative, and technical obstacles have to be faced. In some cases these obstacles will prove unmovable. However, the more attention economists pay to this objective, the more progress is likely to be made. The rationalization of the budget will have to proceed on several fronts.

In the first place the budget should be as inclusive as possible. Constitutional or legal obstacles often prevent the inclusion of subnational government budgets in a truly national budget. However, a major effort could be made to take as much account of subnational budgetary developments as possible. Brazil, for example, is now able to provide full information on the accounts of the lower governments even though the national government is limited in its influence on them. Also, greater efforts must be made to ensure that subnational governments live within their own means. In the United States most states have constitutional requirements to balance their annual budgets. In other countries, they do not. Some recent research has been useful in indicating whether constitutional limitations on fiscal deficits are helpful in achieving better fiscal policy outcomes.

Second, the view that fiscal policy must be predominantly pursued through *fiscal* instruments must be pushed. In most countries there is still too much use of quasi-fiscal alternatives to taxes and public spending, regardless of the welfare costs of these alternatives. It may be impossible or may not be even desirable to get rid of these alternatives completely, but much can be done. Replacing quasi-fiscal activities and quasi-fiscal regulations with their tax and spending equivalents would greatly increase the transparency of fiscal policy and would make the budget a more rational and useful policy instrument. Research will be helpful in establishing the costs and the benefits of the changes. As already indicated, it is conceivable that under special circumstances, quasi-fiscal activities may be economically more efficient than the tax and spending alternatives.[27] Research can help to identify these circumstances.

Third, extrabudgetary institutions that exist at the national level must either be eliminated or their budgets must be fully integrated with the budget of the national government. Extrabudgetary institutions have often been one of the main causes of budgetary fragmentation and poor fiscal policy. At times they are defended on the basis of arguments that would protect certain expenditures from political or even economic development. Once again, there may be special circumstances when extrabudgetary institutions or accounts or earmarking are desirable. It would be useful to have some literature that helps us to identify these circumstances.

Fourth, in many countries there is a great need to strengthen fiscal institutions. These institutions are the pillars that sustain policy decisions. If the institutions do not work well, it will be impossible to promote a rational fiscal policy. In this area it is important to encourage individuals with public administration backgrounds to carry out some research and, especially, to integrate this work with that of economists. Questions that could be addressed in research are, for example: How should a tax administration be organized? By tax or by function? Should tax administrations have the same independence as central banks? Should a treasury be completely centralized, as in Brazil, or largely decentralized, as in Australia and New Zealand?

Finally, a lot more attention must be given to a whole range of principal-agent problems that may arise between the making of policy decisions by the government and the actual down-the-line implementation of those decisions. There are many ways in which decisions can be distorted along the line. Tax incentives are good examples of this.[28] Some of these questions are being addressed in the literature on governance and corruption. Others should be addressed in the, hopefully forthcoming, literature on transparency.

Obviously, a rational budget and optimal fiscal policy must also be

27. However, the argument of this paper has been that the preference for quasi-fiscal options is based on political rather than economic considerations.
28. Some economists defend tax incentives on theoretical grounds, but they ignore that these incentives are often distorted or abused at the implementation stage.

based on good economics. At times, even when all the problems mentioned in this paper are absent, fiscal policy decisions may still be distorted by poor policy decisions. However, economics has progressed a lot in the evaluation of these decisions.

References

Arthuis, Jean. 1998. *Dans les coulisses de Bercy: Le cenquieme pouvoir.* Paris: Albin Michel.
Bruni, Franco, Alessandro Penati, and Angelo Porta. 1989. Financial regulation, implicit taxes, and fiscal adjustment in Italy. In *Fiscal policy, economic adjustment, and financial markets,* ed. Mario Monti. Washington, D.C.: International Monetary Fund.
Daniel, James, and Matthew Saal. 1997. Macroeconomic impact and policy response. In *Systemic bank restructuring and macroeconomic policy,* ed. William E. Alexander, Jeffrey M. Davis, Liam P. Ebrill, and Carl-Johan Lindgren. Washington, D.C.: International Monetary Fund.
Fry, Maxwell. 1997. The fiscal abuse of central bank. In *Macroeconomic dimensions of public finance: Essays in honour of Vito Tanzi,* ed. Mario I. Blejer and Teresa Ter-Minassian. London and New York: Routledge.
Hansen, Bent. 1958. *The economic theory of fiscal policy.* London: Allen.
Johansen, Leif. 1965. *Public economics.* Amsterdam: North-Holland.
Krueger, Anne O. 1974. The political economy of the rent-seeking society. *American Economic Review* 64 (June): 291–303.
Lindbeck, Assar. 1997. *The Swedish experiment.* Stockholm: SNS Forlag.
Mackenzie, George A., and Peter Stella. 1996. Quasi-fiscal operations of public financial institutions. IMF Occasional Paper no. 142. Washington, D.C.: International Monetary Fund.
Mueller, Dennis C. 1989. *Public choice II: A revised edition of Public Choice.* Cambridge: Cambridge University Press.
Musgrave, Richard A. 1959. *The theory of public finance.* New York: McGraw-Hill.
Tanzi, Vito. 1994. The political economy of fiscal deficit reduction. In *Public sector deficits and macroeconomic performance,* ed. William Easterly, Carlos Alfredo Rodriguez, and Klaus Schmidt-Hebbel. New York: Oxford University Press.
———. 1996. Fiscal federalism and decentralization: A review of some efficiency and macroeconomic aspects. In *Annual bank conference on development economics, 1995,* ed. Michael Bruno and Boris Pleskovic. Washington, D.C.: World Bank.
———. 1998a. Corruption around the world: Causes, consequences, scope, and remedies. *IMF Staff Papers* 45, no. 4 (December): 559–94.
———. 1998b. Government role and the efficiency of policy instruments. In *Public finance in a changing world,* ed. Peter Birch Sorensen. London: Macmillan.
Ter-Minassian, Teresa, ed. 1997. *Fiscal federalism in theory and practice.* Washington, D.C.: International Monetary Fund.
Tinbergen, Jan. 1952. *On the theory of economic policy.* Amsterdam: North-Holland.

Exchange Rates in Emerging Economies
What Do We Know?
What Do We Need to Know?

Sebastian Edwards and Miguel A. Savastano

13.1 Introduction

For the past two decades exchange rates have been at the center of policy debates in developing and transition economies. Controversies have abounded, and theoretical as well as applied questions have been discussed vehemently among academics and policymakers. Some of the policy issues that have captured analysts' interest include: Should nominal exchange rate anchors be used during the early phases of a stabilization program? Are floating exchange rates viable in emerging economies? Does real exchange rate overvaluation always precede currency crises? Recent developments have contributed to keeping these questions at the forefront of policy discussions. Some of the actors have changed, but the script remains pretty much the same. Examples of the policy questions that occupy much of the attention at present are: Should Mexico abandon its floating exchange rate and adopt a more "predictable" system? Could Russia have avoided the August 1998 devaluation of the ruble? Should the East Asian countries peg their exchange rates to restore price and output stability? Should Argentina exit its currency board and move toward a more flexible regime? There is every indication that questions of this type will remain prominent in the months and years to come.

In this paper we address some important exchange-rate-related issues in

Sebastian Edwards is the Henry Ford II Professor of International Economics at the Anderson Graduate School of Management of the University of California, Los Angeles, and a research associate of the National Bureau of Economic Research. Miguel A. Savastano is a deputy division chief in the Research Department of the International Monetary Fund.

The opinions expressed in the paper are exclusively those of the authors and do not represent the views of the IMF. The authors are indebted to Anne Krueger and to discussants Maury Obstfeld and Ron McKinnon for helpful comments.

developing and transition economies. We critically review the theoretical and, especially, the empirical literature that focuses on these economies, and we identify some of the areas where knowledge is still limited. Our analysis is deliberately selective and concentrates on

- the relation between nominal exchange rate regimes and economic performance,
- the feasibility of adopting floating exchange rates in developing countries,
- the long-run empirical features of real exchange rates in emerging economies,
- the extent to which purchasing power parity (PPP) provides a useful yardstick for assessing exchange rate behavior in these economies, and
- models and methods commonly employed to assess real exchange rate misalignment.

We are, of course, aware that this is a partial list of issues; it would be utterly impossible to deal with every exchange-rate-related question in a limited space. However, in the concluding section of this paper we address briefly some additional problems that have emerged in recent exchange rate debates.

The rest of the paper is organized as follows: Section 13.2 focuses on nominal exchange rate regimes. In it we try to explain the rather abrupt decline in the number of developing countries with formally pegged exchange rates, and we review the evidence on the relation between exchange rate regimes and economic performance. This discussion deals with inflation and economic growth and focuses on some of the methodological shortcomings encountered in this literature. Finally, in this section we also provide some evidence, based on Mexico's recent (post-1994) experience, on the feasibility of floating exchange rates in developing countries. In section 13.3 we deal with the economics of real exchange rates. We start with a discussion of the empirical evidence on the time-series characteristics of real exchange rates in emerging economies. The analysis focuses on stationarity issues and emphasizes the difference between short- and long-term analyses of PPP. We make the point that most of economists' beliefs on the subject are based on limited evidence from advanced nations, and we argue that additional work on developing countries is needed. In this section we also address the issue of the relation between productivity growth and deviations from PPP—the so-called Balassa-Samuelson effect. Section 13.4 deals with the important issue of real exchange rate misalignment. We critically evaluate existing models for assessing whether a country's currency is misaligned, and we argue that most of the popular approaches are subject to serious methodological as well as empirical shortcomings. We argue that future work in this area should aim at integrating real exchange rate analyses with analyses of current account "sustainability." Section 13.5 presents the conclusions. We summarize our main findings and provide a brief discussion of other areas in which, in our view, the economics profession needs to (significantly) improve its knowledge about exchange rates in emerging economies.

13.2 Nominal Exchange Rate Regimes and Macroeconomic Performance

The modern literature on exchange rate regimes has emphasized the existence of important trade-offs between *credibility* and *flexibility* (Frankel 1995; Devarajan and Rodrik 1992; Edwards 1996). In doing this, however, most theoretical analyses have considered two highly simplified extreme cases: (1) a fully flexible (or floating) exchange rate with minimal central bank intervention and (2) an irrevocably (and credibly) fixed nominal exchange rate. According to this bipolar characterization, a flexible exchange rate regime allows a country to have an independent monetary policy, providing the economy with flexibility to accommodate domestic and foreign shocks, including changes in external terms of trade and interest rates. This flexibility, however, usually comes at the cost of some loss in credibility and, thus, tends to be associated (on average) with higher inflation. Alternatively, fixed exchange rates reduce the degree of flexibility of the system but impart (in theory) a higher degree of credibility to policy making. Since the public believes that under fixed rates, the primary goal of monetary policy is to preserve exchange rate parity, they moderate their wage and price expectations, thus allowing the economy to attain a lower rate of inflation. This analysis assumes that under a fixed exchange rate regime the authorities are always more disciplined and, thus, that the fixed exchange rate is never abandoned—that is, devaluations are not an option. This, of course, is an oversimplification. In fact, as history has shown again and again, fixed exchange rates often fail to impose macroeconomic discipline and end in major devaluation crises (see, e.g., Cooper 1971; Kamin 1988; Edwards 1989). For this reason, a number of analysts who favor credibility over flexibility increasingly argue that fixed exchange rates are a necessary but not sufficient condition for achieving macroeconomic stability and that additional institutional constraints on policymakers— even at the constitutional level—have to be devised.

Purely floating and fixed systems are, of course, only two of the possible exchange rate regimes a country can choose. In reality, many layers lie between these two extremes. Table 13.1 contains a list of nine alternative exchange rate regimes, ranked according to the degree of flexibility that they impart to the economy or, in inverse order, according to the relative stability they afford to the nominal exchange rate.[1] The table describes

---

1. Of course, table 13.1 presents one of many possible taxonomies of exchange rate regimes. For alternative classifications along the criteria advanced in the (earlier) literature on the choice of exchange rate regimes, see Isard (1995, chap. 11) and Eichengreen and Masson (1998).

Table 13.1   **Alternative Exchange Rate Regimes**

Regime	Main Features	Main Benefits	Main Shortcomings	Key Episodes/Comments
1. Free float	Value of foreign exchange freely determined in the market. Actual and expected changes in demand and supply of assets and goods reflected in exchange rate changes.	Changes in nominal exchange rate shoulder bulk of adjustment to foreign and domestic shocks. High international reserves not required.	High nominal (and real) exchange rate volatility may distort resource allocation. Monetary policy needs to be framed in terms of nominal anchors different from exchange rate; scope for discretion and inflation bias may be large.	Virtually no country has a pure float. United States, Germany, and Switzerland (and Japan, according to some) come close.
2. "Dirty" float	Sporadic central bank interventions in foreign exchange market. Modes and frequency of intervention vary, as do objectives guiding the intervention. Active intervention (sterilized and nonsterilized) results in changes in international reserves. Indirect intervention (through changes in interest rates, liquidity, and other financial instruments) does not result in changes in reserves.	Same as in a free float, except that higher international reserves may be needed. Dampens "excessive" fluctuations of exchange rates.	Lack of transparency of central bank behavior may introduce too much uncertainty. Effects of intervention are typically short lived (even when intended as a signal) and may be destabilizing.	Many advanced economies have adopted this regime—Canada and Australia (and Japan, according to others). Mexico adopted a system similar to this following the 1994–95 crisis. A dirty float could be thought of as a managed float with wide bands, with the (undisclosed) position of the bands providing the criterion for intervention.
3. Floating within a band (target zone)	The nominal exchange rate is allowed to fluctuate (somewhat freely) within a band. The center of the band is a *fixed rate*, either in terms of one currency or of a basket of currencies. The width of the band varies (in the ERM it was originally ±2.25%). Some band systems are the result of cooperative arrangements; others are unilateral.	System combines the benefits of some flexibility with some credibility. Key parameters (bands, midpoint) help guide the public's expectations. Changes in the nominal rate within the bands help absorb shocks to fundamentals.	In some cases (especially when the band is too narrow and when domestic macroeconomic policies are not consistent with a "horizontal" band) the system can be destabilizing and prone to speculative attacks. Selecting the width of the band is not trivial. Systems that allow for the possibility of realignment of the bands and central parity weaken the credibility afforded by the regime.	The Exchange Rate Mechanism of the European Monetary System is the best known example of this type of regime. The ERM crises of 1992–93 showed clearly that the system can be subjected to severe speculative pressures, and even collapse, when currencies become misaligned and central banks are hesitant to defend the bands.

4. Sliding band	There is no commitment by the authorities to maintain the central parity "indefinitely." Instead, it is clear at the outset that the central parity will be adjusted periodically (e.g., due to competitiveness considerations). The system is an adaptation of the band regime to the case of high-inflation economies.	The system allows countries with an ongoing rate of inflation higher than world inflation to adopt a band without having to experience a severe real appreciation.	The fact that the timing and size of central parity adjustments are unknown introduces considerable uncertainty, which often leads to high interest rate volatility. As in the case of the standard band system, it is difficult to choose the appropriate width for the band.	Israel had a system similar to this from early 1989 to December 1991. The uncertainty and volatility associated with this system make it less attractive than other alternatives, such as the crawling band.
5. Crawling band	A band system whereby the central parity crawls over time. Different rules can be used to determine the rate of crawl. The two most common are backward-looking crawl (e.g., based on past inflation differentials) and forward-looking crawl (e.g., based on the expected, or target, rate of inflation).	System allows high-inflation countries to adopt a band system without having to undertake (large) stepwise adjustments of the central parity.	Chosing the criteria for setting the rate of crawl entails serious risks. A backward-looking approach can introduce considerable inflationary inertia into the system. A forward-looking approach that sets the "wrong" inflation target can produce overvaluation and give rise to speculative pressures.	Israel adopted this system in December 1991. Chile had a widening band system from 1986 to mid-1998. Italy also had, effectively, a system of this type between 1979 and 1991.
6. Crawling peg	The nominal exchange rate is adjusted periodically according to a set of indicators (usually lagged inflation differentials) and is not allowed to fluctuate beyond a narrow range (say, 2%). One variant of the system consists of adjusting the nominal rate by a preannounced rate set deliberately below ongoing inflation (variant known as a "tablita" regime).	Allows high-inflation countries to avoid severe real exchange rate overvaluation. The tablita variant helps to guide the public's expectations and buys a limited amount of credibility.	A pure backward-looking crawling peg (where the nominal rate is mechanically adjusted according to past inflation differentials) introduces inflationary inertia and may eventually cause monetary policy to lose its role as nominal anchor. Equilibrium changes in the real exchange rate are difficult to accommodate. A tablita system will not last if fiscal and income policies are not supportive.	This system became popular in the 1960s and 1970s in Chile, Colombia, and Brazil. It had its longer running in Colombia, which to this date has a high degree of inflationary inertia.
7. Fixed-but-adjustable exchange rate	The regime epitomized by the Bretton Woods system. The nominal exchange rate is fixed, but the central bank is not obliged to maintain the parity indefinitely. No tight constraints are imposed on the monetary and fiscal authorities, who can follow, if they so decide, policies that are inconsistent with preserving parity. Adjustments of parity (devaluations) are a powerful policy instrument.	Provides macroeconomic discipline by maintaining (tradable goods prices) in line with foreign prices in a context of relatively low uncertainty. The built-in "escape clause" (which allows the authorities to devalue in case of need) provides the system with some flexibility.	Realignments (devaluations) under this system have typically been large and disruptive (introducing uncertainty and inflationary pressures) rather than smooth and orderly events. If supplemented by the right institutions (e.g., an independent central bank) the time inconsistency problems embedded in the system could be attenuated.	The most popular regime of this century. Most developing countries held on to (variants of) it after the formal collapse of the Bretton Woods agreement in 1973. Many emerging countries continue to subscribe to this system de facto (e.g., Thailand 1997), if not de jure.

(continued)

Table 13.1 (continued)

Regime	Main Features	Main Benefits	Main Shortcomings	Key Episodes/Comments
8. Currency board	Strict fixed exchange rate system, with institutional (legal and even constitutional) constraints on monetary policy and no scope for altering the parity. The monetary authority only can issue domestic money when it is fully backed by inflows of foreign exchange.	The system maximizes credibility and reduces (eliminates) problems of "time inconsistency."	The system is long on credibility but short on flexibility. Large external shocks cannot be accommodated through exchange rate changes but have to be fully absorbed by changes in unemployment and economic activity. The central bank loses its role as lender of last resort.	Historically, a number of small countries have had systems of this type. Some of them, however, have not been successful. When faced with major external shocks, countries have been forced to abandon the regime. Currently, Hong Kong and Estonia have currency boards. Argentina and Bulgaria have (quasi-)currency board arrangements.
9. Full "dollarization"	Generic name given to an extreme form of a currency board system where the country gives up completely its monetary autonomy by adopting another country's currency.	Credibility is maximized under this regime. Monetary authorities have, in theory, no scope for "surprising" the public.	As in the currency board, the system is long on credibility but short on flexibility. Adverse external shocks have to be absorbed fully by the real economy. The central bank loses its role as lender of last resort. A nontrivial shortcoming of this system is that it is usually resisted on political and nationalistic grounds. Another one is that the rules of the game can be changed under extreme circumstances.	There are few historical episodes of full dollarization. A regime similar to this has worked relatively well in Panama. However, the case of Liberia unmasked a serious shortcoming of this type of system: when faced with an emergency (civil war) politicians decided to change the rules of the game and issued a national currency.

briefly the main features of each regime, summarizes its alleged merits and shortcomings, and mentions a few relevant historical experiences. One thing the table makes clear is that the profusion of exchange rate systems, and the blurred boundaries between many of them, makes any attempt to empirically determine the merits of alternative regimes extremely difficult. We deal with this issue in greater detail below.

13.2.1   The Shift Away from Currency Pegs

Since the late 1970s single currency pegs have become less and less common among developing countries. This feature of the recent evolution of the international monetary system has been amply documented and discussed in the exchange rate literature. The standard way of illustrating this gradual shift toward more flexible exchange regimes by less developed countries has been to trace the evolution over time of the official exchange rate arrangements that countries are obliged to report to the International Monetary Fund (IMF). Table 13.2 (taken from IMF 1997) is a typical example; the table shows a steady fall over the past two decades in the number of developing countries that maintain some type of pegged exchange rates and a concomitant rise in the number of countries with "more flexible" exchange rate regimes.

At least two broad explanations have been offered to account for this trend toward greater exchange rate flexibility. One explanation is that starting in the late 1970s a confluence of factors of external and domestic origin prompted developing countries to rely more heavily on exchange rate changes as part of their process of macroeconomic adjustment. Those

Table 13.2   **Developing Countries: Officially Reported Exchange Rate Arrangements (percent of total)**

Arrangement	1976	1981	1986	1991	1996
Pegged	86	75	67	57	45
U.S. dollar	42	32	25	19	15
French franc	13	12	11	11	11
Other	7	4	4	3	4
SDR	12	13	8	5	2
Composite	12	14	18	20	14
Limited flexibility	3	10	5	4	3
Single	3	10	5	4	3
Cooperative	–	–	–	–	–
More flexible	11	15	28	39	52
Set to indicators	6	3	4	4	2
Managed floating	4	9	13	16	21
Independently floating	1	4	11	19	29
Number of countries	100	113	119	123	123

Source: IMF (1997).

factors obviously vary from country to country (and from region to region) but are typically thought to include the large exchange rate fluctuations among major currencies that followed the breakdown of the Bretton Woods system, the oil shocks of the 1970s and 1980s, the debt crisis of the 1980s, and, especially in Latin America, fiscally driven bouts of high and chronic inflation. A key premise underlying this explanation is that exchange rate changes can (and should) play a central role in restoring and preserving external and domestic equilibrium in shock-prone developing countries (see, e.g., the discussion in Corden 1990; Aghevli, Khan, and Montiel 1991; Little et al. 1993).

An alternative view that has gained prominence in recent years stresses the inherent tensions that arguably exist between high capital mobility and fixed exchange rates. According to this view, the main factors behind the marked shift away from single currency pegs in developing countries have been the dramatic increase in the degree of capital mobility experienced by these economies over the past two decades and the ensuing rise in the (output) costs of preserving and defending a fixed exchange rate system—which is seen as a key determinant of recent episodes of "currency crashes" (see, e.g., Eichengreen 1994; Obstfeld and Rogoff 1995b; Leiderman and Bufman 1996).

Both of these explanations receive some support from a number of recent studies that have examined the factors behind developing countries' shift toward more flexible exchange rate arrangements from a political economy perspective (see Collins 1996; Edwards 1996; Klein and Marion 1997). An important insight emphasized by these studies is that the switch from traditional currency pegs to more flexible arrangements has had the effect of lowering the (perceived and actual) political cost of exchange rate changes that is normally borne by the authorities. By "depoliticizing" exchange rate movements, the argument goes, the authorities of these countries have become better equipped to respond "flexibly" to any given shock—including those that stem from international capital markets—even though, or perhaps precisely because, the switch rarely has entailed the adoption of freely floating exchange rates and, thus, nominal exchange rates in these countries have remained under heavy administrative control (Collins 1996).

Regardless of the relative merits of the explanations put forward thus far, the marked shift away from fixed exchange rates by developing countries has provided the opportunity to gather evidence on the *actual* effects of alternative nominal exchange rate regimes on the macroeconomic performance of these economies. Of course, this option was not available under the Bretton Woods system (where all countries, developing or not, were required to maintain some type of currency peg) and only became feasible as the shift toward more flexible exchange rate arrangements and current account convertibility gained momentum sometime during the 1980s (table 13.2).

13.2.2   Exchange Rate Regimes and Macroeconomic
Performance: Facts and Fantasies

Individual Country Studies

For a number of years, the bulk of the evidence on the relation between
nominal exchange rate regimes and macroeconomic performance in less
developed countries stemmed from largely descriptive accounts and assessments of experiences and experiments of individual countries (or
groups of countries) with various types of exchange rate arrangements.
Two well-known examples of this approach are the numerous studies that
examined the demise of the infamous "tablitas" adopted by Argentina,
Chile, and Uruguay in the late 1970s (for an overview of these episodes
see Calvo 1986; Corbo and de Melo 1987; Edwards 1985, 1986) and, years
later, the evaluations of the (few) experiences with crawling exchange rate
bands—a distant cousin of target zones—in the developing world (e.g.,
Helpman, Leiderman, and Bufman 1994; Williamson 1996). Findings reported in some multicountry comparative studies sponsored by, or conducted at, the World Bank—notably those of Choksi, Michaely, and Papageorgiou (1989) and Little et al. (1993)—also added to the profession's
collective understanding of the relation between exchange rate regimes
and macroeconomic performance in developing countries.[2]

Not surprisingly, this country-specific literature found it very difficult
to pin down the *independent* effects of the nominal exchange rate regime
on the overall macroeconomic performance of developing countries. Every time the profession seemed to be reaching agreement on a feature or
regularity distinctive of a particular regime based on analyses of the experience of a group of countries, developments in another group of countries provided a devastating counterexample that needed to be reckoned
with. The clearest conclusion that this literature seemed capable of reaching was that the nominal exchange rate regime provided no substitute for
sound and consistent macroeconomic policies. In fact, since the early 1990s
it has become customary to end every study of exchange rates in developing countries by stressing that both fixed and flexible exchange rates
"can work" in those economies, provided that policymakers show a sufficiently strong commitment to macroeconomic stability. Of course all of
this is true, but trite.

Multicountry Studies

As the diversity of experiences increased during the 1970s, and especially during the 1980s, researchers were able to use larger samples—both
in terms of countries and years—to evaluate performance under alterna-

---

2. See Edwards (1997) for a related evaluation of the World Bank's contribution to the
profession's understanding of the processes of trade liberalization and structural reform in
less developed countries.

tive exchange rate systems. Edwards (1993), for example, used a sample of fifty-two developing countries to investigate whether a fixed exchange rate regime indeed delivered lower rates of inflation than more flexible regimes. Edwards noted that this type of cross-country analysis was potentially subject to a serious "survival bias." The problem is that only countries that have successfully defended their pegs are included in the "fixed exchange rate" category. On the other hand, countries that adopted a fixed exchange rate but failed to sustain it are usually classified as having a "flexible regime." This means that high inflation rates generated by exchange rate crashes are incorrectly (or unfairly) attributed to the flexible rate system. This problem had been noted also by Aghevli et al., who, after arguing that "the inflation performance of the countries that have operated under a fixed exchange rate regime has been, on the whole, superior to that of the group operating under more flexible arrangements," added that this type of conclusion "neglects the experience of countries that initially adopted a pegged arrangement, but were forced to abandon it" (1991, 13). Edwards (1993) attempted to address this survival bias by examining whether, after controlling for other variables, countries that had a fixed exchange rate during the first year (1980) of a ten-year period (1980–89) had a lower average rate of inflation for the decade as a whole. He found that countries with a fixed exchange rate indeed experienced a lower average rate of inflation (the regression coefficient of the dummy variable for a fixed exchange rate in 1980 was -0.7). This effect, however, seemed to depend on the country's inflation history: the inclusion of an interactive regression term suggested that at levels of past (historical) inflation equal to or higher than 20 percent, fixed exchange rates lost their macroeconomic discipline effect.

Little et al. also investigated whether fixed exchange rates discouraged inflation in their comprehensive study of experiences with macroeconomic adjustment in a group of eighteen developing countries. Although they recognized the "reverse causality" problem, they conducted their analysis at a simple descriptive level, without making a formal attempt at dealing with the problem. After looking at the data from different angles they came to the perhaps obvious but nonetheless valuable conclusion that it was not possible to make generalizations. While in some countries a fixed exchange rate had been associated with a lower rate of inflation, in other "episodes the exchange rate was clearly not an effective 'nominal anchor'" (Little et al. 1993, 245). In addition, they made the important point that all analyses of country performance under alternative exchange rate regimes should take into account the role of capital mobility. In fact, they suggested that their conclusions were most relevant for countries where the degree of capital mobility was somewhat limited.

One of the most comprehensive multicountry studies to date was conducted by Ghosh et al. (1995). The study examined the effects of the nominal exchange rate regime on inflation and growth using data from 136 countries during the period 1960–89—more than 3,600 annual observations. The authors computed unconditional and conditional means for the rates of inflation and output growth in the countries in the sample grouped and classified according to the degree of flexibility of their nominal exchange rate, as well as by their level of income. The conditional means were obtained from OLS estimates of simple equations for inflation and growth that included as regressors an exchange rate regime dummy and a set of other potential determinants. The authors checked whether (a subset of) their results suffer from a problem of reverse causation (simultaneity bias) and also examined the effects that the regime may have on the volatility of inflation and output growth.

The study found that the inflation rate is indeed significantly lower and less volatile under pegged exchange rates than under more flexible arrangements, even after controlling for the effects of money growth and interest rates. When it comes to output growth, however, the study found little systematic differences across exchange rate regimes, except for the fact that output growth (and employment) were more volatile under pegged exchange rates than under flexible rates. Another interesting finding of the study was that the "inflation bias" of flexible exchange rate arrangements does not seem to be present among the "pure floaters" in the sample—especially among the high- and upper-middle-income ones, a result that suggests that the positive correlation between exchange rate flexibility and inflation detected in the study may not be monotonic.

A more recent IMF study that extended the period of analysis to the mid-1990s reported similar findings: over the past two decades, inflation has been consistently lower and less volatile in developing countries with pegged exchange rates than in those with more flexible arrangements, but there are no clear differences in the growth performance across the two groups (IMF 1997). Although those conclusions were based on rather crude comparisons of the evolution of the median rates of inflation and output growth in countries with "pegged" and "flexible" exchange rate arrangements from 1975 to 1996, the evidence presented in this study suggests that the main findings reported by Ghosh et al. (1995) were not greatly affected by the increased access to international capital markets gained by developing countries in the 1990s. Indeed, it appears that the differences in macroeconomic performance across nominal exchange rate regimes in developing countries continue to boil down to differences in the inflation performance of the countries in each group and that those differences seem to be getting smaller over time.

The apparent superiority of fixed exchange rates for delivering lower and more stable rates of inflation in developing countries is tempered even further when one takes into account the methodological compromises that are common—and oftentimes unavoidable—in cross-country comparisons of nominal exchange rate regimes.[3] First of all, most studies classify the nominal exchange rate regime following the country's official description of its exchange rate system (typically the one it reports to the IMF) rather than on the basis of the *actual* degree of flexibility of its nominal exchange rate. Discrepancies between de jure and de facto (performance based) classification of regimes, however, are often substantial; moreover, the sign and size of those discrepancies vary across countries and over time. Furthermore, to make things tractable, studies have to condense the twenty-odd de jure categories of exchange rate arrangements reported in IMF sources into two or three broad types of regime (e.g., "pegged" and "flexible"), which can lead to important differences in the classification of the same regime across studies.[4]

Second, and as pointed out above, many of these studies implicitly assume that all exchange rate regimes in their samples were sustainable (in the sense of being consistent with other macroeconomic policies) and that all changes in regime (often, though not always, in the direction of greater exchange rate flexibility) were voluntary. A consequence of this assumption is that the macroeconomic effects of all "regime switches" tend to be ascribed to the successor regime; in developing countries, however, changes in exchange rate regime are rarely smooth events and tend to have short-run adverse effects on inflation and output, especially when they involve a large devaluation (Edwards 1989; Edwards and Montiel 1989; Eichengreen and Masson 1998). Another consequence is that the duration of the exchange rate regime is assumed to be immaterial for macroeconomic performance. Thus, for instance, observations corresponding to countries that somehow managed to hold on for a year or two to clearly inconsistent and unsustainable currency pegs are, for the purpose of the tests conducted in the studies, treated no different by observations pertaining to currency pegs that have been in place for several decades (e.g., the countries in the Communauté Financière Africaine zone).

And third, there is the long-standing and earlier noted problem of endogeneity of the choice of exchange rate regime or reverse causation. The key question is whether fixed exchange rates deliver low inflation by adding discipline and credibility to the conduct of macroeconomic policies. Or is it that countries with low inflation choose pegged exchange rates, perhaps to signal their intention to maintain their anti-inflationary stances? A similar problem arises in the case of output growth, despite the difficulties of

3. This applies both to studies that focus on the relation between nominal exchange rate regimes and macroeconomic performance and to those mentioned earlier that attempt to explain the increased demand for more flexible exchange rate arrangements from a political economy angle.
4. E.g., countries with a de jure exchange rate system of "single currency peg with frequent changes in parity" were classified as "pegged" by Ghosh et al. (1995) and as "flexible" in a related study by Cottarelli and Giannini (1997).

empirical studies for finding any clear link between growth and the exchange rate regime. Do fixed exchange rates foster economic growth—say, by delivering an environment of low inflation and low relative price variability? Or do fast-growing countries choose fixed exchange rates so as to further reduce relative price variability and, hence, increase the horizon and efficiency of investment decisions? Of course, these questions have been at the core of the debate between fixed and flexible exchange rates since the beginning. However, the expectation that more systematic analyses of the empirical evidence could shed more light on them than what could be asked from analyses of individual country experiences may have been too optimistic. Although some recent studies (notably Ghosh et al. 1995 and Edwards 1993, 1996) have made serious attempts to control or check for a possible simultaneity bias in their estimates stemming from an endogenous choice of exchange rate regime, the above-noted problems in the classification of those regimes and in the treatment of regime switches are just two of many possible sources of sample selection bias that remain largely unaddressed. All considered, it seems that a satisfactory solution to the reverse causation problem in studies of the relation between exchange rate regimes and macroeconomic performance in developing countries will require, at a minimum, many more, longer, and better defined episodes of fixed and flexible exchange rates in those economies than what is currently available.

13.2.3   What We Need to Know

A key message of the foregoing discussion is that what the literature on exchange rate regimes in developing countries calls "flexible exchange rates" are, in reality, quite a mixed bag. The problem goes beyond the known but often downplayed fact that the great majority of nominal exchange rates considered "flexible" in empirical studies were—and in some cases remain—heavily managed or directly set by the authorities and, hence, that groupings based on de jure classifications of regimes will tend to exaggerate the shift toward exchange rate flexibility in those economies. It has to do also with the difficulties (some would say futility) of trying to capture the independent effects of exchange rate regimes on macroeconomic performance using data and techniques that are not up to the task. For example, empirical studies will often lump together in the flexible exchange rate category countries with nominal exchange rates that are as stable as de jure pegs (i.e., the case of many East Asian countries in the years before the 1997 crises), as well as countries undergoing high inflation, where exchange rates can do little else than move more or less in tandem with the other nominal variables of the economy (e.g., most Latin American countries in the 1980s). But there can be no presumption that the biases that these various subgroups of countries will impart to the *average* indicators of performance of the flexible category will be mutually offsetting or time invariant. Cross-regime comparisons of performance that rely on those average indicators are therefore likely to remain seriously flawed.

A corollary of the above is that the extensive literature on exchange rate regimes in developing countries does not really have much to offer when it comes to defining and characterizing a "flexible" exchange rate. What does nominal exchange rate flexibility entail in practice? What is it supposed to accomplish? And over what horizon? These are some of the important questions for which the literature on the subject has yet to provide even approximate answers. The evidence available does not shed much light either on whether floating exchange rates represent a feasible or desirable option for developing countries. Most of what has been said about this falls somewhere between a priori theorizing and sheer speculation. To our knowledge, there have been no serious attempts at establishing an economically based divide between a flexible and a floating exchange rate in developing countries. Moreover, given the dearth of episodes with floating exchange rates in those economies,[5] it is not entirely clear whether such a distinction is even possible and, therefore, what countries or experiences outside the developing world should provide the yardstick for evaluating this option.

The current state of affairs is, in many ways, unsatisfactory. The newly emerging consensus on the gains that developing countries will reap from moving toward more flexible exchange rate regimes and on the imminent extinction of the middle-of-the-road exchange rate arrangements of the fixed-but-adjustable variety (Eichengreen 1994; Obstfeld and Rogoff 1995b) looks less persuasive when one tries to pin down the notion of exchange rate flexibility that underlies those conclusions. Nonetheless, it seems that the case for greater flexibility has received a further boost from the recent currency crises in Mexico, East Asia, and now Russia and Brazil. A perusal of the rapidly expanding literature on the origins and (short run) consequences of those currency crashes reveals that the calls for greater exchange rate flexibility come in fact from two different camps: (1) those who continue to ascribe a key role to the exchange rate as a nominal anchor of the economy and, thus, see the increased flexibility as consistent with some form of nominal exchange rate targeting (IMF 1997; Eichengreen and Masson 1998) and (2) those who stress the perils of relying on an asset price (the exchange rate) as a nominal anchor or a source of monetary policy credibility in a world of expanding global capital markets (Obstfeld 1995; Obstfeld and Rogoff 1995b). Of course, as is typical in exchange rate matters, there is also an influential group of dissenters who extract the exact opposite conclusions from the recent crises and ar-

---

5. For an early analysis of a brief episode of floating exchange rates in a developing country (Peru) during the Bretton Woods years, see Edwards (1983) and also Lyons (1992).

gue that the time is ripe for a generalized adoption of currency-board-type arrangements by developing countries, for their (unilateral) move to full dollarization, or for the return to some type of gold (dollar) standard for the world as a whole (e.g., Dornbusch 1998; McKinnon 1998).

The debate is up for grabs and probably would be difficult to settle solely on the basis of further (and better) evidence on the relation between nominal exchange rate regimes and aggregate macroeconomic outcomes (i.e., inflation and growth). Better theoretical models of regime choice and exchange rate determination in less developed countries will of course help, but at least in the near term, we think that the most pressing questions will remain empirical in nature. Take, for example, the need to give a more precise operational meaning to the concept of exchange rate flexibility that is "appropriate" for developing countries. We would argue that the differences between the two broad camps identified above lie in their differing views regarding three key features of exchange rate policy in a context of high capital mobility: (1) the scope for (and effectiveness of) sterilized and unsterilized intervention as a means for attaining (and preserving) a degree of nominal exchange rate stability, (2) the costs that "excessive" fluctuations of the nominal exchange rate may impose on the economy's performance, and (3) the *time dimension* of their analysis—that is, the horizon over which monetary policy, the exchange rate, capital flows, and the rest of the economy are assumed to interplay. All of these are empirical issues about which little, if anything, is known for the case of developing countries—not even for the relatively advanced ones. Unless the discussion starts to focus on those types of questions, our understanding of the effects of greater exchange rate flexibility on the economic performance of these countries will remain as tentative and speculative as it is today.

Mexico's experience after the 1994 peso crisis provides an opportunity to gain some insights into the behavior of floating exchange rates in emerging economies. Of course, it is not possible to extract general conclusions from a single episode, but in the absence of other experiences with anything that resembles a floating rate, analyses of Mexico's foray into exchange rate flexibility should prove very useful. One of the most commonly voiced objections to floating rates in developing nations is that they will be "excessively" volatile—indeed much more than in advanced countries.[6] Figure 13.1 presents weekly data on the nominal exchange rate of the Mexican peso vis-à-vis the U.S. dollar for the period January 1992–May 1998; the top panel depicts the nominal peso-dollar rate, while the bottom panel presents the weekly rate of devaluation of the Mexican peso

---

6. For a brief discussion of the feasibility and viability of floating exchange rates in developing and transition economies, see Corden (1990), IMF (1997), and Eichengreen and Masson (1998).

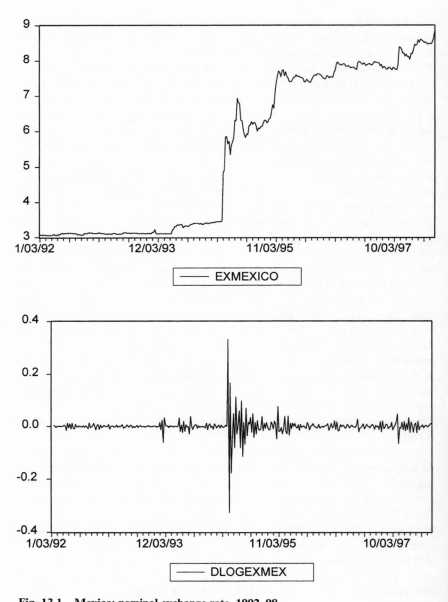

Fig. 13.1   Mexico: nominal exchange rate, 1992–98
Note: Top panel shows the nominal peso-dollar rate; bottom panel shows weekly rate of devaluation of the peso.

during that period. In a recent study, Edwards and Savastano (1998) used high-frequency data similar to that in figure 13.1 to analyze the behavior of the peso-dollar rate during the period January 1995–November 1997. They used a series of indicators to compare the volatility of the peso-dollar rate with that of the rates of the German mark, Japanese yen, British pound, Australian dollar, Canadian dollar, and New Zealand dollar vis-à-vis the U.S. dollar, as well as that of the rate between the French franc and the German mark. They showed that with the exception of 1995, the peso had not been excessively volatile. More specifically, using a battery of indicators they found that the peso was more volatile than the French franc and New Zealand, Australian, and Canadian dollars and less volatile than the yen, mark, and pound. Interestingly enough, an extension of these computations to the first five months of 1998 indicated that in spite of all the turmoil in emerging markets, the peso-dollar rate was still not the most volatile of these nominal exchange rates!

A particularly interesting aspect of the Mexican experience during the 1996–97 period is that the relative lack of volatility of the peso-dollar rate was not due to direct central bank intervention in the foreign exchange market. In fact, during 1996–97, the Banco de Mexico did not sell reserves and only bought them through an options mechanism that did not put undue pressure on the exchange rate. According to Edwards and Savastano, however, during this period the central bank adopted a feedback rule for monetary policy that took into consideration the short-run behavior of the nominal exchange rate. More specifically, using weekly data they were able to identify a reaction function that shows that the monetary authorities tightened liquidity (base money) below its preestablished target when the peso lost value vis-à-vis the dollar and eased liquidity when the peso appreciated. Although preliminary, and based on only a few months of the floating exchange rate experiment, these results suggest that middle-income countries can have a reasonably well functioning floating exchange rate system. As more and more developing countries join Mexico in the flexible rate camp, as we believe they will, it will be possible to expand on analysis of the Edwards and Savastano type and even begin seriously to examine evidence on macroeconomic performance under alternative regimes.

13.3 Long-Run Real Exchange Rate Behavior in Emerging Economies

The distinction between equilibrium and disequilibrium real exchange rates (RERs) is at the core of all empirical analyses of exchange rate behavior. Among the various concepts of equilibrium RER utilized in these analyses, those related to the theory of purchasing power parity, in its many variants, have proved to be the most resilient. Just a few years ago, this assertion would have seemed totally unwarranted. Models built on (or consisting of) PPP-based definitions of the equilibrium exchange rate performed poorly when confronted with data of the early years of the post–Bretton Woods system of generalized floating among the major currencies (e.g., Frenkel 1981; Adler and Lehman 1983; Meese and Rogoff 1983a, 1983b). PPP was therefore rapidly, and rightly, discredited—at least in academic circles—as a guide for assessing the behavior of the RER in both the short and the medium term.

More recently, however, the notion that PPP provides a meaningful benchmark for assessing RER developments over the (very) long term has resurfaced, at least in the case of industrial countries. A number of excellent recent surveys on the subject explain this somewhat surprising revival of PPP as the result of three related factors: "looser" interpretations of the PPP doctrine, longer data samples, and better (and more powerful) empirical tests (see Breuer 1994; Froot and Rogoff 1995; Rogoff 1996).[7] These studies further argue that the interplay of those factors has helped to produce a body of evidence that exhibits a remarkable degree of conformity with four "stylized facts" of RER behavior in advanced economies: (1) The hypothesis that the (bilateral) RER follows a random walk is strongly rejected when tested over sufficiently long horizons—typically spanning six or seven decades. (2) RER series exhibit strong but slow mean reversion properties—with most estimates of the half-life of PPP deviations falling somewhere between three and five years. (3) Hypotheses about the existence of a long-run equilibrium relation between the nominal exchange rate and relative (domestic and foreign) prices are difficult to reject—especially when the tests do not impose restrictions of symmetry or proportionality. (4) With the exception of the yen-dollar rate, there is no compelling evidence of "permanent" deviations from PPP that can be accounted for by other (structural) factors—that is, the Balassa-Samuelson effect is not borne out by the data (Froot and Rogoff 1995; Rogoff 1996).

It is not readily apparent which, if any, of the long-run regularities of the RER noted above also hold in the case of developing countries. However, this type of information could significantly enhance (and even refocus completely) the myriad of analyses and discussions of equilibrium and disequilibrium RER that are conducted for emerging economies. In particular, knowledge of the relative validity of PPP as a (very) long-run benchmark for the equilibrium RER—or, equivalently, of the speed of convergence to long-run PPP—could help refine the horizon for which standard assessments of RER misalignment are most relevant. The review of the evidence on the main features of RER behavior in less developed countries that we undertake below seeks to shed some light on that ques-

---

7. Officer (1976) and Dornbusch (1987) are two earlier and influential surveys of the theory and evidence on PPP up to the mid-1970s and mid-1980s, respectively.

tion. It also sets the stage for the critical evaluation of the literature on RER misalignment that we present in section 13.4.

13.3.1   RER Stationarity and Other Tests of PPP:
Individual Country Studies

The body of empirical literature on PPP focused on developing countries is quite thin, both in absolute terms and when compared to that available for industrial economies (Breuer 1994). This is probably a consequence of developing countries' reluctance to adopt floating exchange rates following the breakdown of the Bretton Woods system. Indeed, the fact that the majority of these countries held on for a while to fixed exchange rate arrangements—as well as to all forms of restrictions on current and capital account transactions—made it both less pressing and less meaningful to use their data to test models that relied on (or consisted of) PPP-based notions of the equilibrium exchange rate.[8]

The situation started to change in the late 1980s. Since then, a growing number of studies have examined the time-series properties of RER in various developing countries, in many cases testing explicitly for some version of PPP. Table 13.3 contains basic information from thirteen of those studies.[9] Specifically, the table contains information on the countries and time period covered by the studies, the measures of exchange rates and (relative) prices they used, the type of test of PPP they conducted, the precise PPP hypothesis they tested, and the results they obtained. To classify the tests employed in the studies we followed the demarcation of the various stages of tests of PPP proposed by Breuer (1994) and Froot and Rogoff (1995), namely, simple tests of PPP as the null hypothesis ("stage 1" tests), univariate tests of the time-series properties of the RER series ("stage 2" tests), and cointegration tests of PPP, both bivariate and trivariate ("stage 3" tests). Notice, however, that none of the studies in the table reported results from stage 1 tests of PPP, probably because the numerous flaws of those OLS-based tests were well known before any serious empirical research on RER in developing countries was undertaken.

The table captures some interesting features of empirical studies of RER and PPP in emerging economies. First, in terms of coverage, far more evidence is available for Latin American economies than for developing countries in other parts of the world. Of the thirteen studies summarized in the table, eight focused solely or primarily on Latin American

8. See, however, Edwards and Losada (1994) and Edwards (1995) for analyses of the time-series properties of inflation differentials (and the RER) in four Central American economies with long-lived fixed exchange rate systems.

9. The sample is intended to be representative, though not exhaustive. In particular, we do not try to present a comprehensive list of all the studies that apply unit-root tests to RER series from less developed countries as a prior step for conducting other tests unrelated to PPP.

Table 13.3   Empirical Studies of PPP in Developing Countries

	Edwards (1989)	McNown and Wallace (1989)	Abeysinghe and Kok-Hong (1992)	León-Astete and Oliva (1992)	Liu (1992)	Gan (199
Sample						
No. of countries	32	4	1	12	9	5
Region	Broad coverage	Latin America and Israel	East Asia	Latin America	Latin America	East Asi
Period covered	1965–85	1976–86	1975–90	1957–90	1948–89	1974–88
No. of years	21	11	15	35	42	15
Data frequency	Quarterly	Monthly	Quarterly	Monthly	Quarterly	Monthly
No. of observations	84	[89, 126]	63	[402, 418]	[120, 170]	[154, 174
Exchange rate and prices						
Price ratio						
CPI		X	X	X	X	
WPI		X	X		X	X
Mixed[a]	X					
Exchange rate						
Bilateral U.S.	X[b]	X	X[c]	X	X	
Multilateral	X					X
Type of test						
Univariate ("stage 2")	X	X	X	X		X
Dickey-Fuller (DF), augmented DF						
(ADF)	X	X	X	X		X
Phillips-Perron (PP)						X
Variance ratios				X		X
Other	Box-Pierce Q			Ljung-Box Q		
Bivariate ("stage 3")		X			X	X
Engle-Granger cointegrating test						
DF, ADF		X			X	X
PP					X	X
Other[d]		ECM			X	BVAR
Trivariate ("stage 3")					X	
Johansen-Juselius cointegrating test						
					X	
PPP version tested	Absolute	Absolute (w/ intercept)	Absolute	Relative	Absolute (w/ intercept)	Absolute (w intercept
Main findings						
Stationarity of						
Real exchange rate	Random walk (RW) rejected (19 of 32 cases)	Found in 2 cases (when p: WPI)	Found for U.S. only (when p: CPI)	RW rejected	Not tested (11 of 12 cases)	Not found
Prices, exchange rate vector	Not tested	Found in 3 cases	Not tested (when p: WPI)	Not tested	Bivariate: 3 yes; 2 no Trivariate: 9 yes	Not found
Mean reversion	Slow (no formal test)	Not tested	Not tested	Strong; long run[e]	Not tested	On another RER
Symmetry (of p and p^*)	Imposed	Imposed	Imposed	Imposed	Found in few cases	Imposed
Proportionality (between p and e)	Imposed	No formal test (apparent)	Imposed	Imposed	Bivariate: 2 cases Trivariate: 4 cases	No formal test (not apparent

Table 13.3   (continued)

	Bahmani-Oskooee (1995)	Calvo, Reinhart, and Végh (1995)	Coes (1995)	Edwards (1995)	Seabra (1995)	Devereux and Connolly (1996)	Montiel (1997)
Sample							
No. of countries	22	3	1	4	11	4	5
Region	Broad coverage	Latin America	Latin America	Latin America	Latin America	Latin America	East Asia
Period covered	1971–90	1978–92	1964–91	1957–82	1970–89	1973–90	1960–94
No. of years	20	15	27	25	20	18	35
Data frequency	Quarterly	Quarterly	Monthly	Quarterly	Quarterly	Quarterly	Annual
No. of observations	80	52	324	101	78	72	35
Exchange rate and prices							
Price ratio							
CPI	X	X		X			X
WPI			X				
Mixed[a]					X	X	
Exchange rate							
Bilateral U.S.			X	X	X		
Multilateral	X	X				X	X
Type of test							
Univariate ("stage 2")	X	X	X	X		X	X
Dickey-Fuller (DF), augmented DF (ADF)	X	X	X	X		X	X
Phillips-Perron (PP)	X	X				X	X
Variance ratios		X					
Other				Ljung-Box Q			
Bivariate ("stage 3")					X		
Engle-Granger cointegrating test							
DF, ADF PP					X		
Other[d]					X		
Trivariate ("stage 3")							
Johansen-Juselius cointegrating test					X		
PPP version tested	Absolute	Absolute	Absolute[f] (quasi)	Relative	Relative	Absolute	Absolute
Main findings							
Stationarity of							
Real exchange rate	Found in 8 cases (PP test)	Not found	Not found	Found in 3 cases	Not tested	Rejected in levels (first-difference stationary)	Rejected (exc. Singapore)
Prices, exchange rate vector	Not tested	Not tested	Not tested	Not tested	Bivariate: 8 yes	Not tested Trivariate: 9 yes	Not tested
Mean reversion	Not tested	Slow (Beveridge-Nelson)	Not tested	Not tested	Suggestive evidence	Not tested	Not tested
Symmetry (of p and p^*)	Imposed	Imposed	Imposed	Imposed	Imposed	Imposed	Imposed
Proportionality (between p and e)	Imposed	Imposed	Imposed	Not applicable[g]	Bivariate: 4 cases Trivariate: 4 cases	Imposed	Imposed

[a]Ratio of foreign WPI to domestic CPI.

[b]Parallel market U.S. dollar rate.

[c]Bilateral rates vis-à-vis the United States, United Kingdom, Germany, Japan, and Malaysia.

[d]ECM, error correction model; BVAR, bivariate vector autoregression model.

[e]Less than five years in five cases; more than five years in seven cases.

[f]Test applied to PPP ratio multiplied by tradables share in WPI.

[g]No changes in the nominal exchange rate during the sample period.

countries and the other three on East Asian economies. Only two studies (Edwards 1989 and Bahmani-Oskooee 1995) examined RER data from (a few) developing countries in other regions of the world. Second, the periods covered by the studies are quite short. The majority of studies conducted tests on data series that covered less than thirty years—and four of them did so on series that covered less than fifteen years. Only three studies (León-Astete and Oliva 1992; Liu 1992; Montiel 1997) used data series that covered thirty-five years or more. To overcome the "small sample problem" all studies but one used either quarterly or monthly data to test their hypotheses; this produced samples that ranged from 50 to 400 observations. Third, studies relied a bit more heavily on consumer price indexes (CPIs) than on wholesale price indexes (WPIs) to construct their measure of relative (domestic to foreign) prices. Three studies (Edwards 1989; Seabra 1995; Devereux and Connolly 1996) used a measure of relative prices that combined both the CPI (domestic prices) and the WPI (foreign prices).[10] Also, in striking contrast with empirical tests on PPP for industrial countries, only seven of the studies in the table used a bilateral exchange rate vis-à-vis a major currency (typically the U.S. dollar) as the measure of the nominal exchange rate.[11] The other six used a multilateral (trade weighted) indicator—what the IMF calls the "nominal effective exchange rate."[12] Fourth, the majority of studies relied on some type of univariate (stage 2) test to examine the main properties of the RER—and the PPP hypothesis. Only four of the thirteen studies (McNown and Wallace 1989; Liu 1992; Gan 1994; Seabra 1995) conducted bivariate cointegration (stage 3) tests of PPP, and just two of those four also tested PPP using trivariate cointegration techniques. And fifth, studies were generally unclear about the precise PPP hypothesis that was being tested. It could be argued, however, that the majority of them were testing for some variant of absolute PPP (in most cases using a somewhat peculiar measure of the foreign price level consisting of a weighted average of price levels in the country's main trading partners). Only three studies (León-Astete and Oliva 1992; Edwards 1995; Seabra 1995) made it clear that they were testing the hypothesis of relative PPP.

An obvious consequence of the predominance of univariate (stage 2) tests of PPP is that the bulk of the findings obtained by the studies in table 13.3 revolve around the stationarity of various measures of the RER. By

10. This measure is commonly used in empirical work as a proxy for the relative price between tradable and nontradable goods, i.e., the concept of the RER that follows from the "dependent economy model" (see Edwards 1989; Corden 1990).

11. Counting the study by Edwards (1995), which focused on countries that maintained a fixed exchange rate vis-à-vis the U.S. dollar during the sample period.

12. Edwards (1989) also constructed an RER series that used the parallel market exchange rate vis-à-vis the U.S. dollar instead of the official exchange rate as the indicator of the value of the domestic currency.

and large, the hypothesis that the RER is stationary in developing countries (and, thus, that some form of PPP condition holds in the long run) *does not* receive much support from these studies. In forty out of fifty-four individual country tests of RER stationarity, the hypothesis that the RER series contained (at least) one unit root could not be rejected. Interestingly, however, the hypothesis that the RER series followed a random walk did not fare much better. In fact, Edwards (1989) and León-Astete and Oliva (1992) tested the random walk hypothesis for a combined total of forty-four series and rejected it in about two-thirds of the cases.

Results from the (few) studies that used cointegration tests were somewhat more supportive of the PPP hypotheses. The four studies that tested for bivariate cointegration between the nominal exchange rate and the ratio of domestic to foreign prices found that the residuals of the estimated regressions were stationary in about 50 percent of the cases (fifteen of thirty-three). The two studies that conducted trivariate tests of cointegration (Liu 1992 and Seabra 1995) found even stronger evidence of an equilibrium relation between the exchange rate and domestic and foreign prices (eighteen of twenty cases). Notably, all the support for PPP obtained from these stage 3 tests stemmed from data on Latin American countries; in fact, Gan (1994) did not find evidence of cointegration between the exchange rate and prices in any of the five East Asian countries in his sample.

A somewhat disappointing aspect of the studies in table 13.3 is that they do not reveal much about the mean reversion properties of the RER series they examined (and, hence, about the speed of convergence to long-run PPP in those economies). Only three studies conducted formal tests of mean reversion—and found some evidence of its presence—and two others simply mentioned mean reversion as a feature of the RER series they used when discussing their findings. Last, again reflecting the predominance of stage 2 tests, most studies ended up imposing rather than testing the restrictions of proportionality and symmetry on the coefficients of the price terms in the RER—or PPP—equation (Breuer 1994).

Seeing what the studies in table 13.3 have to offer, one gets the distinct feeling that our knowledge of the basic time-series properties of RERs in developing countries and, in particular, of the relevance of PPP as a long-run benchmark for equilibrium RERs in these economies is fairly rudimentary. The most serious shortcoming is, without question, the low power of the tests (especially of stage 2 tests) to distinguish among alternative hypotheses in the short periods covered by the studies—a deficiency that cannot be fixed by the common practice of increasing the number of observations through the use of quarterly or monthly data (Froot and Rogoff 1995; Oh 1996). But this is hardly the only problem. The overrepresentation of Latin America in the sample of developing countries examined in the studies, the lack of clarity with regard to the variant of the PPP theory that is supposedly being tested, and the dearth of empirical work aimed at testing a well-defined PPP hypothesis using cointegration techniques, both bivariate and trivariate, also contribute to the above feeling. The pervasive and severe data problems that one encounters in developing countries may well be at the root of these shortcomings, and it is quite possible that for many countries this constraint will not disappear for many years. But this does not alter the basic conclusion that the evidence on RER stationarity and long-run PPP contained in studies of individual developing countries does not enable us to discern which, if any, of the regularities of the long-run RER that have been found for industrial economies are also applicable to (or relevant for) the developing world.

13.3.2   Other Evidence: Panel Estimates and Cross-Country Studies

Recent studies that use panel data from industrial and developing countries to examine various hypotheses related to PPP (e.g., Frankel and Rose 1996; Oh 1996; O'Connell 1998) provide additional insights into the time-series properties of RERs in emerging economies. The studies represent one of the two lines of work that emerged in the 1990s to enhance the power of conventional tests of PPP (Rogoff 1996).[13] They achieve this by taking advantage of the cross-country variation of the data on exchange rates and prices while at the same time reducing the (potentially serious) bias introduced by the many changes in the exchange rate regime that most countries undergo during periods of several decades (Frankel and Rose 1996).

The results from these studies are broadly supportive of PPP as a long-run benchmark for the RER. In particular, the studies reject the hypothesis that the RER follows a random walk in the sample as a whole, as well as in a wide array of subsamples, and find estimates of convergence to PPP similar to those obtained with long-run horizon data sets—that is, PPP deviations with a half-life of about three to five years. The link between these findings and the long-run behavior of the RER in developing countries follows directly from the composition of the sample, which is amply dominated by observations from less developed countries.[14] In fact, an important question is whether developing country data may not be influencing "too much" the overall findings of the studies. Possible sources of bias include the predominance of monetary shocks in many high-inflation developing countries (Rogoff 1996), the cross-sectional dependence stemming from using the U.S. dollar as the base currency for all calculations (O'Connell 1998), and the aggregation across (and frequent

13. The other approach, testing PPP using several decades of data on exchange rates and prices, is not a realistic option for the great majority of less developed countries. However, see Froot and Rogoff (1995) for an illustrative application of this approach to Argentine data covering the period 1913–88. See also Edwards and Losada (1994).

14. The share of developing country data in the panels goes from 50 percent of the observations (Oh 1996, table 3) to about 90 percent (Parsley and Popper 1998, table 1).

switches of) nominal exchange rate regimes within the sample. While the influence of those factors is fairly apparent in many results reported in the studies (see, e.g., Frankel and Rose 1996, tables 2, 3; Oh 1996), the size of the bias that they impart to the overall findings and, hence, the extent to which those findings can be deemed representative of the behavior of the RER in developing countries remains unclear and should be addressed in future work.

Using a completely different methodology, a recent cross-country study by Goldfajn and Valdés (1999) represents a significant addition to the empirical literature on RERs in emerging economies. The authors compiled a large sample of monthly data from ninety-three countries during the period 1960–94 (more than 39,000 observations) and proceeded to identify the main empirical regularities of episodes of RER appreciation and the mechanisms that make those appreciations disappear—that is, the forces that explain the apparent mean reversion of RERs. The episodes of appreciation (or overvaluation) were defined as one-sided, short- and medium-term departures of the actual from the "equilibrium" RER. Concretely, they were defined as the difference between the actual multilateral RER and one of two proxies for the equilibrium RER: one obtained from a regression of the logarithm of the RER on two time trends (linear and square) and the other from a regression that also includes as explanatory variables three RER "fundamentals" (terms of trade, government spending, and openness).[15] The authors assumed, rather than tested, that all the RER series are trend-stationary stochastic processes that tend to revert to their means and, based on this central assumption, claimed that the residuals obtained from their two PPP-based equations for the equilibrium RER provide reasonable boundaries for the "true" overvaluation of the domestic currency.

Goldfajn and Valdés combined their two regression-based estimates of overvaluation with arbitrary thresholds for the "critical" degree of appreciation (which they assumed falls somewhere between 15 and 35 percent) to identify the main regularities of episodes of RER appreciation in the thirty-five years covered in their sample. Specifically they calculated, for different configurations of those key parameters, the number of appreciation episodes, their average duration, and their distribution over five-year intervals and across different exchange rate regimes. They found that depending on the parameters they used, their sample contains between 20 and 173 episodes of appreciation that, on average, last between one and two years each; that the time profile of those episodes exhibits a

---

15. To use these annual frequency fundamentals in their monthly regressions the authors interpolated yearly observations using June as the base month. Of interest for our discussion of RER misalignment in the following section is that the authors alluded to the joint determination of the RER and the current account as the reason for not including a measure of capital flows as an additional fundamental in the RER regression.

pronounced asymmetry (in the sense that their "buildup" phase lasts almost twice as long as their reversal phase); that episodes of appreciation have been more common in the second half of the sample (1980–94); and that they have been much less likely to occur in regimes with (de jure) flexible or floating exchange rates.

To identify the factors that explain the end of appreciation episodes, Goldfajn and Valdés then calculated the contribution of changes in the nominal exchange rate and changes in relative (domestic and foreign) prices to the actual depreciation of the RER that marks the end of those episodes. What they found is that in most cases (between 50 and 70 percent, depending on the parameters used) the appreciations were undone primarily, when not solely, by changes in the nominal exchange rate as opposed to changes in inflation differentials.[16] Moreover, they showed that the probability of undoing an appreciation without a nominal devaluation is inversely related to the size of the appreciation—that is, changes in inflation differentials rarely suffice to make large appreciations disappear. Last, the authors constructed transition matrices in order to examine the relation between the size of the appreciation, the probability of its reversal, and time. They found evidence that this relation is highly nonlinear. Specifically, they found that the probability of undoing a given appreciation is higher, the longer the horizon considered, but that when the horizon is kept fixed, there is a U-shaped relation between the probability of reversal and the size of the appreciation—that is, as the size of the appreciation increases, the forces that make the RER return to its equilibrium path through a real depreciation start to dominate. Goldfajn and Valdés claimed that these findings are consistent with (and supportive of) the recent results on mean reversion and long-run convergence to PPP that we discussed earlier. Although this claim seems a bit of a stretch and, together with a few other conjectures and rough edges,[17] deserves a fuller examination, on the whole we believe that the stylized facts documented in this study and summarized above provide fertile ground for future research on the long-run regularities of RER behavior in developing countries.

13.3.3   Structural Deviations from PPP: The Balassa-Samuelson Effect

A wholly different strand of literature has aimed at documenting and explaining the existence of "structural" (permanent) deviations from absolute PPP across countries. Building on seminal work by Balassa (1964) and drawing primarily on data sets constructed for the UN-sponsored In-

---

16. Edwards (1989, chap. 7) obtained similar results for a sample of thirty-nine devaluation episodes in developing countries during the period 1960–82.

17. These would include, in our view, the lack of explicit tests of the hypotheses of nonstationarity of the RER series, not reporting a breakdown by income level or geographical location of the countries driving the main results of the study, and several issues related to the choice and construction of RER fundamentals.

ternational Comparison Program (ICP),[18] numerous studies have provided evidence of sizable differences between a country's exchange rate and its PPP (defined as the ratio of a country's price level to the price level in a reference country, the United States, both constructed using the same set of weights for individual commodity groups)[19] and have examined empirically what factors may account for the differences.

Table 13.4 presents information for fifteen of those studies.[20] The table shows clearly that up to the early 1990s the empirical approach followed by this strand of the literature consisted of estimating cross-sectional regressions of some countries' "real price level" (the PPP index defined above divided by the nominal exchange rate) or variants thereof (e.g., "real prices" for a subset of commodity groups such as services or nontradables) on a relatively small number of explanatory variables, using samples with a length and coverage that were largely dictated by the latest ICP data available. The rationale for including as regressors a measure of per capital income jointly with proxies for various other "structural" features of the economy (e.g., the share of primary sector output in total GDP, the openness ratio, and indicators of educational attainment) was threefold: test the robustness of Balassa's findings, increase the explanatory power of the regression equation, and ascertain the relative contribution of the competing hypotheses that were being offered to explain large and sustained deviations from absolute PPP—namely, productivity differentials between tradable and nontradable sectors (Balassa 1964; Samuelson 1964), differences in relative factor endowments (Bhagwati 1984; Kravis and Lipsey 1983), differences in the degree of factor mobility (Clague 1985), or differences in consumer preferences (Bergstrand 1991).

On the whole, the cross-country studies in table 13.4 were far more successful in showing that the direct relation between real price levels and per capita income found by Balassa was robust to increases in the sample size, changes in the base year, and inclusion of additional regressors than in their other two objectives. In particular, the goal of distinguishing among competing explanations for the existence of such a link between real prices and income levels proved quite elusive (see Bergstrand 1991; Heston, Nuxoll, and Summers 1994). Also, there were indications that the results were not as strong when the sample was confined to, or dominated by, observations from developing countries (Salazar-Carrillo 1982; Kravis and Lipsey 1988), but the data constraints proved too severe to deal with this problem satisfactorily.

18. See Kravis et al. (1975), Kravis, Heston, and Summers (1982), and Summers and Heston (1988, 1991) for discussions of the objectives, methodology, and data coverage of the ICP.
19. Formally, the purchasing power of any given country is defined as PPP $= \Sigma d_i(p_i/p_i^*)$, where p_i and p_i^* are prices for individual commodity group i in the home country and the reference country measured in each country's currency and the d_i are a set of weights.
20. Not counting Balassa's (1964) study, which is included solely for comparative purposes.

Table 13.4   **Cross-Sectional Studies of PPP Deviations (real price levels)**

	Balassa (1964)	Clague and Tanzi (1972)	Isenman (1980)	Salazar-Carrillo (1982)	Kravis and Lipsey (1983)	Kravis and Lipsey (1987)
Sample						
Cross section	Yes	Yes	Yes	Yes	Yes	Yes (3-year avgs)
No. of countries	12	17–19	16	16, 22	16, 26, 34	25
No. of developing countries	0	17–19	8	16	19	15
Year(s) covered by data	1960	1960	1970	1973, 1970	1975, 1970	1975, 1960–83[a]
Source(s) of price data[b]	ICP (OECD)	ECLA	ICP	ICP, ECLA	ICP	ICP
Specification						
Dependent variable(s)[c]	PPP/e	PPP/e	e/PPP	PPP/e	PPP/e Pn/e; Pt/e	PPP/e Pn/e; Pt/e
No. of regressors[d]						
Min	1	3	2	1	1	3
Max	1	4	5	1	4	4
Per capita income						
Expected sign	Yes	Yes	Yes	Yes	Yes	Yes
Statistical significance	(?)	Yes	Yes	1 of 2	Yes	Yes
(Pseudo) dynamics	No	No	No	No	Yes[e]	Yes[e]

	Kravis and Lipsey (1988)	Clague (1986)	Clague (1988a)	Clague (1988b)	Officer (1989)
Sample					
Cross section	Yes (3-year avgs)	Yes	Yes	Yes	Yes
No. of countries	44, 60	31	59	19	31
No. of developing countries	33	18	32	13	n.a.
Year(s) covered by data	1980, 1960–84[a]	1975	1980	1970	1975
Source(s) of price data[b]	ICP	ICP	ICP	ICP	ICP
Specification					
Dependent variable(s)[c]	PPP/e Pn/e; Pt/e	PPP/e	PPP/e	PPP/e	PPP/e Pn/Pt
No. of regressors[d]					
Min	1	2	2	1	2
Max	4	8	6	4	5
Per capita income					
Expected sign	OECD: yes LDCs: no	No	Yes	Yes	Yes
Statistical significance	Yes	No	Yes	Yes	Yes
(Pseudo) dynamics	Yes[f]	No	No	No	No

	Bergstrand (1991)	Falvey and Gemmell (1991)	Heston, Nuxoll, and Summers (1994)	Connolly and Devereux (1995)	Dollar (1992)
Sample					
Cross section	Yes	Yes	Yes	No[g] (panel)	No[h] (panel)
No. of countries	21	52	16, 34, 61, 64	17	117
No. of developing countries	9	49	n.a.	17	95
Year(s) covered by data	1975	1980	1970, 1975, 1980, 1985	1960–85	1976–85
Source(s) of price data[b]	ICP	ICP	ICP	S&H (PWT)	S&H (PWT)
Specification					
Dependent variable(s)[c]	Pn/Pt	Pn, j/Pn,us[i] Ps, j/Ps,us	Pt/Pn Pt/PPP; Pn/PPP	PPP/e	PPP/e

Table 13.4 (continued)

	Bergstrand (1991)	Falvey and Gemmell (1991)	Heston, Nuxoll, and Summers (1994)	Connolly and Devereux (1995)	Dollar (1992)
No. of regressors[d]					
Min	1	7	1	13	1
Max	3	8	1	14	6
Per capita income					
Expected sign	Yes	Some	Most	Yes	Yes
Statistical					
significance	Yes	Yes	Yes	Yes	Yes
(Pseudo) dynamics	No	No	Yes[j]	Year dummies	?

[a]Annual price data for individual years (and three-year averages) obtained by interpolation.

[b]ICP: International Comparison Program. Country coverage increased over time (in several "phases"). Latest phase is Penn World Table, Mark 5 (PWT5), Summers and Heston (S&H 1991). ECLA: UN Economic Commission for Latin America.

[c]PPP/e: real price level; ratio of "purchasing power parities" to the official exchange rate. Purchasing power parity defined as the ratio of the national price level in country j to the national price level in the United States. Pn/e: U.S. dollar price of nontradables in country j. Pt/e: U.S. dollar prices of tradables in country j. All price categories (Pn, Pt) derived from national accounts data compiled for the ICP.

[d]Excluding the intercept.

[e]Compares coefficients obtained from estimating the same equation using data for different periods (years). Includes as regressor in the equation for period T, the residuals obtained in the estimation for period T − 1 to assess the "persistence" of PPP deviations.

[f]Computes trend regressions for prices and per capita income and gauges the relation between trend changes in those variables.

[g]Six observations per country, each of them representing a five-year period.

[h]Ten annual observations per country (from Penn World Table, Mark 4).

[i]Pn, j/Pn,us [Ps, j/Ps,us]: relative price of nontradables [services] in country j to nontradables [services] in the United States.

[j]Compares per capita income coefficient obtained from estimating the same equation with data for different samples and periods.

Findings of large and seemingly structural deviations from absolute PPP like those obtained from the cross-country studies in table 13.4 are essentially of a static nature and, hence, have only limited value as benchmarks for the medium- and long-run behavior of the RER in a given country or group of countries. That gap has to be filled with time-series evidence or with more systematic analyses of the origin (and duration) of those deviations from PPP, preferably using data not taken from (or related to) the ICP.[21] For many OECD economies such analyses exist.[22] For developing countries, however, that type of evidence is quite rare.

Wood (1991) was among the first (and few) to examine systematically the factors behind "secular" movements in the RERs of a large group of

21. Despite the extended coverage and other methodological improvements of the later phases of the ICP—i.e., the Penn World Tables Marks 4 and 5—those data continue to suffer from a number of limitations that are particularly serious for time-series analyses, such as the reliance on methods of extrapolation to calculate observations from nonbenchmark years and countries and the fixed five-year frequency of the benchmark surveys (Summers and Heston 1988, 1991; Rogoff 1996). Results from studies that use those time series for panel estimations of PPP hypotheses (e.g., Dollar 1992; Connolly and Devereux 1995; Oh 1996) should, therefore, be interpreted with caution and, to the extent possible, cross-checked with evidence obtained from other data sets.

22. The standard references are Hsieh (1982) for Japan and Germany and Marston (1987) for Japan. More recent studies that examine deviations from PPP in a larger sample of OECD countries (using OECD data) include Asea and Mendoza (1994) and de Gregorio, Giovannini, and Wolf (1994); see Froot and Rogoff (1995) for a fuller list of references.

developing countries. Using World Bank data, measures of the RER and its structural determinants closely related to those employed by the studies on the real price level in table 13.4, and a peculiar empirical methodology (wherein, e.g., all variables were expressed in terms of the ratio of their average value in the years 1980–84 to their average value in the years 1960–64), Wood's study showed that from the early 1960s to the early 1980s the RERs of less developed countries had *depreciated* relative to those of industrial countries by an amount that ranged from 20 to 40 percent, depending on the individual developing country's level of income. He then concluded, based on the results obtained from several cross-country regressions, that the main cause for the common trend in the RERs of less developed countries during those twenty-five years was "an unusually large trend increase in the price of nontraded to traded goods within the developed countries" (Wood 1991, 331)—that is, a strong Balassa-Samuelson effect in the RERs of the industrial economies.

Isard and Symansky (1996) followed a more conventional approach to examine long-run movements in the RERs of the member countries of APEC.[23] They constructed four measures of the bilateral RER (one based on ICP data and the other three consisting of exchange-rate-adjusted ratios of GDP deflators, CPIs, and export price indexes) and showed that from 1973 to 1993, only Japan, Korea, and Taiwan experienced substantial real appreciations vis-à-vis the U.S. dollar; most of the other fast-growing APEC countries experienced *depreciation* of their RERs—which was particularly large in the cases of China and Indonesia. Isard and Symansky interpreted these results as prima facie evidence of lack of robustness of the relation between output growth and real appreciation commonly associated with the Balassa-Samuelson hypothesis.

To identify the causes for the absence of a Balassa-Samuelson effect in the majority of APEC countries, Isard and Symansky used national account data from the World Bank to decompose the ratio of real GDP deflators (their preferred measure of the RER) into five "proximate determinants": the relative price of domestic and foreign tradable goods (proxied by the price of manufactures), the domestic and foreign ratios of nontradable goods prices (proxied by the price of services) to tradable goods prices, and the shares of nontradables in the domestic and foreign price indexes. They examined the behavior of those determinants over the sample period and computed their cumulative changes from 1973 to 1993. They found that the relative price of tradables "explained" rather well the year-to-year variation of the RER in the majority of APEC countries and

23. APEC (Asia Pacific Economic Cooperation) comprises eighteen Pacific Basin countries including Japan and the United States; Australia, Canada, and New Zealand; China; the (former) East Asian "tigers"; and Chile and Mexico from Latin America. Isard and Symansky's analyses of RER trends excluded Brunei, for lack of data, and the United States, which was used as the numéraire country.

accounted for the bulk of the trend changes in the RER in about half of the cases. For the other half, they found that the trend movements in the RER over the twenty-year period had been driven by large changes in the relative price of nontradable to tradable goods that were of the opposite sign from what the Balassa-Samuelson hypothesis would have predicted. Isard and Symansky advanced three possible explanations for their finding of trends in the relative price of tradable goods across APEC countries— changes in the composition of tradable goods, changes in the terms of trade across different categories of tradable goods, and changes over time in the costs of "goods arbitrage"—but offered no formal test of these conjectures. Nonetheless, they claimed that their results provide a number of clear counterexamples to the Balassa-Samuelson hypothesis among the APEC countries, which, in their view, challenged the presumption that fast-growing economies should generally be expected to experience sustained real appreciations of their currencies.

All in all, a review of this literature makes it rather easy to fully endorse Rogoff's (1996) critique of the empirical evidence on structural deviations from PPP and the Balassa-Samuelson effect for OECD economies. Support for the various hypotheses offered to explain "permanent" deviations from absolute PPP is even weaker for the case of emerging economies and stems mostly from static comparisons between rich and poor countries obtained from ICP-based data, rather than from analyses focused on more homogeneous groups of less developed countries or on long time-series data for individual countries. The few studies that follow these alternative approaches suffer from a number of shortcomings but nonetheless obtain results that cast further doubts about the presence of a strong Balassa-Samuelson effect in developing countries during the past two to three decades (Wood 1991; Isard and Symansky 1996). Until this evidence is refuted, we think that it would be prudent not to take for granted any assumption or conjecture about the relation between output or income (growth) and RERs (changes) in emerging economies.

13.3.4   What We Need to Know

The main finding of this review of the literature on the long-run properties of RERs in emerging economies has been amply foreshadowed. Briefly put, the evidence in support of various hypotheses related to PPP is generally weaker for less developed countries than for industrial countries; at the same time, however, the evidence on structural deviations from PPP— the Balassa-Samuelson effect and related hypotheses—is as flawed and inconclusive for developing countries as it is for industrial economies, with the exception of Japan. As noted before, for the case of industrial countries a consensus has been reached in recent years regarding the (approximate) answer to questions such as: Does PPP hold in the long run? How long is the long run? What is the half-life of PPP deviations? And which are the effects of productivity differentials on the RER? For developing countries, individually or as a group, no such consensus exists. Severe data problems have undoubtedly contributed to this outcome, but other factors (such as the heavy concentration on Latin American experiences to the detriment of other regions of the world) also have played a role. In any event, the agenda is quite clear: we need to know much more than we currently do about the long-run properties of RERs in emerging economies.

A better grasp of the long-run regularities of RER behavior in developing countries, and, in particular, of the relative validity of PPP as a (very) long-run benchmark for the RER, would help give the appropriate time dimension to the assessments of RER misalignment that as we show in the following section, have become commonplace in emerging economies. In this regard, it is important to stress that firmer evidence of long-run convergence to PPP in developing countries (say, comparable to that available for industrial economies) need not be incompatible with the notion of a time-varying equilibrium RER determined by the interplay of a set of foreign and domestic fundamentals, nor would it make less pressing the need to improve the methods currently used to assess RER misalignment in those countries. Evidence of (slow) convergence to PPP would, at best, provide support for an "ultra-long-run" concept of the equilibrium RER—that is, the rate that would result after all real and (transitory) nominal shocks have dissipated, a process that may take *several decades* (Breuer 1994). The relevant yardstick for the medium to long run, however, will continue to be a time-varying, fundamental-driven RER consistent with the attainment of internal and external balance. Some notion of the horizon over which the equilibrating forces pertaining to each of these dynamic processes should be expected to dominate the other one is precisely what is missing from our collective understanding of RER behavior in developing countries.

13.4   Assessing Real Exchange Rate Misalignment

Questions related to the appropriateness of RERs have for a number of years been at the center of discussions on emerging economies. In particular, analysts have been interested in understanding whether, at a given moment in time, a country's RER is (roughly) in equilibrium or whether it is facing a situation of misalignment. There are at least two reasons why these issues have become increasingly prominent in recent times: first, persistent overvaluation is seen as providing a powerful early warning of currency crises (Kaminsky, Lizondo, and Reinhart 1998; Merrill Lynch 1998). And second, situations of protracted or recurrent RER misalignment have been associated with lower economic growth over the medium and long runs (see, e.g., Edwards 1988a; Cottani, Cavallo, and Khan 1990; Ghura and Grennes 1993).

Assessing whether a country's RER is out of line with its long-run equilibrium is not easy, however. In fact, attempts to construct misalignment indexes have tended to be highly controversial in both academic and policy circles. First, as we argued in the preceding section, PPP-based models of exchange rate misalignment are, more often than not, highly misleading in short- and medium-term horizons. Second, the equilibrium RER is not an observable variable. And third, more sophisticated models are difficult to interpret and, many times, lack a minimal degree of robustness. Mexico provides a clear illustration of these problems. When, in 1994, independent analysts argued that the peso had become dangerously overvalued, the authorities replied that the strong real appreciation experienced by the peso during the previous four years was fully justified by changes in "fundamentals." From there they went on to argue emphatically that the substantial strengthening of the peso should not be a cause for concern and that there would be no crisis. As it turned out, they were wrong.[24]

In this section we evaluate the empirical literature on RER misalignment. We begin with a discussion of single-equation models for evaluating long-run RER sustainability. We then review an approach based on general equilibrium simulation models that has been associated with Williamson's (1985) "fundamental equilibrium exchange rates." As in previous sections, we end with the question: given what this literature has to offer, what do we need to know?

13.4.1 Single-Equation Models of Real Exchange Rate Misalignment

Most empirical approaches to assessing RER misalignment are based on small—usually single equation—econometric models. In these models the RER is defined as the relative price of tradable to nontradable goods that, simultaneously, is compatible with the attainment of internal and external equilibrium.[25]

As a backdrop for those analyses many authors have developed theoretical models (representative agent, intertemporal frameworks, with price flexibility, perfect competition, and rational expectations have become the most popular ones) from which a reduced form for the equilibrium RER is derived.[26] This reduced form relates the long-run equilibrium RER to a

24. On the debates surrounding the Mexican 1994 devaluation, see, e.g., the essays collected in Edwards and Naim (1997).
25. A concept of the RER that, as noted earlier, has its theoretical foundation in the "dependent economy model."
26. On theoretical models of RER behavior, see, e.g., Edwards (1989) and Obstfeld and Rogoff (1995a). On the derivation of reduced forms to derive the long-run equilibrium RER, see Hinkle and Montiel (1997).

set of variables, called the RER "fundamentals." These fundamentals usually include terms of trade, output growth (or productivity differentials), the country's openness to international trade, import tariffs, and government spending. While some authors have tried to use a relatively large number of fundamentals in their regression equations, others have restricted their analyses to a small number of variables.

In this framework the RER is said to be "misaligned" if its actual value exhibits a (sustained) departure from its long-run equilibrium. This situation can arise, for example, when there are changes in fundamentals that trigger a change in the equilibrium RER but that are not reflected in changes in the actual RER. A different type of misalignment takes place when macroeconomic policies become incompatible with maintaining internal and external equilibrium and give rise to a sustained appreciation of the actual RER (see Dornbusch 1989; Edwards 1989; Hinkle and Montiel 1999). From a theoretical standpoint, the concept of misalignment requires assuming that there exist institutional or other type of rigidities that prevent the RER from adjusting rapidly toward its medium- to long-run equilibrium level.[27]

The majority of single-equation models follow a four-step approach for assessing RER misalignment.[28] In the first step, historical data are used to estimate a (reduced form) RER equation:[29]

$$(1) \qquad\qquad RER_t = \sum a_i x_{it} + \varepsilon_t,$$

where the x_{it} are the fundamentals, the a_i are their corresponding regression coefficients, and ε_t is an error term. Most recent studies that estimate equations like (1) have done so using cointegration techniques.

The second step usually (but not always) consists of computing normal or sustainable values for the fundamentals. This is typically done by decomposing the x_{it} into "permanent" and "transitory" components using various techniques, including the methodology suggested by Beveridge and Nelson (1981):

$$(2) \qquad\qquad x_{it} = xp_{it} + xt_{it},$$

where xp_{it} and xt_{it} are the permanent and transitory components of fundamental i in period t. Baffes et al. (1999) have argued that because deficiencies in the data of many developing countries make it problematic to apply

27. Most authors, however, either ignore or do not specify clearly the source of these rigidities. See the discussion below.

28. This methodology was suggested in Edwards (1988a) and applied in Edwards (1988b). In a related discussion, Baffes, Elbadawi, and O'Connell (1999) identified three steps in the single-equation methodology.

29. We have chosen a linear functional form for eq. (1) for expository purposes. Naturally, this need not be the case. Baffes et al. (1997) also considered a linear representation of the equilibrium RER in their analysis.

the Beveridge-Nelson decomposition, analysts should rely on alternative procedures, including ex ante (i.e., judgment based) estimates of the sustainable level of the fundamentals.

The third step consists of using the xp_{it}—which are interpreted as the long-run sustainable values of the fundamentals—and the estimated regression coefficients $\hat{a}_i$ to construct an "equilibrium" path for the RER:

$$(3) \qquad\qquad RER_t^* = \sum \hat{a}_i xp_{it}.$$

An important property of equation (3) is that in contrast with simple PPP-based calculations, it generates an estimated equilibrium RER that does not have to be constant over time. Indeed, to the extent that there are changes in fundamentals, the estimated index of the equilibrium RER obtained from equation (3) will vary through time.[30]

In the fourth, and final, step the degree of misalignment is computed as the difference, at any moment in time, between the equilibrium and the actual (or observed) RER:

$$(4) \qquad\qquad MIS = RER_t^* - RER_t.$$

If $RER_t^* > RER_t$, the model would suggest that the currency is *overvalued;* conversely, if $RER_t^* < RER_t$, the model would indicate that the domestic currency is *undervalued.*

Table 13.5 presents information on sixteen empirical studies that have used the single-equation approach to assess the extent of misalignment in a score of developing and transition economies.[31] The second column of the table indicates the countries and time period covered by each study; the third column provides a list of the fundamentals; the fourth column describes the techniques used to calculate the equilibrium RER; and the last column contains some general comments about each study. A number of features emerge from this table. First, interest in assessments of RER misalignment has gone well beyond academic circles and has captured the attention of the multilateral institutions, government agencies, and the private sector. Second, most studies have relied on cointegration techniques to estimate the long-run equilibrium RER. Third, as noted, the

30. As is argued below, however, computations based either on the single-equation approach (eq. [3]) or on some version of PPP require defining a within-sample benchmark for the equilibrium RER.

31. As in the case of the empirical literature on PPP presented in table 13.3, the list of studies in table 13.5 is intended to be representative, not exhaustive. In particular, we do not include studies that estimate an equation for the RER for a given country (or countries) but do not produce, assess, or use for other purposes a measure of RER misalignment. Also, we have not included the study by Goldfajn and Valdés (1999; which we discuss extensively in section 13.3), even though it conforms with "steps" 1, 3, and 4, because the scope of that study (i.e., identify the "stylized facts" of appreciation episodes using the largest database available) is much broader than that of the "typical" study on RER misalignment.

Table 13.5   Empirical Studies of Real Exchange Rate Misalignment in Less Developed Countries

Author	Countries and Period	Fundamentals	Technique	Comments
Edwards (1989)	Twelve countries: Brazil, Colombia, El Salvador, Greece, India, Israel, Malaysia, the Philippines, South Africa, Sri Lanka, Thailand, and Yugoslavia 1962–84	Terms of trade, capital flows, import tariffs, government spending, productivity differentials (trend), excess domestic credit, and nominal devaluation	Panel data; fixed-effects instrumental variables. Dynamic adjustment equation that allows short-run effects of nominal variables, including the rate of devaluation; long-run RER only influenced by "real" fundamentals. Beveridge-Nelson technique used to calculate permanent and transitory components of fundamentals	Equilibrium RERs calculated No attempt made to compute misalignment due to "benchmark" problem Compares estimated equilibrium RER with simple PPP extrapolations
Cottani, Cavallo, and Khan (1990)	Twenty-four countries, including Argentina, Bolivia, Chile, Colombia, Jamaica, Peru, Uruguay, Côte d'Ivoire, Ethiopia, Mali, Somalia, Sudan, and Zambia 1960–83	Terms of trade, openness (inverse), net capital flows, excess domestic credit, GDP growth, foreign inflation, and time trend	Pooled OLS estimation Three-year moving average for some fundamentals as proxy for permanent component	Compute RER misalignment from three sources: degree of openness, sustainable capital inflows, and domestic credit creation (internal equilibrium) Composite measure of RER misalignment used as regressor in equations of economic performance
Ghura and Grennes (1993)	Thirty-three countries from sub-Saharan Africa 1970–87	Terms of trade, capital inflows, openness (inverse), excess domestic credit, nominal devaluation, and time trend	Instrumental variables estimation of pooled time-series and cross-sectional data; includes country-specific dummies (fixed effects)	Compute three measures of misalignment: one based on excess money creation and excess government borrowing, another based on a measure of "sustainable" capital inflows, and a third based on the black market premium Composite measures of RER misalignment used as regressor in equations of economic performance
Elbadawi (1994)	Three countries: Chile, Ghana, and India 1967–90	Terms of trade, capital inflows, openness, government spending, import tariffs, productivity differentials (trend), domestic credit, and nominal devaluation	Cointegration and error correction models Beveridge-Nelson technique used to calculate permanent component of some fundamentals; for others, five-year moving average	Misalignment is calculated as the difference between the estimated "equilibrium" RER and the actual RER RER assumed to be, on average, in equilibrium during sample period
Calvo, Reinhart, and Végh (1995)	Three countries: Brazil, Chile, and Colombia 1978–92 (quarterly)	Terms of trade, GDP per capita, and inflation tax	Beveridge-Nelson technique to obtain permanent and transitory components of fundamentals Cointegration between permanent components of RER and fundamentals	No estimate of equilibrium RER or of misalignment is provided Compare cyclical and permanent component of RER and fundamentals with predictions of an optimizing model

Study	Sample	Fundamentals	Methodology	Comments
Ades (1996)	Twelve countries: Argentina, Brazil, Chile, Colombia, Ecuador, Indonesia, Mexico, the Philippines, Thailand, Turkey, South Africa, and Venezuela 1980:1–96:4 (quarterly)	Long-run fundamentals: terms of trade, openness, capital inflows, government spending, foreign interest rate, and technology (trend) Short-run determinants: transitory changes in terms of trade, monetary conditions relative to those abroad, risk premium, and international reserves coverage	Cointegration Dynamic error correction model Exponential moving-average procedure to obtain permanent and transitory components	Compares estimates of equilibrium RER with simple PPP extrapolations Stresses differences between long-run and short-run determinants of the equilibrium RER
Soto (1996)	Chile 1978:1–94:4 (quarterly)	Terms of trade, government spending, capital inflows, import tariffs, external debt, financial distortion index, and interest rate differential	Beveridge-Nelson decomposition of fundamentals Cointegration and error correction model Model of endogenous transition	Tries to capture nonlinear behavior of RER Compares linear and nonlinear models; concludes that linear models tend to overreact to shocks to fundamentals Misalignment is computed as the percentage difference between the actual and the equilibrium RER
Montiel (1997)	Five countries: Indonesia, Malaysia, the Philippines, Singapore, and Thailand 1960–94	Terms of trade, openness, government spending, public investment, foreign interest rate, foreign inflation, dependency ration, and time trend	Nonstationarity used as criterion to classify "fundamentals" as permanent Cointegration (modified Johansen) Error correction model	Estimation procedure allows sum of residuals between actual and estimated RER to be different from zero Compares estimated with actual RER over sample and subsamples using confidence intervals
Warner (1997)	Mexico 1979:1–97:1 (quarterly)	Crude oil price, government spending, import tariffs, interest rate on external debt, ratio of nontradable to tradable prices, capital account balance, relative money supplies (Mexico vs. U.S.), relative GDP growth, and interest rate differential	OLS (Stock and Watson) Cointegration (Johansen)	Stresses the importance of capital flows for determining the equilibrium RER Compares monetary model with "real" model; finds little improvement from the addition of "monetary fundamentals"
Soto (1997)	Chile 1960–97 (annual); 1978–97 (quarterly); 1986–97 (monthly)	Terms of trade, government spending, public investment, TFP, capital inflows, openness, import tariffs, and interest rate differentials	Three methods for decomposing permanent and temporary components: Beveridge-Nelson, Hodrick-Prescott, and moving average Cointegration Error correction model	Defines a "benchmark" case by computing a three-period moving average of normalized differences between permanent and temporary components of fundamentals

(continued)

Table 13.5 (continued)

Author	Countries and Period	Fundamentals	Technique	Comments
Razin and Collins (1997)	Ninety-three countries (Penn World Tables data) 1975–92	Terms of trade, long-term capital inflows, resource balance, growth of output per worker, excess money growth Short-run shock to output, absorption, and money supply	Panel data; fixed effects	Misalignment constructed as the difference between the RER and the linear combination of variables that proxy a "flex-price" RER
Broner, Loayza, and Lopez (1997)	Seven Latin American countries (Argentina, Brazil, Chile, Colombia, Mexico, Peru, and Venezuela) and the United States 1960–95	Ratio of relative prices of nontradable to tradable goods (CPI/WPI) and net foreign assets	OLS, GLS, and instrumental variables Gonzalo-Granger decomposition Cointegration (Johansen)	Misalignment constructed as the difference between actual RER and estimates from cointegrating vector
Elbadawi and Soto (1997)	Seven countries: Côte d'Ivoire, Ghana, Kenya, Mali, India, Chile, and Mexico 1960–93	Terms of trade, openness, long-run capital inflows, government spending, public investment, foreign interest rate, and country risk	Newbold's version of Beveridge-Nelson technique Cointegration Phillips-Loretan's error correction model	Scale estimates of equilibrium RER by a scoring function, based on the distance of fundamentals to their sustainable level For Chile, they compare reduced-form estimate of equilibrium RER with forward RER projections
Halpern and Wyplosz (1997)	Six transition economies: Croatia, the Czech and Slovak Republics, Hungary, Poland, and Slovenia 1990–95 (sample size varies depending on data availability)	Real aggregate producer wages, marginal productivity in tradable sector, unemployment, rate of exchange rate appreciation, and interest rate differentials.	Error correction model Fixed country effect in constant, and in constant and slope	Use three measures of RER: doubly deflated nominal exchange rate, ratio of nontraded to traded goods prices, and dollar wages
Baffes, Elbadawi, and O'Connell (1997)	Two countries: Côte d'Ivoire and Burkina Faso	Terms of trade, openness, resource balance, investment share, and foreign price level	Error correction model Three-step procedure: order of integration, estimation (Engle-Granger, Johansen), calculation of equilibrium RER using Beveridge-Nelson	Both countries members of Communauté Financière Africaine zone
Soto and Valdés (1998)	Chile 1977:1–97:4 (quarterly)	Terms of trade, productivity differentials between tradable and nontradable sectors, net foreign assets, and public absorption	Three decomposition techniques: Beveridge-Nelson, Hodrick-Prescott, and Gonzalo-Granger Cointegrated VARs	Use net foreign assets as proxy for terminal condition on foreign indebtedness; do not take into account "supply" effects No "benchmark" considerations

studies have used as regressors a wide variety of fundamentals. However, almost all of them included as regressors the terms of trade and a measure of net capital flows, and about half of the studies included in their set of fundamentals measures of government spending, openness, and output growth—that is, the determinants of the equilibrium RER typically suggested by variants of the dependent economy model. Fourth, the studies have followed very different approaches to decompose the RER fundamentals into permanent and transitory. For example, in their study on Chile, Soto and Valdés (1998) used four alternative decomposition techniques; Warner (1997), in contrast, did not attempt to decompose the fundamentals in his analysis of Mexico's RER. Fifth, whereas some studies have tried to capture the short-run dynamics of RERs through the estimation of error correction models, or other types of dynamic specifications that allow nominal variables to play a role in explaining the RER, others have concentrated exclusively on medium- to long-term "real" determinants of the equilibrium RER. And finally, and perhaps not surprisingly, the studies have obtained all types of results concerning the degree and direction of RER misalignment across countries and over time and often have reached opposite conclusions in their ex post assessments of misalignment of a particular currency. For example, Montiel's (1997) estimates suggest that the Thai baht was significantly *overvalued* from 1981 to 1987, and then again from 1992 to 1994, whereas the model of Ades (1996) shows that the baht was persistently *undervalued* from 1985 to 1993. Similarly, the estimates of Broner, Loayza, and Lopez (1997) suggest that the overvaluation of the Mexican peso that preceded the 1994 crisis started around 1990, and those of Ades (1996) that it had started even earlier, in 1988; however, the results obtained by Warner (1997) indicate that the peso was slightly *undervalued* until mid-1993.

Figure 13.2 depicts estimates of equilibrium and actual RERs for twenty-four countries obtained from the Goldman-Sachs model developed by Ades (1996).[32] The figure captures a number of interesting features. For instance, the estimates from this model indicate quite clearly that the Mexican peso was overvalued in the period prior to the 1994 crisis. The same estimates show that following the devaluation Mexico's RER overshot its equilibrium level, but only for a brief period. The estimates of this model also suggest that since the third quarter of 1996 the currencies of all East Asian countries were overvalued, albeit the size of their misalignment was rather small.

In spite of its relative simplicity and popularity, the single-equation approach sketched above is subject to some important limitations that may,

---

32. The figure presents estimates of the model as of the first quarter of 1997. RER is the actual exchange rate, while GSDEEMER is the estimated equilibrium exchange rate; a higher value represents a real depreciation.

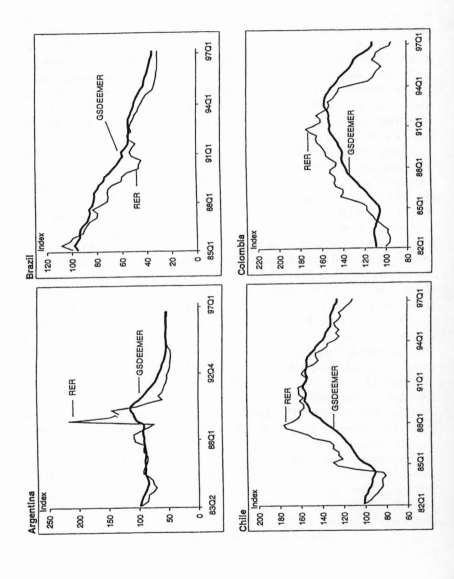

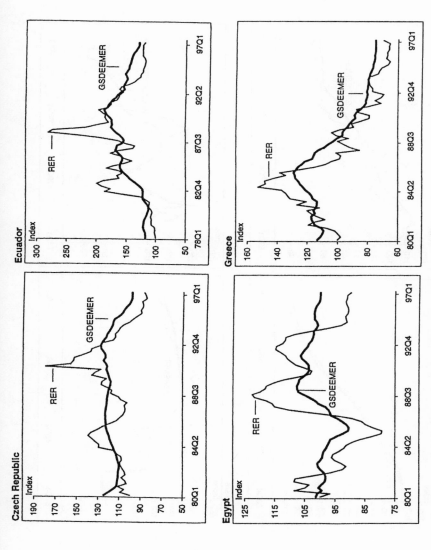

Fig. 13.2   Actual (*RER*) and predicted (*GSDEEMER*) real exchange rates

Source: Goldman-Sachs estimates.

Note: Higher value implies weaker exchange rates.

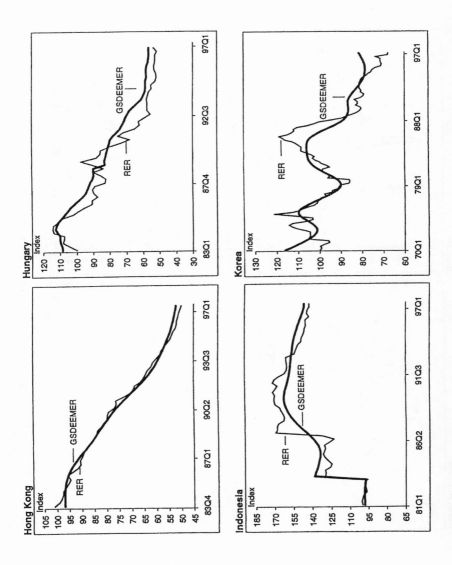

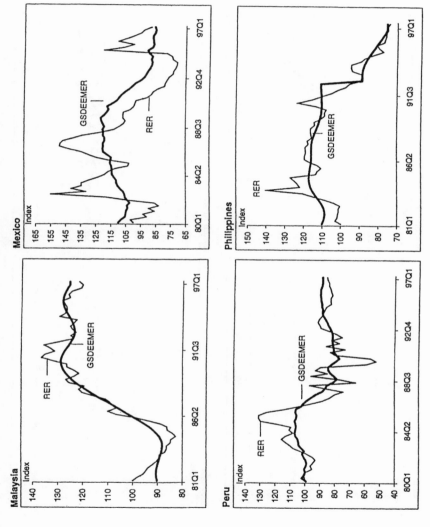

Fig. 13.2 (cont.)

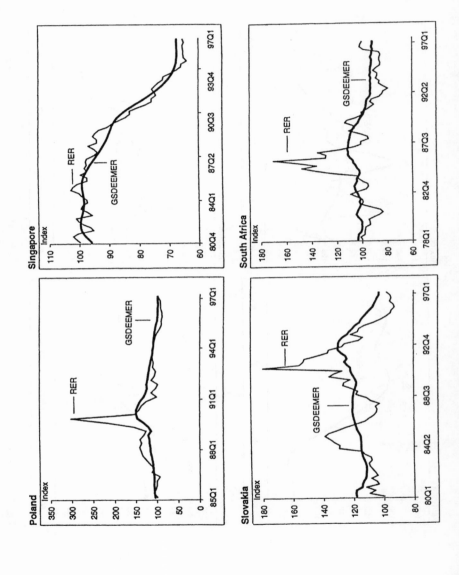

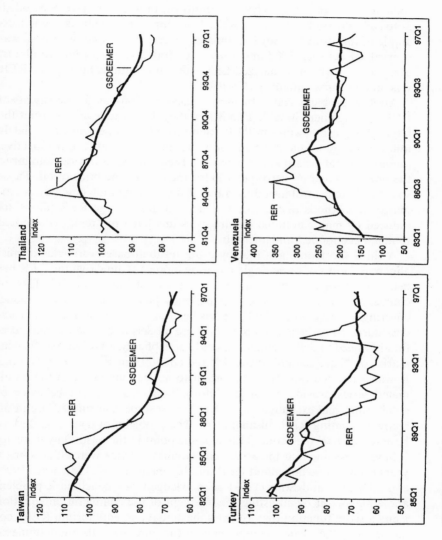

Fig. 13.2 (cont.)

in specific historical circumstances, generate highly misleading results. For example, as noted above, many of the indexes of RER misalignment calculated in the studies presented in table 13.5 suggest disequilibrium patterns that contradict each other or do not conform with what historical or episodic analyses of the country (or countries) in question have concluded. Soto's (1996) study of Chile's RER behavior in the 1990s is a good example of this problem: Soto's estimates suggest that the Chilean peso was overvalued between 1987 and 1989, a period when according to almost every scholar who has analyzed Chile's recent economic history, the RER was, in fact, substantially *undervalued.*[33]

Another problem shared by most single-equation-based assessments of RER misalignment in table 13.5 is that they do not take into account the large (short term) swings in RERs that take place in periods immediately following large nominal devaluations. From an econometric perspective, (large) nominal devaluations generate a break in the time series similar to the one examined by Perron (1989) for the case of the price of oil. Those structural breaks will introduce a bias if the cointegration equation is estimated by methods that ignore the fact that many large RER jumps are induced by major nominal disturbances unrelated to "real," as opposed to macroeconomic, fundamentals.

A third shortcoming is that by using residual-based estimates of misalignment, most of these single-equation models assume that the RER has been, on average, in equilibrium during the estimation period. This, of course, need not be the case. It is perfectly possible to estimate a model covering a period when the RER has been persistently overvalued or undervalued. Nonetheless, in order for these models to be operationally useful, they need to define, either implicitly or explicitly, an in-sample "benchmark" or "base period" (year) for the equilibrium RER. On this issue, Edwards pointed out: "It is important to notice that although these estimated series provide important information regarding the behavior of equilibrium real exchange rates, they have a somewhat limited use in directly computing RER misalignment. The problem, of course, is that we have to 'anchor' the actual RER at some point in the past. Only if we are willing to assume that the actual and equilibrium rate were equal some x years back can we talk about RER misalignment" (1989, 158). Soto (1997) and Elbadawi and Soto (1997) acknowledged this benchmark problem and addressed it by adjusting the intercept of the cointegration equation using a score function that assumes the actual and equilibrium RERs coincide when the cyclical components of the fundamentals are minimized.

---

33. See, e.g., Fontaine (1992) and Dornbusch and Edwards (1994). Also, notice that the estimates for Chile in Ades (1996) do indicate that the RER was undervalued during 1987–89.

Halpern and Wyplosz (1997) also recognized this problem in their estimation of RER indexes for a group of transition economies.

A fourth limitation of these models is that they are based on analytical frameworks that do not incorporate explicitly the sources of rigidities and thus do not provide convincing stories about why, in the first place, the RER should ever be misaligned. Future work on the subject, then, would benefit from explicitly introducing (nontradable) price stickiness and thus providing testable hypotheses on the (potential) sources of RER misalignment.[34]

A fifth problem of the models summarized in table 13.5 is that they do not establish a clear link between the equilibrium RER and the current (or capital) account, nor do they specify a direct relation between the estimated RER* and measures of internal equilibrium, including the level of unemployment. This lack of formal connection between RER* and external and internal equilibrium represents, in fact, a violation of the definition of RER used in the theoretical models employed to derive the empirical RER equation.

Sixth, most of these models use regression specifications that concentrate on "flow" variables and hence ignore the role of stocks, such as the international (net) portfolio demand for the country's assets. Even studies such as those of Soto and Valdés (1998) and Broner et al. (1997), which have explicitly tried to incorporate both stock and flow considerations in their theoretical discussions, suffer from this shortcoming.[35]

Finally, and related to the above, because they rely on historical data from each country to construct the permanent and transitory components of the fundamentals, studies based on this approach run the risk of missing some important changes in the equilibrium RER. Consider, for example, the case of a country that for some reason (say, because it has undertaken a successful reform program) experiences an easing of its external credit constraint toward the end of the estimation period. In this case, the country will be able to "sustain" an equilibrium net foreign asset ratio (and an RER*) that is larger (lower) than what would have been observed during the sample period.

Not every study on RERs—not even all those included in table 13.5—has aimed at assessing whether the actual RER in a country or group of countries is in line with its long-run equilibrium. In fact, a number of studies have calculated indexes of RER misalignment as an intermediate step in analyses of economic performance, or currency crises.[36] Edwards

---

34. Small economy versions of models in the spirit of Obstfeld and Rogoff (1995a) could be used to analyze these issues.

35. These analyses are (partially) based on the flow-stock approach suggested by Faruqee (1995).

36. Some authors, however, have relied on crude estimates of misalignment in their analyses of currency crises. E.g., some have focused on straightforward PPP-based estimates; oth-

(1988a), for example, used a misalignment index constructed with panel data for twelve countries to analyze the effect of RER misalignment on economic growth. Dollar (1992) used deviations from a PPP-based RER equation as a generated regressor in his analysis of growth in a score of countries, and many others computed misalignment indexes to include them as regressors in their analyses of the determinants of growth in developing countries (Cottani et al. 1990; Ghura and Grennes 1993; Razin and Collins 1997).

13.4.2   General Equilibrium Simulation Models

In an effort to capture the complex interactions between different variables, some authors (notably Williamson 1985, 1991) have built general equilibrium simulation models (GESMs) to analyze RER behavior. These models define the equilibrium RER—oftentimes called the fundamental equilibrium exchange rate (FEER)—as the price of tradables relative to nontradables compatible with the achievement of internal and external equilibrium. The former is defined as a situation where output is equal to potential output, while the latter is "defined in terms of a sustainable level of the current account" (Bayoumi et al. 1994, 23).

In a recent review of RER misalignment analyses for the G-3 countries, Clark and MacDonald (1998) have characterized the basic GESM model by the following set of equations:

(5) $$CA = -KA,$$

(6) $$CA = b_0 + b_1 q + b_2 y_d + b_3 y_f = -KA^*,$$

(7) $$FEER = (-KA^* - b_0 - b_2 y_d - b_3 y_f)/b_1,$$

where CA is the current account, KA^* is the *exogenously given* equilibrium capital account, q is the real exchange rate, and y_d and y_f are domestic and foreign aggregate demand levels compatible with full employment (or internal equilibrium). Equation (7) determines the equilibrium RER as a function of the exogenous capital account and of domestic and foreign aggregate demands. In this setting the more traditional fundamentals, such as terms of trade, government spending, and import tariffs, play a role only to the extent that they affect KA^*, y_d, or y_f.

Although the model represented by equations (5), (6), and (7) is a highly simplified version of the GESM approach, it does capture some important features of most efforts in that tradition. First, the sustainable level of the capital account is determined exogenously. In most practical applications the researcher chooses a value for KA^* on the basis of historical evidence.

---

ers, such as Sachs, Tornell, and Velasco (1996) and Milesi-Ferretti and Razin (1998) have defined misalignment as the difference between the actual RER and some in-sample average or base period.

This means that as in the case of the single-equation models, many GESMs require defining some type of base period (year) linked to the country's past experience. And second, most GESMs are largely based on flow considerations and say little about the stock demand for net foreign assets, or the evolution of capital flows over time.

Devarajan (1997) developed a small GESM to assess the degree of RER misalignment in Africa's Communauté Financière Africaine (CFA) franc zone in the early 1990s. In this model the equilibrium RER is defined as the rate "which is consistent with a particular current account target" (Devarajan 1996, 6) and depends, fundamentally, on the terms of trade. The analysis starts by defining a base year in which the current account, and thus the RER, was in equilibrium in each of the twelve CFA countries. Next, the divergence between this backward-looking "equilibrium" current account and the actual current account at the moment of the evaluation is calculated. Finally, the change in the RER required to restore current account equilibrium is computed under a set of assumptions regarding a number of relevant elasticities. Devarajan then extended this simple model to the case where there are changes in the sustainable level of capital flows, and in import tariffs. His results suggest that by early 1993, the RER was overvalued in eleven of the twelve CFA countries, the only exception being Chad.

In many ways Devarajan's model is an extension of the basic elasticities approach, and its appeal resides in its simplicity. On the other hand, it has a number of shortcomings that seriously limit its wider applicability. First, as Devarajan himself recognized, the results are highly sensitive to the choice of the base year. In the case of Benin, for example, if 1981 is chosen as the base year, the calculations indicate an *undervaluation* of 22 percent; if, on the other hand, 1984 is the base year, the calculations suggest an *overvaluation* in excess of 10 percent! Second, like most GESM analyses this model ignores stock considerations and concentrates exclusively on the role of flows. It should be noted, however, that although ignoring asset equilibrium may generate misleading results, the ensuing bias is likely to be relatively small in countries with limited access to international capital markets (as is the case of most African nations, which continue to rely almost exclusively on official capital flows).

In an ambitious undertaking, Serven and Schmidt-Hebbel (1996) developed a dynamic general equilibrium model to analyze the behavior of the RER in Chile. Although their main interest was identifying and understanding the effects of fiscal policy on the RER, their model is general enough to address a battery of policy questions, including assessing whether a country's RER is in equilibrium. The model considers an economy that produces one good that is an imperfect substitute for foreign goods and can be consumed domestically or exported. There are four assets, and a fraction of consumers are subject to a borrowing constraint.

Due to the existence of rigidities, labor markets do not clear and there is unemployment. Agents have rational expectations, and government spending falls entirely on domestic goods. An appealing feature of this model is that in contrast with most of the studies in this tradition, it allows for an explicit interaction between stocks and flows. For example, in steady state equilibrium the "current account deficit is equal to the exogenous flow of foreign investment which, in turn, is equal to the level required to maintain the stock of foreign-held assets constant" (Serven and Schmidt-Hebbel 1996, 99). Additionally, this model has the virtue of tracing the dynamic adjustment of the RER and other variables of interest following a specific shock.

After calibrating the model for the case of Chile, Serven and Schmidt-Hebbel used it to evaluate the effect of changes in fiscal policy on the RER and other macroeconomic variables. In particular, they studied the effects of a "balanced budget" reduction in fiscal spending equivalent to 2 percentage points of GDP. The cases of both a temporary and a permanent fiscal adjustment are considered. The results obtained suggest that this change in fiscal policy will have a very small effect on the RER: a reduction in government spending of 1 percentage point of GDP will induce a *1 percent* depreciation of the RER and will result in a small deterioration of the current account deficit. Interestingly enough, these results are not very different from those obtained in other studies based on different (and simpler) methodologies and suggest that from a political economy perspective, fiscal policy may not be the most effective tool for altering the equilibrium RER.

13.4.3   What We Need to Know

The vast majority of the papers reviewed in this section—Serven and Schmidt-Hebbel being the main exception—emphasize the estimation of misalignment at a specific moment in time and are subject to a number of limitations, including the base-year problem, the limited attention to dynamic issues, and the fact that stock equilibrium issues are largely ignored. An additional limitation of the papers reviewed in this section is that they do not deal in detail with the relation between capital flows and RERs. This issue, however, has become increasingly important in debates on the optimal strategy for economic reform. Some authors have argued that in addressing the sequencing of reform, policymakers should consider the fact that capital inflows generate an RER appreciation. This, in turn, reduces the degree of competitiveness of exports and has important political economy effects. In fact, to the extent that exporters are usually among the early supporters of a reform effort, a reduction in export competitiveness may frustrate the whole reform effort itself (see Edwards 1992 for a discussion in these issues). In the aftermath of the East Asian currency crises a number of authors have argued that controls on capital inflows, similar to those implemented by Chile during 1991–98, would help to avoid inflow-induced RER appreciation. Although this issue is still not fully resolved at either the theoretical or the empirical level, recent evidence suggests that in those countries where they have been implemented, controls on capital mobility—and in particular controls on inflows—have not been effective in reducing the extent of RER appreciation (see Edwards 1999 for this discussion).

Another limitation of most of the misalignment models reviewed in this section is the lack of a well-defined relation between the equilibrium RER and the current account balance. While the single-equation models completely ignore the issue, those in the general equilibrium simulation tradition tend to deal with it in a rather simplistic and mechanical way. Future policy analysis and evaluation would greatly benefit, however, from an explicit understanding of the way in which these two key variables interact. Two aspects of this problem are particularly important: first, the intertemporal implications of the way in which the current account and the RER interact and, second, the role (if any) played by RERs in analyses of current account sustainability (see Milesi-Ferretti and Razin 1998).

13.5 Summary and Conclusions

In this paper we have discussed some of the most important exchange-rate-related issues in emerging economies. We have concentrated our discussion on three broadly defined issues: (1) the relative performance of alternative exchange rate regimes; (2) the long-run behavior of real exchange rates, including whether there is any evidence suggesting that there is long-run convergence to PPP in emerging economies; and (3) the assessment of situations of real exchange rate misalignment.

Throughout the paper we have argued that although the field has experienced tremendous progress in the past few years, a number of issues are still unresolved. In particular, we argue that the debate on the optimal exchange rate regime in emerging countries has been hampered by the lack of genuine experiences with floating exchange rates. In fact, most exchange rate regimes classified as "floating" correspond to some kind of managed system. We have also argued that there are still major gaps in our understanding of the long-run behavior of real exchange rates in emerging countries. In contrast with the case of the advanced nations, the time series available for emerging countries are relatively short, and in many cases, the quality of the data is suspect. An issue that has been the subject of considerable debate is whether there is a (negative) relationship between productivity differentials and real exchange rate behavior—the so-called Balassa-Samuelson effect. The works reviewed in this paper provide some preliminary (and weak) evidence in support of this effect. Better measures of productivity differentials would greatly benefit our understanding of this issue. Our analysis in section 13.4 dealt with alternative methods for assessing real exchange rate misalignment in developing countries. Here, as in the previous sections, we argued that in spite of evident progress in the past few years, existing models are still subject to a number of limitations. Chief among these are the absence of explicit intertemporal considerations in empirical applications of these models, a (still) superficial understanding of the effects of capital inflows on real exchange rates, and the lack of a general equilibrium connection between the equilibrium real exchange rate and the current account position of a particular country.

As we stated in the introduction, in writing this paper we have been forced to be selective, concentrating on only a subset of exchange-rate-related issues. Some of the important issues that we have not covered include (1) the relation between real exchange rates—both misalignment and well as volatility—and economic performance, including growth; (2) the role of nominal exchange rate anchors in stabilization programs; (3) the economics of full dollarization or common currency areas; (4) the role of exchange rates—both nominal and real—in the spreading of crises across countries; and (5) the anatomy of currency crises in emerging economies. While there is an extensive literature on some of these subjects, such as currency crises, others are only beginning to attract attention among scholars.

References

Abeysinghe, T., and L. Kok-Hong. 1992. Singapore's strong dollar policy and purchasing power parity. *Singapore Economic Review* 37 (April): 70–79.

Ades, A. 1996. GSDEEMER and STMPIs: New tools for forecasting exchange rates in emerging markets. New York: Goldman Sachs, Economic Research.

Adler, M., and B. Lehman. 1983. Deviations from purchasing power parity in the long run. *Journal of Finance* 39:1471–78.

Aghevli, B., M. Khan, and P. Montiel. 1991. *Exchange rate policy in developing countries: Some analytical issues.* IMF Occasional Paper no. 78. Washington, D.C.: International Monetary Fund, March.

Asea, P., and E. Mendoza. 1994. The Balassa-Samuelson model: A general equilibrium appraisal. *Review of International Economics* 2, no. 3 (October): 244–67.

Baffes, J., I. Elbadawi, and S. O'Connell. 1999. Single equation estimation of the equilibrium exchange rate. In *Exchange rate misalignment: Concepts and measurement for developing countries,* ed. L. Hinkle and P. Montiel. New York: Oxford University Press.

Bahmani-Oskooee, M. 1995. Real and nominal effective exchange rates for 22 LDCs, 1971:1–1990:4. *Applied Economics* 27 (July): 591–604.

Balassa, B. 1964. The purchasing power parity doctrine: A reappraisal. *Journal of Political Economy* 72 (December): 584–96.

Bayoumi, T., P. Clark, S. Symansky, and M. Taylor. 1994. The robustness of equilibrium exchange rate calculations to alternative assumptions and methodologies. In *Estimating equilibrium exchange rates,* ed. J. Williamson. Washington, D.C.: Institute for International Economics.

Bergstrand, J. 1991. Structural determinants of real exchange rates and national price levels: Some empirical evidence. *American Economic Review* 81, no. 1 (March): 325–34.

Beveridge, S., and C. Nelson. 1981. A new approach to decomposition of economic time series into permanent and transitory components. *Journal of Monetary Economics* 7, no. 2 (March): 151–74.

Bhagwati, J. 1984. Why are services cheaper in poor countries? *Economic Journal* 94 (June): 279–86.

Breuer, J. B. 1994. An assessment of the evidence on purchasing power parity. In *Estimating equilibrium exchange rates,* ed. J. Williamson. Washington, D.C.: Institute for International Economics.

Broner, F., N. Loayza, and J. Lopez. 1997. Misalignment and fundamentals: Equilibrium exchange rates in some Latin American countries. Washington, D.C.: World Bank, November. Unpublished draft.

Calvo, G. 1986. Fractured liberalism: Argentina under Martinez de Hoz. *Economic Development and Cultural Change* 34 (3): 511–35.

———. 1999. On dollarization. College Park: University of Maryland, April. Mimeograph.

Calvo, G., C. Reinhart, and C. Végh. 1995. Targeting the real exchange rate: Theory and evidence. *Journal of Development Economics* 47 (June): 97–133.

Choksi, A., M. Michaely, and D. Papageorgiou, eds. 1989. *Liberalizing foreign trade.* Vol. 7, *Lessons of experience in the developing world.* Oxford and New York: Blackwell.

Clague, C. 1985. A model of real national price levels. *Southern Economic Journal* 51 (April): 998–1017.

———. 1986. Determinants of the national price level: Some empirical results. *Review of Economics and Statistics* 68 (May): 320–23.

———. 1988a. Explanations of national price level. In *World comparison of incomes, prices and products,* ed. J. Salazar-Carrillo and D. S. Prasada Rao. Amsterdam: North-Holland.

———. 1988b. Purchasing power parities and exchange rates in Latin America. *Economic Development and Cultural Change* 36:529–41.

Clague, C., and V. Tanzi. 1972. Human capital, natural resources and the purchasing power parity doctrine: Some empirical results. *Economia Internazionale* 25, no. 1 (February): 3–18.

Clark, P., and R. MacDonald. 1998. Exchange rates and economic fundamentals: A methodological comparison of BEERs and FEERs. IMF Working Paper no. 98/67. Washington, D.C.: International Monetary Fund, May.

Coes, D. 1995. *Macroeconomic crises, policies, and growth in Brazil, 1964–1990.* Washington, D.C.: World Bank.

Collins, S. 1996. On becoming more flexible: Exchange rate regimes in Latin America and the Caribbean. *Journal of Development Economics* 51:117–38.

Connolly, M., and J. Devereux. 1995. The equilibrium real exchange rate: Theory and evidence for Latin America. In *Fundamental determinants of exchange rates,* ed. J. Stein et al. Oxford: Clarendon.

Cooper, R. 1971. Currency devaluation in developing countries. Princeton Essays in International Finance, no. 86. Princeton, N.J.: Princeton University.

Corbo, V., and J. de Melo. 1987. Lessons from the Southern Cone policy reforms. *World Bank Research Observer* 2 (July): 111–42.

Corden, W. 1990. Exchange rate policy in developing countries. Working Paper no. WPS 412. Washington, D.C.: World Bank, Country Economics Department, April.

Cottani, J., D. Cavallo, and M. S. Khan. 1990. Real exchange rate behavior and economic performance in LDCs. *Economic Development and Cultural Change* 39 (October): 61–76.

Cottarelli, C., and C. Giannini. 1997. *Credibility without rules? Monetary frameworks in the post–Bretton Woods era.* IMF Occasional Paper no. 154. Washington, D.C.: International Monetary Fund, December.

de Gregorio, J., A. Giovannini, and H. Wolf. 1994. International evidence on tradables and nontradables inflation. *European Economic Review* 38, no. 6 (June): 1225–44.

Devarajan, S. 1997. Real exchange rate misalignment in the CFA zone. *Journal of African Economies* 6, no. 1 (March): 35–53.

Devarajan, S., and D. Rodrik. 1992. Do the benefits of fixed exchange rates outweigh their costs? The CFA zone in Africa. In *Open economies: Structural adjustment and agriculture,* ed. Ian Goldin and L. Alan Winters, 66–85. Cambridge, New York, and Melbourne: Cambridge University Press.

Devereux, J., and M. Connolly. 1996. Commercial policy, the terms of trade and the real exchange rate revisited. *Journal of Development Economics* 50:81–99.

Dollar, D. 1992. Outward-oriented developing economies really do grow more rapidly: Evidence from 95 LDCs, 1976–85. *Economic Development and Cultural Change* 40 (April): 523–44.

Dornbusch, R. 1987. Purchasing power parity. In *The new Palgrave dictionary,* ed. J. Eatwell et al. New York: Stockton.

———. 1989. Real exchange rates and macroeconomics: A selective survey. *Scandinavian Journal of Economics* 91 (2): 401–32.

———. 1998. After Asia: New directions for the international financial system. Cambridge: Massachusetts Institute of Technology, July. Unpublished draft.

Dornbusch, Rudiger, and S. Edwards. 1994. Chilean trade and exchange rate policy. In *The Chilean economy: Policy lessons and challenges,* ed. B. Bosworth et al. Washington, D.C.: Brookings Institution.

Edwards, S. 1983. Floating exchange rates in less developed countries: A monetary analysis of the Peruvian experience, 1950–54. *Journal of Money, Credit, and Banking* 15 (February): 73–81.

———. 1985. Stabilization and liberalization: An evaluation of ten years of Chile's experiment with free market oriented policies. *Economic Development and Cultural Change* 33:223–54.

———. 1986. Monetarism in Chile, 1973–1983: Some economic puzzles. *Economic Development and Cultural Change* 34:535–59.

———. 1988a. *Exchange rate misalignment in developing countries.* Baltimore: Johns Hopkins University Press.

———. 1988b. Real and monetary determinants of real exchange rate behavior: Theory and evidence from developing countries. *Journal of Development Economics* 29:311–41.

———. 1989. *Real exchange rates, devaluation and adjustment: Exchange rate policy in developing countries.* Cambridge, Mass.: MIT Press.

———. 1992. *The sequencing of structural adjustment and stabilization.* ICEG Occasional Paper no. 34. Panama City: International Center for Economic Growth.

———. 1993. Exchange rates as nominal anchors. *Weltwirtschaftliches Archiv* 129 (1): 1–32.

———. 1995. Exchange rates, inflation and disinflation: Latin American experiences. In *Capital controls, exchange rates and monetary policy in the world economy*, ed. S. Edwards. New York: Cambridge University Press.

———. 1996. The determinants of the choice between fixed and flexible exchange-rate regimes. NBER Working Paper no. 5756. Cambridge, Mass.: National Bureau of Economic Research.

———. 1997. Trade liberalization reforms and the World Bank. *American Economic Review Papers and Proceedings* 87, no. 2 (May): 43–48.

———. 1999. A capital idea? *Foreign Affairs* 78, no. 3 (May/June): 18–22.

Edwards, S., and F. Losada. 1994. Fixed exchange rates, inflation, and macroeconomic discipline. NBER Working Paper no. 4661. Cambridge, Mass.: National Bureau of Economic Research, February.

Edwards, S., and P. Montiel. 1989. Devaluation crises and the macroeconomic consequences of postponed adjustment in developing countries. *IMF Staff Papers* 36, no. 4 (December): 875–903.

Edwards, S., and M. Naim. 1997. *Mexico 1994: Anatomy of an emerging-market crash*. Washington, D.C.: Carnegie Endowment for World Peace.

Edwards, S., and M. Savastano. 1998. The morning after: The Mexican peso in the aftermath of the 1994 currency crisis. NBER Working Paper no. 6516. Cambridge, Mass.: National Bureau of Economic Research, April.

Eichengreen, B. 1994. *International monetary arrangements for the 21st century*. Washington, D.C.: Brookings Institution.

Eichengreen, B., and P. Masson. 1998. Exit strategies: Policy options for countries seeking greater exchange rate flexibility. IMF Occasional Paper no. 168. Washington, D.C.: International Monetary Fund, September.

Elbadawi, I. 1994. Estimating long-run equilibrium real exchange rates. In *Estimating equilibrium exchange rates*, ed. J. Williamson. Washington, D.C.: Institute for International Economics.

Elbadawi, Ibrahim A., and Raimundo Soto. 1997. Real exchange rates and macroeconomic adjustment in sub-Saharan Africa and other developing countries. *Journal of African Economies* 6 (3): S74–S120.

Falvey, R., and N. Gemmell. 1991. Explaining service-price differences in international comparisons. *American Economic Review* 81 (December): 1295–1309.

Faruqee, H. 1995. Long-run determinants of the real exchange rate: A stock-flow perspective. *IMF Staff Papers* 42, no. 1 (March): 80–107.

Fontaine, J. A. 1992. Politica macroeconomica en Chile. *Estudios Publicos*, no. 46 (fall): 187–207.

Frankel, J. 1995. Monetary regime choice for a semi-open country. In *Capital controls, exchange rates and monetary policy in the world economy*, ed. S. Edwards. New York: Cambridge University Press.

Frankel, J., and A. Rose. 1996. A panel project on purchasing power parity: Mean reversion within and between countries. *Journal of International Economics* 40: 209–24.

Frenkel, J. 1981. The collapse of purchasing power parities in the 1970s. *European Economic Review* 16:145–65.

Froot, K., and K. Rogoff. 1995. Perspectives on PPP and the long-run real exchange rate. In *Handbook of international economics*, vol. 3, ed. G. Grossman and K. Rogoff. Amsterdam: North-Holland.

Gan, W. B. 1994. Characterizing real exchange rate behaviour of selected East Asian economies. *Journal of Economic Development* 19, no. 2 (December): 67–92.

Ghosh, A., A. Gulde, J. Ostry, and H. Wolf. 1995. Does the nominal exchange rate regime matter? IMF Working Paper no. 95/121. Washington, D.C.: International Monetary Fund, November.

Ghura, D., and T. Grennes. 1993. The real exchange rate and macroeconomic performance in sub-Saharan Africa. *Journal of Development Economics* 42 (October): 155–74.

Goldfajn, I., and R. Valdés. 1999. The aftermath of appreciations. *Quarterly Journal of Economics* 114 (February): 229–62.

Halpern, L., and C. Wyplosz. 1997. Equilibrium exchange rates in transition economies. *IMF Staff Papers* 44, no. 4 (December): 430–61.

Helpman, E., L. Leiderman, and G. Bufman. 1994. A new breed of exchange rate bands: Chile, Israel and Mexico. *Economic Policy* 19 (October): 260–306.

Heston, A., D. Nuxoll, and R. Summers. 1994. The differential-productivity hypothesis and purchasing power parities: Some new evidence. *Review of International Economics* 2, no. 3 (October): 227–43.

Hinkle, L., and P. Montiel, eds. 1999. *Exchange rate misalignment: Concepts and measurement for developing countries.* New York: Oxford University Press.

Hsieh, D. 1982. The determination of the real exchange rate: The productivity approach. *Journal of International Economics* 12 (May): 355–62.

International Monetary Fund (IMF). 1997. Exchange rate arrangements and economic performance in developing countries. In *World economic outlook,* chap. 4. Washington, D.C.: International Monetary Fund, October.

Isard, P. 1995. *Exchange rate economics.* Cambridge: Cambridge University Press.

Isard, P., and S. Symansky. 1996. Long run movements in real exchange rates. In *Exchange rate movements and their impact on trade and investment in the APEC region,* ed. T. Ito et al. IMF Occasional Paper no. 145. Washington, D.C.: International Monetary Fund, December.

Isenman, P. 1980. Inter-country comparison of "real" (PPP) incomes. *World Development* 8 (January): 61–72.

Kamin, S. 1988. Devaluation, exchange controls and black markets for foreign exchange in developing countries. Occasional Paper no. 334. Washington, D.C.: Board of Governors of the Federal Reserve System, October.

Kaminsky, G., S. Lizondo, and C. Reinhart. 1998. Leading indicators of currency crises. *IMF Staff Papers* 45, no. 1 (March): 1–48.

Klein, M., and N. Marion. 1997. Explaining the duration of exchange-rate pegs. *Journal of Development Economics* 54:387–404.

Kravis, I., A. Heston, and R. Summers. 1982. *World product and income: International comparisons of real gross product.* Baltimore: Johns Hopkins University Press.

Kravis, I., Z. Kenessy, A. Heston, and R. Summers. 1975. *A system of international comparisons of gross product and purchasing power.* Baltimore: Johns Hopkins University Press.

Kravis, I., and R. Lipsey. 1983. Towards an explanation of national price levels. Princeton Studies in International Finance, no. 52. Princeton, N.J.: Princeton University.

———. 1987. The assessment of national price levels. In *Real-financial linkages among open economies,* ed. S. Arndt and J. D. Richardson. Cambridge, Mass.: MIT Press.

———. 1988. National price levels and the prices of tradables and nontradables. *American Economic Review* 78, no. 2 (May): 474–78.

Leiderman, L., and G. Bufman. 1996. Searching for nominal anchors in shock-prone economies in the 1990s: Inflation targets and exchange rate bands. In *Securing stability and growth in Latin America,* ed. R. Hausmann and H. Reisen. Paris: Organization for Economic Cooperation and Development; Washington, D.C.: Inter-American Development Bank.

León-Astete, J., and C. Oliva. 1992. Componente no-estacionario y la paridad del poder de compra en 12 países Latinoamericanos. *Cuadernos de Economía* 29 (88): 481–504.

Little, I., R. Cooper, W. Corden, and S. Rajapatirana. 1993. *Boom, crisis, and adjustment: The macroeconomic experience of developing countries.* New York: Oxford University Press.

Liu, P. 1992. Purchasing power parity in Latin America: A cointegration analysis. *Weltwirtschaftliches Archiv* 128 (4): 662–80.

Lyons, R. 1992. Floating exchange rates in Peru, 1950–54. *Journal of Development Economics* 38 (January): 99–118.

Marston, R. 1987. Real exchange rates and productivity growth in the United States and Japan. In *Real-financial linkages among open economies,* ed. S. Arndt and J. D. Richardson. Cambridge, Mass.: MIT Press.

McKinnon, R. 1998. Exchange rate coordination for surmounting the East Asia currency crises. Stanford, Calif.: Stanford University, July. Unpublished draft.

McNown, R., and M. Wallace. 1989. National price levels, purchasing power parity and cointegration: A test of four high inflation economies. *Journal of International Money and Finance* 8:533–54.

Meese, R., and K. Rogoff. 1983a. Empirical exchange rate models of the seventies: Do they fit out of sample? *Journal of International Economics* 14:3–24.

———. 1983b. The out-of-sample failure of empirical exchange rate models. In *Exchange rates and international macroeconomics,* ed. J. Frenkel. Chicago: University of Chicago Press.

Merrill Lynch. 1998. Global currency and Interest rate outlook. New York: Merrill Lynch.

Milesi-Ferretti, G., and A. Razin. 1998. Current account reversals and currency crises: Empirical regularities. NBER Working Paper no. 6620. Cambridge, Mass.: National Bureau of Economic Research, July.

Montiel, P. 1997. Exchange rate policy and macroeconomic management in ASEAN countries. In *Macroeconomic issues facing ASEAN countries,* ed. J. Hicklin et al. Washington, D.C.: International Monetary Fund.

Obstfeld, M. 1995. International currency experience: New lessons and lessons relearned. *Brookings Papers on Economic Activity,* no. 1:119–96.

Obstfeld, M., and K. Rogoff. 1995a. Exchange rate dynamics redux. *Journal of Political Economy* 103:624–60.

———. 1995b. The mirage of fixed exchange rates. *Journal of Economic Perspectives* 9, no. 4 (fall): 73–96.

———. 1996. *Foundations of international macroeconomics.* Cambridge, Mass.: MIT Press.

O'Connell, P. 1998. The overvaluation of purchasing power parity. *Journal of International Economics* 44:1–18.

Officer, L. 1976. The purchasing power theory of exchange rates: A review article. *IMF Staff Papers* 23:1–60.

———. 1989. The national price level: Theory and estimation. *Journal of Macroeconomics* 11, no. 3 (summer): 351–73.

Oh, K. Y. 1996. Purchasing power parity and unit root tests using panel data. *Journal of International Money and Finance* 15 (3): 405–18.

Parsley, D., and H. Popper. 1998. Exchange rate arrangements and PPP. Nashville, Tenn.: Vanderbilt University, February. Unpublished draft.

Perron, P. 1989. The great crash, the oil price shock, and the unit root hypothesis. *Econometrica* 57 (November): 1361–1401.

Razin, O., and S. Collins. 1997. Real exchange rate misalignments and growth. NBER Working Paper no. 6174. Cambridge, Mass.: National Bureau of Economic Research, September.

Rogoff, K. 1996. The purchasing power parity puzzle. *Journal of Economic Literature* 34, no. 2 (June): 647–68.

Sachs, J., A. Tornell, and A. Velasco. 1996. Financial crises in emerging markets: The lessons from 1995. *Brookings Papers on Economic Activity,* no. 1:147–215.

Salazar-Carrillo, J. 1982. Purchasing power estimation of equilibrium exchange rates. *Economia Internazionale* 35 (February): 79–89.

Samuelson, P. 1964. Theoretical notes on trade problems. *Review of Economics and Statistics* 46 (May): 145–64.

Seabra, F. 1995. Short-run exchange rate uncertainty in Latin America. *Applied Economics* 27 (May): 441–50.

Serven, L., and K. Schmidt-Hebbel. 1996. Ajuste fiscal y tipo de cambio bajo expectativas racionales en Chile. In *Analisis empirico del tipo de cambio en Chile,* ed. F. Morande and R. Vergara. Santiago: Centro de Estudios Publicos and Instituto Latinoamericano de Desarrollo Economico y Social.

Soto, Claudio, and Rodrigo Valdés. 1998. Desalineamiento del tipo de cambio real en Chile. Santiago: Central Bank of Chile. Mimeograph.

Soto, Raimundo. 1996. El tipo de cambio real de equilibrio: Un modelo no lineal de series de tiempo. In *Analisis empirico del tipo de cambio en Chile,* ed. F. Morande and R. Vergara. Santiago: Centro de Estudios Publicos and Instituto Latinoamericano de Desarrollo Economico y Social.

———. 1997. Estimation del desequilibrio del tipo de cambio real en Chile. Santiago: Instituto Latinoamericanos de Desarrollo Economico y Social.

Summers, R., and A. Heston. 1988. A new set of international comparisons of real product and price levels: Estimates for 130 countries, 1950–85. *Review of Income and Wealth* 34, no. 1 (March): 1–25.

———. 1991. The Penn World Table, mark 5: An expanded set of international comparisons. *Quarterly Journal of Economics* 106 (May): 327–68.

Warner, A. 1997. Mexico's 1994 exchange rate crisis interpreted in light of the nontraded model. NBER Working Paper no. 6165. Cambridge, Mass.: National Bureau of Economic Research, September.

Williamson, J. 1985. The exchange rate system. Policy Analysis in International Economics, no. 5. Washington, D.C.: Institute for International Economics.

———. 1991. The great exchange rate controversy: Trade balances and the international monetary system: Comment. In *International adjustment and financing: The lessons of 1985–1991,* ed. C. Fred Bergsten, 239–44. Washington, D.C.: Institute for International Economics.

———. 1996. *The crawling band as an exchange rate regime: Lessons from Chile, Colombia and Israel.* Washington, D.C.: Institute for International Economics.

Wood, A. 1991. Global trends in real exchange rates, 1960–84. *World Development* 19 (4): 317–32.

Financial Market Reform

Frederic S. Mishkin

14.1 Introduction

Financial market reform has risen to the forefront of public policy debates in recent years. The burgeoning literature on economic growth has come to recognize the crucial role that well-operating financial markets play in promoting rapid economic growth.[1] Indeed, it is now well recognized that the structure of financial markets helps to explain why many countries remain poor while others grow richer. Financial market reform to produce an efficient financial system is thus now seen as a key element in raising countries out of poverty.

The banking and financial crises of recent years in emerging market and transition countries (and even in such industrialized countries as Japan) have also demonstrated that when things go wrong with the financial system, severe economic contractions can be the result. Thus another impetus behind the recent interest in financial market reform is the desire to prevent banking and financial crises so that the worst business cycle contractions can be avoided. Furthermore, banking crises impose substantial costs on taxpayers, often in excess of 10 percent of GDP (see Caprio and Klingebiel 1996). Financial reform to avoid these costs has thus also become a central issue for public policy.

This paper examines financial market reform by first outlining an asym-

Frederic S. Mishkin is the Alfred Lerner Professor of Banking and Financial Institutions in the Graduate School of Business at Columbia University and a research associate of the National Bureau of Economic Research.

The author thanks Anne Krueger; his discussant, Ronald McKinnon; and an anonymous referee for helpful comments. Any views expressed in this paper are those of the author only and not those of Columbia University or the National Bureau of Economic Research.

1. See Levine (1997) for a recent survey of this literature.

metric information framework that provides a rationale for government intervention in the financial system. This framework is then used to outline what direction governments should take in financial market reform.

14.2 Asymmetric Information and the Rationale for Government Intervention in Financial Markets

In order to understand why there is a special need for the government to play a prominent role in financial markets, we must first examine how asymmetric information can interfere with the efficient functioning of the financial system. Then we can explore the two basic rationales for government intervention in the financial system: promoting economic efficiency and preventing financial crises.

14.2.1 The Role of Asymmetric Information in the Financial System

Financial markets and institutions are critical to the health of the economy because they perform the essential function in an economy of channeling funds to those individuals or firms who have productive investment opportunities. If the financial system does not perform this role well, then the economy cannot operate efficiently and economic growth will be severely hampered. A crucial impediment to the efficient functioning of the financial system is asymmetric information, a situation in which one party to a financial contract has much less accurate information than the other party. For example, borrowers who take out loans usually have much better information than lenders do about the potential returns and risk associated with the investment projects they plan to undertake. Asymmetric information leads to two basic problems in the financial system: adverse selection and moral hazard.

Adverse selection is an asymmetric information problem that occurs before the transaction occurs when potential bad credit risks are the ones who most actively seek loans. Thus the parties who are the most likely to produce an undesirable (adverse) outcome are most likely to be selected. For example, those who want to take on big risks are likely to be the most eager to take out loans because they know that they are unlikely to pay them back. Since adverse selection makes it more likely that loans might be made to bad credit risks, lenders may decide not to make any loans even though there are good credit risks in the marketplace. This outcome is a feature of the classic "lemons problem" analysis first described by Akerlof (1970). Clearly, minimizing the adverse selection problem requires that lenders screen good from bad credit risks.

Moral hazard occurs after the transaction takes place because the lender is subjected to the hazard that the borrower has incentives to engage in activities that are undesirable from the lender's point of view: that is, activities that make it less likely that the loan will be paid back. Moral hazard occurs because a borrower has incentives to invest in projects with high risk in which the borrower does well if the project succeeds but the lender bears most of the loss if the project fails. Also the borrower has incentives to misallocate funds for her own personal use, to shirk and just not work very hard, or to undertake investment in unprofitable projects that increase her power or stature. The conflict of interest between the borrower and the lender stemming from moral hazard implies that many lenders will decide that they would rather not make loans, so that lending and investment will be at suboptimal levels.[2] In order to minimize the moral hazard problem, lenders must impose restrictions (restrictive covenants) on borrowers so that borrowers do not engage in behavior that makes it less likely that they can pay back their loans; then lenders must monitor the borrowers' activities and enforce the restrictive covenants if the borrowers violate them.

Another concept that is very important in understanding the impediments to a well-functioning financial system is the so-called free-rider problem. The free-rider problem occurs because people who do not spend resources on collecting information can still take advantage of (free-ride off) the information that other people have collected. The free-rider problem is particularly important in securities markets. If some investors acquire information that tells them which securities are undervalued and then buy these securities, other investors who have not paid for this information may be able to buy right along with the well-informed investors. If enough free-riding investors can do this, the increased demand for the undervalued securities will cause their low price to be bid up to reflect the securities' full net present value given this information. As a result of all these free riders, investors who have acquired information will no longer be able to earn the entire increase in the value of the securities arising from this additional information. The weakened ability of private firms to profit from producing information will mean that less information is produced in securities markets, so that the adverse selection problem, in which overvalued securities are those most often offered for sale, is more likely to be an impediment to a well-functioning securities market.

More important, the free-rider problem makes it less likely that securities markets will act to reduce incentives to commit moral hazard. As we have seen, monitoring and enforcement of restrictive covenants are necessary to reduce moral hazard incentives for borrowers to take on risk at lenders' expense. However, because monitoring and enforcement of restrictive covenants are costly, the free-rider problem discourages this kind

---

2. Asymmetric information is clearly not the only source of the moral hazard problem. Moral hazard can also occur because high enforcement costs make it too costly for the lender to prevent moral hazard even when the lender is fully informed about the borrower's activities.

of activity in securities markets. Once some investors know that other securities holders are monitoring and enforcing the restrictive covenants, they can free-ride on the other securities holders' monitoring and enforcement. When these other securities holders realize that they can do the same thing, they also may stop their monitoring and enforcement activities, with the result that not enough resources are devoted to monitoring and enforcement. The outcome is that moral hazard is likely to be a severe problem for marketable securities.

One important feature of financial systems explained by the asymmetric information framework is the prominent role played by banking institutions and other financial intermediaries that make private loans. These financial intermediaries play such an important role because they are well suited to reduce adverse selection and moral hazard problems in financial markets. They are not as subject to the free-rider problem and profit from the information they produce because they make private loans that are not traded. Because the loans of financial intermediaries are private, other investors cannot buy them. As a result, investors are less able to free-ride off financial intermediaries and bid up the prices of the loans, which would prevent the intermediary from profiting from its information production activities. Similarly, it is hard to free-ride off these financial intermediaries' monitoring activities when they make private loans. Financial institutions making private loans thus receive the benefits of monitoring and so are better equipped to prevent moral hazard on the part of borrowers.

Banks have particular advantages over other financial intermediaries in solving asymmetric information problems. For example, banks' advantages in information collection activities are enhanced by their ability to engage in long-term customer relations and issue loans using line-of-credit arrangements. In addition, their ability to scrutinize the checking account balances of their borrowers may provide banks with an additional advantage in monitoring the borrowers' behavior. Banks also have advantages in reducing moral hazard because, as demonstrated by Diamond (1984), they can engage in lower cost monitoring than individuals and because, as pointed out by Stiglitz and Weiss (1983), they have advantages in preventing risk taking by borrowers since they can threaten to cut off lending in the future to improve a borrower's behavior. Banks' natural advantages in collecting information and reducing moral hazard explain why banks have such an important role in financial markets throughout the world.

The asymmetric information framework explains why banks play an even more important role in the financial systems of emerging market and transition countries, because of the greater difficulty of acquiring information on private firms in these countries.[3] When the quality of information

---

3. Rojas-Suarez and Weisbrod (1994) documented that banks play a more important role in the financial systems in emerging market countries than they do in industrialized countries.

about firms is worse, asymmetric information problems will be more severe, and it will be harder for firms to issue securities. Thus the smaller role
of securities markets in emerging market and transition countries leaves a
greater role for financial intermediaries such as banks.[4]

14.2.2 Promoting Economic Efficiency

As we have seen, minimizing adverse selection and moral hazard problems requires production of information through screening and monitoring, and yet not enough information will be produced because of the free-
rider problem. Thus the existence of asymmetric information problems
provides a strong rationale for the government to both regulate and supervise the financial system. By imposing regulations on the financial system
that encourage information production, the government can reduce asymmetric information and improve the efficiency of financial markets and
thus overall economic efficiency. For the securities markets, these regulations can take the form of requiring firms issuing securities to adhere to
standard accounting principles and to publicly disclose information about
their sales, assets, and earnings. In addition, the presence of asymmetric
information provides a rationale for the government to directly engage in
ensuring the safety and soundness of financial institutions, particularly
banks. As we have seen, financial institutions that make private loans,
such as banks, have a special role in promoting efficiency of the financial
system because they are especially well suited to minimize adverse selection and moral hazard problems. If many banks fail, then the information
capital residing in these institutions disappears and asymmetric information problems in the financial system become worse.

One way for the government to promote safety and soundness of these
institutions is to require that each disclose a wide range of information
that helps the market assess the quality of the financial institution's portfolio and the amount of the institution's exposure to risk. More public information about the risks incurred by financial institutions and the quality
of their portfolios can better enable stockholders, creditors, policyholders,
and depositors to monitor these institutions and so act as a deterrent to
their engaging in risky activities that might lead to failure.

Although disclosure requirements of this type help to increase market
discipline of these institutions, the free-rider problem will result in insufficient monitoring of financial institutions by the individuals who provide them with funds. Thus governments can play a role in imposing re-

---

4. As pointed out in Edwards and Mishkin (1995), the traditional financial intermediation
role of banking has been in decline in both the United States and other industrialized countries because of improved information technology, which makes it easier to issue securities.
Although this suggests that the decline in the role of traditional banking that has been occurring in the industrialized countries may eventually occur in the developing countries as
well, the barriers to information collection in developing countries are so great that the dominance of banks in these countries will continue for the foreseeable future.

strictions on the asset holdings of these institutions to prevent them from taking on too much risk. One such restriction is capital requirements, particularly for banking institutions, which can reduce the incentives of these institutions to take on risk. When a financial institution is forced to have a large amount of equity capital, it has more to lose if it fails and is thus less likely to engage in risky activities. In addition, equity capital in itself reduces the probability of failure because it provides a cushion to withstand adverse effects on the institution's balance sheet.

In addition, governments need to guard against the adverse selection problem arising from the fact that people who are inclined to take on risks or engage in fraud at the depositors' expense are the most eager to get their hands on a banking franchise. Chartering (licensing) banks is one method for preventing this adverse selection problem; through chartering, individuals who want to buy or set up a bank can be screened to prevent undesirables from controlling banks.

However, even these measures may be insufficient to prevent excessive failures of financial institutions, thus requiring the government to provide a safety net. This is especially important for banking institutions that have demandable deposits and private loans that are difficult for depositors to monitor. Without a safety net, a bad shock to the economy can cause depositors to withdraw funds not only from insolvent banks but also from healthy institutions because asymmetric information prevents depositors from sorting out the good from the bad banks. Indeed, because banks operate on a first-come-first-served basis (the so-called sequential service constraint), depositors have a very strong incentive to show up at the bank first because if they are last in line, the bank may run out of funds and they will get nothing. Therefore, uncertainty about the health of the banking system in general in the face of an economywide shock can lead to "runs" on banks, both good and bad, and the failure of one bank can hasten the failure of others, leading to a contagion effect. If nothing is done to restore the public's confidence, a bank panic can ensue in which both solvent and insolvent banks go out of business.

A government safety net for depositors can short-circuit runs on banks and bank panics. Deposit insurance is one form of the safety net in which depositors, sometimes with a limit to amount and sometimes not, are insured against losses due to a bank failure. With fully insured deposits, depositors do not need to run to the bank to make withdrawals—even if they are worried about the bank's health—because their deposits will be worth 100 cents on the dollar no matter what. Even with less than full insurance, the incentive for depositors to run to withdraw deposits when they are unsure about the bank's health is decreased.

Deposit insurance is not the only way in which governments provide a safety net to depositors. Governments often stand ready to provide support to domestic banks when banks face runs even in the absence of explicit deposit insurance. This support is sometimes provided by lending from the central bank to troubled institutions and is often referred to as the lender-of-last-resort role of the central bank. In other cases, funds are provided directly by the government to troubled institutions, or these institutions are taken over by the government and the government then guarantees that depositors will receive their money in full.

Although a government safety net can be quite successful at protecting depositors and preventing bank panics, it is a mixed blessing. The most serious drawback of a safety net stems from moral hazard, which arises because depositors expect that they will not suffer losses if a bank fails. Thus depositors are less likely to impose the discipline of the marketplace on banks by withdrawing deposits when they suspect that the bank is taking on too much risk. Consequently, banks that are provided with a safety net have incentives to take on greater risks than they otherwise would. The existence of a government safety net thus creates an additional impetus for governments to impose regulations to restrict risk taking by financial institutions.

Therefore, not only are government regulations needed to restrict risk taking, but supervision is required as well. Regular bank examinations, which allow regulatory authorities to monitor whether the bank is complying with capital requirements and restrictions on asset holdings, also function to limit moral hazard. In addition, bank examiners can assess whether the bank has the proper management controls in place to prevent fraud or excessive risk taking. With this information about a bank's activities, bank examiners can enforce capital requirements and force a bank to revise its management practices if these practices are jeopardizing the safety and soundness of the bank. Not only must supervisors enforce regulations, but they must be ready to close down insolvent institutions promptly because the incentives for insolvent institutions to take huge risks in order to get themselves out of the hole become extremely high.

An important impediment to successful government regulation and supervision of the financial system arises from the relation between voters-taxpayers on the one hand and regulators and politicians on the other. This creates a particular type of moral hazard problem, the principal-agent problem. The principal-agent problem occurs because the agent (a politician or regulator) does not have the same incentives as the principal (the taxpayer he works for) and so acts in his own interest rather than in the interest of the principal.

To act in the taxpayer's interest, regulators have several tasks, as we have seen. They must set restrictions on holding assets that are too risky, impose sufficiently high capital requirements, and close down insolvent institutions. However, because of the principal-agent problem, regulators have incentives to do the opposite and engage in regulatory forbearance. One important incentive for regulators that explains this phenomenon is their desire to escape blame for poor performance by their agency. By loosening capital requirements and pursuing regulatory forbearance, regulators can hide the problem of an insolvent bank and hope that the situation will improve, a behavior that Kane (1989) characterized as "bureaucratic gambling." Another important incentive for regulators is that they may want to protect their careers by acceding to pressures from the people who strongly influence their careers, the politicians.

14.2.3   Preventing Financial Crises

Not only is there a need for the government to improve the efficiency of financial markets by intervening to promote information production and to restrict financial institutions from taking on too much risk, but there is also a need for government intervention to prevent financial crises. To understand what role the government can play in preventing financial crises, we must first understand what a financial crisis is and why it is so damaging to the economy. In recent years, an asymmetric information theory of financial crises has developed that provides a definition of a financial crisis (Bernanke 1983; Calomiris and Gorton 1991; Mishkin 1991, 1996b). A financial crisis is a nonlinear disruption to financial markets in which asymmetric information problems of adverse selection and moral hazard become so much worse than normal that financial markets are unable to efficiently channel funds to economic agents who have the most productive investment opportunities. A financial crisis thus prevents the efficient functioning of financial markets, which therefore leads to a sharp contraction in economic activity.

In most financial crises, and particularly in the recent Mexican and East Asian crises, the key factor that causes asymmetric information problems to worsen and launch a financial crisis is a deterioration in balance sheets, particularly those in the financial sector. An important precipitating factor in these crises is financial liberalization that results in a lending boom. Once restrictions are lifted on both interest rate ceilings and the type of lending allowed, lending increases rapidly. The problem is not that lending expands but that it expands so rapidly that excessive risk taking is the result, with large losses on loans in the future.

There are two reasons that excessive risk taking takes place after financial liberalization. The first is that managers of banking institutions often lack the expertise to manage risk appropriately when new lending opportunities open up after financial liberalization. In addition, with rapid growth of lending, banking institutions cannot add the necessary managerial capital (well-trained loan officers, risk assessment systems, etc.) fast enough to enable these institutions to screen and monitor new loans appropriately. The second reason is that the rapid credit growth in the lending boom stretches the resources of bank supervisors. Bank supervisory agencies are also unable to add to their supervisory capital (well-trained examiners and information systems) fast enough to enable them to keep up with their increased responsibilities because they have to monitor new activities of the banks but also because these activities are expanding at a rapid pace. The inadequacy of bank supervision, both because of the rapid credit growth and because of the principal-agent problem discussed above, exacerbates the loan loss problem. With inadequate bank supervision, banks have increased incentives to take on greater risk because they know that the government safety net makes it unlikely that depositors and other creditors will sufficiently monitor the banks to prevent them from excessive risk taking.

The outcome of the lending boom arising after financial liberalization is huge loan losses and a subsequent deterioration of bank balance sheets. In the case of Mexico, the share of nonperforming loans in total loans rose from less than 5 percent in 1990 to over 15 percent by 1996, while in the East Asian crisis countries, this ratio has risen recently to between 15 and 35 percent (Mishkin 1996b; Goldstein 1998). The deterioration in bank balance sheets is the key fundamental that has driven emerging market countries into their financial crises, and this was particularly true for both Mexico and East Asia recently. One way deterioration in bank balances promotes a financial crisis is that it leads banks to restrict their lending in order to improve their capital ratios or it can even lead to a full-scale banking crisis that forces many banks into insolvency, thereby directly removing the ability of the banking sector to make loans.

Although Japan has not yet experienced a full-fledged financial crisis, the story leading up to the financial instability that country has been experiencing in the 1990s is similar. With the liberalization of Japanese financial markets in the 1980s, Japanese banks suddenly found themselves in a more competitive environment. In an attempt to maintain adequate profit levels, a natural response was to take on riskier loans with high profit margins, such as those in the real estate sector.[5] The incentives to do this were also enhanced by the presence of a government safety net that protected depositors and even large creditors if these risky loans turned sour and led to bank insolvencies.

The second way deterioration in bank balance sheets can lead to a financial crisis is that it can promote a currency crisis because deterioration in bank balance sheets makes it very difficult for the central bank to defend its currency against a speculative attack. Any rise in interest rates to keep the domestic currency from depreciating has the additional effect of weakening the banking system further because the rise in interest rates causes additional damage to bank balance sheets. This negative effect of a rise in interest rates on bank balance sheets occurs because of their ma-

---

5. A similar phenomenon has occurred in the United States and in other countries. See Edwards and Mishkin (1995).

turity mismatch and their exposure to increased credit risk when the economy deteriorates. Thus, when a speculative attack on the currency occurs in an emerging market country, if the central bank raises interest rates sufficiently to defend the currency, the banking system may collapse. Once investors recognize that a country's weak banking system makes it less likely that the central bank will take the steps to successfully defend the domestic currency, they have even greater incentives to attack the currency because expected profits from selling the currency have now risen. Thus, with a weakened banking sector, a successful speculative attack is likely to materialize and can be triggered by any of many factors, a large current account deficit being just one of them. In this view, deterioration in the banking sector is the key fundamental that causes the currency crisis to occur.

In emerging market countries, a devaluation in the aftermath of a currency crisis can help trigger a financial crisis because of two special institutional features of credit markets in these countries. Because of past experience with high and variable inflation rates these countries have little inflation-fighting credibility, and debt contracts are therefore of very short duration and are often denominated in foreign currencies. This structure of debt contracts is very different from that in most industrialized countries, which have almost all of their debt denominated in domestic currency, with much of it long term, which explains why the response to a devaluation in emerging market countries is so different from that in industrialized countries. While a devaluation in emerging market countries can be disastrous because it triggers a financial crisis, in industrialized countries a devaluation often benefits the economy, as occurred in the United Kingdom after the September 1992 foreign exchange crisis. Thus the debt structure in emerging market countries leaves them far more vulnerable to financial crises.

There are three mechanisms through which a currency crisis causes a financial crisis to occur in emerging market countries. The first involves the direct effect of currency devaluation on the balance sheets of firms. With debt contracts denominated in foreign currency, when there is a devaluation of the domestic currency the debt burden of domestic firms increases. On the other hand, since assets are typically denominated in domestic currency, there is no simultaneous increase in the value of firm assets. The result is that a devaluation leads to a substantial deterioration in firm balance sheets and a decline in net worth, which, in turn, worsens the adverse selection problem because effective collateral has shrunk, thereby providing less protection to lenders. Furthermore, the decline in net worth increases moral hazard incentives for firms to take on greater risk because they have less to lose if the loans go sour. Because lenders are now subject to much higher risks of losses, there is now a decline in lending and hence a decline in investment and economic activity.

The damage to balance sheets from devaluation in the aftermath of the foreign exchange crisis has been a major source of the contraction of the economies in East Asia, as it was in Mexico in 1995. This mechanism has been particularly strong in Indonesia, which has seen the value of its currency decline by over 75 percent, thus increasing the rupiah value of foreign-denominated debts by a factor greater than four. Even a healthy firm with a strong balance sheet initially is likely to be driven into insolvency by such a shock if it has a significant amount of foreign-denominated debt.

An additional mechanism linking currency crises with financial crises in emerging market countries occurs because the devaluation can lead to higher inflation. Because many emerging market countries have previously experienced both high and variable inflation, their central banks are unlikely to have deep-rooted credibility as inflation fighters. Thus a sharp depreciation of the currency after a speculative attack that leads to immediate upward pressure on prices can lead to a dramatic rise in both actual and expected inflation. Indeed, Mexican inflation surged to 50 percent in 1995 after the foreign exchange crisis in 1994, and we are seeing a similar phenomenon in Indonesia, the hardest hit of the East Asian crisis countries and the one that had earlier experienced the highest rate of inflation. A rise in expected inflation after a currency crisis exacerbates financial crisis because it leads to a sharp rise in interest rates. The interaction of the short duration of debt contracts and the interest rate rise leads to huge increases in interest payments by firms, thereby weakening firms' cash flow positions and further weakening their balance sheets. Then, as we have seen, both lending and economic activity are likely to undergo a sharp decline.

A third mechanism linking financial crises and currency crises arises because the devaluation of the domestic currency can lead to further deterioration in the balance sheets of the banking sector, provoking a large-scale banking crisis. In emerging market countries, banks have many liabilities denominated in foreign currency that increase sharply in value when a depreciation occurs. On the other hand, the problems of firms and households mean that they are unable to pay off their debts, also resulting in loan losses on the asset side of bank balance sheets.[6] The result is that bank balance sheets are squeezed from both the asset and the liability side,

---

6. An important point is that even if a bank has a matched portfolio of foreign-currency-denominated assets and liabilities and so appears to avoid foreign exchange market risk, a devaluation can nonetheless cause substantial harm to its balance sheet. The reason is that when a devaluation occurs, the offsetting foreign-currency-denominated assets are unlikely to be paid off in full because of the worsening business conditions and the negative effect that increases in the value, in domestic currency terms, of these foreign-currency-denominated loans have on the balance sheets of the borrowing firms. Another way of saying this is that when there is a devaluation, the mismatch between foreign-currency-denominated assets and liabilities on borrowers' balance sheets can lead to defaults on their loans, thereby converting a market risk for borrowers into a credit risk for the banks that have made the foreign-currency-denominated loans.

and the net worth of banks therefore declines. An additional problem for banks is that many of their foreign-currency-denominated debt is very short term, so that the sharp increase in the value of this debt leads to immediate liquidity problems for the banks because this debt needs to be paid back quickly. The result of the further deterioration in bank balance sheets and their weakened capital base is that they cut back lending. In the extreme case in which the deterioration of bank balance sheets leads to a banking crisis that forces many banks to close their doors, thereby directly limiting the ability of the banking sector to make loans, the effect on the economy is even more severe.

The asymmetric information analysis of financial crises provides a rationale for government intervention in the financial system. As argued above, a key factor leading to financial crises is the deterioration of balance sheets in the financial sector, particularly in banks. Emerging market countries are particularly prone to financial crises if their banking sectors are weak because, as we have seen, a banking crisis can provoke a currency crisis that tips the economy into a full-fledged financial crisis. The fact that the deterioration of bank balance sheets can promote a financial crisis provides an even stronger rationale for the government to provide adequate regulation and prudential supervision to limit the risks that banks and other financial institutions take, especially in emerging market countries.

The asymmetric information analysis of financial crises also provides an additional rationale for why the government should provide a safety net to the banking system. A government safety net, whether it is provided by deposit insurance or by a lender-of-last-resort operation by the central bank or government, can help to stop a financial crisis by preventing a run on financial institutions.

Although it sees an important role for bank panics, an asymmetric information view of financial crises does not see bank panics as the only financial disturbances that can have serious adverse effects on the aggregate economy. Financial instability can have negative effects over and above those resulting from banking panics, and analysis of such episodes as the Penn Central bankruptcy in 1970 and the stock market crash in October 1987 suggests that a financial crisis that has serious adverse consequences for the economy can develop even if there is no threat to the banking system (Mishkin 1991). The asymmetric information analysis thus suggests that a lender-of-last-resort role may be necessary to provide liquidity to nonbanking sectors of the financial system in which asymmetric information problems have developed.

Although a government safety net, or a central bank standing ready to exercise its role as a lender of last resort, has the benefit of preventing financial crises, it does create the moral hazard problem described earlier. If a bank's depositors expect that the government or the central bank will come to its rescue, then they have less incentive to monitor the bank and withdraw their deposits if the bank takes on too much risk, thus giving the bank the incentive to take on excessive risk. This moral hazard problem is most severe for large banks if they are the beneficiaries of the somewhat misnamed "too big to fail" policy in which depositors at a large bank in trouble are protected from any losses by a lender-of-last-resort policy. ("Too big to fail" is something of a misnomer because, although depositors are completely protected from losses, the bank is in fact allowed to fail with losses to equity holders.)[7]

Similarly, the lender-of-last-resort role to prevent a financial crisis arising outside of the banking sector may encourage other financial institutions and borrowers from them to take on too much risk. Knowing that the central bank will prevent a financial crisis if it appears imminent will encourage them to protect themselves less against systemic risks, that is, those that occur systemwide that will trigger a lender-of-last-resort response. There is thus a trade-off between the moral hazard cost of the lender-of-last-resort role and the benefits of a lender-of-last-resort role in preventing financial crises.

14.3 Recommendations for Financial Market Reform

Now that we have developed a framework for understanding what role government intervention should play in financial markets we can look at what direction governments should take in financial market reform. We examine twelve basic areas of financial reform: (1) banking supervision, (2) accounting and disclosure requirements, (3) restrictions on connected lending, (4) legal and judicial systems, (5) market-based discipline, (6) entry of foreign banks, (7) capital controls, (8) inappropriate government interventions in financial markets, (9) restrictions on foreign-denominated debt, (10) financial liberalization, (11) monetary policy, and (12) choice of exchange rate regimes.

14.3.1 Banking Supervision

As we have seen, banks play a particularly important role in the financial systems of both industrialized and emerging market and transition countries, and thus problems in the banking sector are a particularly important source of financial instability. Indeed, we have seen that deterioration in bank balance sheets are an important precursor of financial crises, especially in emerging market countries. There, problems in the banking sector can make a foreign exchange crisis more likely, which in turn leads to a full-blown financial crisis. Our asymmetric information framework

---

7. Evidence suggests that the cost of the too-big-to-fail policy has indeed been quite high in the United States after it was announced with the failure of Continental Illinois in 1984. See Boyd and Gertler (1993).

suggests that there is an important need for a government safety net for the banking system in order to prevent bank panics. However, a safety net increases the moral hazard incentives for excessive risk taking on the part of the banks. All governments therefore need to pay particular attention to creating and sustaining strong bank regulatory and supervisory systems to reduce excessive risk taking in their financial systems.

Encouraging a strong bank regulatory and supervisory system takes six basic forms.

1. *Adequate Resources and Statutory Authority for Bank Regulators and Supervisors.* Bank regulatory and supervisory agencies need to be given adequate resources and the statutory authority (the ability to issue cease and desist orders and to close insolvent banks) to do their job effectively. Without these resources, the bank supervisory agency will not be able to monitor banks sufficiently to keep them from engaging in inappropriately risky activities, to have the appropriate management expertise and controls to manage risk, or to have sufficient capital that moral hazard incentives to take on excessive risk are kept in check. Indeed, this inability to monitor banking institutions sufficiently has not surprisingly occurred in many emerging market and transition countries (Mexico and East Asia being recent examples), but it has also been a very serious problem in industrialized countries. Resistance by the U.S. Congress to providing S&L supervisory agencies with adequate resources to hire enough bank examiners was a key factor in making the S&L crisis in the United States in the 1980s much worse. The inadequacy of bank supervision in Japan and the problems it has caused are well known, with the lack of resources for bank supervision exemplified by the fact that the number of bank examiners in Japan is on the order of 400 in contrast to around 7,000 in the United States.

2. *Prompt Corrective Action.* Quick action by bank supervisors to stop undesirable bank activities and, even more important, to close institutions that do not have sufficient capital is critical if banking crises and financial crises are to be avoided. Regulatory forbearance that leaves insolvent institutions operating is disastrous because it dramatically increases moral hazard incentives to take on excessive risk because an operating but insolvent bank has almost nothing to lose by taking on colossal risks and "betting the bank." If it gets lucky and the risky investments pay off, it escapes insolvency. On the other hand, if, as is likely, the risky investments do not pay off, the insolvent institution's losses will mount, weakening the banking system further and leading to higher taxpayer bailouts in the future. Indeed, this is exactly what occurred in the S&L industry in the United States when insolvent S&Ls were allowed to operate during the 1980s, and it has been a feature of the situation in East Asia and Japan recently.

An important way to ensure that bank supervisors do not engage in regulatory forbearance is through implementation of prompt corrective action provisions that require bank supervisors to intervene earlier and more vigorously when a bank gets into trouble. Prompt corrective action is crucial to preventing problems in the banking sector because it creates incentives for banks not to take on too much risk in the first place, knowing that if they do so, they are more likely to be punished.

The outstanding example of prompt corrective action is the provision in the Federal Deposit Insurance Corporation Improvement Act (FDICIA) legislation implemented in the United States in 1991. Banks in the United States are classified into five groups based on bank capital. Group 1, classified as "well capitalized," are banks that significantly exceed minimum capital requirements and are allowed privileges such as insurance on brokered deposits and the ability to do some securities underwriting. Banks in group 2, classified as "adequately capitalized," meet minimum capital requirements and are not subject to corrective actions but are not allowed the privileges of the well-capitalized banks. Banks in group 3, "undercapitalized," fail to meet risk-based capital and leverage requirements and so are required to submit a capital-restructuring plan. Banks in groups 4 and 5 are "significantly undercapitalized" and "critically undercapitalized," respectively, and are not allowed to pay interest on their deposits at rates that are higher than the average and are given only a short period of time to correct their problems or they will be closed. Regulators retain a fair amount of discretion in their actions to deal with undercapitalized banks and can choose from a smorgasbord of actions, such as restrictions on asset growth, requiring the election of a new board of directors, prohibiting acceptance of deposits from correspondent depository institutions, prohibiting capital distributions from any controlling bank holding company, and termination of activities that pose excessive risk or divestiture of nonbank subsidiaries that pose excessive risk.[8] On the other hand, FDICIA mandates that regulators require undercapitalized banks to submit an acceptable capital restoration plan within forty-five days and implement the plan. In addition, the regulatory agencies must take steps to close critically undercapitalized banks (tangible equity capital less than 2 percent of assets) by putting them into receivership or conservatorship within ninety days, unless the appropriate agency and the FDIC concur that other action would better achieve the purpose of prompt corrective action. If the bank continues to be critically undercapitalized, it must be placed in receivership unless specific statutory requirements are met.

A key element of making prompt corrective action work is that bank supervisors have the financial resources to close institutions when they

---

8. See Sprong (1994) for a more detailed discussion of the prompt corrective action provisions in FDICIA.

become insolvent. It is very common that politicians and regulatory authorities engage in wishful thinking when their banking systems are in trouble, hoping that a large injection of public funds into the banking system will be unnecessary.[9] The result is regulatory forbearance with insolvent institutions allowed to keep operating, which ends up producing disastrous consequences. The Japanese authorities have engaged in exactly this kind of behavior, but this was also a feature of the American response to the S&L crisis up until 1989.

Not only must weak institutions be closed, but it must be done in the right way: Funds must not be supplied to weak or insolvent banking institutions to keep them afloat. To do so will just be throwing good taxpayer money after bad. In the long run, injecting public funds into weak banks does not restore the balance sheets of the banking system because these weak banks continue to be weak and have strong moral hazard incentives to take on big risks at taxpayer expense. This is the lesson learned from the U.S. experience in the 1980s. The way to recapitalize the banking system is to close all insolvent and weak institutions and sell their assets to healthy institutions with public funds used to make the assets whole. If this is not possible, a public corporation, like the Resolution Trust Corporation in the United States, needs to be created that will have the responsibility to sell the assets of these closed banks as promptly as possible, so that the assets can be quickly put to productive use by the private sector.

It is also imperative that stockholders, managers, and large uninsured creditors be punished when banks are closed and public funds are injected into the banking system. Protecting managers, stockholders, and large uninsured creditors from the consequences of excessive risk taking increases the moral hazard problem immensely and is thus highly dangerous, although it is common. The FDICIA legislation also has addressed this issue by providing new legislative guidelines for the resolution of bank failures to minimize costs to the taxpayer and to impose costs on large uninsured creditors, as well as on stockholders and managers. FDICIA generally requires that the FDIC resolve bank failures using methods that produce the least cost to the deposit insurance agency. In its report to the comptroller general, the FDIC must document the assumptions used in evaluating the different alternatives for resolution of the failure and show that it chose the least cost method. This has resulted in substantial changes in the resolution methods pursued by the FDIC. As pointed out in Kaufman (1997), in 1991 the FDIC imposed losses on uninsured depositors of only 17 percent of failed banks undergoing costly resolutions (which held

---

9. In addition, banking institutions often lobby vigorously to prevent the allocation of public funds to close insolvent institutions because this allows them to stay in business and, they hope, get out of the hole. This is exactly what happened in the United States in the 1980s, as is described in Mishkin (1998b).

only 3 percent of total assets in failed banks). By 1993, the percentage of failed banks with costly resolutions in which uninsured depositors suffered losses had climbed to 88 percent (with the percentage of total assets of failed banks equaling 95 percent). In 1990, uninsured depositors at all large banks that failed were fully protected, while in 1993 all uninsured depositors at the largest of the banks that failed—none were particularly large—were subject to losses.

These changes in resolution methods do appear to alter the incentives for uninsured depositors (those with over $100,000 in an account) to monitor banks because they are now subject to losses. This may in part help explain why U.S. banks have increased their capital in recent years and appears to be a successful feature of FDICIA. On the other hand, the FDIC did not have lower losses as a percentage of failed bank assets in 1992 and 1993, possibly because of losses incurred by the banks before the establishment of these new procedures. Thus the jury is not completely in on whether the least cost resolution provisions substantially reduce moral hazard incentives in the future.

3. *Focus on Risk Management.* The traditional approach to bank supervision has focused on the quality of the bank's balance sheet at a point in time and whether the bank complies with capital requirements. Although the traditional focus is important for reducing excessive risk taking by banks, it may no longer be adequate. First is the point that capital may be extremely hard to measure. Furthermore, in today's world, financial innovation has produced new markets and instruments that make it easy for banks and their employees to make huge bets quickly. In this new financial environment, a bank that is quite healthy at a particular point in time can be driven into insolvency extremely rapidly by trading losses. This was forcefully demonstrated by the failure in 1995 of Barings, which, although initially well capitalized, was brought down by a rogue trader in a matter of months. Thus an examination that focuses only on a bank's position at a point in time may not be effective in indicating whether a bank will in fact be taking on excessive risk in the near future.

For example, bank examiners in the United States are now placing far greater emphasis on the soundness of a bank's management processes with regard to controlling risk. This shift in thinking was reflected in a new focus on risk management in the Federal Reserve System's 1993 guidance to examiners on trading and derivative activities. The focus was expanded and formalized in the *Trading Activities Manual* issued early in 1994, which provided bank examiners with tools to evaluate risk management systems. In late 1995, the Federal Reserve and the comptroller of the currency announced that they would be assessing risk management processes at the banks they supervise. Now bank examiners give a separate risk management rating from 1 to 5, which feeds into the overall management rating as part of the CAMEL system.[10] Four elements of sound risk management are assessed to come up with the risk management rating: (1) the quality of oversight provided by the board of directors and senior management, (2) the adequacy of policies and limits for all activities that present significant risks, (3) the quality of risk measurement and monitoring systems, and (4) the adequacy of internal controls to prevent fraud or unauthorized activities on the part of employees. Bank examiners get to see what best practice for risk management is like in the banks they examine, and they can then make sure that best practice spreads throughout the banking industry by giving poor rankings to banks that are not up to speed.

This new focus on management processes is also reflected in recent guidelines adopted by the U.S. bank regulatory authorities to deal with interest rate risk. As required by FDICIA, U.S. regulators were contemplating requiring banks to use a standard model to calculate the amount of capital a bank would need to allow for the interest rate risk it bears. Although bank examiners will continue to consider interest rate risk in deciding on the bank's capital adequacy, the regulatory agencies decided to adopt guidelines for how banks manage interest rate risk, rather than a one-size-fits-all formula. These guidelines require the bank's board of directors to establish interest rate risk limits, to appoint officials of the bank to manage this risk, and to monitor the bank's risk exposure. The guidelines also require senior management of a bank to develop formal risk management policies and procedures, to ensure that the risk limits set by the board of directors are not violated, and to implement internal controls to monitor interest rate risk and compliance with the board's directives. Clearly, bank supervisors in countries outside the United States need to adopt similar measures to ensure that risk management procedures in their banks are equal to the best practice in banking institutions elsewhere in the world.

4. *Independence of Bank Regulatory and Supervisory Agency.* Because prompt corrective action is so important, the bank regulatory and supervisory agency needs to be independent enough from the political process that it is not encouraged to sweep problems under the rug and engage in regulatory forbearance. One way to ensure regulatory forbearance does not occur is to give the bank supervisory role to a politically independent central bank. This has desirable elements, as pointed out in Mishkin (1991), but some central banks might not want the supervisory task thrust upon them because they fear it might increase the likelihood that the central bank would be politicized, thereby impinging on its independence.

10. The acronym stands for the five areas assessed: capital adequacy, asset quality, management, earnings, and liquidity.

Alternatively, bank supervisory activities could be housed in a bank regulatory authority that is independent of the government.

5. *Accountability of Bank Supervisors.* It is also important to make bank supervisors accountable if they engage in regulatory forbearance, in order to improve incentives for them to do their job properly. For example, as pointed out in Mishkin (1997b), an important but very often overlooked part of FDICIA that has helped make this legislation effective is the mandatory report that the supervisory agencies must produce if a bank failure imposes costs on the FDIC. The resulting report is made available to any member of Congress and to the general public upon request, and the General Accounting Office must do an annual review of these reports. Opening the actions of bank supervisors to public scrutiny makes regulatory forbearance less attractive to them, thereby reducing the principal-agent problem. In addition, subjecting the actions of bank supervisors to public scrutiny reduces the incentives of politicians to lean on supervisors to relax their supervision of banks.

6. *Limiting Too-Big-to-Fail.* Because the failure of a very large bank makes it more likely that a major, systemic financial disruption will occur, bank supervisors are naturally reluctant to allow a big bank to fail and cause losses to depositors. The result is that most countries either explicitly or implicitly have a too-big-to-fail policy in which all depositors at a big bank, both insured and uninsured, are fully protected if the bank fails. As we have seen, the problem with the too-big-to-fail policy is that it reduces market discipline on big banks and thus increases their moral hazard incentives to take on excessive risk. How can bank supervisors deal with the quandary of not wanting to allow a large bank failure to destabilize the financial system while keeping the moral hazard problem created by too-big-to-fail under control?

One proposal outlined in Mishkin (1998a) is for supervisory agencies to announce the strong presumption that in the event of a bank failure, uninsured depositors will not be fully protected unless this is the cheapest way to resolve the failure. It is important to recognize that although large banking institutions may be too big to liquidate, they can be closed with losses imposed on uninsured creditors. Indeed, this is exactly what FDICIA suggests should be done by specifying that except under the very unusual circumstances in which a bank failure poses "serious adverse effects on economic conditions or financial stability," a least cost resolution procedure will be used to close the bank. Ambiguity is created about the use of this systemic risk exception to the least cost resolution rule because invoking it requires a two-thirds majority of both the Board of Governors of the Federal Reserve System and the directors of the FDIC, as well as the approval of the secretary of the treasury.

An important concern is that the systemic risk exception to least cost resolution will always be invoked when the failing bank is large enough because the Fed, the FDIC, and the secretary of the treasury will be afraid to impose costs on depositors and other creditors when a potential financial crisis is looming. Thus too-big-to-fail will still be alive, with all the negative consequences for moral hazard risk taking by the largest institutions. One way to cope with this problem is for the authorities to announce that although they are concerned about systemic risk possibilities, there will be a strong presumption that the *first* large bank to fail will not be treated as too-big-to-fail and costs will be imposed on uninsured depositors and creditors when the bank is closed. Rather than bail out uninsured creditors at the initial large bank that fails, the authorities will stand ready to extend the safety net to the rest of the banking system if they perceive that there is a serious systemic risk problem.

The advantage of announcing such a stance is that it creates constructive ambiguity for large banks because uninsured depositors and creditors now have to worry that if their bank is the first to fail, they will not be bailed out. (The phrase "constructive ambiguity" may have a somewhat negative connotation because it seems to advocate randomness in the supervision process. The constructive ambiguity advocated here is closer to a contingent rule, but one in which some judgment needs to be applied by supervisors.) As a result these depositors and creditors now have an incentive to withdraw their funds if they worry about the soundness of their bank, even if it is very large, and this will alter the incentives of the bank away from taking on too much risk. Clearly, moral hazard remains in the system because the authorities stand ready to extend the safety net to the rest of the system after the initial large institution fails if its failure creates potential for a banking crisis. However, the extent of moral hazard is greatly reduced by the use of this form of constructive ambiguity. Furthermore, the cost of this remaining moral hazard must be balanced against the benefits of preventing a banking crisis if the initial bank failure is likely to snowball into a systemic crisis.

One potential criticism of a presumption toward allowing the first large bank to fail is that there is a substantial risk of contagion through the payments system.[11] The payments system relies on substantial extensions

---

11. Another potential criticism of the presumption that only the first large bank to fail will impose costs on uninsured depositors and creditors is that creditors have incentives to pump capital into a failing institution to prop it up long enough that it will not be the first to fail. There are several reasons to discount this criticism. First is that the free-rider problem strongly mitigates the incentive for creditors to prop up the bank: each creditor individually is quite happy to let other creditors pump funds into the bank in order to delay the failure, and so the incentive of creditors to prop up the bank is greatly weakened. Second is that constructive ambiguity does not guarantee that delaying the failure of the bank will do any good. If the regulatory authorities decide that the failure of a second bank does not present the financial system with systemic risk, they may decide not to protect the creditors. Thus the incentive for creditors to prop up the bank temporarily will be further weakened.

of intraday, overnight, and longer term credit between banks. Failure of a large bank or one that is intimately involved in the large-dollar payments system could then lead to a systemic shock that causes the payments system to freeze up or, at a minimum, lead to substantial losses at other banks. Thus attention needs to be paid to reduction of potential payments system and contagion problems.

Indeed, the FDICIA legislation of 1991 has done exactly this by taking important steps to deal with these problems through several provisions. FDICIA directed the Board of Governors of the Federal Reserve to develop a regulation that would limit interbank credit exposure, and the Board of Governors responded with Regulation F, which restricts the interday exposure to an inadequately capitalized correspondent to less than 25 percent of the bank's capital. To prevent a systemic liquidity problem from developing because other financial institutions might not have immediate access to their funds at a failed bank, FDICIA also authorizes the FDIC to make a final settlement with creditors when it assumes receivership of a failed bank. The settlement rate is based on the FDIC's average recovery experience. In addition, FDICIA explicitly recognizes contractual netting agreements and holds them legally binding, thereby reducing short-term credit exposure and making the clean-up after a bank failure substantially easier.

Not only do these FDICIA provisions to limit interbank risk make it more likely that a large bank failure will not produce a systemic problem, but they also improve the incentives for regulatory agencies to allow the first large bank to fail because the failure has less potential to damage the banking system. Thus provisions of this type increase the credibility of the presumption that the first big bank will be allowed to fail and incur costs on its depositors and creditors, an essential feature of constructive ambiguity.

14.3.2 Accounting Standards and Disclosure Requirements

Accounting standards and disclosure requirements for financial institutions, which are often particularly lacking in emerging market and transition countries but also in a number of industrialized countries (Japan being the most prominent example), need to be beefed up considerably. Without appropriate information, both markets and bank supervisors will not be able to adequately monitor banks in order to deter excessive risk taking.[12] One prominent example is that accounting and supervisory conventions in many countries, Japan being an example, allow banks to make nonperforming loans look good by lending additional money to the

---

12. The importance of disclosure is illustrated in a recent paper, Garber and Lall (1996), which suggested that off-balance-sheet and offshore derivative contracts were used by Mexican banks before the "tequila" crisis to get around regulations intended to prevent them from taking on foreign exchange risk and that this played an important role in the Mexican crisis.

troubled borrower, who uses the proceeds to make the payments on the nonperforming loan, thus keeping it current, a practice known as "evergreening."[13] The result is that nonperforming loans are significantly understated, which makes it harder for markets to discipline banks or for supervisors to decide when banks are insolvent and need to be closed. Many countries also do not require individual financial institutions to report key financial data, including their consolidated financial exposure, which makes it hard to sort out healthy from unhealthy banks. Implementing proper accounting standards and disclosure requirements is an important first step in promoting a healthy financial system.[14]

An interesting example of an attempt to beef up disclosure requirements and raise their prominence in prudential supervision is the system put in place in New Zealand in 1996.[15] New Zealand scrapped its previous system of regular bank examinations and replaced it with one based on disclosure requirements that uses the market to police the behavior of banks. Every bank in New Zealand must supply a comprehensive, quarterly financial statement that provides, among other things, information on the quality of its assets, capital adequacy, lending activities, profitability, and ratings from private credit-rating agencies and whether it has one. These financial statements must be audited twice a year, and not only must they be provided to the central bank but they must also be made public, with a two-page summary posted in all bank branches. In addition, bank directors are required to validate these statements and state publicly that their bank's risk management systems are adequate and being properly implemented. A most unusual feature of this system is that bank directors face unlimited liability if they are found to have made false or misleading statements.

The New Zealand example illustrates that disclosure requirements can be strengthened appreciably. However, suggesting that relying solely on disclosure requirements to police the banking system is a workable model for other countries is going too far. Depositors are unlikely to have the sophistication to understand fully the information provided and thus may not impose the necessary discipline on banks. Furthermore, unlimited liability for directors might discourage the best people from taking these positions, thereby weakening the management of banks. Although disclosure requirements might be sufficient in New Zealand because almost all New Zealand banks are foreign owned, so that bank supervision has been

13. Poor accounting and supervisory conventions in Japan are one reason nonperforming loans have been grossly understated: currently, official estimates of nonperforming loans in Japan are between $500 and $600 billion, while private estimates range as high as $1 trillion.

14. See Goldstein and Turner (1996) and Goldstein (1997) for further discussion of what steps need to be taken to beef up accounting standards and disclosure requirements.

15. See Mortlock (1996) and Nicholl (1996) for a more extensive discussion of the New Zealand system.

in effect outsourced to the supervisors of the foreign banks that own the New Zealand banks, it is unlikely to work in countries where most of the banking system is domestically owned.

14.3.3   Restrictions on Connected Lending

A particular problem in the banking sector, especially in emerging market and transition countries, is connected lending: lending to banks' owners or managers or their business associates. Banks clearly have fewer incentives to monitor loans to their owners or managers, thus increasing the moral hazard incentives for the borrowers to take on excessive risk, thereby exposing the bank to potential loan losses. In addition, connected lending in which large loans are made to one party can result in a lack of diversification for the bank, thus increasing the risk exposure of the bank.

Regulations against connected lending are clearly necessary to reduce the risk exposure of banks. These can take several forms. One is mandatory disclosure of connected lending. Indeed, one prominent feature of New Zealand's disclosure requirements is that the amount of lending to connected persons is mandatory. In addition, limits must be put on the amount of connected lending as a share of bank capital. Indeed, although New Zealand has discarded many traditional regulatory guidelines, it has chosen to keep prudential limits on the amount of connected lending. Most countries have regulations limiting connected lending, and many emerging market countries have stricter limits than in industrialized countries. However, a key problem in emerging market and transition countries is that connected lending limits are often not enforced effectively. Folkerts-Landau et al. (1995) have pointed out that bank examiners in Asia have often not been able to assess the exposure of banks to connected lending because dummy accounts are used or examiners lack the authority to trace where funds are used. Strong efforts to increase disclosure and increased authority for bank examiners to examine the books of banks to root out connected lending are crucial if this source of moral hazard is to be kept under control.

14.3.4   Legal and Judicial Systems

Legal and judicial systems are very important for promoting the efficient functioning of the financial system, and the inadequacies of legal systems in many countries are a serious problem for financial markets. If property rights are unclear or hard to enforce, the process of financial intermediation can be severely hampered. Collateral can be an effective mechanism to reduce adverse selection and moral hazard problems in credit markets because it reduces the lender's losses in the case of a default. However, in many developing countries, the legal system prevents the use of certain assets as collateral or makes attaching collateral a costly and time-consuming process, thereby reducing the effectiveness of collateral to solve asymmetric information problems (e.g., see Rojas-Suarez and Weis-brod 1996). Similarly, bankruptcy procedures in developing countries are frequently very cumbersome (or even nonexistent), resulting in lengthy delays in resolving conflicting claims. Resolution of bankruptcies in which the books of insolvent firms are opened and assets are redistributed can be viewed as a process to decrease asymmetric information in the market-place. Furthermore, slow resolution of bankruptcies can delay recovery from a financial crisis because only when bankruptcies have been resolved is there enough information in the financial system to restore it to healthy operation.

14.3.5 Market-Based Discipline

There are two problems with relying on bank examiners to control risk taking by banks. First, banks have incentives to keep information from bank examiners so that they are not restricted in their activities. Thus even if bank examiners are conscientious they may not be able to stop banks from engaging in risky activities. Second, because of the principal-agent problem, bank supervisors may engage in regulatory forbearance and not do their jobs properly.

An answer to these problems is to have the market discipline financial institutions if they are taking on too much risk. We have already mentioned that disclosure requirements can help provide information to markets that may help them to monitor financial institutions and keep them from taking on too much risk. Two additional steps may help increase market discipline. One is to require that banks have credit ratings. Part of the BASIC (which stands for bonds, auditing, supervision, information, and credit ratings) supervisory system implemented in Argentina in December 1996 is the requirement that every bank have an annual rating provided by a rating agency registered with the central bank.[16] Institutions with more than $50 million in assets are required to have ratings from two rating agencies. As part of this scheme, the Argentinean central bank is responsible for performing an after-the-fact review of credit ratings to check that the rating agencies are doing a reasonable job. As of January 1998, these credit ratings must be published on billboards in the banks and must also appear on all deposit certificates and all other publications related to obtaining funds from the public. As part of New Zealand's disclosure requirements, all banks must prominently display their credit ratings on their long-term senior unsecured liabilities payable in New Zealand or, alternatively, indicate that they do not have a credit rating. Clearly, the lack of a credit rating or a poor credit rating is expected to make depositors and other creditors reluctant to put their funds in a bank,

---

16. See Banco Central de la Republica Argentina (1997) and Calomiris (1998) for a description of the Argentine BASIC system.

thus giving the bank incentives to reduce its risk taking and boost its credit rating. This has a higher likelihood of working in Argentina and New Zealand because neither country has government deposit insurance.

Another way to impose market discipline on banks is to require that they issue subordinated debt (uninsured debt that is junior to insured deposits, but senior to equity). Subordinated debt, particularly if it has a ceiling on the spread between its interest rate and that on government securities, can be an effective disciplining device. If the bank is exposed to too much risk, it is unlikely to be able to sell its subordinated debt. Thus compliance with the subordinated debt requirement will be a direct way for the market to force banks to limit their risk exposure. Alternatively, deposit insurance premiums could be charged according to the interest rate on the subordinated debt. Not only would the issuance of subordinated debt directly help to reduce incentives for banks to engage in risky activities, but it can also provide supplemental information to bank examiners that can help them in their supervisory activities. In addition, information about whether banks are successful in issuing subordinated debt and the interest rate on this debt can help the public to evaluate whether supervisors are being tough enough on a particular banking institution, thus reducing the scope of the principal-agent problem.

Argentina has implemented a subordinated debt requirement in its BASIC program, although without an interest rate cap, which took effect on January 1998. As reported in Calomiris (1998), initially about half of the banks have been able to comply with this requirement. Interestingly, as expected, it is the weakest banks that have had trouble issuing subordinated debt. Thus the subordinated debt requirement looks like it will have the intended effect of disciplining banks. However, it remains to be seen how the Argentinean authorities will respond to the fact that many banks are not in compliance with this regulation. Thus it is too early to tell how successful the subordinated debt requirement will be.

14.3.6   Entry of Foreign Banks

Many countries have restrictions on the entry of foreign banks. Rather than seeing foreign banks as a threat, their entry should be seen as an opportunity to strengthen the banking system. In all but a few large countries, domestic banks are unable to diversify because their lending is concentrated in the home country. In contrast, foreign banks have more diversified portfolios and also usually have access to sources of funds from all over the world through their parent companies. This diversification means that these foreign banks are exposed to less risk and are less affected by negative shocks to the home country's economy. Because many emerging market and transition economies are more volatile than industrialized countries, having a large foreign component to the banking sector is especially valuable because it helps to insulate the banking system from domestic shocks. Encouraging entry of foreign banks is thus likely to lead to a banking and financial system that is substantially less fragile and far less prone to crisis.

Another reason for encouraging entry of foreign banks is that this can encourage adoption of best practices in the banking industry. Foreign banks come with expertise in areas like risk management. As mentioned earlier, when bank examiners in a country see better practices in risk management, they can spread these practices through their country's banking system by downgrading banks that do not adopt these practices. Having foreign banks to demonstrate the latest risk management techniques can thus lead to improved control of risk in the home country's banking system. Clearly, there are also benefits from the increased competition that foreign bank entry brings to the banking industry in the home country. Entry of foreign banks should thus be encouraged because it will lead to improved management techniques and a more efficient banking system.

14.3.7 Capital Controls

In the aftermath of the financial crises in Mexico and East Asia in 1994 and 1997–98, in which the crisis countries experienced large capital inflows before the crisis and large capital outflows during the crisis, much attention has been focused on whether international capital movements are a major source of financial instability. The asymmetric information analysis of the crises suggests that international capital movements can have an important role in producing financial instability, but as we have seen this is because the presence of a government safety net with inadequate supervision of banking institutions encourages capital inflows that lead to a lending boom and excessive risk taking on the part of banks.[17] Consistent with this view, Gavin and Hausman (1996) and Kaminsky and Reinhart (1996) have found that lending booms are a predictor of banking crises, yet it is by no means clear that capital inflows will produce a lending boom that causes a deterioration in bank balance sheets. Indeed, Kaminsky and Reinhart (1999) found that financial liberalization, rather than balance-of-payments developments, appears to be a more important predictor of banking crises.

Capital outflows have also been pointed to as a source of foreign exchange crises, which, as we have seen, can promote financial instability in emerging market countries. In this view, foreigners pull their capital out of a country and the resulting capital outflow is what forces the country to devalue its currency. However, as pointed out earlier, a key factor leading to foreign exchange crises are problems in the financial sector that lead to a speculative attack and capital outflows. In this view, the capital outflow associated with the foreign exchange crisis is a symptom of under-

---

17. See Calvo, Leiderman, and Reinhart (1994) for a model of this process.

lying fundamental problems rather than a cause of the currency crisis. The consensus from many empirical studies (see the excellent survey in Kaminsky, Lizondo, and Reinhart 1997) supports this view because capital flow or current account measures do not have predictive power in forecasting foreign exchange crises, while a deeper fundamental such as problems in the banking sector helps to predict currency crises.

The analysis here therefore does not provide a case for capital controls such as the exchange controls that have recently been adopted in Malaysia. Exchange controls are like throwing the baby out with the bathwater. Capital controls have the undesirable feature that they may block from entering a country funds that will be used for productive investment opportunities. Although these controls may limit the fuel supplied to lending booms through capital flows, over time they produce substantial distortions and misallocation of resources as households and businesses try to get around them. Indeed, there are serious doubts as to whether capital controls can be effective in today's environment in which trade is open and where there are many financial instruments that make it easier to get around these controls (e.g., see Edwards 1999).

On the other hand, there is a strong case for improving bank regulation and supervision so that capital inflows are less likely to produce a lending boom and excessive risk taking by banking institutions. For example, banks might be restricted in how fast their borrowing can grow, and this might substantially limit capital inflows. These prudential controls could be regarded as a form of capital controls, but they are quite different from typical exchange controls. They focus on the sources of financial fragility rather than the symptoms, and supervisory controls of this type can enhance the efficiency of the financial system rather than hamper it.

14.3.8   Reducing Inappropriate Government Interventions in Financial Markets

A feature of many countries' financial systems, particularly in emerging market and transition countries, is intervention by the government to direct credit either to itself or to favored sectors or individuals in the economy. Governments do this either by setting interest rates at artificially low levels for certain types of loans, by creating development finance institutions to make specific types of loans, by setting up state-owned banks that can provide funds to favored entities, or by directing private institutions to lend to certain entities. Private institutions clearly have an incentive to solve adverse selection and moral hazard problems and lend to borrowers who have productive investment opportunities. Governments have less incentive to do so because they are not driven by the profit motive and so their directed credit programs or state-owned banks are less likely to channel funds to those borrowers who will help to produce high growth in the economy. This type of government intervention in credit markets therefore likely results in less efficient investment and slower growth and should be curtailed.

The absence of a profit motive also means that state-owned banks are less likely to manage risk properly and be efficient. Thus it is not surprising that state-owned banks usually end up having larger loan loss ratios than private institutions, and countries with higher shares of state-owned banks, on average, are also the ones with higher percentages of nonperforming loans and higher operating costs (see Goldstein and Turner 1996). Thus the presence of state-owned banks can substantially weaken the banking system. The inefficiency of state-owned banks and their higher loan losses strongly argue for privatization of the banking sector. However, even privatization must be managed properly or it can lead to disaster. If purchasers of banks are those who are likely to engage in excessive risk taking or even fraud, the likelihood that banking problems will arise in the future is high. Also if purchasers of banks are allowed to put very little of their own capital into the banks, they may also have strong incentives to engage in risky activities at the expense of depositors and taxpayers. These potential downsides of privatization do not indicate that privatization should be avoided but rather that the chartering or licensing process should be sufficiently stringent to screen out bad owners, making sure that bank ownership goes to individuals who will improve bank performance over the previous government managers.

14.3.9   Restrictions on Foreign-Denominated Debt

The asymmetric information view of financial crises indicates that a debt structure with substantial foreign-denominated debt, as is typical in many emerging market countries, makes the financial system more fragile. Currency crises and devaluations do trigger full-fledged financial crises in countries with foreign-denominated debt, while this is not the case in countries whose debt is denominated in domestic currency.

The presence of foreign-denominated debt also makes it far more difficult for a country to recover from a financial crisis. Industrialized countries with debt denominated in domestic currency can promote recovery by pursuing an expansionary monetary policy that injects liquidity (reserves) into the financial system. Injecting reserves, either through open market operations or by lending to the banking sector, causes the money supply to increase, which in turn raises the price level. Given that debt contracts are denominated in domestic currency and many debt contracts are of fairly long duration, the reflation of the economy causes the debt burden of households and firms to fall, thereby increasing their net worth. As outlined earlier, higher net worth then leads to reduced adverse selection and moral hazard problems in financial markets, undoing the increase in adverse selection and moral hazard problems induced by the financial crisis. In addition, injecting liquidity into the economy raises asset prices such as land and stock market values, which also improves net worth and reduces adverse selection and moral hazard problems. Also, as discussed in Mishkin (1996a), expansionary monetary policy promotes economic recovery through other mechanisms involving the stock market and the foreign exchange market.

A second method for a central bank to promote recovery from a financial crisis is to pursue the so-called lender-of-last-resort role in which the central bank stands ready to lend freely during a financial crisis. By restoring liquidity to the financial sector, the lender of last resort can help shore up the balance sheets of financial firms, thereby preventing a systemic shock from spreading and bringing down the financial system. There are many instances of successful lender-of-last-resort operations in industrialized countries (e.g., see Mishkin 1991); the Federal Reserve's intervention on the day after the 19 October 1987 stock market crash is one example. Indeed, what is striking about this episode is that the extremely quick intervention of the Fed not only rendered negligible the impact on the economy of the stock market crash but also meant that the amount of liquidity the Fed needed to supply to the economy was not very large (see Mishkin 1991).

However, if the financial system has a large amount of foreign-denominated debt it may be far more difficult for the central bank to promote recovery from a financial crisis. With this debt structure, a central bank can no longer use expansionary monetary policy to promote recovery from a financial crisis. Suppose that the policy prescription for countries with little foreign-denominated debt—that is, expansionary monetary policy and reflation of the economy—were followed in a country with a large amount of foreign-denominated debt. In this case the expansionary monetary policy is likely to cause the domestic currency to depreciate sharply. As we have seen before, depreciation of the domestic currency leads to a deterioration in firm and bank balance sheets because much of their debt is denominated in foreign currency, thus raising their burden of indebtedness and lowering their net worth.

The net result of an expansionary monetary policy in a country with a large amount of foreign-denominated debt is damage to the balance sheets of households, firms, and banks. Thus expansionary monetary policy has the opposite result to that found in industrialized countries after a financial crisis: it causes a deterioration in balance sheets and therefore amplifies the adverse selection and moral hazard problems in financial markets caused by a financial crisis, rather than ameliorating them as in the industrialized country case.

For similar reasons, lender-of-last-resort activities by a central bank in an emerging market country with substantial foreign-denominated debt may not be as successful as in an industrialized country. Central bank lending to the financial system in the wake of a financial crisis that expands domestic credit might lead to a substantial depreciation of the domestic currency, with the result that balance sheets will deteriorate, making recovery from the financial crisis less likely. Use of the lender-of-last-resort role by a central bank is therefore much trickier in countries with a large amount of foreign-denominated debt because central bank lending is now a two-edged sword.

The above arguments suggest that the economy would be far less prone to financial crises and could recover far more easily if the issuance of foreign-denominated debt were discouraged. Because much foreign-denominated debt is intermediated through the banking system, regulations to both restrict bank lending and borrowing in foreign currencies could greatly enhance financial stability. Similarly, restrictions on corporate borrowing in foreign currency or tax policies to discourage foreign currency borrowing could help to make the economy better able to withstand a currency depreciation without undergoing a financial crisis.

14.3.10   Financial Liberalization

Deregulation and liberalization of the financial system have swept through almost all countries in recent years. Although deregulation and liberalization are highly desirable objectives, the asymmetric information framework in this paper indicates that if this process is not managed properly, it can be disastrous. If proper bank regulatory and supervisory structures, accounting and disclosure requirements, restrictions on connected lending, and well-functioning legal and judicial systems are not in place when liberalization comes, the appropriate constraints on risk-taking behavior will be far too weak. The result will be that bad loans are likely, with potentially disastrous consequences for bank balance sheets at some point in the future.

In addition, before liberalization occurs, banks may not have the expertise to make loans wisely, and so opening them to new lending opportunities may also lead to poor-quality loan portfolios. We have also seen that financial deregulation and liberalization often lead to a lending boom, because of both increased opportunities for bank lending and financial deepening in which more funds flow into the banking system. Although financial deepening is a positive development for the economy in the long run, in the short run the lending boom may outstrip the available information resources in the financial system, helping to promote a financial collapse in the future.

The dangers of financial deregulation and liberalization do not mean that countries should not pursue liberalization strategies. To the contrary, financial liberalization is critical to the efficient functioning of financial markets so that they can channel funds to those with the most productive investment opportunities. Getting funds to those with the most productive investment opportunities is especially valuable in emerging market countries because these investments can have especially high returns, thereby stimulating rapid economic growth. However, proper sequencing of financial deregulation and liberalization is critical to its success. It is important that policymakers put in place the proper institutional structures before liberalizing their financial systems, especially if there are no restrictions on financial institutions seeking funds abroad or issuing foreign-denominated debt. Before financial markets are fully liberalized, it is crucial that the precepts outlined above be implemented: provision of sufficient resources and statutory authority to bank supervisors, adoption of prompt corrective action provisions, appropriate focus on risk management, independence of bank regulators and supervisors from short-run political pressure, increased accountability of bank supervisors, limitations on too-big-to-fail, adoption of adequate accounting standards and disclosure requirements, sufficient restrictions on connected lending, improvements in legal and judicial systems, encouragement of market-based discipline, and encouragement of entry by foreign banks.

Because the above measures are not easy to install quickly and because of the stresses that rapid expansion of the financial sector puts on both managerial and supervisory resources, policymakers probably need to restrict the growth of credit when financial liberalization is put into place. This can take the form of upper limits on loan-to-value ratios or, for consumer credit, maximum repayment periods and minimum down payment percentages. Banks could also be restricted in how fast certain types of loan portfolios are allowed to grow. In addition, at the beginning of the liberalization process, restrictions on foreign-denominated debt and prudential controls that might limit capital inflows may be necessary to reduce the vulnerability of the financial system. As the appropriate infrastructure is put into place, these restrictions could and should be reduced. The bottom line is that although eventually a full financial liberalization should be the goal, financial liberalization needs to proceed at a measured pace, with some restrictions imposed along the way.

14.3.11 Monetary Policy

Although this paper's focus is on financial reform, it is also important to recognize that monetary policy can play an important role in promoting financial stability. Indeed, I have argued elsewhere that central bankers need to focus as much on financial stability as on price stability (Mishkin 1997a). Price stability is a worthy goal in its own right. Not only do public opinion surveys indicate that the public is very hostile to inflation, but there is also mounting evidence from econometric studies that inflation is harmful to the economy.[18]

---

18. Inflation, particularly at high levels, is found to be negatively associated with growth. At lower levels, inflation is found to lower the level of economic activity, although not necessarily the growth rate. See the survey in Anderson and Gruen (1995) and Fischer (1993), one of the most cited papers in this literature.

The asymmetric information analysis of financial crises provides additional reasons why price stability is so important. As was mentioned earlier, when countries have a history of high inflation, debt contracts are often denominated in foreign currencies. As we have seen, this feature of debt contracts makes the financial system more fragile because currency depreciation can trigger a financial crisis. Achieving price stability is a necessary condition for having a sound currency, and with a sound currency, it is far easier for banks, nonfinancial firms, and the government to raise capital with debt denominated in domestic currency. Thus another method for reducing an economy's dependence on foreign-denominated debt and enhancing financial stability is the successful pursuit of price stability.

Furthermore, central banks that have successfully pursued price stability have enough credibility that expansionary monetary policy or a lender-of-last-resort operation in the face of a financial crisis is less likely to result in a rise in inflation expectations and a sharp depreciation of the currency that would harm balance sheets. Thus countries that have successfully pursued price stability have enhanced ability to use monetary policy tools to promote recovery from financial crises.

14.3.12   Choice of Exchange Rate Regimes

Although we have seen that the pursuit of price stability can enhance financial stability and is thus desirable, some methods of pursuing price stability can unfortunately promote financial instability. One method commonly used to achieve price stability is to peg the value of the currency to that of a large, low-inflation country. In some cases, this strategy involves pegging the exchange rate at a fixed value to that of the other country's currency so that the domestic inflation rate will eventually gravitate to that of the other country. In other cases, the strategy involves a crawling peg or target in which one country's currency is allowed to depreciate at a steady rate against that of another country so that its inflation rate can be higher than that of the country to which it is pegged.

Although a fixed or pegged exchange rate regime can be a successful strategy for controlling inflation, the asymmetric information framework in this paper illustrates how dangerous this strategy can be for an emerging market country with a large amount of foreign-denominated debt. Under a pegged exchange rate regime, when a successful speculative attack occurs the decline in the value of the domestic currency is usually much larger, more rapid, and more unanticipated than when a depreciation occurs under a floating exchange rate regime. For example, during the Mexican crisis of 1994–95, the value of the peso fell by half in only a few months, while in the recent Southeast Asian crisis, the worst hit country, Indonesia, saw its currency decline to less than one-quarter of its precrisis value, also in a very short period of time. The damage to balance sheets after these devaluations has thus been extremely severe. In Mexico, there was a severalfold increase in the net debtor position of business enterprises from before the devaluation in December 1994 till March 1995, while in Indonesia the over fourfold increase in the value of foreign debt arising from the currency collapse has made it very difficult for Indonesian firms with appreciable foreign debt to remain solvent. Deterioration in nonfinancial firm balance sheets led to deterioration in bank balance sheets because borrowers from banks became less likely to be able to pay off their loans. The result of this collapse in balance sheets was sharp economic contractions. In Mexico, real GDP growth in the second and third quarters of 1995 fell to rates around -10 percent, while current forecasts predict similar rates of decline for Indonesia over the coming year.

Another potential danger from an exchange rate peg is that by providing a more stable value of the currency, it might lower risk for foreign investors and thus encourage capital inflows. Although these capital inflows might be channeled into productive investments and thus stimulate growth, they might promote excessive lending, manifested by a lending boom, because domestic financial intermediaries such as banks play a key role in intermediating these capital inflows (Calvo et al. 1994). Indeed, Folkerts-Landau et al. (1995) found that emerging market countries in the Asia Pacific region with large net private capital inflows also experienced large increases in their banking sectors. Furthermore, if the bank supervisory process is weak, as it often is in emerging market and transition countries, so that the government safety net for banking institutions creates incentives for them to take on risk, the likelihood that a capital inflow will produce a lending boom is that much greater. With inadequate bank supervision, the likely outcome of a lending boom is substantial loan losses and a deterioration of bank balance sheets and a possible financial crisis.

A flexible exchange rate regime has the advantage that movements in the exchange rate are much less nonlinear than under a pegged exchange rate regime. Indeed, daily fluctuations in the exchange rate in a flexible exchange rate regime have the advantage of making clear to private firms, banks, and governments that there is substantial risk involved in issuing liabilities denominated in foreign currencies. Furthermore, a depreciation of the exchange rate may provide an early warning signal to policymakers that their policies may have to be adjusted in order to limit the potential for a financial crisis.

The conclusion is that a pegged exchange rate regime may increase financial instability in emerging market and transition countries. However, this conclusion does not indicate that fixing or pegging an exchange rate should never be used to control inflation. Indeed, countries with a history of poor inflation performance may find that only with a very strong commitment mechanism to an exchange rate peg (as in a currency board) can inflation be controlled (see Mishkin 1998a). However, the analysis does suggest that a country using this strategy to control inflation must actively pursue policies that will promote a healthy banking system. Furthermore, if a country has a fragile banking system and substantial debt denominated in foreign currencies, using an exchange rate peg to control inflation can be a very dangerous strategy indeed.[19]

14.4 Conclusions and Directions for Future Research

Getting the financial system to do properly its job of channeling funds to those with productive investment opportunities is crucial to the well-being of the economy. This paper has outlined a large number of financial market reforms that can help to achieve this goal. Clearly, much further research remains to be done on additional reforms that can help to make the financial system more efficient and stable. Research is extremely active on how to improve bank supervision. A particular challenge here is that traditional forms of bank supervision focusing on bank capital may be less relevant in the future because of the speed with which banks can lose capital in today's world with financial instruments that make it easy for financial institutions to make huge bets quickly. Research is therefore needed to refine risk management procedures and to help supervisors to assess whether appropriate risk management procedures are in place. In addition, research is also needed on how to make greater use of the market to discipline financial institutions so that they do not take on excessive risk. The use of subordinated debt is one way to provide market discipline, and research on how subordinated debt requirements might work to deter excessive risk taking will be very valuable. Indeed, subordinated debt requirements are being tried in Argentina, and important research will almost surely result from the success or failure of this experiment.

Although the basic outline of what reforms are needed in emerging market countries is reasonably clear, it is striking how difficult it is to get these countries to adopt them. Indeed, no matter what regulations are written down on paper, they are unlikely to succeed if political institutions do not support their effective application. We have seen that the principal-agent problem created by the political process has often resulted in inadequate bank supervision that has led to disaster. Thus an extremely important direction for future research is to focus on the political economy of financial sector reform to see which institutional setups are likely to promote and sustain reforms that encourage financial stability.

This paper has tried to show that implementing the right set of financial market reforms is crucial to the health of the economy. Recent events

---

19. See Obstfeld and Rogoff (1995) for additional arguments as to why pegged exchange rate regimes may be undesirable.

demonstrate that not implementing these financial market reforms at a minimum can retard growth but can also leave the economy susceptible to financial disasters that impose extreme hardship on the public. Therefore, although implementing these reforms successfully is far from a trivial task, governments must put the highest priority on doing so.

References

Akerlof, G. 1970. The market for lemons: Quality uncertainty and the market mechanism. *Quarterly Journal of Economics* 84:488–500.

Anderson, P., and David Gruen. 1995. Macroeconomic policies and growth. In *Productivity and growth,* ed. Palle Anderson, Jacqui Dwyer, and David Gruen, 279–319. Sydney: Reserve Bank of Australia.

Banco Central de la Republica Argentina. 1997. Main features of the regulatory framework of the Argentine financial system. Buenos Aires: Banco Central de la Republica Argentina, April. Mimeograph.

Bernanke, Ben S. 1983. Non-monetary effects of the financial crisis in the propagation of the Great Depression. *American Economic Review* 73:257–76.

Boyd, John, and Mark Gertler. 1993. U.S. commercial banking: Trends, cycles and policy. In *NBER macroeconomics annual 1993,* ed. Olivier Jean Blanchard and Stanley Fischer, 319–68. Cambridge, Mass.: MIT Press.

Calomiris, Charles W. 1998. Evaluation of Argentina's banking sector, 1991–1998. New York: Columbia University, Graduate School of Business. Mimeograph.

Calomiris, Charles W., and Gary Gorton. 1991. The origins of banking panics: Models, facts, and bank regulation. In *Financial markets and financial crises,* ed. R. Glenn Hubbard, 109–73. Chicago: University of Chicago Press.

Calvo, Guillermo A., Leonardo Leiderman, and Carmen M. Reinhart. 1994. The capital inflows problem: Concepts and issues. *Contemporary Economic Policy* 12 (July): 54–66.

Caprio, Gerald, and D. Klingebiel. 1996. Bank insolvency: Bad luck, bad policy, or bad banking? In *Annual World Bank conference on development economics 1996,* ed. M. Bruno and B. Pleskovic, 29–62. Washington, D.C.: World Bank.

Diamond, Douglas. 1984. Financial intermediation and delegated monitoring. *Review of Economic Studies* 51:393–414.

Edwards, Franklin, and Frederic S. Mishkin. 1995. The decline of traditional banking: Implications for financial stability and regulatory policy. *Federal Reserve Bank of New York Economic Policy Review* 1, no. 2 (July): 27–45.

Edwards, Sebastian. 1999. How effective are capital controls? *Journal of Economic Perspectives* 13 (4): 65–84.

Fischer, Stanley. 1993. The role of macroeconomic factors in growth. *Journal of Monetary Economics* 32:485–512.

Folkerts-Landau, David, Gary J. Schinasi, M. Cassard, V. K. Ng, C. M. Reinhart, and M. G. Spencer. 1995. Effect of capital flows on the domestic financial sectors in APEC developing countries. In *Capital flows in the APEC region,* ed. M. S. Khan and C. M. Reinhart, 31–57. Washington, D.C.: International Monetary Fund.

Garber, Peter M., and Subir Lall. 1996. The role and operation of derivative markets in foreign exchange market crises. Providence, R.I.: Brown University, Mimeograph. February.

Gavin, Michael, and Ricardo Hausman. 1996. The roots of banking crises: The macroeconomic context. In *Banking crises in Latin America,* ed. Ricardo Hausman and Liliana Rojas-Suarez, 27–63. Washington, D.C.: Inter-American Development Bank; Baltimore: Johns Hopkins University Press.

Goldstein, Morris. 1997. *The case for an international banking standard.* Washington, D.C.: Institute for International Economics.

———. 1998. *The Asian financial crisis: Causes, cures, and systemic implications.* Washington, D.C.: Institute for International Economics.

Goldstein, Morris, and Philip Turner. 1996. *Banking crises in emerging economies: Origins and policy options.* BIS Economic Paper no. 46. Basel: Bank for International Settlements, October.

Kaminsky, Graciela, S. Lizondo, and Carmen M. Reinhart. 1997. Leading indicators of currency crises. IMF Working Paper no. 97/79. Washington, D.C.: International Monetary Fund.

Kaminsky, Graciela L., and Carmen M. Reinhart. 1999. The twin crises: The causes of banking and balance-of-payments problems. *American Economic Review* 89 (3): 473–500.

Kane, Edward J. 1989. *The S&L insurance mess: How did it happen?* Washington, D.C.: Urban Institute Press.

Kaufman, George G. 1997. FDICIA after five years: What has worked and what has not? *Research in Financial Services: Private and Public Policy* 9:35–43.

Levine, Ross. 1997. Financial development and economic growth: Views and agenda. *Journal of Economic Literature* 35, no. 2 (June): 688–726.

Mishkin, Frederic S. 1991. Asymmetric information and financial crises: A historical perspective. In *Financial markets and financial crises,* ed. R. G. Hubbard, 69–108. Chicago: University of Chicago Press.

———. 1996a. The channels of monetary transmission: Lessons for monetary policy. *Banque de France Bulletin Digest,* no. 27 (March): 33–44.

———. 1996b. Understanding financial crises: A developing country perspective. In *Annual World Bank conference on development economics 1996,* ed. M. Bruno and B. Pleskovic, 29–62. Washington, D.C.: World Bank.

———. 1997a. The causes and propagation of financial instability: Lessons for policymakers. In *Maintaining financial stability in a global economy,* 55–96. Kansas City: Federal Reserve Bank of Kansas City.

———. 1997b. Evaluating FDICIA. In *FDICIA: Bank reform five years later and five years ahead,* ed. George Kaufman, 17–33. Greenwich, Conn.: JAI.

———. 1998a. The dangers of exchange rate pegging in emerging-market countries. *International Finance* 1, no. 1 (October): 81–101.

———. 1998b. *The economics of money, banking and financial markets,* 5th ed. Reading, Mass.: Addison Wesley Longman.

Mortlock, G. 1996. A new disclosure regime for registered banks. *Reserve Bank of New Zealand Bulletin,* March.

Nicholl, P. 1996. Market-based regulation. Paper presented at IBRD conference on Preventing Banking Crises, April.

Obstfeld, Maurice, and Kenneth Rogoff. 1995. The mirage of fixed exchange rates. *Journal of Economic Perspectives* 9, no. 4 (fall): 73–96.

Rojas-Suarez, Liliana, and Steven R. Weisbrod. 1994. Financial market fragilities in Latin America: From banking crisis resolution to current policy challenges. IMF Working Paper no. 94/117. Washington, D.C.: International Monetary Fund, October.

———. 1996. Building stability in Latin American financial markets. In *Securing stability and growth in Latin America,* ed. Ricardo Hausman and Helmut Reisen.

Paris: Organization for Economic Cooperation and Development Development Center; Washington, D.C.: Inter-American Development Bank.

Sprong, Kenneth. 1994. *Banking regulation.* Kansas City: Federal Reserve Bank of Kansas City.

Stiglitz, Joseph E., and Andrew Weiss. 1983. Incentive effects of terminations: Applications to credit and labor markets. *American Economic Review* 73:912–27.

V

Conclusion

15

Reflections on the Theory and Practice of Reform

Joseph E. Stiglitz

It is now almost a quarter-century since the modern economic reform movement—the movement away from state control to a market orientation—got under way. The concept of "reform," of course, dates from much further back (at least to the political reforms of nineteenth-century England). In recent years, the term has evolved to take on "politically correct" overtones: reforms are now those changes that "we" approve of, while changes that we do not condone can be labeled with terms of censure such as "backsliding" and "antireform." Of course, technically reform can mean any change, or at least any change perceived by those perpetrating it to be an improvement on the status quo. And almost by definition, at least from the perspective of some—those who advocate and expect to benefit from it—this would be true of virtually any change.

This simple observation, banal as it may seem, provides an important warning and can help to explain some of the failures of the reform process. There is, especially in nondemocratic societies, a process of self-selection of reforms: the ruling elite has taken advantage of the reform process and the asymmetries of information—both between themselves and the citizenry and between the international aid community and themselves—to push those reforms that would benefit them. These policy changes have been cloaked in the rhetoric of reform and justified to their own populations as externally imposed conditions for receiving assistance, but they

Joseph E. Stiglitz is senior vice president for development economics and chief economist at the World Bank. He is currently on leave from Stanford University, where he is professor of economics.

This paper represents the views of the author, and not necessarily those of the institutions with which he is or has been affiliated. The author would like to acknowledge the helpful comments and assistance of Halsey Rogers and Noemi Giszpenc.

have sometimes been used to entrench the power of elites to enrich themselves and their associates. Western authorities failed to anticipate this dynamic when designing the reform programs that they so ardently advocated, and that failure is one of the reasons that today the reform movement seems, to put it euphemistically, so precarious.

To be sure, the recent wave of market-oriented reforms has had notable successes, particularly in Latin America. In that region, reforms have restored macroeconomic stability, reduced inflation, lowered tariffs and other trade barriers, and led to large-scale privatizations. Yet this list of often-cited successes mixes together means and ends.[1] Privatization and trade liberalization are not ends in themselves, but means to ends—ends such as more rapid, more sustainable, and more equitable growth and improved living standards. Viewed from this perspective, the success of market-oriented reform is more mixed. Some countries have followed all of the reform agenda but have failed to attain significantly faster growth. In some cases, privatization and trade liberalization have failed to lead to lower prices and more competition. Indeed, in some instances, following the privatization of telecommunications increases in prices have effectively reduced access to the Internet—thus impeding the ability of the country to participate in the telecommunications revolution.

The events of recent weeks have thrown further doubt on these reforms, on their ability both to raise living standards and to prove sustainable.[2] Latin American countries, many of which have made remarkable strides in addressing virtually every aspect of the reform agenda, have been buffeted by the international capital markets. One could make a reasonable case that had these countries not opened themselves so far and so fast, they would have been buffeted less. They have had to respond by raising interest rates. If the high rates are sustained, they threaten to bring about further increases in unemployment—beyond the high levels that persist in the wake of the responses to earlier crises.[3] Argentina's unemployment rate has remained high (in excess of 13 percent) since the 1995 bout with the "tequila" crisis,[4] while Brazil's unemployment has soared to 8 percent in the wake of its encounter with the October contagion from East Asia.

1. As another example of such confusion, consider the focus on repressing inflation. While the intent was at least partly to improve the efficiency of resource allocation, to the extent that monetary restraint contributed to an excessive reliance on barter, it may actually have undermined that objective.

2. This paper was delivered shortly after the Russian crisis of August 1998 sparked a global financial crisis.

3. As of July 1999, there is widespread economic slowdown, if not outright recession, in much of the region.

4. Argentina's unemployment rate had been 12.2 percent in 1994, before the crisis; it then soared to 18.4 percent; by October 1997, it had been brought down to 13.7 percent. Since then it has fallen a bit to 13.2 percent in the first quarter of 1998. Brazil's unemployment rate, by contrast, has been, and has remained, much lower. In September 1997, before the East Asian crisis, it was 5.6 percent. Since then, it has gradually increased to about 8 percent.

But far more troubling have been the experiences in Eastern Europe. The past decade in Russia has shown that moving away from central planning to a more decentralized, price-driven economy, from state ownership to private ownership, can be accompanied by huge decreases in GDP, leaving a smaller pie more unequally distributed. From 1991 to 1994, Russian GDP plummeted by some 33 percent (World Bank 1995), and it has since stagnated. But at the same time, income distribution worsened dramatically: between late 1992 and late 1996, the Gini coefficient for Russia increased from about 0.40 to 0.49 (see Lokshin and Popkin 1999). Perversely, the equity-efficiency trade-off seems to have been turned on its head. And in the Czech Republic, the attempt to create people's capitalism through voucher privatization has backfired. The government introduced a capital market that demonstrated that private rent seeking can be even more destructive than public rent seeking, for it failed to perform the essential functions of raising and allocating capital and monitoring enterprises (see Ellerman 1998; Weiss and Nikitin 1998; Czech Ministry of Finance 1997; Coffee 1996).

The weaknesses in the Washington consensus,[5] which stood as the intellectual basis of the so-called reform movement, have already been widely discussed (see Stiglitz 1998b). The countries that pursued its dictums but failed to reap the promised rewards amply demonstrated its insufficiency. Advocates of this religion, like those of any ideology, would point out that the dictums were not perfectly observed. Like the practitioners of medieval medicine, including bloodletting, failures were attributed to the patient's not precisely sticking to the regimen ("failing to stay the course"). According to this near tautology, had the dictums been followed, the policies would have borne fruit. But from today's perspective, there is growing agreement that the Washington consensus left out many elements of a successful development strategy. While fighting inflation is important, so too is establishing a sound financial system, a lesson that has been painfully brought home by the experience of East Asia. This example highlights the frequent failure of the Washington consensus to draw attention to some of the trade-offs that had to be faced; as noted below, an oversimplistic approach to achieving a market economy actually resulted in actions that weakened the market economy. Financial and capital market openness—conventionally viewed as essential components of the reform or liberalization movement—often contributed significantly to financial

---

5. Throughout this chapter, I have in mind a somewhat different conception of the Washington consensus from the one originally outlined by my colleague John Williamson (1990), who coined the term. As Williamson (1997) himself noted, the term has evolved over time to signify a set of "neoliberal" policy *prescriptions,* rather than the more descriptive usage he originally intended in discussing reforms undertaken by Latin American economies in the 1980s. The policies that now fall under the "Washington consensus" rubric are often—and, as I argued in Stiglitz (1998b), incorrectly—taken to be both necessary and sufficient for substantial development.

market weaknesses, which in turn led to financial crises, lower growth, and increased inequality.[6]

While trade liberalization and privatization are important, so too is competition—indeed, the standard model of a market economy requires *both* private property and competitive markets if efficiency is to be attained.[7] And while accumulation of physical and human capital, stressed in earlier models of development, is surely necessary, so too is the transfer of knowledge and the maintenance and reinforcement of social capital.[8] Governments can and have engaged in distortionary policies that impede development. But in many cases, the failure to grow and develop arises from market failures, combined with the failure of government to address those limitations effectively and to establish the preconditions for markets. It is not too *large* a government that is the problem in these instances, but a government that fails to undertake those functions that are uniquely its responsibility. People increasingly recognize that lack of government action—particularly, inadequate prudential regulation of the financial sector—led more to the financial crises of East Asia than an overabundance of government action.[9] The failure of the reform movement to focus on how to improve the government and refocus its attention is increasingly receiving attention (see, e.g., World Bank 1997b).

The failure to establish the institutional infrastructure—including legal and financial—so necessary for a market economy perhaps explains best the failures in so many of the economies in transition. A few countries, such as Poland, deliberately and openly abandoned the strategy of reform

---

6. The link between financial and capital market liberalization and financial fragility has now been established in cross-country econometric studies, which have buttressed detailed analyses of particular episodes (especially that in the United States and Japan) and theoretical analyses. See, e.g., Bhattacharya (1982), Demirgüç-Kunt and Detragiache (1998a, 1998b), Hellman, Murdock, and Stiglitz (1996, 1997), Cole, McKenzie, and White (1995), Demsetz, Saidenberg, and Strahan (1996), Dewatripont and Tirole (1994), Fischer and Chénard (1997), Gennotte and Pyle (1991), Giammarino, Lewis, and Sappington (1993), Kane (1989), Lam and Chen (1985), Rochet (1992), Stiglitz (1992, 1993), and Weisbrod, Lee, and Rojas-Suarez (1992). For an impression of the adverse effects of financial sector crises on economic growth, see Caprio (1997).

7. One key issue (which we emphasize below) is that the reform movement, while it may have mentioned a host of desirable changes, tended to stress only a limited set of changes. Thus competition policy or institutional development may have received passing references, but they hardly had the standing of trade liberalization and privatization. In the early days of reform, even investments in human capital often seemed shortchanged.

8. The particular importance of knowledge and information for development was the focus of the 1998 *World Development Report,* which observed that the ways in which knowledge differs from standard commodities leads to important market failures. Government action can help to rectify such market failures, and indeed many governments, in both developed and less developed countries, have successfully taken steps to address these issues. The report further discussed the many important imperfections of information in less developed countries, as well as the role that these failures play in impeding the functioning of markets and the development of the economy; here too the report illustrated ways in which governments can and have addressed these concerns.

9. For a fuller discussion of this, see Furman and Stiglitz (1998).

advocated by the Washington consensus (without abandoning some of its key ideas) and worked hard to establish this institutional infrastructure at the same time that they emphasized competition over privatization.[10]

There is little doubt about the *insufficiency* of the Washington consensus dictums of reform. The *necessity* of those dictums has also been questioned. Certainly, governments that attempt to ignore the constraints imposed by economic laws—including the limitations imposed by the scarcity of resources—will find themselves in trouble. But the success of countries that have paid little attention to one or another of the dictums should at least raise eyebrows. Turkey has managed to achieve sustained rapid growth in an environment of sustained high inflation, which has exceeded 50 percent per year on average.[11] Even more telling is the experience of China. That country gave a higher priority to competition and the establishment of new enterprises than to privatization; indeed, it has yet to endorse fully the idea of privatization. China has liberalized trade to some extent, but it still has seemingly not achieved the minimum standards set by the United States and other members of the World Trade Organization as a precondition for accession. Despite this behavior, China's growth over the past two decades has been the most remarkable in the world: nearly two-thirds of the entire increase in the GDP of the world's low-income countries between 1978 and 1995 occurred in China, though it accounted for but a quarter of the population and but 40 percent of output at the beginning of the period. If the thirty different provinces of China were treated as separate data points—and the provinces are large, far larger in many cases than the typical African country—then the twenty fastest growing economies in the world between 1978 and 1995 would all have been Chinese.[12]

10. See Kolodko (1997, 1998). As always, there are often multiple interpretations of the facts, especially since there is a fundamental problem of underidentification. Was Russia's failure due to the fact that unlike the countries of Eastern Europe, it had no experience in the interwar period with market economics? (To be sure, some countries with no history of market experiences, such as Mongolia, made great strides in reform.) Was Estonia's success attributable to the speed of its reforms, or to its close ties with its neighbor Finland? Was Hungary's success based on its strong privatization program, or did it follow from the fact that even before the end of Soviet domination, it had been experimenting with market socialism? While systemic judgments seem difficult, this much seems clear: the Czech capital market, with inadequate laws incompletely enforced and with a voucher privatization scheme that left much room for abuses, has been thoroughly discredited; the Polish capital market, which paid attention to issues of institutional infrastructure, functions far more effectively.

11. See World Bank (1998). Looking across the Eastern and Central European economies in transition, it appears that there is even a positive relation between inflation and performance in the real sector (see Stiglitz 1999c).

12. World Bank (1997a). While dramatic, and while clearly illustrating the enormous success of China, such statistics need to be interpreted with caution. For comparison, the subunits of the other large countries (Brazil and India) need to be entered, in which case Chinese domination would almost surely remain, though the statistics would be somewhat less favorable.

The history of reform is even more mixed than this discussion indicates: some reform movements have been left to wither, even before it became clear whether they would yield their promised fruit. As I have already noted, advocates of the reform process claim that the countries simply failed to stay the course. The problem was not with the reforms, according to this view, but with their implementation (or lack thereof). I shall argue that these "excuses" will not do. A reform agenda is not a statement of what an ideal economy might look like—if that were all there were to a reform agenda, then Debreu's theory of value would qualify as an important policy document. Rather, a reform agenda is a view of changes in a country's rules of the game (institutions and policies) that one might reasonably expect to be implemented, taking into account the capacity of its governments and its political processes. Implementation and political sustainability are not sideshows but the main event in a reform agenda. I shall argue that all too often, reformers paid too little attention to these issues. While paying lip service to democracy, they hardly tried to convince voters that the reforms would improve their lives and livelihoods, let alone ensured that the reforms actually did so. There is a certain irony in this failure, for many of the reforms were based on political economy arguments; many attempted to reduce the role of government on the grounds that *political* pressures on government (such as rent seeking) distorted decisions in the public sector. As we shall see, this is only one of several "political economy" mistakes frequently associated with the reform movement.

From our current vantage point we can ask, To what do we attribute this record of—to put it mildly—mixed success? This paper sets forth some general principles of *reform* (or change), principles that in many cases were ignored by the reform movements of the past twenty-five years. After setting forth each principle, I shall detail some of the common mistakes related to that principle made by the reform movement. The principles relate to the *goals* of reform, both long-run goals and intermediate targets; the *strategies* for attaining those goals, the pacing and sequencing of reform; and the *political processes* by which reforms are attained.

Principle 1   While it may be appropriate to have ambitious goals, set reasonable intermediate objectives.

The reform movement failed by setting goals based on a misunderstanding of the fundamental attributes of a market economy.

Failure 1A   The reform movement had as its goal the creation of an idealized market economy based on simplistic and misleading conceptions.

For this, economists in particular need to take much of the blame. In the Arrow-Debreu model, the standard formulation of the competitive market economy, institutions play no role (or perhaps more accurately, they are put "behind the scenes").[13] That model places the focus on private property and prices. In an Arrow-Debreu world, prices convey all the relevant information. Elsewhere, I have argued that if this conception of the market economy were accurate, market socialism would have had a much better chance of succeeding (Stiglitz 1994b). But the model ignores many of the essential features of a market economy—the institutions that underlie it, the richness of the information that is required in order for it to function well, and the processes by which that information is conveyed.[14]

To its credit, the reform movement recognized that even its limited conception of what was required for a well-functioning market economy could not be attained overnight. But it did not think through carefully the appropriate intermediate targets.

Failure 1B   The reform movement set as its intermediate-run goal the establishment of a highly privatized economy with macroeconomic stability and trade liberalization, an intermediate goal that was too ambitious on some counts and not ambitious enough on others.

The reformers were correct in realizing that in the intermediate run, it would be difficult for a developing country to establish a fully working market economy of the kind seen in the United States. They would have to make compromises. The question was, if the baby had to be split in two, where was the best place to put the knife?

As I noted earlier, even in the oversimplified depiction of the market economy provided by the Arrow-Debreu model, efficiency requires more than macroeconomic stability and openness: at a minimum, both private property and competition are also necessary. Yet the Washington consensus hardly addressed how to achieve the latter, except to mention the promise that trade liberalization and the elimination of government monopoly would lead to competition. Yet the experience in the West, not only with natural monopolies (in many of the areas that were being privatized) but with markets more generally, has shown that strong and constant surveillance by antitrust authorities is required to safeguard a competitive environment. Even early advocates of the market economy recognized

13. Indeed, one of the doctrines was that institutions did not matter: one could see behind them to the underlying laws of economics.
Few policy economists would admit to blindly following the Arrow-Debreu model (indeed, the expression is hard to find in the policy literature!). But the question is, whence are derived the theoretical underpinnings of the policy prescriptions?
14. These are not the only limitations of the Arrow-Debreu model that make it particularly inappropriate as a "benchmark" for thinking about development: it is fundamentally a static model, in which there is no learning, no technical change, no absorption of new knowledge, no adaptation—essential elements of the changes that mark the development process. There is no attention to legal institutions, to intellectual property rights, to bankruptcy laws, to contract enforcement—because these deal with problems that simply cannot arise, *given the assumptions of the model.*

these problems. As Adam Smith put it so eloquently more than two hundred years ago:

> To widen the market and to narrow the competition is always the interest of the dealers. . . . The proposal of any new law or regulation of commerce which comes from this order, ought always to be listened to with great precaution, and ought never to be adopted, till after having been long and carefully examined, not only with the most scrupulous, but with the most suspicious attention. It comes from an order of men, whose interest is never exactly the same with that of the public, who have generally an interest to deceive and even to oppress the public, and who accordingly have, upon many occasions, both deceived and oppressed it. (1986, 267)

This experience should have raised caution flags. In developing economies, which generally have far less robust markets than those of OECD countries, firms will recognize that establishing a monopoly stranglehold offers a surer route to profits than does providing new and better products.

Similarly, while the price mechanism is important, capital is not sold to the highest bidder even in advanced market economies. Banks (which still account for the vast majority of flows of new investment funds, beyond which firms finance themselves out of retained earnings; see Myers 1977; Mayer 1989, 1990; Rajan 1992; Rajan and Zingales 1995) allocate much capital, and banks do not lend simply to those who are willing to pay the highest interest rate (Stiglitz 1988). Screening mechanisms are vital. It is ironic that in this respect, the reform movement made the same error that the earlier planning paradigm had made. The latter assumed that all that was required to allocate capital efficiently was to have a good programming model; the shadow prices that emerged from those models would serve as a reliable guide to the allocation of investment, just as the prices that emerge from the market process serve as a reliable guide to the allocation of investment in the reform paradigm. In fact, the informational requirements are far greater than either assumed, and the development of market-based financial institutions is essential to meeting those requirements. This point should have been stressed as an essential part of the intermediate-run goals of reform.

The lack of emphasis on competition and the lack of understanding of the importance of financial institutions (and policies to help strengthen them) are but two of the lacunae of the *intermediate* targets set by the reform agenda. No less important was the lack of attention to the social safety net and to other aspects of the institutional infrastructure (and especially the legal structure, including bankruptcy and contract law).

Intermediate targets with greater emphasis on competition and regulatory policy, the creation of strong financial institutions, a better institutional infrastructure, and more effective safety nets would not obviously have required compromising on the objectives of the other intermediate targets of the reform movement. But even if they had, in my mind the trade-off would have been well worth it. Indeed, I would go further, in a way that is highlighted by the third failure.

Failure 1C   The reform movement failed to pay sufficient attention to the "theory of the second best," which emphasizes that if there are distortions in some part of the economy, it may not be desirable to eliminate certain other distortions (see Lancaster and Lipsey 1996).

More broadly, the market economy can be thought of as a finely honed system, the success of which as a whole depends on the performance of each of its major parts. Without competition policy, privatization may well fail to deliver its promised benefits. Without well-functioning financial systems, macroeconomic stability may not be attainable, even if governments themselves maintain sound fiscal balances and monetary authorities do an effective job in curbing inflation. (The financial side of the economy is important and is not summarized effectively in the money demand and supply equations! See, e.g., Stiglitz 1988, 1992; Greenwald 1998.) Capital and financial market liberalization *may* eventually be desirable; it *may* be an essential feature of a successful, advanced, industrial economy. The elimination of distortionary regulations that serve no purpose other than to create rents for certain special interests seems a reasonable, in some cases even an essential, part of more intermediate goals. Yet as we have learned so painfully from the experience of East Asia, full liberalization prior to the establishment of an effective regulatory system is an invitation to disaster.[15] Econometric studies show, indeed, that such liberalization is a key factor contributing to the "boom in busts"[16] that the world has experienced over the past decade (see Demirgüç-Kunt and Detragiache 1998a). (According to some estimates, there have been banking crises in sixty-nine countries since the late 1970s—and in twenty more countries if the transition economies are added. See Caprio and Klingebiel 1997.)

The information and public goods problems that give rise to the necessity for strong and effective government regulation had been extensively discussed prior to the latest set of crises.[17] But policymakers (at least one

15. See Furman and Stiglitz (1998) and the references cited in n. 6.

16. To use Jerry Caprio's memorable phrase (see Caprio 1997). Caprio and Klingebiel (1997) documented this boom. Not only have financial crises become more frequent, but they have imposed huge budgetary costs (the United States—where costs were somewhere between 2 and 4 percent of GDP—no longer makes the top twenty-five of the past two decades!) and are systematically associated with slower growth (see Caprio 1997). The slowdown generally continues during the five years following the crisis.

17. See, e.g., Arnott, Greenwald, and Stiglitz (1994), Hellman et al. (1997), Caprio and Summers (1996), Kane and Yu (1994), and Akerlof and Romer (1993). These studies emphasize, e.g., the importance of maintaining franchise value (the present discounted value of banks' future profits). Franchise value is often eroded in the process of liberalization, and with its erosion greater regulatory oversight is required to prevent excessive risk taking or looting.

of whom had actually contributed to this literature) somehow failed to absorb the discussion's lessons or hoped that there were simple ways around it. For example, some suggested increasing capital adequacy standards, without recognizing that implementing capital adequacy standards itself requires a strong regulatory agency,[18] that the appropriate risk adjustments for a fully effective capital adequacy standard are not even undertaken in the most advanced economies,[19] that there might be reasons to believe that these failures would be even more severe in less developed countries (because the risks they face are often greater),[20] and that tightened capital adequacy standards are not an efficient substitute for the loss of franchise value and may even be counterproductive.[21] Indeed, there is a growing recognition that *imperfect* capital adequacy standards (and all existing capital adequacy standards are, according to the above discussion, imperfect) may well result in increased riskiness of portfolios.[22]

The importance of the relations among reforms, here financial market liberalization and the strength of the regulatory system, comes home most forcefully when one thinks about the consequences of putting a racing engine into a car with bald tires and inadequate suspension: even a good driver might encounter problems.

While the theory of the second best emphasizes that one set of reforms may not have the desired consequences unless accompanied by reforms elsewhere, the theory need not be a cause of paralysis: one can have tightened regulatory oversight *and* some forms of financial market liberalization. Our intermediate-run goals, however, have to be nuanced: they may not entail monotonic adjustments in all variables. More competition in

18. And indeed, even in advanced countries, regulatory authorities have not adopted accounting principles designed to enhance transparency (e.g., marking to market).

19. E.g., risk is typically viewed on an asset-by-asset basis, which fails to take into account correlations: the focus is on credit risk, not market risk (thus, in the late 1980s, after the S&L debacle, the Fed explicitly made a decision not to treat long-term U.S. bonds as risky assets, even though it seemed obvious—to any economist—they should have been), and not surprisingly, then, no account is taken of the correlation between credit and market risk (a factor that contributed to the recent crises, as the hedges that many banks thought they had placed to cover themselves failed in exactly the circumstances where they were needed). See Dooley (1998).

20. E.g., because their economies are often less diversified and because they have less institutional capacity.

21. See Hellman et al. (1997). The intuition behind their result is simple: increases in capital beyond which the bank would voluntarily undertake reduce the franchise value of the bank. Incentives for prudential behavior are provided by both franchise value and capital requirements; the net benefit of an increase in capital requirements is thus undermined by the loss in franchise value—the net benefit may in fact be negative.

22. See, e.g., Besanko and Kanatas (1996). This is especially true when inadequate accounting practices (such as a failure to mark to market) are used. A bank trying to improve its capital adequacy ratio can sell assets that have increased in value (entering the gain on its books) and retain assets that have decreased in value. Thus market value provides a biased estimate of true value. Worse still, knowing that they may have to engage in such ruses to satisfy the capital adequacy standards induces banks to invest in assets with greater price volatility. Tighter capital adequacy standards (and especially rigorous enforcement in the face of an economic downturn) exacerbate these problems.

the financial sector erodes franchise value and will lead to a tendency for greater risk taking, unless regulatory oversight is strengthened. The government may need to accompany increased liberalization in one direction (say in financial competition) with increased intervention in others (e.g., restricting the opportunities for undertaking high-risk investments, such as speculative real estate).[23]

Having appropriate final and intermediate goals, however desirable, is insufficient for a successful reform movement.

Principle 2   Policymakers must pay careful attention to the sequencing and pacing of reforms.

The *dynamics* of the reform process are important, for both economic and political reasons. Even if we know which mountain we are climbing, even if we know where we want to take our first rest stop (our intermediate goal), the way we set out to attain that goal—the path we take, the sequencing of steps, and the pace at which we proceed—may determine not only the costs of attaining it but even whether we make it. Economic theory has advanced much further in *equilibrium* analysis than in *dynamics,* and it is therefore not surprising that there have been many missteps on the path of reform.

The first failure I wish to discuss is a variant of failure 1C. Balance in reforms must be reflected in the pacing and sequencing of reforms.

Failure 2A   In many cases, the reform agenda pushed ahead with those reforms that could be easily and quickly achieved, without recognizing that complementary reforms, which took longer, would be necessary to keep general economic welfare, or at least the welfare of significant subgroups within the population, from being adversely affected (in some cases significantly so).

Reforms take more time in some areas than in others. There is a tendency to push ahead with the reforms that can be made quickly—the "quick wins" or "low-hanging fruit"—without paying adequate attention to the systemic nature of the reform process. Thus institutional reforms, in some cases at least, take longer than, say, privatization. Clearly, with a simple stroke of a pen, a national enterprise can be privatized by turning it over to some oligarch; it takes far more effort to establish an effective regulatory agency. But the implication of this is not necessarily to push ahead with what can be done quickly—privatization—while leaving the rest for later.

The theory of the second best warned us that reducing distortions in one area may make matters worse if distortions remain in others. So too here: privatizing a public monopoly without simultaneously creating an

23. I shall return to these issues in somewhat greater detail later.

effective regulatory authority may lead to higher prices, and less overall efficiency (even if "profits" are increased). Liberalizing trade without adequate insurance markets—and insurance markets are typically woefully inadequate in most developing countries—exposes market participants to increased risk that not only makes them worse off (assuming that they are risk averse) but also leads to risk avoidance behaviors that can actually lower overall economic efficiency. Liberalizing trade without insurance markets can lead to a Pareto-inferior outcome (see Newbery and Stiglitz 1982).

As noted before, the theory of the second best is not an excuse for inaction: there are carefully balanced strategies that at least hold out the promise of significant overall gains, if not gains for every group. In some cases, reforms went even further.

Failure 2B   In the name of reform, the government's ability to deal with a market failure was undermined at the same time that the consequences of the market failure grew.

An important set of market failures in all economies, but with especially strong consequences in less developed economies, is the absence of risk markets. Richer countries have established social safety nets to compensate for this market failure; but in less developed countries, where risks are more pervasive, the social safety nets are weaker. This is especially true of some economies at "intermediate" stages of development—at stages where traditional risk-sharing mechanisms of the family and community have been weakened, before publicly provided mechanisms of the form found in more developed countries have taken hold. The issue goes beyond just redistribution: all individuals can be worse off because of the additional risks resulting from liberalization. But while reforms often thus increased the need for government safety nets (as partial substitutes for market insurance), the elimination of many subsidy programs (which might be desirable if there were no other distortions or market imperfections) left those affected more vulnerable.

Several other explicitly dynamic effects must be taken into account in the analysis of the pacing and sequencing of reforms. These have to do with not only adverse economic efficiency effects—specifically, exacerbating existing distortions—but also with adverse distributional consequences and, possibly most important, adverse political consequences.

Failure 2C   The pacing and sequencing of reforms often paid insufficient attention to the impact of reforms on capital asset values, and the effect of those asset value changes on economic activity.

A central aspect of reform is the elimination of rents. Sometimes, those rents serve an important economic function—as in the case of a bank's franchise value—and their elimination, prior to the establishment of off-setting improvements in supervision, leads to excessive risk taking and looting, which weakens financial institutions. But even when rents do not serve an important economic function, their elimination needs to be carefully paced. For instance, the United States has highly distorted tax and agricultural policies, the effect of which is to increase real estate values. Reformers rightly point out that these cost the American economy dearly, and they should be eliminated. But timing is everything. Consider the U.S. S&L crisis of the 1980s. It was partly caused by distortionary real estate policies; one might have therefore argued that they should be eliminated as part of the overall reform of the financial sector. But had policymakers taken this course of action, they might well have converted the mild economic downturn of 1991 into a full-scale and deep recession. Eliminating distortions at that time would have led to further collapse in real estate prices, so that even banks that had acted prudently—on the assumption that those special provisions would be continued—would have found themselves under water. The collapse of the financial system would have been deep and widespread, with concomitant effects on the economy.

More broadly, it is increasingly being recognized that wealth redistributions—even if motivated by sound long-run concerns—can have large, adverse short-run effects.[24] Thus to introduce these reforms when the economy is going into a recession may simply exacerbate the downturn. These concerns take on special significance when countercyclical instruments are not available or are weak.

The subtlety of capitalization effects cannot be ignored: in some cases, the effects arise at the time of the announcement of the reform. Gradual implementation of reforms may thus only mitigate the capital asset effects slightly. Indeed, gradual implementation with a strong announcement yields high up-front costs (in terms of the economic disruption generated by the changes in asset values) with a lower present discounted value of benefits (as a result of delayed implementation). Such concerns are of particular importance in the context of financial and capital market liberalization. The announcement of such liberalization will lead to an immediate decrease in franchise value, leading to increased risk taking and looting behavior; offsetting improvements in risk management and regulatory performance may take a long time, and capital market imperfections may imply that an offsetting increase in capital adequacy standards would either be unfeasible or lead to a significant economic contraction (as a result of the forced contraction in lending). The initial stages of liberalization sometimes result in increased opportunities for risk taking, exacerbating the problem. Thus the appropriate response is sequencing in which, ac-

---

24. See Greenwald and Stiglitz (1988). As we will see later, they can also have adverse long-run consequences.

companying the announcement, there must be *stricter* regulations.[25] (Alternatively, the government should hold off the announcement of liberalization until after capital standards have been increased and regulatory oversight been improved.)[26]

The impacts on capital asset values—and the consequences of those impacts—were not the only aspect of capital that received inadequate attention.

Failure 2D   The pacing and sequencing of reforms often ignored adverse effects on social and organizational capital and wealth distribution.

Today, we recognize that aggregate output is not just a function of human and physical capital and the labor supply. Knowledge and organizational and social capital are important too. While precise definitions of the concepts of social and organizational capital have proved elusive, the concepts have demonstrated their usefulness in explaining both differences in levels of productivity across countries and changes over time (see Coleman 1988; Putnam 1993). It is much easier to destroy such capital than it is to recreate it. Yet often in the early stages of reform, such capital does get destroyed. Recent discussions of the failures in the economies in transition attribute at least part of that failure to the destruction of social and organizational capital (see Blanchard and Kremer 1997; Stiglitz 1999b, 1999c). The country within the Commonwealth of Independent States that has seen the smallest drop in its GDP—Uzbekistan—is also the country that has made the greatest efforts not only to protect but actually to enhance its social capital.

The destruction of social capital in many countries led, in turn, to the destruction of physical capital; but the pacing and sequencing of reforms exacerbated the problem. In many cases, given the illegitimacy associated with the manner in which privatization occurred and the absence of sound corporate governance, the new owners thought it more profitable to strip assets than to create wealth; the open capital account made it easy for them to ship their wealth abroad, where it would be protected against any political backlash. Providing this easy "exit" strategy altered the dynamics of the game; had such an easy exit not been available, it might have paid each firm to invest within the country, and as each made such investments, it would have made it more attractive for others to do so. As it was, each

25. It is sometimes suggested that as an alternative to stricter regulation, capital adequacy standards should be strengthened, with the government providing the finance. But government-provided capital may not offer the same incentives for prudential behavior that manager-financed capital would provide; and there is little reason to believe that the government-as-owner could improve significantly on prudential behavior compared to the impact of the government-as-regulator.

26. These observations suggest that there may not be a unique reasonable set of sequencing and pacing decisions; and just as there are a variety of sensible ways of proceeding, there are a variety of ways that undermine the reform process.

saw that others were stripping assets and shipping their wealth abroad; this both conveyed information about others' judgments concerning the future of the economy and reduced the return to their investing within the country.

Similarly, the reformers, too often relying on simplistic neoclassical models, ignored agency costs, which the reforms themselves might unintentionally have exacerbated. In many poor developing countries, the most important agency costs are associated with the disparity between the distribution of wealth and labor (reflected in institutions like sharecropping). Eliminating fertilizer subsidies might, in a static sense, increase efficiency; but if credit-constrained poor farmers become poorer, the inequality in landholdings might increase, exacerbating the underlying agency cost inefficiency.

This is an example of a more general problem with many of the reforms that undermined their long-term sustainability: they focused on aggregate impacts, paying too little attention to distributional consequences.

Failure 2E   The pacing and sequencing of reforms was often such that sizable groups were made worse off in the transition; the changes were not Pareto-improvements, even if they increased overall national income. The compensation systems that would be required to make them even near Pareto-improvements were not put into place.

Governments often promised that in the future everyone would be better off. But these promises were often not credible, partly because the reform process itself was not credible or did not appear to be so.

In some cases, the reform process directly contributed to the weakening of the economy—at least in the short run—and the exacerbation of the problems it was meant to address. This was partly because of a key failure in economic analysis and partly because of key failures in political analyses. Here I address the former, postponing the latter to the next section:

Failure 2F   The pacing and sequencing of reform raised doubts about its long-term credibility, its political sustainability, and its time consistency.[27]

In early stages of reform, reputation and credibility—on the part of both government and entrepreneurs—must be created. A lack of confidence that the reforms are permanent not only undermines the commitment to reform but it also leads to steps that make the reforms less likely to succeed. Thus, if those who succeeded in gaining control of privatized firms in the former Soviet Union and Eastern Europe did not believe that

27. A government's announcement of a plan for some future actions is "time consistent" if, at the time for those actions to occur, it remains in the government's interest to carry out those plans.

the market economy—or their positions of control—were sustainable, they had strong incentives to strip the companies of their assets (before laws were put into place restricting their abilities to do so) and to transfer their wealth abroad. There is here, of course, a vicious circle: capital flight combined with asset-stripping rather than wealth-creating activities made the failure of the market strategy more likely and thus provided even greater incentives to engage in these nefarious activities.

Capital market liberalization would, in the best of circumstances, be expected to lead to some capital flight, as domestic investors seek to diversify their portfolios. If the reforms are not fully credible, then investors may expect a decrease in expected returns and an increase in risk for domestic assets, exacerbating the outward flow. And the flow itself, as we have noted, enhances these risks.

My concerns about capital market liberalization are reinforced by the fact that investors (and others) often remain unconvinced, sometimes rightly so, of the validity of the economic theory of reform and its empirical bases. Economic theory, for instance, provides clear arguments for why a perfectly competitive economy with perfect information and a complete set of markets is Pareto-efficient, but it has far less to say about the imperfect world that confronts those in the less developed countries. And most investors may be less concerned about Pareto-efficiency than about the returns on their own investments. They are Bayesians in that their assumptions about the world will partly be based on what they have experienced. When they see economic performance weakening during the early stages of reform, they may infer that future returns will be lower and that the economic reforms will not succeed, or they may infer that others will make these inferences, with similar consequences.[28] Therefore, a government that took account of the *learning* process by implementing a gradual sequence of reforms would allow investors to build confidence. That in turn would bolster the ability of the reform process to withstand setbacks.

More aspects of "credibility" related to the political process will be discussed in the next section. Nonpolitical ways exist by which the government can attempt to convince others that it will in fact carry out its promises. For instance, some have argued that if the government issues indexed bonds, then the incentive to inflate—to reduce the real value of its obligations—would be reduced, and thus the credibility of a low-inflation policy would be enhanced.[29]

28. This is not always the case. There may be circumstances where the prereform regime is such a failure that *relative to that baseline,* the public retains confidence in the reform process, regardless of initial setbacks. Other factors affect the extent to which priors may be revised in the face of negative initial outcomes; below I discuss how the success or failure of similar reforms in other countries can be one such factor.

29. There is a similar argument for the advantage of short-term bonds over long-term bonds. These issues are complex. People have raised the counterargument that indexed bonds, by reducing the "pain" of inflation, reduce popular resolve to fight inflation. This

We have argued that the reform process is more likely to be successful if market participants believe that the reforms are likely to be sustained. Under gradual reform, market participants need to be convinced that the reform process will continue; under quick and rapid reforms, market participants need to be convinced that the market reforms will not be reversed. Governments can undertake actions that increase the credibility of continuation or nonreversal: actions that increase the costs of reversal or of not continuing reforms become such commitment devices.[30]

But the most important part of credibility of reforms has to do with political processes. Whatever the political process, it is likely that the credibility of reforms will be enhanced if there are early successes in a gradual reform process, or if the failures are quickly dealt with; conversely, credibility will be undermined if early on there appears to be a significant risk of failure.

There are externalities to the reform process: failures in one country convey lessons for others. Today, not only is there virtually no support in Russia for the form of reforms that characterized the 1990s there, but the perceived failures in Russia have also discredited that entire reform strategy. To be sure, the reasons for the failures may be many and only partly related to the reform strategy; yet as good Bayesians, those in other countries draw the inference that the form of the reforms was at least partly to blame. Similarly, the perceived failures in the Czech (and other) voucher privatization schemes have largely discredited that form of privatization. This then represents one of the risks associated with rapid reforms: their very pace makes midcourse correction more difficult, and failures have consequences not only for the countries involved but for others as well.

To the extent that economic systems consist of highly interdependent parts, it is difficult to reform one part without reforming others. The experience with revolutionary changes is not a happy one; in a sense, those who advocated a near instantaneous transition to a market economy were as revolutionary as the Bolsheviks had been three-quarters of a century earlier. The burden of revolutionary reform is that all of the parts have to be redesigned de novo, a daunting task.

Costs of adjustment matter a great deal. For instance, capital cannot be shifted instantaneously from one sector into another,[31] and "learning"

---

argument played some role in the opposition to issuing indexed bonds in the United States. Thus some individuals may interpret the issuance of indexed bonds as reducing the government's anti-inflation credibility, others as strengthening it. See Wilcox (1998).

30. Some countries (Britain) did pay attention to the issue of time consistency and irreversibility in designing their privatizations. One argument for the way in which some British enterprises were privatized—with large numbers of individuals being entitled to buy the shares at below fair market prices—was to create a vested interest that would resist renationalization. See, e.g., Vickers and Yarrow (1988).

31. One could not correct overnight the misallocation of capital that characterizes many less developed countries. Resources should be moved out of, say, inefficient coal or steel

about and adaptation to markets takes time.[32] Most difficult of all is the creation of the kind of social capital and institutional infrastructure required to make a market economy work. Those who advocated quick reform also believed that these would quickly follow. This did not occur, and I shall argue in the next section that the dynamics of the political process in fact impeded the creation of the social capital and institutional infrastructure.

Economic success and political credibility of reform are, as we have seen, inextricable intertwined. This brings me to the third general principle.

Principle 3   Pay sufficient attention to the political economy of reform.

Many market reforms have been accompanied by political reforms that have increased democracy and public accountability. Thus the pacing and sequencing of reforms has to maintain public confidence in the reform process. Some advocates of reform took it as self-evident that everyone would accept the virtues of the market economy; in their view, at most what might be at question was how to attain these goals. But among reputable economists there is no agreement about the nature of many aspects of the market economy that were taken as doctrine (such as the desirability of full capital account convertibility and financial market liberalization without regard to the state of the associated regulatory system). Even in the bastions of market economics, there are constant calls for protectionism and industrial policy.

I have already called attention to one failure of many reform efforts: the failure to recognize that the pacing, sequencing, and design of reforms must be such as to create a widespread perception that most individuals will gain from the reforms reasonably soon and that the reforms are, in some sense, equitable. Part of the strong adverse reaction to market reforms that is setting in throughout the developing world is based not only on the vulnerability to shocks to which those reforms have exposed it (even in those Latin American countries that for the past five years or more, have maintained exemplary economic policies) but also on the distribution

---

enterprises, but the marginal product of an unemployed worker may be even less than that of a worker working in an inefficient steel mill. Underlying the "shock therapy" approach to structural reallocations was the belief that open unemployment would generate more rapid creation of new enterprises than would occur in a process by which workers were bid away from existing enterprises. There was little empirical support for this hypothesis, and indeed the literature on hysteresis effects in Europe has emphasized the attrition of skills that comes from extended unemployment. See Blanchard and Summers (1988).

32. The Japanese compare the time-consuming process of organizational and institutional change to the painstaking process of transplanting a tree. "It is a time-honored Japanese gardening technique to prepare a tree for transplanting by slowly and carefully binding the roots over a period of time, bit by bit, to prepare the tree for the shock of the change it is about to experience. This process, called *nemawashi*, takes time and patience, but it rewards you, if it is done properly, with a healthy transplanted tree" (Morita 1986).

of the impacts. When those shocks occur, the brunt of the costs is borne by innocent bystanders—those who did not participate at all in the international financial markets, including workers and small businesses. While the international community spoke often of the "pain" that must be borne as part of reform, they far less often took note of *who* experienced the pain. The advocates of painful medicines often ignored the seeming inequities of division of pain between the international bankers and developing country workers. The former, although perhaps better able to bear such shocks, often benefited most from the bailouts; the latter were all too likely to suffer extended unemployment in economies lacking safety nets and, ultimately, to bear most of the costs of the bailouts.

The failure to pay attention to the politics of reform runs deeper than just the obvious observation that success breeds commitment and that perceived failure undermines future reforms.

In this section, I wish to emphasize several aspects of the *political* processes by which reform was undertaken that undermined not only its economic success but its political credibility, and thus its sustainability. Ironically, political economy considerations often were put forward as central arguments both for reform itself and for its pace. Reform was necessary to stop public rent seeking associated with, say, protectionist policies, and rapid reform was necessary to take advantage of a "window of opportunity." Reform was necessary to curtail the role of special interest groups. Yet why should those special interests that abused the political process to advance their economic interests suddenly have a change of heart and allow a change in policy that would clearly put them at a disadvantage?[33]

Thus the reform movement should have been more wary of the possibility of abuse.

Failure 3A   The reform process sometimes failed to be sensitive to the vested interests of those who supported pieces of the reform agenda.

Outside reformers were often gratified by governments' sudden embrace of privatization reforms. In fact, policymakers hardly seemed to need convincing. Although they talked extensively about "politics," outside reform enthusiasts typically failed to ask what was driving these political figures—whose ability and desire to conduct policies in the national interest was so often maligned—to launch privatizations *now*. Had they really reformed? The answer in all too many cases was no: they had simply discov-

---

33. Much of the literature emphasizing the key role that crises play in enabling reform to occur can be interpreted as providing an answer to that question: the sudden change in circumstances could cause new coalitions to form, whose interests differ from those of the old groups, and for whom reform would be advantageous. However, such changes in coalitions can occur even outside of crises: some interpret the recent successful trade liberalization represented by the North American Free Trade Agreement and the Uruguay Round as the result of a new militancy of exporters, who, because of growth in exports, saw these trade agreements as vital to their interests. See Bruno and Easterly (1996).

ered that there were more rents, or at least more secured rents, to be achieved through privatization than through rent collection associated with government ownership. Government officials could, through privatization, appropriate a share not only of this year's profits but of future profits as well. Even if the fraction of total profits they could appropriate under privatization might be lower, the total amounts that current governments could appropriate might be larger. And the way in which privatization is conducted might be designed to maximize not the long-run profitability or efficiency of the enterprises but the magnitude of the rents that could be extracted in the privatization process. How well do these considerations explain the failure (in, say, the Czech Republic or Russia) of the privatization process either to generate popular perceptions of its equity and effectiveness or to lead to the increased economic efficiency that might be expected from such substantial privatization? This is a question that I am sure will be the subject of extensive debate in coming years.[34]

The fact that there is a self-selection process at work in reform—those that got adopted may reflect the self-interest of the elites and vested interests, not the broader sense of public interest—is only one of the factors that make policy analysis difficult. Equally complicated are the dynamics of the political process; but despite these complications, it is possible to identify some strategies that seem more likely to succeed than others.

Failure 3B   The reform sequence often failed to pay attention
       to political dynamics.

When privatization (especially of natural monopolies) predated regulatory reforms and the establishment of competition, a vested interest was created with incentives and resources to resist that next stage of reform.[35] In one West African country, for example, sale of the state telecommunications monopoly to a major Western telecommunications firm set up a constituency ready to fight increases in competition in the sector. More generally, vested interests spawned by the very process of reform can impede further advances in the reform process.

Earlier, we emphasized the importance of economic dynamics. Political dynamics are no less important. The reform process should have been more cognizant not only of how political dynamics might undermine reforms but also of how they might have tried to steer the political process in ways that would have enhanced long-term success.

---

34. For a more extended discussion of the issues of privatization and the failures in the economies in transition, see Stiglitz (1999b, 1999c).

35. Some have argued that privatization must precede competition because without privatization government subsidies create an unlevel playing field, which new firms will hesitate to enter. But if privatization cannot be achieved simultaneously with the creation of a competition policy, other strategies can deal with this problem: a commitment to future privatization and the passage of strong competition laws.

The political process can be viewed as a dynamic game. Actions taken at one period may affect coalition formation, and therefore the set of admissible reforms at later stages. Participants in the political process recognize this. Indeed, elsewhere I have argued that these political dynamics help to explain why reforms that seem to be Pareto-improvements are sometimes resisted: the vested interests are not myopic, and they recognize that the political dynamic that today's reform will set in place will eventually make them worse off (Stiglitz 1998c). (And the government may have no way to commit itself effectively to actions that avoid damaging those vested interests.)

Perhaps the most important part of the political process of reform in democratic societies is the creation of political support for the reforms.

Failure 3C   All too often the reform process paid insufficient attention to the consensus building required for political sustainability.

Indeed, in many cases, the reform strategies actually undermined consensus-building democratic processes:

With burdens unequally and unfairly shared, it was hard for the many losers in the reform process to become supporters of the reform.

The imposition of reforms from the outside, in the form of conditionalities—requirements imposed in order to receive financial support—not only undermined country "ownership" but made the reforms appear to be a new form of Western colonialism.

In my discussion of credibility and the pacing and sequencing of reform, I noted one way that early failures undermine future successes. A similar dynamic may be observed on the political level: rather than ensuring early successes that benefited wide segments of society and could serve as a basis for further reforms, many reforms demanded high up-front investment in "pain." Citizens were left simply to trust the reformers' assertions that there would be gains down the road. And while there was much discussion about developing policies of inclusion, the *costs* of reform were shared more inclusively than the *benefits*—a seeming policy of shared pain without shared gain.

More broadly, the process of reform paid too little attention to the political process required for sustainability. Instead of attempting to develop a consensus behind the reform efforts, the reforms often originated outside the country, as conditions on an "adjustment" package from the international financial institutions. All too often the reform packages were adopted (or imposed, depending on one's point of view) in the middle of a crisis, when one could argue there was simply not time to engage in broad consensus building. But neither the governments nor the international financial institutions made sufficient attempts, either at the time or subsequently, to develop widespread popular support for the reforms.

There are many instances where consensus could have been developed, had there been a more open, democratic, participatory process of reform. My predecessor as chief economist at the World Bank, Michael Bruno (1993), emphasized the important role that these consensual processes played in the success of macroeconomic stabilization efforts, especially in Ghana and Israel.

More alarmingly, it could be argued that the way the reform process was conducted in many countries not only undermined the sustainability of the reforms but also undermined democratic processes. The countries, rather than seeing these essential elements of society arrived at through debate and discussion, saw them imposed from above—no longer by colonial masters with a gunboat sitting in the harbor, but under a no less compelling threat, that of the loss of aid. Without this aid, countries' development plans would be thwarted; in some cases, they might starve.

The reform movement failed not only to build a consensus behind it, but the reform agenda (as it was implemented) often served to undermine confidence in reform.

Failure 3D   All too often the reform agenda overreached: it included elements that were not central to the immediate problems of the country and, indeed, behind which there was not even consensus within the economics profession.

Not surprisingly, when reforms failed to deliver as promised, confidence in the overall reform agenda was undermined.

The limited scientific evidence in support of the desirability or efficacy of some of the long-advocated reforms suggested that some of the reforms were at least partly motivated by ideology and by the self-interest of the more advanced countries.

Many of the "reforms" were essentially political, the kinds of changes that in more developed countries are the subject of intense debate; yet the reformers tried to push such political reforms as mere technocratic changes designed to enhance the performance of the economy

Suspicions about the desirability of reforms were reinforced by hypocritical actions of the more advanced countries, which have often themselves pursued policies in contradiction to the advice they give.

Failed Reforms: Corruption and Privatization. The privatization process, as it occurred in many of the economies in transition, illustrates how the reforms undermined themselves. Earlier, we noted that a process of self-selection was at work: corrupt governments undertook privatizations that increased rents available to them.

Corruption in the privatization process did not just reduce the gains from privatization. In many countries it contributed to the perception that the privatization process was fundamentally unfair—it was strengthening vested interests rather than contributing to political reform—and so privatization helped to undermine the credibility of the entire reform process. Indeed, this failure interacted with some of the earlier noted failures: where the privatization entailed a conversion of a public monopoly into a private monopoly without sufficient regulatory oversight, prices did not come down and the public received few benefits.

Undermining Confidence in Reform: Inappropriate Responses to Crises. In many cases, the reforms went well beyond what was required to address the crisis, into longer term structural issues; the issues certainly needed addressing, but not without a more democratic strategy of building understanding and support for structural reforms. In some cases, the reforms even went beyond the consensus within the economics profession: many economists would have argued that the reforms were political, not economic, in nature, or that their benefits—given the country's stage of development—were at best questionable.[36]

Consider, for instance, a provision included in Korea's reform package in December 1997: the establishment of an independent central bank whose sole mandate was to limit inflation. While such a policy *might* be appropriate for a country with a long history of inflation, this was not the case for Korea. In some cases, independent central banks have been effective in controlling inflation, but the evidence on whether such independence is either necessary or sufficient is far from definitive. India, where there is a broad societal consensus against inflation, keeps inflation under control without an independent central bank, while Russia's independent central bank was a major force contributing to inflation, and its independence limited the government's ability to seize control of the situation. Furthermore, econometric analyses suffer from identification problems: are countries that are more committed to limiting inflation more likely to create independent central banks? The evidence on the benefits of targeting inflation is also ambiguous. In particular, there is little evidence that countries that have adopted such policies have either grown faster or had less volatility in real economic output (Alesina and Summers 1993).

The point is that except when inflation is a pressing economic issue, the question of whether to change the governance structure and objectives of the central bank is an intensely political one. It strays well beyond economics into the issue of democratic accountability. In the United States, the Clinton administration strongly resisted pressure from some Republican senators to change the charter of the Fed to make inflation its sole target; indeed, the administration would have made the issue a focus of the political campaign of 1996, had the pressure remained. These are not

36. See Feldstein (1998) for a telling criticism in the case of the recent East Asian crisis.

issues of a purely technical nature, to be relegated to international bureaucrats, but involve real political choices.[37]

Undermining Confidence in Reform: Hidden Agendas. Incorporating such issues in reform packages when they were not germane to the problems at hand undermined confidence in the reform process more generally. Many observers raised questions: did outside interests have a broader agenda than simply resolving the weaknesses in the economy that had led to the current crisis? For instance, including in the conditions for Korea an acceleration of trade liberalization—a reform unrelated to the crisis—suggested that the reform agenda included items more directed at satisfying interests in the developed countries than at correcting problems in the crisis countries. The high-interest-rate policies helped collapse asset prices; this result, combined with the insistence that the borrowing countries sell their assets to foreigners, naturally led to questions about motives.

Undermining Confidence in Reform: Misguided Reforms. A host of more technical issues embraced by overzealous advocates of the reform process also served to undermine confidence in the reforms. In one extremely poor African country, the reform agenda included at an early stage financial market liberalization, including the creation of a treasury bill market—this in an economy that hardly had a capital market at all, and in which the government feared that the reforms would lead (as they had done in neighboring African countries) to higher interest rates facing poor peasants, with little increase in overall economic efficiency. The government, whose political support was agrarian based, refused to go along with the reforms, and an international meeting of economists provided strong support to the government's position concerning financial liberalization at that stage of development, especially in the manner being suggested by the advocates of reform. Such misguided policies make it difficult, if not impossible, to develop a consensus behind reform.

Undermining Confidence in Reform: Ideology versus Evidence. In many cases, the misguided reforms were dictated more by ideology than by economic science. And as more individuals in the developed countries received training in modern economics, they came to recognize more clearly the distinction.

Consider, for instance, the recent debate over capital market liberalization. Given the prominence accorded to the issue, one would presume that this reform was based on a wealth of studies demonstrating its advantages. On the contrary, while cross-country studies demonstrate forcefully the

---

37. See Stiglitz (1997) for a fuller articulation of the issues concerning the governance of central banks in democratic society.

gains that come from trade liberalization, similar studies show that neither growth nor investment seems enhanced by capital market liberalization (Rodrik 1998). Research (reinforced by the recent experiences in East Asia) *has* established that there are substantial risks: capital (and financial) market liberalization increases the risk of a financial crisis,[38] and financial crises have severely adverse consequences not only for government budgets but for economic growth (Caprio and Summers 1996).

These empirical results should not come as a surprise: a large literature explains why capital markets differ from other markets, and why they are replete with market failures that can be and have been effectively addressed by appropriate government regulation (see, e.g., Stiglitz 1988; Arnott et al. 1994; Hellman et al. 1997; Greenwald, Stiglitz, and Weiss 1984). The systemic and contagion effects associated with financial and currency crises naturally and systematically give rise to government action; the existence of such interventions themselves as well as the systemic and contagion effects imply that there are large externalities, that there are significant discrepancies between social and private risks, and that ex ante actions will be necessary to narrow those discrepancies.

Another compelling reason for government action is suggested by more recent analyses of the Asian crisis, which have pointed out that countries may need to maintain reserves equal to their short-term liabilities.[39] Consider a company in a poor developing country that borrows $100 million short term from a U.S. bank and pays 18 percent interest on the loan. According to the dictates of prudential reserve policy, the government should set aside $100 million in reserves, say, purchasing $100 million in U.S. treasury bills. While one can understand why the United States might like such a strategy—lending at 18 percent and borrowing at 4 percent—it is hard to see how this is supposed to be a growth-enhancing strategy for a less developed country![40] The advocacy for capital market liberalization typifies how a policy position may be more extreme than is justified by the scientific evidence.

Undermining Confidence in Reform: Inconsistency between Advice and Action. Another factor that has undermined confidence in the reforms is a seeming gap between the policies pursued internally by some of the coun-

---

38. Kaminsky and Reinhart (1998) pointed out that "in 18 of the 26 banking crises studied here, the financial sector had been liberalized in the past five years, usually less." See also Demirgüç-Kunt and Detragiache (1998a).

39. E.g., Furman and Stiglitz (1998) pointed out that this variable is the only one they studied that is systematically related to the crises of 1997. See also Radelet and Sachs (1998).

40. The necessity of the government's increasing reserves in response to such borrowing implies an externality. The required level of reserves is a function of the aggregate level of borrowing; while the cost of the reserves is borne collectively, the benefits of the borrowing clearly accrue to the borrower.

tries advocating reform and the policies they have pushed on others—a gap that led to accusations of hypocrisy. Consider what was happening in the United States while the Washington consensus was being formulated: trade liberalization was being pushed on others, while nontariff barriers were extended to cover what was estimated by some accounts to be a fifth of all imports (see Low and Yeats 1994). The United States expanded its use of such protectionist instruments as "voluntary" export restraints on automobiles, and it "perfected" the use of unfair "fair trade laws" (antidumping and countervailing duties) to protect other essential industries, such as steel (see Boltuck and Litan 1992; Finger and Artis 1993; Stiglitz 1997). Later, when the former Communist countries attempted to enter world markets, these same laws were used to raise barriers against the few commodities that they could successfully market (such as aluminum and uranium). While the Uruguay Round was widely applauded for opening trade still further, the agricultural sector—the comparative advantage of many less developed countries—remained highly protected. Partly as a result of this protection, some of the poorest of the less developed countries received hardly any benefit from the Uruguay Round and may have actually emerged worse off than before.[41]

By the same token, the message of "getting the prices right" was not heard very clearly by the senders of the message. For example, agricultural subsidies and price supports soared to the point that in the early and mid-1980s, between 30 and 100 percent of net farm income each year came from the government (General Agreement on Tariffs and Trade 1994). Corporate welfare expanded with the growth of the economy—from hidden subsidies for corporate jets to inland waterways to a vast array of real estate subsidies buried in the tax code.[42] And the role of the government in the credit market continued to increase, with government guarantees covering a significant fraction of all outstanding loans.[43]

To be fair, the United States did suffer some of the same consequences that other countries did from the lack of balance: financial sector deregulation led to the S&L debacle, which cost U.S. taxpayers an amount estimated between 2 and 4 percent of GDP and is widely viewed as an important contributor to the economic recession of 1991. But what is remarkable is that *after* that experience, the central reform message did not change: proponents continued to advocate financial market liberalization, without a corresponding emphasis on the importance of strengthen-

41. A World Bank study has estimated, e.g., that Africa's net gain from the Uruguay Round was slightly negative (Harrison, Rutherford, and Tarr 1995). This was in part because many African countries failed to liberalize sufficiently during the Round.

42. For discussions of corporate welfare, see Webre (1995) and Moore and Stansel (1996).

43. In the United States the ratio of federal and federally assisted lending to total lending reached a peak of 22.6 percent in 1980. In 1986, the ratio was 14.5 percent. See U.S. Office of Management and Budget (1988, F-30).

ing the regulatory oversight structure. The lessons from the experience of the United States, and of so many other countries, should have been clear: rather than advocating rapid financial market liberalization, advocate strengthening the financial sector. Had this lesson been incorporated into the reform message, some of the disaster of East Asia might have been avoided.[44]

Thus, by failing to develop a consensus behind the economic reforms, and by reaching for reforms (some of which may in fact have been ill grounded) that went beyond those for which a consensus could be developed, the reformers undermined the political sustainability of their handiwork. As I have traveled around the world, I have been struck by the antipathy expressed toward the Washington consensus; it has become a lightning rod for opposition in the countries where reforms were imposed from the outside. In contrast, many countries have initiated reforms on their own and have developed widespread support for reform. In these countries, the basic elements of reform are matters of bi- (or multi-) partisan support, with slight nuances across parties, but with a commitment to the basic thrust of reforms regardless of which party wins the election. (E.g., several countries in Latin America fall within this group.)

Reform in democratic society is not easy, and remaining ignorant of the sources of difficulty constitutes still another important failure.

Failure 3E   Many of the reformers failed to recognize the difficulty of reform in a democratic context and the impediments to reform.

This failure was perhaps understandable: few development economists engaged in the reform process had in fact participated actively in democratic reform movements in their own countries. I spent from 1993 to 1997 attempting to promote a variety of economic reforms in the United States as a member, and then chairman, of the Council of Economic Advisers. While we had a number of successes, it was often strikingly difficult to achieve even reforms that seemed to be Pareto-improvements; surely there should have been unanimity for such changes. In my Chicago Society of Government Economists lecture, I put forward several hypotheses for why this was so, including the suggestion that the political process needs to be

44. See Furman and Stiglitz (1998). In the case of other messages—such as the importance of ensuring vigorous competition—that were not such a central part of the Washington consensus but that are essential for the success of a market economy, interpreting what was going on in the United States in the 1980s was more complicated. At one level, the government stressed competition policy: there were more price-fixing cases than in previous administrations, and the single largest case, that of the telephone system, reached closure with the breaking up of the telephone monopoly. At another level, however, the government was lax in enforcement of laws against vertical restraints, and there was some cause for concern about the loosening of standards for mergers. It was not until 1993 that these trends began to be reversed.

viewed as a sequential game, rather than a one-shot affair (Stiglitz 1998c). Actions today may have effects tomorrow; reforms that are Pareto-improvements in this period may lead in subsequent periods to changes that may make some groups worse off—so that in this dynamic game they are not in fact Pareto-improvements. Moreover, governments' limited ability to make commitments weakens their ability to provide assurances to those who might be hurt that they eventually will recover. But among the other reasons I cited is that the economic system is very complex: there are real disagreements about the consequences of policies, real concerns about the motives of those advocating reform. If this is true in the United States, with a highly educated population well versed in market economics, imagine how much truer it will be in less developed countries. Those countries are even more likely to make inferences based on limited information; the initial failures of reform may accordingly have disproportionate weight. And when the reforms are driven from the outside or by political elites whose interests are not seen to coincide with those of the average citizen, or are launched through processes that are not open and transparent, questions about key actors' motives can reinforce the doubts raised by the lack of results.[45]

Reform in the Aftermath of the Global Financial Crisis

Today, the world crisis, and especially the recession (or depression, depending on one's vantage point) in East Asia, poses an even greater challenge to restoring confidence in the reform movement, and not just in the countries affected by the crisis. For it is affecting how countries—government officials, students, intellectuals, economists, even businessmen—throughout the world view the role of market-based reforms in the development process.

Let me try to describe briefly what I am picking up from conversations throughout the developing world. In doing so, it is useful to put today's events into a historical context. We in the United States would like to put our history of slavery and oppression of Native Americans into the distant past but have gradually come to recognize that those who have been affected by those actions—and we as a nation—cannot do so. In the same way, we should recognize that in many developing countries, the memory of the colonial experience has not fully faded. Indeed, many former colonies achieved their independence just a few decades ago, after years of political (and in many cases economic) oppression. Consider the unfolding of events as seen through the eyes of someone with such an experience: First, the West insists that a country open its economy to foreign

---

45. In my Oxford Amnesty lecture, I described the corrosive effect of secrecy—as well as the incentives on the part of politicians to maintain it (Stiglitz 1999a).

capital. A flood of capital quickly enters—before the country has developed the full institutional capacity to cope with it. Many of the recipient countries already had very high saving rates—in excess of 30 percent—and so were hardly capital starved in the first place. Not surprisingly, then, marginal investments were of marginal value. Then, just as suddenly, the Western capitalists demand their money back. When a country cannot pay, the Western bankers succeed in having their "agents" extract their pound of flesh—like the unfair, asymmetric treaties opening some developing countries in the nineteenth century. But the agents do not stop there: they insist on raising interest rates to usurious levels (levels that in many of their own countries would not be legal), compounding the economic downturn and causing a further crash in asset values. Further, they insist that these countries sell those assets—at fire-sale prices—to international investors, including some of the same people who precipitated the crisis in the first place by withdrawing their money. (To many developing country observers, this behavior is reminiscent of the loan sharks that prey on the poor throughout the world, first dragging them into heavy debt, and then forcing them either to pay usurious rates that keep them immiserated or else to forfeit the goods purchased with the loans.) And while talk of equity accompanies the billions of dollars of assistance that flows to these countries, instead—as I discussed above—somehow the burden of adjustment seems borne largely by workers and small businessmen, who had little to do with the international borrowing in the first place, and much of the outside money seems to go toward mitigating the losses of the lenders. (Moreover, it is the workers in the country who will have to bear much of the burden of repaying the loans that their governments undertook to bail out foreign lenders!) Viewed through the lens of the colonial experience, this picture is coherent and highly disturbing.

It would be easy to draw out of this picture a conspiracy story, and such stories are indeed circulating. I do not think there was a conspiracy, but rather a sequence of decisions, each reasonable (from at least some perspective) at the time. But the overall picture is not pretty—at least as seen by those now facing the consequences of the crises and the responses. Those of us who believe that the reform process needs to go forward must confront these perceptions; we simply cannot pretend that they are not there. Our task in the coming years will not be easy.

Concluding Remarks

From the current vantage point, the reform movement—at least the reform movement based on the narrow conception of the Washington consensus—seems in shambles, from Russia and Eastern Europe to East Asia to Latin America. Voucher privatization in the Czech Republic and the loans-to-share privatizations in Russia have enriched a few but failed to provide the basis of a market economy, let alone restore growth and prosperity. In Russia, confidence in market reforms has been deeply undermined; in the Czech Republic, fortunately, government and citizens recognize that they must, at last, create the institutional infrastructure required for a market economy. Parts of East Asia are in a depression that at least in some instances, is beginning to rival the Great Depression. Latin America, in spite of its remarkable reforms during this decade, has been badly battered by the markets. If the wondrous markets can do this even to economies that are taking all the right measures, why should people in these countries have confidence in the markets? Why should the workers who will be thrown out of work continue to support reforms that have delivered vulnerability instead of growth?

Those of us who are committed to improving the lives of the poor in less developed countries and who believe that markets are the best way of enhancing growth and alleviating poverty will be facing an enormous challenge in the coming months and years. Throughout the developing world, a backlash against the market-based strategy is gathering strength. But the failures that these people see around them represent not a failure of markets but a failure of *balance* and *strategy*. The overzealousness of some advocates of market reform, their underappreciation of the institutional infrastructure and the important role that government plays in helping to create it, their failure to recognize the importance of competition and new enterprises—all these point the way toward important lessons as we go forward. Societies are complex, and development entails the transformation of whole societies. Focusing on fiscal balances and low inflation, but ignoring financial institutions, can lead to macroeconomic instability just as surely as misguided monetary and fiscal policies can; rent seeking can be just as devastating in the private sector as in the public. Our task will be to stop the pendulum from swinging too far to the other side: the excesses of one side should not be matched by excesses on the other. If we can achieve a sense of balance, if we can learn the lessons from the failures of the reform agenda of the past, there is at least a glimmer of hope. This half-century has seen remarkable improvements in living standards for hundreds of millions of people in the developing world. Our hope is to see those successes—the benefits of democratic, equitable, and sustainable development—shared by the billions more who have yet to taste their fruits.

References

Akerlof, G., and P. Romer. 1993. Looting: The economic underworld of bankruptcy for profit. *Brookings Papers on Economic Activity,* no. 2:1–60.

Alesina, A., and L. Summers. 1993. Central bank independence and macroeconomic performance: Some comparative evidence. *Journal of Money, Credit, and Banking* 25, no. 2 (May): 151–62.

Arnott, R., B. Greenwald, and J. E. Stiglitz. 1994. Information and economic efficiency. *Information Economics and Policy* 6, no. 1 (March): 77–88.

Besanko, D., and G. Kanatas. 1996. The regulation of bank capital: Do capital standards promote bank safety? *Journal of Financial Intermediation* 5, no. 2 (April): 160–83.

Bhattacharya, S. 1982. Aspects of monetary and banking theory and moral hazard. *Journal of Finance* 37 (May): 371–84.

Blanchard, O. 1988. Unemployment: Getting the questions right—and some of the answers. NBER Working Paper no. 2698. Cambridge, Mass.: National Bureau of Economic Research, September.

Blanchard, O., and M. Kremer. 1997. Disorganization. *Quarterly Journal of Economics* 112:1091–1126.

Blanchard, O., and L. Summers. 1988. Hysteresis and the European unemployment problem. In *Unemployment, hysteresis and the natural rate hypothesis,* ed. R. Cross, 306–64. Oxford: Blackwell.

Boltuck, R., and R. E. Litan. 1992. Down in the dumps: Administering America's "unfair" trade laws. *Brookings Review* 10 (spring): 42–45.

Bruno, M. 1993. *Crisis, stabilization, and economic reform: Therapy by consensus.* Oxford: Clarendon.

Bruno, M., and W. Easterly. 1996. Inflation's children: Tales of crises that beget reforms. *American Economic Review Papers and Proceedings* 86, no. 2 (May): 213–17.

Caprio, G. 1997. Safe and sound banking in developing countries: We're not in Kansas anymore. *Research in Financial Services: Private and Public Policy* 9:79–97.

Caprio, G., and D. Klingebiel. 1997. Bank insolvency: Bad luck, bad policy, or bad banking? In *Annual World Bank conference on development economics 1996,* ed. M. Bruno and B. Pleskovic. Washington, D.C.: World Bank.

Caprio, G., and L. Summers. 1996. Financial reform beyond laissez-faire. In *Stability of the financial system,* ed. Dmitri Papadimitriou. London: Macmillan.

Coffee, J. 1996. Institutional investors in transitional economies: Lessons from the Czech experience. In *Corporate governance in Central Europe and Russia.* Vol. 1, *Banks, funds, and foreign investors,* ed. Roman Frydman. Budapest: Central European University Press.

Cole, A., J. A. McKenzie, and L. J. White. 1995. Deregulation gone awry: Moral hazard in the savings and loan industry. In *The causes and costs of depository institution failures,* ed. A. F. Cottrell, M. S. Lawlor, and J. H. Wood, 29–73. Innovations in Financial Markets and Institutions Series. Norwell, Mass.: Kluwer.

Coleman, J. S. 1988. Social capital in the creation of human capital. *American Journal of Sociology* 94 (suppl.): S95–S120.

Czech Ministry of Finance. 1997. Current aspects of the Czech capital markets. Prague: Ministry of Finance. Unpublished manuscript.

Demirgüç-Kunt, A., and E. Detragiache. 1998a. The determinants of banking crises in developing and developed countries. *IMF Staff Papers* 45 (1): 81–109.

———. 1998b. Financial liberalization and financial fragility. Paper presented to the annual World Bank conference on development economics, Washington, D.C., 20–21 April.

Demsetz, R. S., M. R. Saidenberg, and P. E. Strahan. 1996. Banks with something to lose. *Federal Reserve Bank of New York Economic Policy Review* 2, no. 2 (October): 1–14.

Dewatripont, M., and J. Tirole. 1994. Theory of debt and equity: Diversity of securities and manager-shareholder congruence. *Quarterly Journal of Economics* 109 (November): 1027–54.

Dooley, Michael. 1998. Indonesia: Is the light at the end of the tunnel oncoming traffic? Frankfurt: Deutsche Bank Research, Emerging Markets Research, June.

Ellerman, D. 1998. Voucher privatization with investment funds: An institutional analysis. Policy Research Working Paper no. 1924. Washington, D.C.: World Bank.

Feldstein, M. 1998. Refocusing the IMF. *Foreign Affairs* 77 (March–April): 20–33.

Finger, M., and N. T. Artis. 1993. *Antidumping: How it works and who gets hurt.* Ann Arbor: University of Michigan Press.

Fischer, K., and M. Chénard. 1997. Financial liberalization causes banking system fragility. Working Paper no. 97-14; Faculté des Sciences de l'Administration. Working Paper no. 97-12; Centre de Recherches en Economie et Finance Appliquées, 16 June.

Furman, J. and J. E. Stiglitz. 1998. Economic crises: Evidence and insights from East Asia. *Brookings Papers on Economic Activity,* no. 2:1–135.

General Agreement on Tariffs and Trade. 1994. *Trade policy review: United States, 1994.* Geneva: General Agreement on Tariffs and Trade.

Gennotte, G., and D. Pyle. 1991. Capital controls and bank risk. *Journal of Banking and Finance* 15, no. 4–5 (September): 805–24.

Giammarino, R. M., T. R. Lewis, and D. E. Sappington. 1993. An incentive approach to banking regulation. *Journal of Finance* 48, no. 4 (September): 1523–42.

Greenwald, B. 1998. International adjustments in the face of imperfect financial markets. Paper presented to the annual World Bank conference on development economics, Washington, D.C., 20–21 April.

Greenwald, B., and J. E. Stiglitz. 1988. Financial market imperfections and business cycles. NBER Working Paper no. 2494. Cambridge, Mass.: National Bureau of Economic Research, January.

———. 1993. Financial market imperfections and business cycles. *Quarterly Journal of Economics* 108 (1): 77–114.

Greenwald, B., J. E. Stiglitz, and A. Weiss. 1984. Informational imperfections in capital markets and macro-economic fluctuations. *American Economic Review* 74:194–99.

Harrison, G. W., T. Rutherford, and D. G. Tarr. 1995. Quantifying the Uruguay Round. In *The Uruguay Round and the developing economies,* ed. Will Martin and L. Alan Winters. Washington, D.C.: World Bank.

Hellman, T., K. Murdock, and J. Stiglitz. 1996. Deposit mobilisation through financial restraint. In *Financial development and economic growth,* ed. N. Hermes and R. Lensink, 219–46. London: Routledge.

———. 1997. Liberalization, moral hazard in banking and prudential regulation: Are capital requirements enough? Graduate School of Business Research Paper no. 1466. Stanford, Calif.: Stanford University.

Kaminsky, G. L., and C. Reinhart. 1998. The twin crises: The causes of banking and balance of payments problems. Washington, D.C.: Board of Governors of the Federal Reserve System; College Park: University of Maryland, February.

Kane, E. 1989. Changing incentives facing financial-services regulators. *Journal of Financial Services Research* 2, no. 3 (September): 265–74.

Kane, E., and M. Yu. 1994. How much did capital forbearance add to the tab for the FSLIC mess? NBER Working Paper no. 4701. Cambridge, Mass.: National Bureau of Economic Research.

Kolodko, G. 1997. The Polish alternative: Old myths, hard facts and new strategies in the successful transformation of the Polish economy. Instytut Finansow Working Paper no. 55. Poland: Instytut Finansow.

———. 1998. Russia should put its people first. *New York Times,* 7 July.

Lam, C. H., and A. H. Chen. 1985. Joint effects of interest rate deregulation and capital requirements on optimal bank portfolio adjustments. *Journal of Finance* 40, no. 2 (June): 563–75.

Lancaster, K., and R. Lipsey. 1996. The general theory of second best. In *Trade, markets and welfare,* by K. Lancaster, 193–220. Cheltenham, England: Elgar.

Lokshin, M., and B. Popkin. 1999. The emerging underclass in the Russian Federation: Income dynamics, 1992–1996. *Economic Development and Cultural Change* 47 (4): 803–29.

Low, P., and A. Yeats. 1994. Nontariff measures and developing countries: Has the Uruguay Round leveled the playing field? Policy Research Working Paper no. 1353. Washington, D.C.: World Bank.

Mayer, C. 1989. Myths of the West: Lessons from developed countries for development finance. Policy Research Working Paper no. 301. Washington, D.C.: World Bank.

———. 1990. Financial systems, corporate finance, and economic development. In *Asymmetric information, corporate finance, and investment,* ed. R. G. Hubbard, 307–32. Chicago: University of Chicago Press.

Moore, S., and D. Stansel. 1996. How corporate welfare won: Clinton and Congress retreat from cutting business subsidies. Cato Policy Analysis no. 254. Washington, D.C.: Cato Institute, 15 May.

Morita, A. 1986. *Made in Japan.* New York: Dutton.

Myers, S. C. 1977. Determinants of corporate borrowing. *Journal of Financial Economics* 5:147–75.

Newbery, D., and J. E. Stiglitz. 1982. The choice of techniques and the optimality of market equilibrium with rational expectations. *Journal of Political Economy* 90:223–46.

Putnam, R. D. 1993. *Making democracy work: Civic traditions in modern Italy* (with R. Leonardi and R. Y. Nanetti). Princeton, N.J.: Princeton University Press.

Radelet, S., and J. Sachs. 1998. The onset of the East Asian financial crisis. Paper presented at USAID seminar, Washington, D.C., 29 January.

Rajan, R. G. 1992. Insiders and outsiders: The choice between informed and arm's length debt. *Journal of Finance* 47:1367–1400.

Rajan, R. G., and L. Zingales. 1995. Is there an optimal capital structure? Evidence from international data. *Journal of Finance* 50:1421–60.

Rochet, J. C. 1992. Capital requirements and the behaviour of commercial banks. *European Economic Review* 36, no. 5 (June): 1137–70.

Rodrik, D. 1998. Who needs capital-account convertibility? Essays in International Finance, no. 207. Princeton, N.J.: Princeton University, Department of Economics, International Finance Section, May.

Smith, A. 1986. *Glasgow edition of the works and correspondences of Adam Smith.* Oxford: Clarendon.

Stiglitz, J. E. 1988. Money, credit, and business fluctuations. *Economic Record* 64 (187): 307–22.

———. 1992. Capital markets and economic fluctuations in capitalist economies. *European Economic Review* 36:269–306.

———. 1993. The role of the state in financial markets. In *Annual World Bank conference on development economics 1993,* ed. M. Bruno and B. Pleskovic. Washington, D.C.: World Bank.

———. 1994. *Whither socialism?* Cambridge, Mass.: MIT Press.

———. 1997. Dumping on free trade: The U.S. import trade laws. *Southern Economic Journal* 64 (2): 402–24.

———. 1998a. Central banking in a democratic society. *De Economist* (Netherlands) 146 (2): 199–226.

———. 1998b. More instruments and broader goals: Moving towards the post-Washington consensus. United Nations University World Institute for Development Economics Research (WIDER) Annual Lectures 2, Helsinki.

———. 1998c. The private uses of public interests: Incentives and institutions. Distinguished Lecture on Economics in Government. *Journal of Economic Perspectives* 12 (2): 3–22.

———. 1999a. On liberty, the right to know, and public discourse: The role of transparency in public life. Paper given as the 1999 Oxford Amnesty International Lecture. Available at http://www.worldbank.org/knowledge/chiefecon/index.htm.

———. 1999b. Quis custodiet ipsos custodes (who is to guard the guards themselves)? Corporate governance failures in the transition. Keynote address, 1999 Annual World Bank Conference on Development Economics—Europe.

———. 1999c. Whither reform? Ten years of the transition. Keynote address, 1999 Annual World Bank Conference on Development Economics. Available at http://www.worldbank.org/research/abcde/washington.html.

U.S. Office of Management and Budget. 1988. *Special analysis budget of the United States government, fiscal year 1988.* Washington, D.C.: Government Printing Office.

Vickers, J., and G. Yarrow. 1988. *Privatization: An economic analysis.* Cambridge, Mass.: MIT Press.

Webre, P. 1995. Federal financial support of business. Congressional Budget Office Report.

Weisbrod, S. R., H. Lee, and L. Rojas-Suarez. 1992. Bank risk and the declining franchise value of the banking systems in the United States and Japan. IMF Working Paper no. 92/45. Washington, D.C.: International Monetary Fund, June.

Weiss, A., and G. Nikitin. 1998. Performance of Czech companies by ownership structure. Paper presented at the International Workshop in Transition Economics, Prague, July.

Wilcox, D. 1998. The introduction of indexed government debt in the United States. *Journal of Economic Perspectives* 12 (winter): 219–27.

Williamson, J. 1990. What Washington means by policy reform. In *Latin American adjustment: How much has happened?* ed. John Williamson. Washington, D.C.: Institute for International Economics.

———. 1997. The Washington consensus revisited. In *Economic and social development into the XXI century,* ed. L. Emmerij, 48–61. Washington, D.C.: Inter-American Development Bank.

World Bank and Government of Russian Federation. 1995. *Russian Federation: Report on the national accounts.* Washington, D.C.: World Bank.

World Bank. 1997a. *China 2020: Development challenges in the new century.* Washington, D.C.: World Bank.

———. 1997b. *World development report 1997: The state in a changing world.* New York: Oxford University Press.

———. 1998. *World development indicators 1998.* Washington, D.C.: World Bank.

———. 1999. *World development report 1998: Knowledge for development.* New York: Oxford University Press.

Agenda for Future Research
What We Need to Know

Anne O. Krueger

The consensus on the need for far-reaching economic policy reform began emerging in the mid-1980s and gained momentum for at least a decade. Much was learned during that decade, as country after country began undertaking "reforms," some far-reaching and serious, some largely window dressing.[1] But as experience grew, many questions arose about the efficacy of some of the reforms that had been undertaken. It was widely recognized that some—such as the entire set of reforms in Russia and the privatization of banks in Mexico—had simply not worked, or had worked only very poorly. This already gave opponents of reform as well as other observers a basis from which to question entire reform programs, as Joseph Stiglitz observes in the preceding chapter. Other reforms were seen to have had smaller payoffs than had been anticipated, either because of difficulties in implementation or because of the absence of complementary reforms that would have greatly increased economic efficiency. And questions were raised about the income distribution consequences of reforms, as well as about political reactions to them that in some countries seem to have impeded a continuation of the reform process.

Moreover, there was a manifest need to find better ways of achieving

Anne O. Krueger is the Herald L. and Caroline L. Ritch Professor of Economics, senior fellow of the Hoover Institution, and director of the Center for Research on Economic Development and Policy Reform at Stanford University, and a research associate of the National Bureau of Economic Research.

The author is indebted to Sajjid Chinoy for thoughtful suggestions as well as research assistance, and to T. N. Srinivasan for many helpful comments.

1. Some countries, of course, began their reforms before the 1980s. South Korea in the 1960s and Chile in the 1970s were prominent among them. But attention did not focus on questions of reform until the 1980s, when policymakers in many countries began contemplating shifts in their policy regimes.

goals and especially of mitigating the impact of reforms on the poor. But as if these issues were not sufficiently serious, the financial currency crises in Asia in 1997–98 further called reforms into question. On one hand, one of the appeals of reforms had been the apparent success of the East Asian countries with rapid growth (and relatively egalitarian income distributions) under policies that had been thought to differ from the interventionist regimes of many developing countries. With the Asian crises, questions arose both as to whether the East Asian countries had indeed had less interventionist regimes and as to the desirability of the East Asian model, whatever it was. On the other hand, additional questions about the need for, and types of, reform also arose. The importance of appropriate incentives and frameworks in the financial sector came into sharp focus, as did the question of the type of currency regime most conducive to development.

Despite the recent East Asian experience, it is fair to say that even before the beginning of the turnarounds of these countries, most analysts—even the critics—agreed that *if* one could achieve a setting with the sorts of market-based policies and institutions that have worked so well in many Western countries, *then* economic growth would accelerate, with concomitant increases in living standards for all, including the poor. Most critics have focused either on the failure of particular reforms or on the high costs (sometimes to particular groups such as the poor) and potential infeasibility of doing everything perfectly as reasons for not undertaking them.

For most economists, however, experience with reforms has demonstrated the need to find means to achieve a healthy framework for economic growth more effectively. The search can be pursued in a number of ways, including analyses of experiences to date. The need for further thinking about reforms is evident, both because of these sorts of popular reactions in the development community and among policymakers in developing countries and because reforms have not lost their desirability. Rather, analysis of experience with reforms can offer insights for future economic policy reformers that will permit even larger payoffs in the future.

Interestingly, the theme of this volume is: What have we learned, and what do we need to learn? Yet the papers seem to converge neatly into two sets of areas where research can inform future policy decisions. On one hand are areas where reforms have been attempted and where there appears to be considerable scope for improving performance by addressing "nuts and bolts" and implementation issues. It is not, as Aaron Tornell points out, that one should not privatize; it is that mechanisms must be found to assure that the new managers can, and have incentives to, manage and that the old stakeholders cannot block measures that need to be taken if newly privatized firms are to achieve productivity gains. And as Vito Tanzi notes, achieving better fiscal performance is a matter of implementation, of designing processes and incentives that control costs and allocate expenditures in efficient ways. "The devil is in the details," too, for achieving an appropriate financial regulatory regime, reforming education, ensuring that the benefits of growth reach the poor, and in all other areas of reform.

The second set of issues is associated with the "hard cases"—areas where reforms have not yet been undertaken and where key inefficiencies are yet to be addressed, or where, as Anjini Kochar notes in her comment on Michael Kremer, reforms have not been undertaken because even researchers disagree about what should be done. In these instances, "big think" questions arise both about why it is so difficult to address these issues and about how to approach them. It is no exaggeration to say that initial reform efforts were based on (largely well founded) big think ideas—liberalization of trade, control of fiscal expenditures, privatization, and so forth. The "easy" ones seem to have been undertaken, leaving only these hard cases. Questions arise both about why they are so hard and about how to go about them.

The need for reforms in other sectors, even in countries where many reforms have been undertaken, calls for a different agenda. Some critical big think issues arise, as well as questions about the payoffs of various partial reforms. There are also interesting questions about the interactions between reforms. Finally, there are issues, such as the appropriate policy stance with regard to capital flows, that urgently need additional research.

In addressing the remaining large questions and in studying the nuts and bolts of how to undertake reforms more effectively, research results can inform both the "advanced reformers," as they move on to refine their reforms and address new issues, and the laggards, whose reforms are only beginning. It is of course to be hoped that the experience of the first generation will enable later reformers to move more smoothly from the control regimes under which they continue to operate to incentive regimes more conducive to satisfactory economic performance.

16.1   Nuts-and-Bolts Issues

Once we recognize that many second-stage issues involve questions of how-to-do-it in an imperfect world, it is clear that the research agenda is enormous. The challenge is to find ways of estimating the potential costs and benefits of reforms more precisely ex ante and to persuade politicians (and those who influence politicians) that the benefits are large relative to the costs. What is needed is an understanding of the relative quantitative payoffs from different reforms. That, in turn, requires good quantitative estimates of underlying parameters, as well as an understanding of the ways differing institutional and policy contexts affect responses to particular types of policy reform.

Some of these issues call for careful empirical research. In a number of sectors—education, health, labor markets, and the like—quantitative estimates of payoffs from, say, reducing classroom size versus providing more textbooks, or removing minimum wage legislation, or relaxing job tenure requirements would enable policymakers to push for at least some reform in areas where resistance is strong. Quantitative estimates (or empirical regularities as to which policies yield higher returns) would provide an improved base from which policymakers could undertake reforms and achieve more satisfactory results with their limited political capital. This is especially important for countries only now embarking on policy reforms.

At the same time, since different countries are at very different points in their reform processes, it is important to understand when reforms that have achieved significant positive results in countries well along the reform path will or will not work in countries just embarking on reform programs: among other things, failures at early stages of reform can lead to the reversal of the entire process. Equally, demonstrable benefits from the first phases of reform can build support for continuation and for further reform. Comparative analysis of reforms in particular sectors or economic activities, both analytical histories and econometric efforts, should have a high payoff for these purposes.

One question is what sorts of mechanisms can achieve the desired ends, especially in a world where "perfect reforms" will never be possible. Aaron Tornell poses this question starkly: What should policymakers do when they cannot insulate new owner-managers of enterprises from the claims of stakeholders in the former regime? Do they do nothing, knowing it will not be completely successful, or do they move to privatize anyway, knowing that risks of capture by employees, towns, and other interest groups are considerable? As in so many of the papers, the question is well posed and is second best in nature. Tornell concludes that it is probably better to privatize even when stakeholders' influence cannot be removed, but he recognizes that it is a difficult call and that analysis of other privatizations will shed further light on the issue.

Understanding which reforms may still have high returns requires an increasingly good base of knowledge as the reform process progresses, and it is in this regard that a research agenda for second-stage reforms is long and rich. As Anjini Kochar points out in her observations on Michael Kremer's paper, in some instances reforms have not proceeded largely because researchers themselves are divided on the best way to proceed. The role of knowledge, and consensus among professionals as to best practice, is often underestimated as an input to reforms (Cooper 1989).

Julie Schaffner, in her comments, also highlights the need for careful empirical assessment of the effects of particular policies. As she points out, "Surprisingly little research to date pays attention to the details of labor market policies. Even studies of labor market regulation tend to make only broad-brush comparisons across countries. Policymakers undertaking labor market reforms . . . write legislation that changes many specific policy parameters. . . . If research is going to become more useful to policymakers, it must start by paying more attention to detail." She means such questions as: If you could "only" abolish the minimum wage *or* cut the social insurance tax by 10 percentage points, which would have a larger payoff? And how do either of these compare with removal of laws providing that those who have been employed for a specified period (often a year) may not be fired regardless of circumstances, requirements for worker training, and a variety of other mandated labor market interventions? These are questions for which there is almost no empirical evidence. Providing even rough but reliable orders of magnitude would be of great value to policymakers who know that, despite the ideal world of labor market flexibility, they cannot remove all distortions and must focus on the critical view with their limited political capital.

Paralleling Schaffner's assessment of the work on labor markets, Noll observes that the relatively small literature on telecommunications reform consists either of relatively crude regressions of aggregate performance measures (subscriber penetration, average costs, etc.) on dummies indicating the date of reform or of detailed case studies, both of which contain little or no cross-country comparisons of the details of reforms. Part of the problem has been that until the late 1990s, too few countries had embarked on significant reform to generate enough information for comparative institutional analysis; however, since the implementation of the WTO Basic Telecommunications Agreement in 1998, this situation is now changing, so that more comprehensive empirical studies are now becoming feasible. The challenge to reformers is to adopt pricing rules that neither penalize nor subsidize interconnection among competing carriers and to eliminate cross-subsidies in the rate structure so that entry decisions are based on the right price signals. As in many other areas, differences among countries in initial conditions of the telecommunications carriers, in the income levels and density of the populations, and in the initial regulatory framework all influence the manner in which various policy changes affect service quality and cost. Comparative empirical work to understand better the interaction of these variables and their effects on the outcomes of reform efforts could serve not only to enable greater benefits of reforms where attempted but could also help to provide a blueprint for further reform efforts, again strengthening the knowledge base of reforms.

Far and away the largest single category of calls for research in this volume urges much more empirical work on the costs and benefits of alternative techniques for improving outcomes. Kremer's call for research on the determinants of educational quality and the trade-offs between different ways of improving quality is one clear example. So, too, is Matusz and Tarr's suggestion that additional research on the microeconomics of adjustment may facilitate further trade liberalization. Schultz's call for additional survey data in order that we might better understand the linkages between a variety of worker attributes, wage differentials, and labor market regulations also falls into the category of comparative microeconomic analysis.

For regulation of all sorts of economic activities that were previously regarded as public utilities, there is a huge gap in understanding of many aspects of reform. Comparative studies of water system reforms are called for by Noll, Shirley, and Cowan, whose contrast of experience in six countries is a first with regard to water. Likewise, Noll calls for an analysis of comparative experience with telecommunications reform. Although not covered in this volume, undoubtedly a similar situation pertains to provision of electricity.

16.2   Big Think Issues: Neglected Sectors and Questions

For the issues discussed in section 16.1, careful empirical analysis of interactions between incentives and institutions, of behavioral responses, and of benefits and costs is called for. However, there is a range of important issues for which research may well shed light, yet for which hypotheses and questions are not sufficiently well formulated to make them amenable to careful empirical estimation.

One such issue is the determinants of resistance to reform. Stephan Haggard's question, about the relative importance of interests and institutions, is an example. While better understanding of the ways in which interests and institutions support or thwart efforts at reform is highly desirable, it is also very challenging, as Abhijit Banerjee's comment on Haggard's paper suggests. But as with other big questions, any evidence that helps us to better understand how small interest groups (perhaps even with very little, if anything, to lose) can be influenced to support reforms, or how reform structures can be altered to reduce their opposition, will be invaluable. Studies of who actually benefited and lost from various reform episodes may well begin to inform policymakers in this regard.

There are also significant questions regarding political support for reform. Despite concerns with the hardships and losses that reforms may impose, a surprising political fact of life has been the extent to which reforms, once started, seem to gain acquiescence, if not support, from a broad segment of the public. Better understanding of those aspects of reform that command support, and of ways in which policymakers can increase support for reforms, could be invaluable in preventing the adoption of partial reform programs or the abandonment of programs with few benefits (as seems to have happened with some water reforms).

It is often pointed out that the first wave of reforms—exchange rates, trade liberalization, and the like—had as its hallmark the ease with which administrative branch policymakers in reforming countries could carry them out. Changing the exchange rate, reducing or eliminating quantitative restrictions, removing price controls, and similar measures can often be undertaken by administrative decree. A recurring theme of analyses of policy reforms has been that the first-stage reforms were "easy" in other ways as well. Not only could governments undertake reforms by administrative decree, but changing exchange rate regime or curbing public expenditure growth can normally be achieved with a few key actors. The second stage may be harder in at least three ways. First, it may be harder in that the political decision-making processes that must be used to decide on change and reform are slower and less monolithic than is the case with the initial reforms. Second, these reforms seem to require much more careful planning and implementation than do first-stage reforms. Third, it may be that there is more political resistance to those reforms that have not yet been undertaken. Analysis yielding insights into any of the three aspects of this issue would be invaluable. The questions of why reforms are resisted and by whom, of the sorts of mechanisms that would permit the attainment of Pareto-superior outcomes, and of approaches to reforms that reduce resistance are clearly crucial.

Another set of big think questions centers on the proposition, pointed out by T. N. Srinivasan, that the benefits from any one set of reforms are significantly enhanced when other markets are well functioning. Clearly, reforms to the real sector will have bigger payoffs when the financial system is efficient, and reforms in the financial system will have greater payoffs when the real sector is operating in an economically efficient manner. Thus, even in countries where reforms have progressed a considerable distance, the payoff from reforms already in place may be enhanced when other reforms are undertaken or fine-tuned. Vittorio Corbo estimates that in Latin America, additional reforms could accelerate growth rates by up to 2.5 percentage points annually. But, again, not all reforms are equal in their payoffs, and in a context where reforms are politically difficult, estimates of relative payoffs and where interactions are highest would be of great value.[2] Carefully calibrated estimates of these interactions are probably not feasible given the large number of possible policy combinations relative to the number of reform episodes. But comparative analysis of policy changes in countries where policies toward other sectors vary may yield valuable insights.

In a large number of papers, a recurring theme is the desirability and

---

2. It goes without saying that the trade-offs may not be the same across countries, so understanding is needed not only of the trade-offs but also of what aspects of the institutional environment affect the trade-offs and how.

high payoff of research that pays attention to the institutional context in which particular markets function. Calls for attention to details of labor market legislation, telecommunications regulation, judicial systems, institutional aspects of decision-making processes, process and implementation procedures within governments, and incentives confronting agents in particular settings (such as companies after privatization) emerged in all the papers. This is an area where detailed empirical work will probably count for less than well-structured cross-country comparisons or good analytical histories of particular events. But in such areas as banking regulation, privatization, and health and education, focusing on institutions and their role and interaction with markets is clearly an area where insights can have a high payoff for effective policy making.

As the experience with the Asian financial crises amply demonstrates, there are some key issues on which researchers still disagree and on which further research is called for. Because capital flows and financial relations impinge so heavily on all aspects of economic activity, these issues can more appropriately be regarded as big think than as detail issues, although as Frederic Mishkin points out, there are many details to be analyzed as well. As Edwards and Savastano note, considerable disagreement remains over exchange rate regimes in relation to capital flows and domestic monetary and fiscal policy. In part, these issues are technical, but there are also behavioral questions: Are governments operating a floating (or fixed) exchange rate regime more likely to be restrained in their fiscal-monetary policy stance? If so, how so? And if not, why not? These questions are central to any analysis of the major issues regarding exchange rate regimes and capital flows. How large are the benefits from an open capital account relative to the costs of a sudden capital outflow? Is it possible to have an open trade regime and maintain a relatively closed capital account? How quickly does one liberalize the capital account if liberalization is to be undertaken? These are areas where understanding is crucial, and where research has begun in earnest after the financial crises of the mid-1990s.

There are also key issues that still require empirical research. These include the many exchange rate questions raised by Edwards and Savastano, especially on the functioning of more flexible exchange rate regimes in developing countries. Experience with these regimes is mounting rapidly and should provide fertile ground for empirical researchers. Major issues have also arisen about both causes and remedies for the sorts of crises that afflicted East Asia in 1997–98. These include the role of capital flows, and especially short-term capital flows. On one hand, these flows can be viewed as an endogenous response to incentives established by the combination of a relatively weak banking system and a fixed exchange rate regime. On the other hand, they can be viewed as an exogenous trigger to crises. Research designs that enable better differentiation between these two hypotheses will clearly inform economic policy design in developing countries. For as reflected in the discussion in several papers, the potential role—positive or negative—for capital controls hinges crucially on understanding this question.

Related to that question is the important policy question of foreign-currency-denominated debt in developing countries. Research that better identifies, both analytically and empirically, the relation between exchange rate regime, monetary policy, and incentives to borrow abroad and incur foreign-currency-denominated debt is badly needed. As Mishkin, Edwards and Savastano, and Corbo all note, the existence of this debt was one factor underpinning the Asian financial crisis (and that in Mexico in earlier years as well).

Another important aspect of reforms noted by many of the authors concerns legal and judicial systems and the ways in which property rights and contracts are or are not enforced. Yet little is known systematically, from the perspective of economics, about how to reform such systems in the presence of constraints, and quantitative treatment of these issues has not yet been achieved. Corbo notes the need for better understanding of judicial systems, as does Srinivasan. An improved system is vitally important for privatization, as Tornell and Noll point out; and Mishkin's list of considerations for financial reform also gives legal and judicial systems a key role. Clearly, in some cases of failures (as in Mexican privatization and in Russia), the absence of a legal system that permits bankruptcy but enforces repayment by debtors, and property rights more generally, is a huge obstacle to improved economic performance, yet little is known about improving the legal context in which economic activity takes place.

There are also the issues raised by Mishkin regarding the financial sector. There seems to be little disagreement about the desirable properties of an efficient financial system, and the need for such a system for sustainable economic growth. But achieving appropriate incentives and regulatory and supervisory arrangements in countries with different institutional structures, possibly weak legal systems, and so on, is exceptionally difficult. Better understanding of the constraints that these settings place on alternative regulatory modes and experience with different types of regulations and incentives will evidently contribute significantly to improved policy design.

Finally, there are the many key questions raised by Tanzi: How does one achieve desired fiscal results in second-best settings? While implementation is often the issue, some big think issues lie behind failures to implement policies. What are the determinants of corruption, and what institutional or other changes affect its presence and intensity? How does the institutional setup, including such key parameters as the inclusiveness of the budget, regulatory activities, and tax collection mechanisms, become established, and how can constraints (such as the pervasiveness of corruption) be loosened or altered in ways that permit better performance? How can better bureaucratic performance (more aligned with the intent of policymakers) be achieved?

Those deciding to undertake reforms today must do so based on existing knowledge. Even when research advances have improved understanding significantly, reformers will always be taking steps into the unknown, and outcomes cannot be certain. In some instances, pressure groups or other constraints will lead reformers to undertake reforms that are inadequate to achieve desired goals, or deter reformers from undertaking any actions in particular policy arenas. But in other instances, insufficient understanding of the determinants of reforms, or the relative importance of different reforms and their linkages to each other, may impair effectiveness. Researchers cannot affect policymakers today, but research results on these issues can provide future reformers with larger expected payoffs from their reform efforts.

Reference

Cooper, Richard. 1989. International cooperation in public health as a prologue to macroeconomic cooperation. In *Can nations agree? Issues in international economic cooperation,* by Richard Cooper et al. Washington, D.C.: Brookings Institution.

Contributors

Abhijit V. Banerjee
E-52-252d, Sloan Building
50 Memorial Drive
Massachusetts Institute of Technology
Cambridge, MA 02139

Mario I. Blejer
International Monetary Fund
700 19th Street NW
Washington, DC 20431

Vittorio Corbo
Instituto de Economia
Universidad Católica
Casilla 76, Correo 17
Santiago, Chile

Simon Cowan
Worcester College
Oxford OX1 2HB, United Kingdom

Sebastian Edwards
Anderson Graduate School of
　Management
University of California, Los Angeles
110 Westwood Plaza
Los Angeles, CA 90095

Stephan Haggard
Graduate School of International
　Relations and Pacific Studies
University of California, San Diego
9500 Gilman Drive
La Jolla, CA 92093

Nicholas C. Hope
Center for Research on Economic
　Development and Policy Reform
Stanford University
Landau Economics Building
579 Serra Mall, Room 153
Stanford, CA 94305

Takatoshi Ito
2-9-11 Higashiyama
Meguro-ku, Tokyo 153-0043 Japan

Anjini Kochar
Department of Economics
Stanford University
Landau Economics Building
579 Serra Mall
Stanford, CA 94305

Michael Kremer
207 Littauer Center
Department of Economics
Harvard University
Cambridge, MA 02138

Anne O. Krueger
Center for Research on Economic
   Development and Policy Reform
Stanford University
Landau Economics Building
579 Serra Mall, Room 153
Stanford, CA 94305

Steven Matusz
Department of Economics
Eli Broad College of Business
Michigan State University
East Lansing, MI 48824

Frederic S. Mishkin
Graduate School of Business
Uris Hall 619
Columbia University
New York, NY 10027

Jonathan Morduch
220 Bendheim Hall
Woodrow Wilson School
Princeton University
Princeton, NJ 08544

Roger G. Noll
Department of Economics
Stanford University
Landau Economics Building
579 Serra Mall
Stanford, CA 94305

Miguel A. Savastano
Research Department
International Monetary Fund
700 19th Street NW
Washington, DC 20431

Julie Schaffner
22 Bridge Street
Lexington, MA 02421

T. Paul Schultz
Yale University
27 Hillhouse Avenue
PO Box 208269
New Haven, CT 06520

Mary M. Shirley
World Bank
Room MC 3-473
1818 H Street NW
Washington, DC 20433

T. N. Srinivasan
Economic Growth Center
Yale University
PO Box 208269
New Haven, CT 06520

Joseph E. Stiglitz
World Bank
1818 H Street NW
Washington, DC 20433

Vito Tanzi
Fiscal Affairs Department
International Monetary Fund
700 19th Street NW
Washington, DC 20431

David Tarr
World Bank
1818 H Street NW
Washington, DC 20433

Aaron Tornell
Harvard University
Department of Economics
317 Littauer Center
Cambridge, MA 02138

Author Index

Subject Index

Neoliberalism, 201
Netherlands: reduction of unemployment
in, 308; school voucher system, 351,
353–54
New Zealand: legal requirements for banking system, 532–33; regulations related
to connected lending, 533
Nongovernmental organizations: Bangladesh, 137; in microfinance, 424

Organizational capital, 564–65
Outcomes, education related, 356–61
Ownership: under neoliberal reform, 201–4;
shifts in, 7

Pakistan: corruption and governance issues
in, 147–48; development strategies, 99–
100; economic performance, 110; economic reform (1990s), 101; infrastructure reform, 134–35; macroeconomic
indicators (1992–99), 102–3t; privatization, 124; social policy reform, 144–45;
trade policy reform, 116–17
Path dependence: in chaos theory, 187; of
developing countries, 185–86; outcomes with unchanged preferences,
187; political version, 187
Pension systems: reforms in Latin America,
82
Peru: inflation strategy, 70–71; water system
in Lima, 244–45, 259–85
Planned economies: transition to market
economies, 317–20
Political systems: influence on judiciary,
167–68; influences on policy reform,
37–48, 57–59; party fragmentation and
strength, 44–46; polarized and nonpolarized parties, 44–46
Poverty: alleviation strategies in South
Asia, 135–46; attitudes toward alleviation of, 406–7; focus of India's National Planning Committee, 408, 411;
headcount measures of, 422–23; impact of trade liberalization on, 387–89;
measurement of, 421–22; policies in India related to, 137–39; reduction strategies in Latin America, 91
PPP. *See* Purchasing power parity (PPP)
Principal-agent theory: corruption as example of, 449; moral hazard as problem in, 517–18; the state in, 39–44
Private sector: health care in developing

countries, 414–15; in Latin American
reform policies, 90–91; public sector
wages different from, 312–14
Privatization: Bangladesh, 118; India,
118–23; institutional reform with, 49;
in Latin American countries, 65, 72,
80; outcome of unrestrained, 201–2; Pakistan, 124; problems of and solutions
to, 8–9; property rights issue in, 178;
of public utilities in Latin America, 90;
recommendations for South Asia, 152;
reforms to increase efficiency of, 178;
soft budget constraints after, 165–72;
South Asian initiatives, 118–24; Sri
Lanka, 124
Productivity: losses from trade liberalization, 369–89; in state-owned enterprises, 315–16
Property rights: as issue in privatization,
178; libertarian concept, 201; in privatized state-owned firms, 157–64; in
state-owned firms, 159–64; in transition from planned to market economy,
317. *See also* Ownership
Public choice theory: application to behavior of policymakers, 446–47
Public policy: effect of party fragmentation
on conduct of, 45; effect of party preferences on, 44–46; factors influencing
outcomes, 40–44; influence of keepers
of the gate on, 447–48; influences on labor markets, 306–20; labor market research to inform, 325–28, 335–38; options in labor market, 321–25; reforms
for education, 358–63
Public sector: Bangladesh, 104; private sector wages different from, 312–14; provision of unemployment insurance, 308;
reforms in Latin America, 72, 86
Purchasing power parity (PPP): in assessment of short-, medium-, and long-
term RER, 469–81; in Balassa-
Samuelson effect, 454; in developing
countries, 471–76; in evaluation of exchange rate behavior, 454, 478–83;
panel data to examine hypotheses
about, 476–78; structural deviations
from, 478–83; tests of, 471–76

Rao, Narasimha, 100
Real exchange rate (RER): equilibrium and
disequilibrium, 469; long-run move-